# PRODUCTION AND INVENTORY MANAGEMENT

**DONALD W. FOGARTY, Ph.D., CPIM***
Professor, Management Systems and Science
Southern Illinois University at Edwardsville

**THOMAS R. HOFFMANN, Ph.D., CPIM***
Professor of Operations Management
University of Minnesota

For the
**AMERICAN PRODUCTION AND INVENTORY CONTROL SOCIETY**

*Published by*

G04 **SOUTH-WESTERN PUBLISHING CO.**

CINCINNATI WEST CHICAGO, ILL. DALLAS PELHAM MANOR, N.Y. PALO ALTO, CALIF.

ISBN: 0-538-07040-4
Library of Congress Catalog Card Number: 80-53541

6 D 8 7 6

Printed in the United States of America

# PREFACE

The objective of this text is to aid beginning students of Production and Inventory Management (PIM) to attain competency. They may be in the second half of their undergraduate work or beginning graduate level studies in either Business Administration or Industrial Engineering. Some also may be changing careers and entering the PIM field with considerable business experience. Thus, the text may be used for formal classes in colleges and universities, and selected chapters may be used in professional training and development programs.

The book is divided into five major parts. The sequence of chapters and topics in Parts 1 and 3 generally follows the chronological order in which these activities take place in practice. Long-, medium-, and short-range planning, for example, are treated in that order. Following that logic, order release planning is examined in Chapters 4, 5, and 7; and actual order release is covered in Chapters 12 and 13. Although planning for all time horizons, execution, and control are all occurring at any time in an organization, these concurrent, diverse activities usually concern different periods. Treating PIM activities in the sequence in which they apply to a given time period facilitates the explanation, and hopefully the reader's understanding, of these activities.

Inventory management and production planning and control are interwoven inextricably. Although Part 2 concerns primarily inventory management, the relationship of inventory management and production planning activities is emphasized throughout Parts 1, 2, and 3. In fact, a full understanding of the principles and concepts presented in any part of a chapter is difficult to attain without having studied the others. This organization allows each part of the text to focus on a particular area of PIM while giving due recognition to the relationships of principles, techniques, and decisions.

Part 4 covers decision methods that are applicable to PIM on a rather broad scale. Applications of project management techniques, mathematical programming, and simulation to PIM is widespread and growing. Potential decision situations for applying these techniques are pointed out in Parts 1, 2, and 3.

The last part of the text contains a treatment of the bill of materials, derivations, tables, computer programs, selected readings, and a glossary. The computer programs illustrate the relative ease given a certain computer programming capability of computerizing decision models and techniques. Using these programs enables the planner to study the likely effect of various decisions and the sensitivity of various decisions to variations in uncontrolled variables since less time is spent performing calculations. The readings include many examples of the variety and complexity of real world problems. The methods presented for coping with these decision situations are not necessarily the only ones, but, for the most part, they represent good practice and application of basic principles.

In this era of education being viewed as a lifelong activity, it was appropriate for the American Production and Inventory Control Society (APICS) to encourage the writing of a textbook that would both serve its members and college students preparing to enter the profession. It is impossible to single out specific individuals without neglecting a great number who also aided us. The authors, however, are deeply grateful for the financial support from the organization and the encouragement received from the Executive Director, past and present officers, and many different members.

*Donald W. Fogarty*
*Thomas R. Hoffmann*

# CONTENTS

## PART FIVE Appendixes 585

# INTRODUCTION

Interest in production and inventory management (PIM) has skyrocketed! In the last decade, membership in the American Production and Inventory Control Society (APICS) has quadrupled, there has been an exponential growth in the number of applicants for its PIM certification, there are a growing number of prosperous consultants in the field, and well-attended PIM seminars have proliferated. The profusion of commercially available PIM software packages, the increased use of computers for PIM, and the increased demand for professionals in industry and the academic community also testify to this rising interest.

What has led to this surge in interest and corresponding investment by corporate management and individuals? Decline in the productivity improvement rate, industries operating at less than full capacity, developments in PIM technology, better educated personnel, and the availability of less expensive and improved information processing have been primary factors. Oliver Wight has noted that, "When the computer came along, the production and inventory manager was suddenly in a position to do some of the things he had never been able to do before."[1] These developments have provided management with the opportunity to have the best of two worlds: a net reduction in capital investment and decreased operating costs. Whereas reducing production costs frequently requires increased equipment investments, improved PIM frequently results in a reduction in inventory investment, lower inventory expenses, and improved equipment utilization. For example, John Anderson and Roger Schroeder found in their survey of 326 companies that implementation of Material Requirements Planning (MRP) increased annual inventory turns from 5.6 to 9.5 times.[2] Larry McClain of the Rawlings Sporting Goods Company reported an inventory reduction of 25 percent while inventory turns were increased from 2.9 to 5.4 times per year by improving both inventory control procedures and warehouse locations.[3] Robert J. Fesmier reported more than a 20 percent improvement in the productivity of several departments through improved work flow

---

[1]Oliver W. Wight, *Production and Inventory Management in the Computer Age*(Boston: Cahners Books, 1974), p. 4.

[2]Roger Schroeder and John Anderson, "A Survey of MRP Implementation Results," *Materials Requirements Planning Conference Proceedings* (APICS Twin Cities Chapter and University of Minnesota, 1978), pp. 6-42. See also Chapter 6 of this book for a treatment of inventory turns.

[3]Larry McClain, "Inventory Management at Rawlings" (APICS Presentation, St. Louis Chapter, February, 1979).

scheduling.[4] Ernest C. Huge reported how the NCR Corporation's plant in San Diego increased inventory turns while meeting schedules by combining Management By Objectives (MBO) and MRP procedures.[5] These examples are typical of the savings many firms have achieved through improved PIM. George Plossl stated it well, "Dramatic benefits have been achieved in small, medium, and large companies. . . . How else can you increase profit and reduce investment at the same time?"[6]

Developments in PIM concepts and techniques have made improvements in PIM feasible. The increased value of inventory, the high cost of capital, and the reduced costs of electronic data processing (EDP) make improved PIM a very attractive management goal.

Management's interest in hiring and rewarding PIM professionals also has fostered both the quantitative and qualitative growth of the profession. The primary conditions nurturing this growth show no indication of abating. In fact, all signs point to continued development of PIM concepts and techniques as well as the cost of capital remaining high. Add to these facts another, namely that there is an ongoing expansion in the types of organizations that are now able to apply these principles and techniques and one can understand the consequent requirement for up-to-date PIM information. It is the purpose of this book to help meet this new and growing need for extensive PIM information in a consolidated fashion.

The generic definition of *production* as the process that converts or transforms inputs into goods or services is well established in economics and management. We will use that broad meaning of the term here and use the term *manufacturing* when referring to part fabrication or assembly. It is not possible to design a precise classification system for all production proesses. There always will be some processes that overlap categories and some categories will contain processes only vaguely similar at best.

The major process types based on the nature of the process are defined for our use as (1) extraction, (2) refinement, (3) manufacturing, (4) distribution, and (5) service. *Extraction* here is the obtaining of materials from their natural source. These processes, such as mining, fishing, etc., usually require heavy concentrations of capital investment, material handling often is paramount, and long-range planning that requires a longer lead time than other processes is often a necessity. *Refinement* describes processes primarily concerned with changing the chemical properties of materials although physical properties also may be changed. Again, here, material handling plays an important role. Tending to be either a continuous flow or a large batch process, it differs from extraction in that the procurement and

[4]Robert J. Fesmier, "Productivity and Manufacturing Control," *Production and Inventory Management* (4th Quarter, 1978), pp. 37-46.

[5]Ernest C. Huge, "How to Obtain Your Inventory Objective," *Production and Inventory Management* (4th Quarter, 1978), pp. 1-16.

[6]George W. Plossl, *Manufacturing Control–The Last Frontier for Profits* (Englewood Cliffs: Prentice-Hall, Inc., 1973), p. 2.

management of raw materials is a major task. In general, refinement means little flexibility because of the specialized nature of the equipment. Quantitative techniques such as linear programming have proved useful in assisting management in selecting the proper mix of raw materials to achieve an output with optimal cost, chemical properties, and demand fulfillment. Network planning and control techniques also have proved very useful in scheduling teardown, cleanup, and restart of refining processes. *Manufacturing* usually is defined as changing the physical form of material. Manufacturing industries have been the primary focus of production and inventory literature because they usually contribute the largest share of the gross national product in a mature industrialized society, and they are the most complex industry to plan and control. Traditionally, *distribution* is defined as the process of changing the location of an item. In some cases, the distribution task may be more substantial and costly than the process generating the final product. Thus, in such situations it is not surprising that the attention management gives to distribution is greater than that given to the apparent primary process. *Service* provides transformations. For example: psychological, aesthetical, physiological, and educational transformations for individuals; informational, organizational, and technological transformations for organizations; and functional and aesthetical transformations for equipment and structures. Although problems of the service industries will not be the primary focus of this book, some examples are included and potential applications will be noted.

The nature of a product, volume of demand, and competitive pressures may warrant production of some items to stock while other items produced, perhaps by the same form, are manufactured and merchandized most profitably if built to order. Whether a product is built to order or to stock will influence the nature of the PIM system; frequently the system must be capable of handling both and evaluating their relative priorities. A firm's product positioning is a major manufacturing policy decision that top management usually makes and must be consistent with its process technology.

Process technologies frequently are categorized as flow, intermittent (job shop), or fixed position production. The manufacture of discrete parts or assemblies using a continuous process is frequently called *repetitive manufacturing* or *mass production* and the manufacture of nondiscrete products using a continuous process sometimes is called *flow production*.[7] Using a continuous process on an intermittent basis constitutes *batch continuous production* and overlaps the continuous flow and intermittent flow classifications. The spatial and administrative organization of similar equipment by functions such as milling, drilling, turning, forging, and assembly is characteristic of a job shop. Work flows from work center to work center with a different type operation performed in each department. Orders may

---

[7]Robert W. Hall, "Repetitive Manufacturing," *Production and Inventory Management* (2d Quarter, 1982), pp. 78-86.

tend to follow a similar path through the plant allowing the location of departments to be based on the dominant operation flow thus minimizing material handling distances. The identifying characteristic of the fixed position (project shop) type process is that material, tools, and personnel are brought to the location where the product is being fabricated. The order control system is applicable to the job shop and fixed position type production. Inventory management is most complex in the job shop. Although important in all types of processes, availability of material is critical in the continuous process and fixed position production for efficient personnel and equipment utilization. Batch flow processes require the application of both order control and flow control principles and techniques.

The objectives of production and inventory management are to contribute to the overall corporate net profit and return on investment by establishing and achieving customer service, inventory investment, and plant utilization objectives consistent with corporate objectives. PIM objectives are attained through the processes of planning, implementing, and controlling PIM decisions over the long-, medium-, and short-range planning horizons.

PIM policies and procedures should be developed and then operationalized through management systems based on decision rules and guidelines consistent with PIM objectives. Furthermore, PIM should measure the success of these policies and management systems. These ideas are developed further throughout the text.

The importance to the firm of achieving PIM objectives is clear. The customer service level influences sales; and as noted earlier, inventory investment and equipment utilization have an impact on capital requirements and operating costs.

Accounting and finance interface with PIM in at least three ways. First, it is with the cooperation of finance and the approval of general management that time-phased budgets are established for aggregate inventory in relation to the production-inventory plan. Second, accounting can be a source of cost data and a collaborator in developing information systems that will provide meaningful cost data to PIM. And third, the plan for physically counting inventory to validate the count and value of inventory on accounting records must be acceptable to accounting as well as inventory management. In fact, the procedure usually must be acceptable to the external auditor as well.

Marketing and PIM interface in several ways. If marketing does not have prime responsibility for physical distribution, it certainly will be a collaborator in decisions concerning the nature of the physical distribution system, the location of warehouses, and the customer service objectives of the system. Although long-range capacity requirements plans are approved by top management, marketing usually develops the long-range forecasts whose production implications must be determined by PIM. Final resolution of the long-range capacity plan is usually a joint marketing and production activity requiring top management approval, and the medium-range master production schedule should have marketing concurrence.

Personnel requirements planning is an activity that brings together Industrial Relations and PIM. If additional personnel with the required skills are to be added to the payroll, it is normally the task of the Personnel Department (viewed here as an Industrial Relations activity) to determine if people with such skills are available, to recruit them, and to participate in their selection. Plans to hire additional personnel, lay off personnel, or schedule overtime in specific departments for an extended period usually must be reviewed with the Personnel Department to assess the relation of these plans to corporate policy, labor relations, and community impact. If a proposed change in requirements is substantial, top management's review also may be required.

The impact of engineering changes on inventory obsolescence and parts availability make communication between Engineering and Production and Inventory Management essential. The timing of changes in product design must reflect not only the desire for product improvement, but also the cost of obsolete inventory or the added costs of expediting changes in purchased parts or fabrication practices. Added inventory and production expenses due to scrap or product modifications may be justified by customer safety requirements, reliable product functioning, or increased sales; but increased costs for these reasons should result from decisions made with marketing and production involvement and not made unilaterally by engineering. In some cases the impact of the change on costs and the schedule may require top management approval.

Many recent presentations and publications have treated the outstanding productivity of Japanese manufacturers. Their accomplishments and the reasons for them help illustrate much of the foregoing. The accomplishments of the Japanese are due to multiple factors including a shortage of space, a lack of natural resources, a post-World War II recognition and acceptance of the need to improve productivity, a heritage that emphasizes the group rather than the individual, and top management and production management approaches that differ from typical Western approaches.

The goals of Japanese top management, for example, usually focus on the long-term growth of the firm, its global market share, and full employment whereas the goals of Western firms frequently focus on short-term growth, quarterly profits, and minimizing labor costs. Japanese top management concerns itself with the budget, fostering and monitoring conditions that support a consensus decision process, and personnel selection.

Japanese manufacturing management strives for minimum inventory, maximum utilization of a continuous (repetitive) flow process, a uniform flow (balanced load) throughout the plant and its suppliers, and relatively small and focused factories. Small factories of fewer than 1,000 employees enhance the probability of a consensus-developing environment. *Focused factories* (plants that specialize in a limited number of tasks) enhance the likelihood of efficient production of a quality product.

The Japanese integrate these factories into a network of plants some of which are subsidiaries of the firm producing the final product while others are independently owned suppliers or subcontractors. Japanese suppliers and their customers work assiduously at developing a relationship of confidence and trust. The customer's production and inventory control system may encompass the supplier and schedule its production. (This practice is followed in the United States in some cases when the outputs of the MRP are sent to suppliers. See Chapter 13.)

Having succeeded in adapting selected ideas from other areas of the world, the Japanese have also added their own innovations. For example, they have not accepted the inevitability of long setup times; instead, they have concentrated on developing tooling and fixtures that are easily removed and replaced. Reduced setup times decrease their production lot sizes, cycle stock for all items, and capacity requirements. Developments such as this help make PIM a lively field of study.

Summarizing, production and inventory management has taken on added importance in the last 10 to 15 years due to improved technology, the cost of capital, and the search for productivity improvements. The willingness of management to invest resources to achieve the improvements now possible in this field has enhanced career opportunities in it.

# PART ONE

## PLANNING

Planning is the first step in management; it consists of selecting measurable objectives and deciding how to achieve those objectives. Planning is a prerequisite for meaningful execution and control as illustrated in Figure P1-1.

FIGURE P1-1
SCHEMATIC RELATIONSHIP OF MANAGEMENT FUNCTIONS

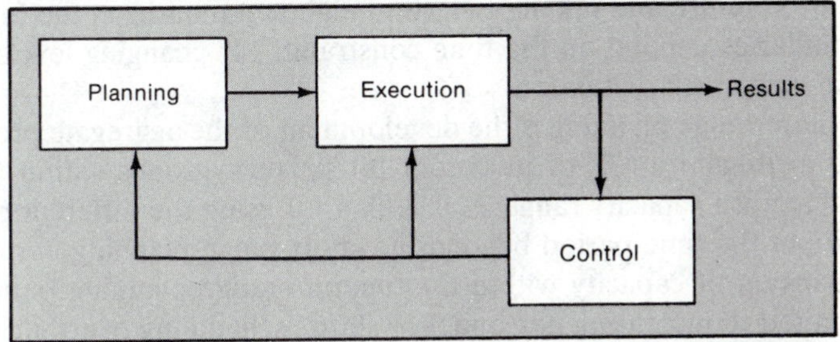


In this schema organization and staffing are viewed as two activities that are planned, executed, and controlled by management. *Execution* is the carrying out (performance) of plans. *Control* is comparing actual results with desired results and deciding whether objectives or methods of execution should be revised. Later in this text, execution and control will be discussed.

Without plans there is no basis for action and no basis for evaluating the results achieved. Planning not only provides the path for action, it also enables management to evaluate the probability of successfully completing the journey. Diligent planning often reveals the pitfalls and shortcomings of decisions which appear to the casual observer as the natural course to follow.

Planning, execution, and control are iterative processes that should occur continuously. Initiation of control does not require that plans actually be executed—only that their results be simulated and evaluated. Thus, at times it is difficult to identify an activity as uniquely planning or uniquely control. However, describing planning and control separately leads to a better understanding of these activities.

Planning activities frequently are classified on the basis of the two related dimensions: (1) the length of the planning horizon and (2) the strategic-tactical dimension.

## LENGTH OF THE PLANNING HORIZON

Plans can be long range, medium range, or short range depending on the length of time from planning to final execution. The time spans of these different ranges depend on the operational environment of a given organization. The period covered by the long-range plan should be equal to or greater than the composite lead time required to implement changes in the product line, to design changes in the manufacturing process, and to acquire new facilities and equipment. In some cases these changes will constitute a change in the direction of the business. This may require ten years or longer for organizations involved in the extraction process where new mines must be developed to increase capacity, or it may be as short as eighteen months for the machine shop where product and process design times are minimal and equipment and facilities are catalog items.

Medium-range planning usually covers a period beginning one to two months in the future and ending twelve to eighteen months in the future. Its exact boundaries depend on the time constraints for changing levels of production in a particular situation.

Medium-range planning is the development of the aggregate production rates and aggregate levels of inventory for product groups within the constraints of a given capacity range. It is a plan for using the different elements of capacity in the time period beyond the short-range planning horizon.

Expansion of capacity within the medium-range planning period typically is limited to increasing personnel or shifts, scheduling overtime, acquiring more efficient tooling, subcontracting, and perhaps adding some types of equipment that can be obtained on short notice.

There is no magical number of days or weeks prior to production at which short-range planning begins. Although detailed schedules and assignments of men and machines to tasks usually do not occur until well within the short-range period, the development of the production schedule frequently bridges the medium- and short-range planning periods. Planning is a continuous activity, and refinement of medium-range forecasts and plans to the detail required in preparing the first draft of a short-range version of the production schedule may take place gradually over a number of weeks.

## STRATEGIC VERSUS TACTICAL PLANS

*Strategic planning* is the process of establishing corporate goals and objectives along with the plans to accomplish them. This process usually includes responses to such questions as: What is the organization's business? What should it be? What is the function of the firm's output? What needs do the company's products and services fill? What are the primary factors that will enable the organization to survive and prosper? What are the quality and pricing level targets? What are profit and return on investment objectives? What is the present position of the firm? What is the company's desired position at some future point in time? What are the milestones on the route from the organization's present position to its long-range strategic goals?

Expanding marketing activities into a new geographic territory, such as the decision of Coca-Coca Bottling Company to enter China, and the entering of a new product or service field, such as the decision of McDonnell Douglas Corporation to market EDP software systems, are two examples of strategic decisions. Building a plant to fabricate components presently purchased is also a strategic decision.

Tactical planning is the process of selecting the methods of achieving organizational objectives. There is no clear demarcation between strategic and tactical plans. The strategic-tactical dimension is a continuum with classification sometimes depending on the vantage point. For example, an organizational decision to diversify is strategic, while a resulting decision to enter a specific market may be tactical with respect to the diversification strategy. However, the decision to enter a specific market normally is classified as strategic, although at a lower level than the general diversification decision. Similarly, the president of a multidivision corporation may view the purchase of a bank of numerically controlled machines by a division as tactical, while the plant manufacturing manager may view the same decision as strategic.

Although production inventory management personnel participate in long-range and strategic planning by specifying the capacity requirements for proposed plans, they devote most of their time and effort to tactical decisions in the medium and short range. While recognizing the strategic impact of some decisions, this book examines production inventory management (PIM) activities in the context of the long-, medium-, and short-range time spans as does most literature in this field.

PIM activities classified by time horizon follow (see Figure P1-2).

Long Range
- Business Forecasting
- Product and Market Planning
- Production Planning
- Resource Planning
- Financial Planning

Medium Range
- Distribution Requirements Planning (DRP)
- Demand Management
- Master Production Scheduling (MPS)
- Rough-Cut Capacity Planning (RCP)
- Material Requirements Planning (MRP)
- Capacity Requirements Planning (CRP)

Short Range
- Demand Management

Final Assembly Scheduling (FAS)
Input/Output Planning and Control
Production Activity Control (PAC)
Purchase Planning and Control

**FIGURE P1-2**
**SCHEMATIC OF PLANNING ACTIVITIES**

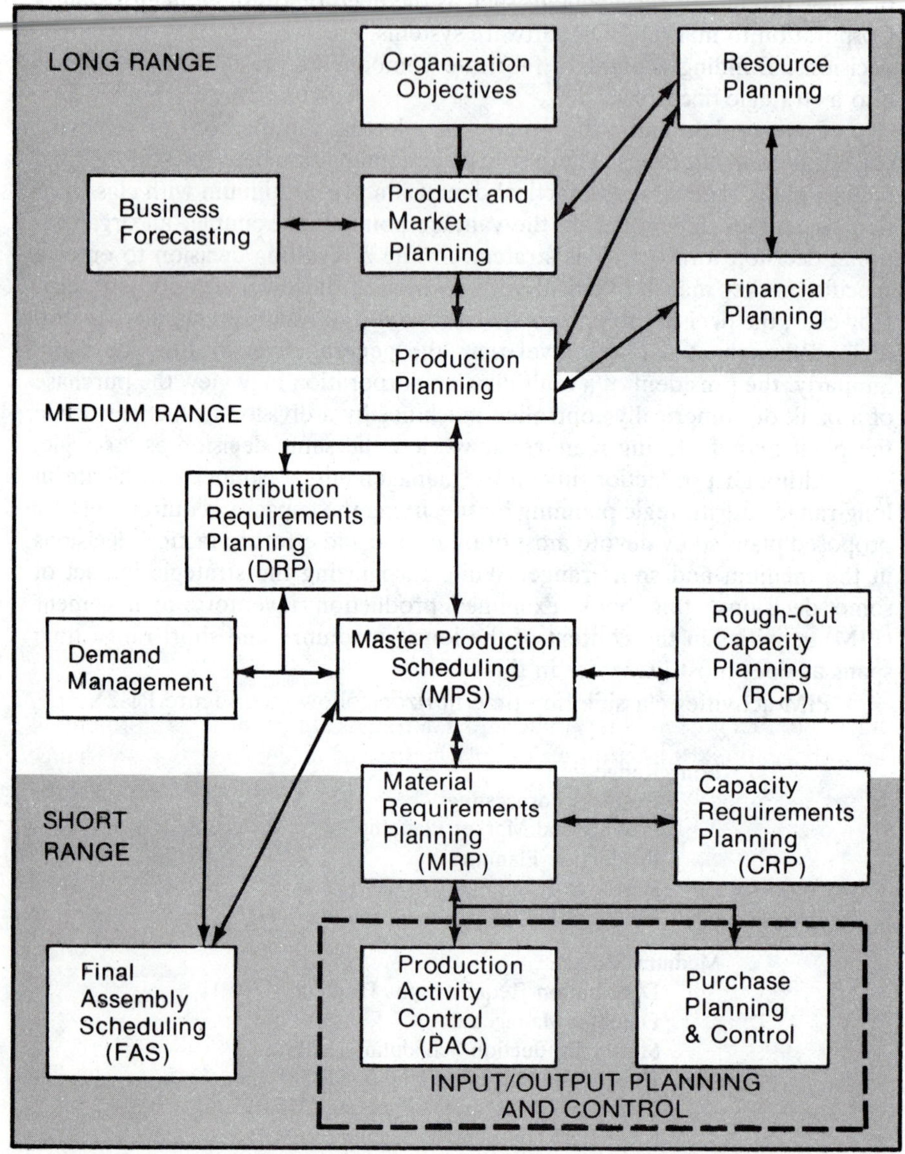


These activities frequently take place in more than one time frame. For example, resource planning for facilities may be required years in advance of production while some equipment can be purchased a few months before needed. In addition, the master production schedule frequently covers both the medium-range and short-range planning periods. A brief overview of these activities is presented here before we examine them in detail in subsequent chapters.

## Long-Range Planning

Long-range planning activities include business forecasting, product and market planning, production planning, resource planning, and financial planning. These activities are interdependent; none is completed until the feasibility of each and the compatibility of all have been established.

**Business Forecasting.** Business forecasting evaluates political, economical, sociological, technological, and competitive factors that will affect the demand patterns to be experienced by a firm's products and the organization's ability to produce.

Top management should assume responsibility for this activity; it is not unusual to have a long-range planning task force reporting directly to the chief executive officer and also to employ the services of external consulting firms that specialize in this activity.

The organization's objectives and the business forecast are the basis for product and market planning.

**Product and Market Planning.** Product and market planning refers here to macrolevel decisions concerning the product lines the company plans to produce, the markets to be served (including the target population and geographic areas), and the levels of demand anticipated for the various product lines. Product line and market planning decisions are explicit commitments to an organizational direction. It usually is difficult in the short run to change them. Organizational growth and prosperity will be influenced substantially by the wisdom of these decisions.

**Production Planning.** Production planning uses the information from product and market planning to plan the aggregate rates of production and the inventory levels by time period for groups of products. In long-range planning output levels are specified in the broadest terms possible: tons, barrels, yards, dollars, and standard man-hours of production. The specificity of product line and product differentiation required at this level depends on the nature of the product and the equipment required to manufacture it. For example, automotive engine blocks usually are machined on a specially designed high-speed, automated or semi-automated line. A line built for the manufacture of four-cylinder engines ordinarily cannot be used to manufacture six-cylinder engines. Thus, in this example, the long-range production plan must separate four- and six-cylinder engine requirements to obtain a valid estimate of facility and equipment requirements. This may be accomplished merely by multiplying the estimated total demand by the anticipated proportion of the various engine sizes.

In the long range and at the far end of the medium planning horizon, it makes sense for plans to be in a production plan broad-gauged format of dollars in inventory, bulk storage requirements, personnel requirements, and work center hours required by product group. Smoothing of production to compensate for varying seasonal demand rates is planned in this time frame.

Different approaches that might be followed successfully in various situations are discussed in Chapter 1, "Long- and Medium-Range Planning." The important point is that it is the production plan which establishes customer service level goals, target inventory levels, size of the backlog, production rates, size of the work force, levels of hiring and firing, and plans for overtime and subcontracting. The production plan can't be a "wish list"; it must not violate capacity constraints.

The production plan spans the long- and medium-range planning horizons; it serves as a basis for medium-range planning. Some organizations refine the plan gradually until at some point it is more of a master production schedule (see Chapter 3, "The Master Production Schedule") than a production plan.

**Resource Planning.** Long-range planning is a complex matter. Product, market, and production planning should be conducted interactively with resource planning. Decisions concerning products, markets, and the output levels should be consistent with planning for facility, equipment, and personnel resources. The availability of facilities, equipment, and personnel depends on the lead time for acquiring the facilities and equipment, the organization's financial strength, technological difficulty of the tasks, and the availability of the required engineering and other type personnel.

**Financial Planning.** Product, market, and production plans frequently require additional resources that in turn require financing. Normal operations require working capital and sales generate income. The financial capability of the organization to carry out the long-range plans should be verified. After the availability of the required resources is assured, a commitment can be made to the production plan.

## Medium-Range Planning

Chapters 1 through 5, 9 and 11 examine the problems of medium-range planning and the techniques available to deal with them. An overview of medium-range planning and its constituent activities of distribution requirements planning, demand management, master production scheduling, rough-cut capacity planning, material requirements planning, and capacity requirements planning are presented in the following paragraphs.

**Distribution Requirements Planning (DRP).** The DRP is the time-phased replenishment needs of branch warehouses summed by period. These requirements are based on the difference between customer demand and the on-hand and in-transit inventory. In a branch warehouse environment the DRP provides a solid link between distribution and manufacturing via the master production schedule.

**Demand Management.** The function of demand management is to determine aggregate demand. This determination reflects forecasts and includes customer orders received, branch warehouse orders, interplant orders, special promotions that might include product or packaging modifications, safety stock requirements, service parts, and the possibility of building inventory for later high volume demand periods. The outputs of demand management are a summation of demand by planning period, grouped in families of products using the same or similar manufacturing facilities and personnel, and the forecast demand for each item by time period.

**Master Production Schedule (MPS).** The MPS is a time phased plan of the items and the quantity of each which the organization intends to build (or purchase) to meet an anticipated Final Assembly Schedule (FAS) and other requirements established by demand management. It is a commitment to meet marketing requirements and to utilize production capacity. The MPS should be approved by production, marketing, and top management.

In some cases the items included on the MPS are the same as those on the FAS; in other cases, the items on the MPS are at a lower level in the bill of materials. This and other aspects of master scheduling are covered in depth in Chapter 3.

The MPS covers anything from the present to one to eighteen months or more in the future. It is used as both a short-range and medium-range planning device. In the medium range the MPS may serve as the production plan or as a more detailed development of that plan. The MPS should be consistent with the production plan. It drives the short-range planning system by providing the input to material requirements planning.

**Rough-Cut Capacity Planning (RCP).** Capacity planning and production planning are interactive at all levels. Before management approves the production plan or the MPS, the organization's ability to carry out the plan must be ascertained. Rough-cut capacity planning includes the following:

1. Determining if sufficient working capital will be available to meet the cash flow requirements of planned inventory and employment levels (a finance function)
2. Verifying that production and warehouse facilities, equipment, and personnel have capacity to handle the plan
3. Determining if key vendors have the required capacity and obtaining commitment of that capacity

If sufficient capacity is not available and cannot be obtained within the planning horizon, the MPS must be altered to fall within capacity constraints.

**Material Requirements Planning (MRP).** Time phased MRP begins with the items listed on the MPS and determines (1) the quantity of all components and materials required to fabricate those items and (2) the time that the components and materials are required.

Time phased MRP is accomplished by "exploding" the bill of materials and offsetting requirements by the appropriate lead times. This process is described in detail in Chapter 4, "Material Requirements Planning."

**Capacity Requirements Planning (CRP).** The time phased requirements obtained from MRP are used in conjunction with the operational sequences of each job and the estimates of time required for each operation to determine the capacity requirements. These requirements are compared to available capacity and corrective action is taken if necessary.

When available capacity is insufficient, the master scheduler reviews relative priorities and, working with marketing and production, makes the difficult decisions required in revising a schedule.

Revisions in the MPS will require the MRP to be rerun and its output used to verify that capacity requirements are now within constraints.

## Short-Range Planning

Short-range planning and control involve both priorities and capacities. Demand management provides the gross requirements' inputs to the MPS, which drives the short-range planning system. The MPS and MRP provide priority planning. The output of the MPS and MRP must be within capacity constraints as determined by CRP. Capacity control is obtained via input/output controls; and priority control is achieved through production activity and purchasing controls.

**Demand Management.** The description of demand management included in medium-range planning is largely applicable in the short-range planning horizon also. Differences in demand management activities for the medium- and short-range planning periods in most organizations include an incorporation in the short range of a greater number of customer orders, the time phasing of order points, a final assembly schedule, and the consumption of all or part of the forecast by orders received.

**Final Assembly Schedule (FAS).** The FAS is a statement of those end item configurations that are to be assembled. In an assembled-to-order environment, the FAS frequently is stated in terms of individual customer orders; and in an assemble-to-stock environment, it is a commitment to provide a specific quantity of different end product catalogued items.

**Input/Output Planning and Control.** Completion of the iterative MPS, MRP, and CRP processes with a schedule of requirements within capacity constraints leads to order release planning. It controls the work-in-process and lead times by planning the flow of work into the shop. If a facility is operating efficiently at full capacity, the release of orders to the shop in terms of workload can be no greater than the output of the plant without increasing work-in-process and likely decreasing efficiency. An increase in capacity via overtime or additional equipment and personnel will make increases possible in both input and output. Order release planning principles and techniques are covered in detail in Chapters 5 and 12.

**Production Activity Control (PAC).** Input/Output control, order sequencing, reporting performance, and determining appropriate corrective action are all part of PAC. The function of order sequencing is to determine that the sequential order in which tasks are to be performed is consistent with their relative priority. A system of establishing valid priorities and updating them in a timely fashion is a necessary prerequisite. Techniques for establishing priorities will be presented in Chapters 5 and 12. Part of the task of the master scheduler (and the shop planner and purchasing agent) is to analyze situations that do not lend themselves to a "priority rule" and to determine the priorities of the jobs involved. Sequencing decisions are executed by order releases and the dispatch list. The *dispatch list,* which includes jobs in or soon to arrive in a department and their relative priorities, is the term commonly used to identify the report used to transmit priorities to the production unit.

Reports of actual departmental output, which reveal actual capacity and anticipated late completion of specific jobs, provide the feedback that "closes the loop." This enables management to exercise control by taking the necessary corrective action.

**Purchase Planning and Control.** Planning and controlling the priorities of purchased items (see Chapter 13) are equally important. Some of the approaches may be different from those used for internal production but the principles are the same.

This overview of planning attempts to reveal the primary functions of the major PIM activities involved in planning capacity and priority. The thrust of planning and controlling capacity and priority is consistent with the discussion of system concepts: goals are established, methods of achieving these objectives are operationalized, actual results are compared with desired results, and corrective action is taken if necessary.

# —1—

# LONG- AND MEDIUM-RANGE PLANNING

As described in the Introduction to Part One, long-range plans concern changes in the product line and the marketing plan, major changes in the manufacturing process, and acquisition or relocation of facilities and equipment. Long-range planning may take place from one to ten or more years prior to execution depending on the nature of the business. Medium-range planning concerns aggregate employment, inventory, and production levels within long-range planning constraints. Although long- and medium-range planning activities can overlap, each has distinct characteristics, and this chapter emphasizes those characteristics.

## LONG-RANGE PLANNING

Long-range planning begins with a corporate strategic plan, a statement of the major goals and objectives of the organization over the next, say, two to ten years with a general plan for achieving those objectives. The strategic plan indicates which product lines, geographic market areas, and services the firm hopes to provide to the public. Development of the strategic plan begins with an analysis of the present position of the firm and its environment. It examines the social, political and economical environment and seeks answers to such questions as: What are the output objectives (products and services) of the organization? What are the quality and pricing level targets? What are profit and return on investment objectives? What is the present position of the firm? What are the financial, marketing, and manufacturing milestones on the route from its present position to its long-range goals?

Questions concerning growth in volume and scope must be addressed. As Peter Drucker[1] has pointed out, all growth is not necessarily good. He noted that some growth is analogous to fat and only adds to the weight that the organization's vital systems must carry. Other growth is analogous to cancer gradually destroying vital functions such as engineering, marketing, and production by dissipating these resources on unrelated tasks, each requiring substantial effort. Desirable growth is that which increases the efficiency of functional activities by adding complementary product lines which utilize present strengths and reduce fixed costs per unit of output.

Ideally such growth should increase the financial strength of the organization, develop personnel and equipment capabilities, and increase the organization's ability to serve present and future markets. Analysis and decisions concerning growth must be made in terms of the unique strengths and weaknesses of each organization. The competitive strategy decision should extend through the manufacturing facilities, processes, and management systems.[2]

It should be noted that a decision to maintain the status quo and not strive for growth in volume, product or market scope, or financial return is also a strategic plan.

Figure 1-1 depicts the major long-range level planning activities and their interaction. Although production and inventory management (PIM) personnel play a major role only in production planning and resource planning, an understanding of their role is enhanced by a discussion of all five activities:

Business Forecasting
Product and Market Planning
Production Planning
Resource Planning
Financial Planning

**FIGURE 1-1**
**SCHEMATIC OF STRATEGIC AND LONG-RANGE PLANNING ACTIVITIES**

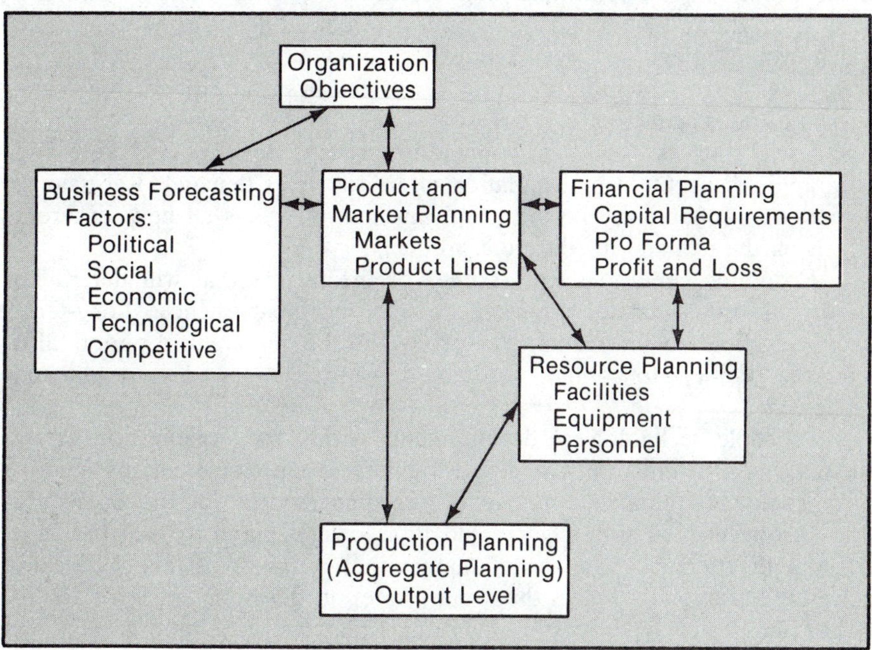

Commitment to a strategic plan does not occur until the long-range planning cycle, including preparation of the business forecast, product and market planning, production planning, resource planning, and financial planning, has been completed.

## Business Forecasting

Long-range planning begins with a business forecast that reflects the total predicted business environment including political, social, economic, technological, and competitive factors. In some organizations preparing this forecast is a formal process conducted by an economic planning, business research, or marketing department; in other organizations it is an informal process carried out by top management.

Political developments affect not only sources of supply for raw materials but also productive capacity in foreign countries. The impact of political developments on the availability of petroleum products is clear to even the casual observer. A reduction in Mideast oil exports can place a constraint on the production of many products and also increase consumer demand for products such as diesel automobiles and insulating materials.

The firm should attempt to anticipate formal action by executive, legislative, and regulatory bodies at the local and national levels. What is the probability of price and wage controls being in effect one to five years from today? What specific actions are federal agencies likely to take which would affect an organization? Is the United States Congress or State Legislative Assembly likely to revise tax laws or expand (limit) the powers of their agencies?

Social factors, such as population growth, the age bracket, and geographic distribution of population affect customer demand. Recessions, depressions, inflationary periods, and business upswings all have different effects on the demand for different products.

Economic conditions are another of the factors that will determine an organization's capital structure two to five years hence. Long-term debt reduction commitments and profits in the intervening period also influence ability to obtain additional capital required for planned expansion.

Probable technological developments within the organization or by competitors also must be assessed. Modularized electronic circuits, microwave cooking equipment and video recording devices for the home are three products that not only created their own demand pattern but also affected the demand patterns of many other items. Will the electrically powered automobile reach the same state of development and acceptance? This is the type question long-range planners in some organizations are asking in the first half of the 80's.

Few of these issues are easy to confront. Nevertheless, solving too many of these problems incorrectly can lead to disaster. In most cases a sensitivity analysis can be performed and contingency plans developed. For example, although the long-range planning task force might base product line demand forecasts on a most likely prediction—moderate long-run economic prosperity combined with an inflation rate of approximately 10 percent—the impact of the other possible combinations of inflation and economic growth levels should be examined also. Answers to such *What if?* type questions will reveal how sensitive predicted outcomes are to vagaries in the total business environment and resulting demand patterns. Contingency plans can be developed then to the degree suggested by the sensitivity of results to conditions. Some firms use computerized, corporate planning, simulation models to assist in this phase of analysis. [3]

The output of the business forecast is a statement of the aggregate annual demand anticipated by product groups, including a forecast of demand for products that may be added to the product line at a future date. The business forecast also may differentiate between new and established market areas, and it is not unusual for these forecasts to be stated in a statistical fashion. They usually are made for each quarter of years 1 and 2 and for each year thereafter.

## Product and Market Planning

The demarcation between business forecasting and product and market planning is not easily discernible in all cases, and information flows in both directions. Using the inputs received from the business forecast, product and market planning determines which markets and products are viable in terms of demand and organizational objectives.

The establishment of market goals and objectives begins with the analysis of corporate objectives, the business forecast, and product life cycles. Although the life spans of different products vary, the demand for all products goes through the stages of growth, stability, and decay; the lengths of these stages for a particular product line are determined by public acceptance, social and economic conditions, and the rate of development of competing technical and styling innovations. For example, a product in the decay stage of its life may be buoyed slightly by healthy economic conditions and merchandising; but, unless it is redesigned, its demand is likely to decrease at an increasing rate. By the same token, the right new product at the propitious moment in a technological-social sense may experience greater demand than economic conditions alone would warrant. This type of analysis leads to recommendations concerning the development of new product lines and the phasing out of some existing products.

Final product line and market planning decisions are not made until the long-range planning loop is closed by verification of manufacturing and financial feasibility as illustrated in Figure 1-1.

The product and market plan is a list of the product lines the company plans to produce, the markets to be served, including the target population and geographic areas, and the levels of demand anticipated for the various product lines.

## Production Planning

*Production planning* (sometimes called *aggregate planning*) is the process of establishing the level of output and the inventory levels by broad product groups usually in monthly or quarterly buckets covering at least a year. It is general management's control on aggregate factors such as the size of the labor force, the aggregate inventory level, resource requirements, and meeting customer demand.

The production plan is specified in the broadest terms possible given the data requirements for resource requirements planning. Terms such as tons, barrels, yards, dollars, and standard man-hours of production are used frequently. The specificity of product line and product differentiation required at this level depends on the nature of the product and the equipment required to manufacture it. In the manufacture of gears, for example, differentiation must be made between types, such as spur and bevel gears, which require different manufacturing equipment.

The objective of the production plan is to provide sufficient finished goods by period to meet the marketing plan objectives while staying within financial and production capacity constraints. When demand varies from period to period, planning production to exceed demand in one period can provide inventory to fill excessive demand in a following period. The following model defines the relationship of inventory, production, and shipments.

$$\text{Ending Inventory} = \text{Beginning Inventory} + \text{Production} - \text{Shipments}$$

Table 1-1 illustrates a production plan for three product groups. The number of product groups used to encompass all products should be no greater than that required to determine resource requirements. Individual production plans may be required for divisions or plants within a firm. As the production period approaches, planning becomes more refined and a Master Production Schedule (MPS) is developed. The MPS is a statement of all anticipated manufacturing by planning period (see Chapter 3). In some firms the production plan is developed in greater detail into what is called a medium-range plan and later refined into an MPS. In others, the production plan is unfolded directly into the MPS at some point, nine months prior to execution, for example; while in some firms the production plan and the MPS are one and the same. The approach selected by a specific organization

**TABLE 1-1**
**24-MONTH PRODUCTION PLAN**
**PRODUCT GROUPS A, B, AND C**

| | Month | | | | | | | Quarter | | | | | |
|---|---|---|---|---|---|---|---|---|---|---|---|---|---|
| **Period** | **Sept.** | **Oct.** | **Nov.** | **Dec.** | **Jan.** | **Feb.** | **March** | **2** | **3** | **4** | **1** | **2** | **3** |
| **Weeks/Period*** | **5** | **4** | **4** | **5** | **4** | **4** | **5** | **13** | **13** | **13** | **13** | **13** | **13** |
| **Prod. Days/Period** | | **20** | **18** | **22** | **19** | **19** | **25** | **64** | **63** | **60** | **63** | **64** | **63** |
| Group A | | | | | | | | | | | | | |
| Prod. Rate: Units/Day | | 36 | 36 | 36 | 36 | 36 | 36 | 36 | 40 | 40 | 40 | 40 | 40 |
| Production | | 720 | 648 | 792 | 684 | 684 | 900 | 2304 | 2520 | 2400 | 2520 | 2560 | 2520 |
| Shipments | | 700 | 760 | 850 | 500 | 500 | 875 | 2500 | 2500 | 2300 | 2600 | 2700 | 2700 |
| Ending Inventory | 180 | 200 | 88 | 30 | 214 | 398 | 423 | 227 | 247 | 347 | 267 | 127 | −53 |
| Group B | | | | | | | | | | | | | |
| Prod. Rate: Units/Day | | 12 | 12 | 12 | 12 | 4 | 4 | 4 | 4/12 | 12 | 12/4 | 4 | 4/12 |
| Production | | 240 | 216 | 264 | 228 | 76 | 100 | 256 | 444 | 720 | 404 | 256 | 444 |
| Shipments | | 250 | 300 | 350 | 250 | 60 | 60 | 180 | 370 | 900 | 370 | 180 | 370 |
| Ending Inventory | 250 | 240 | 156 | 70 | 48 | 64 | 104 | 180 | 254 | 74 | 108 | 184 | 258 |
| Group C | | | | | | | | | | | | | |
| Prod. Rate: Units/Day | | 8 | 8 | 8 | 8 | 20 | 20 | 20 | 22/9 | 9 | 9/22 | 22 | 22/9 |
| Production | | 160 | 144 | 176 | 152 | 380 | 500 | 1280 | 1034 | 540 | 1060 | 1408 | 1034 |
| Shipments | | 110 | 115 | 120 | 180 | 400 | 460 | 1340 | 1060 | 500 | 1100 | 1450 | 1000 |
| Ending Inventory | 50 | 100 | 129 | 185 | 157 | 137 | 177 | 117 | 91 | 131 | 91 | 49 | 83 |

Production Rates:

Group A—36 units per day for first three quarters, 40 units per day thereafter; level production throughout the year; rate change due to long-term positive demand trend.

Group B—12 units per day September through January and 4 units per day February through August due to seasonal sales.

Group C—8 units per day September through January and 20 units per day February through August. These rates increase to 9 and 22 units per day respectively due to long-term positive demand trend.

*The weeks per month in each quarter are assigned arbitrarily as 4,4,5. For example, April and May have 4 weeks, June has 5. The plant does not close for vacation.

depends upon the diversity of its product lines, manufacturing processes, and data processing capabilities.

The production plan is a final output of long-range planning. Commitment to a given plan should not be made until the planned availability of the required financial and production capacity resources is confirmed. This check constitutes control and is known as *closing the loop* because it closes the long-range planning and control cycle (see Figure 1-1). It ties together financial and operational planning, linking marketing, financial, resource and business planning activities. Thus, planned dollar, work force, and facility requirements are related directly to planned production and to forecast sales.

## Resource Planning (Capacity Planning)

New products may require additional personnel such as design and process engineers as well as additional manufacturing capacity. Geographic expansion of the market usually requires additional distribution facilities, and an increased aggregate volume does increase manufacturing capacity requirements.

The determination of personnel requirements in areas such as engineering and marketing is the task of the management of those functional areas. Calculation of manufacturing capacity requirements is the point at which PIM usually enters long-range planning while distribution capacity requirements may be calculated by marketing, PIM, or a joint task force of those two departments.

The necessary inputs for determining long-range manufacturing capacity requirements are:

1. The long-range production plan
2. The manufacturing processes for the different product groups
3. Work center efficiency and utilization
4. Identification of the bottleneck work centers

Capacity requirements should be determined in units applicable to the mix of products to be produced in a facility. The unit of measure may be pieces, gallons, tons, standard work hours, feet, etc. *Actual* capacity may be measured by observing and recording the output of a facility over a typical production period. In some cases recording output over a four- or five-week period may be sufficiently representative to use the weekly average of that period as an estimate of actual weekly capacity. For example, consider the case of a numerically controlled milling machine work center with the output listed for a recent five-week production period as shown at the top of page 17.

These data indicate that actual capacity is 145 standard hours per week. We would want to be sure that these five weeks were typical with regard to characteristics such as job difficulty, setup time, machine downtime, operator

| Week | Output in Standard Hours |
|---|---|
| 1 | 154 |
| 2 | 141 |
| 3 | 138 |
| 4 | 148 |
| 5 | 144 |

Total = 725 Standard Hours
Average = 725 ÷ 5 = 145 Standard Hours

absenteeism, and material shortages. Observations of output over a longer period would increase the accuracy of this measure which can be expressed as an interval estimate of the population mean. For example, the five sample data points in the above illustration have a standard deviation of 6.25. Based on this sample then, actual output should average 145 standard hours and fall between 132.75 and 157.25 (plus or minus two standard deviations) approximately 95 percent of the time.

*Calculated* capacity[1] is equal to the product of available machine time, average work center efficiency, and average work center utilization. Take the case of the work center with five machines each available 40 hours per week, an average efficiency of .80 of standard, and an average utilization of 85 percent:

$$\text{Calculated Capacity} = 5 \times 40 \times .80 \times .85 = 136 \text{ Standard Hours}$$

*Efficiency* is a measure of the standard hours of output produced per operating hour; *utilization* is a measure of the percentage of working hours a machine is being set up or run. Downtime for maintenance or repair, and idle time due to lack of parts or operator absenteeism are included in the nonutilization percentage. If the efficiency and utilization factors of a work center are based on observations of work center performance and not subjective estimates, calculated capacity should approximate the true available capacity. If actual and calculated capacity for the same work center differ widely, either the period during which measurements of actual capacity were made was not representative or one or both of the work center efficiency and utilization factors are inaccurate.

Both actual and calculated capacity, as mentioned, pertain to available capacity. Such information usually is known at the time capacity requirements are calculated. Capacity requirements and available capacity should be expressed in the same terms for purposes of comparison. As mentioned

[1] *Nominal, standing,* or *rated capacity* are terms also used to refer to capacity calculated indirectly from manufacturing data. See the APICS Certification Program Study Guide: Capacity Planning and Control, p. 6.

previously, capacity should be measured in units common to all products processed by a facility. Measures such as pounds, gallons, feet, and pieces provide for straightforward comparison of required and available capacity. Measuring required capacity in standard work hours, a method used in many organizations, involves multiplying the product volume by standard time requirements for each operation.

In many situations there are certain facilities whose capacity historically has been far greater than required capacity, and examination of future requirements is only necessary when substantial changes in volume occur. There also are *bottlenecks*: work centers where available capacity often has been inadequate or barely adequate. It makes sense to determine the required capacity for these work centers first, since they are the most likely constraints on output. In fact, manufacturing requirements planning is another activity in which the ABC Principle (see Chapter 6) can be applied. Application of the ABC Principle in this case would involve classifying facilities on the basis of their historical ratio of required to available capacity. The attention devoted to each classification would then be directly related to the magnitude of that ratio.

Although medium-range planning examines the smoothing of production under seasonal demand conditions, long-range planning must recognize this factor. In such cases it is not unusual for available capacity to be more than sufficient in the slack production periods and insufficient, at least for some work centers, during high production periods. In such cases requirements planning should concentrate on analysis of the required to available capacity match during high output periods.

For example, forecast output for a group of products peaks in the third quarter at a weekly rate of 3,000 units. Work Center 13 is the only bottleneck work center through which this group of items is produced; all other work centers have sufficient capacity. The product group consists of five items with a weighted average standard time of 1.25 minutes calculated in the following manner.

| I | II | III | IV |
|---|---|---|---|
| Item | Proportion of Total Group Volume | Work Center 13 Standard Time | (II) × (III) |
| A | .45 | 1.28 | .576 |
| B | .20 | 1.24 | .248 |
| C | .16 | 1.10 | .176 |
| D | .11 | 1.30 | .143 |
| E | .08 | 1.34 | .107 |
| Total | 1.00 | | 1.25 |

Multiplying the average standard time by the weekly group volume, 1.25 × 3,000 (3,750 standard minutes) gives the required capacity of Work

Center 13 for this product group during the peak production period. If this is the only product group produced in Work Station 13, the next step is to compare this 62.5 standard hours required to the standard hours available. However, this is often not the case.

Any number of product groups may be processed in a work center. The efficiency and utilization rates of the work center may be the same for all groups but that is unusual. When it does occur, the standard hours required can be summed for all groups and compared with the available capacity. When efficiency and utilization rates are not the same for all groups, the standard hour capacity requirements of each group is converted to clock hours and summed for all groups. This total then is compared with available work center clock hours. Conversion of standard time to clock hours is accomplished by dividing standard time by the efficiency and utilization rates applicable to the product group. Continuing with the previous example, Work Center 13 operates on an incentive plan, and efficiency on production of this product group is approximately 110 percent and utilization is 85 percent. Thus,

$$\begin{aligned}\text{Actual Required Clock Hours} &= \frac{\text{Standard Hours}}{\text{Efficiency Rate} \times \text{Utilization Rate}}\\ &= 62.5 \div (1.10 \times .85)\\ &= 66.8 \text{ hours.}\end{aligned}$$

In determining actual clock hours, one should be sure that the setup time is included either in the 15 percent nonutilization rate as a separate category or in the required production time.

Comparison of required capacity to that which is available enables PIM to specify what additional work force personnel, facilities, and equipment, if any, are required to produce the planned output. The time normally required to obtain these resources determines the minimum length of the long-range planning horizon.[2]

## Financial Planning

Once the manufacturing feasibility of the production plan is verified and additional manufacturing resources, if any, specified, the financial feasibility of the plan must be evaluated. Additional facilities and equipment, hiring and training personnel, and opening new markets require capital. Increased output requires additional working capital for added inventory and labor.

The controller's office or a special financial planning group working in concert with top management usually makes this analysis. If the necessary

[2]See Chapter 3, "Master Production Scheduling," and Chapter 5, "Short-Range Planning," for discussions of rough-cut capacity planning and capacity requirements planning.

capital is not likely to be available, marketing and production plans must be modified. The manufacturing and financial feasibility of the revised marketing and production plans must be checked. This cycle must be repeated until the marketing and production plans are feasible in terms of all required resources.

# MEDIUM-RANGE PLANNING

The medium-range production plan is a common intermediate step between the production plan and the master production schedule. It may be a distinct activity at a point in time six to 18 months prior to production or it may be a refinement in the production plan that takes place gradually over a number of months. Whereas long-range planning involves decisions which take a long time to implement or undo, medium-range planning involves capacity modification decisions usually concerning such things as employment levels, overtime budgets, production rates, inventory levels, subcontracting, additional tooling, allocation of facilities to product lines, and the purchase of short lead time equipment for bottleneck centers.

Three major tasks face production and inventory management in the medium range.

1. Planning aggregate inventory and production levels to attain a desired level of customer service and to have the sum of the costs of carrying inventory and those of changing production rates approach a minimum. This is called the *aggregate planning problem*.
2. Dissaggregation, planning the production rates and inventory levels for the different product groups. The sum of these values must be equal to the aggregate values.
3. Planning the allocation of the different production resources among the product groups to be produced.

By definition an *aggregate plan* is the totality of all production plans for the various product groups an organization produces. Monetary units, dollars for example, are the only meaningful method of corporate aggregate planning in a large complex organization producing many different types of products. Thus, individual aggregate production plans usually are made across divisions or plants producing similar products allowing each plan to be stated in such terms as units, pounds, and gallons. These plans then can be converted to dollars and production, inventory, and demand aggregated across all divisions.

The sum of the production requirements and the changes in inventory levels of the individual plans must agree with the corporate aggregate plan. If this is not the case, adjustments must be made either in the aggregate plan or in the plans for the specific product groups; the whole must equal the sum of the parts.

Not all plants have the same capacity; and all products cannot be produced in each facility. The capacity of some plants varies by product line; the aggregate plan must be allotted by time period to the different facilities available. Not only must the aggregate plan fall within available aggregate capacity, but the assignment of product families to different facilities must be consistent with both the technological and capacity load constraints of individual facilities.

Further disaggregation, scheduling the production, and planning the inventory levels of individual items takes place in the short range or in the gray area between the middle and short-range periods. These activities are described in Chapter 5, "Short-Range Planning," and in the chapters discussing inventory management.

In some firms the same or similar forms are used for production planning in all three time horizons. Details and refinements are added to the long-range production plan as it gradually becomes the medium-range aggregate plan which in turn is developed gradually into a full-blown Master Production Schedule (see Chapter 3). The lines of demarcation between the long- and medium-range plans and between the medium- and short-range plans are not precise.

Events do not always unfold as anticipated; abrupt changes in the cost of energy, the actions of competitors, and shifts in political and economic climates can alter demand patterns considerably. In addition, opportunities due to research and design developments or the availability of existing production or distribution facilities at the right price can take place unexpectedly. Under such conditions a decision might be made six months or less prior to production and have long-term, strategic significance for the firm.

## The Aggregate Planning Problem

Not only does the demand for snow blowers and lawn mowers follow a seasonal pattern; but furniture, appliances, automobiles, clothing, small tools, and many other items have demand patterns which reflect seasonal variations rather consistently year after year. Variations in the demand for consumer goods generate varying demand for the raw materials, components, and supplies used in their manufacture. Coping with these variations in demand is one of the most challenging problems confronting manufacturing management. The economic consequences of planning aggregate production and inventory levels can be substantial.

Aggregate planning is the dominant activity at the far end of the medium-range period where the long and medium ranges overlap. In fact, the argument can be made that aggregate planning begins in the long range with the development of the production plan. We do not disagree with that view, especially when production requirements must be forecast five to ten years in the future to calculate resource requirements. However, the development of a production plan, which addresses the problem of smoothing production output and inventory in response to anticipated varying demand per period for specific product lines, usually does not take place more than 18 to 24 months prior to production, and takes place most frequently 12 months prior to production.

Although a uniform production rate is desirable to minimize production costs, seldom is customer demand a nice steady rate. Demand tends to fluctuate from week to week and month to month due to seasonal and business factors. Maintaining a steady production rate while demand varies increases inventories and their carrying costs. The objective of the aggregate plan is to fill a desired percentage of customer requirements while minimizing the sum of production rate change and inventory carrying costs.

Before examining the costs affecting these decisions, let us look at some typical situations. Figure 1-2, Typical Aggregate Monthly Demand Patterns, represents three typical situations: relatively stable demand, one high and one low demand cycle annually, and dual high and low cycles annually. Other seasonal variations in demand are possible, but examination of these three patterns will provide a basis for studying the concepts and techniques useful for aggregate planning under all situations (see Chapter 9).

The challenge in the case of a single period of high demand is also one of product planning: finding and marketing products that will complement the present line and utilize capacity in the off season. For example, some lawn mower companies have been successful in marketing snow blowers while swimsuit manufacturers have entered the ski apparel business. Development of complementary product lines frequently helps considerably but a dual high and low requirements production planning type problem frequently remains. In addition, not all firms are successful in the search for product lines to balance requirements and available capacity.

**FIGURE 1-2**
**TYPICAL MONTHLY AGGREGATE DEMAND PATTERNS**

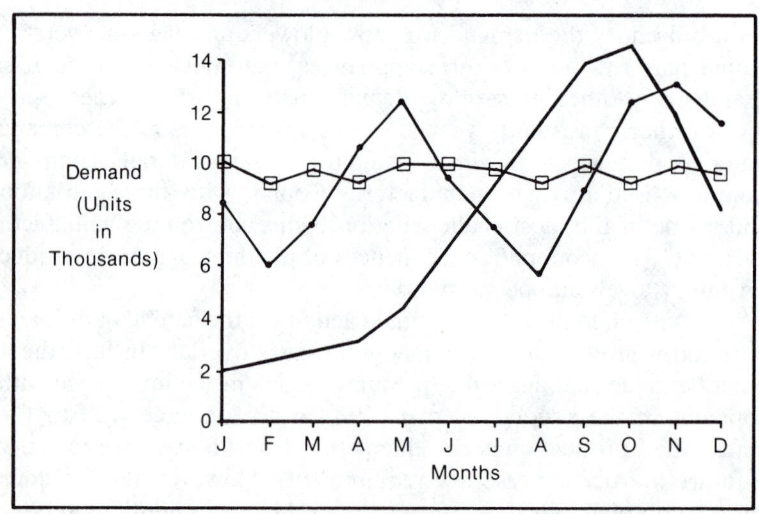

Demand may be smoothed somewhat by offering price reductions or deferred payments for purchases made during periods of low demand.

There are two basic or pure approaches to solving the aggregate planning problem. One possibility, the *chase strategy,* is to have sufficient capacity and flexibility to allow production output to be related directly to demand and thus vary widely. In some cases, such as agriculture, this is a necessity. Harvesting must take place when the crop is ready. Real Christmas trees must be cut shortly before Christmas to avoid deterioration. However, this usually is not economical when deterioration is not a factor.

The other extreme possibility, the *level production strategy,* is to have the same production rate throughout the year and have inventory absorb variations in demand as illustrated in Figure 1-3. This makes sense when demand is relatively stable; but following this approach in some cases, such as the manufacture of artificial Christmas trees, would incur extremely high inventory carrying costs.

The rational choice usually lies somewhere between the two extreme approaches. Figure 1-4, Seasonal Demand with Changing Production Levels,

**FIGURE 1-3**
**INVENTORY VERSUS TIME,**
**SEASONAL DEMAND, AND LEVEL PRODUCTION**

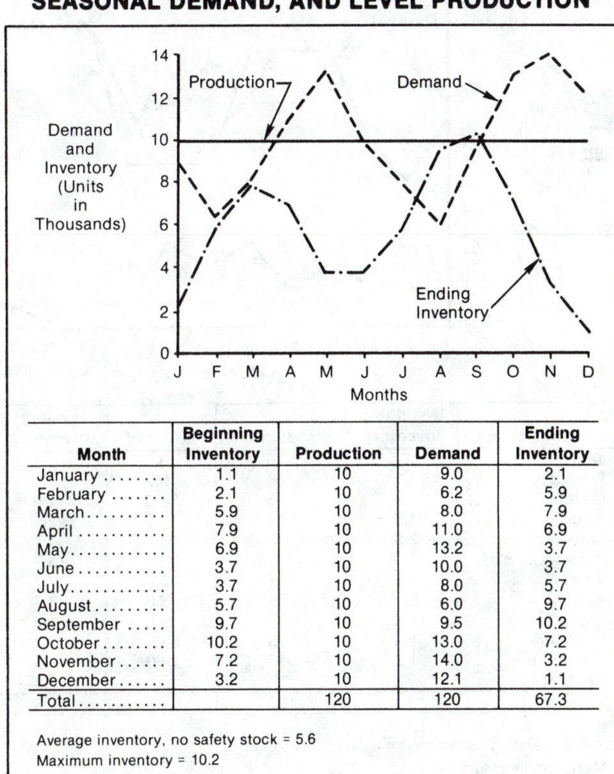


| Month | Beginning Inventory | Production | Demand | Ending Inventory |
|---|---|---|---|---|
| January ........ | 1.1 | 10 | 9.0 | 2.1 |
| February ....... | 2.1 | 10 | 6.2 | 5.9 |
| March.......... | 5.9 | 10 | 8.0 | 7.9 |
| April ........... | 7.9 | 10 | 11.0 | 6.9 |
| May............ | 6.9 | 10 | 13.2 | 3.7 |
| June ........... | 3.7 | 10 | 10.0 | 3.7 |
| July............ | 3.7 | 10 | 8.0 | 5.7 |
| August......... | 5.7 | 10 | 6.0 | 9.7 |
| September ..... | 9.7 | 10 | 9.5 | 10.2 |
| October........ | 10.2 | 10 | 13.0 | 7.2 |
| November...... | 7.2 | 10 | 14.0 | 3.2 |
| December...... | 3.2 | 10 | 12.1 | 1.1 |
| Total........... | | 120 | 120 | 67.3 |

Average inventory, no safety stock = 5.6
Maximum inventory = 10.2

illustrates a compromise solution. Comparison of Figures 1-3 and 1-4 reveals the different ending inventories resulting from a level production rate and from a production rate change each quarter. The demand is the same in both cases. Maximum inventory is 10,200 units, and average inventory is 5,600 units with level production (Figure 1-3); changing the production rate quarterly (Figure 1-4) results in a maximum inventory of 3,700 units and an average inventory of 1,860 units. The inventory carrying cost savings (see Chapter 6) attained by varying the production rate are counterbalanced, at least to some extent, by the costs of changing the production rates. This is the problem that the aggregate planner faces. He or she must plan periodic (usually monthly) production rates that meet demand requirements and which also minimize the sum of inventory carrying costs and production rate change costs. Computer planning models can be very helpful in planning complex situations involving many products, plants, processes, distribution centers, and changing demand.[3, 4]

**FIGURE 1-4**
**INVENTORY VERSUS TIME,**
**SEASONAL DEMAND, AND CHANGING PRODUCTION LEVELS**

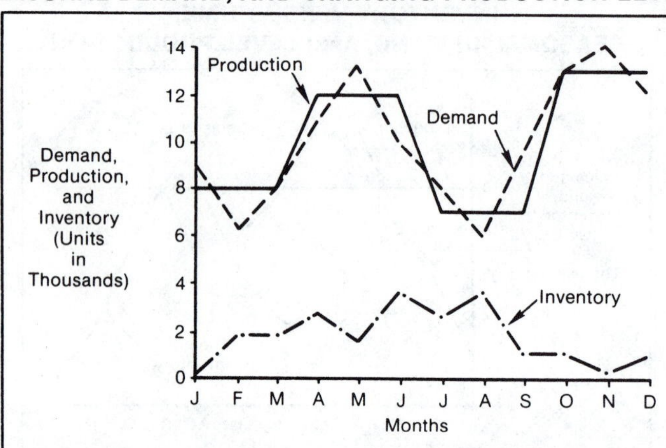


| Month | Beginning Inventory | Production | Demand | Ending Inventory |
|---|---|---|---|---|
| January ........ | 1.1 | 8 | 9.0 | .1 |
| February ....... | .1 | 8 | 6.2 | 1.9 |
| March.......... | 1.9 | 8 | 8.0 | 1.9 |
| April ........... | 1.9 | 12 | 11.0 | 2.9 |
| May............ | 2.9 | 12 | 13.2 | 1.7 |
| June........... | 1.7 | 12 | 10.0 | 3.7 |
| July............ | 3.7 | 7 | 8.0 | 2.7 |
| August......... | 2.7 | 7 | 6.0 | 3.7 |
| September ..... | 1.2 | 7 | 9.5 | 1.2 |
| October........ | 1.2 | 13 | 13.0 | 1.2 |
| November...... | 1.2 | 13 | 14.0 | .2 |
| December...... | .2 | 13 | 12.1 | 1.1 |
| Total........... | | 120 | 120 | 22.3 |

Average ending inventory, no safety stock = 1.86
Maximum inventory = 3.7

## Controlling the Aggregate Plan

Comparing actual cumulative demand and production with forecast demand and planned production enables us to determine if the situation is under control. Either unexpected high demand or actual production substantially below the plan will result in insufficient inventories to fill all orders during subsequent peak demand periods. Unusually low demand or production exceeding the plan can result in excessive inventory. Tabulating and plotting actual results enables us to determine if the spread between planned and actual requires remedial action.

Figure 1-5(A) illustrates a situation in which demand for the initial periods is below the forecast, production is as planned, and inventories are becoming excessive. Management must decide if the low demand levels will continue or if purchases have been postponed and will increase in the future.

**FIGURE 1-5**
**ENDING INVENTORY AND CUMULATIVE DEMAND VERSUS PRODUCTION PERIOD**

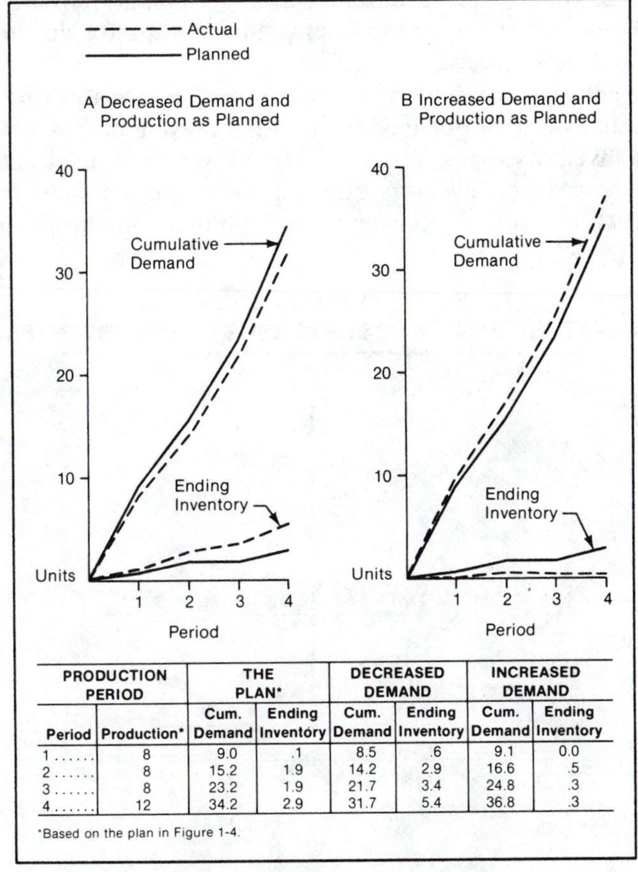


| PRODUCTION PERIOD | | THE PLAN* | | DECREASED DEMAND | | INCREASED DEMAND | |
|---|---|---|---|---|---|---|---|
| Period | Production* | Cum. Demand | Ending Inventory | Cum. Demand | Ending Inventory | Cum. Demand | Ending Inventory |
| 1 ...... | 8 | 9.0 | .1 | 8.5 | .6 | 9.1 | 0.0 |
| 2 ...... | 8 | 15.2 | 1.9 | 14.2 | 2.9 | 16.6 | .5 |
| 3 ...... | 8 | 23.2 | 1.9 | 21.7 | 3.4 | 24.8 | .3 |
| 4 ...... | 12 | 34.2 | 2.9 | 31.7 | 5.4 | 36.8 | .3 |

*Based on the plan in Figure 1-4.

Figure 1-5(B) depicts a situation in which demand has exceeded the forecast for the first few periods, production is as planned, and inventories are precariously low. They are insufficient to meet the forecast peak demand in the immediate future. Management must decide if this increased demand will continue or if purchases were made early and demand in the immediate future will be less than forecast.

## Aggregate Planning Decision Costs

The two major cost categories involved in the aggregate planning decision are the costs of inventory and the costs associated with production rate changes.

**Inventory Costs.** Building inventory for later periods in which anticipated demand exceeds planned production results in inventory carrying costs. These costs, which are described in detail in Chapter 6, include the cost of storage, capital invested, insurance, taxes and the possibility of deterioration or obsolescence. In addition to different average monthly inventory carrying costs, different plans require different storage capacity due to different maximum inventory levels.

Although it is difficult to calculate inventory costs exactly, sufficient accuracy usually can be obtained for decision making purposes. Figure 1-6, Aggregate Inventory Costs versus Inventory Investment, depicts the general nature of the costs of inventory affecting the aggregate planning decision. Carrying costs increase at a constant rate from that point at which inventory

**FIGURE 1-6**
**AGGREGATE INVENTORY COSTS VERSUS INVENTORY INVESTMENT**

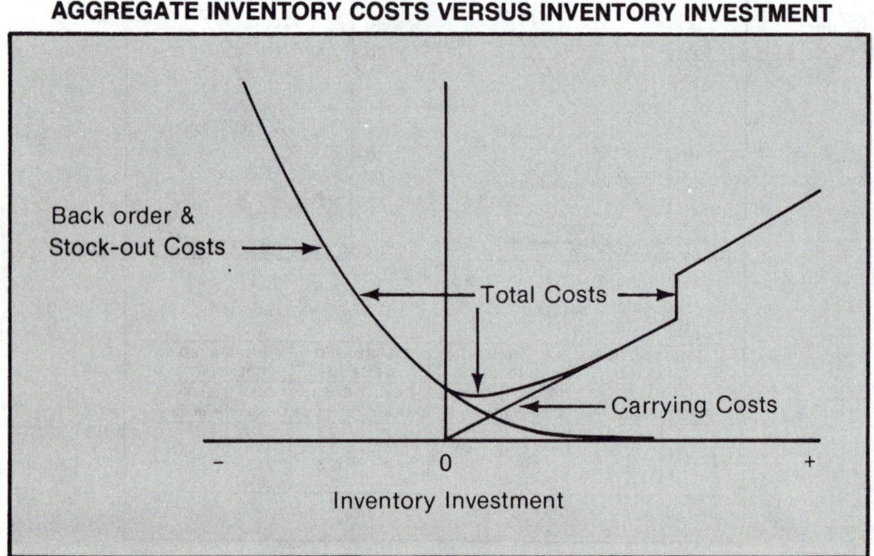

exists. Discontinuities occur at quantities at which storage capacity must increase.

Increasing inventory beyond certain points in some situations requires increases in storage capacity beyond that available. There may be increases in storage facilities and equipment, administrative capabilities, or capital costs. The latter occurs when debt limits are exceeded and interest rates are increased due to the altered capital structure of the organization. Figures 1-3 and 1-4 demonstrate the possibility of different maximum inventory requirements given different production plans with the same demand pattern. The maximum inventory level is 10,200 units in one case and 3,700 units in the other. If inventory storage capacity is less than that required for 10,200 units, the aggregate plan with the higher maximum inventory will require added investment in equipment and facilities or the renting of storage facilities.

Figure 1-6 depicts increased inventory capacity costs as a one-time expense, a step function. This is reasonable for the incremental jumps in facility or administrative costs. However, an increase in cost of capital or renting additional capacity would be reflected more accurately by a carrying cost line with a greater slope and no step increase.

As discussed in Chapter 6, "The Introduction to Inventory Management," the magnitude of back order or stock-out costs depends on many factors including variation in demand and safety stock level in addition to the inventory held above the safety stock level.

The graph in Figure 1-6 represents a *balanced* aggregate inventory condition. If the inventory were out of balance, containing relatively large quantities of some items and few or none of the other items, the worst of two worlds would exist: both back order and carrying costs would be high. Linear programming, goal programming, and simulation (described later) can provide guidance in these situations—if not the answer.

**Production Rate Change Costs.** The total cost of changing the production rate is not minor either. Hiring and training new employees is expensive. New employees usually require more supervision than experienced employees; in general they are more susceptible to accidents, more likely to generate scrap, and generally less productive. In a tight market new employees tend to be marginal, and the situation is worsened. Even in a labor market with an abundance of skilled labor, hiring and training costs are substantial.

Increasing labor capacity by scheduling overtime avoids the costs of hiring and training and does not increase the costs of fringe benefits such as holidays, vacations, and insurance. However, direct costs increase and productivity tends to decrease. This decrease is especially true when overtime becomes excessive or lasts for more than a month or so.

Decreasing the work force also is expensive. Frequently unemployment claims must be paid and the firm's unemployment insurance rate increases. Morale suffers and skilled employees tend to look for more permanent positions. Employees anticipating a layoff frequently decrease their productivity to stretch the work and postpone layoffs as long as possible.

Changing production rates also changes the rates at which materials are required. In some cases this nullifies the cost savings from blanket orders, quantity purchases, and transportation economies. The benefits of shifting the inventory function to the supplier diminish as suppliers tend to increase material costs to include their added inventory costs.

An aggregate plan with changes in the production rate also requires greater equipment capacity to meet higher maximum production rate periods. The relevancy of these costs depends of course on what equipment and facilities are already available.

The Japanese have increased productivity by minimizing production changeover time and inventory. Improved tooling design has reduced setup time; and tight planning and control of inventory is achieved by accurate and timely communication. The KANBAN system at Toyota is an example of the latter.

**Factors Affecting Production Rate Change Costs.** The total incremental costs of a production rate change and the rate at which these costs increase in relation to the magnitude of the change are influenced by the status of certain parameters at the time of the change:

1. Utilization of capacity factors such as
   a. Labor
   b. Facilities and equipment
   c. Administrative structure
2. The manufacturing process

If an increase in the production rate occurs when the firm is operating at less-than-normal capacity with labor on undertime, an increase in the production rate can reduce unit costs and increase aggregate productivity. *Undertime* is the condition that exists when the labor force is greater than that usually required to produce scheduled production. This occurs when a work force level has been retained to avoid layoffs.

If, on the other hand, the present labor force is scheduled at full capacity, an increase in the production rate necessitates either overtime or hiring additional employees. A production rate decrease and resulting layoff when the labor force already has been reduced to the senior and most skilled employees incurs a greater cost than the same magnitude of change when less experienced and less productive employees are laid off. The impact of existing labor utilization is clear. Other factors such as the available labor supply, the skill level required, and social-economic conditions influence the cost. For example, in some situations a summer layoff is appreciated by women who desire to spend time with their children or assist their husbands on the family farm.

A proposed change in the production rate which requires additional production, storage, or transportation equipment is more expensive than one that does not require additional investment. In most cases administrative functions such as accounting, plant engineering, and purchasing have been developed to operate efficiently over the normal range of production rate changes. Production above the range will require adjustment in administrative capacity. Continued gross overloading of the administrative systems increases the probability of system malfunction and collapse. A long-term underloading of the system reduces its efficiency even more than might be expected because idle employees tend to become restless and careless.

The nature of the manufacturing process influences the cost of a production rate change. For example, automobile assembly lines usually are designed to operate at a specific output, say, 60 cars per hour; and management has the choice of producing at the rate of 60 cars per hour or not producing. Overtime and additional shifts are an option, but the weekly output rates available to management do not form a continuous graph. For practical purposes the minimum scheduled weekly output possible is 2,400 units. Many assembly lines are designed with similar limitations on the possible variations in output rates. Various "wet processing" firms have similar output variation limitations. They must be either run or shut down. Refineries or modular portions thereof frequently fit this description.

**Other Considerations.** Production for inventory during periods of low demand should focus on producing items that generate the lowest inventory carrying cost per hour of production capacity used. This is a function of the ratio of setup time to run time for a given item and the carrying cost of the item.

The examples in Figures 1-3 and 1-4 can give the impression that once an aggregate planning decision is made, it is cast in concrete. This is misleading. To review the aggregate plan less than quarterly is courting disaster. This includes formulating the plan for the quarter added since the last review, and making changes in the existing plan where flexibility still exists and recent data indicate adjustments are required. This practice is examined further in the master production scheduling chapter. This process is facilitated by computerization. Take the case in which actual demand during the first three months is 2,000 units higher than forecast in the Figure 1-4 example. This would leave the first quarter ending inventory at zero and decrease safety stock by 100 units, assuming there were 100 units in safety stock. A change in the plan should be considered.

Differences between forecast and actual demand raise interesting questions concerning revising the forecast. Methods of determining when these changes warrant a revision in the forecast are treated in Chapter 2, "Forecasting." Another basic question is whether an upswing in demand will continue in the following periods. Was it due to a single short-term cause, such as a strike at a competitor's firm, was it advanced buying which will be reflected in demand lower than originally forecast for the next quarter, or is it the beginning of a lasting increase in demand? Application of mathematical models will not produce the answer to this set of questions; knowledge of the marketplace, the economy, and the business environment will provide some clues.

We also might ask the question: Are there not occasions when dramatic changes require the review of an aggregate plan before an entire quarter has passed? Sure there are. Statistical limits can be established for detecting upturns or downswings in demand which are greater than normal variations and which, on the upswing, cannot be handled by safety stock. Figure 1-5, illustrates how cumulative demand can be recorded and checked for unusual increases or decreases. Again computer based forecasting, order entry, and planning software packages can assist management in this analysis.

Thus, costs related to production rate changes will vary from firm to firm and even from time to time within the same firm.

## AGGREGATE PLANNING MODELS AND DECISION TECHNIQUES

Different approaches are available for obtaining solutions to the aggregate planning problem:

1. Trial and Error (Heuristic) Methods (T&E)
2. Linear Programming Cost Minimization (LP)
3. Linear Decision Rules (LDR)
4. Search Decision Rules (SDR)
5. Hierarchical Planning and Disaggregation (HPD)
6. Goal Programming (GP)

Trial and error probably is still the most commonly used method, but methods 2 through 6 are gaining greater acceptance as the situations in which each works well are pinpointed. Frequently one or more is used in concert with a trial-and-error approach with each serving as a check on the other. The aggregate planning problem is complex and aggregate planning decisions have a major impact on the success of the firm. Thus, study of this problem continues at an accelerated pace.

The objectives of aggregate planning support overall organizational objectives such as profit, return on investment, growth, and market penetration. Aggregate planning objectives usually include:

1. Achieving a customer service at or above a specified level
2. Maintaining the inventory investment below a specified maximum level[3]
3. Maximizing production efficiency within the constraints of customer service and inventory cost objectives[4]
4. Minimizing total inventory decision related costs while achieving the desired production efficiency and customer service objectives
5. Maintaining a specified level of employment and minimizing labor costs

---

[3]See Chapters 6 and 9 on inventory management.

[4]See Chapters 6 and 9 on inventory management.

Customer service, inventory investment, production efficiency, inventory cost, and labor costs are interrelated. For example, production of large quantities at one time increases production efficiency but also increases inventory investment. Trade-offs among inventory investment, customer service, production efficiency and employment level objectives must be made to achieve profit, return on investment, and market penetration objectives. The purpose of aggregate planning models is to determine the specific trade-offs which best achieve corporate objectives.

## Trial and Error (Heuristic) Methods

Almost all organizations have developed a set of aggregate planning rules based on their experience. These rules of thumb include information and guidelines such as:

1. Identification of bottleneck work centers and their capacities.
2. The point at which overtime produces diminishing results; for example, working the fifth 6-day week in succession usually is followed by at least 25 percent of the work force being absent at least one day in the following week.
3. Reducing the work force below 75 percent of the normal results in a permanent loss of skilled and efficient workers.
4. Changing the work force level more than four times a year overloads the administrative capability of the organization; the industrial relations department has insufficient time for handling grievances, negotiating the labor contract, and promoting labor productivity through cost reduction and profit sharing plans.

The archetype trial-and-error method consists of

1. Preparing an initial production plan on the basis of forecast demand and established guidelines
2. Determining whether the plan is within capacity constraints
3. Costing the plan
4. Preparing an alternative plan, performing Steps 2 and 3 on it, and comparing the costs of the two plans
5. Continuing the above process until a satisfactory plan is developed
6. Performing sensitivity analysis to evaluate the effect of changes in parameters

This approach leads to a feasible solution but not necessarily the optimum solution. Frequently the two extremes, a constant production rate and production levels changed to approximate demand, are developed first. Compromises within these extremes then are developed.

Let's examine the cost of the two production plans illustrated in Figures 1-3 and 1-4. This will enable us to compare the costs of level production to the costs of changing production rates quarterly under seasonal demand conditions. We also will determine the sensitivity of the results to changes in the values of certain parameters.

The following information is added:

Unit costs = \$50.00 (Labor = \$8.00; material = \$30.00; overhead = \$12.00)
Overtime unit costs = \$53.50 (Labor = \$12.00; material = \$30.00; overhead = \$11.50)
Carrying cost rate = .30 per year
Hiring cost = \$600.00 per man (This is a weighted average of hiring and rehiring costs.)
Layoff costs = \$200.00 per man
Labor cost per hour = \$10.00
Capacity per man month = 160 hours

Two hundred units are produced monthly per direct laborer when the company produces between 5,000 and 12,000 units per month. Overtime must be used to produce additional units. Management policy limits overtime to 40 hours per man per month. This results in a maximum capacity of 15,000 units (12,000 units in regular time + 60 direct laborers × 1.25 units per man-hour × 40 overtime hours per man month).

Three different aggregate plans are compared here to exemplify the process. Plan I levels production throughout the year and incurs high inventory carrying costs but no overtime or production rate change costs. Plan II uses a chase strategy with production rates changed quarterly to approximate the quarterly demand. It incurs lower inventory carrying costs but does result in production rate change and overtime costs. Plan III is a compromise between the level production and chase strategies. The production rate changes only three times a year and the magnitudes of the changes are less than those of Plan II. The three plans and their costs are tabulated in Tables 1-3 through 1-5 and summarized in Table 1-2.

**TABLE 1-2**
**SUMMARY OF AGGREGATE PLAN COSTS**

| Costs | I | II | III |
|---|---|---|---|
| Overtime costs | — | \$10,500 | — |
| Production rate change costs | — | 37,000 | \$ 8,000 |
| Inventory carrying costs | \$84,125 | 27,875 | 50,375 |
| | \$84,125 | \$75,375 | \$58,375 |

These three plans certainly do not exhaust all possibilities. An examination of additional plans may reveal a more economical approach. Costs of additional analyses must be compared with possible savings.

**TABLE 1-3**
**COST OF AGGREGATE PRODUCTION PLAN I**
**LEVEL PRODUCTION**
**PRODUCING 10,000 UNITS PER MONTH**

| Month | Beginning Inventory | Production | Demand | Ending Inventory | Overtime Costs | Production Rate Change Costs | Inventory Carrying Costs |
|---|---|---|---|---|---|---|---|
| Jan. | 1.1* | 10* | 9.0* | 2.1* | — | — | $ 2,625 |
| Feb. | 2.1 | 10 | 6.2 | 5.9 | — | — | 7,375 |
| March | 5.9 | 10 | 8.0 | 7.9 | — | — | 9,875 |
| April | 7.9 | 10 | 11.0 | 6.9 | — | — | 8,625 |
| May | 6.9 | 10 | 13.2 | 3.7 | — | — | 4,625 |
| June | 3.7 | 10 | 10.0 | 3.7 | — | — | 4,625 |
| July | 3.7 | 10 | 8.0 | 5.7 | — | — | 7,125 |
| Aug. | 5.7 | 10 | 6.0 | 9.7 | — | — | 12,125 |
| Sept. | 9.7 | 10 | 9.5 | 10.2 | — | — | 12,750 |
| Oct. | 10.2 | 10 | 13.0 | 7.2 | — | — | 9,000 |
| Nov. | 7.2 | 10 | 14.0 | 3.2 | — | — | 4,000 |
| Dec. | 3.2 | 10 | 12.1 | 1.1 | — | — | 1,375 |
| | — | 120 | 120.0 | 67.3 | — | — | $84,125 |

*Item quantities are in thousands.

**TABLE 1-4**
**COST OF AGGREGATE PRODUCTION PLAN II**
**PRODUCTION VARIED QUARTERLY TO**
**APPROXIMATE QUARTERLY DEMAND**

| Month | Beginning Inventory | Production | Demand | Ending Inventory | Overtime Costs | Production Rate Change Costs | Inventory Carrying Costs |
|---|---|---|---|---|---|---|---|
| Jan. | 1.1* | 8* | 9.0* | .1* | — | $ 5,000 (−25 men) | $ 125 |
| Feb. | .1 | 8 | 6.2 | 1.9 | — | — | 2,375 |
| March | 1.9 | 8 | 8.0 | 1.9 | — | — | 2,375 |
| April | 1.9 | 12 | 11.0 | 2.9 | — | 12,000 (+20 men) | 3,625 |
| May | 2.9 | 12 | 13.2 | 1.7 | — | — | 2,125 |
| June | 1.7 | 12 | 10.0 | 3.7 | — | — | 4,625 |
| July | 3.7 | 7 | 8.0 | 2.7 | — | 5,000 (−25 men) | 3,375 |
| Aug. | 2.7 | 7 | 6.0 | 3.7 | — | — | 4,625 |
| Sept. | 3.7 | 7 | 9.5 | 1.2 | — | — | 1,500 |
| Oct. | 1.2 | 13 | 13.0 | 1.2 | $ 3,500 | 15,000 (+25 men) | 1,500 |
| Nov. | 1.2 | 13 | 14.0 | .2 | 3,500 | — | 250 |
| Dec. | .2 | 13 | 12.1 | 1.1 | 3,500 | — | 1,375 |
| | — | 120 | 120.0 | 22.3 | $10,500 | $37,000 | $27,875 |

*Item quantities are in thousands.

**TABLE 1-5**
**COST OF AGGREGATE PRODUCTION PLAN III**
**COMPROMISE SOLUTION**

| Month | Beginning Inventory | Production | Demand | Ending Inventory | Overtime Costs | Production Rate Change Costs | Inventory Carrying Costs |
|---|---|---|---|---|---|---|---|
| Jan. | 1.1* | 9* | 9.0* | 1.1* | — | $2,000 (−10 men) | $ 1,375 |
| Feb. | 1.1 | 9 | 6.2 | 3.9 | — | — | 4,875 |
| March | 3.9 | 9 | 8.0 | 4.9 | — | — | 6,125 |
| April | 4.9 | 10 | 11.0 | 3.9 | — | 3,000 (+5 men) | 4,875 |
| May | 3.9 | 10 | 13.2 | .7 | — | — | 875 |
| June | .7 | 10 | 10.0 | .7 | — | — | 875 |
| July | .7 | 10 | 8.0 | 2.7 | — | — | 3,375 |
| Aug. | 2.7 | 10 | 6.0 | 6.7 | — | — | 8,375 |
| Sept. | 6.7 | 10 | 9.5 | 7.2 | — | — | 9,000 |
| Oct. | 7.2 | 11 | 13.0 | 5.2 | — | 3,000 (+5 men) | 6,500 |
| Nov. | 5.2 | 11 | 14.0 | 2.2 | — | — | 2,750 |
| Dec. | 2.2 | 11 | 12.1 | 1.1 | — | — | 1,375 |
| | — | 120 | 120.0 | 40.3 | — | $8,000 | $50,375 |

*Item quantities are in thousands.

The actual carrying cost rate, hiring and layoff costs, item costs, and overtime costs may differ from the estimates. Investigating the effect of changes in these costs parameters on the total costs of alternate plans will reveal the sensitivity of our decision to such changes. The data in Table 1-2 indicated that Plan III will result in the lowest total cost. We will examine the impact of changes in the carrying cost rate and hiring and layoff costs on the total costs of the three plans.

If all other factors remain the same and the carrying cost rate is .20 rather than .30, the total costs of Plans I, II, and III are $56,083, $66,083, and $41,583 respectively.

If all other factors remain the same and the cost of laying off an employee is $400 rather than $200 and the cost of hiring is $1,000 rather than $600, the cost of Plan I does not change but the costs of Plans II and III increase to $108,375 and $64,375 respectively.

If the above changes occur concurrently, the costs of Plans I, II, and III will be $56,083, $99,083, and $47,583 respectively as shown in Table 1-6.

Thus, Plan III has the lowest total costs under all the preceding conditions. But if unit cost were $20, the carrying cost rate 0.30 per year and layoff and hiring costs $400 and $1,000 respectively, Plan I would have the lowest total cost.

**TABLE 1-6**
**COST OF AGGREGATE PLANS I, II, AND III, REVISED CARRYING COST RATE, AND PRODUCTION RATE CHANGE COSTS**

| Costs | I | II | III |
|---|---|---|---|
| Overtime costs | — | $10,500 | — |
| Production rate change costs | — | 70,000 | $14,000 |
| Inventory carrying costs | $56,083 | 18,583 | 33,583 |
| | $56,083 | $99,083 | $47,583 |

## Linear Programming Approach

The general form of a linear programming model is a set of linear relationships (equations) defining the trade-offs for each resource which may be allocated to production and an equation defining the contribution of each decision variable to the objective (see Chapter 17, "Mathematical Programming"). The following model illustrates the salient characteristics of linear programming models used in the aggregate planning process.

$$Z = \sum_{t=1}^{T} \sum_{i=1}^{N} (C_{i1}Q_{it} + C_{i2}I_{it} + C_{i3}W_{it} + C_{i4}\varnothing_{it} + C_{i5}H_{it} + C_{i6}L_{it} + C_{i7}B_{it})$$

Subject to the following for all periods and all products (for $t = 1, 2, \ldots T$ and $i = 1, 2, \ldots N$)

$$I_{it} = I_{i,t-1} + Q_{it} - D_{it}$$
$$W_{it} = W_{i,t-1} + H_{it} - L_{it}$$
and $Q_{it}, I_{it}, W_{it}, \varnothing_{it}, H_{it}, L_{it}$ and $B_{it} \geq 0$ dor all $i, t$

Where:

- $N$ is the number of product groups
- $T$ is the number of planning periods
- $Q_{it}$ is the quantity of product $i$ produced in period $t$
- $D_{it}$ is the quantity of product $i$ shipped in period $t$
- $I_{it}$ is the inventory of product $i$ at the end of period $t$
- $W_{it}$ is the work force level for product $i$ during period $t$
- $\varnothing_{it}$ is the overtime in hours for product $i$ during period $t$
- $H_{it}$ is the increase in personnel required for product $i$ production in period $t$ (new hires)
- $L_{it}$ is the decrease in personnel required for product $i$ production in period $t$ (layoffs and terminations)
- $B_{it}$ is the number of units back ordered during period $t$

$C_{i1}$ is the overhead and material cost for product $i$
$C_{i2}$ is the cost of carrying one item of product $i$ in inventory one period
$C_{i3}$ is the cost of an hour of labor on product $i$
$C_{i4}$ is the cost of an hour of labor overtime for product $i$
$C_{i5}$ is the cost of hiring an additional employee for product $i$
$C_{i6}$ is the cost of laying off an employee for product $i$
$C_{i7}$ is the cost of back ordering one unit of product $i$

This model calculates the total cost $(Z)$ for a given set of production quantities by period for each product. It includes the major costs of production: labor, material, overtime, hiring, terminating, and back orders. Applying a linear programming approach to these equations will result in a set of production quantities per period for each product $(Q_{it})$ which minimize total costs.[5] Solving the equations usually is not difficult, since most computer systems have LP software packages easily applied by the experienced computer user. However, developing a set of equations which adequately represents a specific situation requires considerable study and judgment. The planner must determine sufficiently accurate cost coefficients and recognize other constraints which may exist. For example, hiring or layoffs may be limited or not permitted. In addition, there is usually a limit to overtime and back orders.

The linear programming approach does have shortcomings. Cost functions are frequently not linear and are sometimes discontinuous (there are cost breaks). For example, the overtime cost per hour may increase as overtime increases due to a decrease in production efficiency. Larger production quantities may result in a lower unit cost at certain points due to quantity discounts or changes in the manufacturing process—justified by the larger quantity. Nonetheless, LP models can provide a reasonable estimate of costs for different plans and also provide valuable insights and guidance to management as reported by Markland[4] and by Greene et al.[5]

## Linear Decision Rules

Holt, Modigliani, Muth, and Simon[6, 7] raised the level of interest in the aggregate planning problem with their description of the Linear Decision Rule (LDR) in 1955. The LDR represents the costs associated with production rate changes, inventory, and overtime as quadratic functions of the production and work force level. Linear decision rules for determining the work force levels and production rates are derived by differentiating the aggregate quadratic cost function.

Although this approach was a valuable step in the continued development of aggregate planning models, it has not had widespread acceptance due to certain inherent limitations. It requires that cost functions be quadratic—for differentiating—and this is often not a valid assumption. It also

[5] See Chapter 17, "Mathematical Programming."

places no constraints on the decision variables, which in practice frequently are constrained.

## Search Decision Rules (Simulation and Search Approaches)

The inherent difficulty of developing a realistic analytic model that is easily solved invites the application of simulation techniques to the aggregate planning decision (see Chapter 18). Analytical aggregate planning models rigidly assume specified relationships between decision variables. For example, some require that costs are linear in relation to the production quantity; others require that the cost-quantity relationship is quadratic; and none allow these relationships to change over the planning horizon. In a given situation some costs may vary linearly while others vary in a quadratic or other fashion in relation to production quantities. In addition, labor and material costs may change over a 12- to 18-month period due to the labor contract and due to inflationary increases in the prices of purchased materials. The arrival of new equipment may be scheduled during the planning horizon with a resulting increase in setup costs, an increase in capacity, and a reduction in unit processing costs. Analytical approaches usually can't handle these changes without a prohibitive increase in model complexity.

Simulation enables the planner to formulate a model with a variety of cost relationships and with relationships that change at specific points in time. Thus, simulation models can approximate reality more closely than their analytical counterparts in most situations. Analytical models such as linear programming, however, guarantee an optimum solution—albeit to an oversimplification of reality—while *running* a simulation model does not guarantee an optimum solution (see Chapter 18).

Search Decision Rules (SDR) combine a very general aggregate planning simulation model and solution search techniques.[8] The general SDR simulation model represents the aggregate planning situation by a set of models each representing the set of conditions existing during one or more planning periods. Thus, changes in conditions such as labor and material costs can be incorporated in the model.

The following symbols are used in the SDR approach:

$S_i$ = a stage, a time period; points in time when decisions are made concerning employment levels, production quantities, overtime, etc.

$P_{ij}$ = the parameters, factors such as material costs and demand which are not controlled by the organization. The values of parameters may be different at different stages.

$D_i$ = the decision variables, those variables such as the production quantities which are controlled by the organization.

$R_i$ = the return, the result of a set of decisions in a planning period with a given set of conditions. Return may be measured in terms of costs, profit, rate of return, etc.

The general form of the simulation model can be expressed as:

$$\Sigma R_i = f\Sigma(Q_i, I_i, W_i, O_i, T_i, B_i)$$

Where:

$Q$, $I$, $W$, $O$, $T$, and $B$ represent the variables described earlier in the linear programming section

The variables included in the model of a particular situation depend on the nature of that situation.

Using simulation, we can develop a different model for each period. If no changes in parameters are anticipated throughout the planning horizon, a single model will suffice. However, if the labor contract calls for wage increases at the seventh and 19th months of a 24-month planning period, at least three different models will exist. One will apply to months one through six; another to months seven through 18, and the third to months 19 through 24. This situation, schematically represented in Figure 1-7, is rather uncommon in practice, since changes in demand or material costs likely will occur in one or more of the three groups of periods. The ability to incorporate parameter changes is one of the cardinal virtues of simulation.

**FIGURE 1-7**
**MULTIPERIOD SEARCH DECISION RULE PROCESS**

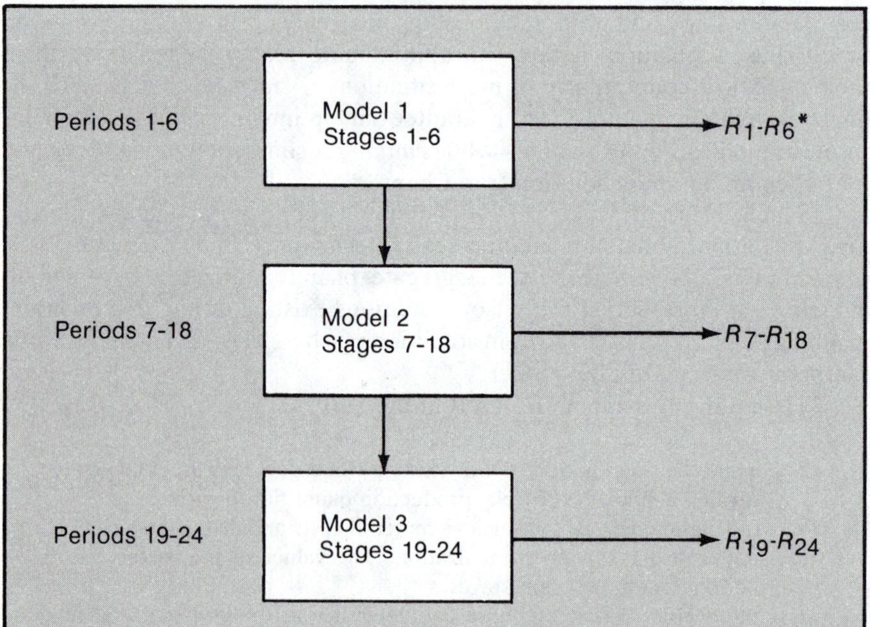

Periods 1-6
Model 1
Stages 1-6
$R_1$-$R_6$*
Periods 7-18
Model 2
Stages 7-18
$R_7$-$R_{18}$
Periods 19-24
Model 3
Stages 19-24
$R_{19}$-$R_{24}$

*All other parameters, including demand, remain constant within each set of periods, an uncommon situation in practice.

Running a simulation model does not reveal the optimum decision; it reveals what outcome will result from choosing specific values for the decision variables (see Chapter 18, "Simulation"). Thus, the decision maker can select the best decision among the alternatives being compared which may not include the best possible decision. If there are many interacting decision variables, each with numerous possible settings, running a simulation of all possible combinations can be time-consuming and expensive.

The trick is to examine and try those decision variable values that have the most promise, and ignore those with a small probability of a high payoff. In practice there are relatively few aggregate planning situations in which observation and intuitive judgment can narrow likely optimum decisions to a relatively few; situation complexity usually makes efficient selection of trial settings of decision variable values less than straightforward. However, various methods (search techniques) are available for selecting trial variables in a simulation.[9]

# Hierarchical Planning and Disaggregation

Hax and Meal[10] have developed an approach which integrates long-range (production) planning decisions, aggregate planning decisions (smoothing production to meet seasonal demand), the planning of item and family production run quantities, and the scheduling of individual items. The hierarchical segregation of these decisions [9], illustrated in Figure 1-8, is compatible with an organizational environment in which they are made by different groups.

The four levels in their planning hierarchy are:

1. Assign items and families to plants.
2. Develop the monthly production plan and inventory position for each product group and plant.
3. Determine the product run quantities for product groups (families) and individual items.
4. Schedule the production of individual items lots (runs).

Hax and Meal developed this approach for a "process industries" type firm with batch production characteristics whereas Britan and Hax[11] developed it for a discrete parts manufacturing organization. They selected different decision techniques for making planning decisions at each step. For example, they used a linear programming approach for the aggregate planning type decisions of Step 2. Neither the decision technique they used at each step nor the number of steps in the process likely will be most appropriate for all organizations, but a hierarchical approach is universally applicable. It recognizes that different decisions are made by different groups and that consistency should exist between the decisions at different levels. Let's examine the steps further.

**FIGURE 1-8**
**BLOCK DIAGRAM OF HIERARCHICAL DECISION PROCESS**

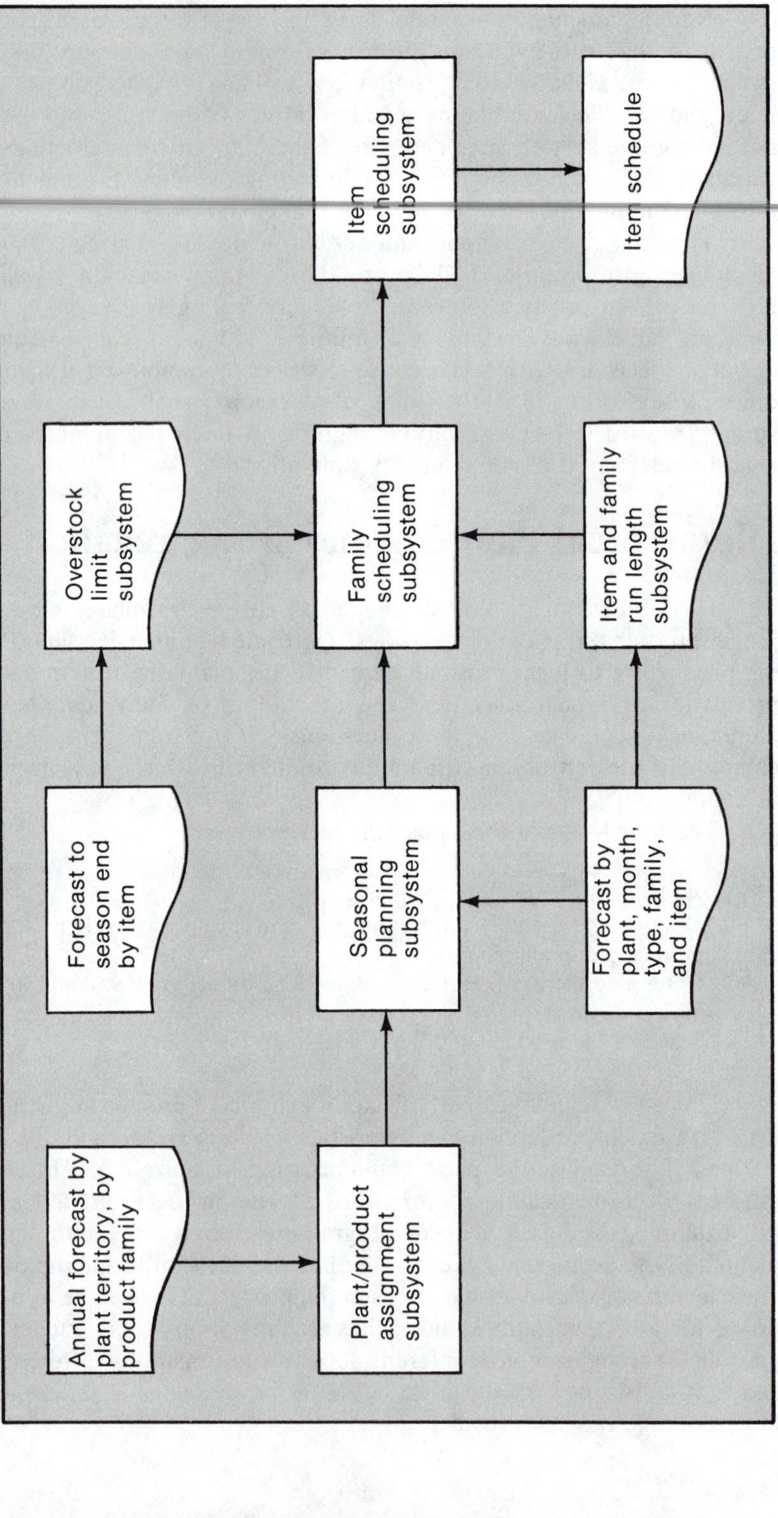

Annual forecast by plant territory, by product family

Plant/product assignment subsystem

Forecast to season end by item

Seasonal planning subsystem

Forecast by plant, month, type, family, and item

Overstock limit subsystem

Family scheduling subsystem

Item and family run length subsystem

Item scheduling subsystem

Item schedule

*Step 1.* Assigning product families and items to specific plants is necessary when individual plants have different production capabilities for raw materials or finished products. The organization with a single production facility must determine if available or planned manufacturing resources are adequate to execute the long-range plan. This step is an important part of resource requirements planning and evaluation of the adequacy of available capacity. Assignment of products must be based on an aggregate planning strategy; for example, level production.

*Step 2.* This is medium-range (aggregate) planning. Production rates by major product lines, inventory levels, work force levels, overtime, and so on are planned to meet demand requirements. These plans should be made within the confines of the Step 1 results. The planning process of some firms has long recognized this relationship. Hax and Meal have performed a service by explicitly stating the requirement for those who tend to forget.[10]

*Step 3.* Development of the planned production or purchased quantities by period for product groups and individual items is the next step. This step is analogous to the development of the Master Production Schedule (MPS), the Final Assembly Schedule (FAS), and the schedule of individual items required by the MPS and FAS (see Chapters 3 and 4). Quantities are based on orders received and/or the forecast plus the lot-sizing decision factors discussed in Chapters 4, 5, 7, 8, 9, and 10.

*Step 4.* The release of production or purchase orders for individual items is scheduled and executed using the techniques discussed in Chapters 5, 12 and 13. Material requirements planning generates the input requirements for this step.

The decisions at each of these steps usually are not made by the same individuals or departments within an organization. Hierarchical planning recognizes the different goals and levels of these sets of decisions while requiring consistency between the steps.

# GOAL PROGRAMMING

There usually are multiple goals when developing the master production schedule for the medium range. A typical set of such goals might include the following:

1. The schedule must be within productive capacity.
2. Production should be sufficient to meet demand requirements.
3. Production and inventory costs should be minimized.
4. Inventory investment should not exceed a specified limit.
5. Overtime costs should be within a specified limit.
6. Any decrease in employment levels will be handled by attrition.

Since most mathematical programming methods require that all goals be expressed in a single dimension, these goals either are formulated in terms of dollars or converted to constraints when that is not possible. This approach has two shortcomings. The constraints may not be as rigid as indicated in a linear programming formulation and not all goals have the same priority. For example, there may be no objection to exceeding either the overtime cost or inventory investment limits on occasion if substantial improvements in delivery performance are achieved.

Goal programming[6] overcomes these objectives. It allows the different goals to be expressed in their natural form—for example, delivery of 14,000 units in Period 4—and provides a solution which achieves the goals in priority order. Since some of the goals are in opposition to each other, frequently it is not possible to achieve all of them. For example, a goal of stable employment may be inconsistent with minimized production costs. Goal programming enables us to analyze the deviations from a given goal required to achieve another.

Sang Lee and Lawrence Moore[12] have described the application of goal programming to the development of a schedule for a manufacturer of large electric transformers. The goals and their priority in that situation were:

1. Operate within the limits of productive capacity.
2. Meet the contracted delivery schedule.
3. Operate at a minimum level of 80 percent of regular time capacity.
4. Keep inventory to a maximum of three units.
5. Minimize total production and inventory costs.
6. Hold overtime production to a minimum.

The first four goals were achieved while overtime production and greater-than-minimum production and inventory costs were allowed in one month to meet the delivery schedule, a higher priority goal. Goal programming provides for a straightforward analysis of such trade-offs.

In summary, many methods have been suggested for making aggregate planning decisions. Not all have been discussed in this chapter. For example, Jones[13] has proposed a parametric production planning method and Mellichamp and Love[14] have developed a production switching heuristic method, neither of which is discussed here. Although more recent methods, such as simulation and goal programming, do not have the limitations of earlier methods, none have been applied in industry on a broad scale. In fact, reported cases of continuing use of formal aggregate planning methods are scarce. Trial-and-error simulation type approaches prevail.

There are a number of probable reasons for this. Many of the mathematical approaches have underlying assumptions that limit their applicability,

[6]See Chapter 17 for a discussion of goal programming.

and the mathematical nature of most of the approaches also discourages love at first sight. However, the dominant causes are:

1. The broad applicability of the various techniques is unproven; most organizations have approaches that provide satisfactory results.
2. Production results frequently are evaluated by a dominant criteria such as meeting the delivery schedule, a stable work force, or low production costs. When such dominance does exist, decisions tend to be less complicated.
3. Tailoring of a given method to function effectively in a specific situation usually requires considerable analysis, time, and patience.

Use of aggregate planning models in industry is the exception rather than the rule. Continued development, testing, and validation of the applicability of these models in many types of situations are prerequisites for widespread acceptance.

## PROBLEMS AND QUESTIONS

**1.** The Valley Springs Lumber Mill manufactures door and frame assemblies for a number of hardware store chains and building supply wholesalers. They have forecast sales of 40,000 doors per month for the next 6 months. Recent production data reveal that 4 doors are produced per day for each production employee. If there are 20 production days each month, how many employees should they have?

**2.** The following information is available concerning Department A. The department runs one shift, 8 hours a day, 5 days each week. There are 4 machines with one man assigned to each machine. During a recent 5-week period, considered typical in all respects, the standard hours of output listed below were achieved. What capacity in man-hours was achieved? What capacity in man-hours should be used for planning or (asking the question another way) what is the normal capacity of the department?

| Week | Output (Standard Hours) |
|---|---|
| 1 | 145 |
| 2 | 170 |
| 3 | 130 |
| 4 | 150 |
| 5 | 135 |

**3.** Describe the aggregate planning decision including:

a. What does it decide?
b. How long a period does it usually cover and how often is it made?
c. What are the alternative pure strategies? Describe briefly.
d. What cost factors affect the decision?
e. What other factors (some perhaps indirectly related to costs) may affect the decision?

4. Conesto Ltd. uses a 13-month per year calendar with 4 weeks per month and 5 working days per week for planning purposes. The plant closes for holidays as shown below and for two weeks' vacation in late July.

| | |
|---|---|
| New Year's Day ....... | 1 day |
| President's Day........ | 1 day |
| Memorial Day......... | 1 day |
| Independence Day .... | 1 day |
| Labor Day............. | 1 day |
| Thanksgiving.......... | 2 days |
| Christmas............. | 2 days |

a. How do you recommend that the planning calendar be revised?
b. Last year 25% of the production crew had a third week of vacation which they took the first week in August. How does this affect capacity?
c. Management is considering a proposal to have vacation time spread evenly throughout the year; the union seems agreeable. How does this affect planning and the work force?
d. The table below gives the expected number of unskilled laborers required in each month. If the normal attrition rate is 1 to 2 men per month and the present number of unskilled laborers on the payroll is 30, what plans do you recommend for hiring and firing? Graphically record the plan.

| Month | Laborers Required |
|---|---|
| 1 | 35 |
| 2 | 35 |
| 3 | 40 |
| 4 | 40 |
| 5 | 38 |
| 6 | 35 |
| 7-10 | 30 |

5. The Neptune Manufacturing Company has an inventory of 3,000 units at the beginning of Period 3. Stock-outs are not allowed; demand is certain; and units must be ordered in thousands. Forecast demand for the next eight periods is:

| Period | Forecast* |
|---|---|
| 3 | 10 |
| 4 | 12 |
| 5 | 13 |
| 6 | 15 |
| 7 | 12 |
| 8 | 8 |
| 9 | 7 |
| 10 | 9 |

*Units (in thousands)

a. Management prefers to follow a level strategy in production during the next eight months while incurring minimum inventory costs under this policy. At what production rate should the plant operate?
b. If an item in inventory at the end of a period costs $1.00, what are the inventory costs of the policy selected in *a* during the 8-month period?

c. Is it economically advantageous to change the production rate if the cost of a rate change is $15,000? If it is advantageous, how often will you change the rate? What production level do you recommend in each period? Justify economically.

**6.** The following data are available concerning Work Center 185:

15 machines with essentially the same capacity
8 hours/shift, 2 shifts/day, 5 days/week
5 operators on first shift, 3 operators on second shift
3 machines run by each operator
90% employee efficiency, 75% machine utilization

a. What is the normal machine limited capacity?
b. What is the normal operator limited capacity?
c. What is the nominal (rated) capacity of the department?

**7.** Part 972501 is processed in Work Center 185, described in Problem 6. The standard setup time is 2.5 hours, and the standard machining time is 1.3 hours per 100 pieces. If 6 machines are used simultaneously to produce 600 parts, what is the workload on the department in standard hours? How many machine hours do you expect processing of the part to take?

**8.** The Labor Report of the final assembly department for the last 10 weeks includes the following data:

| Week | Labor Hours Expended | Standard Hours of Work Completed |
|---|---|---|
| 1 | 2000 | 1873 |
| 2 | 1600 | 1650 |
| 3 | 1840 | 1827 |
| 4 | 1820 | 1782 |
| 5 | 1760 | 1583 |
| 6 | 2000 | 2017 |
| 7 | 1880 | 1890 |
| 8 | 1920 | 1900 |
| 9 | 1880 | 1878 |
| 10 | 2000 | 1950 |

a. If there were no equipment failures or line downtime during these ten weeks, what was the efficiency of the department?
b. If the department lost an average of 100 man-hours each week due to machine failures, power outages, and material shortages, what were the utilization and efficiency rates of the department?

**9.** Items A through F belong to a family of parts. Determine the average standard time for use in calculating the load due to this family in Department 829.

| Item | Typical Proportion of Total Group Volume | Work Center 829 Standard Time (Hours/100 units) |
|---|---|---|
| A | .15 | .62 |
| B | .08 | .18 |
| C | .33 | .25 |
| D | .27 | .07 |
| E | .10 | 1.10 |
| F | .07 | .52 |

10. If department efficiency is .90 and department utilization is .95, how many actual clock hours of capacity are required in Work Center 829 for production of 5,000 units of the family of parts described in Problem 9 assuming a typical distribution of items?

11. Given the data below for Week 17, which are the bottleneck work centers?

WORK CENTER 927
PROCESSING TIME (ACTUAL HOURS)
PRODUCT GROUPS I-IV

| Work Center | Available Capacity (Hrs.) | Capacity Required I | II | III | IV |
|---|---|---|---|---|---|
| Turret Lathe | 60.0 | 27.2 | 13.3 | 16.4 | — |
| Horizontal Mills | 60.0 | 11.4 | — | 14.5 | 31.9 |
| Gear Cutting | 40.0 | 16.8 | 8.3 | — | 8.5 |
| Subassembly | 40.0 | 22.0 | 6.4 | 9.4 | 12.1 |
| Assembly | 60.0 | 17.0 | 5.1 | 8.5 | 18.4 |

12. Using the data applicable to Tables 1-3 through 1-5 (pages 33-35), propose an alternate plan with lower costs. (Hint: Try overtime in October, November, and December rather than a production rate change.)

13. Using the data applicable to Tables 1-3 through 1-5, except that the cost of hiring an employee is $1,500 and the cost of laying off an employee is $500, what is the most economical plan?

14. Using the data applicable to Tables 1-3 through 1-5, except that the regular time cost of an item is $10.00 and overtime cost is $11.00, what is the most economical plan?

15. Using the data applicable to Tables 1-3 through 1-5, except that back orders are now permissible at a cost of $1.00 per unit, what plan do you recommend?

16. Referring to the data in Table 1-3, an unexpected slowdown in the economy has occurred. Actual demand in January is 8,000 units; the forecast for February and March has been revised downward by 1,000 units for each month. The forecasts for April through December have not been changed. What change in the plan do you recommend?

17. Referring to the data in Table 1-5, demand in January was 10,000 units, and an increase of 1,000 units in both February and March to 7,200 and 9,000 units is now forecast. There is no agreement yet on any change in the forecast for April through December. What change in the plan do you recommend?

18. Forecast demand for the next 12 months is given below. Beginning inventory is 50 units; an ending inventory (December 31) between 99 and 150 is desired; and space and capital constraints limit inventory to 400 units at any time. The plant is closed 2 weeks in July for vacation. If a level production strategy is followed, what should the weekly production rate be? Graphically represent cumulative demand, production and inventory. Assume January, May, August, and October have five weeks and all other months have four weeks.

Forecast Demand (Units)

| Month | Demand |
|---|---|
| January | 400 |
| February | 370 |
| March | 350 |
| April | 340 |
| May | 370 |
| June | 410 |
| July | 440 |
| August | 460 |
| September | 470 |
| October | 450 |
| November | 430 |
| December | 410 |

**19.** Circumstances are the same as those in Question 18, except that the forecast is:

Forecast Demand (Units)

| Month | Demand |
|---|---|
| January | 410 |
| February | 440 |
| March | 460 |
| April | 470 |
| May | 450 |
| June | 430 |
| July | 410 |
| August | 400 |
| September | 370 |
| October | 350 |
| November | 340 |
| December | 370 |

What types of options are feasible? What is your short run recommendation? your long run recommendation?

# SELECTED READINGS


1. Peter F. Drucker, *Management: Tasks, Responsibilities, Practices* (New York: Harper & Row, Publishers, Inc., 1974), p. 775.
2. Wickham Skinner, *Manufacturing in the Corporate Strategy* (New York: John Wiley and Sons, Inc., 1978).
3. W. B. Lee and C. P. McLaughlin, "Corporate Simulation Model for Aggregate Materials Management," *Production and Inventory Management*, Vol. 15, No. 1, First Quarter (1974).
4. R. E. Markland, "Improving Fuel Utilization in Steel Mill Operations Using Linear Programming," *Journal of Operations Management*, Vol. 1, No. 2 (November, 1980).

5. J. H. Greene, K. Chatto, C. R. Hicks, and C. R. Cox, "Linear Programming in the Packing Industry," *Journal of Industrial Engineering,* Vol. 10, No. 5 (September/October, 1959), pp. 364–372.
6. Charles C. Holt, Franco Modigliani, and Herbert Simon, "A Linear Decision Rule for Production and Employment Scheduling," *Management Science,* Vol. 2, No. 1 (October, 1955), pp. 1–30.
7. Charles C. Holt, C. R. Modigliani, J. F. Muth, and H. A. Simon, *Planning Production Inventories and Work Force* (Englewood Cliffs, N. J.: Prentice-Hall, Inc., 1960).
8. Elwood S. Buffa and Jeffrey G. Miller, *Production-Inventory Systems: Planning and Control,* 3rd ed. (Homewood, Ill.: Richard D. Irwin, Inc., 1979).
9. William Taubert, "A Search Decision Rule for the Aggregate Scheduling Problem," *Management Science,* Vol. 14, No. 6 (February, 1968), B343–B359.
10. Arnoldo C. Hax and H. C. Meal, "Hierarchical Integration of Production Planning and Scheduling," *Studies in Management Sciences, Logistics,* Vol. 1, M. A. Geisler, ed. (New York: North Holland Publishing Co., 1973).
11. Gabriel R. Britan and Arnoldo C. Hax, "On the Design of Hierarchical Planning Systems," *Decision Sciences,* Vol. 1, No. 8 (January, 1977).
12. Sang M. Lee and L. J. Moore, "A Practical Approach to Production Scheduling," *Production and Inventory Management,* First Quarter (1974), pp. 79–92.
13. Curtis H. Jones, "Parametric Production Planning," *Management Science,* Vol. 13, No. 11 (July, 1967), pp. 843–866.
14. Joseph Mellichamp and Robert Love, "Production Heuristics for the Aggregate Planning Problem," *Management Science,* Vol. 24, No. 12 (August, 1978), pp. 1242–1251.
15. Paul N. Alvey and George H. Zimmer, "Capacity Planning," *Industrial Engineering,* Vol. 6, No. 4 (April, 1974).
16. Robert N. Anthony, *Planning and Control Systems: A Framework for Analysis* (Cambridge, Mass.: Harvard University Graduate School of Business Administration, 1965), pp. 26–47.
17. APICS *Certification Program Study Guide: Capacity Planning and Control* (Washington D.C.: APICS, 1980).
18. E. H. Bowman, "Consistency and Optimality in Managerial Decision Making," *Management Science,* Vol. 9 (January, 1963), pp. 310–321.
19. ———, "Production Scheduling by the Transportation Method of Linear Programming," *Operations Research,* Vol. 4 (February, 1956), pp. 100–103.
20. Gabriel R. Britan and Arnoldo C. Hax, "On the Design of Hierarchical Planning Systems," *Decision Sciences,* Vol. 1, No. 8 (January, 1977).
21. D. K. Corke, "Long-Range Planning for Production," *Long-Range Planning* (December, 1970), pp. 27–31.
22. Samuel Eilon, "Five Approaches to Aggregate Production Planning," *AIIE Transactions,* Vol. 7, No. 2 (June, 1975), pp. 118–131.
23. Jack A. Fuller, "A Linear Programming Approach to Aggregate Scheduling," *Academy of Management Journal,* Vol. 18, No. 1 (March, 1975), pp. 129–137.
24. Jay R. Galbraith, "Solving Production-Smoothing Problems," *Management Science,* Vol. 15, No. 12 (August, 1969), B665–B673.
25. Vincent J. Graziano, "Production Capacity Planning—Long Term," *Production and Inventory Management,* Vol. 15, No. 2, Second Quarter (1974).

26. F. Haussmann and S. W. Hess, "A Linear Programming Approach to Production and Employment Scheduling," *Management Technology,* Vol. 1 (January, 1960), pp. 46–52.
27. C. W. Hofer and D. Schendel, *Strategy Formulation: Analystical Concepts* (St. Paul, Minn.: West Publishing Co., 1978).
28. D. W. Karger and F. A. Malik, "Long-Range Planning and Organizational Performance," *Long-Range Planning* (December, 1975).
29. Larry J. Kretz and Arthur S. Bryant, "Production Planning—An Old Solution to a New Problem," *1978 Conference Proceedings, American Production and Inventory Control Society* (Washington, D.C.).
30. W. B. Lee and B. M. Khumawala, "Simulation Testing of Aggregate Production Planning Models in an Implementation Methodology," *Management Science,* Vol. 20 (February, 1974), pp. 903–911.
31. Leroy B. Schwarz and Robert E. Johnson, "An Appraisal of the Empirical Performance of the Linear Decision Rule for Aggregate Planning," *Management Science,* Vol. 24, No. 8 (April, 1978), pp. 844–849.
32. Edward A. Silver, "A Tutorial on Production Smoothing and Work Force Balancing," *Operations Research* (November-December, 1967), pp. 985–1011.
33. ————, "Medium-Range Aggregate Production Planning: State of the Art," *Production and Inventory Management,* First Quarter (1972).
34. R. C. Vergin, "Production Scheduling under Seasonal Demand," *Journal of Industrial Engineering,* 17 (May, 1966).
35. Thomas E. Vollmann, "Capacity Planning: The Missing Link," *Production and Inventory Management,* First Quarter (1973), pp. 61–73.

# 2

# FORECASTING

The foundation for any production activity is either an actual order or the forecast of an order. While some systems may build to stock or follow a master schedule, implicitly or explicitly underlying these bases is a forecast.

Generally the literature on forecasting focuses almost exclusively on techniques, primarily quantitative techniques. But before discussing the means of manipulating data to yield informative forecasts, let's look at the origin of that data, the data's dimensions and time characteristics, and the inherent quality and accuracy of the data itself. Following that we can discuss forecasting techniques and forecasting accuracy. We will also examine the relationship of forecasting to other business functions and review some managerial considerations in determining a forecasting system.

## DATA SOURCES

Most production forecasting systems are built upon extrapolating time series data—that is, an historical record of the past activity (sales or use of a product or component) is made and used to project future demand or need. A fundamental assumption for this to be a useful approach is that the future is related to the past in some, possibly complex, way. Since, even in a rapidly changing environment such as we have today, fundamental relationships still hold, this is a reasonable assumption as long as the look backwards is not too far back and the look forwards is not too far distant. It does not necessitate that tomorrow be just like today (although in weather forecasting one can observe a very high correlation of just this sort); it only requires a stability of relationships. Some typical time series are shown in Table 2-1. Some of the obvious characteristics to note are the time intervals (weeks, months, years, etc.), the dimensions (units, dollars, kilograms, etc.), and variability or lack thereof.

Before turning to an examination of formal techniques for extrapolating time series historical data, let's first look at some other sources of data besides those intrinsic to the item we wish to forecast.

Foremost among the external data sources are various types of market intelligence such as survey information, test panel data, and sales force feedback. Frequently this type of data is considered of questionable value to production control, but the fault in its use is often not in the quality nor in

**TABLE 2-1**
**TYPICAL TIME SERIES DATA**

| | **Weekly Demand for Item 05880—Red Desk Lamp** | | | | | | |
|---|---|---|---|---|---|---|---|
| Week Number | 122 | 123 | 124 | 125 | 126 | 127 | 128 |
| Demand | 9 | 7 | 8 | 13 | 18 | 22 | 27 |
| | **Monthly Shipments of Part 5149—Detergent 127** | | | | | | |
| Month | March | April | May | June | July | August | |
| Kilograms | 10 | 15 | 10 | 25 | 10 | 30 | |
| | **Net Sales of XYZ Corporation** | | | | | | |
| Year | 1973 | 1974 | 1975 | 1976 | 1977 | 1978 | 1979 |
| Dollars ($000) | 437,626 | 475,998 | 480,700 | 641,283 | 711,193 | 765,818 | 802,295 |
| | **Japanese Imports of Manufactured Goods** | | | | | | |
| Year | 1972 | 1973 | 1974 | 1975 | 1976 | 1977 | |
| $ (in billions) | 6.0 | 9.2 | 11.3 | 9.4 | 10.9 | 12.0 | |
| | **Number of Jobs Run per Hour on Computer A** | | | | | | |
| Time | 1000 | 1100 | 1200 | 1300 | 1400 | 1500 | |
| Quantity | 78 | 85 | 40 | 75 | 105 | 120 | |

the accuracy of the data itself but rather in its interpretation and timeliness. Market survey data are primarily obtained to aid in sales, promotion, and product introduction decisions. The specific procedures for selecting proper samples, designing questionnaires, and conducting interviews will not be covered in this text. Rather, we wish to point out that, since the data obtained by these methods are intended primarily for marketing purposes, they must be viewed carefully rather than ignored in making production decisions. Specific recognition of the time dimensions of the data should be noted; for example, a survey that establishes an intent to increase purchases may be more useful in planning production capacity than in establishing production schedules. It also behooves the production people to know the characteristics of the sample as well as the number of items the people in the sample say they will purchase. This may shed light on the marketing mix (size, color, configuration) of the demand—these attributes being of more importance in determining manufacturing units than in establishing aggregate sales dollar estimates.

Another source of data is sales force feedback. As salespeople contact customers or potential buyers, they accumulate information about what customers say they want and what competitors are offering or plan to offer (or withdraw from) the market. The difficulty in using these data for production decisions are several. Since these types of data are not obtainable in an orderly and regular manner, their comparability to other information is difficult to establish. Does the reported fact that customer *X* intends to buy 15 percent more next month represent demand over that already scheduled, or does it just compensate for the unreported decline by customers *Y* and *Z*? Since it is quite common to use already forecast sales to set sales force goals and hence compensation, the incentive exists to manipulate and/or withhold data to influence personal pay. The nature and extent of this modification are difficult to determine or control and thus results in questionable, but not altogether unusable, data from this source.

One type of difficulty that sometimes arises between marketing and manufacturing is caused by sales promotions or new advertising campaigns. While it is obvious that production should be aware of any such activities, it nevertheless happens that such activities are not communicated adequately. But perhaps of greater concern is that the effects of such campaigns or promotions cannot be estimated accurately. It is necessary that marketing and manufacturing personnel agree in advance on both a forecast and a schedule in order to share responsibility for those decisions. Too often marketing estimates that *X* units will be sold; manufacturing, in the belief that marketing's estimates are always optimistic, makes *X* less 10 percent. When the results are in, each blames the other for excess inventories or shortages. A mutually agreed upon master schedule (discussed in Chapter 3) will reduce these kinds of problems.

Most market research is intended to yield information about new products, new packages, or new promotion strategies. It is not directed towards ongoing demand for existing products. Some demand research is directed towards detecting fundamental changes in demand patterns; this is often called *econometric forecasting* and usually addresses itself to aggregate demand for product lines or groups. The techniques often employ very elegant statistical and mathematical methods. But, since the underlying relationships are poorly understood, the accuracy of such forecasts is often not good. Also, the time frame and level of detail of such forecasts make them of use in production and warehouse capacity planning but not particularly well suited for scheduling decisions.

# TIME FRAME AND DATA DIMENSIONS

One source of confusion that is sometimes related to marketing data is that for certain purposes demand should be expressed in dollars, while for others only units or kilograms or meters are of any use. Care must be exercised in converting data between these dimensions. Cost dollars are not sales dollars; 20 one-liter bottles neither cost nor sell for the same amount as 40 half-liter bottles, but do contain the same amount of liquid. Problems arise here because correct conversion ratios may not be developed or detailed product mix data (needed to obtain the 40 half-liter containers rather than the 20 one-liter bottles) are unavailable. Also, the dollar data may be subject to price changes which have no effect on units demanded.

The other dimension aspect is time. Total demand is not sufficient for scheduling, since the timing and rate of demand must be accounted for. Often the duration or length of the forecast period will be significant. While it is well recognized that the accuracy of detailed forecasts diminishes the further ahead in time they are projected, it is also true that the exact timing of orders may be difficult to predict even in the short run. Thus, it is probably most easy to predict aggregate demand over a moderate time period. The significance of this is that explicit recognition of these timing issues should be considered and inventory policies established which recognize the nature of these timing problems.

A further aspect of the time dimension of data is the forecast period length as it relates to inventory reordering policies, particularly those based on periodic review. Obviously the forecast horizon must equal or exceed the review period in order for the system to function. Care must be exercised in the extrapolation of forecasts for short periods of time which are used to cover long review intervals.

For forecasting systems based on historical data—and most are—the amount of past data available and/or needed is of great significance. For some systems—adaptive exponential smoothing, for example—substantial histories may be desirable (required) to get them started; but very little historical data are required to keep them functioning in the future. When little historical data are available, then data on similar products or market research data may be used.

Another aspect of the data's dimensions is its level of detail. As has already been pointed out with the one-liter versus the half-liter example, aggregate (20 liters of demand) data may be satisfactory for some uses but insufficient for others. This conflict is further aggravated by the fact that aggregate data are usually easier to forecast than detailed data; hence, forecasts are more often obtained by decomposing aggregate data than by aggregating detailed data. In addition, a number of top level decisions (work force, plant, cash needs, etc.) can best be made by predicting aggregate dollar sales without the necessity for detailed unit demand. As an example of what the relationship between aggregate and composite data might be, examine Table 2-2. The four model types, *A, B, C,* and *D,* have dollar values of 10, 9, 8, and 7 respectively. Each of the models varies considerably from period

**TABLE 2-2**
**AGGREGATE AND COMPOSITE DATA RELATIONSHIPS**

| | Units of Model Type | | | | Aggregate Units of | Aggregate Dollar Value |
|---|---|---|---|---|---|---|
| Period | A | B | C | D | Demand | of Demand |
| 1 | 28 | 79 | 46 | 91 | 244 | 1,996 |
| 2 | 79 | 70 | 49 | 29 | 227 | 2,015 |
| 3 | 82 | 26 | 56 | 76 | 240 | 2,034 |
| 4 | 77 | 77 | 44 | 35 | 233 | 2,060 |
| 5 | 28 | 98 | 79 | 41 | 246 | 2,081 |
| 6 | 87 | 38 | 84 | 31 | 240 | 2,101 |
| 7 | 95 | 56 | 44 | 45 | 240 | 2,121 |
| 8 | 86 | 79 | 35 | 41 | 241 | 2,138 |
| 9 | 68 | 47 | 50 | 94 | 259 | 2,161 |
| 10 | 48 | 63 | 70 | 82 | 263 | 2,181 |

to period, but the aggregate units of demand per period have a relatively small variation. A careful examination of the dollar values shows that they are growing at a fairly uniform one percent per period. Depending on the decisions being made and the technological differences between the models, these data may present a difficult or easy forecasting problem. For production planning purposes, each level of product aggregation from stockkeeping units, to assemblies, to product groups, and total demand have significance in different scheduling and planning decisions.

# DATA QUALITY AND ACCURACY

The byword in data processing is *GIGO*, Garbage in-Garbage out. This is equally true in forecasting. Not only must we concern ourselves with the validity and appropriateness of the data sources and the physical and time dimensions of the data, but we must control the data for errors and make appropriate modifications for recognized changes in such things as price or product.

A most obvious source of errors is in recording. These errors may be with regard to numeric quantity (recording 71 instead of 11) or in identification (part 6A5Z instead of 6A52) or in dimensionality (seven dozen in place of seven gross). The data processing system, whether manual or computerized, should be developed to find such errors, if possible, and to correct them, or at least point them out for further investigation as to cause.

Various techniques such as check sums, cross tabs, dual entries (possibly in dollars and quantity), and so on, can be built into the data entry system. Verifying that a part number actually exists before accepting an order should be standard procedure. Reasonableness checks should also be used. For example, if order quantities are normally (say, 95 percent of the time) for 50 or less, then any order in excess of 50 should be questioned. (This type of check would have caught the 71 in place of the 11.) The imposition of such a *demand filter* to check for reasonable input data will highlight any *outliers*, that is, values outside normal expectations. Whether these are correct values or errors must be determined through specific examination of each instance. To avoid too much manual intervention, we must establish appropriate limits as a compromise between chasing down nonexistent errors and allowing erroneous data to enter the system. At the very least detected errors must be corrected and, if the error is caused by using units instead of dozens, then modified to reflect correct dimensions.

Many forecasting errors and hence many scheduling errors have been made through failure to recognize the difference between orders and shipments. For example, they differ in timing. Orders precede shipments by manufacturing lead time or at least by order filling time. Quantities shipped may be less than quantities ordered for a variety of reasons; partial shipments may be made over a period of time to fill one order. Shipments may exceed orders because spare parts or allowances for defects may be included. Whatever the reason, the distinction between orders and shipments must be taken into account when using historical data for forecasting.

Another factor to consider is that price changes may cause increased sales dollars but not increased unit sales. Historical variations in unit prices are frequently overlooked, and errors arise because a single conversion factor is used in translating past sales dollars into past unit sales. For example, a price increase from $2.50 to $2.75 last July means that the first six months' sales of $30,000 and the second half sales of $32,000 actually represent a decline in unit sales. Similarly, past product changes may have resulted in aggregate shipments which do not reflect constant ratios of component parts and subassemblies. Thus, a current package which contains five subassemblies of type Z20 may have had only three such components and two of type Y17 six months ago. Care must be exercised in making conversions, or erroneous forecasts will result.

To summarize, before one can look at forecasting techniques and the accuracy of forecasts, one must examine the source and accuracy of the data on which forecasts will be built. No amount of ordinary photographic developing techniques can transform a fuzzy negative into a clear, sharp picture. Similarly, elegant (or simplistic) forecasting techniques applied to poor data cannot yield good forecasts. The first place to look for forecasting inaccuracies is in the quality and accuracy of the source data and transformations (e.g., dollars to units) applied to that data. Explicit recognition of the purpose for collecting the data and the inclusion of techniques to point out possible errors will enhance the likelihood of producing good forecasts.

# BASIC FORECASTING TECHNIQUES

Forecasting techniques can be divided into two categories: qualitative and quantitative. The former, which may involve numbers, uses methodology which is basically not mathematical. Qualitative techniques rely on judgment, intuition, and subjective evaluation. Among the major techniques within this category are market research (surveys), Delphi (panel consensus), historical analogy, and management estimation (guess). The other class of techniques, quantitative, can be divided into intrinsic and extrinsic types.

The intrinsic techniques are often referred to as *time series analysis* techniques. They involve mathematical manipulation of the history of demand for an item; that is, they make use of the historical period-by-period (time phased) series of numeric values of the demand for an item. These techniques are the most commonly used in forecasting for production and inventory control. The other group of quantitative techniques, extrinsic methods, attempts to relate demand for an item to data about another item, a group of items, or outside factors (such as general economic conditions) to create a forecast for the item of interest.

## Qualitative Techniques

We have previously mentioned some aspects of market research in discussing data sources. The important factor to keep in mind is that, while the techniques are based on good theory and can yield valuable information for marketing decisions, they are not intended directly to support inventory decisions. An intent-to-buy survey, or a market research project to determine preferred packaging or product characteristics, is intended to support product development and promotion strategies. Data gathered by these methods can and should be considered in some aggregate inventory or capacity planning decisions, but should not be the sole data source for such decisions.

The Delphi, or panel consensus, method may be useful in technological forecasting; that is, in forecasting the general state of the market, economy, or technological advances five or more years from now based on expert opinion. (The name for this method comes from the ancient Greek oracles of Delphi who forecast future events.) The process of creating a Delphi forecast is a variation of the following. A panel of futurists is asked a question: In the next ten years which consumer products do you envision containing microcomputers as an integral part? Each specialist independently submits a list of such items to the panel coordinator. The combined lists are then sent back to each panel member for evaluation and rating of likelihood of occurrence. Panel members may see something that they hadn't thought of and rate it highly; also members may have second thoughts about items they themselves previously submitted. This evaluated list is condensed by removing items not rated highly, and the shortened list is recycled. After a sufficient number of cycles—generally two or three—the result is a list with high consensus and usefulness for new product ideas, long-range corporate strategy, and the like. It is not a suitable technique for short-range forecasting, certainly not for individual stockkeeping units.

When attempting to forecast demand for a new item, one faces a shortage of historical data, he may look to the history of demand for an analogous product. If the related product is very similar, quantitative techniques may be used, but if the relationship is tenuous it may be more appropriate to relate the products only qualitatively in order to get an impression of demand patterns or aggregate demand. For example, the seasonal demand pattern for an established product such as tennis balls may be used to estimate the expected demand for tennis gloves. The actual levels and trends for the latter cannot be determined in this manner with any precision, but the demand pattern may be expected to be similar.

Finally, we must not overlook management estimation (intuition) as a forecasting method. It is widely practiced, often successfully by talented people, with regard to new products or unexpected changes in demand for established product lines. Not everyone has such talent, however. Some studies have shown that a mathematical technique consistently followed will lead to better results than the "expert modification" of those forecasts. Nonetheless, many mathematical techniques need significant quantities of historical data which may not be available. When substantial data are lacking, subjective management judgment may be better than objective manipulation of poor quality data.

# Quantitative Techniques

Intrinsic techniques use as source data the time sequenced history of activity for a particular item to forecast future activity for that item. Such a history is commonly referred to as a time series. Some typical time series patterns are shown in Figure 2-1. The characteristics of such series can be labeled in various ways, and the algebraic representation of such graphs can be accomplished by a variety of methods.

**FIGURE 2-1**
**TYPICAL TIME SERIES PATTERNS**

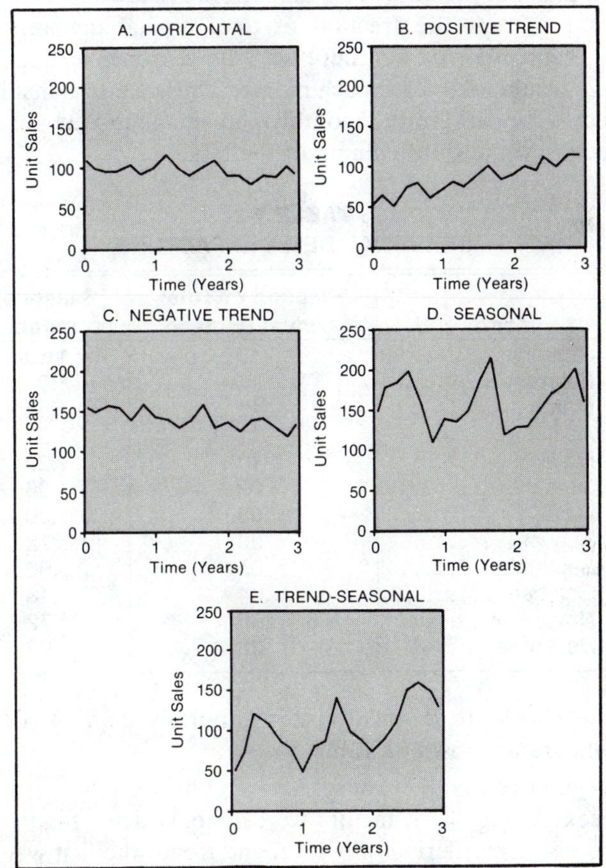

While a series is actually only a set of point values, it is common to connect those points and thus to imply continuous variables. For example, quantities are really 6, 8, and 104, not 5.917, 8.003, and 104.172 units; time is expressed in whole days or weeks, not in fractions thereof. This is of significance in trying to determine aggregate demand, in converting forecasts to orders, or in interpolating for values between two points in time.

Generally a time series can be thought of as consisting of up to five components or underlying factors: (1) level, (2) trend, (3) seasonal, (4) cyclical, and (5) random (or irregular). These factors are sometimes represented as *L, T, S, C,* and *R* respectively. In other words, the components which give rise to a particular pattern of demand consist of an average demand or level which may be modified by a trend, which may be further modified by a seasonal or cyclical phenomenon, all of which are somewhat muddied by a random, irregular, or otherwise unpredictable variation.

To illustrate this, let us construct a set of underlying factors and then observe the resulting time series. First, let us pick an initial level of 100 units per week; then we will presume that this is increasing at a rate of one unit per week, its trend. A possible seasonal pattern is shown in Table 2-3, where the numbers represent the fraction of total annual demand that occurs each month. Remember that if there were *no* seasonal or trend effect 8.33 percent (1/12) would take place each month. Thus, the seasonal index values are computed as the ratio of the monthly percentage to 8.33 percent and are usually shown as in the third column of the table.

**TABLE 2-3**
**SEASONAL DEMAND FACTORS**

| Month | Fraction of Total Annual Demand | Seasonal Index |
|---|---|---|
| January......... | .10 | 1.20 |
| February........ | .11 | 1.32 |
| March .......... | .12 | 1.44 |
| April............ | .11 | 1.32 |
| May............ | .10 | 1.20 |
| June ........... | .09 | 1.08 |
| July ............ | .08 | .96 |
| August ......... | .06 | .72 |
| September...... | .05 | .60 |
| October......... | .04 | .48 |
| November ...... | .06 | .72 |
| December ...... | .08 | .96 |

Within each month demand is not uniformly distributed so that the cyclical factors are as shown in Table 2-4.

The irregular component causes about a plus or minus ten-unit fluctuation each week. Using these factors we can construct a time series by the following process. Considering only level and trend, the first week's demand will be 100, the second 101, the third 102, and the fourth 103 for a cumulative

**TABLE 2-4**
**CYCLICAL DEMAND FACTORS**

| Week | Fraction of Monthly Demand | Cyclical Index |
|---|---|---|
| 1 | .10 | .40 |
| 2 | .15 | .60 |
| 3 | .25 | 1.00 |
| 4 | .50 | 2.00 |

total of 406. Since January represents 10 percent of the total (from the seasonal factor table) January base demand will be multiplied by a factor of 1.20 to adjust for seasonality. Similarly, taking into account the cyclical factors, by week the demand will be as follows:

| Week | Quantity |
|---|---|
| 1 | 48 |
| 2 | 73 |
| 3 | 122 |
| 4 | 244 |

With the additional modification for random fluctuations it may be as follows:

| Week | Quantity |
|---|---|
| 1 | 42 |
| 2 | 63 |
| 3 | 115 |
| 4 | 250 |

Similarly, considering all factors, for October the values may be the following:

| Week | Quantity |
|---|---|
| 1 | 29 |
| 2 | 49 |
| 3 | 72 |
| 4 | 143 |

Mathematically this process is based on a combination multiplicative and additive model of the following sort:

$$D = (L + T) \times S \times C + R$$

where $D$ is demand.

A pure multiplicative model would express both the trend and random components as percentages, so that the model could be expressed as:

$$D = L \times T \times S \times C \times R$$

**Time Series Decomposition.** Before considering in detail specific methods of time series forecasting, let us consider an overview of the various methods. One set of approaches to time series analysis attempts to examine the series and manipulate the numbers to determine these underlying components of trend, seasonal, and cyclical factors. The foremost embodiment of this approach is contained in the United States government computer programs known as CENSUS II and CENSUS X-11. These are commonly used in Federal forecasts of economic factors (unemployment, cost of living, and so on) and are used by a few firms in aggregate sales forecasting.

Another set of approaches tries to include these factors implicitly through various curve-fitting techniques. Other techniques view the series as a statistical set of numbers related to one another through correlation. Still others seek a combination of these techniques.

While it may seem straightforward to use the approach of determining the components of the series, sometimes referred to as decomposition, that is not always possible nor practical. It is a lot easier to create the series knowing the components than it is to deduce the components given the series, as can be seen by examining Table 2-5. In actuality, in order to determine seasonal component factors from intrinsic data only, at least two years of data are required. However, several years of data are desirable in order to sort out random variations within these factors (such as weather pattern fluctuations from year to year). Furthermore, the pattern would have to be stable over that period; if the trend itself were increasing, a single value would not suffice. Obtaining sufficient data to do this may not be possible, since the average life of a product may be only one to three years. The result is that seasonal factors are often determined for a family of items by assuming groupings based on judgments. In addition, the accuracy of the data and the large random components for individual items, which work to cancel each other out when aggregated over a family of items, tend to make these decomposition techniques appropriate for high-level forecasts and aggregate planning, but not for SKU forecasts.

**TABLE 2-5**
**TABLE OF TYPICAL TIME SERIES FOR ONE YEAR**

| **Week** | 1 | 2 | 3 | 4 | 5 | 6 | 7 | 8 | 9 | 10 | 11 | 12 | 13 |
|---|---|---|---|---|---|---|---|---|---|---|---|---|---|
| **Quantity** | 42 | 63 | 115 | 250 | 59 | 83 | 143 | 279 | 69 | 75 | 117 | 184 | 357 |
| **Week** | 14 | 15 | 16 | 17 | 18 | 19 | 20 | 21 | 22 | 23 | 24 | 25 | 26 |
| **Quantity** | 61 | 93 | 158 | 307 | 46 | 75 | 150 | 279 | 54 | 65 | 108 | 137 | 298 |
| **Week** | 27 | 28 | 29 | 30 | 31 | 32 | 33 | 34 | 35 | 36 | 37 | 38 | 39 |
| **Quantity** | 49 | 70 | 115 | 238 | 40 | 51 | 86 | 200 | 37 | 37 | 70 | 81 | 180 |
| **Week** | 40 | 41 | 42 | 43 | 44 | 45 | 46 | 47 | 48 | 49 | 50 | 51 | 52 |
| **Quantity** | 29 | 49 | 72 | 143 | 46 | 67 | 107 | 203 | 51 | 75 | 112 | 149 | 237 |

The second category of techniques, those which have implicit seasonal and other factors, in some manner assumes a mathematical equation such as:

$$D = a + bt + ct^2 + r, \text{ or}$$
$$D = a + bt + ct^2 + dt^3 + r, \text{ or}$$
$$D = a + bt + c(\sin wt + \cos wt) + r$$

The first two equations are called *polynomials* and may have only the $a$ (average) and $r$ (random component) terms, or the $t$ (time) term may be added for higher powers. The third equation is primarily the so-called Fourier series and makes use of *sin* (sine) and *cos* (cosine) terms to handle cyclical and seasonal factors. While the level and trend factors are often identified as equivalent to the $a$ and $b$ coefficients in these equations, that is not always the case, and care should be exercised or arguments may result. To illustrate this point, consider the difference between saying that demand is 100 and increasing at 10 units per month versus saying that it is increasing at a 10 percent rate. The former results in the following trend:

| | | | | | |
|---|---|---|---|---|---|
| 100 | 110 | 120 | 130 | 140 | 150 |

The latter creates the trend:

| | | | | | |
|---|---|---|---|---|---|
| 100 | 110 | 121 | 133 | 146 | 161 |

since the magnitude of the increase is itself increasing even though the rate is constant. The equations for the two series involving demand and trend respectively follow:

$$D^1{}_T = 100 + 10(T - 1)$$

and

$$D^2{}_T = 100 \times (1.1)^{T-1}$$

The first equation is a polynomial, but the second is an exponential equation.

The third set of techniques attempts to determine the correlation between successive values in the series, including those separated by various time intervals, and thus to build a predictive model. While these techniques are very promising, they are not widely used as yet in SKU forecasting.

Finally, it should be pointed out that, since the polynomials do not handle seasonality very well, it is common and quite useful to establish seasonal factors through analyses of groups of items, to "deseasonalize" or modify the series for a particular item accordingly, and then to apply a simple polynomial approach to the resulting series. Also, one must not overlook judgmental approaches such as visual examination of graphs or looking at a series of numbers to get a *feel* for the data.

**Moving Averages.** Perhaps the simplest of all time series forecasting techniques is a moving average. To use this method, we calculate the average of, say, three periods of actual demand and use that to forecast the next period's demand. For example,

$$D_{5,6,7} = \frac{D_5 + D_6 + D_7}{3}$$

forecasts the demand for Period 8. Since each average is moved ahead one period each time, this is referred to as a *moving average.* The number of periods to use in computing the average may be anything from 2 to 12 or more, with 3 or 4 periods being common. If the time series is essentially like that in Figure 2-1A, in other words, if $D = a + r$, then this is a satisfactory technique from an accuracy standpoint. If, however, there is any trend or seasonal effect, then it will not work very well since it lags behind any changes as illustrated in Figure 2-2.

**FIGURE 2-2**
**MOVING AVERAGE LAGS BEHIND ACTUAL DATA**

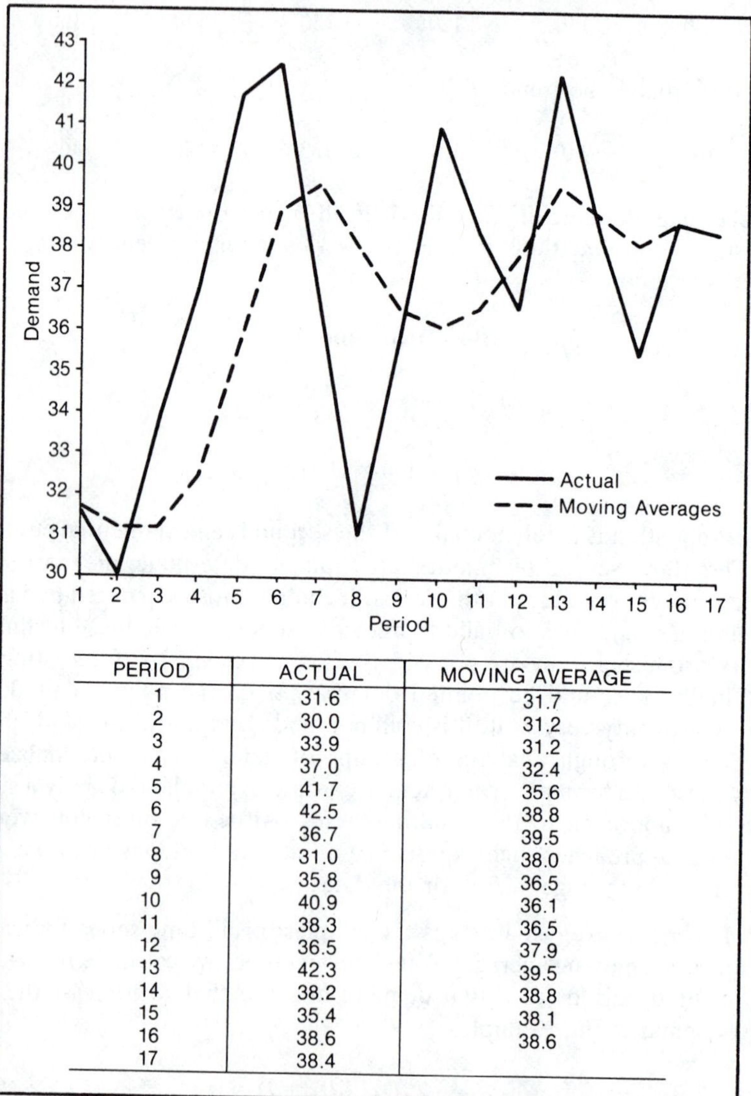


| PERIOD | ACTUAL | MOVING AVERAGE |
|---|---|---|
| 1 | 31.6 | 31.7 |
| 2 | 30.0 | 31.2 |
| 3 | 33.9 | 31.2 |
| 4 | 37.0 | 32.4 |
| 5 | 41.7 | 35.6 |
| 6 | 42.5 | 38.8 |
| 7 | 36.7 | 39.5 |
| 8 | 31.0 | 38.0 |
| 9 | 35.8 | 36.5 |
| 10 | 40.9 | 36.1 |
| 11 | 38.3 | 36.5 |
| 12 | 36.5 | 37.9 |
| 13 | 42.3 | 39.5 |
| 14 | 38.2 | 38.8 |
| 15 | 35.4 | 38.1 |
| 16 | 38.6 | 38.6 |
| 17 | 38.4 | |

The standard approach to determining seasonality coefficients makes use of a 12-month average. This works because it is assumed that the seasonal pattern is constant over the period of interest. In order to use this approach to produce 12 months of indexes it is necessary to have at least 24 months, and preferably 3 or more years, of data available. The procedure is quite straightforward. The moving average of each twelve months is calculated and placed on a line centered between the central months, that is, six (June) and seven (July). For example, in Table 2-6, the average for the 12 months March through February is 123.42, and this figure is entered between August and September. The average of the months April through the following March is 123.00, which is placed between September and October. Now the average of these two values is computed (123.21) and placed opposite their common period, September. Next, the ratio of September actual to this *centered 12-month moving average,* as it is called, is computed. This process is repeated for each month. If several years of data are available, the average of all July monthly indexes is computed and used as the index value for July and similarly for each other month. This process works fairly well, and better if the random component is small.

**TABLE 2-6**
**SEASONAL COEFFICIENTS THROUGH A CENTERED MOVING AVERAGE**

| | Actual Demand | 12-Month Moving Average | Centered Average | Seasonal Index |
|---|---|---|---|---|
| January | 149 | | | |
| February | 167 | | | |
| March | 180 | | | |
| April | 161 | | | |
| May | 148 | | | |
| June | 129 | | | |
| | | 124.08 | | |
| July | 117 | | 124.08 | 0.94 |
| | | 124.08 | | |
| August | 89 | | 123.75 | 0.72 |
| | | 123.42 | | |
| September | 78 | | 123.21 | 0.63 |
| | | 123.00 | | |
| October | 61 | | 123.13 | 0.50 |
| | | 123.25 | | |
| November | 87 | | 123.08 | 0.71 |
| | | 122.92 | | |
| December | 123 | | 123.33 | 1.00 |
| | | 123.75 | | |
| January | 149 | | 124.04 | 1.20 |
| | | 124.33 | | |
| February | 159 | | 124.50 | 1.28 |
| | | 124.67 | | |
| March | 175 | | 124.79 | 1.40 |
| | | 124.92 | | |
| April | 164 | | 124.83 | 1.31 |
| | | 124.75 | | |
| May | 144 | | 124.75 | 1.15 |
| | | 124.75 | | |
| June | 139 | | 124.75 | 1.11 |
| | | 124.75 | | |
| July | 124 | | | |
| etc. | etc. | | | |

On the assumption that the most recent actual data are more indicative of the future than are older data, a weighted moving average can be computed. A typical equation for this might be

$$D_{5,6,7} = \frac{2 \times D_5 + 3 \times D_6 + 4 \times D_7}{2 + 3 + 4}$$

where $D_{5,6,7}$ is used to forecast demand for Period 8.

Weighting factors can be any values, and the denominator is the sum of the weights. The average is moved just as in a simple moving average system. As a comparison, examine Table 2-7 and Figure 2-3 (page 65). Although here the average differences indicate that the second weighted moving average had the least average error, it does not mean it will for all series of data.

**TABLE 2-7**
**COMPARISON OF MOVING AVERAGES**

| | | Forecast | | | | | |
|---|---|---|---|---|---|---|---|
| | | 3-Period Moving Average | | 3-Period Weighted Average Weights—2, 3, 4 | | 3-Period Weighted Average Weights—1, 5, 9 | |
| Period | Actual Demand | Forecast | Error | Forecast | Error | Forecast | Error |
| 1 | 98 | | | | | | |
| 2 | 85 | | | | | | |
| 3 | 86 | | | | | | |
| 4 | 89 | 90 | 1 | 88 | 1 | 86 | 3 |
| 5 | 93 | 87 | 6 | 87 | 6 | 88 | 5 |
| 6 | 88 | 89 | − 1 | 90 | − 2 | 91 | − 3 |
| 7 | 73 | 90 | −17 | 90 | −17 | 90 | −17 |
| 8 | 74 | 85 | −11 | 82 | − 8 | 79 | − 5 |
| 9 | 80 | 78 | 2 | 77 | 3 | 75 | 5 |
| 10 | 82 | 76 | 6 | 76 | 6 | 78 | 4 |
| 11 | 76 | 79 | − 3 | 80 | − 4 | 81 | − 5 |
| 12 | 72 | 79 | − 7 | 79 | − 7 | 78 | − 6 |
| 13 | 71 | 77 | − 6 | 76 | − 5 | 74 | − 3 |
| Sum of Errors | | | −30 | | −27 | | −22 |

A major difficulty in using moving averages to forecast thousands of stockkeeping units is that *N*-1 periods (*N* being the number of demand periods used in the average; three in our example) of data must be retained; and *N* multiplications, *N*-1 additions, and one division must be performed for each forecast. This amounts to a great deal of data and many calculations.

**Exponential Smoothing.** Probably the most popular methods for forecasting stockkeeping units are various exponential smoothing techniques. Simple or first order exponential smoothing can be viewed several ways. One approach is to build a forecasting technique based on the forecasting errors. If the forecast, $F$, for Period $n$ is $F_n$ and the actual demand for Period $n$ is $D_n$, then one can forecast the next period as being $F_n$ plus some fraction, $(a)$, of the current error $(D_n - F_n)$.

**FIGURE 2-3**
**RELATION OF ACTUAL TO MOVING AVERAGES**

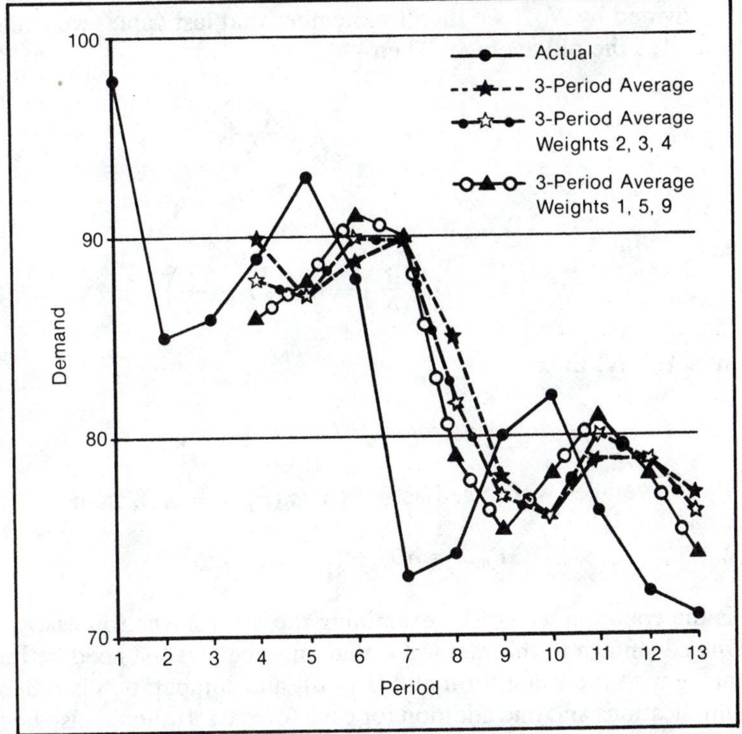


$$F_{n+1} = F_n + a(D_n - F_n)$$

or

$$F_{n+1} = aD_n + (1 - a)F_n$$

The same formula can be arrived at by looking at the simple moving average equation.

$$A_n = \frac{D_n + D_{n-1} + \cdots + D_{n-N+1}}{N}$$

Now

$$A_{n-1} = \frac{D_{n-1} + D_{n-2} + \cdots + D_{n-N}}{N}$$

or

$$A_n = A_{n-1} + \frac{D_n}{N} - \frac{D_{n-N}}{N}$$

that is, the new average, $A$, equals the old average plus the new actual demand divided by $N$ minus the oldest actual demand used in computing the previous average, divided by $N$. If we didn't remember that last value, we could estimate it as $A_n$, the old average. Then

$$A_n = A_{n-1} + \frac{D_n}{N} - \frac{A_{n-1}}{N}$$

or

$$A_n = D_n\left(\frac{1}{N}\right) + A_{n-1}\left(1 - \frac{1}{N}\right)$$

and if $a = 1 \div N$, then

$$A_n = aD_n + (1 - a)\,A_{n-1}$$

and if these averages were used as forecasts ($F_{n+1} = A_n$), then

$$F_{n+1} = aD_n + (1 - a)F_n$$

which is the equation we got by examining the error in the forecast.

One advantage to this method is that only the forecast need be remembered along with the value for $a$ and $(1 - a)$, and computation is reduced to two multiplications and one addition for each forecast. It should also be noted that this is really a weighted moving average type of relationship. Large values of $a$ place heavy weight on the most recent actual demand data and lesser weight on historical values. To see why this is true, note the following derivation:

$$A_n = aD_n + (1 - a)A_{n-1}$$

but

$$A_{n-1} = aD_{n-1} + (1 - a)A_{n-2}$$

and

$$A_{n-2} = aD_{n-2} + (1 - a)A_{n-3}$$

Therefore, combining the last two equations,

$$A_{n-1} = aD_{n-1} + (1 - a)[aD_{n-2} + (1 - a)A_{n-3}]$$

or

$$A_{n-1} = aD_{n-1} + a(1-a)D_{n-2} + (1-a)^2 A_{n-3}$$

Similarly, this last equation can be substituted in the original formula:

$$A_n = aD_n + (1-a)[aD_{n-1} + a(1-a)D_{n-2} + (1-a)^2 A_{n-3}]$$

and by combining terms

$$A_n = aD_n + a(1-a)D_{n-1} + a(1-a)^2 D_{n-2} + (1-a)^3 A_{n-3}$$

Since $a$ must be between zero and one, this amounts to a moving average with decreasing weights of

$$a \qquad a(1-a) \qquad a(1-a)^2$$

and so on.

These latter forms of the equations are never used, but they are logically equivalent to the first form. As shown in Table 2-8, the weights decrease rapidly for $a$ close to one and slowly for values close to zero. In practice, the relationship between $a$ and an equivalent moving average of $N$ periods may be approximated by

$$a = \frac{2}{N+1}$$

**TABLE 2-8**
**DECREASING WEIGHTS FOR OLDER TIME PERIODS**

| Period | 1 | 2 | 3 | 4 | 5 |
|---|---|---|---|---|---|
| Weights | a | a(1 − a) | a(1 − a)$^2$ | a(1 − a)$^3$ | a(1 − a)$^4$ |
| a = .9 | .9 | .09 | .009 | .0009 | .00009 |
| a = .6 | .6 | .24 | .096 | .0384 | .01536 |
| a = .1 | .1 | .09 | .081 | .0729 | .06561 |

The problem with simple exponential smoothing is that, as with any simple average technique, it lags behind changes in the series. To compensate for this, several variations have been devised. Each looks different and some really are different. They generally are referred to as smoothing with trend correction or second order smoothing.

As an example of this, we can calculate the current trend, $t_n$, as

$$t_n = A_n - A_{n-1}$$

Next, apply the smoothing concept to get a new average trend, $T_n$, by

$$T_n = at_n + (1-a)T_{n-1}$$

We can now "correct" the average by applying this trend factor to yield an estimate of the new average as

$$A_n + \frac{1 - a}{a} T_n$$

Now to forecast for a period ($N$) in the future, we multiply this average by $N$ and multiply the trend by the sum of the increases so that the forecast becomes

$$F_{n+N} = N\left(A_n + \frac{1 - a}{a} T_n\right) + \frac{N(N + 1)}{2} T_n$$

If $N = 1$, then

$$F_{n+1} = A_n + \frac{(1 - a)}{a} T_n + T_n = A_n + \frac{T_n}{a}$$

As a comparison of these equations with single smoothing, look at Table 2-9. The data series is the same as was used in comparing moving averages.

**TABLE 2-9**
**SMOOTHING WITH TREND CORRECTION**

| | | Forecasts | | | | | | | |
|---|---|---|---|---|---|---|---|---|---|
| | | First Order a = .9 | | First Order a = .6 | | Trend Corrected a = .9 | | Trend Corrected a = .6 | |
| Period | Actual Demand | Fore-cast | Error | Fore-cast | Error | Fore-cast | Error | Fore-cast | Error |
| 1 | 98 | | | | | | | | |
| 2 | 85 | | | | | | | | |
| 3 | 86 | | | | | | | | |
| 4 | 89 | 87 | 2 | 88 | 1 | 82 | 7 | 84 | 5 |
| 5 | 93 | 89 | 4 | 89 | 4 | 90 | 3 | 88 | 5 |
| 6 | 88 | 93 | −5 | 91 | −3 | 97 | −9 | 92 | −4 |
| 7 | 73 | 89 | −16 | 89 | −16 | 85 | −12 | 87 | −14 |
| 8 | 74 | 75 | −1 | 79 | −5 | 60 | 14 | 68 | 6 |
| 9 | 80 | 74 | 6 | 76 | 4 | 71 | 9 | 68 | 12 |
| 10 | 82 | 79 | 3 | 78 | 4 | 83 | −1 | 77 | 5 |
| 11 | 76 | 82 | −6 | 80 | −4 | 85 | −9 | 81 | −5 |
| 12 | 72 | 77 | −5 | 78 | −6 | 72 | 0 | 76 | −4 |
| 13 | 71 | 73 | −2 | 74 | −3 | 68 | 3 | 69 | 2 |
| Sum of Errors | | | −20 | | −24 | | 5 | | 8 |

NOTE: Initial forecasts based upon using average of Periods 1 and 2 as old average and Period 3 actual demand in the respective formulas; e.g., Period 4 forecast, first order smoothing, $a = .6$, no trend correction: $.6(86) + (1 + .6)(98 + 85) \div 2 = 88.2 \approx 88$.

**Double or Second Order Smoothing.** The concept of smoothing can be applied more generally to many series. As an example, we can apply it not only to the observed values as in

$$A_n = aD_n + (1 - a)A_{n-1}$$

but we could also smooth the smoothed averages by

$$A'_n = aA_n + (1 - a)A'_{n-1}$$

As Brown [1] has shown, these can then be used in a linear trend model of the form

$$F_{n+T} = m + s \times t$$

Where

$$m = 2A_n - A'_n$$

and

$$s = \frac{a}{1 - a}(A_n - A'_n)$$

This approach is referred to as second order exponential smoothing or double smoothing. Unfortunately, some of the literature has identified the equation

$$F = 2A_n - A'_n$$

as double smoothing but that is only the estimate of the average and doesn't fully account for the trend component. It has been shown by Brown [2] that this formulation is equivalent to first order smoothing with trend correction. An example of the application of second order smoothing is shown in Table 2-10.

**TABLE 2-10**
**SECOND ORDER SMOOTHING**

| Period | Actual Demand | Forecast a = .6 | Error |
|---|---|---|---|
| 1 | 98 | | |
| 2 | 85 | | |
| 3 | 86 | | |
| 4 | 89 | 84 | 5 |
| 5 | 93 | 87 | 6 |
| 6 | 88 | 93 | −5 |
| 7 | 73 | 88 | −15 |
| 8 | 74 | 69 | 5 |
| 9 | 80 | 68 | 12 |
| 10 | 82 | 77 | 5 |
| 11 | 76 | 82 | −6 |
| 12 | 72 | 75 | −3 |
| 13 | 71 | 70 | 1 |
| Sum of Errors | | | 5 |

Another exponential smoothing type model which tries to apply the smoothing concept more broadly is the so-called Winter's Model. [3] It attempts to incorporate in one equation separately smoothed average, trend, and seasonal factors. The basic equation is

$$A_t = a\frac{D_t}{S_{t-L}} + (1 - a)(A_{t-1} + T_{t-1})$$

where $L$ is the length of the season (number of periods per year). Trend is updated by

$$T_t = b(A_t - A_{t-1}) + (1 - b)T_{t-1}$$

and seasonality by

$$S_t = c\frac{D_t}{A_t} + (1 - c)S_{t-L}$$

The forecast for period $m$ is then

$$F_{t+m} = (A_t + mT_t)S_{t-L+m}$$

Note that different smoothing coefficients ($a$, $b$, and $c$) may be used in these relationships. While the computations for this seem much more complex than for simple smoothing, the technique has proved feasible in practice and appears to work quite well.

Over the years many variations on the simple exponential smoothing concept have appeared in the professional literature and have been incorporated into different companies' computer programs for forecasting. One of those is termed *adaptive smoothing* by its developer, R. G. Brown. [4] It involves the use of trigonometric functions, *sine* and *cosine*, to fit a time series and exponential smoothing to update coefficients. A typical example is

$$F_t = a + bt + c(\sin wt + \cos wt) + d(\sin 2wt + \cos 2wt)$$

Equations containing these types of trigonometric relationships are known in mathematics literature as Fourier series and have been used for hundreds of years to fit data points just as polynomials have. The Fourier equation has an advantage when seasonal or cyclical phenomena are being represented. The complexities of fitting such functions are beyond the scope of this book (see Brown [5]); but it should be noted that the technique is reported to work quite well in some cases and has been incorporated in an IBM computer package, *Consumer Oriented Goods System,* sometimes referred to as COGS.

In attempting to get better forecasts while still retaining the computational advantages of exponential smoothing, many authors have developed variations on the fundamental process. They often focus on changing the value of $a$ in order to make the forecast more responsive to the current happenings when the situation is rapidly changing, but more stable when it appears that the situation is less volatile. These techniques have been viewed as adapting to the situation by varying $a$, and hence they too have been called adaptive smoothing. The basic concept is to examine the forecast error and to use it in some manner to revise $a$.

**Regression Analysis.** While it is not very useful in forecasting SKU's, regression analysis may be useful in aggregate forecasting. The simplest version of regression analysis is often referred to as *trend line* analysis. In its most elemental form, the trend line involves plotting time series data and "eyeing in" a straight line that shows the general upward or downward trend in the data. In a more sophisticated manner, a *best* (in a statistical sense) line can be calculated.

To observe how a best line might be calculated, consider the data in Table 2-11 and the plotting of this data in Figure 2-4. If a line is drawn through the data in Figure 2-4, it conveys the impression of an upward trend of about seven units per period. Mathematically a best line can be determined by selecting a line in such a manner as to minimize the differences between the observed values and the corresponding values on the line.

**TABLE 2-11**
**TYPICAL SCATTER DATA SET**

| Period | Demand |
|---|---|
| 3 | 34 |
| 4 | 43 |
| 5 | 51 |
| 6 | 54 |
| 7 | 62 |
| 8 | 70 |
| 9 | 73 |
| 10 | 80 |
| 11 | 90 |
| 12 | 97 |

If we compute the average $x$ value and the average $y$ value, we can then plot a line which passes through that point. Regardless of the inclination of that line, we will find some observed values above it and others below it. If we add those differences, they will sum to zero no matter what the slope of the line. Thus, to get the best line, we must do more than just use the sum of the differences. We can attempt to minimize the sum of the absolute values of these differences, but that is computationally difficult. A preferred alternative is to minimize the sum of the squares of these differences. When this is done, we can then use the familiar statistical measure of standard deviation and variance to make statements about the accuracy of our forecasts. (This is true as long as certain statistical assumptions hold true, e.g., the series is stable and the random component is distributed in a normal distribution fashion.)

**FIGURE 2-4**
**SCATTER DIAGRAM AND TREND LINE**

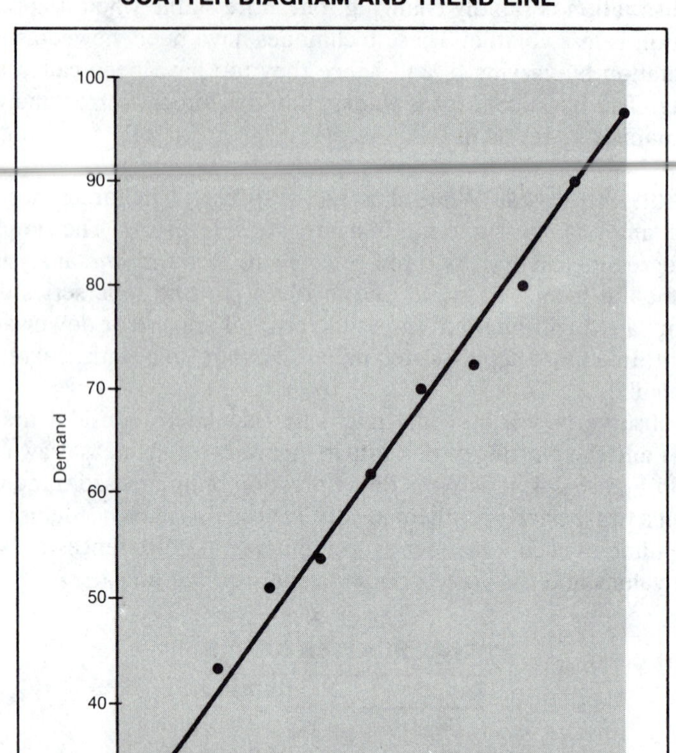


The specific model we use has coefficients of the form:

$$y = a + bx + r$$

where $r$ is a random component and we estimate $a$ and $b$ by

$$b = \frac{n\Sigma xy - \Sigma x \Sigma y}{n\Sigma x^2 - (\Sigma x)^2}$$

and

$$a = \frac{\Sigma y}{n} - \frac{b\Sigma x}{n}$$

where the $x$'s and $y$'s are the observed values and $n$ is the number of values.

The computations for these equations are given in Table 2-12. Substituting in the equations for $a$ and $b$ the following occurs:

$$b = \frac{10 \times 5458 - 75 \times 654}{10 \times 645 - 75 \times 75} = \frac{54580 - 49050}{6450 - 5625}$$

$$b = \frac{5530}{825} = 6.703$$

and, therefore,

$$a = \frac{654}{10} - \frac{6.703 \times 75}{10} = 65.40 - 50.27$$

$$a = 15.13$$

Thus, our equation is

$$y = 15.13 + 6.703x$$

This line does pass through the mean of $x$ and $y$ values; therefore, the sum of the differences is zero. Of all such lines it is the one for which the sum of the squares of the differences is least.

**TABLE 2-12**
**COMPUTATION OF REGRESSION LINE COEFFICIENTS**

| x | $x^2$ | y | xy |
|---|---|---|---|
| 3 | 9 | 34 | 102 |
| 4 | 16 | 43 | 172 |
| 5 | 25 | 51 | 255 |
| 6 | 36 | 54 | 324 |
| 7 | 49 | 62 | 434 |
| 8 | 64 | 70 | 560 |
| 9 | 81 | 73 | 657 |
| 10 | 100 | 80 | 800 |
| 11 | 121 | 90 | 990 |
| 12 | 144 | 97 | 1164 |
| 75 | 645 | 654 | 5458 |

Closely related to regression analysis is statistical correlation. If two phenomena are observed to move in the same or opposite directions consistently, whether that direction be up or down or back and forth, they are said to be correlated. This does not mean that one *causes* the movement of the other, but only that they are related. An example might be that, whenever the Gross National Product (GNP) of the United States moves up one percent, the Jones Company sales increase by $40,000. And, conversely, whenever there is a similar drop in GNP, sales decrease by approximately a corresponding amount.

**Box-Jenkins Method.** In studying time series data, evidence often shows that when sales are up one month they are up the next month also. Such a situation—the relationship of one period's increase (or decrease) to a subsequent period's increase (or decrease)—is called *autocorrelation.* The periods need not be successive, that is, January and March may move together. The direction of movement need not be the same; for example, an increase in July may mean a decrease in August. Because this relationship is generally true in examining the time series for a particular item, it taints the purity of the mathematical assumptions underlying regression analysis. However, it also provides a powerful tool for forecasting time series; for example, the Box-Jenkins [6] method, which follows.

In regression analysis, or in exponential smoothing for that matter, it was necessary to postulate an underlying model such as

$$y = a + bt$$

or

$$y = a + bt + c(\sin wt + \cos wt)$$

or

$$y = a + bt + ct^2$$

In the so-called Box-Jenkins approach we simply examine the autocorrelation between observed values for various time lags—that is, the relationship between adjacent values, those separated by two periods, those separated by three periods, and so on. The mathematical procedure for doing this is quite complex and can only be done effectively with a computer, but the accuracy can be very good. Regardless of whether there are trend, seasonal, or cyclical factors present, if sufficient data are available (more than one cycle), the coefficients relating the time spaced values can be determined. Generalized statistical software, such as MINITAB [7], and other special programs are becoming increasingly available to facilitate use of this powerful technique.

**Extrinsic Techniques.** Extrinsic techniques use data in addition to or instead of the time series of the values being forecast. We previously mentioned regression and correlation analyses, but in those examples we related only the values themselves over time. If we expand on that concept, we can relate the number of repair parts needed next year to the number of new machines sold last year. Or we can relate the number of absentee employees tomorrow to the weather tomorrow. The first example is of a so-called leading indicator: machines sold leads (in time) demand for spare parts. The second example illustrates a less desirable correlation, since to use it to forecast absenteeism we must first have a forecast of the weather. Perhaps a more useful example of the latter is the U.S. Department of Agriculture forecasting crop yields and hence providing information to forecast harvesting work force needs.

But we need not limit this relational concept to just one variable (say, spare parts) tied to one other variable (machines sold). We can extend this to include many factors. For example, spare parts demand could be a funtion of machines sold, dollar cost of the machines, fraction of that cost represented by the part's cost, expected useful life of the machine, etc. In this case, spare parts demand is called the *dependent variable,* and the others are called *independent variables.* A whole body of statistical knowledge is devoted to this concept of *multiple regression/correlation.* Such techniques can be very useful if (1) the indicators lead by enough time so that one can take action, (2) the correlation is strong, and (3) data are available. Primarily these techniques are useful at aggregate planning levels rather than for SKU forecasting.

**Econometric Modeling.** One other technique worth mentioning is econometric modeling. *Econometric modeling,* as its name implies, is most often used in forecasting aggregate economic measures such as GNP. The basic concept is to develop a set of regression equations relating various factors in the economy and then to solve these equations simultaneously, either by analytic methods or simulation, to forecast economic developments. Although the number of equations may be large, numbering in the hundreds, the accuracy of the forecasts is not particularly good because the true causal, as opposed to correlation, relationships are not known. However, these models do find usefulness in examining the direction of change that may occur at the macroeconomic levels.

## FORECAST ERRORS IN INVENTORY SYSTEMS

The only thing almost always correct about forecasts is that they are wrong—sometimes just a little bit, sometimes a great deal. There is almost always some error.

It is common in both literature and practice to label all differences between actual and forecast values as errors. But this is like saying that all poor performances, be they in games, the classroom, or life, are mistakes. Sometimes poor forecasts (those with serious errors), like poor grades, are because of lack of knowledge; other times errors are due to inherent difficulties in the task. Once in a while they are caused by real mistakes, such as adding two and two to get five.

We should recognize real errors. These have been discussed previously in talking about data quality on the input side of forecasting. The same comments can be extended to cover recording and dimension errors and the use of wrong values in writing a forecast. These are real errors and ought to be eliminated.

A variation of these errors is selecting the wrong model to match the phenomenon it is to forecast. For example, if the true series is actually generated by a function of the following kind:

$$D = d + r$$

in other words, a level demand affected only by random fluctuations, then use of a higher order model such as

$$F = a + bt + ct^2 + r$$

will cause the forecasting model to amplify each random fluctuation, since it is looking for a trend and a change in trend that doesn't really exist. Any mismatch between the model and the real world can thus be viewed as a true error and should be eliminated. However, this is often difficult because we don't really know the nature of real world phenomena.

The other type of error is really caused by the random component of the process that is generating the time series. In the simplest case, where

$$D = d + r$$

the best we can hope to do is to identify correctly the value of $d$. If we do so, then our forecast will equal $d$ and hence

$$D - d = r$$

and

$$D - F = r = \text{error}.$$

Thus, the observed error will reflect the true variability of the underlying process, something that cannot be forecast and which we have to make plans to accommodate. Thus, the statistical distribution of these differences, or errors, can be used to establish safety stocks for inventories, safety lead times for scheduling, or other contingency plans to deal with an uncertain future.

The problem in labeling all these differences, whatever their cause, as errors is that the forecasting system is too often the scapegoat for inadequate actions in other areas. For example, controlling the variability of suppliers in meeting delivery dates and specified quantities may be overlooked as a way of reducing forecast errors, or improving quality control on a production process may not be seen as a way to improve forecasts of shipping quantities.

On the other hand, it should be pointed out that many forecasting systems fail to explicitly use forecast errors to improve future forecasts. In contrast to moving average systems, exponential smoothing averages can be viewed as explicitly feeding back into the forecast the forecast error. This can be seen by examining the basic model,

$$F_{n+1} = F_n + a(D_n - F_n).$$

The term $D_n - F_n$ is the error, and thus the new forecast is simply the original one corrected by a percentage of the error.

The uses of forecast errors lie in two directions. One direction is to improve the forecast itself, including selection of the correct model, use of proper coefficients in that model, and elimination of real errors. The other direction is as a measure of the uncertainty in the future caused by inherent fluctuations in the process that generates the time series. The uses of this latter measure in developing plans and procedures for dealing with forecast errors will be covered in later chapters concerning such topics as setting safety stocks, revising schedules, and planning capacity changes.

## Forecast Error Measurement

In Tables 2-7 through 2-10, we computed the algebraic difference between the actual and forecast demand and the sum of those errors. If the function generating such a demand series were of the following form:

$$D = d + r$$

where $d$ is a constant and $r$ is a random component, it is assumed that $r$ is normally distributed with a mean of zero. Thus, if you subtracted $d$ from every observed $D$ and computed the sum of the differences, it should be zero (or close to it). However, the variance estimate

$$s^2 = \sum_{n=1}^{N} \frac{(D_n - d)^2}{N}$$

would not be zero. The best you could hope to accomplish in forecasting such a series would be to predict $d$ correctly, but there would still be an error of size $r$.

A running total of the forecast errors may be used as a measure of accuracy. Thus, the current error, $e_i$, or deviation is defined as

$$e_i = D_i - F_i,$$

and the cumulative error, $E_i$, is

$$E_i = \Sigma e_n \text{ for all } n.$$

The *Smoothed Average Deviation* (*SAD*) is

$$SAD_i = be_i + (1 - b)\ SAD_{i-1}$$

Since, for this measure, positive errors tend to cancel out negative errors, a usually preferred measure is based upon the smoothed *Mean Absolute Deviation* (*MAD*)[1]:

$$MAD_i = \frac{\Sigma|e_i|}{n} = \frac{\Sigma|D_i - F_i|}{n}$$

or, if exponential smoothing is preferred for averaging instead of the algebraic average, then

$$MAD_i = b|e_i| + (1 - b)MAD_{i-1}$$

where $|e_i|$ means the absolute value, that is, the value without regard for the sign. Usually $b$ is chosen as a small value (0.1) so that long-term averaging is in effect.

In order to see how these different measures behave consider the actual and forecast data shown in Table 2-13 and the corresponding error measures.

**TABLE 2-13**
**MEASURES OF FORECAST ERRORS**

| Actual | Forecast | Current Error $e_i$ | Sum of Current Errors $\Sigma e_i$ | SAD ($b$ = .1) | Absolute Error $\lvert e_i \rvert$ | Absolute Error/No. of Values $\frac{\lvert e_i \rvert}{n}$ | Smoothed *MAD* |
|---|---|---|---|---|---|---|---|
| 150.00 | 153.00 | −3.00 | −3.00 | −.30 | 3.00 | 3.00 | .30 |
| 146.00 | 155.00 | −9.00 | −12.00 | −1.17 | 9.00 | 6.00 | 1.17 |
| 156.00 | 147.00 | 9.00 | −3.00 | −.15 | 9.00 | 7.00 | 1.95 |
| 152.00 | 145.00 | 7.00 | 4.00 | .56 | 7.00 | 7.00 | 2.46 |
| 145.00 | 155.00 | −10.00 | −6.00 | −.49 | 10.00 | 7.60 | 3.21 |
| 146.00 | 154.00 | −8.00 | −14.00 | −1.24 | 8.00 | 7.67 | 3.69 |
| 153.00 | 148.00 | 5.00 | −9.00 | −.62 | 5.00 | 7.29 | 3.82 |
| 157.00 | 146.00 | 11.00 | 2.00 | .54 | 11.00 | 7.75 | 4.54 |

Notice in Table 2-13 that the *MAD* is always positive, but the *SAD* may be positive or negative. The algebraic *MAD* is somewhat more difficult to calculate than the smoothed *MAD* because you have to keep track of $n$ for the divisor.

Returning now to the adaptive smoothing models, one example of such a process is that proposed by Trigg and Leach. [8] They propose to calculate

[1]Defined on page 80.

the ratio of *SAD* to *MAD* and use the absolute value of this ratio as the smoothing constant. They have shown this process to work well under some circumstances.

## The Tracking Signal

The *Tracking Signal*, *TS*, is usually computed as the ratio of the cumulative error to the *MAD;* that is

$$TS_i = E_i / MAD_i.$$

This value can, of course, be positive or negative; but if all is going well it should stay within reasonable limits and not be biased (that is, constantly negative or positive). Just as in statistical quality control where values of the mean of a sample beyond plus or minus three standard deviations cause one to look for the manufacturing process to be out of control, so a tracking signal in excess of plus or minus four is often viewed as indicating that the forecasting process is out of control. (Four rather than three is used because of the statistical properties of the *MAD* as opposed to the standard deviation). If the tracking signal exceeds this limit, the signal is said to be *tripped*, and it is assumed that a fundamental change has taken place in the average demand. Two courses of action are possible: (1) searching for a cause (e.g., marketing campaign, data error, etc.) or (2) temporarily revising coefficient *a* to a higher value. The first action may or may not cause a revision in the forecast parameters while the second attempts to allow the system to right itself by placing heavy emphasis on the more recent data. This latter process is another variation of adaptive smoothing. One must remember that this large a tracking signal may only be a statistical aberration and that it is possible that nothing is actually wrong or in need of correction.

Table 2-14 illustrates the previous paragraph. For the same data set as in Table 2-13, note that the initial one or two values are quite large because all errors were initially assumed to be zero.

**TABLE 2-14**
**TRACKING SIGNAL COMPUTATIONS**

| Actual | Forecast | Error $e_i$ | $\Sigma e_i$ | Tracking Signal |
|---|---|---|---|---|
| 150.00 | 153.00 | −3.00 | −3.00 | −10.00 |
| 146.00 | 155.00 | −9.00 | −12.00 | −10.25 |
| 156.00 | 147.00 | 9.00 | −3.00 | −1.54 |
| 152.00 | 145.00 | 7.00 | 4.00 | 1.62 |
| 145.00 | 155.00 | −10.00 | −6.00 | −1.86 |
| 146.00 | 154.00 | −8.00 | −14.00 | −3.79 |
| 153.00 | 148.00 | 5.00 | −9.00 | −2.36 |
| 157.00 | 146.00 | 11.00 | 2.00 | .44 |

# FORECAST ACCURACY

While we have referred to forecast accuracy and mentioned error measurement and the difference between forecast and actual, we have not examined carefully alternative measures of accuracy or what to do about forecast errors.

First, let us look at measures of accuracy. A watch that gains two minutes each day is never correct (except when first set), while a watch that is stopped is correct twice each day. Obviously the former is preferred to the latter; so frequency of correctness alone is not an adequate measure of desirability. Similarly, a forecast that always understates demand by 5 percent is preferred to one that varies above and below the right value and is sometimes correct, but one never knows when. A forecast that is consistently low (or high) is said to be biased; and, if the amount of bias is known, it can be corrected.

Average errors may be useful if the forecast is biased; but, if not, large negatives cancel out large positives and the measure (average error) doesn't indicate that anything is wrong. Statisticians, for a variety of theoretical reasons, prefer to measure errors by examining the average sum of the squares of the errors, called the *variance*.[2] The square root of this quantity is called the *standard deviation* and the Greek letter, $\sigma$ (sigma), is often used to represent it.

Since the advent of exponential smoothing, the average of the absolute values of deviations has been preferred by many people in production and inventory control. This mean absolute deviation is usually referred to as the *MAD*. The standard deviation places equal emphasis on the first error (in time) and on the last. The *MAD* is usually calculated by applying the fundamental exponential smoothing concept to the absolute deviations and hence emphasizes the more recent errors. If one is going to monitor forecast accuracy by computing the standard deviation, some of the concepts of statistical quality control may then be applicable to the forecasting process.

As was pointed out previously, since there is a random component in the actual demand pattern, we cannot hope to achieve perfect, always correct forecasts. Thus, errors (differences) are to be expected and planned for. Keeping more inventory on hand than one forecasts for a need in a particular time span is one way of dealing with forecast errors. Having such safety stock allows the business to continue operations when unexpected (impossible to forecast) demand occurs. Exactly how to compute such stocks is discussed in the chapters on inventory control.

It should be noted that often the consequences of forecast errors are not symmetric with regard to over and under actual values. Overestimating demand with resultant excess production and inventory leads to a whole

---

[2]In accounting practice, any deviation from plan is often termed a *variance*. Both these terms refer to differences, but are not at all the same concept.

different set of problems than underestimating demand and suffering stockouts and lost customers. Thus, $\sigma$ and *MAD* do not reveal the entire story! One should also look for bias, correlation of errors, and other factors that might be used to improve forecast accuracy.

It was pointed out previously that it is often easier to forecast aggregate demand than demand for individual units. In part, this is a product mix problem in that we don't know which varieties customers may order. It is also a statistical problem governed by the fact that variances are additive. If total demand is viewed as consisting of independent component demands, then the variance of the total error is

$$\sigma_t^2 = \sigma_a^2 + \sigma_b^2 + \sigma_c^2 + \cdots$$

This equation means that if we simply add together the forecasts for the individual items, the variance of the total error will be quite large. Hence, it is usually better to forecast the total demand directly than to sum component forecasts.

One additional, important aspect of forecasting often overlooked is timing of demand as opposed to quantity of demand. If individual orders are large relative to total demand, the most important factor to be considered is the time the order is received. This is one aspect of the *lumpy demand problem.* It is not sufficient to forecast monthly demand if only one order is received and the firm doesn't know whether the order will arrive on the first or the 20th of the month. Extrinsic information or knowledge of timing demand patterns by customers is necessary in these situations.

# QUESTIONS

1. Name three different extrinsic types of data that will be useful in forecasting demand for modular home production.
2. The sales and finance departments of the Orange Computer Company estimate total sales of 1,000 computer systems each valued at an average cost of $247,000. Assuming their forecast is correct, of what use is it and how must it be interpreted by the manufacturing division?
3. The following table shows the demand for Honest John's Elixir. Forecast total demand using (a) a three-period moving average, (b) simple exponential smoothing ($a$ = .2), and (c) regression line analysis. What problems are encountered in using each method?

ELIXER DEMAND

| Month | Sales (In thousands) Liters | 750 ml* | 2,500 ml* |
|---|---|---|---|
| January | 122 | 176 | 79 |
| February | 114 | 179 | 90 |
| March | 126 | 189 | 82 |
| April | 114 | 177 | 98 |
| May | 128 | 192 | 89 |
| June | 127 | 187 | 105 |
| July | 138 | 194 | 104 |
| August | 129 | 186 | 95 |
| September | 148 | 207 | 109 |
| October | 140 | 197 | 104 |
| November | 147 | 205 | 104 |
| December | 147 | 198 | 120 |

*milliliter

**4.** Construct monthly seasonal indexes based on the following data using the 12-month centered moving average technique.

| Month | 1977 | 1978 | 1979 |
|---|---|---|---|
| January | 117 | 120 | 146 |
| February | 124 | 126 | 150 |
| March | 133 | 149 | 181 |
| April | 134 | 138 | 164 |
| May | 126 | 127 | 175 |
| June | 144 | 157 | 186 |
| July | 148 | 179 | 199 |
| August | 158 | 184 | 201 |
| September | 144 | 162 | 193 |
| October | 122 | 135 | 163 |
| November | 108 | 120 | 148 |
| December | 118 | 146 | 170 |

**5.** The following set of data purports to be demand for pencils which are boxed 12 to a carton and have a price of 17 cents, or $2 a box. Point out which entries are likely to be wrong. Why? How can such errors be caught and corrected?

| Week | Quantity | Week | Quantity |
|---|---|---|---|
| 27 | 108 | 39 | 256 |
| 28 | 122 | 40 | 242 |
| 29 | 181 | 41 | 45 |
| 30 | 136 | 42 | 218 |
| 31 | 148 | 43 | 220 |
| 32 | 165 | 44 | 3468 |
| 33 | 2016 | 45 | 3502 |
| 34 | 2232 | 46 | 408 |
| 35 | 190 | 47 | 190 |
| 36 | 224 | 48 | 180 |
| 37 | 232 | 49 | 172 |
| 38 | 480 | 50 | 170 |

6. In order to forecast demand for a new product, you may use an existing product for which you have historical data. Identify four such pairs and tell how their demand patterns might be similar.
7. Given the seasonal indexes, level, and trend shown in the text, deseasonalize the data in Table 2-5, page 60. Why isn't each month's deseasonalized value equal to 100?
8. Having corrected the data in Question 5, assume you are at Week 32. Forecast demand for Weeks 33 through 43 using (a) a four-week moving average, (b) first order smoothing ($a = .1$), (c) double smoothing ($a = .1$), and (d) single smoothing with trend correction.
9. Using the computer in Appendix J, page 608, analyze the same set of data as in Question 8 with three different coefficient *a* values ($a = .2, .3, .9$). Prepare a table showing *a* values versus degree of smoothing and showing error measures. Explain the findings in the table.
10. Even though the theory says first order smoothing with trend correction is the same as second order smoothing, why are values in Table 2-9, page 68 and 2-10, page 69, different?
11. Write a computer program to implement Winter's exponential smoothing model. Compare its results with second order exponential smoothing.
12. Using the data in Table 2-9, page 68, compute the *MAD* and the *TS*.
13. Write a computer program to implement the Trigg and Leach model of exponential smoothing.
14. For the data in Table 2-10, page 69, compute the following error measures: (a) *MAD*, (b) cumulative algebraic errors, (c) maximum absolute error, and (d) sign of the errors. Comment on each of these measures.
15. Referring to Question 3, compute a forecast for each size container as well as the aggregate volume using second order smoothing ($a = .15$). Do the aggregate forecast by summing actual demand, forecasting that series, and summing individual forecasts. Which process works better? Why?

# SELECTED READINGS


1. Robert G. Brown, *Smoothing, Forecastings and Prediction of Discrete Time Series* (Englewood Cliffs, N.J.: Prentice-Hall, Inc., 1963), pp. 126–128.
2. ———, pp. 128–132.
3. P.R. Winters, "Forecasting Sales by Exponentially Weighted Moving Average," *Management Science*, Vol. 6 (April, 1960), pp. 324-342.
4. Brown, op. cit., pp. 158–173.
5. ———, pp. 160–164.
6. George E. Box and G. M. Jenkins, *Time Series Analysis: Forecasting and Control* (San Francisco: Holden-Day, Inc., 1970).
7. Thomas A. Ryan, Jr., Brian L. Joiner, and Barbara F. Ryan, *MINITAB Student Handbook* (North Scituate, Mass.: Duxbury Press, 1976).
8. D. W. Trigg and A. G. Leach, "Exponential Smoothing with an Adaptive Response Rate," *Operational Research Quarterly*, Vol. 18 (March, 1967), pp. 53–59.
9. J. Scott Armstrong, *Long-Range Forecasting* (New York: John Wiley & Sons, Inc., 1978).
10. Steven C. Wheelwright and Spryros Makridakis, *Forecasting Methods for Mangagement* (New York: John Wiley & Sons, Inc., 1977).

# —3—

# THE MASTER PRODUCTION SCHEDULE

The Master Production Schedule (MPS) [1] is a statement of the anticipated manufacturing schedule for selected items by quantity per planning period. The items on the MPS plus those on the final assembly schedule should encompass all known requirements. The production plan (sometimes called the *aggregate plan*) sets the overall level of manufacturing output and inventory levels by broad product groups usually per month as described in Chapter 1; the MPS is a manufacturing plan of specific items by quantity usually per week.

The production plan is general management's control knob on aggregate factors such as the size of the labor force, the aggregate inventory level, customer service objectives, and capacity resource requirements; whereas the MPS is the point of disaggregation at which marketing and manufacturing agree to meet specific demand requirements with available resources. It is misleading to label planning at one of these levels more important than planning at the other. Both are important links in the planning chain.

Figure 3-1 illustrates the relationship of the MPS to other manufacturing planning, execution, and control activities. The production plan establishes the broad policy limits for the MPS that is an anticipated build schedule of selected items. The *Final Assembly Schedule* (FAS) is a schedule of the operations required in the production of finished goods. In some cases almost all items on the MPS are final products; thus, the MPS is the FAS. In other cases, the items on the master schedule are combined in various ways at a later date into different final product configurations, are painted or finished differently, or are packaged or bottled differently with each combination constituting a different final product. Thus, the FAS is sometimes called the finishing schedule, mixing schedule, or packing schedule. In such cases the FAS frequently is a distinct but integral part of the MPS.

In a make-to-order environment orders are entered into the FAS; in a make-to-stock environment inventory or products on the FAS must be allocated to orders received.

Material Requirements Planning (MRP) uses the MPS to determine the needs for the components required in the production of items on the MPS.

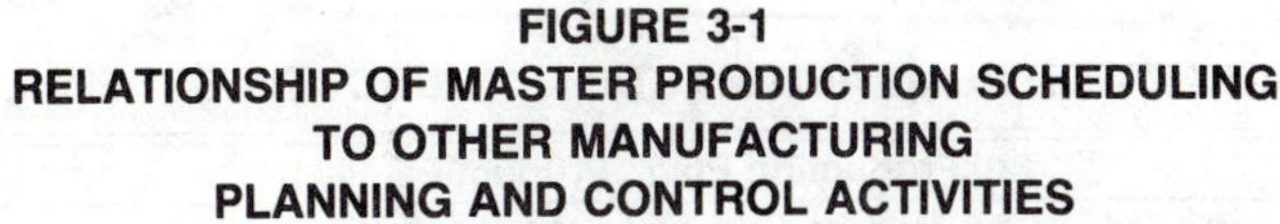
**FIGURE 3-1**
**RELATIONSHIP OF MASTER PRODUCTION SCHEDULING TO OTHER MANUFACTURING PLANNING AND CONTROL ACTIVITIES**

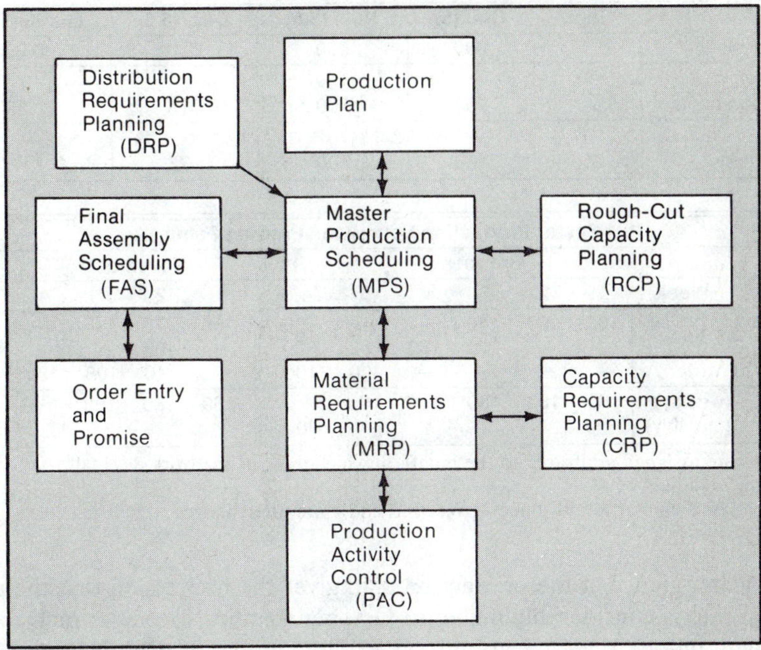


MRP is described in Chapter 4. The relationships of MRP to Capacity Requirements Planning (CRP) and Production Activity Control (PAC) are described in Chapters 5 and 12.

# PRODUCTION PLAN AND MASTER PRODUCTION SCHEDULE ILLUSTRATED

Table 3-1 is an illustration of a production plan and the corresponding master production schedule for a single product group for one quarter. Most production plans cover 12 months with the plan being rolled over at least each quarter and preferably monthly. *Rolled over* means that as one quarter ends, the MPS is extended for another quarter.

Simplifying assumptions: (1) The required production time per unit is the same for all three products, (2) setup time is negligible. Cases in which these assumptions are not made will be examined shortly; however, the example is consistent with the basic relationship that:

$$\begin{array}{ccccccc} \textit{Ending Inventory} & = & \textit{Beginning Inventory} & + & \textit{Production} & - & \textit{Requirements} \\ 75 & = & 200 & + & 2{,}200 & - & 2{,}325 \end{array}$$

**TABLE 3-1**
**PRODUCTION PLAN AND MASTER PRODUCTION SCHEDULE**

**(a) Production Plan: Product Family A**

| | Months (Weeks in the Month)* | | | | |
|---|---|---|---|---|---|
| | **Sept.** | **Oct. (5)** | **Nov. (3.6)** | **Dec. (3.6)** | **Quarter Total** |
| Production | | 900 | 650 | 650 | 2,200 |
| Forecast Requirements | | 950 | 700 | 675 | 2,325 |
| Ending Inventory | 200 | 150 | 100 | 75 | |

**(b) Master Production Schedule: Product Family A**

| | October | | | | | | November† | | | | |
|---|---|---|---|---|---|---|---|---|---|---|---|
| **Week** | **1** | **2** | **3** | **4** | **5** | **Total** | **1** | **2** | **3**** | **4** | **Total** |
| Product 1 | 180 | 180 | 140 | — | — | 500 | 180 | 70 | — | — | 250 |
| 2 | — | — | 40 | 180 | 80 | 300 | — | 100 | — | — | 100 |
| 3 | — | — | — | — | 100 | 100 | — | 10 | 108 | 180 | 298 |
| Totals (weekly) | 180 | 180 | 180 | 180 | 180 | | 180 | 180 | 108 | 180 | |
| (monthly) | | | | | | 900 | | | | | 648 |

*Weeks are assigned arbitrarily to the month in which most of the work days fall.
**Two-day holiday
†December is similar to November—Weeks 3 and 4 are interchanged.

A first glance at the production plan gives the impression that the production rate is considerably higher in October than in November or December when, in fact, the rates are the same. The number of workdays available in these months differ due to holidays and to the convention of assigning weeks to a month, but the production rates are the same. Arbitrary conventions such as the above rule for assigning weeks to months can be altered to match conditions. Other organizations have adopted the 4, 4, 5 convention of assigning 13 weeks to each quarter; 4 weeks are assigned to each of the first 2 months, and 5 weeks to the third month. Holidays, however, and vacation periods require adjustments in planned period output.

An examination of the data in (b) reveals that the production rate per hour is 4.5 units (180 ÷ 40) for all three products. If the hourly production rates of all products are not identical, the product mix will affect capacity requirements. Available capacity constrains the product mix as follows:

$$CR \text{ (Capacity Requirements)} \leq CA \text{ (Capacity Available)}$$
$$CR = \Sigma H_i$$
$$H_i = Q_i \div P_i$$

Where:

$H_i$ is the hours required to produce Product $i$
$Q_i$ is the quantity of Product $i$ required
$P_i$ is the output of Product $i$ per hour

These relationships, the revised production rates given below, and the data in (b) allow us to calculate the capacity requirements for October:

$$P_1 = 4.5 \text{ units per hour}$$
$$P_2 = 5.5 \text{ units per hour}$$
$$P_3 = 3.5 \text{ units per hour}$$
$$Q_1 = 500$$
$$Q_2 = 300$$
$$Q_3 = 100$$
$$H_1 = 500 \div 4.5 = 111.11 \text{ hours}$$
$$H_2 = 300 \div 5.5 = 54.55 \text{ hours}$$
$$H_3 = 100 \div 3.5 = 28.57 \text{ hours}$$
$$CR = \Sigma H_i = 111.11 + 54.55 + 28.57 = 194.23 \text{ hours}$$

Given one 40-hour shift for each of the 5 weeks in October, there are 200 hours of available capacity. Thus, planned output underutilizes capacity slightly by 5.77 hours (200 − 194.23). Now let us look at November which has an available capacity of only 144 hours (3.6 × 40) due to the two-day holiday in Week 3.

$$Q_1 = 250, Q_2 = 100, Q_3 = 298$$
$$H_1 = 250 \div 4.5 = 55.56$$
$$H_2 = 100 \div 5.5 = 18.18$$
$$H_3 = 298 \div 3.5 = 85.14$$
$$CR = \Sigma H_i = 158.88 \text{ hours}$$

Capacity required is greater than capacity available; therefore, one of the following must be done:

1. The product mix must be changed if an aggregate output of 648 units is desired.
2. Approximately 15 hours of additional capacity must be obtained through overtime, adding personnel, subcontracting, or a combination thereof.
3. The planned aggregate output and the MPS for one or more of the three products must be reduced.

The primary point is that the planned aggregate production output places constraints on the MPS. In this case the planned aggregate output, 648 units, is based on an aggregate output average rate of 4.5 units per hour. This rate is consistent with the rate for Product 1 but not with rates for Products 2 and 3. If an aggregate output rate of 4.5 units per hour is to be used in the aggregate plan, the weighted average output rate, $R_i$, of all products in the period must equal 4.5:

$$\text{that is, } \overline{R_i} = \frac{\Sigma H_i R_i}{\Sigma H_i}$$

A case can be made for using work hours as a measure of aggregate production in such situations; but given that 250 units of $Q_1$ and 100 units of $Q_2$ are to be produced, there are approximately 70 hours left for producing $Q_3$; and at a rate of 3.5 units per hour, approximately 245 units of Product 3 can be produced without overtime. However, if an aggregate output of 4.5 units per hour is desired (perhaps the profit and return on investment are the same for each product), then the quantity of Product 2 must be increased and that of Product 3 decreased further to achieve the desired profit and rate of return per hour.

What effect do such decisions have on customer service and inventory levels? Will the required material and tooling be available? These are the types of questions the master scheduler must ask when making the final draft of the master schedule. The mathematical programming methods described in Chapter 17 can provide insight and assistance to the master scheduler in the allocation of resources to achieve specific goals. Simulation techniques described in Chapter 18 also can be helpful.

# ORGANIZATIONAL FACTORS

A number of organizational factors influence the nature of MPS. These will be treated briefly before we deal with the development of an MPS in and of itself.

In a make-to-order company with long lead time where the entire product is fabricated after receipt of the order, the MPS is a schedule of orders. However, in the fabrication of many items with long lead times (such as the fabrication of special truck bodies for the utilities industry), common components are built to stock and special items and the final assembly are built to order. In such cases, there is a master production schedule that has at least two parts, one for components built to stock and one for special components built to order. In addition, there is an FAS. Furthermore, if some orders require engineering and manufacturing process design efforts, engineering and manufacturing process design capacities should be scheduled just as component and assembly fabrication production resources are.

In a make-to-stock company, the MPS is a schedule of those orders generated by inventory requirements. In many such companies a time-phased order point (TPOP) approach is used while in others the traditional order point practice is followed with the timing of production requirements established by the master scheduler working in concert with marketing. Of course, it is not unusual for an organization to have both make-to-order and make-to-stock items on its MPS.

For example, the Hyster Company plant in Portland, Oregon, builds standard components of lift trucks to stock and assembles final product configurations to customer orders. The Elliot Company plant in Jeanette, Pennsylvania, builds apparatus engineered to meet customer specific requirements. For these products they master schedule engineering design, purchasing, and fabrication. [2]

# DEVELOPING THE MASTER PRODUCTION SCHEDULE

The steps required in the development of an MPS are:

1. Select the items, the levels in the Bill of Materials (BOM) structure to be represented by the items scheduled (both components and final assemblies may be included). See Appendix A (page 586) for a description of the BOM.
2. Make the revisions necessary on the BOM to obtain consistency between the BOM and the listing of items on the MPS.
3. Organize the MPS by product groups.
4. Determine the planning horizon, the time fences, and the related operational guides. The *planning horizon* is the span of time from the present covered by the MPS; it must be equal to or longer than the time required to carry out the plan. *Time fences* are boundaries of planning horizon subperiods in which different guidelines govern schedule modifications. Within a typical time fence certain changes are not permitted.
5. Obtain the necessary informational inputs.
6. Prepare the initial draft of the MPS.
7. Calculate the Rough-Cut Capacity Requirements Plan (RCP).
8. Revise the initial draft of the MPS to obtain a feasible schedule. Further revise the MPS so that it approaches an optimum. Mathematical programming approaches to this task are described in Chapter 17. Simulation approaches are discussed in Chapters 5 and 18.

The first four steps are clearly system design activities while the remainder are steps in the on-going master scheduling process.

## Level in the Bill of Materials

Deciding the BOM Level represented on the MPS determines which items will be contained in the master schedule. These MPS items frequently will not be the same as the final product. In fact, some of these items may exist as a set of parts, organized in a planning BOM for scheduling and control purposes only. Four alternative levels of aggregation are illustrated in Figure 3-2. Appendix A provides further information on the BOM. The four levels are described here.

*Case I* illustrates a situation in which the FAS and the MPS are one and the same. This condition exists when final assemblies are built to stock

FIGURE 3-2
MPS ITEM LEVEL — BOM STRUCTURES

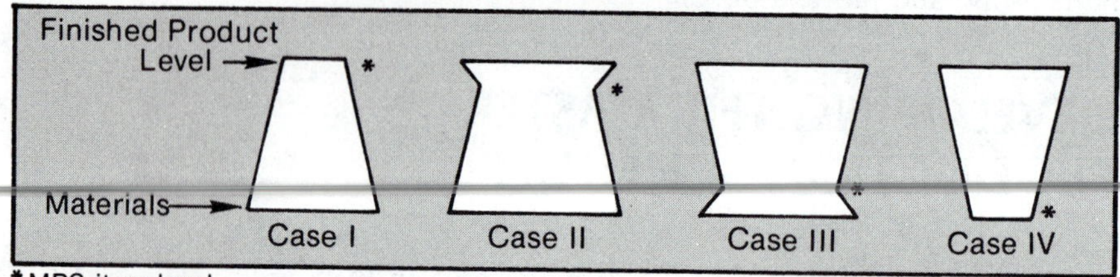


*MPS item level

and sold as catalog items. Consumer goods such as electric drills, sanders and hedge trimmers are examples.

*Case II* represents the fabrication of final products from common subassemblies, components, and materials. Thus, the MPS may list subassemblies, purchased or fabricated parts, paint, and packaging materials. Liquids and other bulk materials marketed in different size containers and perhaps even with different labels frequently are scheduled in this manner. Automobiles built to order from stocked components and subassemblies are other excellent examples of an MPS a level or two below the final product in the BOM.

*Case III* represents the situation where relatively few basic ingredients are combined at an intermediate level in the BOM. These intermediate products then are used in making many different final products. Chemical companies frequently have such a relationship between MPS items and final products. In Case II relatively little processing takes place in converting MPS items into final products; whereas in Case III the conversion of MPS items into final products generates a relatively large portion of the manufacturing activity.

*Case IV* differs from Case III in that the MPS states only the requirements for purchased materials and all production is based on the FAS. This is typical of organizations which purchase materials to stock and perform all fabrication to order. Job shops producing machined parts and tool and die manufacturers are two examples.

## Restructuring the Bill of Materials

Each item of the MPS must be identified by a unique part number on the BOM. This may present some problems since BOMs usually are developed by engineering to reflect the design of the product and not stages necessary in its manufacturing process. In some situations a planning BOM is developed to facilitate manufacturing control. The planning BOM does not alter the engineering specifications; it merely organizes the product definition in some of the ways described as follows.

Numbers are assigned to sets of items not sold or fabricated as an assembly but usually consumed in the production of final products in predictable proportions. This approach may be applied to a group of items, such as hardware, which go into all final products or to optional items which vary from final product to product. The proportions of 4, 6 and 8-cylinder engines demanded in Ford Mustangs is an example.

Specific item numbers may be required to identify assemblies partially completed and stored before the addition of special features which distinguish the many possible variations in the next level of assembly. The objectives of restructuring the bill of material are as follows:

1. Reduce the number of items in the MPS to a manageable level.
2. Unambiguously identify every item on the MPS.
3. Adequately identify semiprocessed parts and assemblies as they move from one step in the manufacturing process to the next.
4. Facilitate observation and control of product mix changes affecting material and production requirements.

Some parts that are not MPS items in terms of final assembly components achieve that status due only to their service parts requirements. For example, a solenoid may be a component part of a switch subassembly which is an MPS item and it also may be a service part with independent demand.

If the number of such parts is large and threatens to clutter the MPS, they may be combined into a few groups for scheduling purposes. If, for example, the demands for three such items (let's call them *S*, *E*, and *R*) have a 1.0:2.0:2.5 ratio (i.e., usually two *E*s are sold for every *S* and for every 2½ *R*s) they can be scheduled as a set in keeping with the principle: minimize the number of items needed to adequately represent the MPS. [3]

# The Planning Horizon

A principle of planning is that a plan must cover a period at least equal to the time required to accomplish it. This means that the MPS planning horizon (the time period which it covers) must be at least as long as the lead time required to fabricate the MPS items. This includes production and procurement time.

Many organizations divide the planning horizon into periods with different controls on schedule changes. The closer a period is to the present, the tighter are the controls on schedule changes. For example, time fences (the boundary between different periods) may be established at the fourth week, and eighth week (two month) boundaries (as in Table 3-2), with the following limitations on changes in the MPS. The location of time fences and the

**TABLE 3-2**
**MPS PLANNING HORIZONS**

| Period | Time Horizon | Conditions | Approval Required |
|---|---|---|---|
| A | 0–4 weeks | Emergency | Top management |
| B | 4 weeks–8 weeks | Dramatic shift in requirements | Marketing-manufacturing negotiation |
| C | Beyond 2 months | Normal | Master scheduler |

nature of the approval required is dependent on the situation. Varying lead times, market conditions and processing flexibility make for different time fences, sometimes at different plants within the same firm. Time fences should be tailored to specific product groups as lead time may vary widely between groups. In all cases, the MPS is the vehicle for coordinating a balanced achievement of marketing and manufacturing goals.

In Period C (beyond 2 months in Table 3-2) the MPS is prepared in harmony with the production plan. A good production plan will make preparation of the MPS straightforward in this time frame. Product families are extended into MPS items, as illustrated in Table 3-1.

In Period B (4 to 8 weeks in our example) things become a bit sticky. What is known as a *Zero Sum Game* exists. Any additions to the schedule must be counterbalanced by comparable deletions. Changes in demand patterns, unusual orders, or equipment failures may warrant changes in the MPS. These changes are usually negotiable between marketing and manufacturing with the master scheduler determining their feasibility before final acceptance. The product mix may change but not the production rate. In Period A only an act of God or top management can change the MPS.

As the time for order execution and manufacturing approaches, labor and material are committed. Change in the schedule can be disruptive and costly. These costs must be compared with the benefits of the change. Following time-fence-control guidelines, which reflect realistic lead time constraints and competitive factors, will result in an MPS that promotes manufacturing stability and productivity while providing reasonable flexibility in meeting marketing demands. The competitive environment may force decisions to restructure the BOM, to develop a modular BOM, to produce to stock at a higher level in the BOM, or to move time fences.

## Data Requirements

The preparation of an achievable and meaningful MPS requires that the following information be available:

1. Knowledge of all production requirements
2. Load profile of each MPS item
3. Capacity available
4. Availability of material and tooling

One of the roles of the master production scheduler is to carry out the demand management function of recognizing and tabulating all sources of demand including these:

1. Forecast and actual
   a. Customer orders
   b. Service parts requirements
   c. Interplant orders

2. International (plant) orders
3. Special promotions
4. Safety stock
5. Seasonal inventory requirements

These requirements should be tabulated for each of the items and the product groupings on the MPS.

A *product load profile* is a list of the time required in each of the critical work centers to produce an item. It is sometimes called a *resource profile* or a *bill-of-labor*. The latter term is appropriate when labor availability is the critical factor. A *load profile* is a statement of the resources required to produce a given mix of a family of items. Engineering time is included if appropriate. Setup time is either allocated to each unit based on the usual lot size or listed separately. The load profile is necessary to calculate resource requirements, as described later. An example of a load profile is presented in Table 3-3.

**TABLE 3-3***
**LOAD PROFILE FILE DATA (EXAMPLE)**
**PRODUCT GROUP A**

| Work Center | | Setup Time (hours) | Operation Time (hours) (100 units) | Week |
|---|---|---|---|---|
| 101 | Turret Lathes | 1.2 | 16.0 | 1 |
| | | .8 | 22.0 | 2 |
| 102 | Vertical Lathes | 2.7 | 30.0 | 2 |
| | | | 18.7 | 3 |
| 201 | Mills | 1.5 | 20.0 | 2 |
| | | .5 | 14.0 | 4 |
| 202 | Bridgeports | 1.3 | 30.0 | 2 |
| | | | 34.3 | 3 |
| 203 | Numerical Control | 2.8 | 23.8 | 3 |
| 601 | Welding | .6 | 19.6 | 4 |
| 701 | Subassembly | 2.50 | 73.5 | 5 |

*Note that Product 1 consists of more than one component, thus the capacity required may be varied.

If the MPS is to be meaningful, the capacity, materials, and tooling required for its execution and quantity of each available must be known. The uses of this information are in the following description of preparing the initial draft of the MPS. Figure 3-3 is a schematic representation of the information required for master scheduling.

FIGURE 3-3
SCHEMATIC, MPS DATA REQUIREMENTS FLOW

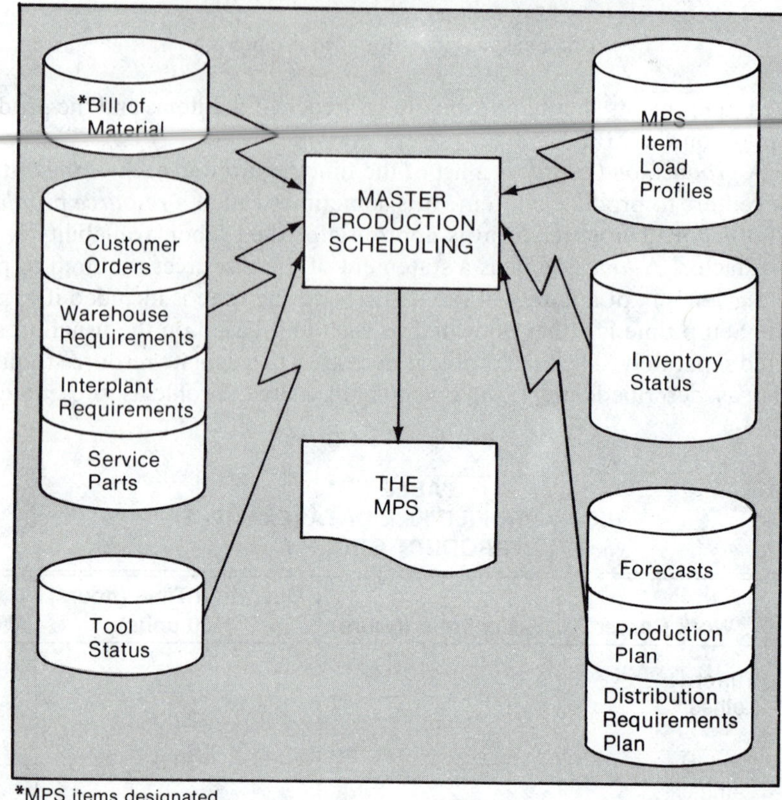


*MPS items designated

# Initial Draft of the MPS

Preparing the first draft of the MPS for a given planning period or group of periods usually takes place when those periods are a considerable distance from the present and there is leeway for schedule revisions. Given that all known requirements have been tabulated and consolidated into the item designations used in the MPS, the requirements on the production resources are calculated by adding (subtracting) the desired adjustments in inventory to (from) the demand requirements. Using the data in Table 3-1 as an example, the total demand requirements are 950 units in October with a desired reduction of 50 units (200 − 150) in inventory leaving a net requirement of 900 units for the month. The initial draft of the MPS then is prepared by listing the net demands for all items in the appropriate periods. The initial schedule of items serves as the basis for rough-cut capacity planning, the determination of the resources required by planning period to achieve the MPS. If the requirements of the MPS do not exceed those of the production plan, the capital requirements, inventory storage requirements, and facility requirements should be available in the aggregate. Given this aggregate availability there is still the possibility that specific item mixes may overtax production or distribution capacities.

## Rough-Cut Capacity Planning (RCP)

RCP is concerned primarily with macro measures of required capacity and should provide an early warning of schedule problems. As such it should measure capacity requirements across broad groups of similar resources and focus on potential work center bottlenecks. In some situations, capacity in some areas—the paint shop, for example—may be known to be well beyond that ever required; while capacity in other areas—welding and heat-treating, for example—may be relatively low and a frequent bottleneck. RCP is concerned primarily with macro measures of required capacity and should provide an early warning of infeasible or difficult schedules.

Calculation of rough-cut capacity requirements requires the availability of a load profile for each MPS item or product group. The load profile is multiplied by the scheduled item quantity per period to determine the capacity required in each critical capacity center for each MPS item. Summing these requirements for all items or product groups will give the capacity requirements per center in each period.

Many organizations have computerized the calculation of rough-cut capacity requirements while others have standard forms and procedures that facilitate manual computations by clerical personnel. In any event the rough-cut capacity required to implement the MPS must be compared to available capacity. Table 3-3 is an example of a tabular load profile that is used in developing work center capacity requirements per period.

A product group load profile is a composite of the capacity requirements of all the components that comprise the individual products in the group. The industrial engineering department usually develops the load profiles from routing file data (see Chapter 5). Figure 3-4 illustrates how a work center load

**FIGURE 3-4**
**WORK CENTER LOAD PROFILE EXAMPLE**

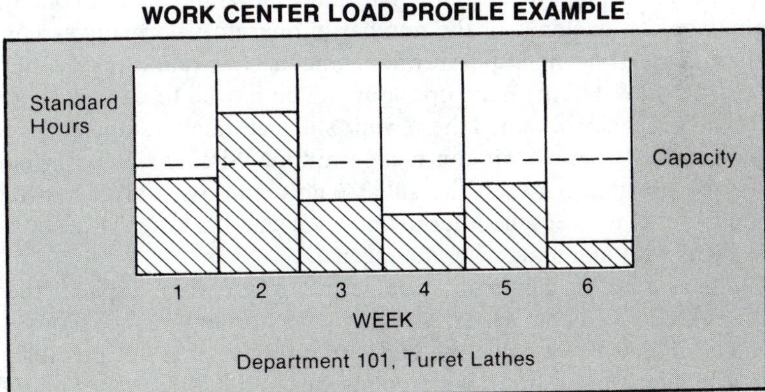

profile can be displayed graphically. Similar profiles can be developed by product for each capacity center.

Multiplying the operation times in Table 3-3 by the October requirements for Product Group A, as stated earlier in Table 3-1, and adding the setup time results in the standard hours of capacity requirements posted in Table 3-4. For example, the total capacity required for Product Group A in Work Center 101 is 2 hours for setup plus 342 (9 × 38) hours for machining, a total of 344 hours. The requirements for two other product groups, B and C, have been added to illustrate the nature of a completed rough-cut capacity plan. The RCP also may be developed by week.

**TABLE 3-4**
**ROUGH-CUT CAPACITY PLAN***
**PERIOD: OCTOBER**

| Work Center | | Product Groups | | | Total | Availability |
|---|---|---|---|---|---|---|
| | | A(900) | B(300) | C(75) | | |
| 101 | Turret lathes | 344 | — | 182 | 526 | 480 |
| 102 | Vertical lathes | 441 | 227 | 41 | 709 | 710 |
| 103 | B & S lathes | — | 309 | 20 | 329 | 620 |
| 201 | Mills | 308 | 281 | 86 | 675 | 750 |
| 202 | Bridgeports | 580 | — | 18 | 598 | 580 |
| 203 | Numerical control | 217 | 106 | 82 | 405 | 460 |
| 601 | Welding | 177 | — | 58 | 235 | 280 |
| 701 | Subassembly | 664 | 104 | 16 | 784 | 930 |
| 801 | Final Assembly | — | 413 | — | 413 | 290 |

* All numbers are rounded to the nearest integer in hours.

# Obtaining a Feasible Schedule

The available hours reflect labor efficiency and machine utilization and are calculated as illustrated in Chapter 1 on long-range planning. A review of Table 3-4 reveals that capacity requirements for the month of October exceed normal availability for the turret lathes, bridgeport mills, and final assembly departments. The question naturally follows: Is capacity constrained by the number of machines or the number of operators normally assigned to the department? If normal operator assignments constrain capacity, perhaps a B & S (Brown & Sharp) lathe operator can be moved to a turret lathe and the necessary capacity obtained there while still maintaining sufficient capacity in Department 103—the labor contract permitting. Similar shifts of personnel also may be possible between the subassembly and assembly departments. It is the job of the master scheduler to know the answers to such questions and resolve them with manufacturing management.

For the sake of further analysis, let us take a case where capacity requirements far exceed available capacity in many departments and reallocation of personnel either will not solve the capacity problem or is not possible. The master scheduler should bring these conditions to the attention of marketing and manufacturing representatives who have the authority to decide which items or orders have priority and which will be postponed to later production periods.

Table 3-4 lists the load for the nine key departments only and not other areas in which capacity is known to be ample. In addition, this RCP does not consider the sequence of operations or the specific weeks or days in which individual lots will be processed in a work center. This occurs later in capacity requirements planning (CRP) as the production period approaches.

## What-If Analysis

Preparation of the MPS and the rough-cut capacity plan presents an opportunity to address a what-if type question such as, What if the sales of Product A increase by 20 percent? The answer can be obtained by simulating the MPS and the RCP for such situations using either a computer program or a manual procedure when the computations are not too laborious.

A review of alternate schedules will enable marketing and manufacturing to agree with the master scheduler in the selection of a feasible MPS. Mathematical programming and simulation techniques are useful for evaluating alternate schedules.

# THE FINAL ASSEMBLY SCHEDULE

The FAS is a statement of those final products which are to be assembled from MPS items. In some organizations, Black and Decker, for example, MPS items and final products are identical and one document serves as both the MPS and the FAS. In many other situations the two are separate and distinct.

In some cases final products differ only by the labeling or packaging of the same MPS item; in others painting or finishes may constitute the difference; while in a third situation vast differences in combinations of MPS items (plus some fabrication) may exist in the transformation of items into a variety of final products. In each of these cases an FAS distinct from but consistent with the MPS must be prepared.

In the manufacture of automatic washers, for example, the motor, transmissions, control units, consoles, tubs, sets of assembly hardware, and various optional accessories may be MPS items with the different models available to the customer being final assemblies. Thus, the manufacture of motors can be authorized long before each motor is committed to the assembly of a particular model. The FAS is constrained by the availability of those items scheduled on the MPS plus those in inventory, the lead time required for assembly, and the assembly capacity.

In an assemble-to-order environment the FAS frequently is stated in terms of individual customer orders and must be consistent with the shipping schedule. In a make-to-stock environment, it is a commitment to produce specific quantities of catalog final products. The shipping schedule depends primarily on available inventory.

In any event, authorization of the final assembly schedule should be held to the last possible moment. This provides the greatest flexibility in meeting actual demand and improves customer service. Since assembly lead time and MPS item availability constrain the FAS, the planning and design, which reduce this lead time and increase flexibility, aid in achieving customer service objectives.

The capacity requirements of the FAS also must be calculated to determine if the plan can be executed. Preparation, measuring of actual output, and control of the FAS should rest with the master scheduler. This enables him to control all demands on resources and coordinate order entry and order-promising activities.

# ORDER ENTRY AND PROMISING

In a made-to-order environment orders are entered in the FAS; in a make-to-stock environment inventory or products on the FAS must be allocated to the orders received. In both cases, items on the MPS or the FAS which are to be used in filling orders must be allocated from those Available to Promise (ATP).

Two principles underlie ATP calculations: (1) make maximum use of all inventory, including safety stock and (2) protect all commitments to customers. [4]

The ATP in a period is calculated as follows:

$$ATP\,(i) = I(i) + MPS\,(i) - (\Sigma cc \mid \text{from period } i \text{ to next MPS receipts})$$

Where:

$i$ is the period
$I$ is inventory on hand
$MPS$ is the receipts scheduled on the MPS
$cc$ is commitments to customers

The term *customers* is used here in the broad sense: any legitimate source of demand including service parts warehouses, other plants, and external customers.

Tables 3-5 and 3-6 illustrate ATP calculations. These tables were adapted from James R. Schwendinger's 1978 presentation concerning master scheduling and order promising at TRW Mission Manufacturing. [5]

The ATP for Period 1 is calculated as follows:

$$\begin{aligned} ATP(1) &= I(1) + MPS(1) - [cc(1) + cc(2)] \\ &= 20 + 20 - (14 + 0) \\ ATP(1) &= 26 \end{aligned}$$

**TABLE 3-5**
**AVAILABLE TO PROMISE (A)**

| Item 110<br>Safety Stock 4<br>Lot Size 20 | Description A-1 Valve<br>Lead Time 2 weeks | | | | |
|---|---|---|---|---|---|
| | P1 | P2 | P3 | P4 | P5 |
| Forecast | — | 10 | 10 | 20 | 20 |
| Inventory on hand | 20 | 26 | 26 | 66 | 66 |
| MPS | 20 | 0 | 40 | 0 | 40 |
| Customer commitments* | 14 | 0 | 0 | 0 | 0 |
| Available to promise | 26 | 26 | 66 | 66 | 106 |

*May correspond to demand

The ATP for Period 2 also equals 26, since there are no scheduled receipts from the MPS or customer commitments in Period 2.

If we commit to ship a new order for 25 units in Period 2, the ATPs will change as illustrated in Table 3-6. The ATP of Period 1 is now one unit, since no receipts are scheduled until Period 3.

**TABLE 3-6**
**AVAILABLE TO PROMISE (B)**

| Item 110<br>Safety Stock 4<br>Lot Size 20 | Description A-1 Valve<br>Lead Time 2 weeks | | | | |
|---|---|---|---|---|---|
| | P1 | P2 | P3 | P4 | P5 |
| Forecast | — | 10 | 10 | 20 | 20 |
| Inventory on hand | 20 | 26 | 1 | 41 | 41 |
| MPS | 20 | 0 | 40 | 0 | 40 |
| Customer commitments | 14 | 25 | 0 | 0 | 0 |
| Available to promise | 1 | 1 | 41 | 41 | 81 |

If another order is received later for shipment of 20 units in Period 1, Week 3 is the earliest possible promised delivery date. All save one of the units available prior to Week 3 have been promised. Of course, if orders for this item continue to pour in at a rate substantially greater than scheduled production, the master scheduler along with marketing and manufacturing representatives should examine the advisability of revising the MPS.

An operational ATP capability will improve order-promising credibility with customers, provide an early warning of customer service problems, and support rational inventory allocation.

## THE PLAN AND THE PERFORMANCE

Some events are known with near certainty:

1. Actual orders will vary from the forecast.

2. Workloads will be unbalanced. Some work centers will be overloaded; others will be operating under capacity in any given period.
3. Vendors will be late in the delivery of key components.
4. Items will be scrapped in the shop.
5. Orders will be canceled.
6. Engineering (or a customer) will decide that an item must be redesigned either for consumer protection or to meet minimum performance requirements.
7. A key piece of equipment will fail.
8. The company president will promise delivery to a favored customer within the frozen planning horizon.

The point is that the master scheduler must have the capability to work with the MPS and capacity planning processes, to measure the impact of such events, and to determine alternative courses of action that will solve or reduce such problems. The master scheduling team, consisting of at least the master scheduler and marketing and manufacturing representatives, can then decide which revised plan is the best.

Two beneficial attributes of MPS and rough-cut capacity planning are: (1) the opportunity they provide to analyze problems and to select a remedial course of action and (2) the what-if analysis capability. The results of such analyses will be enhanced if a capability exists to identify which customer orders result in specific requirements for an MPS item. This capability, illustrated in Table 3-7 is called *pegging*.

Table 3-7, Customer Pegging, is an example of such a record for Item 110, whose MPS and ATP are illustrated in Tables 3-5 and 3-6.

**TABLE 3-7**
**CUSTOMER PEGGING**

**Item 110**
**Description A-1 Valve**

| Period | Quantity | Customer | Order |
|---|---|---|---|
| 1 | 10 | Behomoth Manufacturing | 2798 |
| 1 | 4 | Service Warehouse | 3183 |
| 2 | 25 | Hobnail Diversified | 3275 |

If an order for shipment of five A-1 valves in Period 1 arrives after delivery promises have been made on the three orders listed in Table 3-7, the pegging information reveals the other customer candidates for late or short deliveries. Marketing (or order entry) can check to determine if any of the first three customers will be satisfied with a shipment in Week 3, and can then evaluate the priority of the new order relative to previous commitments.

Previously some predictable events were described. Each one of these events—let's hope all of them don't occur simultaneously—will diminish the chance of accomplishing the goals established in the MPS unless corrective action is taken or the schedule is revised. A complicating aspect of such problems as scrap, late delivery, and engineering changes is that they affect components of MPS items. Without all the components, the MPS items cannot be fabricated. In such event, the MPS items affected by scheduling problems with individual components can be ascertained if requirements are pegged as described in Chapter 4, "Material Requirements Planning." Whenever possible these problems should be resolved without impacting the MPS.

If the problem cannot be rectified, the MPS cannot be met and is no longer realistic. Revision of the MPS should be considered, viewing the priority of all orders, the availability of material and capacity, and the need to utilize capacity. Shop personnel quickly discover when they are working under a schedule that can't be met and, as a result, the MPS loses credibility as a priority planning system. The primary reason for tracing a component with an unsolvable schedule problem to its MPS item(s) using pegged requirements is to reschedule the appropriate MPS items. This will change the priority of the other components that are required to fabricate these MPS items and allow the components to be rescheduled.

This process is especially applicable in the short range when the material requirements plan has been developed and implemented (or will be shortly) through shop orders. The nature and value of this process should become even clearer upon reading those chapters concerned with material requirements planning and production activity control (Chapters 4 and 12).

A pretentious MPS poses another problem. In this case the problem is in the schedule itself. There is a common tendency for the MPS to be overstated, to plan a production output which is greater than capacity in the belief that this will motivate the plant to excel. It seldom works. The MPS should not be a wish list, a dream scheme, or an attempt to motivate manufacturing to improve performance by setting unattainable goals. This lack of credibility will lead to the formal system collapsing and being replaced by an informal system. Priorities and actual production will be established by hastily called conferences, the exhortations of expediters, and ubiquitous lists of hot jobs. The MPS should be a statement of what can and should be produced given normal operating conditions and efficiency. Past performance is a good measure of capacity. The first principle of preparing the MPS is that *the MPS should be realistic*.

Carrying a behind schedule output, in addition to full load for the future periods, also constitutes an overloaded schedule. If there are past-due MPS items (a not uncommon condition), they should be candidates for future schedule periods and compete for capacity along with other items due shortly. To do otherwise generates a meaningless schedule and order promises which are in fact commitments to ship late in proportion to the backlog. Not only the shop but also customers soon begin to pay little attention to the formal system.

## PERFORMANCE EVALUATION

One of the primary purposes of planning is to establish a measure by which performance will be judged. There should be a formal system for reporting actual performance and comparing it with the MPS and the FAS. Differences should be analyzed, causes determined, and future plans and implementation revised accordingly. If planned capacity for a department has been 300 standard hours of output per week but performance reports for the last 10 weeks reveal an average output of 275 standard hours, it makes little sense to continue planning 300. Capacity may have been 300 at one time; it isn't now. The MPS should reflect actual capacity. Other steps should be taken to improve productivity.

If production due dates are missed continually because of late deliveries from specific vendors, future schedules should reflect actual vendor lead times. In the meantime, purchasing should take the steps necessary to decrease lead time.

Measures of available capacity reflect efficiency of shop personnel, equipment utilization, and scrap rates (yield is the complement of scrap). Actual performance differing significantly from the MPS over a number of periods may indicate that one of these factors has changed. The introduction of new products may introduce learning curve type effects; therefore, labor efficiency will be below that achieved in established products.

Vance Dippold [6] reports that Black and Decker's "Productionometer" provides a performance measure by comparing the weekly gross sales value of output with the current MPS and with the MPSs of one year ago and one quarter ago for the same week. This enables an evaluation of both production performance and the validity of schedules made far in advance.

Other measures, such as delivery performance, capacity utilization, inventory turns, inventory investment, back orders, etc., are used by many companies. [7] Performance may differ by facility and product lines within the same company. Separate evaluations for each section of the MPS make sense. The relative importance of performance measures depends on the situation. Chapter 6 discusses many of these measures in detail.

In summary, MPS is the anticipated manufacturing schedule of selected items by quantity per planning period. It includes items that have a substantial impact on low level component requirements and/or resources. Various factors, including product complexity and competitive pressures, determine the BOM level represented on the MPS. MPS items may be final products or they may be low level subassemblies which are combined later into various final products. In the latter case an FAS is a distinct but integral part of the MPS which lists scheduled assemblies by period. Service parts also must be included on the MPS.

Development of the MPS requires information describing production requirements, material and tool availability, the load profile of each MPS item, and available capacity. RCP assures that the MPS does not exceed aggregate capacity constraints.

Tying order entry and order promising to the MPS and the FAS develops order-promising credibility and early warning of delivery problems. The MPS also provides a rational basis for coping with events threatening a schedule disruption and for analyzing what-if questions related to schedule parameters.

The reader may consult the Appendixes and Selected Readings for this chapter for detailed reports on the application of MPS principles. Briefly they are as follows [1]:

1. The MPS must be in concert with the production plan. The sum of the individual parts of the MPS must equal the production plan.
2. The MPS drives the entire manufacturing system. The MPS translates into material requirements which in turn trigger production and purchase orders.
3. Include all known requirements in preparation of the MPS and the FAS.
4. Minimize the number of items that are needed to adequately express the MPS.
5. Treat the MPS as a set of *firm planned orders*. This is MRP terminology that means that the schedule should not be changed by an automatic process but a human assessment and decision should be required.
6. Manage stability in the MPS. Rigid adherence to infeasible schedules will destroy system credibility while continued change will diminish both the plant's ability to respond and its productivity.
7. The MPS should be understandable. It should be understood easily by both management and operating personnel.
8. Close the planning loop. Feedback on shop and vendor performance is required to make revisions in the MPS required by material and capacity shortages. (This is discussed further in the chapters on planning and control.)
9. Safety stock in the MPS should be highly visible to the master scheduler. Safety stock has an inherent lower priority than customer orders and can provide flexibility for schedule revisions.
10. Tie the order-promising activity directly to the MPS. Fill orders either from inventory or the MPS. Realistic promising can take place only if tied to the MPS.
11. Avoid releasing the FAS until the latest possible moment. This provides the greatest flexibility in meeting customer demand.
12. Determine key facility capacity requirements on the basis of the MPS. Only if capacity needs are compared with available capacity can the feasibility of the schedule be determined.
13. Above all, the MPS must be realistic.

## PROBLEMS

**1.** The tree structure BOM for Assembly A follows with the manufacturing or purchasing lead time in parentheses.

a. If all items are made or purchased to order, what is the minimum planning horizon for Assembly A?
b. If management desires to cut the planning horizon in half, what might they do?

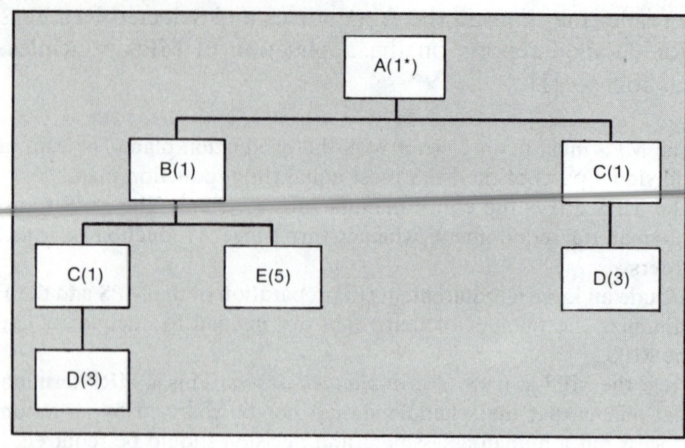


*Weeks

2. Products 1, 2, and 3 constitute Product Group A. The following table gives the number of hours for producing 100 units of each and the typical proportion of total group demand for each product.

| | Product | | |
|---|---|---|---|
| | 1 | 2 | 3 |
| Hours required per 100 units | 20 | 30 | 60 |
| Typical proportion of group demand | .25 | .50 | .25 |

a. How many hours of capacity will be required for 1,000 units of a typical mix of Product Group A?
b. How many hours will be required per 100 units if the mix proportion shifts to .35, .38 and .27 for A, B, and C respectively in a given month?
c. Production of 10,000 units, typical mix, of product group A is planned for each of the next 3 months. How many hours of capacity are required?
d. Given a demand of 10,000 units per month, what changes in the production mix will increase capacity requirements with no change in total volume?

3. Using the data in Table 3-4,
   a. Given that the load represents the typical load expected for the next 6 to 12 months, what department has the greatest need for increased capacity? How much additional capacity is required? How might it be obtained?
   b. What will be the change in capacity requirements if the load for Groups A and B remain the same and the load for Group C increases to 100 units?
   c. What will be the effect if the demand for all groups increases by 10 percent? decreases by 10 percent?
   d. What will be the effect if the demand for A increases to 1,000 units and the demand for B decreases to 200 units? if A decreases to 900 units and B increases to 400 units?
   e. How many weeks does Table 3-4 assume there are in October for planning purposes? Hint: See subassembly in Table 3-3.

**4.** The following data are available for Product 1: Inventory on hand: 15 units. Assembly lead time: 1 week. Available assembly capacity: 15 units per week. Normal safety stock: 5 units. Shipping schedule: Week 1: 15 units; Week 2: 10 units; Week 3: 10 units; Week 4: 12 units. Components are available to assemble 30 units. Normal lead time to obtain components: two weeks. Overtime capability: 5 units each week. Company policy is to guarantee delivery in two weeks or less.

a. What should the FAS be for Weeks 1, 2, 3, and 4?

b. What should it be if an order is received for another five units in Period 2? another 10 units in Period 2?

**5.** A company has 30 units of Product A in inventory. The MPS covers the next 6 periods and calls for production of 40 units each in Periods 2, 4, and 6. Forecast demand is 20 units per period. Promises have been made to customers to deliver 25 units by the end of Period 1 and 15 units by the end of Period 2.

| | PERIOD | | | | | |
|---|---|---|---|---|---|---|
| | 1 | 2 | 3 | 4 | 5 | 6 |
| Forecast | 20 | 20 | 20 | 20 | 20 | 20 |
| Inventory | 30 | | | | | |
| MPS | 0 | 40 | 0 | 40 | 0 | 40 |
| Customer Commitments | 25 | 15 | 0 | 10 | 0 | 0 |
| ATP | | | | | | |

a. What are the projected inventory available at the beginning of each period and the ATP for delivery during each period?

b. Given the above, the company agrees to ship 20 units to another customer in Period 3. What are the projected inventory and ATP in each period now?

c. After the above events occur, an order for 40 units in Period 6 is received from an import company in a foreign country where the company previously had no sales. Determine the projected inventory and the ATP for each period. What action, if any, do you recommend at this time?

**6.** The indented BOMs (without item description) for four final assemblies, B100, B200, B300, and B400 are:

| Item No. | Quantity |
|---|---|
| B100 | 1 |
| B101 | 1 |
| X | 2 |
| Y | 1 |
| Z | 1 |
| B102 | 1 |
| R | 3 |
| Y | 1 |
| Z | 1 |
| B103 | 1 |
| R | 1 |
| S | 3 |
| Z | 3 |

| Item No. | Quantity |
|---|---|
| B200 | 1 |
| B201 | 1 |
| X | 3 |
| Y | 1 |
| Z | 1 |
| T | 2 |
| B103 | 1 |
| R | 1 |
| S | 3 |
| Z | 3 |

| Item No. | Quantity |
|---|---|
| B300 | 1 |
| B201 | 2 |
| X | 3 |
| Y | 1 |
| Z | 1 |
| T | 2 |
| B104 | 1 |
| R | 1 |
| S | 2 |
| Z | 3 |
| Q | 1 |
| T | 1 |

| Item No. | Quantity |
|---|---|
| B400 | 1 |
| B201 | 2 |
| X | 3 |
| Y | 1 |
| Z | 1 |
| T | 2 |
| B101 | 1 |
| X | 2 |
| Y | 1 |
| Z | 1 |

a. Prepare a multilevel tree structure BOM for each of four assemblies. Identify the levels.

b. Prepare a matrix summary BOM combining the four assemblies.
c. The typical ratio of demand among the four assemblies is:
B100 : B200 : B300 : B400 = 4 : 3 : 2 : 1
The forecast demand for this product group is 10,000 units for each of the next 3 months. What is the forecast demand for each assembly during each of these months?
d. Items R, T, X, and Z are purchased parts. How many of each must be purchased each month?
e. the lead time for all items except the following is one week:

| Item | Lead Time |
|---|---|
| 102 | 2 weeks |
| T | 3 weeks |

f. If all items are purchased or produced to order, what is the minimum planning horizon of each assembly?
g. If no items are available, which assembly would be the first scheduled in the final assembly department (for which assembly would the subassemblies be ready first)?
h. B100, B200, B300, and B400 are fabricated in the final assembly department; all other nonpurchased items are fabricated in the subassembly department. The following are the capacity requirements of each item:

| Item | Capacity required per 100 units | Item | Capacity required per 100 units |
|---|---|---|---|
| B100 | 40 work hours | B103 | 15 work hours |
| B200 | 20 | B104 | 25 |
| B300 | 30 | B201 | 25 |
| B400 | 20 | Q | 5 |
| B101 | 15 | S | 5 |
| B102 | 15 | Y | 5 |

How many personnel are required in the assembly department? in the subassembly department (use 160 work hours per month)?
i. If the forecast is stated with a plus or minus 10 percent on the total and on the mix ratio, what are the minimum capacity requirements in the subassembly and final assembly departments?

## SELECTED READINGS

1. William L. Berry, Thomas E. Vollmann, and D. Clay Whybark, *Master Production Scheduling: Principles and Practice* (Washington, D.C.: American Production and Inventory Control Society, 1979).

2. Ibid., pp. 111 and 129.
3. Joseph Orlicky, *Material Requirements Planning* (New York: McGraw-Hill Book Company, 1974), p. 25.
4. Berry, Vollmann, and Whybark, op. cit., pp. 9–16.
5. James R. Schwendinger, "Master Production Scheduling's Available to Promise," *APICS Conference Proceedings* (1978), pp. 316–330.
6. Vance F. Dippold, "Master Production Schedule—The Handle on Business," *APICS Conference Proceedings* (1975), pp. 358–365.
7. Berry, Vollmann, and Whybark, op. cit.
8. Ned W. Brenizer, "The Bottom Line Begins at the Top," *Production and Inventory Management,* First Quarter (1977).
9. C. John Bobeck and Robert W. Hall, "The Master Schedule: New Financial Tool," *APICS Conference Proceedings* (1976).
10. James R. Conlon, "Is your Master Production Schedule Feasible?" *Production and Inventory Management,* First Quarter (1976).
11. Romeyn Everdell, *Master Production Scheduling* (Washington, D.C.: American Production and Inventory Control Society, 1976).
12. Stewart R. Hanson, "The Synergistic Effects of Master Scheduling," *Production and Inventory Management,* Third Quarter (1973).
13. Robert W. Kohankie II, "Master Scheduling: An Ongoing Analytical Process," *APICS Conference Proceedings* (1976).
14. Richard C. Ling and Kemble Widmer II, "Master Scheduling in a Make-to-Order Plant," *APICS Conference Proceedings* (1974).
15. Richard Malko, "Master Scheduling; A Key to Results," *APICS Conference Proceedings* (1976).
16. Paul Maranka, "Master Schedule—A User Applies the Theory," *APICS Conference Proceedings* (1976).
17. Hal F. Mather and George W. Plossl, *The Master Production Schedule* (Atlanta, Ga.: Mather and Plossl, Inc., 1978).
18. Joseph Orlicky, "Closing the Loop with Pegged Requirements and the Firm Planned Order," *Production and Inventory Management,* First Quarter (1975).
19. Gerald A. Sanderson, "Reverse/Balancing Scheduling," *APICS Conference Proceedings* (1981), pp. 76–80.
20. Lars O. Sødahl, "How Do You Master Schedule Half a Million Product Variants?," *APICS Conference Proceedings* (1981).
21. P. B. Spampani, "Executing the Company Game Plan," *APICS Conference Proceedings* (1975).
22. Daniel C. Steele, "The Nervous MRP System: How to Do Battle," *Production and Inventory Management,* Fourth Quarter (1975).
23. Merle D. Ulberg, "Master Scheduling Technique for Rapistan," *APICS Conference Proceedings* (1975).
24. Martin S. Visagie, "Production Control in a Flow Production Plant," *APICS Conference Proceedings* (1975).
25. Oliver W. Wight, *Production and Inventory Management in the Computer Age* (Boston, Mass.: CBI Publishing Co. Inc., 1974).
26. David A. Wilkerson, "Material Requirements Planning and Manpower Planning," *Production and Inventory Management:* Second Quarter (1976).

# —4—

# MATERIAL REQUIREMENTS PLANNING

Material Requirements Planning (MRP) is probably the most significant development in production and inventory control in the last ten or twenty years. It has formed a framework around which other scheduling and control concepts and methods are being developed and against which all other developments are compared. The essence of MRP is Master Production Schedule (MPS) requirements explosion and time-phased planning, both of which we will examine. MRP has fostered a reexamination of topics such as the MPS, aggregate planning, production activity control (PAC), and the general management of inventories. In this chapter, we will explain the rationale and mechanics of MRP including ideas such as independent and dependent demand, gross to net requirements, lead time offset, and lot sizing. Concepts such as the firm planned order (FPO) and net charge versus regenerative updating of the schedule also will be examined. The role of the computer, without which MRP would not be practical, also will be reviewed.

MRP provides the logical tie between the MPS and the detailed inventories and/or purchase or shop orders needed to satisfy the MPS. It is designed to do this on an ongoing basis and to create either new or revised shop or purchase orders as circumstances change. MRP's objectives are (1) to determine what to order, how much to order, when to order, when to schedule delivery, and (2) to keep priorities current for inventory planning, capacity requirements planning (CRP), and shop floor control.

## DATA REQUIREMENTS

MRP is accomplished through a time-phased explosion of the production schedule. To do this (see Figure 4-1) it uses as input the MPS. MRP logic combines this demand information with a description of what components go into a finished product (the product structure file, which is also known as the bill of materials [BOM]), how long it takes to produce or acquire the component, and the current inventory status to determine the quantity and timing of orders to be placed or issued. This process is termed *product explosion* because the demand for one end product breaks up into demand for many component

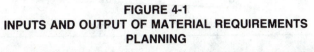

FIGURE 4-1
INPUTS AND OUTPUT OF MATERIAL REQUIREMENTS PLANNING

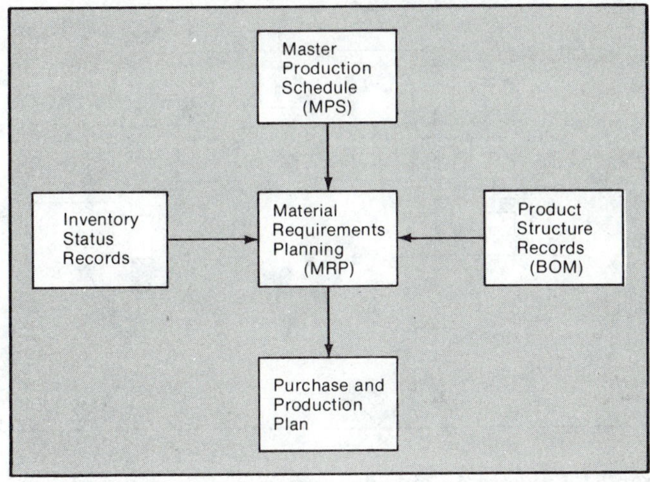


products. It also illustrates the difference between dependent and independent demand; that is, the requirement for table legs is dependent upon the schedule for tables (as is the need for feet on the legs). In contrast there may exist a demand for legs as repair parts independent of the demand for tables. Thus, the MPS might contain a planned production of tables and chairs and separately there would be a forecast for chair legs as spare parts.

# MRP MECHANICS

Individual products may have only a few components, or thousands. Each component itself may be composed of a single item or many sets of items. The relationships can be shown in list or graphic forms. To illustrate two examples, see Figure 4-2, Simple Product Structure, and Figure 4-3, Multilevel Product Structure.

FIGURE 4-2
SIMPLE PRODUCT STRUCTURE

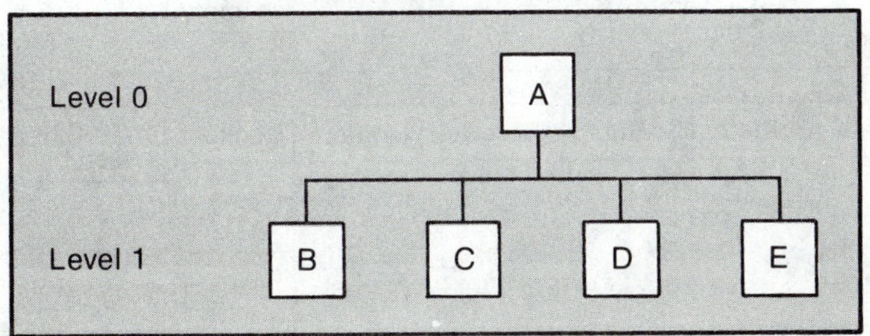

FIGURE 4-3
MULTILEVEL PRODUCT STRUCTURE

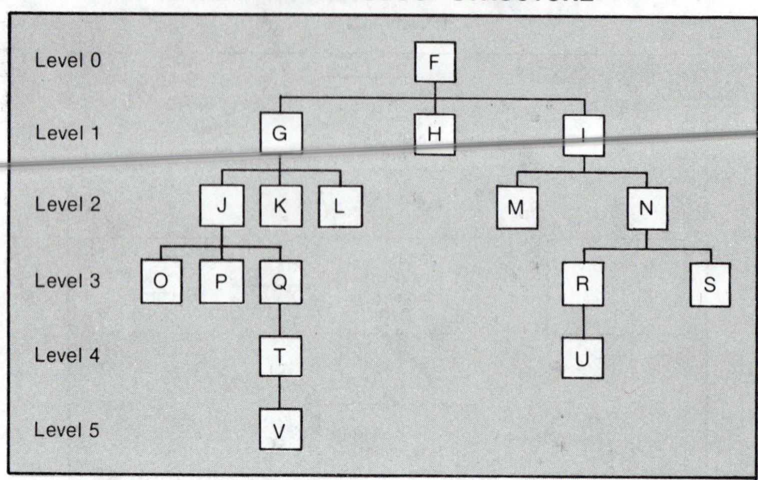


Figures 4-2 and 4-3 illustrate product structure diagrams and what are referred to as product structure levels. The end product is set at Level 0 and its immediate components and/or subassemblies are at Level 1. Each of these levels is similarly divided into successively lower (but by convention, numerically higher) levels down to fundamental components; that is, purchased parts and/or raw materials.

# Gross to Net

In order to understand the basic problem that MRP addresses and how its logic works, consider Figure 4-4, Simplified Product Structure for a Lamp.

FIGURE 4-4
SIMPLIFIED PRODUCT STRUCTURE FOR A LAMP

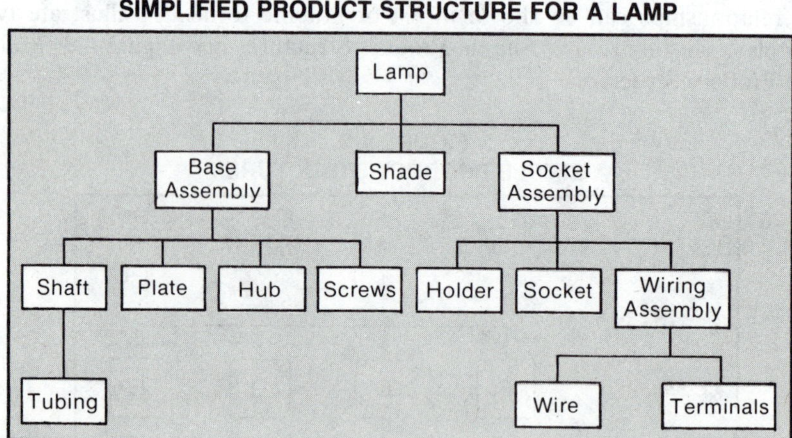

First, let's take an idealized situation where no deviations can cause complications. Consider only the left branch of this diagram: lamp, base assembly, shaft, tubing. Assume we receive an order for 25 of these lamps. We have the following components on hand:

| | |
|---|---|
| Lamps | 3 |
| Base assemblies | 7 |
| Shafts | 4 |
| Tubing | 16 feet |

In this instance each shaft requires two feet of tubing. How much should we order? A simple response would be 22 lamps (25 −3), 18 base assemblies (25 − 7), 21 shafts (25 − 4), and 34 feet of tubing (25 × 2 − 16). This is incorrect, because each unit in a level contains all the components that are below it; that is, each shaft already contains two feet of tubing. Thus, the gross requirement for 25 lamps must be analyzed to get the net requirement at each level. The gross to net logic is as follows:

| | |
|---|---|
| Lamp | |
| Gross requirement | 25 |
| Quantity on hand | 3 |
| Net requirement | 22 |
| Base Assemblies | |
| Gross requirement | 22 |
| Quantity on hand | 7 |
| Net requirement | 15 |
| Shaft | |
| Gross requirement | 15 |
| Quantity on hand | 4 |
| Net requirement | 11 |
| Tubing | |
| Gross requirement (feet) | 22 |
| Quantity on hand | 16 |
| Net requirement | 6 |

These net requirements are considerably less than the previous, simplistically computed ones and represent the true needs to meet the demand for 25 lamps. This preceding process, referred to as *netting* or *gross to net* calculation, must now be combined with a knowledge of how long it takes to either manufacture or purchase the components in order to schedule a start date for each assembly. These time intervals are referred to as the lead times and in this case are as follows:

| | |
|---|---|
| Lamps ............ | 2 weeks |
| Base assemblies .... | 1 week |
| Shafts ............ | 2 weeks |
| Tubing ........... | 3 weeks |

These lead times are used to compute *lead time offsets* for each component.

Assume the order is to be shipped in Week 27, then the offsets are as follows:

| | Week |
|---|---|
| Shipping week........ | 27 |
| Lamp lead time....... | 2 |
| Begin assembly....... | 25 |
| Base lead time........ | 1 |
| Begin assembly ....... | 24 |
| Shaft lead time ....... | 2 |
| Begin manufacture .... | 22 |
| Tubing lead time...... | 3 |
| Order tubing ......... | 19 |

Thus, an order for 6 feet of tubing must be placed in Week 19 in order for the lamps to be shipped in Week 27.

This is the essence of the MRP logic: gross to net and lead time offset. Notice how the net requirement for one level becomes the gross requirement for the next and that the beginning date for one level is the completion or arrival date for the next. The logic for a simple product like this is quite straightforward. When dealing with thousands of items and varying product structures, however, the situation in practice is much more complicated.

## The MRP Chart

As a convenience in visualizing an MRP plan, a diagram or chart such as the following is often used. The Gross Requirements come from the MPS and the On Hand is calculated.

Lead Time: 3 Lot Size: 25

| Period | | 1 | 2 | 3 | 4 | 5 | 6 |
|---|---|---|---|---|---|---|---|
| Gross Requirements | | 10 | 15 | 15 | 10 | 15 | 10 |
| Scheduled Receipts | | | | 25 | | | |
| On Hand | 30 | 20 | 5 | 15 | 5 | −10 | −20 |
| Planned Order Releases | | | 25 | | | | |

Because the quantity on hand would be negative in Period 5, a planned order release is set for Period 2. This is a plan, however, and if gross requirements in Period 3 should fall to 5, then the plan would change as shown at the top of page 113. This illustrates MRP's ability to maintain proper priorities, that is, to work on what is really needed. Note that it is common practice to choose time periods as weeks and to thus lump together or place in each *time bucket* all activities taking place within that week.

Lead Time: 3 Lot Size: 25

| Period | | 1 | 2 | 3 | 4 | 5 | 6 |
|---|---|---|---|---|---|---|---|
| Gross Requirements | | 10 | 15 | 5 | 10 | 15 | 10 |
| Scheduled Receipts | | | | 25 | | | |
| On Hand | 30 | 20 | 5 | 25 | 15 | 0 | −10 |
| Planned Order Release | | | | 25 | | | |

MRP software (computer programs) has been developed by most major computer vendors and some independent software houses. An example output is shown in Figure 4-5. Usually the MRP program is part of a total manufacturing package including forecasting, order entry, inventory and BOM file maintenance, shop floor control, etc. The programs are often separately priced and vary in their capabilities. They generally require modification in order to interface properly with other information systems in a company and may also require fine tuning to operate efficiently with a firm's unique product characteristics.

**FIGURE 4-5**
**TYPICAL MATERIALS PLANNING REPORT**

```
DEVPV220   MV6500    RUN NO. 1                 A. O. SMITH CORPORATION                  12/10/81    18:05    PAGE     1
REVIEW DATE 12/10/81                         INVENTORY PLANNING DETAIL REPORT
2000-3           DESC(24 IN. STD BICYCLE (MODEL 20A)          ) OH(       0) VC(A) LLC( 0) LTC(M) B/A(X)
2000F-1          DESC(FRAME MODEL 21B                          ) OH(       0) VC(B) LLC( 1) LTC(P) B/A(X)
                 PASTDUE  11/10 X 12/10   01/09   02/08   03/10   04/09   05/09   06/08   07/08   08/07   09/06   10/06   FUTURE
GROSS INDEPENDENT                X            100                                                          202
GROSS DEPENDENT                  X
PROJECTED ON-HAND       0       0X      0    -100    -100    -100    -100    -100    -100    -100    -100   -302    -302    -302
PROJECTED AVAIL         0       0X      0       0       0       0       0       0       0       0       0      0       0       0
NET REQUIREMENTS                 X            100                                                          202
PLND ORD REC                     X            100                                                          202

T ---DATES--- --QUANTITIES- ---ORDERS--- C   T ---DATES--- --QUANTITIES- ---ORDERS--- C   T ---DATES--- --QUANTITIES- ---ORDERS--- C
P  REL   DUE   REQD ISS/RCP CUST/PUR/MNF D   P  REL   DUE   REQD ISS/RCP CUST/PUR/MNF D   P  REL   DUE   REQD ISS/RCP CUST/PUR/MNF D
                                                                                          P 10/01 10/01   202
R       01/27   100          CUST-16     I   * 2000-1
R       10/01   202                      D   P 01/27 01/27   100

2000F-1GN        DESC(FRAME MODEL 21B                          ) OH(     680) VC(B) LLC( 1) LTC(P) B/A(X)
                 PASTDUE  11/10 X 12/10   01/09   02/08   03/10   04/09   05/09   06/08   07/08   08/07   09/06   10/06   FUTURE
GROSS INDEPENDENT                X    600     660     820    1450    1180    1340    1500    2100    1860    2020    2750    3000
GROSS DEPENDENT                  X
PROJECTED ON-HAND       0       0X   -600   -1260   -2080   -3530   -4710   -6050   -7550   -9650  -11510  -13530  -16280  -19280
PROJECTED AVAIL         0       0X      0       0       0       0       0       0       0       0       0       0       0       0
NET REQUIREMENTS                 X    600     660     820    1450    1180    1340    1500    2100    1860    2020    2750    3000
PLND ORD REC                     X    600     660     820    1450    1180    1340    1500    2100    1860    2020    2750    3000

T ---DATES--- --QUANTITIES- ---ORDERS--- C   T ---DATES--- --QUANTITIES- ---ORDERS--- C   T ---DATES--- --QUANTITIES- ---ORDERS--- C
P  REL   DUE   REQD ISS/RCP CUST/PUR/MNF D   P  REL   DUE   REQD ISS/RCP CUST/PUR/MNF D   P  REL   DUE   REQD ISS/RCP CUST/PUR/MNF D

R       12/10   100                      I   R       05/27   340                      I   R       11/18   590                      I
R       12/17   110                      I   R       06/03   350                      I   R       11/25   600                      I
R       12/24   120                      I   R       06/10   360                      I   R       12/02   610                      I
R       12/31   130                      I   R       06/17   370                      I   R       12/09   620                      I
R       01/07   140                      I   R       06/24   380                      I   P 12/10 12/10   100
R       01/14   150                      I   R       07/01   390                      I   P 12/17 12/17   110
R       01/21   160                      I   R       07/08   400                      I   P 12/24 12/24   120
R       01/28   170                      I   R       07/15   410                      I   P 12/31 12/31   130
R       02/04   180                      I   R       07/22   420                      I   P 01/07 01/07   140
R       02/11   190                      I   R       07/29   430                      I   P 01/14 01/14   150
R       02/18   200                      I   R       08/05   440                      I   P 01/21 01/21   160
R       02/25   210                      I   R       08/12   450                      I   P 01/28 01/28   170
R       03/04   220                      I   R       08/19   460                      I   P 02/04 02/04   180
R       03/11   230                      I   R       08/26   470                      I   P 02/11 02/11   190
R       03/18   240                      I   R       09/02   480                      I   P 02/18 02/18   200
R       03/20   200          CUST-17     I   R       09/09   490                      I   P 02/25 02/25   210
R       03/25   250                      I   R       09/16   500                      I   P 03/04 03/04   220
R       04/01   260                      I   R       09/23   510                      I   P 03/11 03/11   230
R       04/08   270                      I   R       09/30   520                      I   P 03/18 03/18   240
R       04/15   280                      I   R       10/07   530                      I   P 03/20 03/20   200
R       04/22   290                      I   R       10/14   540                      I   P 03/25 03/25   250
R       04/29   300                      I   R       10/21   550                      I   P 04/01 04/01   260
R       05/06   310                      I   R       10/28   560                      I   P 04/08 04/08   270
R       05/13   320                      I   R       11/04   570                      I   P 04/15 04/15   280
R       05/20   330                      I   R       11/11   580                      I   P 04/22 04/22   290
```

Source: Manufacturing Data System
Courtesy: A. O. Smith Corporation, Data Systems Division

# Lot Sizing

In the preceding example we assumed a lot size of 25, but one of the key questions in implementing MRP is what is the proper lot size. Consider the following situation. (Orders not yet placed are shown in italics on the "Scheduled Receipts" line.)

Lead Time: 2

| Period | | 18 | 19 | 20 | 21 | 22 | 23 | 24 | 25 | 26 | 27 | 28 | 29 | 30 |
|---|---|---|---|---|---|---|---|---|---|---|---|---|---|---|
| Gross Requirements | | | 12 | | | 18 | | | | | 25 | | 12 | |
| Scheduled Receipts | | 15 | | | | *12* | | | | | 22 | | *12* | |
| On Hand | 6 | 21 | 9 | 9 | 9 | 3 | 3 | 3 | 3 | 3 | 0 | 0 | 0 | 0 |
| Planned Order Releases | | | | 12 | | | | | 22 | | 12 | | 15 | |

This is not a properly planned schedule of order releases as evidenced by the seeming lack of correlation between quantities needed and ordered. Assuming that orders can be for any quantity, then ordering the exact quantity that is actually needed (sometimes referred to as the lot-for-lot [L4L] ordering size rule) no on hand inventory should be needed. In practice this doesn't occur for several reasons: orders arrive late (or early), orders are canceled, quantities made (or delivered) are under (or over) those ordered, or the economics or technology dictate constant lot sizes (or multiples thereof).

If we take our previous example, assume that we are planning order releases, and that the lot size must be 15 units, the situation, consequently, will look like the following.

Lead Time: 2 Lot Size: 15

| Period | | 18 | 19 | 20 | 21 | 22 | 23 | 24 | 25 | 26 | 27 | 28 | 29 | 30 |
|---|---|---|---|---|---|---|---|---|---|---|---|---|---|---|
| Gross Requirements | | | 12 | | | 18 | | | | | 25 | | 12 | |
| Scheduled Receipts | | 15 | | | | | | | | | | | | |
| On Hand | 6 | 21 | 9 | 9 | 9 | −9 | −9 | −9 | −9 | −9 | −34 | −34 | −46 | −46 |
| Planned Order Releases | | | | | | | | | | | | | | |

In order to cover the negative On Hand in Period 22, we must plan on Order Releases in Period 20. The result is illustrated in the table at the top of page 115.

Lead Time: 2 Lot Size: 15

| Period | | 18 | 19 | 20 | 21 | 22 | 23 | 24 | 25 | 26 | 27 | 28 | 29 | 30 |
|---|---|---|---|---|---|---|---|---|---|---|---|---|---|---|
| Gross Requirements | | | 12 | | | 18 | | | | | 25 | | 12 | |
| Scheduled Receipts | | 15 | | | | *15* | | | | | | | | |
| On Hand | 6 | 21 | 9 | 9 | 9 | 6 | 6 | 6 | 6 | 6 | −19 | −19 | −31 | −31 |
| Planned Order Releases | | | | 15 | | | | | | | | | | |

Similarly, orders can be planned for release in Periods 25 and 27 as follows:

Lead Time: 2 Lot Size: 15

| Period | | 18 | 19 | 20 | 21 | 22 | 23 | 24 | 25 | 26 | 27 | 28 | 29 | 30 |
|---|---|---|---|---|---|---|---|---|---|---|---|---|---|---|
| Gross Requirements | | | 12 | | | 18 | | | | | 25 | | 12 | |
| Scheduled Receipts | | 15 | | | | *15* | | | | | *30* | | *15* | |
| On Hand | 6 | 21 | 9 | 9 | 9 | 6 | 6 | 6 | 6 | 6 | 11 | 11 | 14 | 14 |
| Planned Order Releases | | | | 15 | | | | | 30 | | 15 | | | |

Notice that in Period 25 we had to place an order for 30 because one lot size of 15 was not enough.

Lot sizing has a number of ramifications in an MRP system. If in the previous example the lot size was 30, our time phasing would be as follows.

Lead Time: 2 Lot Size: 30

| Period | | 18 | 19 | 20 | 21 | 22 | 23 | 24 | 25 | 26 | 27 | 28 | 29 | 30 |
|---|---|---|---|---|---|---|---|---|---|---|---|---|---|---|
| Gross Requirements | | | 12 | | | 18 | | | | | 25 | | 12 | |
| Scheduled Receipts | | 30 | | | | | | | | | *30* | | *30* | |
| On Hand | 6 | 36 | 24 | 24 | 24 | 6 | 6 | 6 | 6 | 6 | 11 | 11 | 29 | 29 |
| Planned Order Releases | | | | | | | | | 30 | | 30 | | | |

Notice that the number of planned orders is decreased, but the average On Hand is increased. On the other hand, if L4L ordering is permitted, then the situation is as pictured in the table at the top of the next page. As can be seen, this results in zero inventory On Hand (after the initial on hand units are depleted). L4L also results in the most orders being placed, orders

Lead Time: 2 Lot Size: L4L

| Period | | 18 | 19 | 20 | 21 | 22 | 23 | 24 | 25 | 26 | 27 | 28 | 29 | 30 |
|---|---|---|---|---|---|---|---|---|---|---|---|---|---|---|
| Gross Requirements | | | 12 | | | 18 | | | | | 25 | | 12 | |
| Scheduled Receipts | | | 6 | | | *18* | | | | | 25 | | 12 | |
| On Hand | 6 | 6 | 0 | 0 | 0 | 0 | 0 | 0 | 0 | 0 | 0 | 0 | 0 | 0 |
| Planned Order Releases | | | | 18 | | | | | 25 | | 12 | | | |

of varying sizes. However, one of the issues raised is trying to balance two opposing costs: ordering cost versus carrying charges.

One approach is referred to as Least Total Cost (LTC). Consider the following demand situation.

Lead Time: 2

| Period | | 1 | 2 | 3 | 4 | 5 | 6 | 7 | 8 | 9 |
|---|---|---|---|---|---|---|---|---|---|---|
| Gross Requirements | | 12 | 15 | 9 | 17 | 8 | 10 | 16 | 7 | 11 |
| Scheduled Receipts | | | 13 | | | | | | | |
| On Hand | 14 | 2 | 0 | −9 | | | | | | |
| Planned Order Release | | | | | | | | | | |

If the cost of holding an item in stock is 5 cents per unit per week and the cost of placing an order is \$5.75, we can attempt to balance these costs of holding and ordering. To do this we compute the cost of ordering for Period 3 just enough to cover needs, that is, 9 units. Then the holding cost will be zero since no inventory will be left. In contrast we could order enough to cover Weeks 3 and 4, that is, 26 units, and incur a holding cost of $17 \times .05 = 85$ cents. Similarly, to cover Weeks 3, 4, and 5, the cost would be $25 \times .05 + 8 \times .05 = \$1.65$. Table 4-1 shows calculations for various coverage periods. The holding costs come closest to balancing the ordering cost if we order to cover Weeks 3 through 7.

A variation of the LTC technique is Part-Period Balancing. [1] It looks ahead (and back) to see whether the inclusion of one or more periods of demand in a planned order might delay a subsequent order and thus reduce the carrying costs. This appears to be a good technique if demand is cyclic but it may not look forward (or backward) far enough.

Another technique,[1] which in theory produces optimal orders, is the Wagner-Whitin dynamic programming algorithm. [2] Given a finite time

[1] See Chapter 10 for a detailed discussion of part-period balancing, the Wagner-Whitin dynamic programming algorithm, and other lot sizing methods.

**TABLE 4-1**
**LEAST TOTAL COST LOT SIZING**

| Coverage Period | Order Quantity | Holding Costs | |
|---|---|---|---|
| 3 | 9 | .05 (0) | = $ 0 |
| 3 and 4 | 26 | .05 (17 + 0) | = .85 |
| 3 thru 5 | 34 | .05 (25 + 8 + 0) | = 1.65 |
| 3 thru 6 | 44 | .05 (35 + 18 + 10 + 0) | = 3.15 |
| 3 thru 7 | 60 | .05 (51 + 34 + 26 + 16 + 0) | = 6.35 |
| 3 thru 8 | 67 | .05 (58 + 41 + 33 + 23 + 7 + 0) | = 8.10 |
| 3 thru 9 | 78 | .05 (69 + 52 + 44 + 34 + 18 + 11 + 0) | = 11.40 |

horizon and known demands, it optimally balances costs. A major problem with it is its complexity and its sensitivity to change. While our planning horizon must be long enough to cover the total lead times for all our items, the dynamics of the real world cause the specific quantities and times to change; hence the optimal solution changes. Small changes at high levels can cause "nervous" changes and instability in dependent demand plans. This is often quite undesirable and is one factor that argues for fixed lot sizes. For example, if the demand changes in our first example with the lot size of 30, there may be no change in planned orders. An illustration of this follows.

Lead Time: 2 Lot Size: 30

| Period | | 18 | 19 | 20 | 21 | 22 | 23 | 24 | 25 | 26 | 27 | 28 | 29 | 30 |
|---|---|---|---|---|---|---|---|---|---|---|---|---|---|---|
| Gross Requirements | | | 12 | 6 | | 18 | | | | | 25 | | 12 | 23 |
| Scheduled Receipts | | | 30 | | | | | | | | *30* | | *30* | |
| On Hand | 6 | 6 | 24 | 18 | 18 | 0 | 0 | 0 | 0 | 0 | 5 | 5 | 23 | 0 |
| Planned Order Releases | | | | | | | | | 30 | | 30 | | | |

In this case, demand over this time horizon has increased by almost 40 percent but planned orders have not changed at all.

The difficulty with each of these fixed lot sizing techniques is that they only look at one level in a multilevel system. The setting of lot sizes for Level 1 of the product structure has impact all the way down through the explosion of that structure. Trying to take into account the carrying and setup costs for all levels simultaneously to establish optimal lot sizes is an area just now being investigated.

## Safety Stock

So long as parts procurement and manufacturing lead time are constant and the MPS is frozen (fixed) for a sufficient period of time to allow for parts procurement or production, no safety stock is required. Competitive pressures frequently prevent the MPS from being fixed for a period as long as the total lead time. Figure 4-6 illustrates a situation in which the MPS must be frozen for at least 16 weeks if there is to be no variability in any requirements. However, if customers expect delivery in six weeks, then subassemblies are planned to a forecast. Parts and materials requirements are based on the schedule of subassemblies; safety stocks are required at the subassembly level if uncertainty in final assembly demand is to be filled within the six-week lead time.

**FIGURE 4-6**
**MASTER PRODUCTION SCHEDULE OF LEAD TIME**

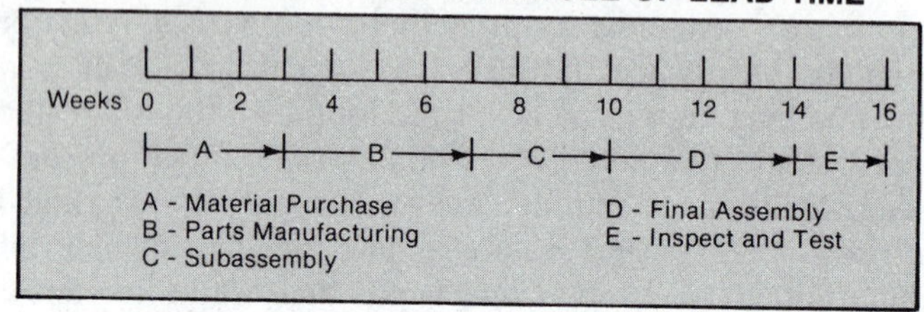


Given a fixed schedule for an assembly (either a final assembly or a subassembly as described previously) both the delivery of purchased material and the manufacturing of parts involve uncertainties. Parts are scrapped late in the manufacturing process, and a new lot cannot be produced within normal lead time. Vendors often do not ship the quantity promised. Vendors also have manufacturing and procurement problems; late delivery and short quantities result. If an item experiences either vendor delivery or manufacturing problems in a regular fashion, safety stock is appropriate. Safety stock requirements are determined as described in Chapter 7.

To illustrate how safety or buffer stocks impact system behavior consider our previous example with a fixed lot size of 15. With a safety stock of 10 units, the plan is illustrated as follows.

Lead Time: 2 Lot Size: 15 Safety Stock: 10

| Period | | 18 | 19 | 20 | 21 | 22 | 23 | 24 | 25 | 26 | 27 | 28 | 29 | 30 |
|---|---|---|---|---|---|---|---|---|---|---|---|---|---|---|
| Gross Requirements | | | 12 | | | 18 | | | | | 25 | | 12 | |
| Scheduled Receipts | | 15 | 15 | | | *15* | | | | | *15* | | *15* | |
| On Hand | 6 | 21 | 24 | 24 | 24 | 21 | 21 | 21 | 21 | 21 | 10 | 10 | 13 | 13 |
| Planned Order Releases | | | | 15 | | | | | 15 | | 15 | | | |

Planned order releases are calculated just as before, except that the trigger point is when the inventory falls below 10 rather than below zero. The direct impact of such safety stock is to raise the average inventory level. This negative aspect is offset by the system's ability to handle unexpected demand increases or time advancements. For example, if demand for 10 units were suddenly to occur in Period 18, it could be accommodated; if the demand of Period 19 were to move up to Period 18, it could be met. And, if a future demand usage occurred, that is, if the demand in Period 22 were to suddenly become 25, no change in the order release for Period 20 would be required with the safety stock. A shortage would have occurred if no buffer stock were present.

An alternative to safety stocks is safety lead times. By overstating the lead time in the plan, the actual deliveries may arrive early and can then be used to satisfy changed demand. Whybark and Williams[3] have shown with a simulation study that, if the uncertainties are in the demand quantities then safety stock quantity is desirable; while, if the uncertainty is in the timing of demand, safety lead times are preferred. Since demand for component items is certain, in the sense that it is dependent demand, in theory there should be no need for safety stock except for independent demand items and end products in the MPS. In practice, however, uncertainty in supply, either purchasing or manufacturing induced, may warrant some type of safety or uncertainty preparedness.

## Firm Planned Orders

One of the difficulties in establishing lot sizes is that the traditional economic order quantity (EOQ) formula looks only at the costs associated with one level in the product structure; but, in the manufacture of multilevel products, as most are, a lot size decision at any level except the bottom results in requirements for items at all levels. For example, the act of producing a gear box assembly necessitates the production of all components at levels below it; that is, gears, castings, shafts, bolts, etc. The impact of the assembly EOQ on these components has usually not been considered until recently.

Consider the following example in which the rotor is a component of the motor assembly.

Motor Assembly    Lead Time: 2    Lot Size: 35

| Period | Past Due | 1 | 2 | 3 | 4 | 5 | 6 | 7 |
|---|---|---|---|---|---|---|---|---|
| Gross Requirements | | | | | 5 | 10 | 10 | 10 |
| Scheduled Receipts | | | | | *35* | | | |
| On Hand | | 0 | 0 | 0 | 30 | 20 | 10 | 0 |
| Planned Order Release | | | 35 | | | | | |

| Rotor | | | Lead Time: 2 | | | | Lot Size: 10 | |
|---|---|---|---|---|---|---|---|---|
| Period | Past Due | 1 | 2 | 3 | 4 | 5 | 6 | 7 |
| Gross Requirements | | | 35 | | | | | |
| Scheduled Receipts | | | *10* | | | | | |
| On Hand | | 25 | 25 | 0 | | | | |
| Planned Order Release | 10 | | | | | | | |

The need for motor assemblies in Period 4 triggers a planned receipt for a lot size of 35. This in turn generates a planned order release in Period 2 and hence a gross requirement for the rotor in the same period. MRP logic causes a past due condition for the planned order release for the rotor. In actuality, the 25 on hand could cover the true need caused by the gross requirements for motor assemblies (5 + 10 + 10), but the lot sizing forces a past due situation. Manual intervention by a production scheduler may be required to either expedite the past due order, change the lot size for the motor assemblies, or introduce what is termed a *Firm Planned Order* (FPO). An FPO is an order entered by the planner that supersedes the computer's MRP logic, that is, the planner does not allow the normal MRP gross to net and lead time offset logic to take place but rather freezes an order in a particular time bucket. In this example, an FPO for 25 could be entered for the motor assembly and then all lower level gross requirements would be determined by its value. The FPO technique can also be used if the planner believes the lead time can be compressed. In this case the planner might decide that the motor assembly can be done in one week instead of two. He therefore enters as an FPO a scheduled receipt of 35 in Week 5 instead of Week 4. This allows the MRP logic to proceed normally in scheduling the rotor. The computer program will probably issue a warning message because it notes the discrepancy between the time the FPO will arrive and when it is logically needed, but the planner just uses this message to prompt expediting.

In practice, it may be possible to have complicated lot-sizing rules although fixed sizes (as illustrated) or minimum lot sizes (for example, order at least 20) are the most common alternatives to L4L ordering. Even the fixed size rule should be subject to reevaluation and periodic recomputation as costs, normal demand levels, or technology change. In addition, human judgement by the production planners should review schedules and use firm planned orders when appropriate.

## Pegging

Next let's complicate our illustration to see one of the other realities of MRP. Frequently engineering designs families of end products that have a common component. MRP must pool the demands for these items. Consider, for example, the two product structures and their time-phased demands shown in Figures 4-7 and 4-8 respectively.

**FIGURE 4-7**
**PRODUCT STRUCTURES**

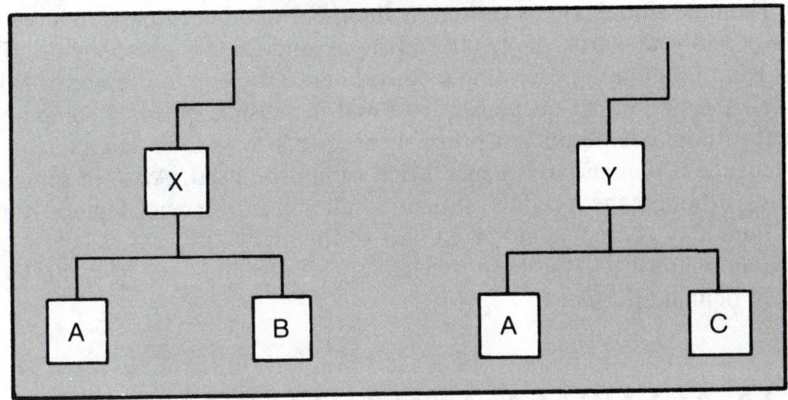


**FIGURE 4-8**
**TIME-PHASED DEMANDS**

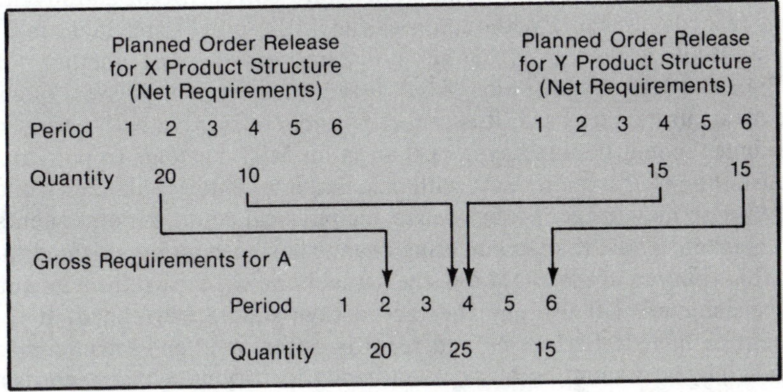


This introduces some interesting complexities. If for some reason the production lot of 25 units of *A* is reduced to 20 units (damage and scrap, low level delays, etc.), what impact should this have on *X* and *Y*? The first question is: Have you kept track of which items gave rise to *A*'s gross requirement of 25 in Period 4? In order to have such a record, valuable computer space must be used to note these parent demands. Furthermore, if this is a multilevel product structure, and it usually is, will you also keep track of succeeding generations (parents, grandparents, etc.) or derive such information from a knowledge of each parent and/or offspring? These are important data processing considerations. This process of keeping track of parents and offspring is termed *pegging* and most systems do *at most* single level pegging (keeping track of parents only) because of the complexities of the data base problem.

More complexity is added by having the same component at different levels or in different branches within the same product; for example, matching decorative hardware on the tables and chairs that constitute a dining room suite of furniture.

The final complexity is caused by the sheer number of parts in a typical firm—possibly upwards of 1,000 end items and 20,000 components. The result is no small data processing task and hence the rise in the use of MRP parallels the pattern of decreasing cost and increasing speed of computers. In fact, without computers it is probably necessary to assume that all demand is independent demand and hence MRP cannot be used. Also, in some instances, although the product structure relationship of the demand for a given item may be dependent, the effect of the many different requirements can be an aggregate demand of a relatively steady rate—in short, an independent demand profile.

## DATA ACCURACY AND DEPENDENCIES

At the base of all MRP computations are correct BOM and inventory status records. In fact, without these the MRP processing logic is quite useless. While it may seem that any company regardless of whether it uses MRP, or EOQ/Re-Order Point (ROP) techniques, or just guesses, ought to have an accurate data base, it is in fact possible to survive with poorer data in an independent demand system than in an MRP system. In part, this is because the MRP system deals with calculated inventory balances while an ROP system may trigger orders because a physical count of components on hand is taken. Thus, if an engineering change has been communicated to the shop floor but not to the BOM file, the actual item withdrawn from inventory will be depleted, not the one the record says should have been. It is not efficient to have actual items and records differ, neither is it uncommon. Periodic physical counting of stock-on-hand to verify data base records aids in maintaining record accuracy and improving data recording procedures. This process is called *cycle counting*. The frequency of counting a particular item depends on many factors. Chapter 10 describes cycle counting in greater detail.

One of the realities of the manufacturing world is change. A critical aspect of any scheduling system is its ability to deal with changes such as shortages, scrap, machine breakdowns, work stoppages by suppliers, absenteeism, engineering changes, etc. When any of these occur, it is necessary to note their impact and to take action accordingly. If any of these actions is going to cause production delays, we should revise our priorities and produce items that are needed rather than those that are not. Returning to the lamp assembly example, if wiring assemblies are going to be delayed because of a shortage of terminals, there is no need to retain the original schedule for base assemblies. We may as well work on another order or we will have an inventory of base assemblies gathering dust while waiting for the socket assemblies. From this example, it can be seen that the key feature of MRP is its ability to de-expedite work when necessary and, hence, to maintain correct priorities so that production can be accomplished on what is really needed.

As information comes in regarding changes, we can immediately revise our schedule; however, this is both unnecessary and undesirable. First of all, notice that MRP provides plans; it does not just issue orders. It is likely that only the plans need be changed, not the orders already issued to the shop floor. Secondly, the time frame of MRP is usually weeks. Changes that cause delays of less than a week aren't recognized by the system. Third, it is preferable to have stability in the system since compensating changes may occur well within the planning horizon. This is a stage at which MRP interfaces with the MPS (discussed in Chapter 3). The planner must decide which changes are feasible and desirable on the basis of customer requirements, material and tooling availability, and the status of work in the shop.

Somewhat associated with change (but equally the result of time passing and hence production being accomplished and new orders received) is the necessity to revise the MRP. This can be done in two ways. One is to start with the current plan and to change it incrementally based upon new information: delays, orders, shipments, etc. This is termed the *net change* approach.

Second, while the net change approach may seem simple, in practice it has usually been found easier to start from the same basic information—the MPS, BOM, and inventory status data—and to regenerate the entire schedule.

A number of factors influence the choice of the firm regarding a net change or a regenerative system. One of these is computer processing time. To effectively perform a net change the program must have pegging and, depending on the computer environment, about 10 parts per minute might be handled. Thus, 2,400 parts could be done in four hours. For a pegged, regenerative system perhaps two or three times as many parts could be handled per unit time, but many more parts must be handled each time the program is run. For a 20,000-part situation, it may take 11 hours to do a complete replanning run. A regenerative system may not contain pegging, in which case processing time is speeded up by a possible factor of 3 or 4. Because product structures, software implementations, and the dynamics of change vary so greatly from company to company it is impossible to state categorically whether net change or regenerative MRP will require less computer time. Inherently a net change system, particularly if it is an on-line system where changes can be input as soon as they occur rather than grouping them for periodic processing, is very responsive to changes. This makes the plan very current, but also causes it to be "nervous." The use of time fences to limit the planning horizon within which changes can be made becomes very critical. Regenerative systems are less responsive but more stable, and hence fewer variations from the plan are noticed. Thus, closer control may be possible with a net change system, but computer costs and stability may argue for a regenerative system. A possible compromise is to net change weekly and to regenerate monthly.

## PROBLEMS

1. Referring to Figyre 4-3, page 110, if there is a gross requirement of 50 units for Product F, what is the net requirement for Part V given the following on hand quantities?

| Part/Assembly | On Hand |
|---|---|
| F | 3 |
| G | 4 |
| J | 2 |
| O | 7 |
| P | 9 |
| Q | 6 |
| T | 4 |
| V | 4 |

2. Referring to Figure 4-3, if 50 units of *F* are to be shipped in Week 30, when must Part V be ordered given the following lead times?

| Part/Assembly | Lead Time (Weeks) |
|---|---|
| F | 3 |
| G | 3 |
| J | 4 |
| O | 2 |
| P | 2 |
| Q | 1 |
| T | 1 |
| V | 3 |

3. For the following situation, determine the planned order releases.

Lead Time: 3 Lot Size: 25

| Period | | 1 | 2 | 3 | 4 | 5 | 6 | 7 | 8 | 9 |
|---|---|---|---|---|---|---|---|---|---|---|
| Gross Requirements | | 15 | 10 | 20 | 5 | 15 | 25 | 10 | 15 | 20 |
| Scheduled Receipts | | 25 | | | | | | | | |
| On Hand | 25 | | | | | | | | | |
| Planned Order Release | | | | | | | | | | |

4. If in Problem 3 the L4L ordering size rule is employed, what are the planned order releases?
5. If in Problem 3 the lot size is 15, what are the planned order releases?
6. For the following situation, determine the planned order releases using the LTC procedure. Ordering cost is $10.00. Holding cost is 15 cents.

Lead Time: 2

| Period | | 1 | 2 | 3 | 4 | 5 | 6 | 7 | 8 | 9 | 10 | 11 | 12 |
|---|---|---|---|---|---|---|---|---|---|---|---|---|---|
| Gross Requirements | | 6 | 4 | 6 | 12 | 8 | 10 | 8 | 8 | 12 | 6 | 8 | 6 |
| Scheduled Receipts | | | | | | | | | | | | | |
| On Hand | 10 | 4 | 0 | | | | | | | | | | |
| Planned Order Releases | | | | | | | | | | | | | |

7. Referring to Problem 1, what is the net requirement for Part V if lot sizes are 15 for all parts/assemblies?
8. What is the significance of the fact that MRP systems refer to planned order releases and scheduled receipts?
9. Many production and inventory control systems are referred to as "order launching systems." In what ways are MRP systems different from these?
10. Why is it critical in MRP systems that BOM and inventory status files be very accurate?

# SELECTED READINGS


1. J. J. DeMatheis, "An Economic Lot-Sizing Technique: The Part Period Algorithms," *IBM Systems Journal,* Vol. 7, No. 1 (1968), pp. 50–51.
2. Harvey M. Wagner and Thomson M. Whitin, "Dynamic Version of the Economic Lot Size Model," *Management Science,* Vol. 5 (October, 1958), pp. 89–96.
3. Clay D. Whybark and J. G. Williams, "Material Requirements Planning under Uncertainty," *Decision Sciences,* Vol. 7, No. 1 (October, 1976), pp. 595–606.
4. Joseph Orlicky, *Material Requirements Planning* (New York: McGraw-Hill Book Company, 1974).

# —5—

# SHORT-RANGE PLANNING

The objectives of short-range planning are to:

1. Fully develop production and purchase requirements by time period
2. Calculate capacity requirements by time period and determine if adequate capacity is available
3. Schedule work assignments (orders) in a manner consistent with job priorities and available capacity
4. Plan order releases

The Master Production Schedule (MPS) and the Final Assembly Schedule (FAS) are the primary inputs to the short-range planning process as illustrated in Figure 5-1. The end item requirements stated in the MPS and

**FIGURE 5-1**
**SHORT-RANGE PLANNING BLOCK DIAGRAM**

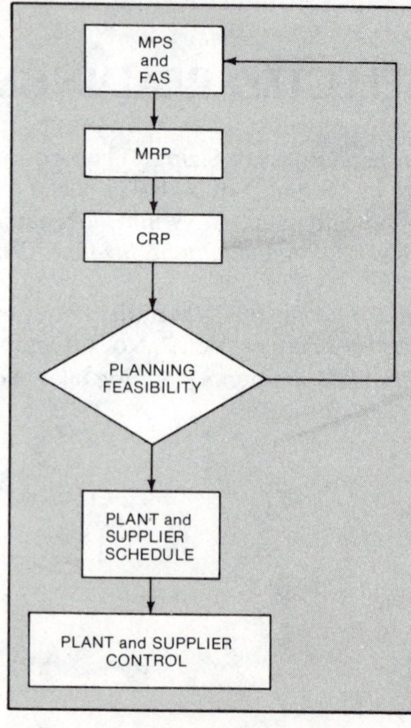

the FAS are the inputs to the Material Requirements Planning (MRP) system which determines the time-phased requirements for individual components and materials. (In some organizations the FAS is an integral part of the MPS.) Thus, MRP is the first step in the short-range planning cycle. (The case also can be made that commitment to a master schedule within the short range is the first step.) Where medium-range planning ends and short-range planning begins is not that important; the continuity, consistency, and integrity of the planning process is. Figure 5-1 illustrates the flow of that process and its iterative nature.

The MPS and the resulting MRP accomplish the priority planning objective of production and inventory management. They determine what is needed and when it is needed. The output of the MRP system is the input to Capacity Requirements Planning (CRP).

# CAPACITY REQUIREMENTS PLANNING

Resource requirements planning and rough-cut capacity planning fulfill the capacity planning function in the long- and medium-range planning horizons. If the MRP is within the constraints of the production plan, no major disparities should exist between short-range capacity requirements and capacity actually available. However, events do not always unfold as planned. Unexpected changes in economic, social, and political conditions as well as the actions of competitors frequently result in short-range requirements substantially different from those anticipated. Even when short-range requirements follow a pattern generally within the bounds of anticipated requirements, seemingly small shifts in the quantity or timing of requirements for different products can affect the match of required and available capacity in specific work centers. Equipment failure and a strike at a key supplier's plant are examples of events which can alter actual available capacity.

The CRP process provides the answers to the following questions:

1. Is sufficient capacity available to fulfill the MRP and thus the MPS?
2. If sufficient capacity is not available, which work centers and vendors have inadequate capacity, and how much additional capacity is required by each?

If the answer to the first question is negative, the answers to the second provide information necessary for evaluating the alternatives of revising the MPS or adding capacity by overtime, subcontracting, and so on.

CRP determines the capacity required in each work center by time period to produce a given output; for example, the MRP generated on the basis of the master schedule. The principles and related examples included in this chapter are described primarily in relation to manufacturing; but they are applicable to planning in any setting including an educational institution, editorial office, hospital, or architectual firm. Measures of output, the process, lead times, and the nature of capacity resources differ but the concepts remain the same; and most of the techniques are applicable with minor adjustments to fit the situation.

## The CRP Procedure

CRP consists of the following steps:

1. Obtaining the requisite data.
2. Backward scheduling each item requirement on the basis of the MRP.
3. Loading all capacity centers in accordance with the schedule without considering capacity constraints (infinite loading).
4. Comparing capacity requirements with available capacity (finite loading).
5. a. If available capacity is sufficient, the planned release of orders conforms to the schedule developed in Step 2.
   b. If available capacity is insufficient, either capacity must be increased or the schedule revised and Steps 3, 4, and 5 repeated.

Each of the steps is discussed in detail in the remainder of this chapter.

**Data Requirements.** Certain data must be available for CRP to take place. Methods of organizing these data are covered in Chapter 14, "Production and Inventory Management Systems." For present purposes these data can be divided into data concerning each required item (from the final assembly to the seemingly least significant purchased part or raw material), data concerning each work center, and data describing supplier capacity and lead time.

Although the data required for short-range planning can be organized in different ways, typically there are three files which contain the necessary information:

1. Routing File
2. Work Center File
3. Purchase File

A routing file exists for each manufactured part. The record for each part includes:

1. The total manufacturing lead time based on a typical lot size.
2. A list of the required processing operations identified normally by number in ascending order: (1) work center number, (2) a brief description, (3) the setup time required, and (4) the run time (time required for processing) per unit.
3. Possibly the foregoing information for alternate routings.

Table 5-1 illustrates the routing file data required for CRP.

**TABLE 5-1**
**ROUTING FILE DATA**

| **Part S1205 Drive Shaft** | | **Lead Time = 31 days (80-unit lot size)** | | |
|---|---|---|---|---|
| **Work Center** | **Operation Number** | **Description** | **Setup Time*** | **Run Time per Part*** |
| 1 | 10 | Turn | .4 | .125 |
| 3 | 20 | Mill | .8 | .075 |
| 5 | 30 | Gear Cut | 1.0 | .25 |
| 8 | 40 | Drill | .3 | .25 |
| 9 | 50 | Heat Treat | | 3** |
| 7 | 60 | Grind Shaft | .6 | .3 |
| 6 | 70 | Grind Gear | 1.0 | .4 |

*Standard Hours
**Total time required for subcontracted process.

The work center file contains a record for each work center in the plant; and each record contains the following data which are required in capacity requirements planning and scheduling.

1. Number of shifts: the number of shifts worked per planning period (usually per week).
2. Machine hours per shift: the number of machines available each shift.
3. Labor hours per shift: the number of labor hours available per shift. The availability of manpower determines the number of machines that can be used.
4. Efficiency: the ratio of actual performance to standard performance in terms of labor or machine hours per unit produced.
5. Utilization: the ratio of hours of effective capacity usage to scheduled work hours. Noneffective usage includes downtime due to machine failure, lack of material, and employee absenteeism. Coffee breaks, cleanup, and fatigue allowances are reflected in standard times and efficiency calculations. For example, with five operators assigned to the first shift and three to the second in a work center with five machines each requiring an operator, 320 hours of capacity are available each week. If an average of 40 hours is lost each week due to machine failure, lack of material, or employee absenteeism, the utilization rate is .875 (280 ÷ 320).
6. Effective Daily Capacity (EDC): the number of standard hours of output that can be expected daily from a department. EDC equals the product of the number of shifts, the number of hours per shift, the number of machines or workers (whichever is the limiting factor), the departmental efficiency, and the department utilization. For example, the EDC of Work Center 2 in Table 5-2 is 25.8 standard hours (2 × 2 × 8 × .95 × .85).
7. Planned queue: the planned average time a lot waits before processing.

Table 5-2 illustrates the work center file data that are required for CRP.

**TABLE 5-2**
**WORK CENTER FILE**
**(8 Hours per Shift)**

| Work Center | Description | Shifts | Number of Machines* | Efficiency | Utilization | EDC** | Planned Queue** |
|---|---|---|---|---|---|---|---|
| 1 | Turret Lathes | 1 | 4 | .80 | .90 | 23.0 | 2 |
| 2 | Screw Machines | 2 | 2 | .95 | .85 | 25.8 | 2 |
| 3 | Horizontal Mills | 1 | 4 | .80 | .90 | 23.0 | 2 |
| 4 | Bridgeports | 1 | 2 | .75 | .95 | 11.4 | 2 |
| 5 | Gear Cutters | 1 | 3 | .80 | .75 | 14.4 | 3 |
| 6 | Gear Grinders | 2 | 1 | .80 | .80 | 10.2 | 3 |
| 7 | External Grinders | 2 | 1 | .85 | .80 | 10.9 | 3 |
| 8 | Drills | 1 | 5 | .70 | .75 | 21.0 | 1 |
| 9 | Heat Treat | — | — | | | | |

*One operator per machine.
**EDC is in hours; planned queue is in days. EDC of a machine ($EDC_m$) equals the EDC of the work center divided by the number of machines in the work center.

The purchase parts file contains, along with other data, the following information required for short-range planning:

1. Alternate sources
2. Lead time of each source
3. Normal yield associated with lots received from each source
4. Vendor's capacity

Short-range planning of purchased items is discussed in Chapter 13.

The MRP reveals when an item is needed to meet the MPS and when an order for that item must be released to produce or procure it on schedule, given normal lead time. It does not reveal necessarily when specific capacity is required to produce the item. Some items, such as small rods, are produced on one machine; a turret lathe or automatic screw machine for example. Production of a lot of such items may be expected to take place in a week or less. However, this is frequently not the case; many items require processing in numerous work centers, and production of these items requires five or more weeks. This is especially true when lot sizes are large, processing time per unit is relatively long, and a particular process—heat treating, for example—is subcontracted. Thus, the nature of the process and the lot size influence when specific types of capacity are required and when an order must be released to be produced on schedule (manufacturing lead time).

The elements of manufacturing lead time can be divided into operation time and interoperation time as described in Figure 5-2.

**FIGURE 5-2**
**LEAD TIME COMPONENTS**

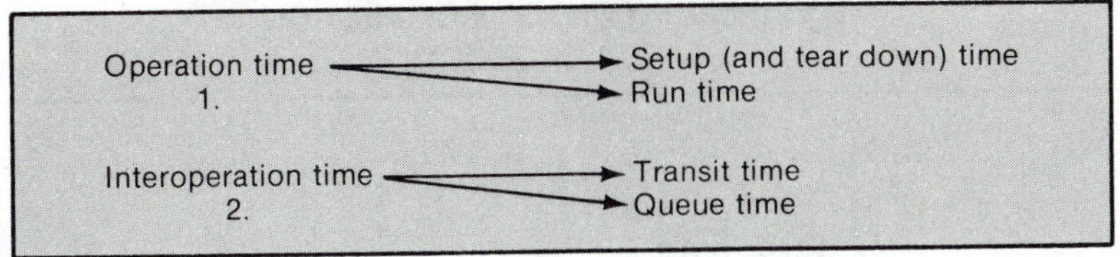


The flow of a job through a production facility is illustrated in Figure 5-3. A lead time profile for each part is necessary in order to determine the time periods when specific elements of capacity are required. This profile is available from the data described earlier; its use will be demonstrated later in the discussion of scheduling.

**FIGURE 5-3**
**MANUFACTURING LEAD TIME PROFILE OF AN ORDER REQUIRING FOUR OPERATIONS**

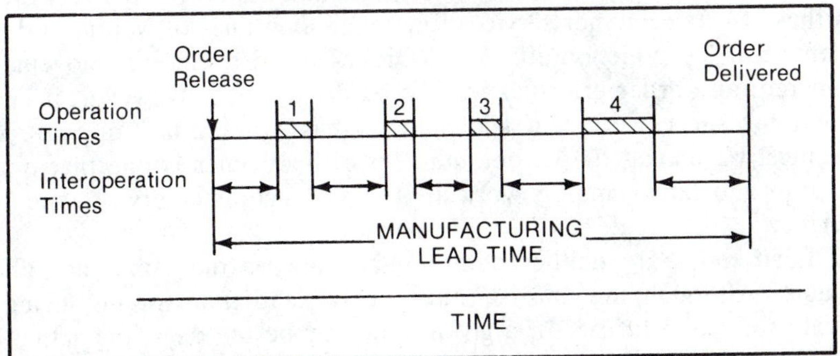


Lead time management is critical to successful production and inventory management. Lead time directly affects the amount of work-in-process and thus affects inventory investment.

The average work-in-process, in finished item equivalent units, equals one half the product of lead time and the weekly output rate as illustrated in Figure 5-4.

$$WIP = .5 \times MLT \times P$$

Where:

$WIP$ = Average work-in-process in finished item equivalent units
$MLT$ = Manufacturing lead time
$P$ = Production output per unit time

For example if the MLT is 3 weeks and P is 20 units per week, the average WIP = 30 units. If MLT increases to 4 weeks, WIP increases to 40 units.

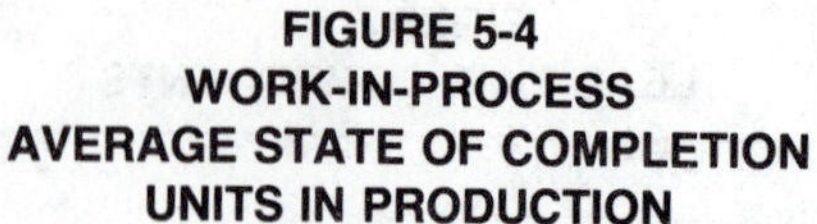

**FIGURE 5-4**
**WORK-IN-PROCESS**
**AVERAGE STATE OF COMPLETION**
**UNITS IN PRODUCTION**

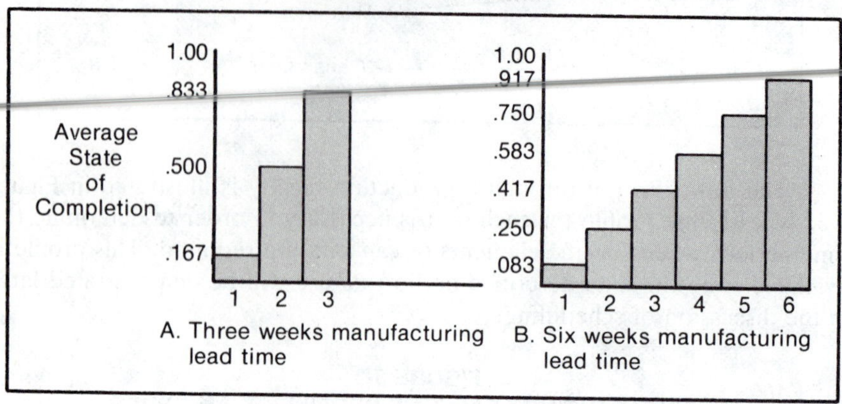


Lead time affects the ability to respond to a customer's delivery request and thus affects customer service. Relatively long lines of waiting orders in a plant reduce production efficiency. Orders are lost; material movement is hampered; and order priorities tend to be disregarded. However, if queues become too short, work center idleness increases due to lack of parts. Lead time must be managed. An optimum set of lead times is one that obtains the proper balance among work-in-process, customer service, and shop efficiency.

Lead times are neither deterministic (always the same) nor uncontrollable. Although the normal (most likely) lead time for producing the typical production lot size of a given item may be ten days, the actual lead time of a specific order for that item may vary from five to twenty days, for example. Machine breakdowns, scrap, shop load, weather conditions, and personnel absenteeism can cause the lead time to be longer than usual. In a similar fashion, a reduced shop load or expediting by either management or shop personnel can result in a shorter than normal lead time. The point is that lead time can be managed, planned, and controlled.

Although there have been methods proposed for optimizing lead times—such as that by Weeks [1]—the practical difficulties of implementing them support Jan Young's recommendation that lead time management begins by assuring that lead times are reasonably balanced among similar items and that work-in-process, queue lengths, and machine utilizations are within established bounds. [2]

The balance of lead time across similar parts can be measured by determining the queue length per operation of each item. This is calculated in the following manner suggested by Young. [3]

$$QTT/O = TQTT/NOP$$
$$TQTT = LT - (SU \text{ and } RT)$$

Where:

$QTT/O$ = Queue and transit time per operation
$TQTT$ = Total queue and transit time
$NOP$ = Number of operations
$LT$ = Lead time
$SU\ and\ RT$ = Setup and run time

Table 5-3 is an example of average queue and transit time for a family of parts.

**TABLE 5-3**
**AVERAGE QUEUE AND TRANSIT TIME FOR A FAMILY OF PARTS**

| Part Number | LT | SU and RT | TQTT | NOP | QTT/O |
|---|---|---|---|---|---|
| C101 | 8.2 | 2.2 | 6.0 | 5 | 1.2 |
| C102 | 11.0 | 2.6 | 8.4 | 6 | 1.4 |
| C103 | 2.4 | 1.2 | 1.2 | 4 | .3 |
| C104 | 14.9 | 1.1 | 13.8 | 3 | 4.6 |
| C105 | 8.1 | 1.8 | 6.3 | 7 | .9 |
| C106 | 8.7 | 2.1 | 6.6 | 6 | 1.1 |

If the parts in this family are in fact produced by similar processes, one would expect their queue and transit time per operation to be roughly equivalent. Examination of Table 5-3 reveals that this is not the case. Part C103 has a QTT/O much smaller than the others, while Part C104 has a much larger QTT/O than the other parts. These two lead times (QTT/O's) are out of balance.

The variation from the norm in the lead time of Part C104 may be due to a unique (in this group) processing requirement, a bottleneck operation usually with a large backlog, or it may be due to a traditional acceptance of a long lead time for this part. Lead time and queue management are discussed further in Chapter 12, "Production Activity Control." In a similar fashion, the QTT/O of Part C103 may be due to a processing sequence involving excess capacity work centers with little or no backlog or to speedy processing motivated by an ease of production and a favorite job status.

An examination of the manufacturing cycle efficiency (Setup and Run Time/Total Lead Time) leads to the same conclusion concerning the balance of the lead times in the family of parts examined earlier. The manufacturing cycle efficiencies of these parts are shown in Table 5-4. The point is that the established lead times of Parts C103 and C104 should be examined to determine if they are justified or if they are merely artifacts of tradition or convenience.

Once balanced lead times have been established, the question of work-in-process, queue lengths, and machine utilization being within reasonable bounds must be addressed. A model for the determination of minimum cost lead times has been presented by James Weeks, but, as he points out,

**TABLE 5-4**
**MANUFACTURING CYCLE EFFICIENCIES**

| Part Number | Total Lead Time | SU and RT | Manufacturing Efficiency |
|---|---|---|---|
| C101 | 8.2 | 2.2 | .27 |
| C102 | 11.0 | 2.6 | .24 |
| C103 | 2.4 | 1.2 | .50 |
| C104 | 14.9 | 1.1 | .07 |
| C105 | 8.1 | 1.8 | .22 |
| C106 | 8.7 | 2.1 | .24 |

substantial, practical problems are encountered in implementation of this model. [4] The management of work-in-process inventory is discussed in Chapter 9.

**Backward Scheduling.** Once the required data are available, backward scheduling of each item is the next step in CRP. It starts with the due date for an item and works backward operation by operation in its routing. It assigns operations and queue times, and determines appropriate time periods on the basis of operation times, lot sizes, and standard queue and transit time allowances.

Table 5-1, page 129, is an example of data contained in a routing record, and Table 5-2, page 130, illustrates data typically contained in a work center file. These data permit the tabulation of manufacturing lead time as illustrated in Table 5-5.

The total SU and RT required for performing an operation on a lot of parts is determined by adding the setup time to the product of the lot size and the run time per unit.

$$T = S + QR$$

**TABLE 5-5**
**TABULATION OF MANUFACTURING LEAD TIME**
**(Drive Shaft, 80 units)**

| Work Center | Operation Number | SU and RT per Lot[1] | SU and RT per Lot[2] | Queue Time[2] | Transit Time[2] | Total Days | Cumulative Days |
|---|---|---|---|---|---|---|---|
| 1 | 10 | 10.4 | 1.8 | 1.5 | .5 | 3.8 | 3.8 |
| 3 | 20 | 6.8 | 1.2 | 1.5 | .5 | 3.2 | 7.0 |
| 5 | 30 | 21.0 | 4.4 | 2.5 | .5 | 7.4 | 14.4 |
| 8 | 40 | 3.5 | .8 | 1.0 | .5 | 2.3 | 16.7 |
| 9 | 50 | | 3.0 | | .5 | 3.5* | 20.2 |
| 7 | 60 | 24.6 | 2.3 | 1.5 | .5 | 4.3 | 24.5 |
| 6 | 70 | 33.0 | 3.2 | 2.5 | .5 | 6.2 | 30.7 |
| | Stores | 99.3 | 16.7 | 10.5 | 3.5 | 30.7 | |

[1]Standard hours.
[2]Days
*Subcontracted operations include queue time.

Where: $T$ = time required to complete an operation on a lot of parts
$S$ = setup time for the operation
$Q$ = lot size
$R$ = operation run time per unit

For example, $T$ of Operation 10 = 10.4 (.4 + 80 × .125)

$D = T/EDC_m$
$D$ of operation 10 = 10.4 ÷ 5.76 = 1.8

Where: $D$ = days required to set up and process a lot on a particular machine and
$EDC_m$ = effective daily capacity of a machine in the work center

For example, the days required by Operation 30 for actual processing are 4.4 (21 ÷ 4.8).

The total manufacturing lead time for the lot of parts in the example is 30.7 days consisting of 13.7 days for actual processing in the shop, 3.0 days for subcontracted work, 3.5 days for transit time, and 10.5 days for queue time. This example is atypical in that the sum of queue and transit time (14.0) is approximately equal to internal processing time (13.7). A more typical ratio in a job shop situation is for the sum of the queue and transit times to be three or four times the actual processing time.

Backward scheduling is illustrated in Table 5-6 using the data from Table 5-5 and based on the drive shafts being required on Day 175. Table 5-6

**TABLE 5-6**
**BACKWARD SCHEDULING***
**(Part S1205 Drive Shaft**
**80 Units, Due Date 175)**

| Operation Number | Work Center | Center Description | Transit to Center** | Arrival in Center | Queue Time** | Start Date | Process Time** | Finish Date | Processing Week |
|---|---|---|---|---|---|---|---|---|---|
| | | *Stores* | .5 | 175 | | | | | |
| 70 | 6 | Gear Grinders | .5 | 168.8 | 2.5 | 171.3 | 3.2 | 174.5 | 35 |
| 60 | 7 | External Grinders | .5 | 164.5 | 1.5 | 166.0 | 2.3 | 168.3 | 34 |
| 50 | 9 | Heat Treat | — | 161.5 | — | 161.5 | 3.0 | 164.5 | 33 |
| 40 | 8 | Drills | .5 | 159.2 | 1.0 | 160.2 | .8 | 161.0 | 33 |
| 30 | 5 | Gear Cutters | .5 | 151.8 | 2.5 | 154.3 | 4.4 | 158.7 | 31/32 |
| 20 | 3 | Horizontal Mills | .5 | 148.6 | 1.5 | 150.1 | 1.2 | 151.3 | 31 |
| 10 | 1 | Turret Lathes | .5 | 144.8 | 1.5 | 146.3 | 1.8 | 148.1 | 30 |

*Five days a week.
**Transit time to center, queue time, and process time are expressed in days. (Arrival in center, start date, and finish date are hypothetical points in time.)

portrays the real world in that Arrival, Start, and Finish Dates do not fall neatly at the beginning of a day. In practice, they normally are rounded down to simplify scheduling. For example, the lot would be scheduled to arrive in Work Center 6 for gear grinding on Day 169 and be finished on Day 174. In addition, center capacity usually is allocated on a weekly basis. Table 5-6 follows the convention of assigning processing requirements to the week in which each takes place. The schedule of Operation 30 bridges processing Weeks 31 and 32. In such a situation, the job may be assigned proportionately to both weeks or to the week in which the major portion of the work takes place depending on the precision required in determining capacity requirements.

**Infinite Loading and Capacity Requirements.** Backward scheduling of each item on the MRP provides the data required to determine capacity requirements by time period for each work center.

Summing the setup and run times required in a work center for an order gives the capacity requirements for that order. Adding these requirements to all other items scheduled for processing during the same period gives the period capacity requirements for that work center as illustrated in Table 5-7. The work center has been loaded as though it possessed infinite capacity.

**TABLE 5-7**
**CAPACITY REQUIREMENTS**
**(Turret Lathe Department)**

**Machines: 4** **Effective Weekly Capacity: 115 hours**

| Week | Order Number | Part Number | Hours Required | Cumulative Hours Required |
|---|---|---|---|---|
| 29 | 718 | S1320 | 32.4 | 32.4 |
| 29 | 684 | S2816 | 18.2 | 50.6 |
| 29 | 735 | R0635 | 26.0 | 76.6 |
| 30 | 726 | S1205* | 10.4 | 10.4 |
| 30 | 804 | P6831 | 57.0 | 67.4 |
| 30 | 962 | R7219 | 31.4 | 98.8 |
| 30 | 829 | G4123 | 12.1 | 110.9 |
| 30 | 784 | S0705 | 17.9 | 128.8 |
| 31 | 876 | S1102 | 15.7 | 15.7 |
| 31 | 973 | P7780 | 30.2 | 45.9 |

*Drive shaft scheduled in Tables 5-5 and 5-6.

**Finite Loading.** Figure 5-5 illustrates infinite loading. It reveals that the capacity required in Week 30 is greater than that available, while surplus capacity is available in Weeks 29 and 31. In this type situation, the planner normally will attempt to move one of the items scheduled for Week 30 into either Week 29 or Week 31. Adjusting the schedule so that loads are within work center capacities constitutes finite loading (see Figure 5-6).

If the material for the drive shaft, Part S1205, will be available, it can be scheduled in the Turret Lathe Department for Week 29 with no changes

**FIGURE 5-5**
**GRAPHICAL REPRESENTATION OF INFINITE LOADING**
**(Turret Lathe Department—Order 726)**

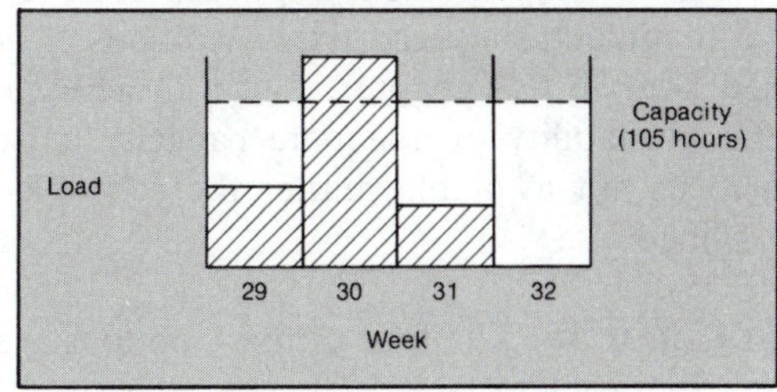


**FIGURE 5-6**
**GRAPHICAL REPRESENTATION OF FINITE LOADING**
**(Turret Lathe Department—Order 726)**

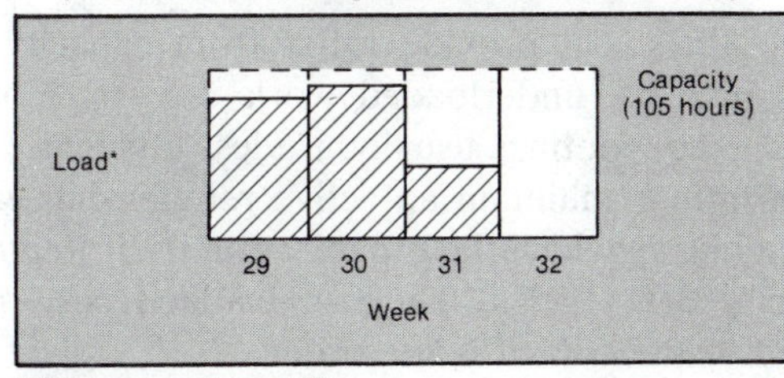


*24.8 hours moved to week 29

required in the schedule of remaining operations. If material will not be available in Week 29, Part S1205 can be scheduled for turret lathe work in Week 31 and the remaining lead time reduced by means described later in this chapter. The latter is less desirable, since it requires greater control of shop activities and may change the timing of capacity requirements in other work centers.

Comparison of required to available capacity must be made for all work centers. Problems often are not as simple as that illustrated by the data in Table 5-7, page 136. Two other conditions are typical:

1. Capacity requirements may exceed that available for an operation occurring midway or beyond in the total manufacturing process. (Our example involved the first operation.) For instance, if the Drilling Department was overloaded in Week 33 but short of work in Week 32, the drilling operation (Operation 40) could be moved to Week 32. This would require that prior operations (30, 20, and 10) be rescheduled and the impact of their rescheduling on capacity requirements evaluated.
2. Backward scheduling may indicate that the order should be released and work begun in Week 30 when, in fact, it is already late in Week 31.

Forward scheduling will reveal when the order will be finished if it is begun on the first day in Week 32 and is processed in the normal manner.

Forward scheduling begins at a given point, the first day in Week 32 in this case, and schedules the order forward from that point in accordance with standard processing, transit, and queue times. If the scheduled completion date resulting from forward scheduling is not acceptable, steps must be taken to reduce the total manufacturing lead time. Methods of accomplishing the latter are discussed later in this chapter. Once an acceptable schedule has been achieved, the availability of adequate capacity must be ascertained. If adequate capacity is not available, either the schedule must be revised or the capacity modified.

**Modification of Capacity.** The four primary options available for coping with short run capacity problems are:

1. Alternate routings
2. Subcontracting
3. Temporary employees
4. Overtime

Alternate routings will provide relief from capacity overload if the alternate process involves underloaded work centers. However, alternate (second or third choice) routings usually are less efficient.

Many organizations maintain an active relationship with vendors possessing those capacities in which the organization itself frequently encounters short term capacity deficiencies. The usual added cost of subcontracting must be compared to the cost of a late order.

Adding temporary employees is an option in some labor constrained situations. The ability to add temporary employees generally is related inversely to the skill level required. For example, material handlers, operators of simple drill presses, salesclerks, office clerks, porters, and waiters or waitresses usually are available in the labor market while gear cutters, numerically controlled machine operators, intensive coronary care nurses, systems programmers, and legal secretaries usually are scarce.

Overtime is another source of added capacity. It can provide limited relief for limited periods. Excessive overtime (over 54 hours a week) or overtime for an extended period (two to three months) usually results in diminishing returns for the added hours.

The work center file also may include the maximum effective weekly capacity (Max. EWC) available as well as the normal EDC illustrated in Table 5-2 (page 130). For example, maximum capacity could be achieved by working a sixth day on all shifts and also by working ten hours per shift, Monday through Friday, in all departments, operating on a one shift basis. Maximum and normal effective weekly capacities contained in Table 5-8 are based on the above arrangement and the data contained in Table 5-2. For example,

$$\text{Max. EWC} = \text{Hours worked} \times \text{number of machines} \times \text{department efficiency} \times \text{department utilization}$$

Max. EWC for Work Center 1 = $58 \times 4 \times .80 \times .90 = 167$
Max. EWC for Work Center 2 = $96 \times 2 \times .95 \times .85 = 155$

**TABLE 5-8**
**WORK CENTER FILE**
**(Addition of Maximum Weekly Capacity)**

| Work Center | Description | Normal Weekly Capacity | Maximum Weekly Capacity |
|---|---|---|---|
| 1 | Turret Lathes | 115 | 167 |
| 2 | Screw Machines | 129 | 155 |
| 3 | Horizontal Mills | 115 | 167 |
| 4 | Bridgeports | 57 | 82 |
| 5 | Gear Cutters | 72 | 104 |
| 6 | Gear Grinders | 51 | 61 |
| 7 | External Grinders | 54 | 65 |
| 8 | Drills | 105 | 152 |

**Schedule Modification.** When backward scheduling reveals that normal lead time provides insufficient time to produce an order on schedule, the planned completion date can be changed to reflect the forward schedule. The penalty for late completion must be compared with the cost of expediting. *Expediting* means assigning top priority to an order which gives it first place in any queue and which may involve operation overlapping or lot splitting (both are described later in this chapter). The Achilles' heel of this approach is the tendency for more and more orders to receive a top priority rating. The designation gradually becomes meaningless and control collapses.

## Limitations of CRP

CRP projects work center loads by time period on the basis of realistic average plant efficiency and utilization, processing times, and queue lengths. However, just as a given family does not have the average 1.4 children, the characteristics of a specific production situation rarely conform to their averages at any given time. The product mix varies; setup and run times and plant utilization and efficiency vary in a probabilistic manner. Parts are scrapped, orders are cancelled, engineering changes are required, and rush orders are promised for special customers. Thus, work center loads and queues cannot be predicted with certainty for a given period. Variations in work center load may be predicted with greater certainty for continuous flow production than for job shop production, but continuous flow processes also are prone to disruptions and rate of flow variations.

An organization must have the capability to plan and control production activity in a dynamic environment. This capability is achieved through lead time management and methods of controlling job and operation priorities. The latter are discussed in Chapter 12, "Production Activity

Control;" a discussion of input/output planning, a key element of lead time management, follows.

## INPUT/OUTPUT PLANNING AND CONTROL

Input/output (I/O) planning and control is an integrated process which involves the following:

1. Planning the input to and output from work centers usually for each time period in the short range
2. Establishing the size of deviations (the difference between planned and actual inputs) and outputs which will be considered normal
3. Controlling release of orders to production
4. Measuring actual inputs and outputs and comparing them to the plan
5. Analyzing variations beyond normal limits for cause and determining the appropriate corrective action

Although it is impossible to separate the planning and control of inputs and outputs, the remainder of this chapter emphasizes I/O Planning and Chapter 12 emphasizes I/O Control.

MRP systems and order point systems frequently call for very erratic release of work to the plant as illustrated in Figure 5-5. Planning order releases without regard to balancing input and output will lead to uncontrolled lead times and excessive work-in-process.

The basic concept of input/output planning and control is that output plus changes in the work-in-process equals input. This relationship is represented schematically in Figure 5-7.

**FIGURE 5-7**
**INPUT/OUTPUT RELATIONSHIP**
**(Single Work Center Process)**

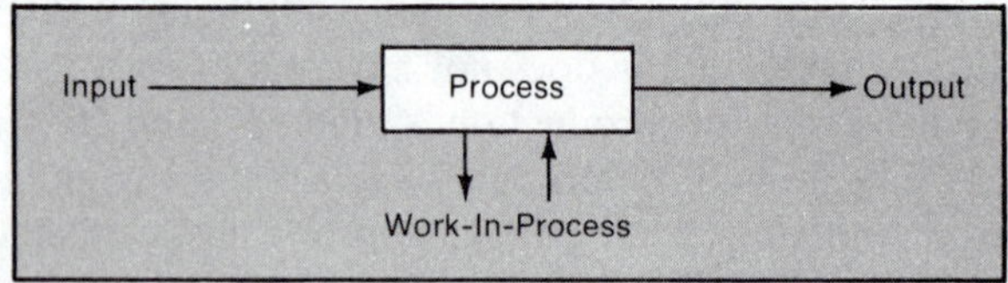


Since input must be absorbed by output, it follows that increasing input when operating at full capacity results in increased work-in-process.

Tables 5-9A through 5-9D reveal the impact of input planning by illustrating the following four situations:

1. Balancing input/output
2. Increasing input, plant operating at capacity
3. Increasing input, bringing operations to capacity
4. Decreasing input, reducing work-in-process

**TABLE 5-9A***
**PLANNED BALANCED INPUT/OUTPUT;**
**SINGLE PROCESS PRODUCTION**
**Beginning Queue: 20 Units**

| Week | Planned Input | Planned Output | Lead Time (Days) | Work-in-Process Material |
|---|---|---|---|---|
| 26 | 100 | 100 | 6 | 120 |
| 27 | 100 | 100 | 6 | 120 |
| 28 | 100 | 100 | 6 | 120 |
| 29 | 100 | 100 | 6 | 120 |

*Tolerance: plus or minus five units

Input and output are measured in the same dimension as capacity requirements: man-hours, machine hours, gallons, tons, or (as with our examples) units.

Table 5-9A exemplifies planned balanced input and output for Weeks 26 through 29. The work center is operating at capacity, 100 units per week. There is a material queue of 20 units, and another 100 units are being fabricated.

Increasing input while operating at full capacity is illustrated in Table 5-9B. Work-in-process and lead time increase, controlling production becomes more difficult, and the plant probably is less efficient. On the other hand, increased input is required to increase the output of a plant operating below capacity. Table 5-9C, illustrates that situation, and Table 5-9D, illustrates decreasing input to bring work-in-process within bounds while maintaining capacity.

**TABLE 5-9B***
**PLANNED INCREASED INPUT; NO CHANGE IN CAPACITY**
**Beginning Queue: 20 Units**

| Week | Planned Input | Planned Output | Lead Time (Days) | Work-in-Process Material |
|---|---|---|---|---|
| 26 | 100 | 100 | 6 | 120 |
| 27 | 120 | 100 | 7 | 140 |
| 28 | 120 | 100 | 8 | 160 |
| 29 | 120 | 100 | 9 | 180 |

*Tolerance: plus or minus five units

**TABLE 5-9C***
**PLANNED INCREASED INPUT; BRINGING OPERATIONS TO CAPACITY**

| Week | Planned Input | Planned Output | Lead Time (Days) | Work-in-Process Material |
|---|---|---|---|---|
| 26 | 60 | 60 | 6 | 80 |
| 27 | 100 | 80 | 6 | 100 |
| 28 | 120 | 100 | 6 | 120 |
| 29 | 100 | 100 | 6 | 120 |

*Tolerance: plus or minus five units

**TABLE 5-9D***
**PLANNED DECREASED INPUT; REDUCING WORK-IN-PROCESS**

| Week | Planned Input | Planned Output | Lead Time (Days) | Work-in-Process Material |
|---|---|---|---|---|
| 26 | 100 | 100 | 8 | 160 |
| 27 | 80 | 100 | 7 | 140 |
| 28 | 80 | 100 | 6 | 120 |
| 29 | 100 | 100 | 6 | 120 |

*Tolerance: plus or minus five units

Input/output planning in a continuous process plant is similar to that described previously for a single process production. Input/output planning and control in a job shop is more complicated since orders follow a variety of paths from start to completion. Figure 5-8 illustrates possible flow patterns in a job shop.

Work centers A1 and A2 in Figure 5-8 frequently are called gateway centers. They are the work centers in which work begins; orders enter the plant at these work centers. Work centers B1, B2, B3, C1, C2, and C3 are intermediate or downstream centers; and D1 and D2 are the finishing or final work centers.

Queues and work-in-process at gateway centers are relatively easy to plan by treating them as single process work centers. Input to these work centers should never be greater than output unless one of the following conditions exist:

1. The work center is operating below actual capacity and increased output is desired.
2. An increased queue is required to reduce idle time due to variations in output exceeding the present planned queue.

Input/output planning and control at downstream and final work centers are discussed further in Chapter 12, "Production Activity Control."

If operating properly, MRP has planned the release of orders on the basis of item due dates and normal lead time. The order release system plans order releases so that

1. In a job shop environment material arrives prior to the release of orders for component production, and the production of components and subassemblies is completed prior to the release of orders for assembly fabrication.
2. In a continuous process environment material and/or components arrive at a rate equal to the rate of the production process and in ample time to avoid its disruption.
3. In a repetitive process environment the required material and/or components arrive prior to the release of production orders. If material and components are bulky and the process is scheduled to run for a relatively long period (two weeks or more), multiple arrivals may be planned.

**FIGURE 5-8**
**FLOW PATTERNS IN A JOB SHOP**

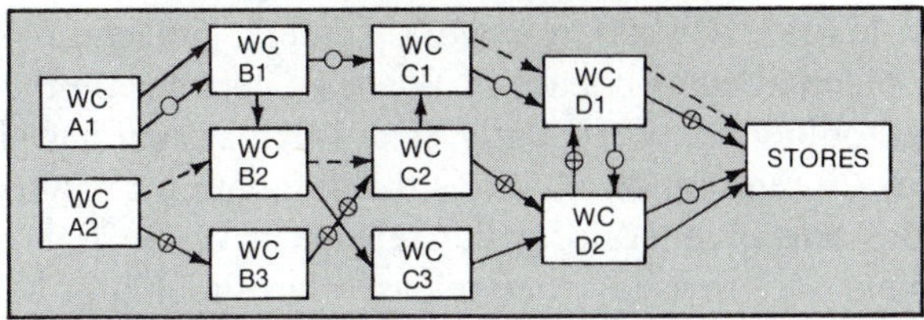


The MRP planned order release dates must be revised when capacity planning reveals that the load in the plant will be outside acceptable tolerances in certain periods.

Planned loads can be (1) balanced and approaching capacity or (2) highly variable, overloading the plant in some periods and underloading it in others.

If planned loads are balanced and near capacity, the planned order releases can be identical to those generated by the MRP system. If not, the MRP planned releases must be revised. If the master schedule is within capacity constraints, the total load over the planned horizon will not exceed capacity, although loads may exceed capacity in some periods and fall short in other periods. If capacity is constant, load adjustments must be made in underloaded and overloaded periods. This is accomplished by early and late releases of orders. If capacity can be varied sufficiently, orders can be released as planned. This is usually not the case.

Table 5-10 illustrates a highly variable load by period requiring revisions in the planned order releases. Planned order releases must be reduced in Weeks 15, 16, and 20 by approximately 15, 30, and 20 hours respectively. This is accomplished by (1) rescheduling some orders from Weeks 15 and 16 to Weeks 17 and 18 and starting them late (2) rescheduiing orders from Week 20 to Week 19 and starting them early.

Selection of orders from Weeks 15 and 16 for later release is based on the priority of orders and the anticipated load on the different downstream work centers where capacit/ is required by the different orders. For example, orders required to replenish a safety stock would be selected for a late start, while an order for a component part required for an assembly would be

**TABLE 5-10**
**PLANNED CAPACITY AND ORDER RELEASES**
**(Gateway Work Center)**

**Date: Week 14**

| Week | Capacity Hours | Cumulative Capacity Hours | Planned Load | Cumulative Planned Load |
|---|---|---|---|---|
| 15 | 80 | 80 | 95 | 95 |
| 16 | 80 | 160 | 110 | 205 |
| 17 | 80 | 240 | 60 | 265 |
| 18 | 80 | 320 | 50 | 315 |
| 19 | 80 | 400 | 60 | 375 |
| 20 | 80 | 480 | 100 | 475 |

started on time. And, other things being equal, orders utilizing underloaded downstream work centers would be planned for release prior to orders requiring fully loaded downstream work centers. Selection of orders in Week 20 for a planned early release in Week 19 depends on the availability of material and tooling one week early. The MRP system has given the beginning of Week 20 (end of Week 19) as the due date for material and tooling required for items planned for order release in Week 20.

Commitment to a revised order release plan should not be made until the latest possible moment. Conditions change and premature revisions of the planned release of orders likely will be followed by other revisions. For example, the decision concerning movement of orders from Week 20 to Week 19 should not be made until Week 18 when updated information concerning order priority, projected work center loads, and material status is available.

In summary, short-range planning sets the stage for execution. It prepares plans that are achievable and coordinated. The right items are scheduled for production at the right time. The availability of the required information, tooling, and capacity is ascertained. Efficient use of available capacity is planned with the given output requirements. Figure 5-9 is a schematic of the flow of information, decision making, and output documents

**FIGURE 5-9**
**FLOW OF DATA, DECISION MAKING, AND OUTPUT DOCUMENTS**
**(Short-Range Planning)**

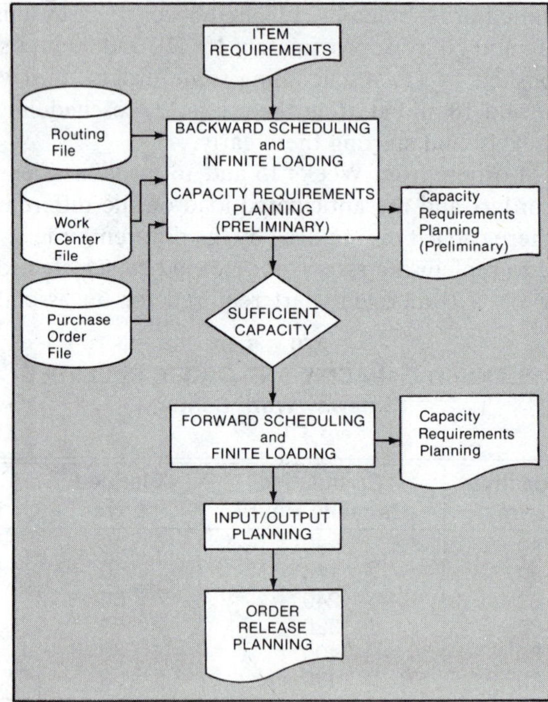

in short-range planning. The impact of these activities on purchasing is examined in Chapter 13 while Chapter 12 concerns the execution of these plans in a dynamic production environment.

## PROBLEMS

1. Given the following data:

| Work Center | Shifts* | Number of Machines | Efficiency | Utilization |
|---|---|---|---|---|
| 101 | 1 | 5 | .90 | .90 |
| 102 | 1 | 4 | 1.00 | .85 |
| 103 | 2 | 3 | .95 | .82 |
| 104 | 1 | 2 | .85 | .88 |

*40 hours per shift; machines are controlling element.

a. Determine the effective daily capacity of each work center.
b. Determine the average effective daily capacity of machines in each work center.
c. Determine the maximum effective weekly capacity in each work center if a ten-hour day can be worked on each shift, plus an eight-hour Saturday shift.
d. Determine the maximum effective weekly capacity of each work center if each has two 8-hour shifts six days a week.

2. Given the following data for the subassembly and assembly departments:

| Department | Shift* | Personnel | Absenteeism Rate | Efficiency | Utilization |
|---|---|---|---|---|---|
| Subassembly | 1st | 20 | .08 | 1.04 | .95 |
| Subassembly | 2nd, 3rd | 12 | .15 | .90 | .98 |
| Assembly | 1st | 16 | .08 | .95 | .96 |
| Assembly | 2nd, 3rd | 12 | .18 | .88 | .94 |

*40 hours per shift

a. Determine the effective weekly capacity of the assembly and subassembly departments.
b. Determine the maximum effective weekly capacity if the second shift personnel level can be raised to the level of the first shift and a sixth day can be scheduled on both shifts.
c. Determine the maximum effective weekly capacity if in addition to the increase described in *b*, a third shift of 20 workers can be added.

3. Given the data for Part B726 shown at the top of page 146:

a. What is the standard total setup and run time for a lot of 120 units in each department? Use only one machine in each department.
b. What is the MLT in days of a lot of 120 No. B726 parts?
c. If the order is required on Operating Day 67, what day should the order be released based on normal lead time?

| Work Center | Operation | Setup Time Hours | Run Time/Unit Hours | Effective Daily Capacity (EDC) | Queue Time |
|---|---|---|---|---|---|
| 1 | 10 | 1.5 | .4 | 14.2 | 2.5 |
| 2 | 20 | .8 | .5 | 20.4 | 3.0 |
| 3 | 30 | 1.6 | .25 | 8.4 | 2.0 |
| 4 | 40 | .4 | .8 | 30.2 | 2.0 |

Transit time = .5 days between departments

d. If the order is released on Day 10, when would you expect it to be completed?
e. If the order is released on Day 10, given normal lead time, when would the order normally reach Department 3?
f. If the time remaining to desired completion is eight days less than the MLT, what do you suggest?

4. Using the data in Problem 3:

a. What is the total queue and transit time (TQTT)?
b. What is the queue and transit time per operation (QTT/O)?
c. What is the manufacturing cycle efficiency of the manufacturing process of Part B726?
d. What will the manufacturing cycle efficiency be if the lot size is 60 units.?
e. What will the manufacturing cycle efficiency be if the lot size remains 120 units and queue time is reduced by 25%?

5. The following data describe the TQTT and SU & RT for a group of parts which go through the same operations.

| Part No. | SU & RT | TQTT |
|---|---|---|
| H297 | 3.8 | 14.07 |
| H542 | 4.1 | 15.17 |
| H389 | 2.7 | 16.42 |
| H572 | 1.8 | 7.02 |

a. Do the above data suggest that the lead time of any of the above items be examined?
b. What questions might be asked in the analyses?

6. The planned input and output—in standard hours—of Department 17 for the next five weeks is given below. The beginning work-in-process is 300 standard hours of work. The department is working a 40-hour week.

| Week | 26 | 27 | 28 | 29 | 30 |
|---|---|---|---|---|---|
| Planned Input | 180 | 180 | 175 | 185 | 180 |
| Planned Output | 175 | 190 | 180 | 185 | 180 |

a. What is the planned work-in-process and lead time at the beginning of each week from Week 27 through Week 31?

b. If the department schedule is changed to include 18 hours of overtime each week, what will be the planned work-in-process and lead time at the beginning of each week?
c. The plant is shut down for two days in Week 26 by a wildcat strike. What will the planned lead time and work-in-process be in each week now?
d. Manufacturing management believes that output will increase by 20% if the work-in-process level is increased by 30 units. Revise the planned input and output per this plan and its assumption.
e. Given the action taken in *d*, what will the planned lead time and work-in-process be each week?

7. From the following data:

Work Center 879 Effective Weekly Capacity = 110 Hours

| | Order No. | Part No. | Standard Hours Required |
|---|---|---|---|
| Week 13 | 419 | B783 | 26.4 |
| | 431 | C813 | 35.8 |
| | 427 | B635 | 18.7 |
| Week 14 | 451 | A713 | 12.6 |
| | 438 | C218 | 48.2 |
| | 444 | C125 | 61.3 |
| | 437 | D613 | 18.5 |
| Week 15 | 448 | D412 | 22.4 |
| | 462 | A319 | 31.7 |
| | 457 | A227 | 25.3 |

a. Graphically represent the load in Department 879 during each week.
b. What changes in order schedules do you recommend?
c. Graphically represent the load as revised by your response to *b*.

8. The following data describe work center loads based on planned order releases.

| Work Center | Effective Weekly Capacity | Loads/Week 1 | 2 | 3 | 4 | 5 |
|---|---|---|---|---|---|---|
| A | 84 | 45 | 40 | 30 | 30 | 30 |
| B | 110 | 95 | 105 | 40 | 40 | 20 |
| C | 70 | 20 | 10 | 10 | 10 | 10 |
| D | 60 | 15 | 15 | 15 | 12 | |
| E | 75 | 20 | 10 | 10 | 10 | |

The following orders all have the same priority and have the following manufacturing processes. In what sequence do you recommend their planned order release?

| Order | Manufacturing Process* |
|---|---|
| 1101 | (A, 1, 15) – (B, 1, 10) – (C, 2, 20) – (D, 2, 12) – (E, 3, 20) |
| 1102 | (C, 1, 15) – (D, 2, 25) – (E, 2, 12) |
| 1103 | (A, 1, 20) – (C, 2, 20) – (D, 2, 12) – (E, 3, 15) |
| 1104 | (A, 1, 15) – (D, 1, 15) – (C, 2, 12) – (E, 3, 18) |

*(*i*, *j*, *k*) where *i* represents the department, *j* represents the week after release in which the order enters the department, and *k* represents the standard hours required by the operation.

# SELECTED READINGS


1. James K. Weeks, "Optimizing Planned Lead Times and Delivery Dates," *Proceedings of the 21st Annual International Conference of the American Production and Inventory Control Society* (1978), pp. 177-188.
2. Jan B. Young, "Understanding Shop Lead Times," *Proceedings of the 22d Annual Conference of the American Production and Inventory Control Society* (1979), pp. 177-179.
3. ———, p. 178.
4. Weeks, loc. cit.
5. Frank S. Covaro and Stephen B. Oresman, "On-Time Deliveries Start with Centralized Dispatching," *Production and Inventory Management*, Vol. 8, No. 2 (April, 1967).
6. Richard W. Foxen, "Scheduling and Loading," *Production and Inventory* Management, Vol. 8, No. 3 (July, 1967).
7. D. Garwood, "Delivery as Promised," *Production and Inventory Management*, Vol. 11, No. 3, Third Quarter (1971).
8. Raymond L. Lankford, "Short-Term Planning of Manufacturing Capacity," *Proceedings of the 21st Annual International Conference of the American Production and Inventory Control Society* (1978).
9. Joseph Orlicky, *Material Requirements Planning* (New York: McGraw-Hill Book Company, 1974).
10. George W. Plossl, *Manufacturing Control: The Last Frontier for Profits* (Reston, Virginia: Reston Publishing Company, Inc., 1973).
11. Edward M. Stiles, "Controlling a Job Shop with EDP Techniques: A Case," *Production and Inventory Management*, Vol. 9, No. 3, Third Qaurter (1968).
12. William Wassweiler, "Material Requirements Planning—The Key to Critical Ratio Effectiveness," *Production and Inventory Management*, Third Quarter (1972).
13. Oliver Wight, "Input/Output Control: A Real Handle On Lead Time," *Production and Inventory Management*, Vol. 11, No. 3, Third Quarter (1970).
14. ———, *Production and Inventory Management in the Computer Age* (Boston, Mass.: CBI Publishing Co. Inc., 1974).

# PART TWO

## INVENTORY MANAGEMENT

The management of inventory is often the keystone of success in a manufacturing firm. Marketing needs finished goods to supply customers; manufacturing needs raw materials and purchased parts to produce finished goods; and work-in-process inventory affects production efficiency.

Inventory usually is a major investment that ties up capital and incurs costs. If selected wisely, inventory increases sales, increases productivity, reduces production costs, and increases profit. Improved inventory management can reduce investment and costs, a rare combination. The trick is to have the right inventory at the right time. Having the wrong inventory results in the worst of all worlds: high investment, high inventory costs, low productivity, high production costs, and poor customer service.

Increasing cost of capital and increased competition in price and delivery service have emphasized the importance of inventory management. Some firms have recognized the significance of these economic facts and have placed management of all inventory under one individual—a materials manager. In some companies the materials manager is responsible for all inventory management activities from purchasing through distribution.

Many individuals in an organization make decisions concerning inventory. These decisions vary widely in scope and significance. For example, a decision on where to store lockwashers is rather narrow in scope while the establishment of the aggregate inventory budget for each of the next four quarters has a broad impact. The scope of a decision depends primarily on its level of aggregation.

The three levels of aggregation frequently used for studying inventory management decisions are the aggregate level, the intermediate level, and the individual item level. Aggregate level decisions concern general inventory management policies, plans, operating objectives, and performance. They include establishing customer service objectives, the inventory investment budget, and the production-inventory strategy; developing the inventory management system specifications; and selecting the method of distribution. Top management is primarily responsible for aggregate level decisions. This is the point at which the objectives and activities of marketing, production, and finance are integrated. If top management ignores this responsibility, inventory decisions are likely to be inconsistent with organization objectives. Some aspects of aggregate level decisions were discussed in Chapter 1; others are treated in Chapter 9.

At a lower level of aggregation, sometimes called *intermediate*, items are grouped to achieve the economies of joint purchases, common setups, joint shipments from common suppliers, common production processes, transportation economics, and individual customer requirements. Management of these items revolves around the grouping of items, the development of production facilities for managing groups, and the establishment of ordering rules or guidelines and their implementation.

*Group technology* is an approach that identifies the sameness of items in order to obtain economies in design and manufacturing. Group technology effects manufacturing economies resulting from the installation of manufacturing "cells" which combine in one location the different functional operations required to produce a group of similar items. Modified equipment dedicated to a group, special tooling, reduced materials handling, and reduced setup time achieve economies in manufacturing. *Intermediate inventory management* relates to the order quantity and order release decision rules for the group and the items within the group. Chapter 8 discusses intermediate level inventory management.

Individual inventory items include assemblies, subassemblies, fabricated components, and purchased materials. For practical purposes every line item is an individual item whose inventory must be managed. Some are managed as part of a group decision. Most are handled as members of a class. Line items are found in finished goods, spare parts, work-in-process, and raw material. The decisions to be made at this level are many. When is the individual item needed? How many should be ordered? When should they be ordered? Where are they to be stored? Is the appropriate inventory management system being used to manage an item? Chapters 7, 10, and 11 discuss these decisions.

When items are made-to-stock, decisions must be made concerning distribution. Will finished goods be shipped only from a factory warehouse, or will remote warehouses be used? If remote warehouses are used, where should they be located? How should they be stocked? What should the distribution safety stock policy be? Can Distribution Requirements Planning be implemented to integrate manufacturing and distribution? Physical control of inventory is essential for raw materials, work-in-process, and finished goods wherever it is located. Chapter 11 discusses these topics.

Consistency should exist among decisions at different levels and throughout the flow of inventory. Decisions at the intermediate level should be made in the context of aggregate policies, objectives, and plans. Individual item decisions should fall within the confines established by intermediate and aggregate level decisions.

Decisions concerning raw materials affect an organization's ability to achieve work-in-process inventory management objectives, and work-in-process decisions affect an organization's ability to achieve finished goods inventory management objectives.

Since the study of individual item decisions provides a sound basis for an understanding of intermediate and aggregate level decisions, this text treats item level decisions first.

Operationalizing management systems that use state-of-the-art technology to achieve inventory management goals requires management commitment, knowledgeable personnel, and electronic data processing capability.

# 6

# INVENTORY MANAGEMENT, AN INTRODUCTION

Inventory includes all those goods and materials that are used in the production and distribution processes. Raw materials, component parts, subassemblies, and finished products—all are part of inventory as are the various supplies required in the production and distribution process.

Inventory ties up capital, uses storage space, requires handling, deteriorates, sometimes becomes obsolete, incurs taxes, requires insurance, can be stolen, and sometimes is lost. If managed properly, however, the benefits outweigh the costs.

The absence of the appropriate inventory will halt a production process; lack of component parts will shut down an assembly line with partially completed assemblies collecting dust; an expensive piece of earth-moving equipment may be idled by lack of a small replacement part; a patient may die due to the unavailability of plasma; the learning process will be hampered by the nonarrival of texts; and, in many cases, a good customer may become irate and take his business elsewhere if the desired product is not immediately available. The availability of the right items at the right time supports the organizational objectives of profit, productivity, and return on investment. This is true in manufacturing, wholesale, retail, health care, and educational organizations. Measures of performance and productivity may differ among organizations, but all need adequate inventory management.

Inventory management encompasses the principles, concepts, and techniques for deciding what to order, how much to order, when it is needed, when to order for purchase or production, and how and where to store it. It supports organizational objectives by (1) defining and attaining desired levels of customer service, and by (2) achieving inventory investment objectives.

In an operational setting, inventory management is accomplished through the use of a set of procedures, frequently called an *inventory management system*. (See Figure 6-1, Inventory Management System Development Flowchart.) An inventory management system embodies a set of decision rules and guides for the various inventory situations the organization is encountering. It utilizes information processing capabilities to determine the nature of different situations as they arise on the planning horizon. Using the information describing the decision variables, the system will make automatic decisions on the basis of explicit models of some situations; and in other less structured situations, the system will provide the relevant information to a decision maker for human action.

This chapter examines the functions of inventory, measures of inventory management performance, classifying inventory by value, and costs relevant to inventory decisions.

**FIGURE 6-1**
**INVENTORY MANAGEMENT SYSTEM DEVELOPMENT FLOWCHART**

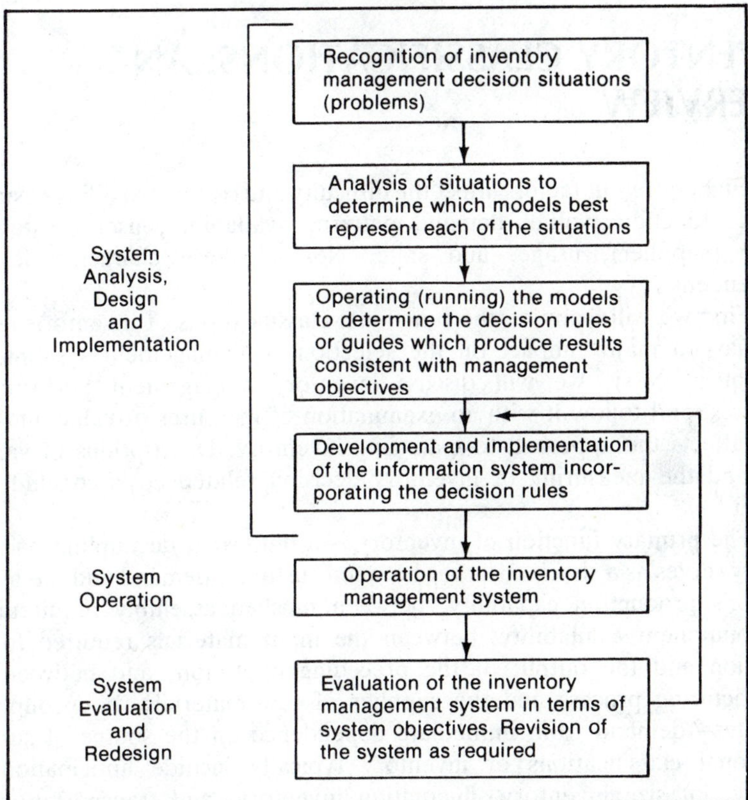


# PREREQUISITES TO INVENTORY DECISIONS

Where should one begin in the management of inventories: calculating economic order quantities (EOQ's); purchasing a computer and a material requirements planning (MRP) software package; or hiring a consultant? Each of these actions may do more harm than good unless an adequate analysis is made beforehand.

The inventory manager must determine the boundaries, magnitude, and composition of the aggregate inventory before she or he can expect to make decisions that are rational in terms of the organization's objectives and the nature of a specific decision situation. The point is that there is no inventory model, set of decision rules, or management system appropriate for all situations even in the same firm. Characteristics such as demand pattern, lead time, delivery requirements, and the various cost factors determine the appropriateness of the inventory management system and the model on which it is based. Let's examine some of these characteristics and their influence on the design of the management system.

## INVENTORY CLASSIFICATIONS: AN OVERVIEW

Eight different factors affect the difficulty and cost of providing customer service: function, value, demand pattern, availability, user (customer), source (supplier), usage, and state. Not all these characteristics are independent.

First we will examine the functional classifications of inventories since they have a major impact on the selection of management systems and techniques. Next, we will discuss inventory management performance measures, and follow it with an examination of measures of value and how value affects the approach to managing inventory. Descriptions of various costs and the measuring of inventory decision related costs conclude the chapter.

The primary function of inventory is a buffering, decoupling one. Inventory serves as a shock absorber between customer demand and the manufacturer's production capability, between finished assembly requirements and component availability, between the input materials required for an operation and the output of the preceding operation, and between the manufacturing process and the supplier of raw materials. It decouples—separates—demand from immediate dependence on the source of supply. Functional classifications of inventory typically include anticipation inventory, lot size inventory, fluctuation inventory, and transportation inventory. Inventory serves as a special type of buffer in each of these cases.

### Anticipation Inventories

Vacation shutdowns, peak sales periods, sales promotions, possible strikes, and the possibility of war—all lead to producing or purchasing finished goods, components, materials, or supplies, so that the organization will be able to cope with either the anticipated surge in demand or the supply drought. George Plossl has defined inventories purchased or built to take advantage of present costs and avoid anticipated substantial price increases as hedge inventories [1] because they are purchased as a hedge against price increases.

Decisions concerning acquisition of anticipation inventory are excellent examples of investment decisions with a risk element. Additional carrying cost is incurred by purchasing the inventory early. This cost must be less than the expected savings to justify acquiring anticipation inventory. For example, a hospital in the Northwest had the opportunity to double its order quantity and purchase an additional three months' supply, 1,000 units, of surgical kits at the present unit price of \$6.50 with an anticipated price increase to \$6.75 in three months. The purchasing agent estimated the probability of a price increase to be 90 percent. He knew that space and capital were available. Policy was to purchase not more than six months' supply. Should he make the purchase? Let's see.

Total expected savings = Cost of placing an order + Expected savings in material costs
Expected material savings = Number of units × Savings per unit × Probability of cost increase
= 1,000 × .25 × .9 = \$225
Order cost savings = 1 order at \$30
Total expected savings = \$255
Total costs = Incremental inventory × Time period × Carrying rate

Using a carrying cost rate of 25 percent a year (we will discuss carrying costs more later) renders the following costs:

Investment = 1,000 × \$6.50
Time = .25 years (3 months)
Rate = 25% a year
Cost = 1,000 × 6.50 × .25 × .25
Cost = \$406.25

Given these facts, the purchase does not pay. But wait, let's change the purchasing agent's figures and allow him to use a carrying cost rate of 10 percent based on out-of-pocket costs resulting from the assumption that the space will not be used for any other purpose and the cost of capital is the primary if not the only incremental cost; then

Cost = 1,000 × 6.50 × .25 × .10 = \$162.50

He will save money by buying.

Ah, yes, a little agility and simple elementary school arithmetic will allow us to support either position; reality, however, will not. The crucial question is: What is the true carrying cost rate? It may be difficult to determine whether the carrying cost rate should be 24 to 26 percent or, say, 10 to 12 percent; but a knowledgeable manager can determine whether a 10 percent or a 25 percent carrying cost rate will be incurred.

Assuming the above calculations do indicate that an early purchase will result in a net savings, there is at least one other question that should be asked before we bound forward to other decisions. Are the savings worthwhile? Is the return on investment adequate? In the second version of the above example the net expected savings are $92.50 ($255.00–$162.50) and the added investment is $6,500 for three months. Return on Investment (ROI) is thus

$$\begin{aligned} ROI &= \text{Savings/Investment} = \$92.50 \div \$6{,}500 \\ &= .0142 \text{ for three months} \\ &= .0568 \text{ on an annual basis} \end{aligned}$$

Is a 5.6 percent return on an investment worthwhile? That's a policy question, but most firms would not be overly excited about an investment with a return approximating (or less than) that available from short-term investments at local financial institutions.

The production manager, although always concerned about costs and monetary savings, should be concerned primarily about storing critical commodities and resources. Manufacturing organizations frequently have inadequate machine capacity of a specific type to meet an above average demand rate. In building anticipation inventory during a less than average demand period, the manager should make those items that require bottleneck machine and work force capacities.

Before leaving anticipation stocks, we should recognize that in those cases involving possible shortages, the cost of not buying can be extremely large when a shortage can shut down a production line, threaten the life of a patient, or damage customer relations.

## Lot Size Inventories

It is very inefficient in most cases to produce or purchase goods at the same rate at which they are consumed; efficient rates of production usually are much greater than the consumption rate. For example, the process producing die castings for carburetor housings generates output at a much greater rate than the sales of automobiles using a specific carburetor housing. To use a slow method of production matching the demand rate—for example, machining the housing in sections from raw materials and then assembling it—is much more expensive than casting the housings on an intermittent basis and holding some in stock as they are used gradually.

The folly of a hospital purchasing gauze on a daily basis is apparent immediately. The costs of writing the purchase order, delivering the gauze, and processing the invoice can very well be greater than the cost of the gauze.

In many cases of this type purchasing a large quantity of material to be used over a period is the economical approach.

The economics of manufacturing and purchasing lead to the intermittent purchasing or production of goods and materials in a quantity (lot size) sufficient to meet relatively stable demand during an extended period. Decisions concerning determination of the lot size and timing of the order will be discussed later as will the crucial issues of selecting the method of determining the lot size and timing the release of orders.

## Fluctuation Inventories

The sales of canned or frozen beans, sweaters, refrigerators, lawn mowers, fountain pens, fertilizer, shoes, and so on—all vary day to day and week to week. It is, therefore, not realistic in most cases to expect the demand for these products to be predictable with anything like 100 percent certainty. At best we know a range within which the demand will fluctuate. When it is economical, inventories are provided to meet the high side fluctuations of finished goods demand just as they are provided to absorb the variations in the requirements for raw materials, components, manufacturing supplies, and office supplies. In addition to demand fluctuations there are supply fluctuations. When vendor lead time or in-process time is greater than average, inventory is required to maintain a steady flow of work through the shop.

Such inventories are called safety stock, buffer stock, or reserve stock. They enable an organization to service its customers when the demand for that service is above average or when delivery of replenishment stocks takes longer than usual. Fluctuation inventory will be examined further when we look at order points and at controlling lead time.

## Transportation Inventories

Stages in the production process are not always physically adjacent. In fact, components frequently are manufactured in one part of the state, country, or world and shipped to another location for assembly. Similarly, finished products often are shipped sizable distances to warehouses, distributors, or customers. Ample inventory, flowing from one stage to the next, must be kept in the pipeline if the production and distribution process is not to be interrupted. Items in movement from one stage to the next are called transportation inventories. They include all items being shipped from finished goods warehouses to the customer as well as those items which an organization is shipping from one of its plants to another.

There is a natural tendency to overlook or not fully recognize the transportation inventory cost (TRIC). Such inventory ties up capital and is subject to spoilage, deterioration, damage, insurance, taxes, pilferage, and handling costs. Transportation inventories do exist and do cost money, and this cost can be measured.

TRIC equals the product of the transportation carrying cost rate, the dollar volume shipping rate, and the transit time.

$$\text{TRIC} = k \times R \times C \times t$$

Where:

$k$ = Transportation carrying cost rate based on cost of capital, insurance, pilferage, and so on (does not include cost of shipment)
$R$ = Requirements (demand) per period
$C$ = Unit cost
$t$ = Transit time

In most cases the actual transportation inventory cost can be determined with sufficient accuracy for decision making purposes. For example, if a manufacturer of automobile frames ships a daily average of a thousand frames that cannot be billed to the customer until received, the frames take a day and a half on the average to reach the assembly plant, the frames have a value of $30 each, and .15 is a good estimate of the transportation carrying cost rate, then

$$\begin{aligned}\text{TRIC} &= \frac{.15}{\text{year}} \times \frac{1{,}000 \text{ units}}{\text{day}} \times \frac{\$30}{\text{unit}} \times 1.5 \text{ days} \\ &= \$6{,}750 \text{ per year}\end{aligned}$$

Although at first it may have seemed that frames in transit for only a day and a half really do not amount to much, still, the question is: What does this cost? The facts of the situation reveal that these frames tie up $45,000. Reduction of transportation time from a day and a half to one day would result in an annual savings of $2,250.

To summarize, the primary function of inventory is to have items available to maintain the flow of goods through the production process to the customer while minimizing the investment required to achieve this service. Achievement of these goals supports the overall organization goals of productivity, profit, and return on investment. Methods of achieving these goals are discussed throughout the text. Inventories can be functionally classified as anticipation, lot size, fluctuation, and transportation inventories. The importance of these types of inventories in a particular organization depends on the firm. However, the management of lot size and fluctuation inventories frequently has the greatest impact on the achievement of organizational objectives. The concepts and decision techniques employed in managing lot size and fluctuation inventories are later discussed in detail.

# PERFORMANCE MEASURES

The levels of customer service achieved and the inventory investment required to achieve those levels are the two primary criteria for evaluating inventory management performance. Establishing target levels and measuring performance against those targets are practices followed by many companies. [2]

This section examines different measures of customer service and inventory investment emphasizing their application to individual item management.[1]

## Customer Service (Service Level)

Operationally *customer service* is the term used to describe the availability of items when needed by the customer. The customer may be the consumer of a finished product, a distributor, a plant in the organization, or the department in which the next operation is performed. Seldom if ever can an organization plan or act so that all items always are available in the proper quantity when desired. Some of the obvious causes of the unavailability of items when desired are an unusually large number of orders, machine failure, and late delivery by suppliers. However, an organization should aim for a target level of customer service and attain a probabilistic result measured in the same terms. Richard Artes stated it well, "A good finished goods inventory system will compare actual performance to planned performance and provide a feedback loop to correct significant deviations."[3]

But measuring delivery performance relative to delivery dates is only part of the story in those situations where back ordering and late deliveries are possible. How good a job the organization does in filling back orders should also be determined.

**Measures of Customer Service.** There is a plethora of ways for measuring customer service. Each has its strengths and weaknesses and appropriate applications. These measures can be divided into those which are percentage measures and those which are absolute values. Both types are suitable for comparison with a standard, perhaps performance in a previous similar period.

The percentage type measures include:

1. Orders shipped on schedule
2. Line items shipped on schedule
3. Total items shipped on schedule

[1]Chapter 9, "Aggregate Inventory Management," describes the application of these measures to aggregate inventory.

4. Dollar volume shipped on schedule
5. Profit volume shipped on schedule
6. Operating item days not out of stock
7. Ordering periods without a stock-out

The absolute value type of measurements include:

8. Order days out of stock
9. Line item days out of stock
10. Total item days out of stock
11. Dollar volume days out of stock
12. Idle time due to material and component shortages

**Percentage Type Measures.** Let us now consider the percentage type measures.

1. *Percentage of orders shipped on schedule.* This is a good measure of service to the external customer if all orders are of equal value. But if 99 percent of the orders constitutes only 50 percent of the volume and profit while the 1 percent shipped months late constitutes the other 50 percent, a 99 percent customer service level achievement is misleading. In short, this is a good measure for finished goods service if all orders and customers have roughly the same value and late deliveries are not excessively late.
2. *Percentage of line items shipped on schedule.* This measure overcomes a deficiency of the previous measure in that it recognizes that different orders may be for different numbers of items. However, it does not recognize the possible dollar differential in line items and the lateness of the order. In addition, the complexity and cost of the measure are increased by having to record the number of items on each order. It also is most appropriate for measuring the service performance of finished goods.
3. *Percentage of total items shipped on schedule.* This measure is better than the preceding in that it recognizes the differences in quantities in orders and line items. But, again, dollar volume and the lateness in delivery variations could distort the picture. For example, if a company sells automotive brake sets and also rivets, the percentage of total items shipped on schedule is not very helpful. The measurement is more costly and complex than the previous measures.
4. *Percentage of total dollar volume shipped on schedule.* This measure removes many of the previous objections and can be calculated easily if the dollar volume of each order is readily available. However, it too will give a distorted picture if some large orders consisted primarily of purchased materials with relatively little value added. In brief, a plant manager can demonstrate a relatively good customer service level by processing such orders on schedule while the delivery performance on the bulk of the work being processed in the factory is poor. Again, the lateness of the late orders is not measured.

5. *Percentage of profit dollar volume shipped on schedule.* The ethics of forever delaying the low profit and negative profit orders certainly can be questioned—not to mention potential legal problems that can arise. However, the legitimacy and importance of shipping the most profitable orders on schedule are difficult to question. This measure is very difficult to implement in most cases, since order profitability is not in the data base readily available to shop and inventory management.
6. *Percentage of operating item days not out of stock.* If a company operates 250 days and has 1,000 line items in its finished goods product line for sale from stock, it has a potential total of 250,000 line item days of desired availability in any year. If the total item days for which all back ordered items are late is 2,500, the service level is then 1 − 2,500 ÷ 250,000 or 99 percent. This is not a bad performance measure for an organization in which the items are of similar value and profit with comparable demand. However, if most items sold for under $5 while ten items sold for $1,000 to $1,500 and the company experienced relatively long stock-outs on these high value items during a period of high demand, the measure certainly would present a distorted picture with this percentage.

   Implementing measures 5 and 6 may not be practical in most cases.
7. *Percentage of ordering periods not out of stock.* If an item is ordered monthly and there is one stock-out during the year, the customer service level according to this measure is 91.67 percent (11 ÷ 12). This method lends itself to the determination of order points (an order is placed when stock on hand reaches the order point) providing specific levels of customer service. It provides a good starting point in many situations for establishing customer service objectives; refined measures then can be implemented on selected items.

**Absolute Value Type Measures.** Since the percentage measures related to absolute value measures 8 through 11 (order days, line item days, total item days, and dollar volume days out of stock) were discussed previously, these measures will not be discussed individually since each possesses shortcomings similar to its counterpart. The combination of a percentage measure and its absolute value counterpart removes the inherent disadvantage of a percentage or absolute value type used individually.

Results obtained using absolute value type measures can be evaluated only if a basis for comparison exists. As mentioned previously, comparison can be made to a standard—for example, 50 order days out of stock per year—or to results obtained in previous periods.

12. *Idle time due to material and component shortages.* This is a very useful measure of production activity control including queue management and input/output control (see Chapter 12). The measure for a period can be compared to the performance in a period of similar plant activity. It is not uncommon for this measure to be taken monthly. Any manufacturing facility operating against standard production times usually maintains a record of productive and nonproductive hours with

> the latter's causes noted. Admittedly in some situations the causes of idle times are multiple and in others it is difficult to judge, but with a little practice, the dominant cause can be determined in most cases. Thus, the data required to measure idle time due to material and component shortages are frequently available.

To see how a single situation can give rise to different values, consider the following data. During a one-year time span, a firm supplied 152,700 units of a particular product. Of the 1,227 orders received, 46 could not be filled from stock. This represented a total of 5,560 units not shipped from stock. Over the 52-week period, the company was out of stock nine times. What was its service level on this one part?

On the basis of the percentage of items shipped on schedule [(152,700 − 5,560) ÷ 152,700] the service level was 96.36 percent; on the basis of percent of orders shipped complete on schedule [(1,227 − 46) ÷ 1,227], it was 96.25 percent; but on the basis of the percent of the periods in which no stockout occurred [1 − (9 ÷ 52)], it was only 82.70 percent.

None of these methods is "right" or "wrong"; circumstances determine which is most appropriate.

**Back Order Delivery Performance.** In the design and manufacture of equipment, zero defects seldom if ever occur. Even when a piece of equipment malfunctions rarely, the customer is concerned with how long it takes to repair. Many inventory management situations are analogous to this. When back orders (late deliveries) are possible, inventory management must be concerned not only with customer service relative to the original goal but also with the organization's ability to rectify the situation. As Henry Jordan has noted, "In addition to measuring delivery performance, the system should provide a means of analyzing delinquent orders."[4] In brief, how fast are the back orders filled? It is one thing if all back orders are shipped the following day, but quite another if it takes weeks or months.

Here again there are many different ways of measuring performance. Goals should be established and performance measured against those goals. Some of the measures are:

1. The percentage of back orders shipped within different time periods. For example, one manufacturer of small tools has a goal of shipping 80 percent of all back orders within five working days and 100 percent within ten working days.
2. The average time and the standard deviation of the time it takes to ship a back order.
3. An aging of back orders similar to an aging of accounts receivable may take place with limits established as goals on the various brackets.
4. The back order turnover rate may be measured and compared to a performance standard. The back order turnover rate is equal to the shipment

of back orders in the appropriate volume measure divided by the average number of back orders.[2]

To measure delivery performance against scheduled shipping dates without measuring the delivery performance on back orders is to possess only half a picture. Confucius must have said something about having half a picture.

**Selecting the Measure of Customer Service.** The foregoing undoubtedly did not exhaust all the possible measures of customer service, but it does indicate the myriad of possibilities. How does management determine which, if any, of the above are cost beneficial and worthy of implementation? Perhaps the most important questions to be asked concerning the selection of a measure of service are the following:

1. Are the data available?
2. Can the results being measured be affected by the manager's decisions?
3. Do the results being measured have an impact on productivity, profit, and return on investment?

Obviously if the data are not available, the measure is not feasible. Estimated costs of obtaining the data must be compared to the benefits of the measure. For example, measuring and recording the profitability of items completed on schedule versus those that are late may cost more than the increase in profit possible to achieve with the added information.

Shortages of scarce purchased items available only from a single source are situations in which the manager may be able to do little to achieve on-time delivery. An accumulation of circumstances similar to the foregoing can lead to measure results not indicative of the manager's performance.

If the measure is not related to productivity, profit, and return on investment, it has little value. An indication of something wrong and where to go to correct it does have value because it does relate to performance.

The fundamental problem is aggregation. A single measure used across all items and orders is bound to be deceptive. Thus, it is necessary to group items and/or orders by their important characteristics. What different types of inventories are being managed? What are the competitive pressures? Are all stock-outs of equal importance? Are some customers more important than others?

First, divide inventories into raw materials, work-in-process, and finished goods. In many organizations it may be necessary to subdivide one or more of these classifications further to achieve the desired measurement and control of performance. At that point the ABC approach can be applied. As will be mentioned in the section describing the principles of ABC analysis,

---

[2]Bayvet, Inc. of Shawnee Mission, Kansas, for example, uses this type of measure.

the fundamental concept is to devote attention to decisions in proportion to their importance, whether that importance is based on the monetary value of the items involved or the difficulty in controlling the situation. Items of high value, long lead times, or critical in the production process are *A* items. Items of intermediate concern are classified *B*, and items that are readily available and whose absence for a day or two would not be missed should be classified *C*. This enables management to implement different measurements of performance on different types of items. The objective is to balance the cost of measuring and controlling service of items with the relative importance and difficulty of achieving customer service for different items in inventory.

In summary, customer service measures are in most cases a surrogate measure of the customer's satisfaction with the organization's late delivery performance. How unhappy a customer is with a specific late delivery depends on how pressing the customer's need is at that time. One measure that is not a surrogate is *idle time due to material and component shortages*. It, in fact, does measure how well a particular type of inventory fulfills its function. Obtaining this measure is not especially difficult when both the items needed for production and the production facility are controlled by the same organization.

Finally, different measures of customer service are appropriate for different sets of circumstances. These circumstances include the nature of the inventory, the availability of data, the use of the measures by management, the relation of the measures to organizational objectives, and their costs.[3]

**Customer Service Objectives.** After an organization selects customer service measures for its different types of inventory, performance objectives must be established. For example, should the organization aim for a 90 percent or a 95 percent level of customer service for finished goods? How much idle time in the plant due to material and component shortages is acceptable? Again, these are not easy questions to answer; but there are rational approaches that can be followed to establish reasonable objectives.

To begin with, different performance objectives are usually appropriate for different types of items. The controlling factors in establishing the customer service objective for an item are the cost of carrying the item and the cost of a stock-out. Inexpensive, easily stored items whose absence results in relatively high costs should have high customer service performance objectives. For example, it doesn't seem unreasonable that a 100 percent customer service level objective be established for all hardware items such as washers, nuts, bolts, screws, pins, and so on, used in assembly operations. Theoretically it is true that a 100 percent customer service level is impossible over an infinite time span or for an infinite number of parts, but the typical organization measures performance on a finite number of parts over a period

[3] Johnson Wax uses a three-week, projected customer service measure by product and by warehouse to enable them to react quickly and reduce the severity of problems. [5]

seldom longer than a year. Elton Throndsen, of General Electric, recommends that customer service level objectives be established on the basis of the delivery service needed to serve the market and obtain the desired return on investment given the inventory investment required to achieve a specific level of service. [6]

In a dependent demand environment with a time phased requirements planning system, a 100 percent service level is necessary for component parts if assemblies are to be fabricated. As Joseph Orlicky pointed out, planned service levels of less than 100 percent at the component level will diminish the assembly service level in a cumulative fashion due to joint probability. [7] The probability of all the assembly being completed on schedule is equal to the product of the probabilities of each of the components being available multiplied by the probability that assembly will be completed within the standard lead time given that the parts are available. For example, if an assembly consists of three parts each with a .95 service level, and if the probability of fabricating the assembly within the standard lead time is .98, the service level—designed into the system—of the assembly being completed on schedule equals .95 × .95 × .95 × .98, or .84. Eighty-four percent may not seem terrible (not too good either), but change the .95's to .90 and the .98 to .95 and the service level of the assembly is .69—certainly not a praiseworthy performance.

Some practical approaches can help in establishing customer service objectives. For finished goods sold from stock, determine the customer service level achieved during the past year. Was it satisfactory? What were the level and intensity of customer complaints? How much business was lost due to shortages or back orders? Estimates, if not exact figures, can be obtained from marketing, the customer service department, or the order entry department. If the data are not available, provisions should be made to collect the information. After such information has been obtained, the acceptability of present performance can be evaluated in terms of competitors' performance, customers' expectations, and the cost of improving the customer service level.

In the same fashion, information concerning machine center downtime and assembly line downtime due to material and component shortages is usually available. If not, it should be. Although it may be necessary to slip the scheduled fabrication of an assembly, it is not unreasonable to have an objective of never shutting down an assembly line for lack of components. In brief, once the assembly fabrication is begun, a 100 percent customer service for items required in the assembly is not unusual.

**Customer Service and Inventory Investment.** In a large organization with inventories of many types, the aggregate customer service level achieved has an exponential relationship to aggregate investment in inventory. For each additional percentage increase in customer service, a greater increase in investment is required than was required to achieve the previous percentage point increase in customer service. Figure 6-2 assumes that all other factors remain the same. Such is not always the case. For example, if the inventory management system is improved, it is not unusual to

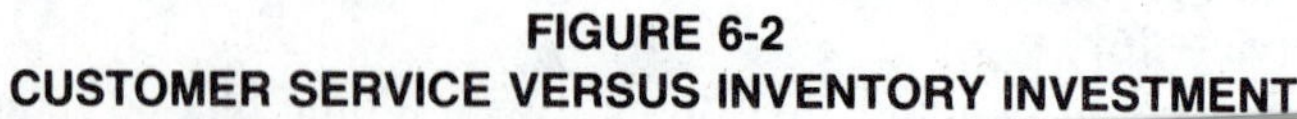

**FIGURE 6-2**
**CUSTOMER SERVICE VERSUS INVENTORY INVESTMENT**

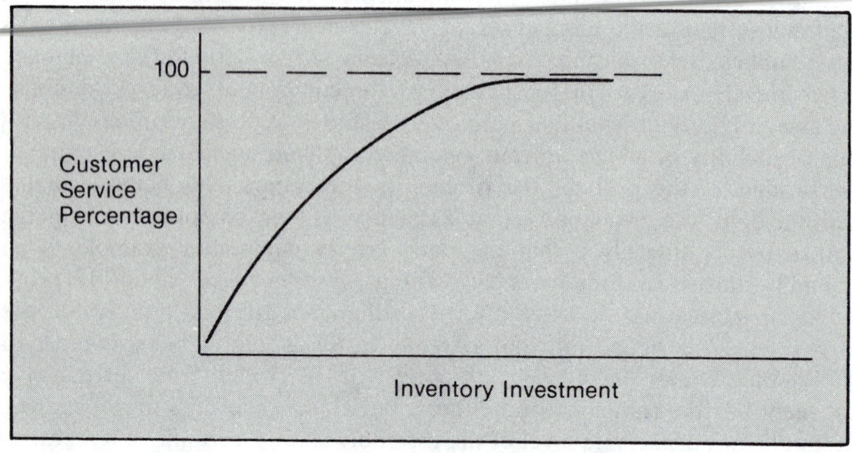


increase the level of customer service while simultaneously decreasing investment in inventory. This possibility is illustrated by the family of curves shown in Figure 6-3.

In addition, it is possible to increase the inventory investment and decrease customer service even when the investment has been made in those items needed most. This happens whenever a system is overburdened physically or administratively. Continual increases in work-in-process eventually will reach the point where all or some of the following conditions result: lots are lost; movement of material through the shop is inefficient; foremen combine lots for setup cost savings and so create more costly scheduling

**FIGURE 6-3**
**CUSTOMER SERVICE VERSUS INVENTORY INVESTMENT WITH DIFFERENT MANAGEMENT SYSTEMS**

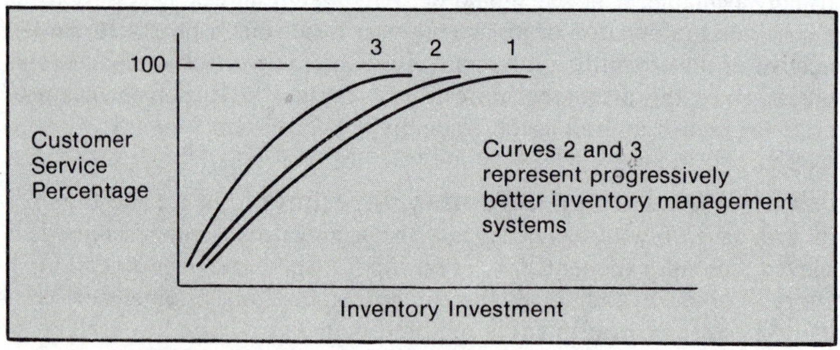

problems; and the information system is not capable of handling the volume. In a similar fashion, exceeding storage capacity may result in some of the following: weather damage due to outside storage; misplacement of lots due to inability to use the normal storage locations; and item damage due to aisle storage. In brief, overloading the system physically and administratively well may reduce customer service and create chaos.

In summary, there are many measures of customer service, each with its strengths, weaknesses, and appropriate applications. Management should establish customer service objectives consistent with market demands and inventory investment objectives. Different performance measures and different objectives frequently will be appropriate for different types of items. Dependent demand items virtually require a 100 percent service level because of the multiplicative effect of joint probabilities. And, finally, to measure delivery performance against scheduled shipping dates without establishing the cause of the problem and measuring the delivery performance on back orders is to do only half the job.

## Inventory Investment

Oliver Wight made an excellent point when he wrote that, "Most people in production and inventory management do not focus enough of their attention on dollars." [8] He was advocating that the raw material, purchase parts input, and fabricated output quantities projected in a materials requirement plan be used to determine the aggregate inventory investment projected for different time periods in the planning horizon; and, thus, our discussion of measuring inventory investment begins.

**Measuring Inventory Investment.** Inventory investment can be measured as of a past date, as of today, or projected to a future date. None of these measures will be exact to the penny, but they will be sufficiently precise for analysis and decision making. Without a measure of inventory investment, management is operating in the dark.

Periodic, say monthly, costing of the aggregate inventory is essential to the management of inventory. Costing inventory only once a year rarely does the job. Annual physical counts of inventories commonly are taken at atypical times, and it's not entirely unknown for organizations to manipulate inventories at that time to obtain desired balance sheet results or to avoid property taxes. Even if that is not the case, an annual evaluation of inventory investment completely misses fluctuations in investment that occur during the year. Periodic, say monthly, accounting evaluations combined with a cycle counting program enable an organization to spot short-term seasonal fluctuations, discern long-term trends early, and avoid end-of-year inventory surprises which perenially haunt some organizations.

Utilizing accounting evaluations requires a system with the capability of measuring finished goods, work-in-process, and raw materials. Confidence in such measures, especially the state of completion of work-in-process, can be developed through sample counts of such items to determine the accuracy of the accounting evaluations. Having obtained a measure of inventory investment, how can we use it?

**Absolute Measures of Investment.** Determination of the total dollars invested in raw materials, work-in-process, and finished goods constitutes an absolute measurement of inventory investment. The value obtained from this measure then can be used for comparisons and to obtain relative measures of investment. First, actual levels can be compared to budgeted target levels and variances analyzed. [2] Are variances (differences between actual and budgeted) due to an increase (decrease) in volume, scrap rate, labor costs, or lead time? The results of such analyses are the basis for corrective action. Projected inventory investments by period are necessary for cash flow analysis and to determine whether inventory investment will be within the financial capability of the organization. If not, management has the option of revising the production plan to bring projected inventory investment within financial constraints. The above decision is one more opportunity for applying the ABC principle of concentrating on the high dollar volume items to achieve the necessary changes.[4]

**Relative Measures of Investment.** Once the inventory investment has been measured, the inventory turnover rate (ITR) can be determined:

$$ITR = \frac{\text{Cost of sales}}{\text{Inventory investment}}$$

To avoid obtaining a misleading value, we must not mix apples and oranges. The ratio of actual cost of sales to actual investment or, as an alternative, the ratio of standard cost of sales to inventory investment at standard cost will produce legitimate and meaningful measures. If total sales, rather than cost of goods sold, are divided by the inventory investment, the measure is distorted by the changing profit percentages contained in the total sales. Use of standard cost data will provide for a more uniform measure, not contaminated by cost variances, and more suitable for period to period comparisons.

Krupp argues that the cost of sales value used in calculating this ratio should be based on an historical smoothed cost of sales (for a period of three months or so) divided by the present value of inventory. [9]

$$DITR = \frac{\text{Sum of last three months cost of sales} \times 4}{\text{Instantaneous inventory}}$$

Where: DITR = Historical inventory turnover ratio

[4] See Chapter 9, "Aggregate Inventory Management."

Close [10] recommends a projected inventory turnover rate (PITR) calculated in the following manner:

$$PITR = \frac{\text{Annualized forecast cost of sales}}{\text{Inventory investment today}}$$

Although their approaches differ, both models have the same objective, providing a meaningful measure of inventory investment in a dynamic environment. One method does this by using forecast cost of sales and the other does it by changing the target turnover rate to reflect planned production and sales.

When using past rather than future sales (as in the DITR model), the inventory turnover rate target will change in response to shifts in the demand forecast as Krupp points out. [9] Turnover targets usually will be lower when high demand is anticipated and vice-versa.
Certainly it is the only meaningful approach under seasonal demand or substantial trends in demand. For example, if a firm is entering the slow season after having just completed its fast sales period, the cost of goods sold annualized for the past three quarters is relatively high while the present inventory investment is relatively low. Using historical volume to calculate the ratio will generate a very low ITR when the inventory was in fact at an appropriate level to meet forecast demand.

What about using an *instantaneous* inventory value; the value of inventory on, say, the 25th of the month? Are there any pitfalls? There usually are. An usually large shipment or receipt of goods on the 24th is an event that will distort the ratio. Professional alertness and integrity will assist in avoiding this problem. If an event of unusual magnitude takes place shortly before inventory investment is measured, then any report including the ITR also should include a statement describing the event and its impact. In accounting, this is called the *principle of full disclosure.*

How are the calculations made? First, the forecast sales must be obtained for a period long enough to provide some stability and at the same time reflect shipments for which the present inventory will be used. Then this forecast must be annualized by multiplying it by the appropriate factor. This factor can be obtained by dividing the number of months in a year, 12, by the length of the forecast period in months. The annualized cost of sales is then divided by the present inventory. For example, forecast cost of goods sold for the next three months is $30 million, and the cost of present inventory is $28 million.

$$\text{Annualized cost of goods sold} = \$30 \text{ million} \times 12 \div 3 = \$120 \text{ million}$$
$$PITR = \$120 \text{ million} \div \$28 \text{ million} = 4.29 \text{ per year}$$

**Sensitivity Analysis.** Sensitivity analysis, especially on the pessimistic side, is appropriate here. What if our forecast is high and the standard cost of actual sales turns out to be only $108 million in the next three months?

Then our PITR will be: *PITR* with 10 percent decrease in sales = \$108 million ÷ \$28 million = 3.86. Such an analysis enables us to predict both a pessimistic PITR and an expected PITR. Inventories exist primarily for future requirements. If the errors in projecting future inventories are relatively small and the HITR experienced is continually lower than the PITR, changes in the cost of goods sold are the likely problem area and not the inventory management system.

The above figures can be used very easily to determine such common measures as weeks of sales on hand. For example,

$$\text{Weeks of sales on hand} = \text{Present inventory} \div \text{Projected average of weekly cost of sales}$$

$$\text{Projected average of weekly cost of sales} = \text{Annualized cost of sales} \div \text{weeks per year} = \$120 \text{ million} \div 52 = \$2.31 \text{ million}$$

$$\text{Weeks of sales on hand} = \$28 \text{ million} \div \$2.31 \text{ million per week} = 12.12 \text{ weeks}$$

Check:

$$PITR = \frac{\text{Weeks/Year}}{\text{Weeks of sales on hand}} = \frac{52}{12.12} = 4.29$$

**Obsolete Inventory.** A company with a large dollar amount of obsolete inventory carried at cost will have an ITR understating inventory management performance. Furthermore, if an unusually large amount of such inventory is purged with the appropriate accounting entries, the increase in the ITR will reflect not a stroke of genius in the inventory management department but more likely an increase in the value of scrap or a belated resolution of an obsolescent inventory problem.

**The Inventory Turn Ratio Objective.** There is no magic ITR goal for all organizations and all periods of activity. In fact, different ratio performance objectives may be appropriate for the different inventories within the same firm. Establishment of the ITR objectives should be a joint venture of inventory management, marketing, and financial management. It should reflect cash flow requirements, customer service objectives, and the individual characteristics of the business. As Plossl and Wight have pointed out, "Two companies in the same business may have extremely different rates of turnover, depending upon the degree of manufactured versus purchased material contained in the end product, whether the business is make-to-stock or make-to-order or both, consignment stocking policies, distance from suppliers, the number of warehouses maintained, and many other considerations that vary substantially affect the companies' ability to turn inventory." [11] In brief, the ITR objective should be based on the customer service objectives, the process cycle time, purchased and fabricated parts ratios, and stocking policies.

Like many management tools, the ITR has been abused and misapplied as Campbell reports. [12] As a result, its credibility has suffered. It is, nonetheless, still a useful technique. It is easy to understand and explain, can be measured and monitored, and reacts with minimum lag in reflecting change.

## ABC ANALYSIS

If not the first certainly one of the first steps in gaining a handle on an inventory situation should be the performance of an ABC Analysis.

Vilfredo Pareto, a nineteenth century Renaissance man, was the first to document the Management Principle of Materiality, which is the basis of ABC Analysis. Pareto, educated as an engineer and renowned as an economist, sociologist, and political scientist, noted that many situations are dominated by a relatively few vital elements in the situation. Thus, he surmised that controlling the relatively vital few will go a long way toward controlling the situation.[5]

Applying the ABC principle to inventory management involves

1. Classifying inventory items on the basis of relative importance
2. Establishing different management controls for different classifications with the degree of control being commensurate with the ranked importance of each classification

The letters *A*, *B*, *C* represent different classifications of descending importance, but there is nothing sacred about having three classes. Criteria for classification should reflect the difficulty of controlling an item and the impact of the item on costs and profitability.

ABC Analysis usually is illustrated using the annual dollar volume criteria as in Table 6-1, but that is only one of many criteria which may affect the value of an item. Factors affecting the importance of an item and that may be criteria for classifying items in an ABC Analysis include the following:

1. Annual dollar volume of the transactions for an item
2. Unit cost
3. Scarcity of material used in producing an item
4. Availability of resources, manpower, and facilities to produce an item
5. Lead time
6. Storage requirements for an item
7. Pilferage risks, shelf life, and other critical attributes
8. Cost of a stock-out
9. Engineering design volatility

[5] Ford Dickie, of General Electric, has illustrated how this principle could be applied to inventory management. [13]

Whether lead time, storage requirements, possibility of pilferage, shelf life, or scarcity of resources such as raw materials, work force personnel or facilities for production should be considered in the classification of a group of items can be determined only by examining the situation. For example,

**TABLE 6-1**
**EXAMPLE OF ABC ANALYSIS**

| Item | Unit Cost | Annual Usage | Annual Dollar Usage | Total Annual Percentage Usage |
|---|---|---|---|---|
| 1 | .05 | 50,000 | $2,500 | 34.3% |
| 2 | .11 | 2,000 | 220 | 3.0 |
| 3 | .16 | 400 | 64 | .9 |
| 4 | .08 | 700 | 56 | .8 |
| 5 | .07 | 4,800 | 336 | 4.6 |
| 6 | .15 | 1,300 | 195 | 2.7 |
| 7 | .20 | 17,000 | 3,400 | 46.7 |
| 8 | .04 | 300 | 12 | .2 |
| 9 | .09 | 5,000 | 450 | 6.2 |
| 10 | .12 | 400 | 48 | .7 |
| | | | $7,281 | |

Paul Conroy discusses the use of average weekly usage at Data General to establish breakpoints for an ABC classification. [14]

## Criteria Other than Dollar Volume

Table 6-2 illustrates how criteria can be applied in a programmed manner with the classification of an item being determined by the yes answer which results in the highest classification.

**TABLE 6-2**
**TYPICAL DECISION TABLE FOR ABC CLASSIFICATION**

| Question | Class Based on a Yes Answer[1] |
|---|---|
| 1. Is annual usage more than $50,000?[2] | A |
| 2. Is annual usage between $10,000 and $50,000? | B |
| 3. Is annual usage less than $10,000? | C |
| 4. Is the unit cost over $500? | A |
| 5. Is the unit cost between $100 and $500? | B |
| 6. Does the physical nature of the item cause special storage problems? | B |
| 7. Is the lead time longer than 6 months? | A |
| 8. Is the lead time between 3 and 6 months? | B |
| 9. Is shelf life less than 3 months? | A |
| 10. Is shelf life greater than 3 months but less than 6 months? | B |

[1] Final classification of an item is based on the highest classification received.
[2] The exact values used in annual usage, unit cost, lead time, and other criteria depend on the situation.

## The Procedure

With one more *caveat* that annual dollar volume alone should not be used to classify an item, the following procedure and simplified examples (Tables 6-1, 6-3, and 6-4) for classifying items on the basis of dollar volume are presented.

1. Determine the annual usage for each item in inventory.
2. Multiply the annual usage of each item by the cost of the item to obtain the total annual dollar usage of each item.
3. Add the total annual dollar usages of all items to determine the aggregate annual dollar inventory expenditures.
4. Divide the total annual dollar usage of each item by the aggregate annual expenditure for all items to obtain the percentage of total usage by each item.
5. List the items in rank order on the basis of the percentage of aggregate usage.
6. Examine annual usage distribution and group items on basis of percentage of annual usage.

**TABLE 6-3**
**ABC ANALYSIS—RANK BY PERCENTAGE OF USAGE**

| Item | Annual Usage | Percentage of Total | Cumulative Percentage | Item Classification |
|---|---|---|---|---|
| 7 | $3,400 | 46.7 | 46.7 | A |
| 1 | 2,500 | 34.3 | 81.0 | A |
| 9 | 450 | 6.2 | 87.2 | B |
| 5 | 336 | 4.6 | 91.8 | B |
| 2 | 220 | 3.0 | 94.8 | B |
| 6 | 195 | 2.7 | 97.5 | B |
| 3 | 64 | .9 | 98.4 | C |
| 4 | 56 | .8 | 99.2 | C |
| 10 | 48 | .6 | 99.8 | C |
| 8 | 12 | .2 | 100.0 | C |

Tables 6-3 and 6-4 typify real world situations in that the classifications of some items are clearly discernible while others are debatable. Items 7 and 1 are clearly *A* items while the classification of Items 2 and 6 could be either *B* or *C*. A graph illustrating *A*, *B*, and *C* items is found in Figure 6-4.

**TABLE 6-4**
**ABC ANALYSIS—RANK BY CLASSIFICATION**

| Item Classification | Items | Percentage | Percentage Value |
|---|---|---|---|
| A | 7, 1 | 20 | 81.0 |
| B | 9, 5, 2, 6 | 40 | 17.5 |
| C | 3, 4, 10, 8 | 40 | 2.5 |

**FIGURE 6-4**
**DISTRIBUTION OF INVENTORY BY VALUE**

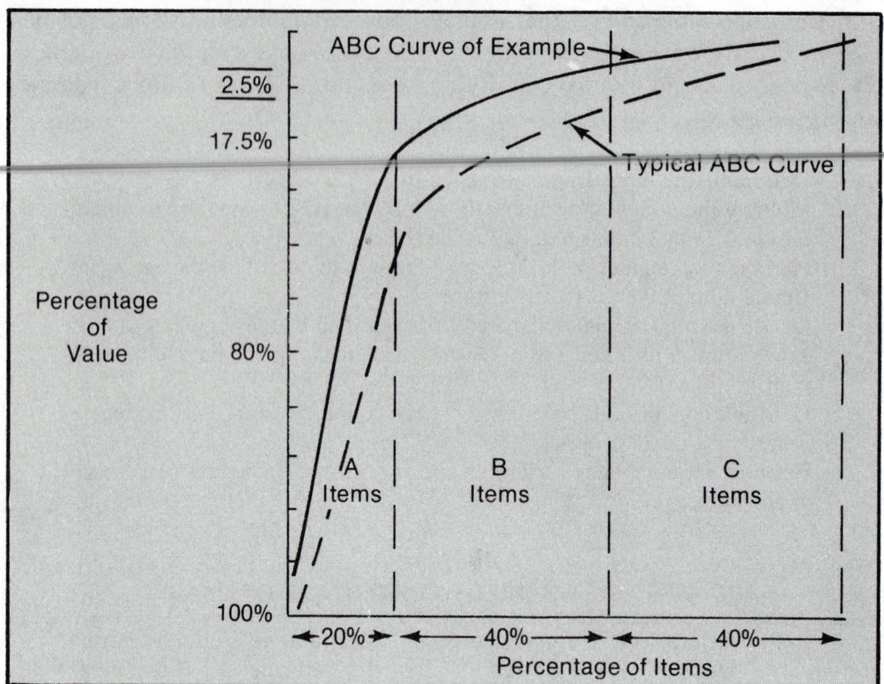


Examples of different controls that might be used for different classifications are:

*A* Items

1. Frequent evaluation of forecasts and forecasting method
2. Frequent, perhaps monthly, cycle counting with tight tolerances on accuracy
3. Daily updating of records
4. Frequent review of demand requirements, order quantities, and safety stock; usually resulting in relatively small order quantities
5. Close follow-up and expediting to reduce lead time

*B* Items

Similar to controls for *A* items with most control activities taking place less frequently

*C* Items

1. Basic rule is to *have them*
2. Simple records or no records; perhaps use a periodic review of physical inventory
3. Large order quantities and safety stock
4. Store in area readily available to production workers or order fillers
5. Count items infrequently, annually or semiannually, with scale accuracy (weighing rather than counting) acceptable

Widespread application of electronic data processing to inventory management has had an impact on some applications of ABC Analysis. Accurate and timely records now can be maintained economically on all items except very low cost ones, such as standard rivets, washers, and other pan stock items. For record-keeping purposes, only *A* and *C* items may exist; but record-keeping procedures are only one aspect of inventory management. Other planning and control procedures such as evaluation of forecasts and cycle counting frequencies still may be influenced by the result of an ABC Analysis.

Application of ABC Analysis principles does not require the use of only three classifications or even that the classifications be designated *A*, *B*, and *C*. In an interesting presentation, Kenneth L. Campbell recommends the adoption of a *descriptive* classification system with five different categories each related to the functional use of the items rather than classification based only on annual dollar volume of transactions. [12]

Before leaving ABC Analysis there are at least two or three other points which should be made. Distinct ABC Analyses should be performed for different product groupings. Purchased items, manufactured items, assemblies, subassemblies, independent demand items, and dependent demand items should be analyzed separately in most situations. The analysis should not ignore trends in demand or future plans. Most items experience what is usually called a product life cycle. Some are on the upswing experiencing an increasing demand; others may have leveled off and be declining. Historical usage patterns can be misleading if followed blindly. In addition, marketing may be planning to drop a product or engineering may be planning to redesign a component. Such information must be obtained by inventory management and used in establishing planning and control procedures.

In addition to inventory management, the principles of ABC Analysis can be applied to many production and inventory control decisions. Gary Zimmerman, of McCormick & Company, Inc., discusses the use of the ABC principle in establishing "trigger limits" for tracking signals in forecasting; evaluating orders in relationship to capacity planning on the basis of the amount of critical capacity (worker or machine hours) required by the order; scheduling by noting those primary operations which provide the bulk of the load on secondary operations; and determining the frequency of cycle counting. [15] Rolf Norbom reports on the use of ABC principles by the Philco-Ford Corporation in controlling purchase part deliveries, inventory levels, and investment at a medium-sized assembly plant. [16]

## INVENTORY COSTS

Costs are the crux of inventory management decisions at all levels. What about profits? Lost profits (profits foregone) can be and, in fact, are viewed as a cost in some inventory management decisions. As mentioned previously, when an organization selects a customer service objective less than 100 percent it does so on the premise that the lost profits which are incurred by lack of inventory on certain occasions are less than the costs of carrying sufficient stock to cover all demand situations. As a result, analyses throughout this text almost always include an examination of the relevant costs. Although different costs may occur in different situations in somewhat different ways and magnitudes, there is a common cost structure applicable to most inventory management decisions.

Before exploring the elements of that common structure, a brief discussion of the following aspects of costs and costing should be helpful.

## Relevant, Opportunity, and Sunk Costs

Full cost accounting procedures record all manufacturing costs and assign these costs to an organization's output. In brief, all costs incurred in the production process end up in cost of goods sold (expense) or in various inventories (assets).

As a general rule, the inventory planners should include only relevant costs in the decision making process. *Relevant costs* are costs that are incurred because of a decision. The ordering costs, setup costs, direct labor and material costs related to a lot size decision are examples of relevant costs. Costs which will be incurred regardless of a decision are not relevant costs. For example, the cost of heating the plant seldom is affected by lot size or order release decisions.

*Opportunity costs* are returns on capital that would have been obtained from an alternate foregone investment. They represent the gains surrendered because one possible venture is neglected due to the use of limited resources for another. Such costs usually are not recorded in financial accounting records, but must be considered by the decision maker. For example, if an organization has large cash reserves, the financial accounting system normally will not record the cost of funds invested in inventory even though the organization could earn income on those funds if invested in treasury bills or another income producing vehicle. The decision maker should recognize opportunity costs. In many cases the average expected return from feasible alternative investment is used as an estimate of opportunity costs.

*Sunk costs* are expenditures which already have been incurred and which will not be affected by a decision. These costs include capital expenditures for equipment and land and training costs for new personnel. Expenditures for raw materials or purchased parts already received usually cannot be considered as sunk costs. The assumption is that, if the materials or parts are not used unless used now to complete a particular order they will be used in the near future for another order. An exception occurs when consideration is being given either to using materials with a fast expiring shelf life or to using scrap. Costs of personnel for whom no alternate tasks are available in a period also may be viewed as sunk costs. For example, the cost of underutilized setup personnel may be considered as sunk cost if no other productive tasks are available and laying them off is not practical. This is a valid, although sometimes hazardous, assessment of setup personnel, production workers, or office staff. The hazard is that this approach may be adopted to justify an emotionally desired decision when in fact resourceful management would have discovered other and more profitable opportunities to employ these resources. Sunk costs should not be included in the decision maker's calculations.

## Incremental Costs, Cost Breakpoints, and Marginal Costs

The change in total costs resulting from a sizable change in output is an *incremental cost*. For example, if output increases from 250 to 500 tons and causes an increase in total costs from $25,000 to $40,000, the incremental cost of this change is $15,000.

Equally important to the decision maker are the *cost breakpoints*, points on the total cost curve where discontinuity exists. Let us add the following information to the example shown under incremental costs.

1. As illustrated, 250 tons will cost $25,000.
2. An increase from 250 to 350 tons will cost $25 a ton.
3. Any increase beyond 350 tons will require a capital investment of $11,000.
4. Additional output from 350 tons to 700 tons will cost $10 a ton.

This cost function is described in Figure 6-5.

**FIGURE 6-5**
**INCREMENTAL COSTS AND COST BREAKPOINTS**

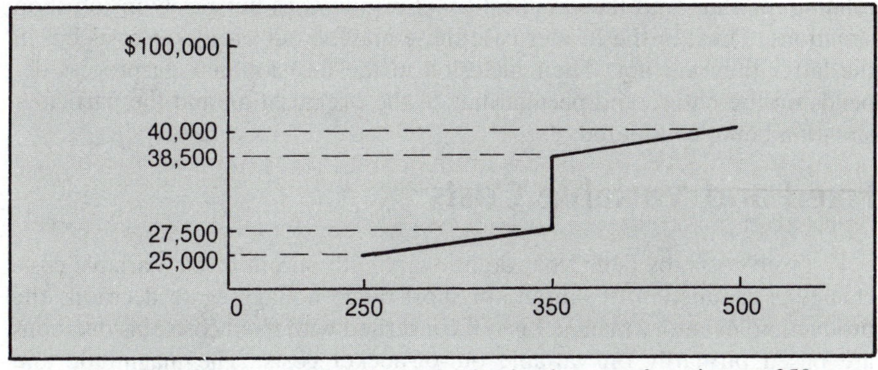


The critical point is the discontinuity in the cost function at 350 tons. Considerations of cost breaks such as this will arise often in our examination of inventory costs.

*Marginal costs* are those incurred to produce one additional unit. In the previous example the marginal cost of the 251st ton was $25; the marginal cost of the 351st ton was $11,010; and the marginal cost of the 352d ton was $10. Marginal cost is a particular type of incremental cost; the two differ by degree. For example, the additional (marginal) cost incurred in building one more supertanker is rather large to be called marginal.

## Direct, Indirect, and Overhead Costs

*Direct costs* are those that can be traced directly to the fact that an order, task, or lot of parts has been produced. Material and labor fall into this category; they are clearly direct out-of-pocket costs in most cases. In fact, most accounting systems call these Direct Material and Direct Labor costs. Relevant and out-of-pocket costs are used synonymously in this text. Even depreciation cost changes may be relevant because of their effect on taxes.

*Indirect costs* are those not directly traceable to a specific item. Frequently they are synonymous with manufacturing overhead. Cutting oils, lubricants, material handling, perishable tools such as drill bits and cutters, plant supervision, and other manufacturing support and services usually are recorded as indirect costs and allocated to products on some common proportional basis such as a multiple of the direct labor hours or material costs of each item. Some of these costs—drill bits, for example—may be out-of-pocket costs, but, for the most part, these costs are not affected by an individual lot size decision. An aggregate level decision to increase or decrease the production output rate usually will affect these costs; thus, they should be included in an aggregate level type decision.

*Overhead costs* are those expenditures for heating, lighting, buildings, equipment, top management, sales, and general services such as plant security and the personnel department. They are affected by individual item level decisions only if that item constitutes a major portion of the production and the decision has aggregate level impact. This situation sometimes exists in refining, mining, and the chemical process industries but rarely in job shop situations. Thus, in the former case these may be out-of-pocket costs but in the latter they are not. Their inclusion in the decision-making process depends on the nature and peculiarities of the organization and the particular situation being considered.

## Fixed and Variable Costs

Fixed costs, by definition, do not vary with output level. Variable costs change as a function of output. In short-range nonaggregate decisions the production inventory manager is not concerned with fixed costs; his decisions are based pirmarily on variable out-of-pocket costs. The magnitude and time horizon of a decision determine what is fixed and what is variable cost. A decision to increase the lot size of one item by 20 percent rarely requires the purchase of additional equipment, the hiring of personnel, or building additional storage space; in other words, these costs are fixed. But the decision to increase the output rate from 100 to 200 gallons an hour may require additional manufacturing and distribution capacity and, hence, these costs are variable. As described here, they are an incremental type of variable cost. Again, what are fixed costs and what are variable costs depend on the nature of the decision.

### Actual Costs and Standard Costs

Expenditures recorded as having been incurred as the result of a decision are *actual costs*. Such costs are available only after products have been made or after a project is completed.

*Standard cost* is a preestablished criterion or norm, based on efficient operating procedures, for what an item should cost to produce or purchase. Material, labor and overhead costs usually are included.

In practice, actual costs seldom are equal to standard costs. In some cases they oscillate about the standard cost; in other situations—for example, where incentive plans exist—they may be consistently below standard cost; while in another situation—for example, a measured day rate nonincentive plant—they may be consistently above standard cost. In those situations where actual costs exhibit a bias with respect to standard cost, that bias should be recognized by the decision maker's calculations. If actual costs vary about the standard costs with no consistent bias, the standard cost may be used in the calculations.

### Intangible Costs

Some costs are very difficult to quantify and some cannot be valued in ordinary economic terms. The cost of a dissatisfied customer due to the unavailability of stock depends on numerous, difficult-to-measure variables such as the degree of the customer's unhappiness and the impact it will have on his future purchases. The value of having the proper blood type for a transfusion or of having life-saving medication when required does not lend itself to economic analysis. In such situations it is common to establish system objectives such as always having certain quantities of various blood types and medicines available.

## INVENTORY DECISION COSTS

There are four types of costs relevant to inventory management decisions: (1) Preparation costs, (2) Carrying costs, (3) Stock-out costs, and (4) Capacity related costs.

## Preparation Costs

These costs include the costs of all activities required in issuing a purchase or production order. They include the cost of writing the order, preparing specifications, recording the order, order follow-up, the processing of invoices or plant reports, and the preparation of payment. Production orders, sometimes called shop orders or manufacturing orders, are orders for internal fabrication of items as opposed to purchases. They usually require a setup, including the mounting of fixtures, adjustment of machine settings, checking the first items produced, and tearing down the setup at the end of the operation. The man and machine costs of these activities are part of the preparation costs. Preparation costs sometimes are called ordering costs or setup costs. Since the connotations of these terms are limited, *preparation cost* is used in this text to indicate the broad nature of these costs.

**Measuring Preparation Costs.** One good way of examining different costing approaches is to look at an example. Let's estimate the cost of issuing a purchase order under the following conditions.

1. During the last three years the purchasing department placed an average of approximately 10,000 purchase orders annually. The total number of personnel and the number per wage classification were constant during that period.
2. Cost of Purchasing Agents (CPA) is the direct and indirect costs of five purchasing agents. This cost is projected as $140,000 next year.
3. Cost of Purchasing Management, Stenographers, and Clerical Personnel (CPMS) is the total direct and indirect costs of these persons. It is forecast as $80,000 next year. This includes $38,000 for a purchasing manager and $42,000 for three stenographers and two clerks.
4. Cost of Services (CSER) is the cost of copying, communications, and miscellaneous supplies. It is forecast as $30,000 next year.
5. Building and equipment amortization charges, building and equipment maintenance, and utilities are grouped under general and administrative overhead. The corporation is considered as an ongoing concern; these costs are viewed as sunk costs, not affecting the purchase lot size decision.
6. Industrial engineering has studied the purchasing department using work sampling and some standard time data for clerical functions. They have found the following:
   The average purchase order requires .1 standard hours of the purchasing manager's time, 1.0 standard hours of the purchasing agent's time, .5 standard hours of stenographic and clerical time, and $2 of copying and communication cost. Paper costs are 25 cents per order. The average monthly direct and indirect compensation of stenographic personnel is $875. Estimates are based on next year's costs.

What does it cost to place a purchase order? "Your guess is as good as mine," is the reaction of many. We can do better than that; much better, in fact. Three alternative approaches to the problem follow. Each approach is demonstrated and its strengths and weaknesses discussed.

**The Aggregate Approach.** This approach consists of dividing the total costs of the activity (purchasing in this case) by the total number of purchase orders to obtain the average cost of an order. Using the data from the foregoing example:

$$\begin{aligned}\text{Total costs} &= CPA + CPMS + CSER \\ &= \$140{,}000 + \$80{,}000 + \$30{,}000 \\ &= \$250{,}000\end{aligned}$$

$$\begin{aligned}\text{Cost per order} &= \text{total costs} \div \text{total orders} \\ &= \$250{,}000 \div 10{,}000 \\ &= \$25 \text{ per order}\end{aligned}$$

**The Standard Cost Approach.** Summing the standard costs of personnel time, materials, and services required for each order is another approach. For the sake of simplicity we will assume that all efficiency factors are 1.00 (for personnel performances and usage of materials and services).

$$\begin{aligned}\text{Standard cost of purchasing manager's time} &= \frac{\$38{,}000 \text{ per year} \times .1 \text{ hour per order}}{50 \text{ weeks per year} \times 40 \text{ hours per week}} \\ &= \$1.90 \text{ per order}\end{aligned}$$

$$\begin{aligned}\text{Standard cost of purchasing agent's time} &= \frac{\$140{,}000 \text{ per year} \times 1.0 \text{ hour per order}}{50 \text{ weeks per year} \times 40 \text{ hours per week} \times 5 \text{ agents}} \\ &= \$14 \text{ per order}\end{aligned}$$

$$\begin{aligned}\text{Standard clerical and stenographic costs} &= \frac{\$42{,}000 \text{ per year} \times .5 \text{ hour per order}}{50 \text{ weeks per year} \times 40 \text{ hours per week} \times 5 \text{ persons}} \\ &= \$2.10 \text{ per order}\end{aligned}$$

Paper costs = \$.25 per order
Copy costs = \$.45 per order
Costs of communication = \$1.55 per order

| | | |
|---|---|---|
| Total costs = | \$ 1.90 | Purchasing manager's time |
| | 14.00 | Purchasing agent's time |
| | 2.10 | Stenographic and clerical time |
| | 2.00 | Copy and communication costs |
| | .25 | Paper costs |
| | \$20.25 | per order |

(Estimated costs equal standard costs since the efficiency factor is 1.00 for all costs.)

**The Marginal Out-of-Pocket Cost Approach.** If placing an additional order does not require an additional purchasing agent, additional stenographic and clerical personnel, additional management, additional accounting or receiving personnel, or additional office equipment, then the added costs of placing the order consist of the paper consumed plus telephone and telegraphic expenses resulting directly from this order. In summary, the cost of the purchase order would be the out-of-pocket costs of paper and communication costs cited earlier in this analysis. The out-of-pocket marginal costs of the purchase order being considered are:

| | |
|---|---|
| Paper costs | = $ .25 |
| Copy and communication costs | = 2.00 |
| | $2.25 |

Thus, we can use $25, $20.25, or $2.25 as the cost of a purchase order. This should enable us to justify whatever action we want to take (the essence of agile management). Will it really though? Not if we analyze the underlying assumptions and premises of each of these approaches.

**Assumptions and Premises of the Aggregate, Standard, and Marginal Cost Approaches.** The aggregate approach assumes that all the purchasing department does is place orders and follow-up orders with vendors and that the rated capacity of the purchasing department is represented by the average production of the last few years. The second assumption is frequently invalid and the first should be if it is not. In addition to issuing purchase orders, an effective purchasing department will be searching for new and additional sources, participating in value analysis activities, participating in material board review of damaged items, developing the purchasing management systems, reviewing developments in decision techniques, and so on.

Assuming that the average purchasing activity of the previous two or three years is an accurate measure of the purchasing department's capacity is precarious. If those years were unusually busy ones in a period of high business activity, the nine-hour day and Saturday morning work in purchasing may have been common with the 10,000 orders being above a reasonable upper limit of the activity the department can maintain without additional personnel, chaos, or disgruntled employees. If the preceding years were a slack period, the 10,000 orders annually may be substantially below what the department can handle.

A major weakness of the standard cost approach to determining the cost of a purchase order is that it assumes, at least in the form presented, that all purchase orders are equally demanding. Such is not the case. Many orders are routine, present little or no problem in vendor selection, and have few if any quality and delivery problems associated with them. Different orders require substantially different commitments of purchasing time. Vendor selection, price and contract negotiations, vendor performance in the fulfillment of the product quality, and delivery promises vary widely for different orders. For example, the introduction of new products or new product lines may involve establishing purchasing relations with new suppliers. If the standard cost approach is used, it makes sense in many organizations to establish rates for at least four types of purchase orders, *A*, *B*, *C*, and *D*.

*A:* Orders for which considerable difficulty in vendor selection, contract negotiation, purchase order approval, supplier quality, delivery performance, or production setup is expected
*B:* Orders for which moderate difficulties are anticipated or have been experienced
*C:* Routine, straightforward orders
*D:* Joint orders

Some purchasing agents will tell you they don't have any of the *C* type situations and few of the *B* types. That may be true if they are the elite of the department and assigned the difficult tasks. However, in most organizations Pareto's principle will hold; a relatively small number of items, 10 to 20 percent, will generate most of the problems. Under such circumstances, different standards can be established for the types of purchase orders with different levels of administrative difficulty. How to establish such standards is more appropriately within the realm of a text on clerical and administrative work measurement. Such standards can be established with the cooperation of the purchasing department. The standards may not represent reality precisely to the third decimal point, but they are precise enough for decision making. In addition, they are more accurate than a single average for all purchase orders. A similar approach can be followed in measuring the clerical and administrative costs of production orders.

As noted in the previous discussion of marginal costs, this approach is of questionable validity except in unusual circumstances. It is valid if the department is operating far below capacity and dismissal of personnel is not desirable for long-term economic reasons or for other reasons. If applied to its logical extreme, it means that lot sizes would be relatively small and a much larger number of orders would be placed. It also means that the organization would eventually reach a point at which an additional order would require the addition of a purchasing agent and to maintain consistency that order would cost thousands of dollars. Such an approach is unrealistic.

What is a valid approach? The standard cost approach modified to include actual costs of personnel time, processing, and forms, while excluding sunk costs such as building and equipment overhead is adopted frequently. The aggregate approach modified to include only those costs related to the number of orders processed should produce similar results. This requires that the proportion of personnel time devoted to activities such as vendor selection and value analysis be excluded from the order preparation costs because they are not related in most cases to the number of orders. If these two approaches result in substantially different results, it suggests that the calculations should be reviewed.

**Setup Costs.** Preparation costs for production orders, the internal fabrication or assembly of items as opposed to purchasing, also include the costs of machine setup which involves activities such as obtaining tools, the mounting of fixtures, receiving instructions concerning the job, adjusting machine settings, checking the first items produced, and tearing down the setup when the job is complete.

Labor costs and machine costs are the components of setup costs. Labor costs can be determined in a straightforward manner by multiplying standard setup times by the applicable efficiency factor and the hourly cost of labor. If standard times are not available, good estimates usually can be obtained from shop supervision.

The determination of machine costs is not quite that straightforward. To begin with, machine costs should not include depreciation costs or any other absorption of sunk costs. The lost profits and foregone contribution to overhead when equipment is being set up rather than operating and producing output are the machine costs. These are opportunity costs and, although usually not readily available in the accounting records, they must be considered by the planner. Such costs exist only if setup activities are consuming time which otherwise would be used for production. This occurs only when equipment is being utilized at or near capacity. A resulting rule of thumb is that during slack periods, other things being equal, orders with relatively large setup times should be run. This increases equipment utilization during the slack period and places fewer material dollars in inventory for a given labor investment and machine utilization. It usually will result in a higher operating (productive) proportion of time and in a lower proportion of setup (nonproductive) time in periods of high demand. Thus, production run sizes will decrease in slack periods and increase in high demand periods. Consider the following setup calculation example.

Setup labor costs = \$15 per hour
Standard time for setup on a particular operation = 1.8 hours
Rated efficiency of setup workers on this task = .80

$$\text{Estimated setup cost} = \frac{\text{Cost} \times \text{average actual time}}{\text{Hours}}$$

$$\text{Average actual time} = \frac{\text{Standard}}{\text{Efficiency}} = \frac{1.8}{.8} = 2.25 \text{ hours}$$

$$\begin{aligned}\text{Estimated setup labor costs} &= \$15.00 \times 2.25 \\ &= \$33.75\end{aligned}$$

When setup personnel do not operate equipment, have substantially less than a full workload, and will be retained on the payroll in any event, setup labor is a sunk cost. It can be treated as free in a lot sizing decision.

The opportunity costs of setup (profit and contribution to overhead lost by not producing output) exist only when a plant or machine center is operating at or near capacity. If a machine center is used to produce many products, these lost profits depend on which product is not being manufactured; for all items are not equally profitable. The equipment to manufacture a particular product may include some machine centers which are rarely utilized fully, some which are loaded to capacity on occasion, and other bottleneck type work centers which usually are utilized fully. These factors make estimating setup machine costs difficult in job shop operations. In such cases, it makes sense to use average profit and overhead contributions but only for those work centers which are usually or frequently operating at full capacity. Continuous flow operations such as those found in paper making, some textile plants, paint factories, and food processing present a less complex picture.

In general, it seems that setup machine costs are not investigated as often as they might be when analyzing production and inventory decisions. In many cases these costs may be negligible and not worthy of inclusion. However, this decision should be a conscious one and not made by default.

Take the following example where a part is processed through five departments—*A*, *B*, *C*, *D*, and *E*. The following conditions exist.

| Department* | Setup Time (Hours) | Percentage of Work Center Utilization |
|---|---|---|
| A | .6 | 60 |
| B | 1.2 | 100 |
| C | 0.0 | 100 |
| D | .5 | 95 |
| E | .4 | 85 |

* Average profit and overhead contribution = $20.50 per hour.

The process of determining the machine opportunity costs of setup involves:

1. Establishing a utilization cutoff point and determining those departments in which such costs are not incurred
2. Adding the setup time for those departments which are utilized above the utilization cutoff point
3. Multiplying total setup hours by overhead and profit contribution per hour
4. Determining if cost is sufficient to include in total preparation costs

Applying these steps to the foregoing data the following occurs:

*Step 1.* Setup time is not required in Department C. Utilization is only 60 percent in Department A. Setup machine costs are not incurred in either of these departments. Setup time is incurred in Departments B and D, and they are fully utilized for all practical purposes. What about Department E? Is 85 percent utilization sufficiently high to believe that additional setup hours will affect productive output? Perhaps not; but, for purposes of this example, a cutoff point of 80 percent for full utilization exists. This is a policy decision which must be based on the number of hours reserved for flexibility to handle rush orders, unplanned scrap, and so on.

*Steps 2 & 3.* Sum the opportunity cost setup hours and multiply them by the contribution rate.

| | |
|---|---|
| Department B | 1.2 |
| Department D | .5 |
| Department E | .4 |
| Total | 2.1 hours |

$$\text{Machine costs} = \text{Total setup hours} \times \text{contribution rate/hour}$$
$$= 2.1 \times \$12.50$$
$$= \$26.25$$

*Step 4.* In this instance, $26 is a cost worthy of including in most lot size decision calculations.

How are overhead and profit contribution costs per hour determined? Accounting can help here if production management does not have such costs available. Sometimes a general model or formula has been established by management for estimating these costs. For example, every dollar of labor expended requires $1.50 of manufacturing overhead and should generate 40 cents profit.

## Carrying Costs

Carrying costs are those costs incurred by the very fact that an item is in stock. Included are the cost of the capital invested; the costs of deterioration, obsolescence, pilferage, insurance, and taxes; and the storage costs due to handling, security, space, and record-keeping requirements. Each of these is a very real cost although their relative importance may vary from item to item. For example, in the manufacturing of men's clothing the probability of obsolescence may be negligible for classic single-breasted blazer jackets but rather high in the manufacture of men's or women's fashion items with abrupt changes in demand.

Costs of pilferage, spoilage, obsolescence, and damage vary from industry to industry and even from product to product. Some costs are incurred to prevent pilferage or spoilage. Experience can be used to estimate these costs as a proportion of the value of inventory. Accounting should be able to provide the cost of insurance. It may be a flat rate based on estimated value of inventory. This easily translates into a percentage of dollar value.

Taxes are different. They usually are paid only once a year on the basis of inventory on hand at that time. Many companies make it a point to reduce inventories to a minimum as the date of assessment approaches. This is accomplished by reducing production and purchases, increasing sales, or moving inventory to a geographic area with a different assessment date. Our present objective is not to evaluate the wisdom of such actions. Rather it is to point out that inventory decisions made 11 months prior to the assessment date rarely will impact the amount of taxes paid while those made in the quarter preceding the assessment date frequently do. Thus, it may make sense to incorporate the corporation property tax rate, usually in the .5 to 3.0 percent of value range, in the inventory decision process only during those months preceding assessment. This approach presents a problem when inventory cycle times (the time interval between orders) range from two weeks to, say, six months. A reasonable approach here is to determine that time period which would include 80 percent of the *A* items, and it probably will include close to 80 percent of the inventory value. If this cycle time turned out to be three months, then the cost of taxes would be included in all inventory decisions made within three months of the assessment date and excluded during the nine months following the assessment.

Some companies include taxes at one half the assessed rate on the rationale that the value of inventory at assessment time is usually only one half that during the remainder of the year. This approach makes little sense when applied either in the period immediately following or the period immediately preceding assessment. It is valid only when the lot obtained has approximately a 50 percent probability of being in stock when assessment takes place.

Others contend that the question of taxes has little impact on the decision and excessive time and worry should not be consumed on it. There is some truth in this; but it is also true that a relatively small time investment normally will provide for a more rational and accurate estimate of the cost of taxes relevant to the inventory lot size decision.

The cost of space again raises the challenge of separating sunk and opportunity costs. An organization with a half full warehouse incurs few if any additional warehouse storage costs if inventory is increased. The cost of the building and utilities plus security will exist whether or not inventory is doubled. This is true regarding warehouse space, but seldom if ever true concerning work-in-process. Even with excellent shop floor control, space in the plant is usually at a premium. In addition, half empty warehouses have a habit of filling up overnight. Except in those cases, where it is very difficult to see storage costs increasing due to increased lot sizes, it is good practice to include the out-of-pocket cost of storage although it may be free for the moment. The product line in some organizations may make it possible to charge for storage at a constant rate of the value of an item. Such is not always the case. Large bulky items with large size per dollar value may cost much more to store per dollar of value than their small size high dollar value counterparts. In the latter situation it is appropriate to use different rates per dollar volume for different size items.

Handling costs are similar to space costs in that many are sunk costs, and others are related to the bulkiness and weight of the item rather than its cost.

The cost of capital can be based on the higher of either the actual cost of capital or the opportunity costs. If a firm is paying two points over the prime rate, the cost of capital is straightforward, although it may vary from time to time as the prime rate changes. If a firm continually earns an ROI of at least 15 percent before taxes, the opportunity costs of capital invested in inventory are at least 15 percent. This assumes that opportunities for further investment exist as in the following:

| | |
|---|---|
| Costs of capital are 15 percent | .150 |
| Insurance costs are .5 percent of value | .005 |
| Taxes are 2.5 percent of value | .025 |
| Pilferage, spoilage, and damage | .010 |
| Obsolescence | .010 |
| Storage space and handling | .040* |
| | .240 |

* See determination which follows.

**Storage Costs.** Storage and handling costs were determined from the following information. Out-of-pocket costs for storage space and handling include the following annual costs:

| | |
|---|---|
| Utilities | $ 25,000 |
| Material handling personnel | 110,000 |
| Equipment maintenance | 12,000 |
| Building maintenance | 13,000 |
| Security personnel | 20,000 |
| | $180,000 |

The average dollar value of inventory in stores is $4,500,000. Dividing $180,000 by $4,500,000 renders an annual rate of .04. These calculations are based on the assumption that all items in storage require essentially the same storage space and services per unit of value. If this is not the case, the ratio of the requirements of the different classes of items must be determined and the costs proportioned accordingly.

Even in the best of situations, these calculations result in an estimated cost. As many have pointed out, the actual carrying cost rate used is a management policy variable whose selection is determined by the financial condition of the firm among other factors. [17, 18] Carrying costs are obtained by multiplying the carrying rate by the cost of the items being stored whether they are purchased or produced internally.

**Item Costs.** The cost of purchased items usually is readily available. The cost of internally produced items traditionally consists of labor, material, and overhead costs. The cost of labor per item can be determined in the usual manner by multiplying the standard hours by the average efficiency level achieved in producing that product and by the labor charge per hour. The cost of material can be obtained from accounting or purchasing.

Occasionally the argument will be presented that, in those cases where material is used for many products and producing a lot of a specific finished product will not require the purchase of an additional lot of material, material costs are sunk costs and need not be included when determining the lot size of the finished item. Unless the material is scrap, or approaching obsolescence or spoilage, this reasoning is fallacious. Eventually an order for a finished item will require ordering additional materials. Consistency then demands that the order which triggers a new order for raw materials be assigned the cost of all the new raw materials. Although the availability of materials must be considered in the release of orders, it makes little economic sense to subject the lot size decision to such vagaries. If the use of materials is lumpy and dependent on demand for finished goods, it would make more sense to use MRP rather than the EOQ approach.[6]

In most firms the cost of an item used in lot size decision making is obtained from accounting and does include allocated manufacturing overhead costs. If sunk costs such as building and equipment depreciation costs can be determined rather easily, they should be excluded from these calculations. Other overhead costs such as expenditures for cutting oils, materials handling, shop supervision, and production management are actual period costs contributing to the output. In many cases, it may not be practical to separate these two types of manufacturing overhead. In this event the fact that the out-of-pocket value of items is overstated should be recognized. This overstatement will result in item costs being estimated on the high side and fixed order quantity lot sizes being lower than they would be if actual out-of-pocket costs were used. An investigation of the models and formulas in the following chapters will confirm the above statements. On the other hand, a correction factor compensating for this overstatement can be established by estimating which portion of overhead is not sunk and multiplying the overhead cost by the corresponding percentage.

## Stock-out Costs

A stock-out occurs whenever insufficient stock exists to fulfill a replenishment order. The sources of stock-out costs are easy to describe but very difficult to calculate. If stock is not available, two possible conditions—back order or no back order—may exist.

---

[6] See Chapters 4 and 7.

In a back order situation, the customer is willing to wait to receive the item. The customer may be the purchaser of the finished product or, in fact, an internal user such as the final assembly department. In a no back order situation, the customer doesn't wait; the order is lost.

In the case of a back order, there are at least the costs resulting from the paperwork of keeping track of the back order and possibly the loss of future sales due to the customer's inconvenience in waiting. Emergency shipment costs also are possible.

When the sale is lost in the no back order situation, there is the loss of the possible profit plus the loss of the contribution to overhead costs. Here, too, there is the possibility of additional losses due to future orders being placed with competitors. Repeated inability to deliver in a competitive manner can generate a poor delivery reputation, loss of goodwill, and loss of sales.

Stock-out costs are virtually impossible to calculate in a straightforward, explicit manner. Part of the cost is lost customer goodwill, an intangible. How lost goodwill transforms into future buying habits of a customer is uncertain. How much adverse publicity results from a stock-out? How does that publicity affect future sales and profits? What impact does lack of parts have on the assembly department's morale and efficiency? No one doubts the results of stock-outs, but direct quantification of these results has not been achieved to any great extent. Instead the approach followed most frequently is for management to establish a desired level of customer service. Since the marginal cost of each level of service can be determined, this approach implicitly assigns a cost to a stock-out. For example, if

1. A part is ordered 20 times per year.
2. A stock-out is defined as any period in which inventory is insufficient to cover demand.
3. Present level of service is 90 percent and management desires to raise the service level to 95 percent. Two stock-outs per year were permitted, now only one will be.
4. An additional $440 in stock must be added to safety stock—and therefore to average inventory—to achieve this goal.
5. The annual carrying rate for inventory is .25.
6. Then implicitly management is stating that the total cost of a stock-out is greater than .25 × $440, or $110.

This example is also an approach to measuring the cost of achieving various levels of customer service.

## Capacity Related Costs

Costs of expanding or contracting capacity are incurred as a result of aggregate planning decisions of either the middle- or long-range type. Short-term decisions to run a work center or an entire facility overtime for a brief period are predominately scheduling problems, although they may result from a poor inventory position relative to demand.

When capacity is increased, costs are increased by some or all of the following:

1. Hiring and training direct laborers
2. Hiring and training supervisors
3. Adding service personnel in receiving, the warehouse, and so on
4. Learning curve experiences
5. Purchasing equipment

A substantial decrease in capacity results in costs due to

1. Layoffs: terminal pay and unemployment compensation
2. Fixed overhead spread across a smaller volume
3. Temporary inefficiency due to change in production rate and reassignment of personnel
4. Low morale

Consideration of the costs of changing output rates were examined in greater detail in Chapter 1, "Long- and Medium-Range Planning."

The primary function of inventory, to summarize briefly, is to decouple customer demand and production capacity. Functionally inventory can be divided into anticipation, lot size, transportation, and fluctuation inventories. Each serves as a buffer between demand and production in a particular type situation.

Inventory management performance is measured in terms of customer service and inventory investment. Measures of customer service are many and varied with back order service an important component of that measure. Measuring customer service by multiple methods is a good idea in any situation. The availability of data, effect of decisions on the measured results, and the relationship of the measured results to profit and productivity influence the selection of customer service measures.

Inventory investment is measured in both an absolute and a relative manner. Absolute values—$1 million, for example—serve as upper limit constraints on inventory while inventory turn ratios measure inventory investment in relation to the cost of goods sold. Both types of measures should be employed in most situations.

ABC Analysis, based on Pareto's Principle of the Vital Few, divides items into ranked categories on the basis of monetary value, scarcity, and other factors influencing the desired degree of control. Different control procedures are established for the different classes.

Inventory costs are easier to describe than calculate. Preparation costs, carrying costs, stock-out costs, and capacity related costs affect inventory management decisions. Capacity related costs are associated with medium-range aggregate type decisions more than with individual item decisions. Cost calculations should include opportunity costs as well as direct costs while sunk costs should be excluded.

Determination of inventory classifications, performance measures, and costing procedures should precede aggregate, intermediate, and individual item inventory management decisions.

## PROBLEMS

1. The Klingenbaum Mortuary has four funeral homes in a large metropolitan area. The most popular casket it sells has an average demand of 30 units per month. They purchase these caskets in truckload quantities of 60 units every two months for shipment to their warehouse. They use a carrying cost rate of .30 per year and an ordering cost of $30, with unlimited storage space for practical purposes. The present cost is $1,200 per unit. They believe that there is a 80% chance that the unit price will be increased to $1,350 each in two months. They are about to place an order. What should the quantity be?
2. A local manufacturer uses 100 gallons of zinc chromate primer a month at a steady rate throughout the year. The present EOQ is 80 gallons. The supplier has a practice of increasing prices each June 1. On May 1 the company estimates that there is a 95% probability that the price of the primer will be increased from $10 to at least $11 per gallon. What quantity should be ordered when the order point is reached on the 15th of May?
Ordering costs are $15 an order and the company policy is to use a carrying cost rate of .25 per year.
3. A division ships a truckload of 1,000 transmissions to its assembly plant twice each week. One shipment leaves the plant around noon on Monday and arrives around noon on Thursday; the other leaves around noon on Thursday and arrives at the assembly plant about noon on Monday. What is the annual cost of transmission transportation inventory if the annual carrying cost rate is .20?
4. A multinational corporation ships components via rail and ship to its European assembly plant at a cost of $1 a unit. Total transit time is one-half month; unit cost is $40; the carrying cost rate is .24. They have the opportunity to ship by air at a cost of $1.80 a part. Air shipment will consume three calendar days. How should they ship?
5. The B & J Home Supply Company carries lighting fixtures that it sells to small contractors and do-it-yourself homeowners. Last year it sold 1,240 of the most popular fixture. Sales of another 50 items were lost when stock-outs caused contractors to find another supplier. On another occasion a contractor waited three days for a shipment from which he received his order for 12 fixtures. What level of customer service did B & J achieve?
6. A manufacturer of roller bearings supplies distributors and manufacturers from its warehouse. The following table describes the sales of five bearings which constitute its most popular items. Items not shipped were back ordered. How many measures of customer service are possible using these data? What measure of customer service did the manufacturer achieve in each?

| Demand | Cost per unit | Profit per unit | Shipped from stock |
|---|---|---|---|
| 8,000 | .90 | .10 | 7,500 |
| 6,000 | 1.25 | .15 | 5,800 |
| 4,000 | 1.00 | .12 | 4,200 |
| 4,500 | .80 | .10 | 3,900 |
| 3,000 | .60 | .12 | 2,850 |
| 25,500 | | | |

7. The South Plains Manufacturing Company produces sporting goods apparel for which demand is seasonal as indicated in the data below. Company forecasts are relatively accurate. The company president wants to know the inventory turnover ratio at the end of Period 3. What will you tell him?

| Months | Forecast | Demand | Inventory |
|---|---|---|---|
| 1 | 6.4 | 6.3 | 8.2 |
| 2 | 6.5 | 6.4 | 9.4 |
| 3 | 6.6 | 6.7 | 10.0 |
| 4 | 9.2 | | |
| 5 | 10.4 | | |
| 6 | 11.4 | | |

8. An electronics component manufacturer produces high precision assemblies for the aeronautics and space industry, controls for kitchen appliances, as well as some items for industrial equipment. Classify the following sample of the company's purchased parts according to ABC principles and the following data.

| Product | Unit Cost | Annual Volume | Other Factors |
|---|---|---|---|
| 575 | $ 93.00 | 3,200 | |
| 607 | 31.00 | 2,500 | |
| 625 | 212.00 | 320 | Single source |
| 811 | 130.00 | 475 | |
| 947 | 618.00 | 300 | |
| 024 | 720.00 | 300 | |
| 413 | .25 | 25,000 | |
| 483 | .60 | 6,800 | Engineering change anticipated in next two months |
| 495 | 1.25 | 15,000 | |
| 211 | 6.30 | 3,000 | Lead time six months |

9. The inventory manager of a chain of department stores is reviewing the carrying cost rates used for small tools, paper products, and small appliances. The controller has told him to treat the cost of capital as 16%. The company is borrowing at a point and one half over the prime rate which is 14%. He collects the following information:

| | Costs as a Percentage of Item Value | | |
|---|---|---|---|
| | Small Tools | Paper Products | Small Appliances |
| Insurance | .5 | .5 | .5 |
| Taxes | 1.0 | 1.0 | 1.0 |
| Pilferage, and damage | 2.0 | .2 | 2.4 |
| Obsolescence | .1 | .3 | .6 |
| Storage space and handling | 5.4 | 11.0 | 5.5 |

What is the carrying cost rate for each of the product groups? Why do you think the storage space and handling costs of the paper products are substantially higher than the other two groups?

10. A pottery manufacturer makes coffee mugs for an international hotel chain. Orders are received throughout the year from new hotels and for replacements from established hotels. These mugs use the same raw materials as other items manufactured by this firm. These mugs account for approximately 20% of the annual use of these materials. The inventory control department has obtained the following data concerning the cost of this item.

| Work Center | Setup Time (Hours) | Process Time (Hours) | Department Utilization | Operators |
|---|---|---|---|---|
| A | 2.4 | .0055 | 100% | 1 |
| B | .6 | .0500 | 65% | 1 |
| C | 0.0 | .0167 | 80% | 1 |

Labor costs are $12.50 an hour, and the hourly contribution of equipment to overhead costs and profit is $25. Raw material costs 2 cents per unit and the yield rate equals 90% (the scrap rate is 10%). If the typical lot size is 2,000 units, what should the item cost used in the lot size calculation be?

11. Product A is assembled from four components, *B*, *C*, *D*, and *E*, by the North Central Fabricating Company. Purchasing and component part machining departments have achieved their objective of a 98% service level relative to supplying the final assembly department. When the assembly department has all the components on time, it has completed the assembly on time 99% of the time. What level of service do you think the company achieves in shipping assemblies to customers? Do you recommend any changes in their objectives?

12. The president of the South Plains Manufacturing Company is unhappy with your answer to Problem 7. He wants to know how many weeks of sales are in inventory. What are you going to tell him?

# SELECTED READINGS

1. George W. Plossl, *Manufacturing Control: The Last Frontier for Profits* (Reston, Va.: Reston Publishing Company, Inc., 1973), p. 98.
2. J. Nicholas Edwards, "Target Level Inventories," *American Production and Inventory Control Conference Proceedings* (1975), p. 309.

3. Richard P. Artes, "Making Some Cents out of Service Level," *Production and Inventory Management,* Vol. 18, No. 4, Fourth Quarter (1977), p. 59.
4. Henry Jordan, "How to Plan and Control Inventories," *APICS Conference Proceedings* (October, 1976), p. 305.
5. C. G. Limpert and C. C. Vacek, "Projecting Customer Services," *Production and Inventory Management,* Vol. 18, No. 4, Fourth Quarter (1977), p. 77.
6. Elton C. Throndsen, "Performance Measurement Criteria for Inventory Management," *American Production and Inventory Control Society Conference Proceedings*, Third Quarter (1971), p. 256.
7. Joseph Orlicky, *Material Requirements Planning* (New York: McGraw-Hill Book Company, 1974), p. 24.
8. Oliver Wight, *Production and Inventory Control in the Computer Age* (Boston, Mass.: Cahner Books, 1974), pp. 184 and 188.
9. James A. Krupp, "Inventory Turn Ratio, as a Management Control Tool" *Inventories and Production*, Vol. 1, No. 4 (September/October, 1981), pp. 18-21.
10. Arthur C. Close, "Projected Inventory Velocity Measurement," *Production and Inventory Management*, Vol. 11, No. 3, Third Quarter (1970), p. 66.
11. George W. Plossl and Oliver Wight, *Production and Inventory Control* (Englewood Cliffs, N.J.: Prentice-Hall, Inc., 1967), p. 332.
12. Kenneth L. Campbell, "Inventory Turns and ABC-Analysis—Outmoded Textbook Concepts?" *American Production and Inventory Control Conference Proceedings* (1975), p. 420.
13. H. Ford Dickie, "ABC Inventory Analysis Shoots for Dollars," *Factory Management and Maintenance* (July, 1951), p. 92.
14. Paul G. Conroy, "Data General ABC Inventory Management," *Production and Inventory Management*, Vol. 18, No. 4, (1977), p. 63.
15. Gary Zimmerman, "The ABC's of Vilfredo Pareto," *Production Inventory Management*, Vol. 16, No. 3, Third Quarter (1975), pp. 1–9.
16. Rolf Norbom, "The Simple ABC's (A Loose Piece Float System)," *Production and Inventory Management*, Vol. 14, No. 1, First Quarter (1973), p. 16.
17. Plossl and Wight, op. cit., p. 56.
18. Robert G. Brown, *Materials Management Systems*, (New York: John Wiley and Sons, Inc., 1977), p. 210.
19. Donald W. Fogarty and Thomas R. Hoffmann, "Customer Service," *Production and Inventory Management*, First Quarter (1980).
20. James H. Greene, *Production and Inventory Control Handbook* (New York: McGraw-Hill Book Company, 1970).
21. _______, *Production and Inventory Control* (Homewood, Ill.: Richard D. Irwin, Inc., 1974).
22. Henry Jordan, *Cycle Counting* (Washington, D.C.: American Production and Inventory Control Society, 1976).
23. _______, "Relating Customer Service to Inventory Control," *American Management Association's Advanced Management Journal*, Vol. 39, No. 4 (October, 1974).
24. John F. Magee and David M. Boodman, *Production Planning and Inventory Control*, 2d ed. (New York: McGraw-Hill Book Company, 1967).
25. George W. Plossl, "How Much Inventory is Enough?" *Production and Inventory Management*, Second Quarter (1971).
26. S. Pursche, "Putting Service Level into Proper Perspective," *Production and Inventory Management*, Third Quarter (1975).

# —7—

# BASIC SYSTEMS FOR INDIVIDUAL ITEM MANAGEMENT

Individual items include assemblies, subassemblies, fabricated components, purchased components, and purchased materials. They are found in finished goods, spare parts, work-in-process, and raw materials.

Prior to analyzing individual items, decisions have been made at the aggregate and intermediate levels concerning such things as constraints on inventory, grouping of items, customer service objectives, and the development and implementation of inventory management information systems. These activities are discussed in Chapters 6, 8, 9, 13, and 14.

Individual item management activities begin with selecting the appropriate inventory management system (decision rules for how much to order and when to release the order) for the different individual items. Table 7-1 lists the names of the basic methods for managing individual items.

**TABLE 7-1**
**NAMES OF**
**BASIC ORDERING AND LOT SIZE RULES**
**(GROUPED BY TYPE OF RULE)**

| When to Order Rules | Quantity to Order Rules |
|---|---|
| Order point | Fixed order quantity |
| Periodic review | Economic order quantity |
| Time-phased order point | Variable order quantity |
| Material requirements planning | Discrete order quantities[1] |

[1]For example, lot-for-lot.

Many different combinations of lot size and order point rules are possible. Different combinations are appropriate under different conditions. In this chapter we will examine the data required for inventory management decisions, the situational characteristics determining the appropriateness of different management systems, and the nature of basic inventory management decision rules and the systems that they constitute.

## DATA REQUIREMENTS

Certain data concerning each item are required for inventory management decisions. In less complex situations (low volume transactions) this data may be processed manually and stored on cards. However, the complexity of most situations and the availability of relatively inexpensive computer hardware has led to increased computerization of inventory management support systems. In either event, the data usually are organized in the following manner:

1. The Inventory Record File, also called the Part Master File or the Item Master File
2. The Bill of Materials (BOM) File also known as the Product Structure File
3. The Master Production Schedule (MPS)

## The Inventory Record File

This file contains a record, identified by part number, for each item. Each record usually contains inventory status and cost data required for cost estimating and production activity control in addition to the following data required for inventory management:

1. Part number—the unique part number assigned to the item
2. Part description—the name of the item
3. On-Hand quantity—the number of units of this item in stock
4. Allocated quantity—the number of units of this item which has been assigned to previously planned future orders
5. Available quantity—the difference between the on-hand quantity and the allocated quantity
6. Lot size quantity—the normal number of units of this item produced at one time (the order quantity), the quantity of which will vary in many situations
7. Lead time—the normal time required to manufacture (or purchase) this item in a typical lot quantity range
8. Item cost—the standard cost of the item
9. Preparation costs—the sum of administrative, clerical, and shop costs incurred in issuing and monitoring the order (Machine setup time is included in these costs for manufactured orders [see Chapter 6].)
10. Carrying cost—the annual cost of carrying one unit of this item in inventory (see Chapter 6)
11. Group code—An indication as to whether this item is to be purchased or produced as one of a group of items in a *joint* lot size decision process (If the indication is positive, the group will be identified [see Chapter 8].)
12. Where used (next assembly)—the identification of the assembly or assemblies in which this item is used
13. Safety stock—a number of units usually held in inventory to protect against fluctuations in demand and/or supply
14. Average demand—the average quantity required per period

## The BOM File

This file contains the relationship of components and assemblies necessary for the accurate determination of component requirements. It is necessary for a requirements planning system; thus, it is required in almost any manufacturing situation. Each record is identified by a unique item number and includes the following data required for inventory management:

1. The item number assigned to the part including the current engineering change letter and its effectivity
2. The parent item number, the next assembly or assemblies of which it is a part
3. The quantity used in each assembly of which it is a part

See Chapter 3, "The Master Production Schedule," for further discussion of the Bill of Materials.

## The MPS

The MPS is a statement of the anticipated manufacturing schedule for MPS items by quantity per period (see Chapter 3). By definition an MPS item is an assembly or component that has been selected for inclusion in the MPS. The MPS is the source of all inventory requirements and reflects customer orders, forecast demand, and available capacity.

# FACTORS IN INVENTORY DECISIONS

The nature of a situation determines the appropriateness of an inventory management system. And, although it is not feasible to examine all the possible combinations of factors each of which can define a unique situation and set of considerations, it is possible to describe those that are most important in selecting an inventory management system and why they are important. Those factors are: (1) demand pattern, (2) source—common suppliers or production process, and (3) customer requirements.

## The Demand Pattern

The nature of the demand pattern has an effect greater than any other possible factor on the appropriateness of the when-to-order decision rules—and thus on the design of the inventory management system. The relation of a demand pattern to the quantity on hand (in stock) is the key factor in classifying demand patterns. Some demand patterns result in a relatively gradual and steady decrease in inventory as illustrated in Figure 7-1 while other patterns cause abrupt and dramatic changes in stock as illustrated in Figure 7-2.

**FIGURE 7-1**
**RELATION OF DEMAND AND STOCK DISSIPATION PATTERNS OVER TIME (INDEPENDENT DEMAND)**

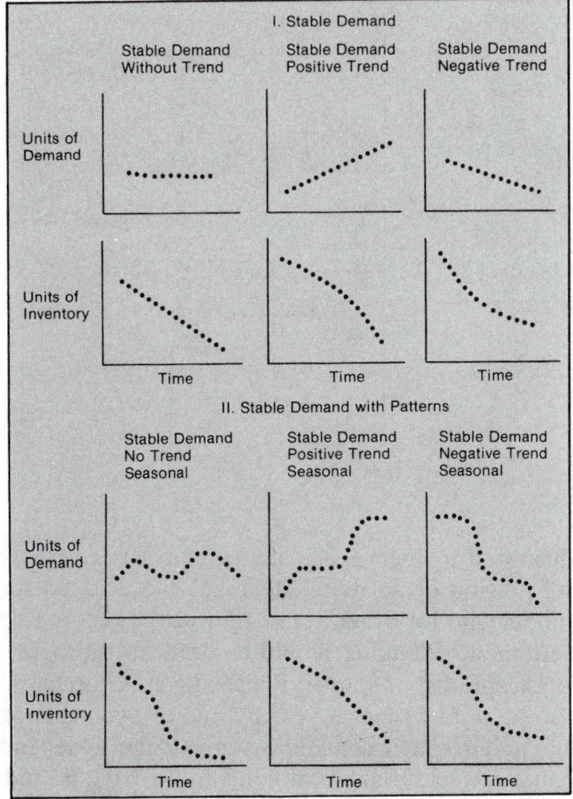


The latter figure is characteristic of dependent demand and the former is characteristic of independent demand.

**Independent Demand.** Distribution inventories (items held as finished goods for sale) and service parts purchased by many different customers in small quantities per time period relative to total annual demand usually experience a relatively stable demand, as illustrated in Figure 7-1. This demand, which may be affected by trends and seasonal patterns, does not depend on demand for other items; it is independent demand.

**Dependent Demand.** Subassemblies, component parts, and raw materials have a demand that is dependent for the most part on the demand for the final products in which they are used. If the final products are fabricated intermittently in lots (batches), which occurs in all situations except continuous production, the demand for these items is relatively abrupt and

**FIGURE 7-2**
**RELATION OF DEMAND AND STOCK DISSIPATION PATTERNS OVER TIME (DEPENDENT DEMAND)**

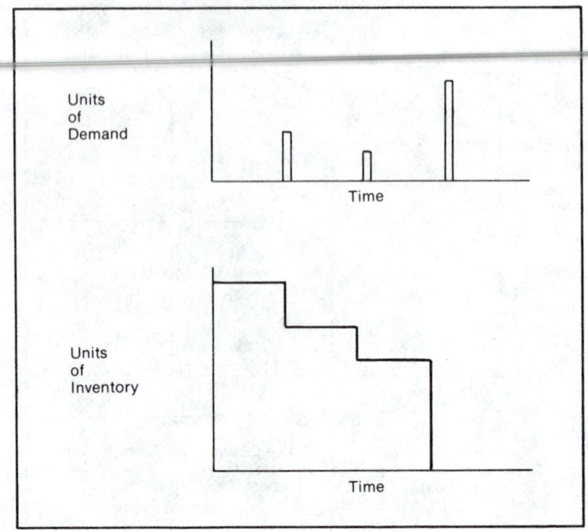


dramatic as illustrated in Figure 7-2. Except for service part requirements (usually a small portion of an item's demand) the demand for these items results from the demand for other items; they are dependent demand items. Materials Requirements Planning should be used for these items.

There are exceptions, of course. Finished goods purchased in relatively large quantities only a few times a year by one or two customers will likely exhibit an abrupt and irregular demand pattern similar to dependent demand. On the other hand, raw materials, common hardware items, and components used in many different final products may experience a relatively stable demand similar to that usually associated with independent demand items. The demand pattern for each item must be evaluated on its own merits. (Later we will examine the impact of demand patterns on the when-to-order question.)

## Source: Common Supplier or Production Process

Inventories also can be grouped on the basis of the supplier, the process, and the departments through which the items are processed. For example, parts that are to be purchased from a single supplier frequently are grouped together to facilitate joint purchase orders, joint product quantity discounts, transportation, and communications with suppliers. Items produced in the same department or on a similar group of machines also should be grouped for analyzing the relationship of the aggregate order quantity capacity requirements to the capacity availability and the possibility of common setups. Methods available for analyzing such situations are discussed in Chapter 8. Items purchased from a common supplier or produced on common facilities are candidates for Periodic Review Inventory Management when the combination of orders or joint orders generates savings greater than the possible increase in inventory investment costs.

### Customer Requirements

When a group of items has been ordered or usually is ordered by a single customer, the production or purchase of these items may be grouped to enable concurrent delivery unless the purchase order specifies different delivery dates for different items. This practice not only enables joint shipping and invoicing, but in many cases none of the items are of value to the customer unless all are delivered, and, in practice, some purchase orders predicate payment upon receipt of all items. This situation may exist when all the items are required in an assembly produced by the customer. Analysis of such situations also is treated in Chapter 8.

### Other Factors

Demand and design stability, shelf life, and lead time also affect inventory decisions. Items susceptible to the whims of fashion or engineering changes may be ordered in quantities smaller than otherwise would be the case. Limited shelf life also imposes limits on the quantity ordered. Dependent demand parts and materials with long lead times relative to final assembly delivery requirements may require an order point system to achieve customer service objectives.

## INVENTORY MANAGEMENT MODELS AND DECISION RULES

A company may manufacture or purchase an item in two instances: (1) after receiving an order for the item (production to order) or (2) in anticipation of customer orders (production to stock).

In the first instance, production to order, the firm may produce the quantity ordered by customers, or it may produce that quantity plus additional units in anticipation of further orders.

The principles and techniques of material requirements planning (MRP), discussed in Chapter 4, are used in determining the order release dates and lot sizes of items produced only to order. In the case of production to stock, the decision rules governing lot size and order release timing are a function primarily of an item's demand characteristics. A fixed order quantity —order point type system or a periodic review type system—usually is most appropriate for managing independent demand items. Dependent demand items usually are managed best by an MRP type system.

Production of customer order requirements plus anticipated requirements upon receipt of an order frequently involves a combination of MRP and order point management systems. In fact, most real world systems are hybrid; they combine features of the different systems to cope with real world complexities. This introduction to lot size and order release decision rules views inventory management situations as relatively simple and neat. The principles and techniques developed under these conditions aid in handling the more complex situations discussed later.

Inventory management system objectives are to provide a level of customer service and to minimize the costs of providing that service. The order release mechanism is the major determinant of customer service while order quantity size is the primary determinant of inventory costs.

First, we examine the fixed order quantity model because it clearly illustrates the cost structure of lot size decisions. Presentation of the statistical order point model follows as the concepts involved are relevant to any demand situation. Treatment of periodic review systems, visual review systems, and the time-phased order point follow. Material requirements planning has been covered in Chapter 4.

## Fixed Order Quantity

The fixed order quantity lot size decision rules specify a number of units that are ordered each time an order is placed for a particular item. This quantity may be arbitrary such as a two weeks supply or 100 units, but is frequently the economic order quantity (EOQ). The EOQ is the most economical under a given set of conditions. The fixed order quantity lot size determination method can be combined with each of the different methods for determining the order release. Later we will examine the conditions appropriate for the different combinations.

The conditions under which the basic fixed order quantity is valid are:

1. Demand is relatively constant and known; thus, there are no stock-outs.
2. Preparation costs, total carrying costs, and lead time are constant and known.
3. Replenishment is instantaneous; items arrive at an infinite rate at a given time.

Situations in which all the relevant factors—demand, lead time, and costs—are known with complete certainty are rare. But assuming deterministic conditions, certainty is a legitimate expectation when analyzing some inventory situations for at least three reasons. First, situations do exist in which the facts are known with near certainty. Second, the effect of the decision frequently is relatively insensitive to small changes in decision factors. And third, understanding the fixed order quantity model can aid in the modeling of more complex situations.

Two graphs are essential in analyzing inventory management situations. One displays the relationship of the quantity on hand to time, and the other illustrates the relationship of lot size and cost. In the case of the fixed order quantity, the quantity versus time relationship takes the sawtooth shape in Figure 7-3.

The straight vertical line in Figure 7-3 represents the arrival of items in inventory just as the stock level reaches zero. The number of units in stock then increases instantaneously by $Q$, the amount ordered and received. This graphic representation of the arrival of an order instantaneously is a very accurate depiction of the arrival of a lot of purchased parts. It is also an

**FIGURE 7-3**
**UNITS IN INVENTORY VERSUS TIME**
**(FIXED ORDER QUANTITY MODEL**
**WITH DEMAND AND LEAD TIME CERTAIN)**

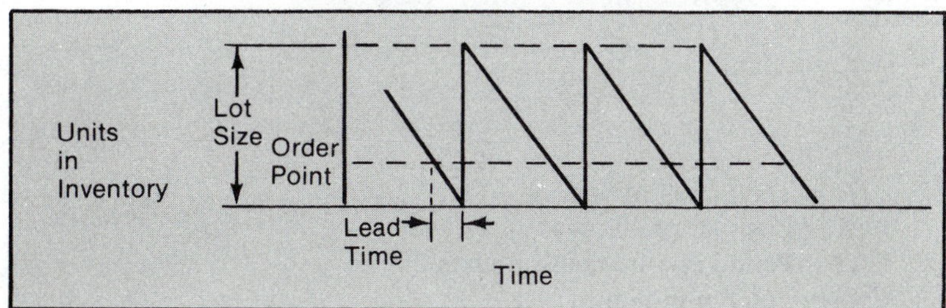


accurate representation of the arrival of parts produced within the organization when the time from the manufacture of the first item to the last is relatively brief.

Withdrawals of items from inventory under constant demand conditions actually take place in an incremental step fashion which is approximated by the straight line slope shown in Figure 7-4.

**FIGURE 7-4**
**CONSTANT WITHDRAWALS FROM INVENTORY OVER TIME**

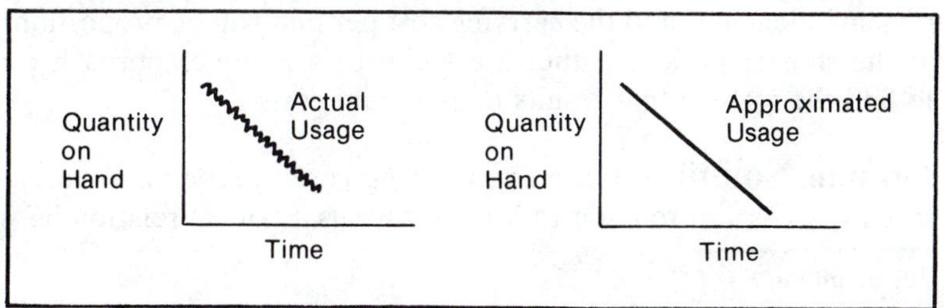

Costs incurred in a lot size decision include carrying costs, preparation costs, stock-out costs, and the cost of the item itself. The cost of the item, the purchase price or the cost of material, and labor and overhead in the case of an item produced internally can change in those situations where purchase or production of larger quantities will achieve economies of scale. For the purpose of this analysis, the cost of an item is treated as a constant and stock-outs do not occur. The impact of changes in the cost of the item and stock-outs on the lot size decision are examined in Chapters 10 and 13. Therefore, the total costs incurred during a period as a result of the lot size decision when using the basic fixed order quantity decision rule are formulated as follows:

Total costs equal preparation costs plus carrying costs.
Preparation costs equal cost per preparation times the number of preparations in the period.
Carrying costs equal the average quantity in inventory times the cost of carrying one unit for the period or the average quantity in inventory times unit cost times the cost rate of carrying one unit for the period.

Therefore, $TC = \frac{SR}{Q} + \frac{QK}{2}$ or $\frac{SR}{Q} + \frac{QCk}{2}$[1]

Where:

$TC$ = Total costs per period
$S$ = Cost per preparation in dollars
$R$ = Period requirements in units
$Q$ = Lot size in units
$K$ = Cost of holding one unit in inventory for the period
$C$ = Cost of one unit
$k$ = Cost rate of carrying one unit in inventory for the period

Figure 7-3 reveals that average inventory equals one half the lot size. Inventory decreases at a constant rate from a maximum lot size to a minimum of zero. Thus, the average inventory equals $(Q + 0) \div 2$ or $Q \div 2$.

The period used for these calculations is usually one year. However, it may be appropriate to use a different length period; for example, the planning period of some items may be only six months. You should note that the requirements, demand, and the carrying cost per unit will be proportionately less for the shorter period. Either a calculus or a graphic approach can be used to find the lot size that results in minimum costs.

**The Graphic Solution.** Graphing carrying costs, preparation costs, and total inventory costs in relation to lot size reveals a critical relation between

[1] By definition $K = kC$.

carrying costs and preparation costs at that point, lot size, where total costs are a minimum. Let's look at an example.

A ball bearing distributor has an item that has an annual demand of 60,000 units at a relatively constant rate throughout the year. Preparation costs are $45 each time an order is placed; the carrying cost rate is 30 cents per dollar of inventory per year; and the units cost $2 each. To graph the relationship of lot size and total costs, it is necessary to calculate the total costs for different lot sizes. The costs for different lot sizes are contained in Table 7-2 and graphed in Figure 7-5.

**TABLE 7-2**
**TABULATION OF INVENTORY COSTS FOR DIFFERENT LOT SIZES**

| **S = $45** | **R = 60,000** | **k = .30** | **C = $2** |
|---|---|---|---|
| **Lot Size (Q)** | **Preparation Costs (SR/Q)** | **Carrying Costs (QCk/2)** | **Total Cost** |
| 10 | $270,000 | $3 | $270,003 |
| 100 | 27,000 | 30 | 27,030 |
| 500 | 5,400 | 150 | 5,550 |
| 1,000 | 2,700 | 300 | 3,000 |
| 1,500 | 1,800 | 450 | 2,250 |
| 2,000 | 1,350 | 600 | 1,950 |
| 2,500 | 1,080 | 750 | 1,830 |
| 3,000 | 900 | 900 | 1,800 |
| 3,500 | 771 | 1,050 | 1,821 |
| 4,000 | 675 | 1,200 | 1,875 |
| 6,000 | 450 | 1,800 | 2,250 |
| 10,000 | 270 | 3,000 | 3,270 |
| 15,000 | 180 | 4,500 | 4,680 |
| 30,000 | 90 | 9,000 | 9,090 |
| 60,000 | 45 | 18,000 | 18,045 |

The tabulated values and the graph reveal two interesting facts: (1) total period costs are lowest at that point where preparation costs equal carrying costs (lot size equals 3,000) and (2) the total costs are approximately the same for a wide range of lot sizes centered on the minimum cost lot size. In fact, preparation costs are equal to carrying costs for the minimum total cost lot size in most continuous demand situations. You may want to tabulate and graph other examples to verify this. The width of the span of lot sizes in which there is little change in total costs depends on the values of the parameters (carrying costs, preparation costs, and annual demand). We will return to this topic later when discussing the sensitivity of the model. The first observation enables us to establish the general procedure for setting preparation costs equal to carrying costs and for solving for the EOQ:

Since the EOQ is that quantity where preparation costs equal carrying costs:

$$\frac{QkC}{2} = \frac{SR}{Q}$$

Thus, solving for $Q$ gives:

$$Q^2 = \frac{2SR}{kC} \text{ and, therefore,}$$

$$Q^* \text{ (optimum value)} = \left(\frac{2SR}{kC}\right)^{1/2}$$

The EOQ can be determined using the above model. Graphing the cost functions versus lot size will also provide valuable insight concerning the increase in total cost as the lot size is increased or decreased in a particular case.

**FIGURE 7-5**
**FIXED ORDER QUANTITY**
**(COSTS VERSUS LOT SIZE: AN EXAMPLE)**

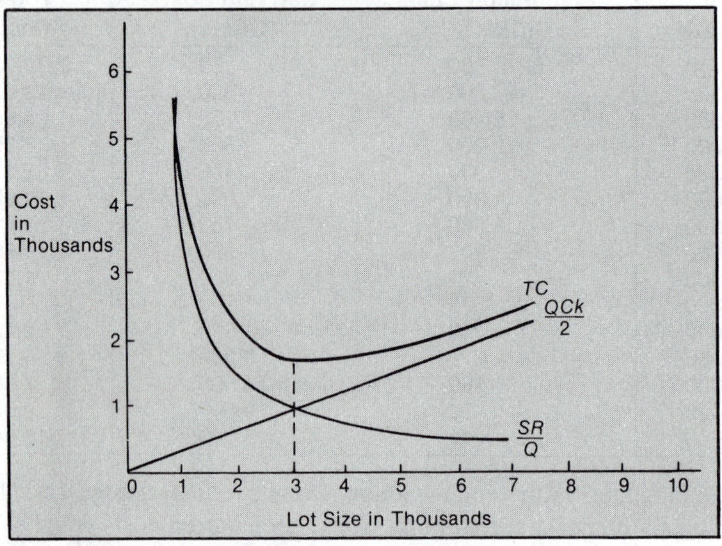


**The Calculus Optimization Approach.** The calculus approach is presented to illustrate a technique useful for deriving a decision rule in many inventory situations. One need not possess a knowledge of calculus to use the resulting decision rule.

Using the basic calculus optimization technique, the first derivative of the total cost expression with respect to $Q$ is set equal to zero. The value of $Q$ which satisfies that equation is an optimum. Taking the first derivative of $TC$ ($TC'$) with respect to $Q$,

$$TC = \frac{RS}{Q} + \frac{KQ}{2}$$

$$TC' = \frac{-RS}{Q^2} + \frac{K}{2} = 0 \text{ and, so, } \frac{K}{2} = \frac{RS}{Q^2}$$

Multiplying both sides of the equation by $Q^2$ and $\frac{2}{K}$ gives:

$$Q^2 = \frac{2RS}{K}$$

$$Q^* = \left(\frac{2RS}{K}\right)^{1/2}$$

This is the same decision rule we obtained using the graphic approach. True, $kC$ has been replaced by $K$, but then $K = kC$.

To determine if this point is a maximum or minimum we must next take the second derivative of $TC$ ($TC''$) and determine if it is positive or negative at $Q^*$. This is formulated as follows:

$$TC'' = \frac{2RS}{Q^3}$$

Since $R$, $S$, and $Q$ are always positive, the test of a minimum solution is met; $TC''$ will be positive for $Q^*$. Therefore, the solution obtained by solving the second derivative is a minimum; i.e., it gives the value of $Q$ that will result in the minimum total period costs.

**Total Period Costs and Sensitivity.** Both approaches result in the same lot size, 3,000 units. The total annual costs resulting from using a lot size of 3,000 are determined in the following manner:

$$\begin{aligned} TC\,(Q^*) &= \frac{SR}{Q^*} + \frac{CkQ^*}{2} \\ TC\,(3{,}000) &= (\$45 \times 60{,}000 \div 3{,}000) + (\$2 \times .3 \times 3{,}000 \div 2) \\ &= \$900 + \$900 \\ &= \$1{,}800 \end{aligned}$$

Let's see what impact a 10 percent increase or decrease in lot size will have on the total costs.

1. Increasing $Q$ by 10 percent to 3,300 yields:

$$\begin{aligned} TC\,(3{,}300) &= (\$45 \times 60{,}000 \div 3{,}300) + (\$2 \times .3 \times 3{,}300 \div 2) \\ &= \$818.18 + \$990 \\ &= \$1{,}808.18 \end{aligned}$$

Increasing the lot size by 10 percent results in a little less than a one-half percent increase in total costs given the parameters of this situation.

2. Next, decreasing $Q$ by 10 percent to 2,700 yields:

$$\begin{aligned} TC\,(2{,}700) &= (\$45 \times 60{,}000 \div 2{,}700) + (\$2 \times .3 \times 2{,}700 \div 2) \\ &= \$1{,}000 + 810 \\ &= \$1{,}810 \end{aligned}$$

A 10 percent decrease in lot size results in slightly more than a one-half percent increase in the total annual inventory costs. Total costs resulting from the lot size decision do not seem to be overly sensitive to changes in the lot size if the foregoing example is any indication. Let's look at the general case.

The relationship of the total cost, *TC*, of a nonoptimum lot size to the total cost, $TC^*$, of the optimum lot size can be determined as follows:

$$TC^* = \frac{SR}{Q^*} + \frac{Q^* K}{2}$$

and

$$TC = \frac{SR}{Q} + \frac{QK}{2}$$

$$\frac{TC}{TC^*}\text{, therefore, } = \left(\frac{SR}{Q} + \frac{QK}{2}\right) \div \left(\frac{SR}{Q^*} + \frac{Q^* K}{2}\right)$$

Substituting $Q^* = \sqrt{\frac{2SR}{K}}$ and then manipulating algebraically to remove $S$, $R$, and $K$ gives:

$$\frac{TC}{TC^*} = \frac{1}{2}\left(\frac{Q^*}{Q} + \frac{Q}{Q^*}\right)$$

Thus, the effects of a specific percentage change in $Q$ can be calculated. For example,

$$\text{let } Q = 1.10Q^* \text{ (a 10 percent increase)}$$

$$\text{Then, } \frac{TC}{TC^*} = \left(\frac{Q^*}{1.10Q^*} + \frac{1.10Q^*}{Q^*}\right) \div 2$$

$$= (.909 + 1.10) \div 2$$

$$= 1.0045$$

These results correspond to those obtained when analyzing the sensitivity of total costs to changes in the lot size of the previous examples. Thus, in general, the percentage difference in inventory costs is relatively small in comparison with the difference in lot sizes around the EOQ.

**Variations of the EOQ Model.** There are literally dozens of ways the basic EOQ model can be modified to fit different situations. At this point we will examine the dollar lot size model and then the noninstantaneous receipt model because of their broad applicability. Other variations are described in Chapters 8, 10, and 13.

The total cost (inventory) model may be formulated to provide the optimum lot size value in monetary units rather than physical units. This approach is especially useful when developing and applying a model to determine the minimum cost lot size of a group of related items. Letting:

$$Q_\$ = \text{lot size in dollars}$$
$$A = \text{period requirements in dollars and, so,}$$
$$TC = kQ_\$ \div 2 + SA \div Q_\$$$

Following the calculus approach to determine the value of $Q_\$$ that results in the minimum total period costs, $TC^*$ yields the following:

$$Q_\$^* = \left(\frac{2AS}{k}\right)^{1/2}$$

And, using data from the previous example:

$$C = \$2$$
$$R = 60{,}000$$
$$k = .3$$
$$S = \$45$$
$$A = CR = \$2.00 \times 60{,}000 = \$120{,}000$$
$$Q_\$^* = \left(\frac{2 \times 120{,}000 \times 45}{.3}\right)^{1/2}$$
$$= \$6{,}000$$
$$Q^* = Q_\$^* \div C = \$6{,}000 \div \$2 = 3{,}000, \text{ the same answer obtained earlier.}$$

Thus, the two answers are equivalent.

**Noninstantaneous Receipt.** Frequently when items are produced internally, they enter inventory gradually on a day-to-day basis during a substantial portion of the consumption period rather than at once as when a purchased lot arrives. Thus, the investment of dollars in inventory takes place day by day during the production run, as illustrated in Figure 7-6, and units continue to be withdrawn from stock as the newly produced items arrive. Thus, in this case of noninstantaneous receipt, known lead time, and no safety stock, the inventory level is never as great as the lot size.

Inventory is both produced and consumed during the period of production ($T_p$). The rate ($P$) at which an item is produced is equal to the production lot size ($Q$) divided by $T_p$; and the demand rate ($D$) is equal to $Q$ divided by the consumption period ($T_c$). These are, then, formulated as follows:

$$P = \frac{Q}{T_p}, \text{ and } D = \frac{Q}{T_c}$$

Both $P$ and $D$ are expressed in units per time period, and $D$ equals $R$ when they relate to the same period. In this case, as in the instantaneous receipt

**FIGURE 7-6**
**INVENTORY VERSUS TIME, FIXED ORDER QUANTITY (NONINSTANTANEOUS RECEIPT)**

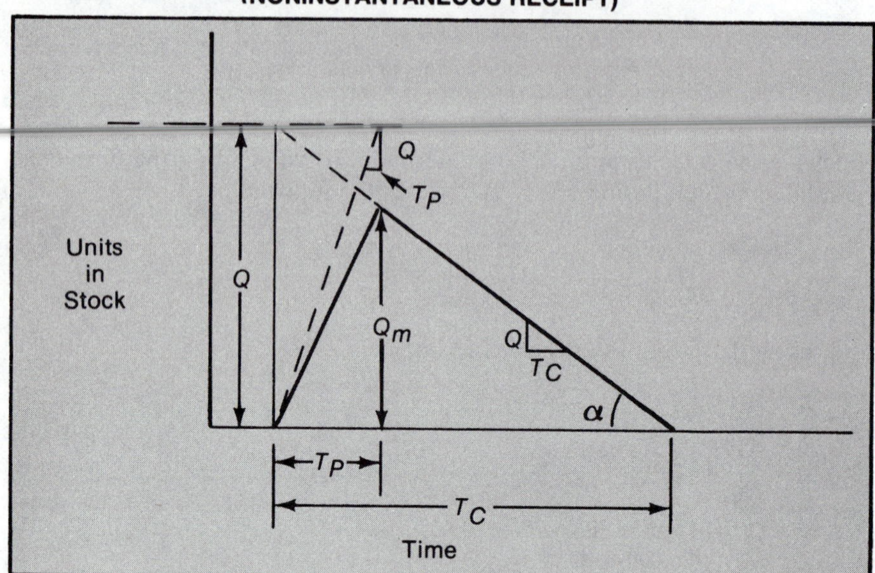


case, the *TC* resulting from the lot size decision is equal to the preparation cost plus the carrying cost. Preparation costs again equal the cost per preparation times the number of preparations in the period as illustrated earlier. Carrying costs again equal average inventory quantity (or value) times the cost (or cost rate) of carrying one unit for the period. The catch is that average inventory is not one half the lot size, $Q \div 2$, in this case. An examination of Figure 7-6 reveals that average inventory is equal to $Q_m \div 2$, but the value of $Q_m$ isn't immediately apparent. A little basic geometry will allow us to determine it from the known parameters. From similar triangles, it can be stated with the following model:

$$\frac{Q_m}{T_c - T_p} = \frac{Q}{T_c}$$

since both ratios describe the angle alpha, $\alpha$. Thus:

$$Q_m = \frac{Q(T_c - T_p)}{T_c}$$

From the earlier definitions of $P$ and $D$, it follows that:

$$T_p = \frac{Q}{P} \text{ and } T_c = \frac{Q}{D}$$

Substituting $\frac{Q}{P}$ for $T_p$ and $\frac{Q}{D}$ for $T_c$:

$$Q_m = \frac{Q\left(\frac{Q}{D} - \frac{Q}{P}\right)}{\frac{Q}{D}}$$

Dividing the numerator on the right side of the equation by the denominator, $\frac{Q}{D}$, gives:

$$Q_m = Q\left(\frac{D}{D} - \frac{D}{P}\right) = Q\left(1 - \frac{D}{P}\right)$$

And thus the average inventory is equal to $Q_m \div 2$ which equals $Q\left(1 - \frac{D}{P}\right) \div 2$. The average inventory, therefore, in the noninstantaneous receipt case is equal to one half the lot size multiplied by one minus the ratio of the consumption rate to the production rate. Intuitively this makes sense: One would suspect the average inventory to decrease in proportion to the ratio of the consumption and production rates due to the fact that units are being withdrawn from stock as they are produced and enter stock.

The purpose of the foregoing is not to stir the embers and ecstasies of high school geometry; rather it is to illustrate an approach useful for determining average inventory under many different circumstances. A graphic analysis can be fruitful in determining the average inventory in many situations that do not correspond exactly to the basic model. Thus, substituting $Q(1 - D \div P) \div 2$ for $\frac{Q}{2}$ in the basic decision rules gives the following:

$$TC = SR \div Q + kCQ(1 - D \div P) \div 2$$

$$Q^* = \left[\frac{2RS}{kC(1 - D/P)}\right]^{1/2}$$

**Noninstantaneous Receipt Example.** Let's return to the previous example of the ball bearings with the same facts except that the situation has changed to one of a manufacturer producing these items for finished goods with a production capacity of 960 units per 8-hour shift. Thus, we have the following:

$R$ = 60,000 units per year
$S$ = \$45 per order
$k$ = .30 per \$ per \$ per year
$C$ = \$2 each
$P$ = 960 units per 8-hour shift
$D$ = 60,000 units per year

If we casually insert the given demand and production rates directly into the decision rule model we have developed for this situation, we will have fruit salad—a mixture of apples and oranges. We must, consequently, first convert either $P$ or $D$ to the same dimension base as the other. They should not be stated in units for different time periods. In this case let's convert $P$ to the same base as $D$, an annual one.

Since the plant works one shift a day, five days a week, and 50 weeks a year, the annual production rate is calculated next as:

$$P = 960 \times 5 \times 50 = 240{,}000 \text{ units/year}$$

and the minimum cost order quantity is:

$$Q^* = \left[\frac{2RS}{kC\left(1 - \frac{D}{P}\right)}\right]^{1/2}$$

$$= \left[\frac{2 \times 60{,}000 \times 45}{2 \times .3\left(1.0 - \frac{60{,}000}{240{,}000}\right)}\right]^{1/2}$$

$$= 12{,}000{,}000^{1/2}$$

$$= 3{,}464.1$$

By its very nature the answer obtained raises practical considerations. First, it's not meaningful to produce 3,464.1 ball bearings; second, it probably makes sense to round off the lot size to 3,500 or 3,400 units. The increased unit costs should be relatively small and the record keeping much easier. Using a lot size of 3,464 or 3,465 is attributing greater precision to the estimated parameter values than is justified in most cases.

In summary, the fixed order quantity model is useful for determining the lot size under relatively stable, independent demand. Total costs are relatively insensitive to the actual lot size differing slightly from the optimum lot size. Modifications to the basic model are required to provide decision rules for more complex situations.

## Statistical Order Point

As mentioned previously, deciding when to release an order for purchase or production and deciding the quantity to order are the two basic problems of individual item management. There are three basic methods of deciding when to order: (1) statistical order point, (2) periodic review, (3) time-phased order point.

When to order an item depends on when an item is needed. The first two methods consider need implicitly while the third recognizes it explicitly.

Traditionally the EOQ, fixed order quantity, lot-sizing approach has been combined most frequently with the statistical order point method of deciding when to order. Thus, we will examine the statistical order point first. The periodic review method of ordering and the variable order quantity are interwoven inextricably; an examination of this method and its most common variations follows. The use of the time-phased order point in conjunction with the EOQ in independent demand situations, a relatively recent development, also is presented.

The statistical order point system places an order for a lot whenever the quantity on hand is reduced to a predetermined level, known as the order point (*OP*), as illustrated in Figure 7-7. This type system can be used effectively for independent demand items with relatively stable demand.

**FIGURE 7-7**
**TYPICAL QUANTITY IN STOCK VERSUS TIME**
**(ORDER POINT SYSTEM)**

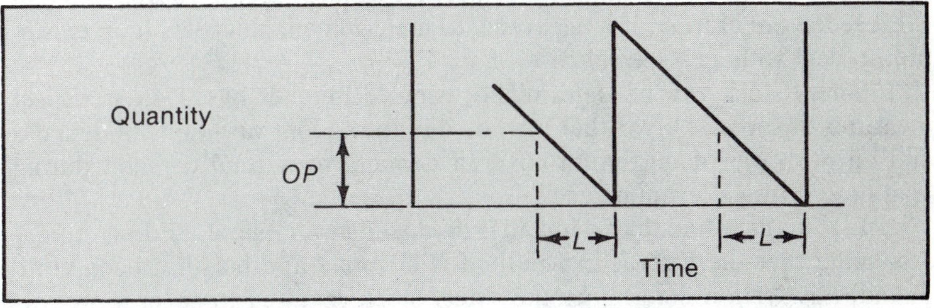


*L* = Lead Time

If the demand rate and the replenishment lead time (*L*) are constant, it is not difficult to determine exactly how low the stock level of an item can drop before an order must be placed to avoid a stock-out. For example, if an automobile parts distribution warehouse experiences a constant demand for 250 ball joint sets every two weeks—month in and month out—and it always takes exactly two weeks to obtain a replenishment order from the factory, the order point should be set at 250 sets, exactly two weeks of stock. However, this is not the common case. More typically the demand would vary, for example, from 200 to 300 sets during lead time. In this more realistic case, the order point is established to cover average usage during average lead time plus some of the expected high side variations in demand or in lead time. Stock held to cover these variations is called safety stock, $Q_S$ (buffer or reserve stock). The degree of variations covered depends on the level of customer service desired. The relationships between order point, lead time, and safety stock are shown in Figure 7-8.

The purpose of carrying a safety stock is to allow routine handling of the normal fluctuations that can be expected in any real situation. Safety stock is not intended to prevent all stock-outs or to eliminate completely the need

**FIGURE 7-8**
**RELATIONSHIP BETWEEN INVENTORY LEVEL, ORDER POINT, SAFETY STOCK, AND LEAD TIME.**

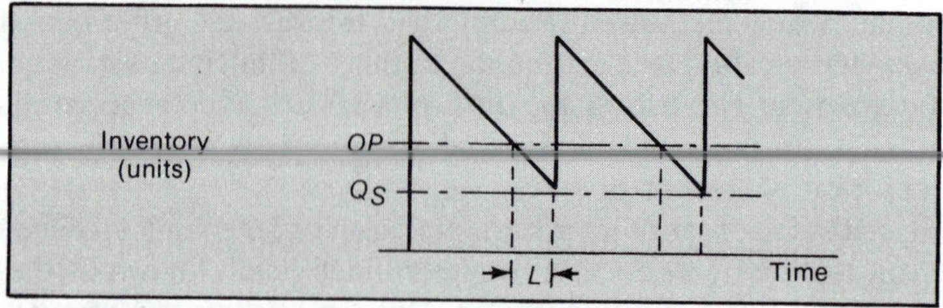


for expediting; that is, emergency follow-up on delayed orders or requests for quick delivery in unusual situations. Safety stock is present to allow management by exception, where the exceptions are truly unusual delays or surges in demand. For most statistical distributions the maximum demand rate can be infinite, but analysis of actual data should suggest a usage rate that is exceeded only rarely; if it is exceeded, management considers it an exception to deal with as a special case.

Safety stock can be determined using techniques based on statistical measures of forecast error that may be due to random variations in demand and on the ratio of maximum covered demand to normal demand during lead time. We will examine each.

Bias in the estimate of demand is discussed in Chapter 2, "Forecasting." Assuming that the forecasting method is adaptive and bias has been eliminated, this section determines the safety stock required to cover a proportion of forecast errors due to variations in demand. Thus, the order point is equal to normal usage during normal lead time plus the safety stock ($OP = DL + Q_S$).

Safety stock is a function of the random variation in demand per forecast period, the desired customer service level, and the ratio of the lead time (L) to the forecast period (FP). Variation in demand may be measured by two different techniques: standard deviation (S), or mean absolute deviation (MAD). The standard deviation of demand per forecast period equals the square root of the sum of the differences per period, between the forecast ($F_i$) and the demand ($D_i$) divided by the number of periods ($n$). Formulated, we have the following:

$$S = \sqrt{\frac{\Sigma(F_i - D_i)^2}{n}}$$

The MAD measure of variation is calculated by summing the absolute values of the recorded forecast demand deviations (forecast errors) and dividing that sum by the number of periods. Thus,

$$MAD = \Sigma|F_i - D_i| \div n$$

As discussed in Chapter 2, a smoothed value of MAD (SMAD) may be preferred in order to place greater emphasis on recent variations as in the following equation (wherein $b$, the smoothing factor, is between zero and 1):

$$SMAD_{i+1} = b|F_i - D_i| + (1.0 - b)SMAD_i$$

The safety factor is a function of the desired customer service level and the measure of variation. By assuming that forecast errors are normally distributed, the safety factor used with the standard deviation can be found in Figure 7-9. For example, the safety factor corresponding to a 92 percent customer service level is 1.40. This is determined by finding the $Z$ value in

**FIGURE 7-9**
**AREAS OF A STANDARD NORMAL DISTRIBUTION FOR Z VALUES**

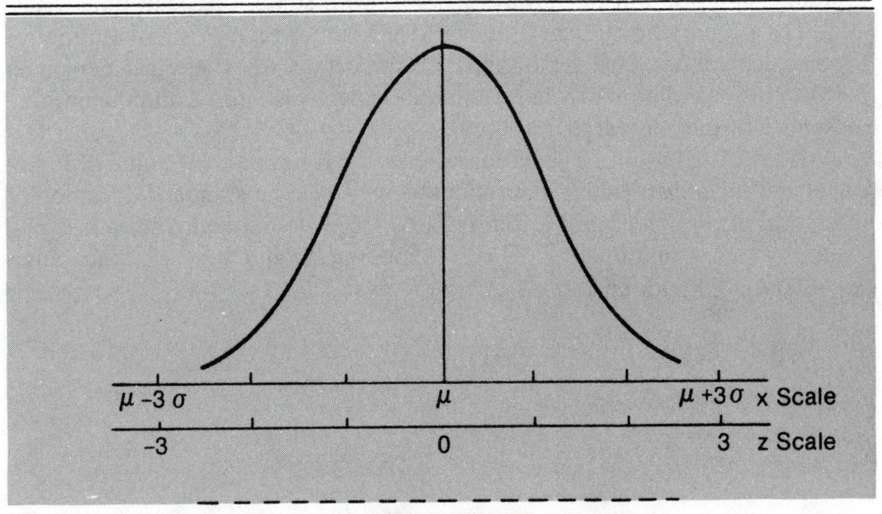


**Cumulative Normal Distribution**

| z | .0 | .1 | .2 | .3 | .4 |
|---|---|---|---|---|---|
| 0.0 | .5000 | .5398 | .5793 | .6179 | .6554 |
| 0.5 | .6915 | .7257 | .7580 | .7881 | .8159 |
| 1.0 | .8413 | .8643 | .8849 | .9032 | .9192 |
| 1.5 | .9332 | .9452 | .9554 | .9641 | .9713 |
| 2.0 | .9773 | .9821 | .9861 | .9893 | .9918 |
| 2.5 | .9938 | .9953 | .9965 | .9974 | .9981 |
| 3.0 | .9987 | .9990 | .9993 | .9995 | .9997 |
| 3.5 | .9998 | .9998 | .9999 | .9999 | .9999 |

the figure that corresponds to .92 (actually .9192). See Figure 7-10, Typical Distribution of Demand during Lead Time. Stock levels required to provide other levels of customer service can be determined in the same fashion.

**FIGURE 7-10**
**TYPICAL DISTRIBUTION OF DEMAND DURING LEAD TIME**

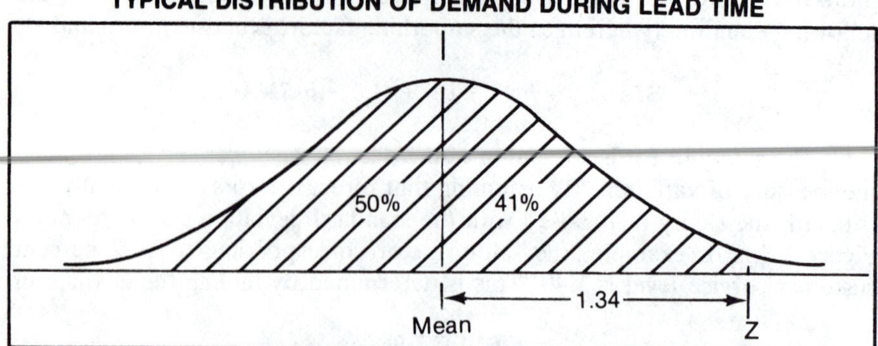


In most cases the forecast period and lead time are equal. This is the desirable situation but not always possible with some long lead time items.

The primary advantage of using MAD rather than $S$ is that it requires fewer calculations. This factor may be important when clerical personnel perform the calculation or when computer capacity is limited and the number of items is extremely large.

If the distribution of deviations ($F_i - D_i$) is normal, the value of MAD calculated for a distribution approximates .8 times the standard deviation of this distribution. Thus, MAD safety factors can be derived from a list of $Z$ values by merely multiplying the corresponding $Z$ value by 1.25. Since this is so, safety stock can be calculated as follows:

$$Q_s = MAD \times SF \times \sqrt{\frac{L}{FP}}$$

or

$$Q_s = S \times Z \times \sqrt{\frac{L}{FP}}$$

and the statistical order point can be calculated next:

$$OP = DL + Q_S$$

We can see how this would work with an example. A demand of 250 ball joint sets was forecast for each of 10 two week periods during the preceding 20 weeks. (For ease of calculation this problem uses data from only 10 periods. In a real world example analysis of more data is desirable.) Lead time equals the forecast period, two weeks. Table 7-3 lists the demand that then occurred in each period.

Inspection of this data reveals that the sum of the absolute deviations for the 10 periods is 150 units. Dividing 150 by 10 (the number of forecasting

**TABLE 7-3**
**DETERMINATION OF DEVIATION IN DEMAND; MAD AND STANDARD VARIATION**

**Forecast = 250 units/period**

| Period | Demand (*D*) | Deviation (Forecast Error) (*F* − *D*) | $(F - D)^2$ |
|---|---|---|---|
| 1 | 262 | 12 | 144 |
| 2 | 276 | 26 | 676 |
| 3 | 240 | −10 | 100 |
| 4 | 252 | 2 | 4 |
| 5 | 236 | −14 | 196 |
| 6 | 282 | 32 | 1024 |
| 7 | 240 | −10 | 100 |
| 8 | 237 | −13 | 169 |
| 9 | 222 | −28 | 784 |
| 10 | 253 | 3 | 9 |

periods covered in the data) yields a MAD of 15. If management desires a customer service level of 95 percent, the safety factor is 2.06 (see Table 7-4). Therefore, the safety stock, calculated next, is:

$$Q_S = 2.06 \times 15\sqrt{\frac{2}{2}} = 30.9$$

$$OP = 250 + 30.9 = 280.9, \text{ or } 281 \text{ for practical purposes}$$

For purposes of comparison, let's determine what OP would result from using the standard deviation as a measure of variation. From the ten periods observed as a sample, the estimated standard deviation is 18.87 and the value of $Z$ corresponding to 45 percent of the area (.95 − .50) is 1.65. Therefore:

$$OP = 250 + 1.65 \times 18.87 \times \sqrt{\frac{2}{2}}$$

$$= 250 + 31.14 = 281.14 \text{ or } 282$$

**TABLE 7-4 COMMON SAFETY FACTORS (MULTIPLES OF MAD AND THE NORMALIZED STANDARD DEVIATION CORRESPONDING TO GIVEN CUSTOMER SERVICE LEVELS AND STOCK-OUT PROBABILITIES)**

| *SF* Values | *Z* Values | Service Level | Stock-out Probability |
|---|---|---|---|
| 1.60 | 1.28 | .90 | .10 |
| 2.06 | 1.65 | .95 | .05 |
| 2.56 | 2.05 | .98 | .02 |
| 2.91 | 2.33 | .99 | .01 |
| 3.75 | 3.0 | .9986 | .0014 |
| 5.0 | 4.0 | .9999 | .0001 |

The results of these two different approaches differ only because the sample distribution is not a perfect normal distribution. The observed measure of variation is based on sample data and is always, therefore, an estimate of the true standard deviation.

For most statistical distributions the maximum demand rate can be infinite. Analysis of actual past data, however, should suggest some usage rate that is exceeded only rarely so that if it is exceeded management treats it as an exception.

Following this approach, the safety stock is simply the difference between the normal usage during the lead time and the maximum usage during the lead time that will be handled routinely, without the necessity of expediting. Figure 7-11 illustrates what happens when demand rises from a normal rate ($D_n$) to a maximum rate ($D_m$) just after an order has been placed, and continues at that level throughout the normal lead time ($L_n$). In that case we have the ensuing formula:

$$Q_S = L_n D_m - L_n D_n = L_n (D_m - D_n)$$

**FIGURE 7-11**
**INVENTORY LEVEL CHANGE**
**(WHEN DEMAND CHANGES FROM NORMAL TO MAXIMUM RATE)**

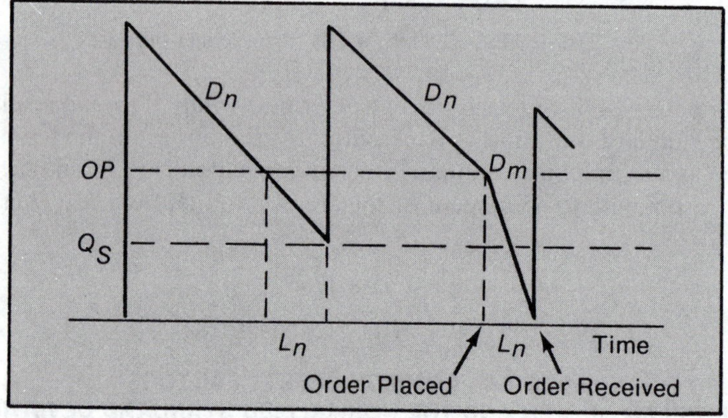


Figure 7-12 shows the case in which the usage rate does not change but the lead time increases to some maximum length, $L_m$. In that instance the following formula obtains:

$$Q_S = L_m D_n - L_n D_n = D_n (L_m - L_n)$$

**Order Point Determination.** Since the order point is equal to the normal usage during the normal lead time plus the safety stock, it can be determined from Figure 7-11 as follows:

$$\begin{aligned} OP &= L_n D_n + Q_S \\ &= L_n D_n + L_n (D_m - D_n) = L_n D_m \\ &= L_n D_n \frac{D_m}{D_n} \end{aligned}$$

Thus, the order point is the normal usage during the lead time multiplied by a safety factor, $D_m/D_n$. And for Figure 7-12:

$$\begin{aligned} OP &= L_n D_n + Q_S \\ &= L_n D_n + D_n (L_m - L_n) = L_m D_n \\ &= L_n D_n \frac{L_m}{L_n} \end{aligned}$$

**FIGURE 7-12**
**SAFETY STOCK REQUIRED DURING MAXIMUM LEAD TIME**

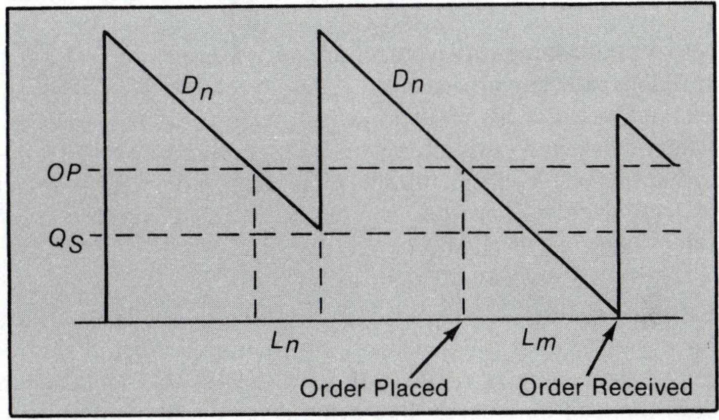


The order point again is equal to normal usage during lead time multiplied by a safety factor, but the safety factor is $L_m/L_n$.

In many situations both demand rate and lead time vary. Protection against stock-out to a maximum tolerable rate of combined demand rate and lead time variations can be obtained using a similar analysis. Figure 7-13 illustrates what happens when demand rises from a normal rate to a maximum rate just after an order has been placed and lead time increases to a maximum length. In that case:

$$\begin{aligned} Q_S &= L_m D_m - L_n D_n, \text{ and} \\ OP &= L_n D_n + Q_S, \text{ thus} \\ &= L_m D_m \end{aligned}$$

In their 1962 article, John Lu, John Toellner, and Norbert Kaufman present an interesting approach using nomographs to establish order points based on maximum lead time and maximum demand. [2] These practical

**FIGURE 7-13**
**SAFETY STOCK REQUIRED TO MEET MAXIMUM DEMAND DURING MAXIMUM LEAD TIME**

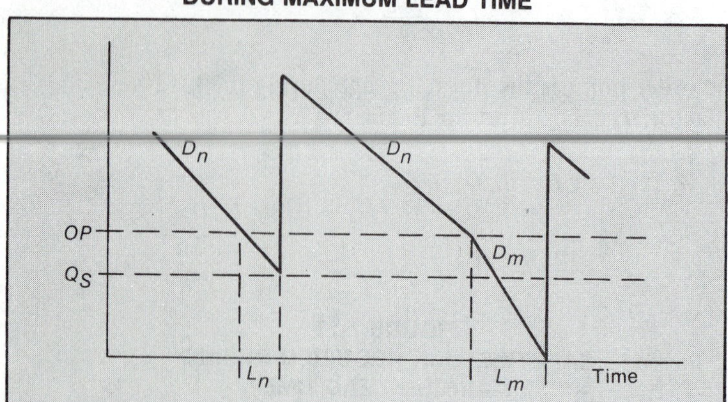


approaches to establishing order points are very useful when statistical data are not available or easily processed.

The above discussions of safety stock apply to a fixed order quantity system. Safety stock in a periodic review system must be provided not only for demand during the lead time but also for demand over the time between reviews as well. This will be examined in the section covering the periodic review system later in this chapter.

**Other Considerations.** A number of questions arise. What measure of customer service is being used in these calculations? What if the forecast period and lead time are not equal? In fact, do not the demand rate and the length of the lead time both vary? What if the distribution of demand is not normal? In the following sections, we will examine these issues.

When using the standard deviation or MAD in calculating safety stock, customer service is defined as the percentage of replenishment periods during which the stock available will be equal to or greater than the demand. Little work has been done in defining order points using other measures of customer service.

**Unequal Lead Time and Forecast Period.** If the lead time is greater than the forecast period then we must modify our calculations accordingly. Let lead time be four weeks (two periods) in the previous example with all other factors remaining the same. Then,

$$OP = 250 \times 2 + 1.65 \times 18.874 \times \sqrt{\frac{4}{2}}$$
$$= 500 + 43.91 = 544$$

In this case, do not overlook the fact that the calculation of normal usage during lead time must reflect the fact that lead time includes multiple forecast periods. If calculations had been carried out to three decimal places, an order point of 544 plus, or 545, would have been obtained. This would have given undue respect to the precision of demand estimates. Whenever practical, the forecast period is set equal to the lead time. This is done by the practice of recording demand during lead time and developing a forecast for that length of time.

**Variations in Lead Time and Demand.** Safety stock is held to cover both the variations in the demand rate and variations in lead time as is illustrated in Figure 7-14. Operationally there are a number of ways of handling these concurrent variations. Perhaps the simplest is merely to record the

**FIGURE 7-14**
**LEAD TIME AND DEMAND DISTRIBUTIONS**

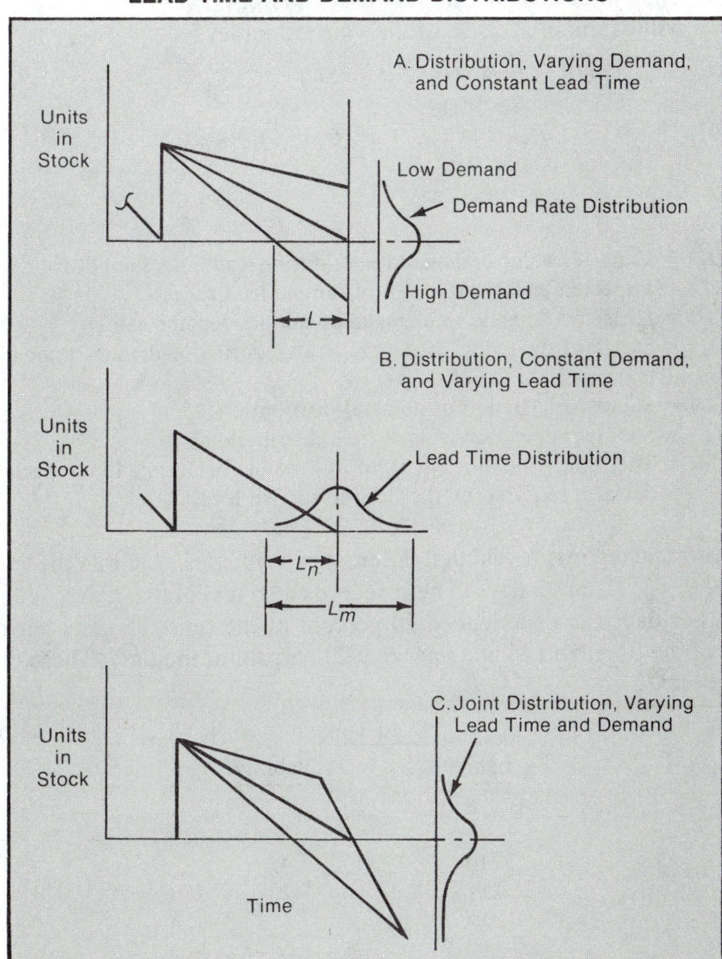

actual joint variations and treat the result as a single distribution. For example, if Table 7-3 contains data for ten periods during which both lead time and demand vary, we have an average demand of 250 units per lead time and a standard deviation of 18.87.

Danish [3] and Jacobs [4], among others, have developed a feasible approach to determining the order point when both the lead time and demand during the lead time vary. Briefly stated, this approach uses the lead time and the demand distributions to determine the mean and stated deviation of the joint distribution.

The list of areas under the normal curve then is used in the traditional manner to determine the safety stock required to obtain the desired customer service level as follows: The order point equals the expected value of demand during the lead time, the mean of the joint distribution, plus the safety factor times the standard deviation of the joint distribution of lead time and demand. This joint probability approach makes two crucial assumptions which we will examine after the following example:

$$OP = E(D_L) + SF \times \sigma(D_L)$$
$$E(D_L) = E(D)E(L)$$
$$\sigma(D_L) = [E(L)\sigma^2(D) + E^2(D)\sigma^2(L)]^{1/2}$$

Where:

$E(D_L)$ = Expected value of demand rates during lead time, joint distribution
$E(L)$ = Expected lead time (mean of sample lead times)
$E(D)$ = Expected demand rate (mean of sample demand rates)
$\sigma(D_L)$ = Standard deviation of demand rates during lead time, joint distribution
$\sigma(D)$ = Standard deviation of demand distribution
$\sigma(L)$ = Standard deviation of lead time distribution
SF = The safety factor; equal to the value of $Z$, standard normal deviate, required by the desired service level

Historical records reveal that different probabilities exist that the lead time will be 8, 9, 10, 11, or 12 days. These records also reveal that a demand rate of 24 units per day was experienced 20 percent of the time, 25 units per day 60 percent of the time, and 26 units per day 20 percent of the time. These data are tabulated next.

| Lead Time | |
|---|---|
| Length | Probability |
| 8 | .1 |
| 9 | .2 |
| 10 | .4 |
| 11 | .2 |
| 12 | .1 |
| | 1.00 |

| Demand Rate | |
|---|---|
| Units/day | Probability |
| 24 | .20 |
| 25 | .60 |
| 26 | .20 |
| | 1.00 |

Applying the preceding model as follows:

$$
\begin{aligned}
E(D) &= \Sigma P(D_i) \times D_i \\
&= .2 \times 24 + .6 \times 25 + .2 \times 26 = 4.8 + 15 + 5.2 \\
&= 25 \\
E(L) &= \Sigma P(L_i) \times L_i \\
&= .1 \times 8 + .2 \times 9 + .4 \times 10 + .2 \times 11 + .1 \times 12 \\
&= .8 + 1.8 + 4 + 2.2 + 1.2 \\
&= 10 \\
E(D_L) &= E(D)E(L) = 25 \times 10 \\
&= 250
\end{aligned}
$$

By definition, the variance of a discrete probability distribution equals $E(x^2) - \mu^2$. Thus, the following:

$$
\begin{aligned}
\sigma^2(D) &= E(D^2) - E^2(D) \\
E(D) &= 25 \\
E^2(D) &= 625 \\
E(D^2) &= \Sigma P(D_i)(D_i)^2 \\
&= .2 \times 576 + .6 \times 625 + .2 \times 676 \\
&= 115.2 + 375 + 135.2 \\
&= 625.4 \\
\sigma^2(D) &= 625.4 - 625 = .4 \\
\sigma^2(L) &= E(L^2) - E^2(L) \\
E(L) &= 10 \\
E^2(L) &= 100 \\
E(L^2) &= \Sigma P(L_i)(L)^2 \\
&= .1 \times 64 + .2 \times 81 + .4 \times 100 + .2 \times 121 + .1 \times 144 \\
&= 6.4 + 16.2 + 40 + 24.2 + 14.4 \\
&= 101.2 \\
\sigma^2(L) &= 101.2 - 100 = 1.2 \\
\sigma(D_L) &= [E(L)\sigma^2(D) + E^2(D)\sigma^2(L)]^{1/2} \\
&= [10 \times .4 + 625 \times 1.2]^{1/2} \\
&= [4 + 750]^{1/2} = [754]^{1/2} = 27.46
\end{aligned}
$$

And thus the order point for a 95 percent service level is calculated next as:

$$
\begin{aligned}
OP &= E(D_L) + SF\,[Z(.45)] \times \sigma\,(D_L) \\
&= 250 + 1.64 \times 27.46 = 250 + 45.03 \\
&= 295.03, \text{ or } 295
\end{aligned}
$$

These calculations may seem rather laborious but, as Krupp has pointed out, they can be performed easily on a programmed calculator. [5] A digital computer also can handle them with little difficulty.

Two crucial assumptions are made when using the previous approach. One is that demand on one day is independent of demand on the preceeding day, and the other is that demand is independent of lead time. Frequently these assumptions are not valid. Low demand one day may be a precursor of high demand the following day. In addition, increases (decreases) in lead time may generate at least temporary increases (decreases) in demand rate. Situations are different. Each organization must determine the relevant characteristic relationships of the items and groups of items that it manages.

Greene presents an excellent discussion of the factors that influence the demand, withdrawal, distribution and the lead time, replenishment, distribution. [6] He also points out—and we should remember—that basing order point calculation on withdrawal and replenishment distributions of historical data assumes that the future will correspond to the past. Changing economic conditions, the actions of competitors, new products, and unusual events such as strikes, wars, and threats of war may make that assumption false.

A recollection of Chapter 2 reminds us that demand forecasts must consider seasonal and trend factors as well as promotions. Order point calculations also should recognize these factors.

**Implementation of an Order Point System.** A statistical order point system requires a mechanism that alerts management when the order point has been reached. There are two basic methods of accomplishing this: (1) a perpetual inventory system and (2) a two-bin inventory system.

**Perpetual Inventory System.** A record is kept of each transaction, receipt or withdrawal from inventory, and the new on-hand balance recorded. Computerized systems of this type usually are programmed to output an *exception* message when the stock balance is at or below the order point. Manual systems require the inventory planner to compare the stock balance to the order point after each transaction.

**Two-Bin System.** The material is physically separated into the order point quantity and the remaining units. The latter are consumed first and an order is placed upon their consumption. Material may be placed in different bins or physically separated within the same bin. The order point quantity may be placed in a special container or designated by a line on the storage bin or drum. When the container is opened or stock reaches the designated line an order is placed. This type system depends on stockroom personnel recognizing that an order point has been reached, but all systems require responsible personnel. The two-bin system is best suited for independent demand and for low value items with short lead times. Office supplies and common hardware items are likely candidates.

## Periodic Review

The characteristics of many items in inventory do not make them amenable to the continuous review inherent in a statistical order point system. Some items, especially dependent demand items, are managed best by a material requirements planning type system while some others are managed more appropriately by a periodic review type system.

Conditions that recommend the adoption of a periodic review system or one of its derivatives include the following:

1. When independent demand is the usual situation.
2. When it is difficult to record withdrawals from stock and continuous review is expensive. Although optical scanning and modern computer systems have reduced this problem—even in some grocery stores—it still exists in many situations including raw materials and finished goods storerooms.
3. When groups of items are purchased from a common supplier and the total preparation costs per item are greatly reduced by combining the items into one order. Small tools; manufacturing supplies; common commercial parts such as nuts, bolts, washers; and office supplies are examples.
4. When items have a limited shelf life (perishables) they are ideal candidates for fixed period review management. Dairy items and fruits and vegetables are the classic examples. Many chemicals, pharmaceuticals, solvents, etc., used directly or indirectly in the manufacturing process, also may be managed most effectively by a periodic review type system.
5. And, perhaps, when there is an economic advantage in generating full carload shipments or fully utilizing available production capacity. This type situation will be examined when discussing joint replenishment.

**The System.** A periodic review system in its basic form involves determining the amount of an item in stock at a specified, fixed, time interval and placing an order for a quantity that, when added to the quantity on hand, will equal the sum of the estimated demand during lead time plus the estimated demand during the review period plus the safety stock (see Figure 7-15). Since the time period between reviews of the quantity on hand is fixed, this approach sometimes is called the fixed review period system.

The sum of the anticipated demand during lead time and the replenishment period plus the safety stock is called the target level inventory or the maximum level. We will use the term *maximum inventory level* ($M$). The inventory on hand never will reach this level unless demand (withdrawals from stock) ceases during the lead time.

This system is described by the following model:

$$M = D(R + L) + Q_S$$

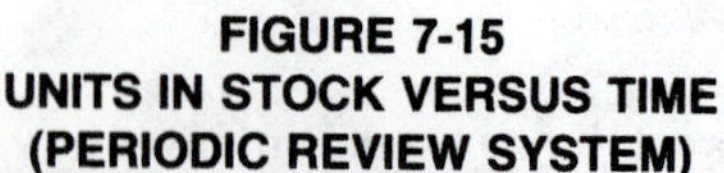

**FIGURE 7-15**
**UNITS IN STOCK VERSUS TIME**
**(PERIODIC REVIEW SYSTEM)**

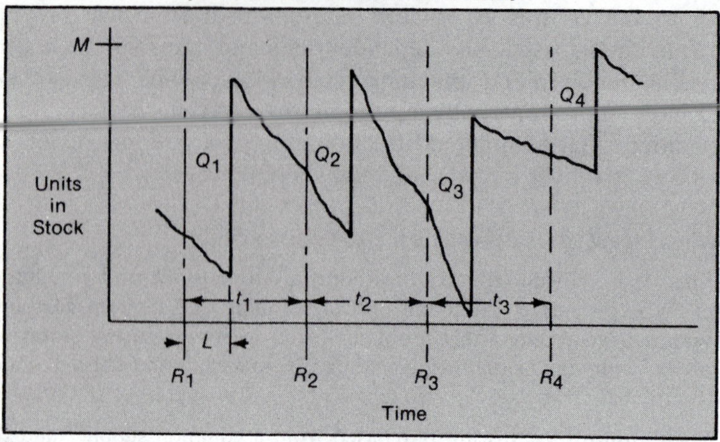


Where:

$M$ = Maximum inventory level
$L$ = Lead time duration
$D$ = Demand per unit of time
$R$ = Review period duration
$Q_S$ = Safety stock

And with:

$I$ = Inventory
$Q$ = Order quantity
$O$ = Quantity on order

The order quantity is equal to the maximum level minus the sum of the quantity on hand (inventory) and the quantity on order:

$$Q = M - (I + O), \text{ or } Q = D(R + L) + Q_S - (I + O)$$

In those cases where the lead time is greater than the review period ($L > R$) there will be some items on order unless $Q$ equaled zero in a previous period.

Figure 7-15 illustrates the relationship of the inventory versus time for a periodic review system. It clearly reveals that $t_1 = t_2 = t_3$ and that $Q_1$, $Q_2$, $Q_3$, and $Q_4$ are not necessarily equal. Thus, the review period is fixed, and the order quantity may vary; whereas in the traditional fixed order quantity order point system the order quantity is fixed, and the period between orders may vary. Let's look at a periodic review example.

A company uses a zinc based primer that is obtained along with other paints, solvents, etc., from a local supplier. Normal usage is three gallons per day; the review period is every two weeks (ten working days); lead time is three days; and safety stock is four gallons. Inventory is reviewed at the appropriate time, and there are 15 gallons in stock. Thus, the maximum inventory level and the order quantity can be calculated as follows:

$$\begin{aligned} M &= D(L + R) + Q_S \\ &= 3(3 + 10) + 4 \\ &= 43 \\ Q &= M - I \\ &= 43 - 15 \\ &= 28 \end{aligned}$$

An order should be placed for 28 gallons.

What if the inventory on hand had been six gallons instead of 15? This is insufficient to cover normal usage during the three-day lead time. In all likelihood, the company will be able to obtain some on short notice by special order. However, if this is not possible, the question of the permissibility of back orders must be addressed. In this example, a stock-out in primer paint can result in a schedule delay and in some items being painted late (after the paint arrives). The order quantity then will be calculated in the normal fashion as follows:

$$\begin{aligned} Q &= M - I \\ &= 43 - 6 \\ &= 37 \text{ gallons} \end{aligned}$$

Let's look at a slightly different situation. When a stock-out occurs, the company uses a substitute primer. In this case the minimum inventory on hand will be nine gallons for practical purposes since the requirements during the lead time are covered by a substitute; and $Q$, then, $= 43 - 9 = 34$ gallons.

A similar situation frequently exists when the periodic reordering system is used in managing finished goods. If the customer usually goes to a second source when an item is not available, the minimum value of $I$ in the calculation is the demand during lead time, $D_L$. Hardware stores, grocery stores, drug stores, and manufacturing supply houses frequently operate under such conditions.

**Safety Stock Considerations.** The purpose of safety stock is to cover high side variations in demand from the placement of an order to the arrival of a subsequent order. In an order point system, unusually heavy demand will trigger another order as soon as the order point is reached. This may occur immediately after the receipt of the first order. In a strictly periodic system (one without an order point mechanism) another order will not be placed until the review period has passed. Therefore, in an order point system, safety stock need cover variations in demand during lead time only; but in a strictly periodic system the safety stock must cover variations in demand during the combined review and lead time period. As illustrated in Figure 7-16, the quantity ordered at $R_1$ must recognize possible variations in demand from $R_1$ to $D_2$ (date of delivery of order No. 2).

**FIGURE 7-16**
**SAFETY STOCK (PERIODIC REVIEW SYSTEM)**

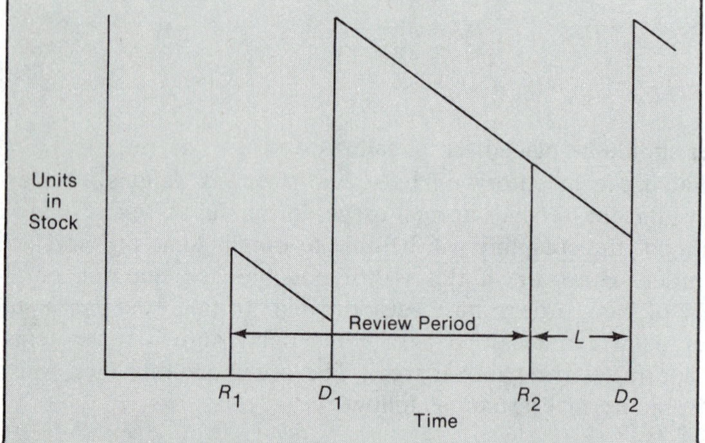

Order size determined at $R_1$ and $R_2$.
Deliveries occur at $D_1$ and $D_2$.

Thus, safety stock is calculated by multiplying the safety factor times the standard deviation of demand during lead time plus the review period. The value of the safety factor depends, of course, on the customer service level desired. For example, the safety factor for a customer service level of 95 percent is 1.645 (see Table 7-4) when using the standard deviation as the measure of variation. *Service level* is defined here as the percentage of periods during which all customer orders are filled (a stock-out does not occur). Without any safety stock, the service level will be 50 percent since demand is less than or equal to the average demand 50 percent of the time.

Returning to our earlier example of the zinc based primer, let the standard deviation of demand during the combined lead time and review period be 2.43 units and the desired service level be 95 percent. Then, safety stock will be equal 2.43 times 1.645, that is, 3.997, or 4 units.

## Hybrid Systems

There are many different ways of combining the features of the periodic ordering system and the order point system. The two most common will be described.

The first (the Order Point-Periodic Review Combination System) combines the order point feature with the periodic review. In brief, if the inventory level drops below a specified level prior to the review date, an order is placed; if not, the order quantity is determined at the end of the period in the basic periodic review manner (see Figure 7-17). This system

**FIGURE 7-17**
**UNITS IN STOCK VERSUS TIME**
**(PERIODIC REVIEW-ORDER POINT COMBINATION)**

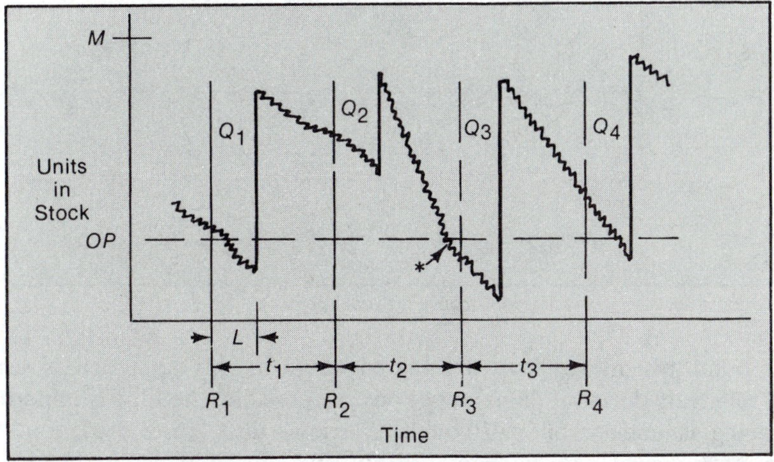


*Order is placed before scheduled review as stock drops below order point.

is appropriate when relatively large variations in demand are common and the costs of safety stocks required to cover these variations during the combined lead time and review period are excessive (greater than the costs of a combination system). A combination periodic review-order point system requires safety stock to cover variations in demand during the lead time only. To function, this system must have a mechanism for indicating when the order point is reached. If perpetual records are not available, then one of the physical forms of the two-bin system, described earlier, must be installed. A combination order point-periodic review type system frequently is used to manage families of independent items.

If an item is frequently reaching the reorder point before the review period has expired, examination of the value of *D*, demand per unit of time, and thus *M*, the maximum, is in order.

The second most common combination is the Optional (s,S) Replenishment System. In this periodic review-order point combination system, an order is placed only if the quantity on hand is below a specific level. See Figure 7-18, Units in Stock versus Time, Optional Replenishment System. This method enables an organization to avoid placing orders for relatively small quantities. It also is known as the *s, S* model where *S* represents the maximum inventory level, which we have called *M,* and *s* represents the

**FIGURE 7-18**
**UNITS IN STOCK VERSUS TIME**
**(OPTIONAL REPLENISHMENT SYSTEM)**

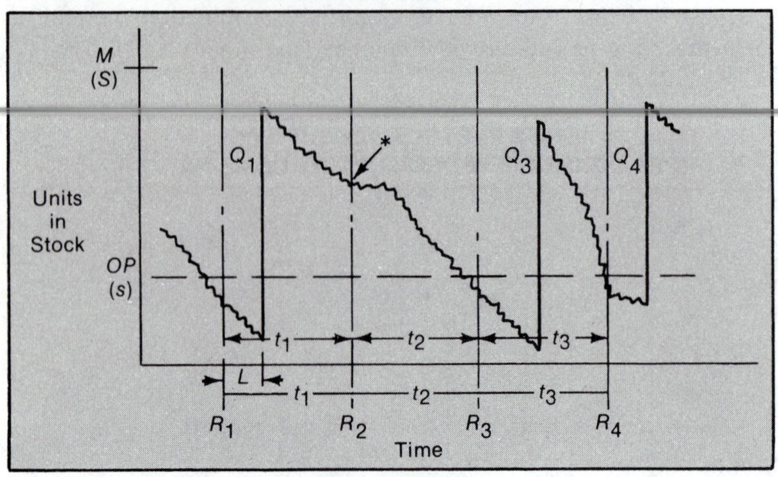


*Order is not placed. Stock level is above the order point.

order point which we have designated as *OP*. This approach is useful when relatively dormant demand periods are possible, shelf life is important, and aging is undesirable. Although staleness, dust, rust, oxidation, and other attributes of age may not prevent an item from being sold if it is needed, they do not enhance customer satisfaction. The optional replenishment system diminishes the probability of these deficiencies, but it does increase the probability of a stock-out.

Establishing the order point in this type system is extremely complex if one desires to have the mathematical assurance that the order point guarantees that the sum of holding costs, ordering costs, and expected stock-out costs are being minimized. [7, 8] This assurance is always tempered by a few assumptions including one concerning the demand distribution.

The main point is that this type system is used and used successfully by different organizations. I suspect many have observed, as we have, the storeroom or supply clerk who reviews commercial items on a periodic basis (such as on the fifth and twentieth of every month) and orders only if an item has reached the order point. In some such cases, the order point may be relatively high since the carrying costs are relatively low compared with the cost of ordering, which includes the costs of writing the order, receiving, moving to stores, and processing the payment.

In other cases, such as fresh food markets, seasonal goods, bookstores, restaurants and pharmacies, the order point may be set relatively low since the cost of a stock-out is balanced against the cost of obsolete, unusable, inventory.

## Visual Review Systems

Both periodic review and order point systems can be implemented using a physical review of the stock on hand rather than a perpetual inventory record system. For example, in many retail outlets the customer is the stock picker and real time records of the quantity on hand do not exist. A periodic physical count of the stock to determine the order quantity is common.

The Two-Bin system of inventory storage is a common method of operating a visual review order point system. It is appropriate for the management of independent demand, low value items with short lead times, such as office supplies and common hardware items.

## Time-Phased Order Point System

The time-phased order point system applies the logic of material requirements planning to independent demand items. The prerequisites for this type system include a forecast of requirements, the lead time of the item, and the order quantity. The sequence for this type system is as follows:

1. Requirements, scheduled receipts, and the on hand quantity are projected by week for the short-range planning period, usually two to six months.
2. The week is determined in which the order quantity falls below zero, or if safety stock is used, below the safety stock level. This is the outage period.
3. An order release is planned for the outage period minus the lead time. For example, if the lead time is two weeks and the projected outage occurs in Week 8, an order release should be planned for Week 6.

Let us see how this works with an example. The following is known about a service part that is not used in currently produced assemblies:

Lead time = 3 weeks
Weekly demand forecast = 20 units
Safety stock = 30 units
Order quantity = 100 units
An order of 100 units is scheduled for receipt in Week 2
On hand quantity = 40 units

The projected gross requirements, scheduled receipts, and on-hand quantity by week are:

| Week | | 1 | 2 | 3 | 4 | 5 | 6 | 7 | 8 | 9 | 10 |
|---|---|---|---|---|---|---|---|---|---|---|---|
| Gross Requirements | | 20 | 20 | 20 | 20 | 20 | 20 | 20 | 20 | 20 | 20 |
| Scheduled Receipts | | | 100 | | | | | | | | |
| On Hand | 40 | 20 | 100 | 80 | 60 | 40 | 20 | 0 | (20) | (40) | (60) |
| Planned Order Releases | | | | | | | | | | | |

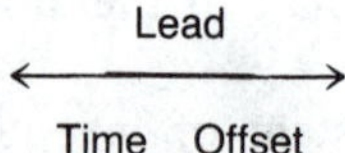


The on-hand quantity will fall below the safety stock level of 30 in Week 6. An order release must be planned for Week 3 to have a scheduled receipt in Week 6. The release of an order in Week 3 and its scheduled receipt in Week 6 is incorporated in the planning document below. We also have determined that an order receipt will be required in Week 11 and have included its planned release and scheduled receipt.

| Week | | 1 | 2 | 3 | 4 | 5 | 6 | 7 | 8 | 9 | 10 | 11 |
|---|---|---|---|---|---|---|---|---|---|---|---|---|
| Gross Requirements | | 20 | 20 | 20 | 20 | 20 | 20 | 20 | 20 | 20 | 20 | 20 |
| Scheduled Receipts | | | 100 | | | | 100 | | | | | 100 |
| On Hand | 40 | 20 | 100 | 80 | 60 | 40 | 120 | 100 | 80 | 60 | 40 | 120 |
| Planned Order Releases | | | | 100 | | | | | 100 | | | |

The time-phased order point system reveals when orders for an item likely will be placed during the entire planning horizon. Thus, it provides the information necessary for projecting capacity requirements and for planning the gross inventory requirements of parts and materials used in the fabrication of the item. Other basic systems do not have this capability.

## Other Considerations

Even the most complex inventory management models only approximate reality; and the cost, demand and lead time values used in calculating lot sizes and order release timing are estimates. The inventory planner should not use the results of lot size and order release calculations without considering practical factors such as rounding off, material usage, tool life, package or container size, and yield, etc.

**Rounding Off.** Lot size and safety stock calculations frequently result in fractional values that are obviously infeasible in the case of discrete parts.

For example, one can not sell 97.2 transmissions. Rounding a number like 97.2 or 98.0 up to 100 makes sense in most cases. Total carrying and setup costs would change little and numbers ending in one or more zeros facilitate human memory and recognition.

**Material Usage.** Frequently it makes sense to increase a lot size to use all of the material available in coil, rod, sheet, or container rather than returning a small leftover amount to stores. The added material and processing costs may be less than the costs of handling and storing small amounts.

**Tool Life.** The required periodic replacement or maintenance of a tool or process such as a dye, cutting blade, filter, or treatment solution may consume as much production capacity (machine downtime) as the machine setup. Increasing production lot sizes so that the end of the production run and the maintenance requirement occur currently will decrease downtime. Since such tools, solutions, and filters must be replaced or cleaned when a different item is run, coordinating required maintenance and setup activities may be equivalent to eliminating a setup.

Care should be taken not to reduce the lot sizes of dependent demand items required for an assembly. The savings in machine downtime and maintenance costs will be small compared to the costs resulting from the missing parts.

**Package or Container Size.** Items often are purchased or stored in standard size containers or packages. Increasing lot sizes to fill containers may be justified by reduced transportation, storage, and handling costs per unit. Quantity discounts are discussed in Chapter 13.

**Yield.** The scrap or yield rate of a process should be considered when calculating lot sizes. In a material requirements system using lot-for-lot order quantities, scrap and yield factors require that the actual order quantity be greater than the net requirements. This quantity can be calculated in the following manner for lot sizes in a given range.

$$Q = \frac{\text{net requirements } (NR)}{1.0 - \text{maximum likely scrap percentage } (MLS)}$$

Or

$$Q = \frac{\text{net requirements}}{\text{yield rate (y)}}$$

Where:

$$\text{y} = 1 - MLS$$

An Example:

$$NR = 500 \qquad Q = 500 \div (1 - .90)$$
$$MLS = .10 \qquad Q = 556$$

(Note: If 550 units were produced with 10 percent scrap, only 495 good units will result.)

The number of units scrapped is more likely a function of the number of setups rather than the direct percentage of the lot size. For example, experience in running a lot of 25 units of Item *A* may indicate a maximum likely scrap of five units, 25 percent, but when running lots of 400 units of Item *A*, a maximum likely scrap of twenty units, five percent has occurred. Joseph Orlicky [1] suggests the following declining percentage formula be used in determining the quantity of a planned order release:

$$Q = Q^* + a\sqrt{Q^*}$$

Where:

$Q$ = the planned order release quantity
$Q^*$ = lot size calculated by the lot sizing method without scrap considered
$a$ = multiplier reflecting the scrap rate incidence

Table 7-5, following, illustrates the procedure with a multiplier of 1.

**TABLE 7-5**
**DECLINING PERCENTAGE**
**SCRAP ALLOWANCE ($a$ = 1.0)**

| Calculated Lot ($Q^*$) Size without scrap allowance | Scrap[1] allowance | Lot Size ($Q$) with scrap allowance[2] | Percentage allowed[3] |
|---|---|---|---|
| 1 | 1 | 2 | 100 |
| 5 | 3 | 8 | 60 |
| 10 | 4 | 14 | 40 |
| 20 | 5 | 25 | 25 |
| 50 | 8 | 58 | 16 |
| 100 | 10 | 110 | 10 |
| 500 | 23 | 523 | 4.6 |
| 1000 | 32 | 1032 | 3.2 |

[1]Scrap allowance is rounded up to an integer value.
[2]The planned order releases of 58, 523, and 1032 likely would be rounded up to 60, 525, and 1040.
[3]Actual allowances depend on the situation.

**Minimums and Maximums.** Floors and ceilings may be established by policy to eliminate overloading of production and order handling capacity by a large number of small orders and to prevent production of quantities greater than required in a reasonable planning horizon. These limits may be stated in absolute terms such as no fewer than 10 units and no more than 100 units or in demand related terms such as no less than two weeks supply and no more than 6 months supply. Rarely does it make sense to produce more than a year's supply.

**Implementation of Multiple Factors.** It is common for more than one practical consideration to affect the order quantity decision. When ordering dependent demand items, top priority is to order at least the net requirements. Maximum and minimum limits usually rank next followed by yield calculations, tool life, and material usage. However, the planner should evaluate each situation on its own merits as the costs related to the various factors can differ widely from case to case.

In summary, individual item management concerns when to order (the order point), and how many to order (the lot size). The dependent demand-independent demand dichotomy is the major determinant of the appropriateness of the different models for a given item. The lot sizing decision rules are based on models that minimize the sum of carrying and preparation costs. Order point decision rules are predicated on a customer service level objective. A timely and accurate information processing system is required to implement these decision rules. Figure 7-19 is a schematic representation of data flow in a typical system.

**FIGURE 7-19**
**SCHEMATIC INVENTORY MANAGEMENT INFORMATION SYSTEM**

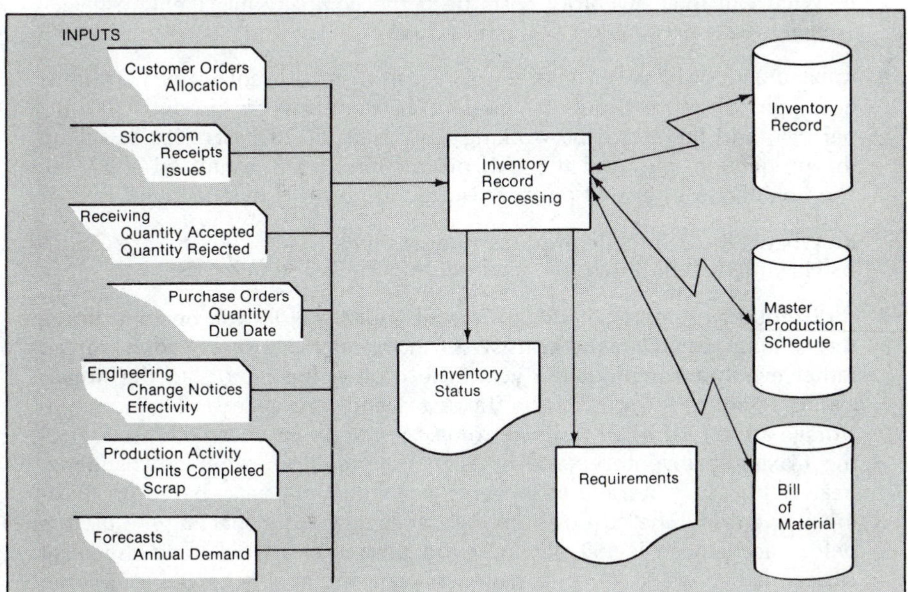

# PROBLEMS

1. A purchased item in the finished goods warehouse has an annual demand of 14,400 units with no seasonality or trend. Unit costs are 40 cents; holding costs are estimated to be 25% of average inventory value; and ordering costs are estimated as $20.

   a. What should the economic ordering quantity be?
   b. How often should an order be placed?
   c. What are the total annual inventory costs?
   d. If the same company decides to produce these items at a cost of 30 cents each with a total preparation cost of $45 per order and its annual capacity is 21,600 units, what is the economic order quantity?

2. The Near East Electronics Sales Company sells 16,000 Model 19A meters every year. There is no seasonality or trend in the demand pattern. They pay $2 for the meters and sell them for $3, $3.50, or $4 depending on the quantity the customer purchases. The company uses a carrying cost rate of .30 and estimates preparation costs as $40. What is the economic purchase lot size?
3. Near East—see Problem 2—discovers that they can assemble these meters for a total labor, material, and overhead cost of $1. Total preparation costs will be $45; annual production capacity is 16,000 units. What is the economical production lot size?
4. A pottery company experiences a rather steady independent demand of 25,000 units annually for an ash tray. They have the capacity to produce 50,000 units each year. Holding costs are estimated to be 10 cents per unit per year, and total preparation costs are $25.

   a. What is the economic production lot size?
   b. What will total inventory costs be if the company mistakenly estimates total preparation costs to be $36?

5. A manufacturer of power take-offs forecasts a steady demand of 1,000 units next year for its most popular model. The company can produce 10 units per day, and there are 250 working days available. It costs $900 to set up the production line, and the unit production cost is estimated at $2,750. The holding cost per unit per year is $750. Demand is independent.

   a. What is the economic production quantity?
   b. How many runs should be made during the year?

6. A distributor estimates that 4,000 Model G198Z motors will be sold during the coming year. Demand consists of many relatively small orders spread rather evenly throughout the year. The cost of the motors to the firm is estimated to be $15 per motor. Taxes (*T*) and insurance (*I*) for motors in storage are a total of 20 cents per motor per year, based on one quarter of the maximum inventory; and costs of deterioration, pilferage, handling, heat, light, etc. (*P*) come to 30 cents per motor per year, based on maximum inventory. The cost of ordering, receiving, and inspecting the motors before acceptance is $50 per lot. Lead time is two weeks and the plant closes for two weeks for vacation each year. The cost of capital is 20% per year.

a. Develop the TC model assuming constant deterministic demand and no stock-outs.
b. Derive the EOQ model and determine the EOQ.
c. What are the total inventory costs for the year?

7. Given the following data for an item with independent demand:

Annual demand = 26,000 units
Economic order quantity = 500 units
Lead time = one week
Mean absolute deviation = 200 units per order interval
Management has set the tolerable number of stock-outs per year at one

Determine:

a. The number of exposures per year
b. The service rate percentage
c. The reserve, safety stock
d. The order point

8. A local distributor sells an average of 100 CB radios, Model 784DJ, each week. The standard deviation of weekly sales is 20 units. Lead time to obtain replacement stock from the manufacturer is one week.

a. What should the reorder point be if a customer service level of 50% is desired?
b. What should it be if a 98% customer service level is desired?
c. What percentage of time would the distributor be out of stock if the order point is 120 units?
d. What should the order point be if the lead time is four weeks and a service level of 95% is desired?

9. An Atlanta equipment supply distributor stocks pumps, valves, and similar items used in the chemical, pharmaceutical, and similar wet processing industries. The average weekly demand for Pump 19X7 is 20 units with a standard deviation of five units. Pumps are ordered from the main warehouse in Chicago every 25 working days, and the company is interested in achieving a 95% service level on these pumps. If lead time is one week, what should the order point be (based on the traditional statistical approach)? What should the order point be if the lead time is two weeks?

10. The parts department of a large automobile dealership uses a combination periodic review-order point system to manage the inventory of a fuel pump, Model 75A, used on many different models of the automobiles it has sold. The following conditions exist:

(1) A review is made late every second Wednesday and an order for many different parts is placed with the regional warehouse. Parts arrive late Monday.
(2) Four Model 75A pumps are used on the average each day, either for repairs in the shop or for purchases by individuals doing their own work. The parts department is open five days a week. The standard deviation of demand is one unit per day.
(3) Special orders can be placed for individual items with delivery in two days.

(4) The firm's customer service objective is to approach 100%.

a. What should the order quantity be if the stock-on-hand is 20 units on a given Wednesday?

b. What should the order point be for special orders?

**11.** The local grocery supermarket uses a fixed interval inventory management system to determine the number of frozen chickens it orders each week. (The policy is to have a stock-out only once every 20 weeks.) The store places an order every Wednesday morning for delivery at 6 a.m. on Monday. It sells 20 chickens on the average each day of the week except Sunday when the store is closed. The mean absolute deviation of daily sales is three chickens. The poultry department manager determines that there are 85 frozen chickens in the store on a Wednesday immediately before opening at 8 a.m.

a. How many chickens should he order?

b. What if there are 65 frozen chickens and back orders are not allowed?

**12.** The Ace Publishing Company is printing a textbook for a course in production control. It estimates the demand to be 5,000 books per year. The production cost of each book is $13, inventory carrying costs are computed using $k = 0.25$, each order requires a fixed setup cost of $500, and up to 15,000 books may be printed and bound a year. No shortages are allowed; if the publisher is out of stock, another printing will be run immediately. Suppose, however, that the publisher is in error, and the actual demand for the book is 7,500 copies a year. To what extent has this lack of perfect information affected the optimal inventory policy? How much would the publisher be willing to pay to have a perfect estimate of demand?

**13.** The Mendell Chemical Company is experiencing expensive stock-outs with an inexpensive compound it uses in relatively small quantities. The compound is essential to many of its manufacturing processes and the president has asked you to suggest an ordering policy to eliminate stock-outs. You check and discover that records of past usage do not exist. The general manager tells you that they use an average of 100 pounds weekly and at most 135 pounds each week. The only supplier is some 500 miles away. The normal lead time is one week; but on one occasion in the last two years it took two weeks for delivery. What order point would you recommend?

**14.** The Great Eastern Electronics Company carries over 3,000 items in its warehouse for sales to local manufacturers and service organizations. Demand varies greatly for many items, and it is impossible to prevent all stock-outs. The company's objective is to achieve a 98% service level on all *A* items, since these items account for 80% of the company's profit. Given the following data concerning a particular electronic control assembly—an *A* item—what is the average lead time demand? What should the order point be?

| Lead Time | |
|---|---|
| Length (Days) | Probability |
| 5 | .30 |
| 7 | .30 |
| 8 | .30 |
| 9 | .10 |

| Demand Rate | |
|---|---|
| Units/day | Probability |
| 5 | .20 |
| 10 | .30 |
| 15 | .40 |
| 20 | .10 |

# SELECTED READINGS


1. Joseph Orlicky, *Material Requirements Planning* (New York: McGraw-Hill Book Company, 1974), pp. 22–25.
2. John Y. Lu, John D. Toellner, and Norbert Kaufman, "A Practical Method of Calculating Reorder Points for Conditions of Stochastic Demand and Lead Time," *The Journal of Industrial Engineering*, Vol. 13, No. 6 (November-December, 1962).
3. Ali Danish, "A Note on Calculating the Reorder Point in a Stochastic Inventory Problem," *Production and Inventory Management*, Vol. 13, No. 3, Third Quarter (1972).
4. Lester W. Jacobs, "Note on Joint Probability Approach," *Production and Inventory Management*, Vol. 14, No. 4, Fourth Quarter (1973).
5. James A. G. Krupp, "Programmable Calculators: The New Materials Management Tool," *Production and Inventory Management*, Vol. 18, No. 4, Fourth Quarter (1977).
6. James H. Greene, *Production and Inventory Control* (Homewood, Ill.: Richard D. Irwin, Inc., 1974), pp. 300–301.
7. K. J. Arrow, Karlin, and H. Scarf, *Studies in the Mathematical Theory of Inventory and Production* (Stanford, Calif.: Stanford University Press, 1958).
8. Joseph Buchan and Ernest Koenigsberg, *Scientific Inventory Management* (Englewood Cliffs, N. J.: Prentice-Hall, Inc., 1963).
9. S. C. Aggarwal and D. G. Dhavale, "An Empirical Sensitivity Analysis of $(s, S)$ Inventory Policies," *Production and Inventory Management*, Vol. 15, No. 4, Fourth Quarter (1974).
10. Kenneth Joseph Arrow, Samuel Karlin, and Herbert Scarf, *Studies in the Mathematical Theory of Inventory and Production* (Stanford, Calif.: Stanford University Press, 1958).
11. Robert Godell Brown, *Materials Management Systems: A Modular Library* (New York: Ronald Press Co., Div. of John Wiley & Sons, Inc., 1977).
12. Elwood S. Buffa and Jeffrey G. Miller, *Production-Inventory Systems: Planning and Control*, 3rd ed. (Homewood, Ill.: Richard D. Irwin, Inc., 1979).
13. James H. Greene, *Production and Inventory Control Handbook* (New York: McGraw-Hill Book Company, 1970).
14. Rein Peterson and Edward A. Silver, *Decision Systems for Inventory Management and Production Planning* (New York: John Wiley & Sons, Inc., 1979).
15. George W. Plossl and Oliver Wight, *Production and Inventory Control* (Englewood Cliffs, N. J.: Prentice-Hall, Inc., 1967).
16. Richard J. Tersine, "Inventory Risk, The Determination of Safety Stock," *Production and Inventory Management*, Third Quarter (1974).
17. ———, *Materials Management and Inventory Systems*, (New York: Elsevier North-Holland, Inc., 1976).

# —8—

# JOINT REPLENISHMENT

By coordinating the lot sizing decisions for related items and treating them as a family of items, it is possible to obtain economies in ordering and setup costs, manufacturing run costs, and transportation costs. Since some items are manufactured using the same equipment and tooling, one major setup frequently serves the entire group with only minor changes required for each item, Other items are purchased from the same supplier, and some products are destined for the same customer. An order combining such a group constitutes a *joint order* and executing such an order is called *joint replenishment*.

Joint replenishment requires decisions concerning:

1. The aggregate size of the order (group lot size)
2. The lot size of each item
3. The order intervals for individual items within a group
4. The timing of order releases

These decisions are used in the management of:

1. Purchased items
2. Production parts manufactured on (a) Equipment dedicated to one group and (b) Equipment used in the production of two or more groups

This chapter first examines group lot size decisions with constant demand and each item ordered every cycle. A discussion of different order intervals for items within a group precedes an explanation of using equal-run-out lot quantities to cope with variations in demand. Models are provided to determine appropriate order quantities for jointly considered items. The second part of the chapter covers the establishment of order release points for joint orders and the evaluation of quantity discounts.

## JOINT PURCHASE ORDER LOT SIZE

The economic order quantity model for groups is derived in the same manner as the economic order quantity for individual items. The equation defining the total costs related to the lot size decision is established; its first derivative with respect to $Q$, the lot size, is found; the first derivative is set equal to zero and solved for $Q^*$, the minimum cost lot size.

The assumptions of the basic (deterministic demand, instantaneous replenishment) EOQ model apply; namely:

1. The demand rate for each item is constant and known with certainty. Thus, there are no stock-outs and no stock-out costs.
2. Replenishment occurs after a fixed, known lead time each cycle; this time is common to all items; all ordered items arrive at one point in time each cycle.
3. The carrying cost rate, individual item costs, and preparation costs are deterministic; they do not vary in a probabilistic manner.
4. Costs are constant. There are no discontinuities in the cost of units (such as quantity discounts), setup costs, and the carrying cost rate.

Figure 8-1 graphically depicts inventory over time in this situation. Under these conditions, the total cost of an aggregate lot size decision is equal to the sum of preparation costs and carrying costs during the period.

**FIGURE 8-1**
**STOCK ON HAND VERSUS TIME**
**(AGGREGATE PURCHASED LOTS)**

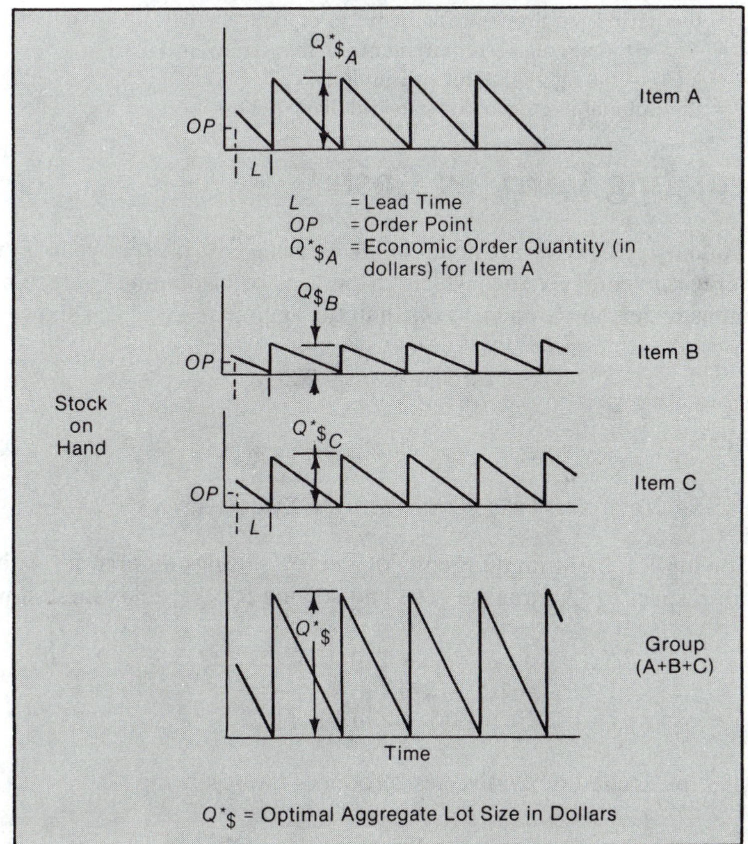

## Calculating Preparation Costs

Total preparation costs equal the number of preparations in the period times the cost of preparation. The latter equals the major cost of processing an order plus the sum of the costs associated with the addition of each item to the order. The number of orders per period equals the aggregate of all item requirements divided by the aggregate lot size. Both aggregate values must be calculated in monetary units for dimensional consistency as shown in the following:

$$\text{Total preparation costs} = (S + \Sigma s_i)A \div \Sigma Q_{\$_i}$$

Where:

$S$ = the preparation costs independent of the number of items (sometimes called major setup costs or header costs)
$s_i$ = the incremental preparation costs incurred by the inclusion of a specific item (These are the clerical, receiving, and expediting costs associated with Item $i$; sometimes called minor setup costs.)
$a_i$ = the period requirement for Item $i$ in dollars
$A = \Sigma a_i$ = the aggregate requirement for the period in dollars
$Q_\$ = \Sigma Q_{\$_i}$ = the aggregate lot size in dollars
$Q_\$^*$ = the optimal aggregate lot size in dollars

## Calculating Carrying Costs

Total carrying costs are equal to the carrying cost rate per year ($k$) times the average inventory value, which in the case of instantaneous receipt and deterministic demand is equal to one half the aggregate lot size as shown next.

$$\text{Total carrying costs} = k(\Sigma Q_{\$_i}) \div 2$$

Therefore:

$$\text{Total costs (TC)} = (S + \Sigma s_i)A \div \Sigma Q_{\$_i} + k(\Sigma Q_{\$_i}) \div 2$$

Solving for the minimum cost lot size by setting the first derivative of TC with respect to $Q_\$$ equal to zero and solving for $Q_\$^*$ yields the following:

$$\text{TC}'\,(Q_\$) = -\,(S + \Sigma s_i)\,A \div (\Sigma Q_\$^*)^2 + k \div 2 = 0$$
$$(\Sigma Q_\$^*)^2 = 2(S + \Sigma s_i)A \div k$$
$$Q_\$^* = \Sigma Q_{\$_i}^* = [2(S + \Sigma s_i)A \div k]^{1/2}$$

Applying the second derivative test produces the following:

$$\text{TC}''(Q^*) = 2(S + \Sigma s_i)A \div (Q_\$^*)^{-3}$$

Since $S$, $\Sigma s_i$, $A$ and $Q^*_\$$ are positive under all conditions, $TC''(Q^*)$ is positive. Thus, TC is a minimum at $Q^*_\$$.

The minimum cost lot size of each item is determined by multiplying the minimum cost aggregate lot size by the ratio of the item's period requirements to aggregate period requirements. Thus, $Q^*_{\$i} = (a_i \div A)Q^*_\$$.

The individual lot size quantity equals the dollar value of the lot size divided by the cost of the item. Thus, we have the following equation:

$$Q^*_i = Q_{\$i}{}^* \div C_i$$

Where: $Q^*_i$ = the minimum cost lot size of Item $i$ in units
$C_i$ = the unit cost of Item $i$

The data in Table 8-1, for example, concern a group of items purchased from a single source.

**TABLE 8-1**
**DATA, AGGREGATE LOT SIZE**
**(DETERMINISTIC DEMAND, INSTANTANEOUS RECEIPT EXAMPLE)**

| Item | Annual Demand | Unit Cost | Annual Dollar Requirements ($a_i$) | Item Preparation Costs ($s_i$) | $a_i \div A$ |
|---|---|---|---|---|---|
| 1 | 1,000 | $ 5.00 | $ 5,000 | $ 5 | .0567 |
| 2 | 2,500 | 6.00 | 15,000 | 10 | .1701 |
| 3 | 800 | 3.50 | 2,800 | 15 | .0317 |
| 4 | 3,200 | 12.00 | 38,400 | 10 | .4354 |
| 5 | 1,800 | 15.00 | 27,000 | 10 | .3061 |
| | | | 88,200 | 50 | 1.000 |

$$k = .30 \text{ and } S = \$70$$

$$Q^*_\$ = \left[\frac{2(70 + 50)\,88{,}200}{.3}\right]^{1/2}$$
$$= (2 \times 120 \times 88{,}200 \div .3)^{1/2} = (21{,}168,\ 000 \div .3)^{1/2}$$
$$= (70{,}560{,}000)^{1/2} = (7{,}056 \times 10^4)^{1/2}$$
$$= \$8{,}400$$

$$Q^*_{\$i} = (a_i \div A)Q^*_\$, \text{ and}$$
$$Q^*_i = Q_{\$i}{}^* \div C_i$$
$$Q^*_{\$1} = .0567 \times \$8{,}400 = \$476.28$$
$$Q^*_{\$2} = .1701 \times \$8{,}400 = \$1{,}428.84$$
$$Q^*_{\$3} = .0317 \times \$8{,}400 = \$266.28$$
$$Q^*_{\$4} = .4354 \times \$8{,}400 = \$3{,}657.36$$
$$Q^*_{\$5} = .3061 \times \$8{,}400 = \$2{,}571.24$$
$$Q^*_1 = \$476.28 \div \$5.00 = 95.26$$
$$Q^*_2 = \$1{,}428.84 \div \$6.00 = 238.14$$
$$Q^*_3 = \$266.28 \div \$3.50 = 76.08$$
$$Q^*_4 = \$3{,}657.36 \div \$12.00 = 304.78$$
$$Q^*_5 = \$2{,}571.24 \div \$15.00 = 171.41$$

Practical aspects must be considered when implementing these results. First, an integer number of units must be ordered. Second, order size is usually rounded to a multiple of 5 or 10; and third, container and package size can affect the order size. Thus, the order sizes for Items 1 through 5 might be 100, 240, 80, 300 and 175 respectively.

Purchasing an optimum aggregate order of items under deterministic conditions results in the order being placed at a constant interval throughout the year. This enables us to approach the same problem in terms of the optimum order interval.

## Optimum Order Interval

The number of orders per year ($N$) equals the aggregate annual demand for the family of items divided by the aggregate lot size. (Thus, $N = A \div Q^*_\$$.)

The interval between orders ($T$) can be expressed as a proportion of the period—a year in most cases—by dividing the period length in years by the number of orders. Thus, $T^* = 1 \div N = 1 \div (A \div Q^*_\$) = Q^*_\$ \div A$.

Practical considerations must be recognized when using this approach to establish the interval between reviews in a periodic review type system. In the preceding example the optimum interval ($T^*$) is .095 years, approximately five weeks. This is a feasible solution. However, the optimum interval could have been .025 years which is equivalent to approximately 6.25 working days. In such a case an interval of either one or two weeks usually would be the practical solution.

## Noninstantaneous Receipt

Selected lots of items produced internally also can be grouped to obtain the economic benefits of joint replenishment. For example, a group of items produced on a screw machine may share a major setup (relatively minor adjustments required for individual items once the major setup is made). In the hot rolling of steel shapes (e.g., angle iron), changing the large mill rolls for a family of sizes is a very major setup. Yet switching from one size to another requires only minor adjustments of guides to direct the steel to the proper grooves in the rolls. Textiles or paper products may be identical except for color. A major setup is made for the entire group with, again, relatively minor changes required as the colors of the final product are changed progressively from light to dark.

Producing an aggregate lot of a group of items internally results in inventory being increased gradually rather than in one large lot at a point in time. Each lot enters inventory gradually as it is completed; in fact, the value of inventory increases hourly as labor is expended during the production period. Figure 8-2 illustrates this relationship.

Average inventory in the case of noninstantaneous receipt of an aggregate order equals $\Sigma Q_{\$_i}\ (1 - \Sigma D_{\$_i} \div \Sigma P_{\$_i}) \div 2$

Where:

$D_{\$_i}$ = the demand rate of individual Product $i$ in dollars
$P_{\$_i}$ = the production rate of Product $i$ in dollars

The minimum cost aggregate lot size model in the case of noninstantaneous receipt is determined in the typical manner. The first derivative of the Total Period Cost Model is set equal to zero and solved for $Q^*_\$$ as follows:

**FIGURE 8-2**
**AGGREGATE PRODUCTION LOT SIZE**
**EXAMPLE DATA AND GRAPHS**
**(STOCK ON HAND VERSUS TIME)**

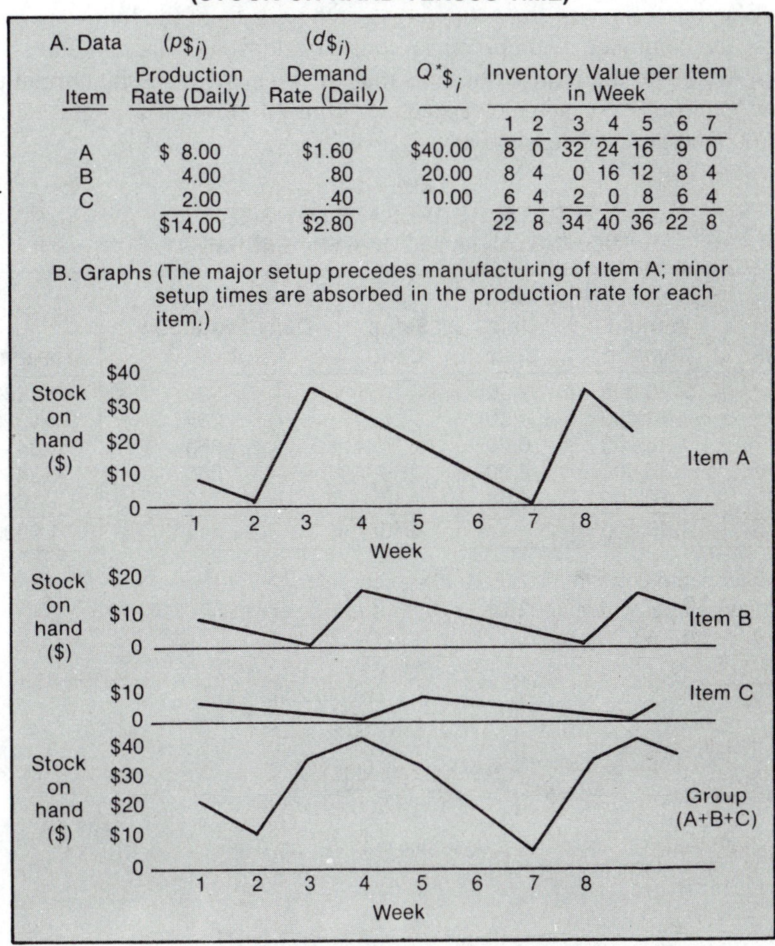

A. Data

| Item | ($p\$_i$) Production Rate (Daily) | ($d\$_i$) Demand Rate (Daily) | $Q^*\$_i$ | Inventory Value per Item in Week 1 | 2 | 3 | 4 | 5 | 6 | 7 |
|---|---|---|---|---|---|---|---|---|---|---|
| A | $ 8.00 | $1.60 | $40.00 | 8 | 0 | 32 | 24 | 16 | 9 | 0 |
| B | 4.00 | .80 | 20.00 | 8 | 4 | 0 | 16 | 12 | 8 | 4 |
| C | 2.00 | .40 | 10.00 | 6 | 4 | 2 | 0 | 8 | 6 | 4 |
| | $14.00 | $2.80 | | 22 | 8 | 34 | 40 | 36 | 22 | 8 |

B. Graphs (The major setup precedes manufacturing of Item A; minor setup times are absorbed in the production rate for each item.)

$$\text{TC}' = \frac{(S + \Sigma s_i)A}{Q_\$} + k(\Sigma Q_\$)(1 - \Sigma D_{\$_i} \div \Sigma P_{\$_i}) \div 2$$

$$\text{TC}' = 0 = -\frac{(S + \Sigma s_i)A}{(\Sigma Q_\$^*)^2} + (k \div 2)(1 - \Sigma D_{\$_i} \div \Sigma P_{\$_i})$$

$$Q_\$^* = \left[\frac{2(S + \Sigma s_i)A}{k(1 - \Sigma D_{\$_i} \div \Sigma P_{\$_i})}\right]^{1/2}$$

$$Q_{\$_i}^* = (a_i \div A)\Sigma Q_\$^*$$
$$Q_i^* = Q_{\$_i}^* \div C_i$$

Table 8-2, for example, contains data regarding a group of items manufactured on the same equipment with one major setup for the group and a minor setup for each item. Production and demand rates in dollars have been calculated by multiplying the unit cost of each item by its production and demand rates in units.

When determining the actual lot size, the results of the following calculations are combined with practical considerations such as container size, process yield and the number of units that can be made from the normal unit of raw material. The actual lot sizes for Items 1 through 5 might be 900, 320, 700, 400 and 400 respectively.

**TABLE 8-2**
**DATA, AGGREGATE LOT SIZE, NONINSTANTANEOUS REPLENISHMENT**

| ($i$) Item | ($a_i$) Annual Demand | $C_i$ Unit Cost | $s_i$ Setup Cost | ($P_{\$_i}$) Daily Production Rate | ($a_i \div A$) |
|---|---|---|---|---|---|
| 1 | $ 20,500 | $2.00 | $10 | $ 500 | .1460 |
| 2 | 14,400 | 4.00 | 6 | 264 | .1026 |
| 3 | 48,000 | 6.00 | 4 | 860 | .3419 |
| 4 | 35,000 | 7.00 | 8 | 560 | .2493 |
| 5 | 22,500 | 4.50 | 12 | 360 | .1602 |
| | $140,400 | | $40 | $2,544 | 1.0000 |

Major setup costs, $S$ = $80; Holding cost rate, $k$ = .3
Daily aggregate demand rate, $\Sigma D_{\$_i} = A$/days per year = $140,400 ÷ 250 = $561.60

$$Q_{\$_i}^* = \left[\frac{2(\$80 + 40)\,140{,}400}{.3(1 - \$561.60 \div \$2{,}544}\right]^{1/2}$$

$$= \left[\frac{2(\$120)(140{,}400)}{.3(1 - .22)}\right]^{1/2}$$

$$= \left(\frac{33{,}696{,}000}{.234}\right)^{1/2}$$

$$= \$12{,}000$$

$$Q^*_{\$1} = .1460 \times \$12{,}000 = \$1{,}752.00$$
$$Q^*_{\$2} = .1026 \times \$12{,}000 = \$1{,}231.20$$
$$Q^*_{\$3} = .3419 \times \$12{,}000 = \$4{,}102.80$$
$$Q^*_{\$4} = .2493 \times \$12{,}000 = \$2{,}991.60$$
$$Q^*_{\$5} = .1602 \times \$12{,}000 = \$1{,}922.40$$
$$Q^*_1 = \$1{,}752 \div \$2.00 = \$876.00$$
$$Q^*_2 = \$1{,}231.20 \div \$4.00 = 307.80$$
$$Q^*_3 = \$4{,}102.80 \div \$6.00 = 683.80$$
$$Q^*_4 = \$2{,}991.60 \div \$7.00 = 427.40$$
$$Q^*_5 = \$1{,}922.40 \div \$4.50 = 427.20$$

## Varying Item Cycles

Frequently it is not economical to order each item every cycle. Aggregate preparation costs equal aggregate carrying costs for the minimum cost aggregate lot size. Although individual item carrying costs and preparation costs approach equality at the minimum cost aggregate lot size, they usually are not equal. Items with relatively large annual dollar demand have a greater influence on the aggregate lot size, especially when minor preparation costs are equal. Items that have a relatively low ratio of annual dollar demand to minor preparation cost ($a_i/s_i$) are likely candidates for ordering less frequently. Any marked lack of balance suggests that multiple cycles be investigated. Using the previous example data in Table 8-1 allows us to calculate in Table 8-3 the ratios of preparation costs to carrying costs per cycle for each item.

**TABLE 8-3**
**DATA, AGGREGATE LOT SIZE, MULTIPLE INTERVALS**

| (1) | (2) | (3) | (4) | (5) | (6) | (7) | (8) |
|---|---|---|---|---|---|---|---|
| Item | Carrying Cost | Minor Preparation Costs ($s_i$) | (3)/(2) | $a_i/A$ | $S(a_i/A)$ | (3) + (6)* | (7)/(2) |
| 1 | $ 6.80 | $ 5 | .74 | .0567 | $ 3.97 | $ 8.97 | 1.32 |
| 2 | 20.00 | 10 | .50 | .1701 | 11.91 | 21.91 | 1.10 |
| 3 | 3.81 | 15 | 3.95 | .0137 | 2.22 | 17.22 | 4.52 |
| 4 | 52.00 | 10 | .19 | .4354 | 30.47 | 40.47 | .78 |
| 5 | 36.83 | 10 | .27 | .3061 | 21.43 | 31.43 | .85 |
| | $119.44 | $50 | .42 | 1.0000 | $70.00 | $120.00 | 1.00 |

*Allocated total preparation costs

Using the carrying cost results obtained when assuming that all items are ordered each cycle gives the ratio of minor preparation costs to carrying costs listed in Column 4 and the ratio of allocated total preparation costs to carrying costs listed in Column 8. The following calculations for Item 1 illustrate how the carrying costs per period are obtained.

Carrying cost per period equals lot size times period length times annual carrying rate divided by two

$$K = Q_{\$_1} T \frac{k}{2}$$

$$= \$476.28 \times .0952 \times \frac{.3}{2} = \$6.80$$

Carrying costs and setup costs approach a balance for all items except Item 3. The data in both Columns 4 and 8 reveal that setup costs far exceed carrying costs for Item 3; the ratios are 3.94 and 4.52. Thus, an investigation of the use of multiple intervals is in order. R. G. Brown and E. A. Silver have recommended different methods of determining the interval multiples ($n_i$) for each item. [1, 2] We will examine each.

**Brown's Approach.** Let us first look at Robert Brown's technique which has a number of steps to obtain a solution:

1. Compute an initial estimate of the order interval ($T$) assuming that all items are ordered each cycle using the model developed earlier; i.e., $T = [2(S + \Sigma s_i) \div (kA)]^{1/2}$.
2. Determine $n_i$'s using the model:

$$n_i = \frac{1}{T}\left[\frac{2s_i}{ka_i}\right]^{1/2}$$

Since $n_i$ is rarely an integer, use Table 8-4 to round off $n_i$'s. If all $n_i$'s equal 1, the solution was obtained in Step 1; if not proceed to Step 3.

**TABLE 8-4**[1]
**ROUND-OFF RULES; MULTIPLE INTERVALS**

| Range of Calculated Multiple $n$* | Use an $n$ of |
|---|---|
| 0 to 1.414 | 1 |
| 1.414 to 2.449 | 2 |
| 2.449 to 3.464 | 3 |
| 3.464 to 4.472 | 4 |
| 4.472 to 5.477 | 5 |
| 5.477 to 6.480 | 6 |
| 6.480 to 7.483 | 7 |

*For calculated values of $n$ greater than 6 use the integer part of ($n$ + .52). For example, if calculated $n$ = 8.9, $n$ + .52 = 9.42. An $n$ of 9 should be used.

3. Determine a new value of $T$ using the following model that incorporates the possibility of different order intervals.

$$T = [2(S + \Sigma s_i \div n_i) \div (k\Sigma n_i a_i)]^{1/2}$$

[1] Robert G. Brown, *Decision Rules for Inventory Management* (New York: Holt, Rinehart & Winston, 1967), p. 49.

4. Return to Step 2 and calculate the new $n_i$'s. If none of the interval multiples, $n_i$'s, change, Step 3 has provided the solution. If one or more of the $n_i$'s has changed, repeat Step 3 with the revised $n_i$'s and continue the process until none of the $n_i$'s change. This process converges rapidly, frequently on the first interation. Let us next see how this would work out using the previous example data in Table 8-1, $T = \frac{1}{10.47}$:

$$n_1 = 10.47[2 \times 5 \div (.3 \times 5{,}000)]^{1/2}$$
$$n_2 = .85 \rightarrow 1 \text{ (referring to Table 4)}$$

Calculating $n_2$ through $n_5$ in the same manner gives:

$$n_2 = .698 \rightarrow 1 \qquad n_4 = .43 \rightarrow 1$$
$$n_3 = 1.97 \rightarrow 2 \qquad n_5 = .52 \rightarrow 1$$

Calculating the new $T$ produces the following:

$$T = \left[\frac{2\left(S + \sum\left(\frac{s_i}{n_i}\right)\right)}{k\sum n_i a_i}\right]^{1/2}$$

$$= \left[\frac{2\left(70 + \frac{5}{1} + \frac{10}{1} + \frac{15}{2} + \frac{10}{1} + \frac{10}{1}\right)}{.3(5{,}000 + 15{,}000 + 2 \times 2{,}800 + 38{,}400 + 27{,}000)}\right]^{1/2}$$

$$= \left[\frac{2(112.5)}{.3(91{,}000)}\right]^{1/2} = .091$$

Calculating the new $n_i$'s gives:

$$n_i = \frac{1}{T}\left(\frac{2s_i}{ka_i}\right)^{1/2} = \frac{1}{.091}\left(\frac{2 \times 5}{.3 \times 5{,}000}\right)^{1/2}$$

$$= 10.99 \times .082 = .9, \text{ i.e., } 1$$

Calculating $n_2$ through $n_5$ in the same manner gives the following:

$$n_2 = .72 \rightarrow 1$$
$$n_3 = 2.07 \rightarrow 2$$
$$n_4 = .44 \rightarrow 1$$
$$n_5 = .55 \rightarrow 1$$

Since none of the $n_i$'s have changed, we have a solution:

$$T = .091;\ n_1,\ n_2,\ n_4, \text{ and } n_5 = 1; \text{ and } n_3 = 2$$

**Silver's Approach.** As opposed to R. G. Brown, Edward Silver employs the following procedure to determine interval multiples for individual items:

1. **Determine the item that has the smallest ratio of minor setup costs to annual dollar demand ($s_i/a_i$), and set its cycle interval equal to one.**
2. **Determine the interval multiple ($n_i$) for each item by rounding the value obtained from the following model to the nearest integer greater than zero. Use the ensuing formula for $n_i$:**

$$n_i = \left(\frac{s_i}{a_i} \cdot \frac{a_j}{S + s_j}\right)^{1/2}$$

Where:

$$j = \text{that item with the lowest } \frac{s_i}{a_i} \text{ ratio}$$

Let us exemplify this, again using data from Table 8-1.

| *Item* | $\frac{s_i}{a_i}$ | $\frac{s_i}{a_i} \cdot \frac{a_j}{S + s_j}$ | $n_i$ |
|---|---|---|---|
| 1 | .00100 | .480 | .69 → 1 |
| 2 | .00067 | .319 | .57 → 1 |
| 3 | .00536 | 2.571 | 1.60 → 2 |
| 4 | .00026* | .124 | .35 → 1 |
| 5 | .00037 | .178 | .42 → 1 |

*Item 4 has the lowest $s_i \div a_i$ ratio; thus $a_j \div (S + s_j) = 480$ [38,400 ÷ (70 + 10)].

These are the same results obtained with Brown's approach. This is not always the case. Silver's method is not iterative and thus slightly less tedious to determine manually; neither approach guarantees the optimum. See Silver's article for further discussion. [2]

# UNCERTAINTY: LOT SIZES AND ORDER RELEASE

In a deterministic situation with known constant demand all items in a purchased group reach their order points simultaneously as illustrated in Figure 8-1. Thus, an order for the optimum item lot sizes (which constitute the optimum aggregate lot size) is placed when the items reach their order point. Items in a production group with deterministic demand reach their order points sequentially in an order corresponding to their production sequence. An order is placed whenever the item produced first reaches its order point. In a situation with known constant demand, the item produced first always will reach its order point prior to other items. This was illustrated by Figure 8-2.

However, independent item demand rates are rarely deterministic; they vary daily; and sporadic surges in demand occur for particular items. Although dependent demand item requirements are calculable, they can change abruptly due to late orders, scrap, order cancellations, etc. Provisions for handling the reality of uncertainty must be incorporated in lot size and order release models and decisions. We will examine the impact of varying demand on lot sizes first.

## Equal-Run-Out Lot Size

Figure 8-3 illustrates the case of one item in a purchased group reaching its order point prior to the other items. The objective in this case is to bring the item stocks back into balance, to attain an equal time supply, days of stock, for each item. It is accomplished by ordering each item's EOQ adjusted by the difference between its expected order point and its

**FIGURE 8-3**
**STOCK ON HAND VERSUS TIME**
**VARYING DEMAND**

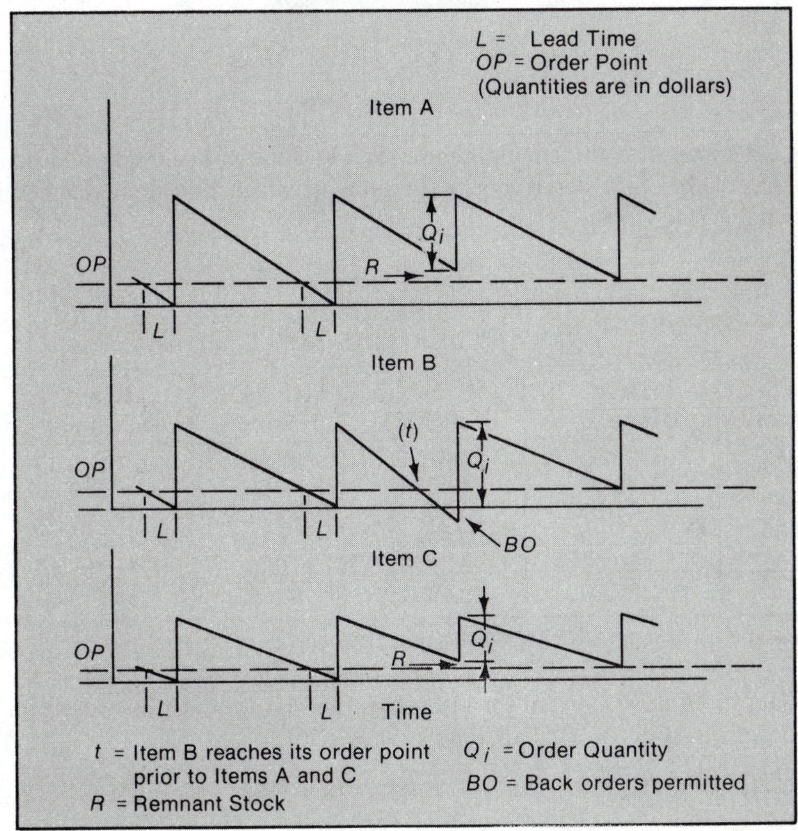

available stock when the order is placed. The resulting modified lot size frequently is called the *equal-run-out quantity*. The following model accomplishes this adjustment.

$$Q_{\$i} = (a_i \div A)(Q^*_\$ + \Sigma I_{\$i}) - I_{\$i}, \text{ or}$$
$$Q_{\$i} = (d_i \div D)(Q^*_\$ + \Sigma I_{\$i}) - I_{\$i}$$

Where:

$Q^*_{\$i}$, $A$, $a_i$ are as defined earlier
$I_{\$i}$ = dollar inventory of Item $i$ when order is triggered
$d_i$ = daily usage, demand, rate of Item $i$
$D = \Sigma d_i$

Since $D = A \div 250$ (working days per year), and

$$d_i = \frac{a_i}{250}$$

Then,

$$\frac{d_i}{D} = \frac{a_i}{A}$$

Let's return to the example described in Table 8-1 and add additional data (see Table 8-5) describing a situation in which one item reaches its order point prior to the rest of the group.

**TABLE 8-5**
**DATA, PURCHASED GROUP**
**VARYING DEMAND EXAMPLE**

| Item | Daily Usage ($d_i$) | EOQ | Order* Point | Quantity on Hand ($I_{\$i}$) |
|---|---|---|---|---|
| 1 | $ 20.00 | $ 476.28 | $ 200 | $ 240.00 |
| 2 | 60.00 | 1,428.84 | 600 | 660.00 |
| 3 | 11.20 | 266.28 | 112 | 168.00 |
| 4 | 153.60 | 3,657.36 | 1,536 | 1,536.00 |
| 5 | 108.00 | 2,571.24 | 1,080 | 1,108.80 |
| | $352.80 | $8,400.00 | $3,528 | $3,712.80 |

*Two weeks, ten working days, is the lead time.

The data in Table 8-5 reveal that Item 4 is the first to reach its order point. The order quantities are calculated as follows:

$$Q_{\$1} = \$20 \div 352.80(8{,}400 + 3{,}712.80) - 240$$
$$Q_{\$1} = \$446.66 \qquad Q_1 = \$446.66 \div \$5 = 89.33$$

The days of stock provided by the inventory on hand plus the order quantity is calculated as follows:

$$t_i = (I_i + Q_{\$_i}) \div d_i$$

Where:

$t_i$ = time period in days covered by the sum of the order quantity plus the inventory on hand of Item $i$

Thus,

$$t_i = (\$446.66 + 240) \div 20 = 34.33 \text{ days}$$

Calculating these values for the other items gives the results in Table 8-6.

**TABLE 8-6**
**EQUAL-RUN-OUT TIME, BALANCED, LOT SIZES**

| (1) | (2) | (3) | (4) | (5) | |
|---|---|---|---|---|---|
| Item | Order Quantity | Daily Usage | Inventory on Hand | (2) + (4) | Days Supply (5)/(3) |
| 1 | $ 446.66 | $ 20.00 | $ 240 | $ 686.66 | 34.33 |
| 2 | 1,400.00 | 60.00 | 660 | 2,060.66 | 34.33 |
| 3 | 216.53 | 11.20 | 168 | 384.53 | 34.33 |
| 4 | 3,737.91 | 153.60 | 1,536 | 5,273.91 | 34.33 |
| 5 | 2,598.92 | 108.00 | 1,108 | 3,707.92 | 34.33 |
| | $8,400.02 | $352.80 | $3,712 | $12,113.02 | 34.33 |

Table 8-6 reveals that the aggregate order quantity is still $8,400 as in the basic case, but item order quantities have been adjusted to provide the same time supply for all items.

## Remnant Stocks and Added Costs

Varying rates of demand and placement of a group order when only one item reaches its order point result in increased costs and *remnant stock,* inventory in excess of an order point when an order is placed as illustrated in Figure 8-3.

Since an order is placed prior to the expiration of the normal order interval ($T$) more orders are placed each year. The stock on hand when the replenishment order arrives equals the remnant stock if expected lead time demand occurs. The increase in cost per year can only be estimated since both the value of the remnant stock and the decrease in the interval length vary. Estimated increased annual carrying costs equal the estimated average remnant stock times the carrying cost rate; and the estimated increased preparation costs equal the cost of a preparation times the estimated increased number of preparations per year. The estimated average remnant stock equals the estimated average inventory on hand when an order is placed minus aggregate demand during lead time, the aggregate order point. The calculation of these estimated costs can be illustrated by using the data in Table 8-6 as the average case in the example given next.

Records of the past two years reveal that:

1. The data in Table 8-5 represent the average position of inventory on hand when an order is placed.
2. Approximately one additional order is placed each year.

Estimated average remnant stock = \$3,712 minus \$3,528 (i.e., \$184).
Increased carrying costs = .3 times \$184 (i.e., \$55.20).
Increased ordering costs = 1 times \$120 (i.e., \$120).
Total increase in costs = \$55.20 plus \$120 (i.e., \$175.20).

The estimated percentage increase in costs equals:

$$= \frac{\text{Estimated Total Annual Increase in Costs}}{\text{Minimum Total Annual Costs} \times 100}$$
$$= \$175.20 \div [(.3 \times \$8{,}400 \div 2 + \$120 \times 10.5) \times 100]$$
$$= \$175.20 \div (\$2{,}520 \times 100) = 6.9 \text{ percent}$$

This calculation provides a rough estimate of the added costs of the increased customer service protection provided by ordering equal-run-out quantities as soon as one item reaches its order point rather than waiting until the aggregate order point is reached.

# ORDER RELEASE

A time-phased order point system, a traditional (statistical) order point system, or a periodic review system can be used to trigger the release of joint orders. An MRP system with time-phased order release is the best system for managing dependent demand items. A periodic review system or a continuous review system incorporating either time-phased ordering logic or a traditional order point approach is appropriate for making order release decisions concerning independent demand items. Situational charactistics influencing the selection of individual item inventory management systems were examined in Chapter 7; the same criteria apply to the release of joint orders. General explicit decision rules have not been developed for releasing joint orders to attain an optimum balance between inventory cost and customer service objectives; but feasible approaches do exist for making rational joint order release decisions in specific situations. An examination of these approaches follows a discussion of the role of safety stock in joint ordering decisions.

## Safety Stock and Joint Orders

Safety stock is used to achieve customer service objectives in the management of individual items with probabilistic demand or supply. Joint ordering, in general, reduces safety stock requirements as an order is typically placed before all items, except one, reach their individual order points. Providing safety stocks for all items in a group can result in excessive carrying costs. Each time an order is received, both remnant stock and safety stock likely will exist for all items, save the item that triggered the order. Conversely, the costs of stock-outs can be expensive. This dilemma can be resolved by applying the ABC Principle, i.e., control the vital few. Application of the ABC Principle in this case requires that safety stock be provided only for those items that meet criteria such as the following:

1. A stock-out is expensive.
2. Carrying costs are relatively low.
3. Surges in demand have a relatively high probability.

The criteria used for determining if safety stock should exist for an item depend on the situation. For example, if back ordering is possible and not expensive, there is little need for safety stock. Dependent demand items managed by a time-phased order point frequently do not require safety stock. This is especially true if they are fabricated from materials and parts for which safety stocks do exist.

## Continuous Review (Order Point) System

In a basic continuous review $(s, Q)$ system a fixed order quantity $(Q)$ is ordered whenever the stock on hand reaches the order point $(s)$. In a variation of this system the quantity ordered equals the difference between an order-up-to-level $(S)$ and the stock on hand $(s)$. This is known as the order point, order-up-to-level $(s, S)$ system. If the stock on hand of an item managed by an $s, S$ system is less than the order point, the quantity ordered is greater than it would be under an $s, Q$ system.

## The $S, c, s$ System

Silver has suggested that an $S, c, s$ system be used for managing coordinated items in a continuous review, coordinated replenishment system. [3] An $S, c, s$ system incorporates an order-up-to-level (S), a can order level (c), and a must order level (s) for each item. A joint order is placed whenever the inventory of any item descends to $s$. Orders are placed for each item whose stock is at or below its $c$ or $s$ to raise its inventory level to $S$. The rationale is that when a joint order is triggered by one item reaching its order point, individual decisions to order (or not to order) the other items can reduce total inventory related costs. An item should be included in the group order only if its inventory is below a predetermined level.

The $S,c,s$ system reduces ordering costs by eliminating the minor ordering costs associated with items not ordered and it reduces inventory carrying costs by reducing remnant stocks. However, total inventory costs may increase if the average interval between joint orders decreases substantially due to items that were not ordered triggering a new order in less than the normal interval.

Implementation of an $S,c,s$ system requires extensive prior study. For example, an item that has not reached its can order level may be experiencing a postponed demand. In such a case demand in the immediate future would be greater than normal and an $S,c,s$ system would be very inappropriate. It is appropriate when minor setup costs are substantial, carrying costs are high, and recent demand is a good predictor of the short-term future demand.

## Periodic Review Systems

In a basic periodic review system each item is ordered in a quantity that, when added to the stock on hand, will equal the safety stock plus the demand during lead time and the demand during the replenishment period (see Chapter 7). Using a periodic review system to manage joint replenishment has inherent problems. A periodic review system requires a larger safety stock than a continuous review system, given the same variations in demand (forecast error), because safety stock must cover variations in demand during the replenishment period as well as during lead time. Accumulation of safety stock across a large number of items ordered jointly can be substantial. IBM's Wholesale IMPACT System includes a service point method of determining whether a joint order should be placed or postponed for a period.[2] The decision is based on a comparison of the expected shortage (if no order is placed) with the allowed average shortage.

## Time-Phased Order Point (TPOP) System

Managing a group of items by a TPOP system can provide a straightforward estimate of the benefits and costs of omitting any item from a group order. A prerequisite of a TPOP system is known requirements, i.e., calculated dependent demand requirements and independent demand requirements consisting of either received or forecast order quantities. In deciding

[2]See IBM, *Wholesale IMPACT—Advanced Principles and Implementation Reference Manual E20-0174-1* (White Plains, N.Y.: 1971) for the development and further discussion.

whether to include any item in the group order, one of three situations can exist as illustrated in Table 8-7:

1. When requirements greater than the quantity in stock do not occur until after a group order is—or likely will be—triggered. Thus, a shortened order interval is not anticipated.
2. When requirement greater than the quantity in stock does occur before the normal order interval, but after an order is triggered by a requirement for another item in the group.
3. When a requirement greater than the quantity in stock does occur before the normal order interval and before an order is triggered by a requirement for any other item in the group.

The savings that are gained by omitting an item when ordering a group are (1) $s_i$—the minor ordering costs associated with the item and (2) $Q_iKt$—the cost of carrying the item order quantity until the next order is placed.

**TABLE 8-7**
**TIME-PHASED ORDER POINT SYSTEM**
**NORMAL INTERVAL BETWEEN ORDERS, T = 5 WEEKS**
**(GROUP CONSISTS OF ITEMS A, B AND C)**

| Ordering Costs | Item Costs | Minimum Lot Sizes |
|---|---|---|
| $S$ = $80<br>$S_A$ = 30<br>$S_B$ = 20<br>$S_C$ = 20 | A = $ 70<br>B = 100<br>C = 60<br>$k$ = .3 | A—50 units<br>B—50 units<br>C—50 units |

**Case 1**

| Period | Items | Past Due | 1 | 2 | 3 | 4 | 5 | 6 | 7 |
|---|---|---|---|---|---|---|---|---|---|
| Planned | A | 0 | 65 | 0 | 0 | 0 | 0 | 0 | 0 |
| Order | B | 0 | 50 | 0 | 0 | 0 | 0 | 50 | 0 |
| Releases | C | 0 | 0 | 0 | 0 | 0 | 0 | 0 | 60 |

**Case 2**

| Period | Items | Past Due | 1 | 2 | 3 | 4 | 5 | 6 | 7 |
|---|---|---|---|---|---|---|---|---|---|
| Planned | A | 0 | 65 | 0 | 0 | 0 | 0 | 50 | 0 |
| Order | B | 0 | 50 | 0 | 50 | 0 | 0 | 0 | 0 |
| Releases | C | 0 | 0 | 0 | 0 | 60 | 0 | 0 | 0 |

**Case 3**

| Period | Items | Past Due | 1 | 2 | 3 | 4 | 5 | 6 | 7 |
|---|---|---|---|---|---|---|---|---|---|
| Planned | A | 0 | 65 | 0 | 0 | 0 | 0 | 50 | 0 |
| Order | B | 0 | 50 | 0 | 0 | 0 | 0 | 50 | 0 |
| Releases | C | 0 | 0 | 0 | 0 | 50 | 0 | 0 | 0 |

Omitting an item results in added costs only if the next group order is placed sooner as a result (the order interval is reduced). This situation is analyzed by determining the least cost option available. The analysis of the data in Table 8-7 illustrates this approach.

Returning to the three situations just mentioned, the following analyses can be made.

*Situation 1*—An order for the item that may be omitted is not planned until after the normal order interval has passed. Case 1 in Table 8-7 illustrates this situation. An order is not planned for Item C for seven weeks; the normal order interval is five weeks. Omitting Item C from the group order in Period 1 will result in no additional costs, only savings. This typifies this situation; Item C should be omitted from the order.

The preceding analysis assumes requirements are known with certainty. Probabilistic requirements can be handled by standard decision making under risk approaches.

*Situation 2*—An order for the item that may be omitted is not planned until after an order is triggered for another item in the group. This analysis is similar to Case 1. There are no added costs; omit Item C from the first order. This situation is illustrated in Case 2 of Table 8-7.

*Situation 3*—An order for the item is planned before the normal order interval and before requirements trigger an order for another item. Table 8-7's Case 3 illustrates this situation. The three available options and their relevant costs are as follows:

1. Order Items A, B, and C in Period 1 as a group and Items A and B in Period 6.

| | | |
|---|---|---|
| Setup Costs | | |
| | Period 1—$150.00 | |
| | Period 6— 130.00 | |
| | $280.00 | |
| Carrying Costs | | |
| | $50 \times \$60 \times .3 \times 3 \div 50 =$ $ 54.00 | |
| | Total = | $334.00 |

2. Order Items A and B in Period 1 and in Period 6, and order Item C in Period 4.

| | | |
|---|---|---|
| Setup Costs | | |
| | Period 1—$130.00 | |
| | Period 4— 100.00 | |
| | Period 6— 130.00 | |
| | $360.00 | |
| Carrying Costs | None | |
| | Total = | $360.00 |

3. Order Items A and B in Period 1 and order Items A, B, and C in Period 4.

| | | |
|---|---|---|
| Setup Costs | | |
| | Period 1—$130.00 | |
| | Period 4— 150.00 | |
| | $280.00 | |
| Carrying Costs | | |
| | 50 × $70 × .3 × 2 ÷ 50 = $ 42.00 | |
| | 50 × $100 × .3 × 2 ÷ 50 = 60.00 | |
| | $102.00 | |
| | Total = | $382.00 |

Option 1 is the minimum cost decision in the illustration contained in Table 8-7. However, not only are the cost differences small but other factors such as capacity must be considered before a final decision is made. These other factors are discussed in the remainder of this chapter and in Chapters 5 and 12.

# Order Release, Joint Production Lots

Demand patterns, production capacity, and production sequence requirements affect decision rules governing order release for joint production lots. A given decision can involve any combination of the demand, production sequence, and capacity factor variations listed in Table 8-8.

**TABLE 8-8**
**FACTORS AFFECTING**
**JOINT PRODUCTION LOT**
**ORDER RELEASE DECISION RULES**

| I. Demand | II. Capacity | III. Production Sequence |
|---|---|---|
| (a) Dependent<br>(b) Independent | (a) Dedicated<br>(b) Nondedicated | (a) Optional<br>(b) Prescribed |

**Demand.** Order releases for dependent demand items are predicated on the Material Requirements Plan (MRP) flowing from the Master Production Schedule (MPS). The MRP seldom calls for the individual item lot quantities suggested by the economic lot size model. Decisions to increase production lot quantities above the MRP quantities depend on available capacity and a comparison of the expected increased carrying costs with expected savings in setup costs as previously described. See Chapter 10 for a further discussion of MRP (discrete requirements) lot sizes.

Order releases for production of independent demand items should be planned on the basis of order releases established in the manner suggested for joint purchased orders. Final release also depends on production sequence and capacity requirements.

**Capacity.** Some multi-item production groups are manufactured by *dedicated facilities*, equipment used exclusively for the production of one group. Other groups are manufactured on equipment used in the manufacture of many different items and groups. In the latter case, the nature of demand, process sequence, and available capacity determine the release of orders. Order release and scheduling problems under these conditions have been examined in Chapter 5.

**Dedicated Equipment.** Decisions concerning groups manufactured on dedicated equipment include the following:

1. Determining the minimum group lot size and the minimum interval between lots to provide the capacity required
2. Determining the maximum quantity of an item to produce when an order has not been released for any other item in the group in order to maintain proper balance among item inventories
3. Establishing order release points for individual items
4. Determining when production of all items should be interrupted

**Minimum Group Lot Size.** Effective capacity, frequently expressed in standard hours, is a function of the standard hours available, production efficiency, and equipment utilization. It usually is obtained by multiplying the actual hours available by a factor that reflects production efficiency and utilization experience. Total setup and production time must not be greater than effective capacity if requirements are to be produced within available capacity. The relationship of the maximum number of cycles per year and the effective available annual capacity is:

$N$ = maximum number of cycles per period
$T_s$ = major setup time
$t_{si}$ = minor setup time for Item $i$
$D_i$ = period demand for Item $i$
$p_i$ = hourly production rate for Item $i$
$C$ = period effective capacity in hours
$T$ = interval between cycles

$$N(T_S + \Sigma t_{si}) + \Sigma(D_i \div p_i) \leq C$$

$$N \leq \frac{C - \Sigma(D_i \div p_i)}{T_S + \Sigma t_{si}}$$

and since $T = \frac{1}{N}$, then

$$T \geq \frac{T_S + \Sigma t_{si}}{C - \Sigma(D_i \div p_i)}$$

If more than $N$ cycles are run per year, there will be insufficient time for the required setups and production runs. Calculation of the upper limit on the number of cycles per year, for example, is illustrated using the data in Table 8-9.

**TABLE 8-9**
**DATA, CAPACITY REQUIREMENTS, EQUIPMENT DEDICATED TO A MULTI-ITEM PRODUCTION GROUP***

| Item | ($t_{si}$) Time per minor Setup (hours) | ($D_i$) Annual Demand | ($p_i$) Hourly Production Rate | ($D_i/p_i$) | ($P_i$) Annual Production Rate** | ($D_i/p_i$) |
|---|---|---|---|---|---|---|
| 1 | 0.2 | 10,000 | 20 | 500 | 36,000 | .28 |
| 2 | 0.3 | 9,000 | 20 | 450 | 36,000 | .20 |
| 3 | 0.2 | 12,000 | 48 | 250 | 86,400 | .14 |
| 4 | 0.3 | 6,000 | 12 | 500 | 21,600 | .28 |
| | 1.0 | 37,000 | | 1,700 | 180,000 | |

*$T_S$ = 9 hours
**Based on 1,800 hours of effective capacity

Effective annual capacity equals the hours available each year multiplied by the decimal fraction reflecting operating efficiency and utilization. In this case there are fifty weeks, five days per week, one eight-hour shift per day and an effective capacity multiplier of .9. This is formulated in the following:

$$C = 50 \times 5 \times 8 \times .9 = 1{,}888 \text{ hours per year}$$

$$N \leq \frac{1{,}800 - (500 + 450 + 250 + 500)}{9 + 1}$$

$$N \leq 10$$

$$T \geq .1 \text{ years}$$

(The optimum lot size for the group is calculated as described on page 246 for noninstantaneous receipt.)

**Maximum Production Run.** On occasion demand may slump for items not being produced, and the optimum lot size of the item being produced will be reached prior to requirements for any other item. Since optimum lot sizes are proportional to demand, continuing to run the item being produced will bring its inventory into balance with other item inventories. However, running the present item for too long a period can result in two or more items reaching their order point simultaneously, resulting in a stock-out. The following decision rule can be used for determining the maximum quantity to run before switching to another item. (Appendix C contains the derivation of the model stated below.)

When item $i$ is being run and no other item has reached—or is near—its order point, continue producing Item $i$ until its inventory reaches the quantity defined by the following model or until another item does reach its order point. [4]

$$I_i^* = \frac{(\Sigma I_i) \times 2D_i(1 - D_i \div P_i)}{\Sigma D_i(1 - D_i \div P_i)}$$

Where:

$I_i^*$ = the maximum inventory of Item $i$
$\Sigma I_i$ = the sum of the inventories of all items
$D_i$ = the demand rate for Item $i$
$P_i$ = the production rate for Item $i$

Let us exemplify this with an extension of the situation described by the data in Table 8-9. The setup costs are \$10 per hour; the carrying cost rate ($k$) is .3; and each item costs \$1 to produce. Table 8-10 contains the minimum cost lot sizes and the present inventory of each item. The situation is:

1. Item 3 is being run and its minimum costs lot size, 1,800, has been produced. Average demand has occurred during production and the inventory of Item 3 equals $Q_3^*(D_i \div P_i)$.
2. Demand has slumped for Items 1, 2, and 4.
3. The question is, How long should we continue to run Item 3?

**TABLE 8-10**
**DATA, MAXIMUM RUN CALCULATIONS**

| Item | $Q_i^*$ | Present Inventory | $D_i(1 - D_i/P_i)$[1] |
|---|---|---|---|
| 1 | 1,500 | 510 | 7,200 |
| 2 | 1,350 | 420 | 7,200 |
| 3 | 1,800 | 1,548 | 10,320 |
| 4 | 900 | 222 | 4,320 |
| | | 2,700 | 29,040 |

[1]See Table 8-9 for values of $D_i$ and $D_i/P_i$.

Since

$$I_3^* = 2{,}700 \times \frac{2 \times 10{,}320}{29{,}040} = 2{,}700 \times .71 = 1{,}917$$

Thus, we should continue producing Item 3 until its inventory reaches 1,917 units. Since its inventory increases at a rate of $1 - D_3/P_3(1 - .14 = .86)$, increasing its inventory by 369 units (1,917 − 1,548) requires production of another 436 units (369 ÷ .86). The increase in inventory equals the quantity produced divided by $1 - D_i/P_i$. Since 48 units of Item 3 are produced each hour, production of Item 3 will continue for another nine hours or until one of the other items reaches its order point.

If the production of a maximum size lot (436 units in this example) requires a relatively long time, a new value of $I_i^*$ should be computed periodically using the updated value of $\Sigma I_i$. Sometimes $\Sigma I_i$ may change abruptly due to demand surges before the calculated maximum of a given item is produced or before any item reaches its order point. Short-term surges in demand and reductions in $\Sigma I_i$ may suggest recalculation of $I_i^*$. Thus, when producing $I_i^*$, production may be switched to another item due to an updated calculation of $I_i^*$.

If we let production of Item 3 continue until its total inventory reaches 1,800 units while the remaining stocks for Items 1, 2, and 4 drop to 400, 200, and 100 units respectively, then the new value of $I_3^*$ will equal 1,775 (i.e., 2,500 × .71). Production should be switched from Item 3 to the item that is closest to its order point.

**Order Release, Dedicated Equipment.** Items manufactured on dedicated equipment can have either dependent or independent demand; and, thus, order releases can be based on an MRP, a TPOP, or a traditional (statistical) order point. The lead time for production equals the setup time plus the time to produce a meaningful quantity. Taking Item 1 from the previous example as an illustration (see Table 8-10), it has a setup time of .2 hours, a 20 per hour production rate, and a 5 per hour demand rate (10,000 units ÷ 2,000 hours). If the minimum movement quantity is a box of 100, the lead time equals 5.2 hours (.2 + 100 ÷ 20). The order point equals 26 units, the minimum lead time multiplied by the demand rate. Of course, capacity or sequencing considerations could alter the lead time (see Chapter 5).

**Production Sequence.** When items may be run in any order without increasing setup costs, order release points are established as described in the preceding section. Using item order points including safety stock based on the individual item demand variations can result in increased inventory costs due to remnant stocks. Practical approaches to diminish this problem include establishing the sequence in which items are run on the following criteria:

1. Other things being equal, run the items with the shortest production time first.
2. Other things being equal, run the items with the largest variation in demand first.

In other cases technological factors such as dyes, ingredients, and tooling require that the items be run in a specific sequence to gain the full benefit of combining setups. Light colors, for example, are run prior to dark; and a product susceptible to contamination by ingredients of another product should be run first also. When there is a required group production sequence, the order point for an item not run first must provide for demand during the lead times of items preceding it in the production sequence.

## Quantity Discounts

Some suppliers offer price discounts based on the total dollar value of an order. The number of different items on the order is not restricted. For example, a 3 percent discount is given on all orders over $10,000. When the $Q^*_\$$ is less than the order size required to obtain the discount, increase the lot size to the discount quantity if the net benefits are positive. Increasing the aggregate lot size to earn a quantity discount will produce the following three results: (1) decrease the costs of material, (2) increase annual carrying costs due to the increase in average inventory, and (3) decrease annual preparation costs due to the fewer number of orders per year.

A decision in a given situation can be made by comparing the savings to the added costs. As an example, let's use the data in Table 8-1 and grant a 2 percent discount to all orders equal to or greater than $15,000. Consequences would be as follows.

$$Q^*_\$ = \$8{,}400$$
$$k = .3$$
$$S = \$120$$
$$A = \Sigma a_i = \$88{,}200$$
$$d\text{, discount} = 2 \text{ percent if } Q^*_\$ \geq \$15{,}000$$

A good rule is to increase the lot size to the discount quantity if the net savings are positive, neither constraints nor practical considerations override the decision, and the rate of return on the increased investment is satisfactory. (See Chapter 13 for a discussion of rate of return on quantity discounts.) We can calculate this in the following manner:

Net Savings = Purchase Price Discount plus Preparation Cost Savings minus Increased Carrying Cost

Purchase Price Discount = Annual Requirements times Discount Percentage
= $88,200 × .02
= $1,764

Preparation Cost Savings = Cost per Preparation times Decrease in number of Preparations per Year
= $120($88,200 ÷ $8,400 − $88,200 ÷ $15,000)
= $554.40

Increased Carrying Cost = Carrying Cost Rate times Increased Average Inventory
= .3($15,000 − $8,400) ÷ 2
= $990

Net Savings = $1,764 + $554.40 − $990
= $1,328.40

If financial and storage constraints are not violated, purchase an aggregate lot size of \$15,000 calculating the individual item lot sizes next in the usual manner:

$$Q_{\$_i} = (a_i \div A) Q_{\$}, \text{ and}$$
$$Q_i = Q_{\$_i} \div C_i$$

Therefore,

$$\begin{aligned}
Q_{\$_1} &= .0567 \times \$15{,}000 = \$850.50 \\
Q_{\$_2} &= .1701 \times \$15{,}000 = \$2{,}551.50 \\
Q_{\$_3} &= .0317 \times \$15{,}000 = \$475.50 \\
Q_{\$_4} &= .4354 \times \$15{,}000 = \$6{,}531.00 \\
Q_{\$_5} &= .3061 \times \$15{,}000 = \$4{,}591.50 \\
Q_1 &= \$850.50 \div \$5.00 = 170.1 \\
Q_2 &= \$2{,}551.50 \div \$6.00 = 425.25 \\
Q_3 &= \$475.50 \div \$3.50 = 135.86 \\
Q_4 &= \$6{,}531 \div \$12.00 = 544.25 \\
Q_5 &= \$4{,}591.00 \div \$15.00 = 306.10
\end{aligned}$$

Practical considerations such as container size and round numbers influence the actual order quantity. Lot sizes for Items 1 through 5 in a specific situation might be 170, 425, 135, 550, and 300.

Capital and storage constraints, shelf life, possible engineering changes, and the return on other possible investments must be considered prior to a final decision.

In summary, items obtained from the same supplier may be purchased as a group with reduced total inventory costs due to the savings in ordering costs being greater than any increases in carrying costs for individual items. Coordinating the production of items that share a major setup can achieve similar savings. The optimum (minimum total cost) group lot size can be calculated for purchased items and production parts with known and steady independent demand. Derivation of the optimum lot size model is similar to derivation of the individual item optimum lot size model. Purchase or production of those items with relatively low demand may take place less than every cycle in some cases. Ordering up to the equal-run-out quantity is one approach for dealing with uncertainties in demand.

Order releases for purchase parts may be based on either a time-phased order point system, a periodic review system, or a statistical order point system. The nature of order releases for joint production lots depends on the type of demand, the group production sequence requirements, and capacity considerations. Explicit decision rules for calculating safety stocks to achieve specified customer service levels have not been developed yet. When producing a group on dedicated equipment, conditions can arise that warrant producing larger than the optimum lot size of an item in order to maintain a balanced inventory.

Decisions concerning purchasing larger than the straightforward EOQ lot sizes to obtain quantity discounts are made on the basis of minimum total costs and the rate of return on the increased investment.

Economies are available through astute management of joint orders. However, establishing order release decision rules in situations with relatively large item demand variations can require lengthy analysis of data regarding a specific situation.

# PROBLEMS

1. A medium size manufacturer of specialized (low volume) construction equipment purchases four sizes of hydraulic hoses. The demand for each is relatively steady throughout the year. Hosing is purchased in a continuous segment and cut to size in the plant where the couplings are added. The company usually buys all five types on one purchase order to save the costs of five separate purchase orders. Given the following information:

   Plant operates 250 days a year. Annual carrying cost rate of .30 has been established by management. The major cost of this type purchase order is estimated as $75.

   Usage and Cost Data

   | Item | Annual Usage | Cost Per Foot | Additional Ordering Cost |
   |---|---|---|---|
   | Hose H25 | $ 600 | $.30 | $4 |
   | Hose H29 | 5,000 | .50 | 4 |
   | Hose H48 | 2,000 | .20 | 8 |
   | Hose H73 | 1,200 | .60 | 4 |

   a. Determine the aggregate order quantity and the order quantity of each type (in dollars and units).
   b. If the company presently orders hoses once a month, what would you estimate the total annual savings to be if the new aggregate order quantity was used?

2. The Demart Locker and Cabinet Company purchases five types of hardware from the same firm. These items are used in many products at a rather steady rate throughout the year. The inventory manager has decided to combine the purchase of these items in a joint order. The following information is available.

   | Item | No. | Annual Requirements (Units) | Unit Cost | Minor Order Costs |
   |---|---|---|---|---|
   | Hook | H95 | 24,000 | $ .50 | $5 |
   | Handle | H122 | 8,000 | 2.00 | 5 |
   | Handle | H197 | 4,000 | 1.50 | 5 |
   | Lock | L79 | 12,000 | 3.00 | 8 |
   | Hinge | H478 | 36,000 | .75 | 5 |

The annual carrying cost rate = .25
Major cost of a purchase order = $40

a. What is the joint economic order quantity?
b. What is the quantity of each item in that order?

3. The lathe department of a company that fabricates material handling equipment produces four pins each of which is used at a relatively steady rate throughout the year. The pins are pan stock items and are required in many standard products as well as special design material handling systems. Manufacturing runs the pins as a joint lot to gain the benefits of a single major setup for all four items. Given the following information make the ensuing determinations:

The company operates 250 days a year.
An annual carrying cost rate of .30 is used.
The major costs of ordering and setup are $60.

| Item | Annual Usage | Unit Cost | Daily Production Rate | Minor Setup Costs |
|---|---|---|---|---|
| P121 | $6,000 | $3 | 48 | $3 |
| P127 | 5,000 | 5 | 32 | 3 |
| P132 | 3,600 | 9 | 24 | 5 |
| P143 | 2,400 | 6 | 40 | 4 |

a. The aggregate lot size should be what?
b. What should the economic quantity of each be?

4. The Rocky Mountain Gear Company manufactures commercial gears to stock. They run similar types jointly to economize on setup costs and production capacity. Data concerning four such gears are given next:

Major setup time = 2 hours, Setup cost = $25 per hour

| Gear | Annual Demand Units | Unit Cost of Production | Minor Setup Time | Production Rate |
|---|---|---|---|---|
| 1 | 10,000 | $ 2.00 | .2 hr | 40/hr. |
| 2 | 8,000 | 3.50 | .1 hr | 20/hr. |
| 3 | 14,000 | 5.00 | .2 hr | 14/hr. |
| 4 | 1,000 | 10.00 | .5 hr | 5/hr. |

The plant operates 250 days a year, one eight-hour shift a day. The carrying cost rate is .25.

a. What is the economic joint lot size?
b. What is the economic lot size of each gear?
c. How many times are the gears run each year?
d. What is the total of the costs related to this decision?

5. An order is being placed for the hydraulic hoses described in Problem 1. The inventory on hand for each item follows:

| Item | Present Inventory |
|---|---|
| Hose H25 | $ 12.00 |
| Hose H29 | 200.00 |
| Hose H48 | 120.00 |
| Hose H73 | 38.40 |

How many feet of each item should be ordered?

6. A decision has been made to run the pins described in Problem 3. The inventory on hand is listed as follows:

| Item | Present Inventory |
|---|---|
| P121 | 30 |
| P127 | 300 |
| P132 | 180 |
| P143 | 54 |

How many of each pin should be run?

7. Use the information concerning the Rocky Mountain Gear Company in Problem 4, and add the following data:

The four gears listed are the only items run on a group of machines. The department has a .95 utilization factor, excluding setup, and the average operating efficiency is .98.

What, then, is the maximum number of joint lots that can be run in a year without exceeding production capacity?

8. Using Brown's method to determine whether each item should be ordered each interval:

a. Use the data in Problem 1 and determine T*.
b. Repeat this process with the data in Problem 2.

9. Determine whether each item should be ordered each interval:

a. Applying Silver's approach to the data in Problem 3.
b. Applying Silver's approach to the data in Problem 4.

10. The following data concern five items that are the only items run on a press that has a utilization rate of .875 and is operated at an average efficiency of .90.

| Item | Time Per Setup (Hours) | Annual Demand | Hourly Production Rate |
|---|---|---|---|
| 1 | 3.0 | 8,000 | 20 |
| 2 | 2.0 | 4,000 | 60 |
| 3 | 1.5 | 15,000 | 30 |
| 4 | 2.5 | 900 | 10 |
| 5 | 1.0 | 9,000 | 25 |

What is the maximum number of runs that can be made per year given an eight hour day, 250 workdays per year?

## SELECTED READINGS


1. Robert G. Brown, *Decision Rules for Inventory Management* (New York: Holt, Rinehart & Winston, 1967), pp. 48–52.
2. Edward A. Silver, "Modifying the Economic Order Quantity (EOQ) to Handle Coordinated Replenishment of Two or More Items," *Production and Inventory Management*, Vol. 16, No. 3 (1975), pp. 26–38.
3. ———, "A Control System for Coordinated Inventory Replenishment," *International Journal of Production Research*, Vol. 12, No. 6 (1974), pp. 647–671.
4. Robert G. Brown, *Management Decisions for Production Operations* (Hinsdale Ill.: Dryden Press, 1971).
5. ———, *Materials Management Systems* (New York: John Wiley & Sons, Inc., 1977).
6. IBM, *Wholesale IMPACT—Advanced Principles and Implementation Reference Manual E20-0174-1* (White Plains, New York: 1971).
7. Lynwood Johnson and Douglas C. Montgomery, *Operations Research in Production Planning, Scheduling and Inventory Control* (New York: John Wiley & Sons, Inc., 1974).
8. John F. MaGee and David M. Boodman, *Production Planning and Inventory Control*, 2d ed. (New York: McGraw-Hill Book Company, 1967).
9. George W. Plossl and Oliver W. Wight, *Production and Inventory Control* (Englewood Cliffs, N. J.: Prentice-Hall, Inc., 1967).

# —9—

# AGGREGATE INVENTORY MANAGEMENT

Aggregate inventory encompasses the raw materials, purchase parts, work-in-process, and finished goods in different stages of the production-distribution process. These components of aggregate inventory fulfill the anticipation, fluctuation, cycle stock, and transportation inventory functions at various stages in the production-distribution process as illustrated in Figure 9-1.

Inventory is an asset. The primary objective usually is to attain a minimum level of achievement in each goal; the secondary objective is to maximize the achievement of each in keeping with its relative priority. Priorities, such as those shown in the set of inventory investment goals, should be established by management.

**A SET OF INVENTORY INVESTMENT GOALS**

1. Return on investment
2. Profit
3. Customer service
4. A stable work force
5. Facility and equipment utilization
6. Keeping the aggregate inventory investment below a specified level
7. Achieving a specified inventory turnover ratio (ITR)

The achievement of these goals is affected by many decisions including:

1. The distribution plan
2. The production (aggregate) plan
3. The master production schedule
4. Purchasing commitments
5. Family (group) lot-sizing decisions
6. Item lot-sizing decisions
7. Safety stock levels
8. Quantity discount and hedge purchases
9. Transportation modes and decisions

Aggregate inventory management concentrates on the trade-offs between the costs of inventory and the benefits it provides. It also develops a consistency between the above decisions and aggregate inventory management objectives.

**FIGURE 9-1**
**THE LOCUS AND FLOW OF INVENTORY THROUGH A PRODUCTION AND DISTRIBUTION PROCESS**

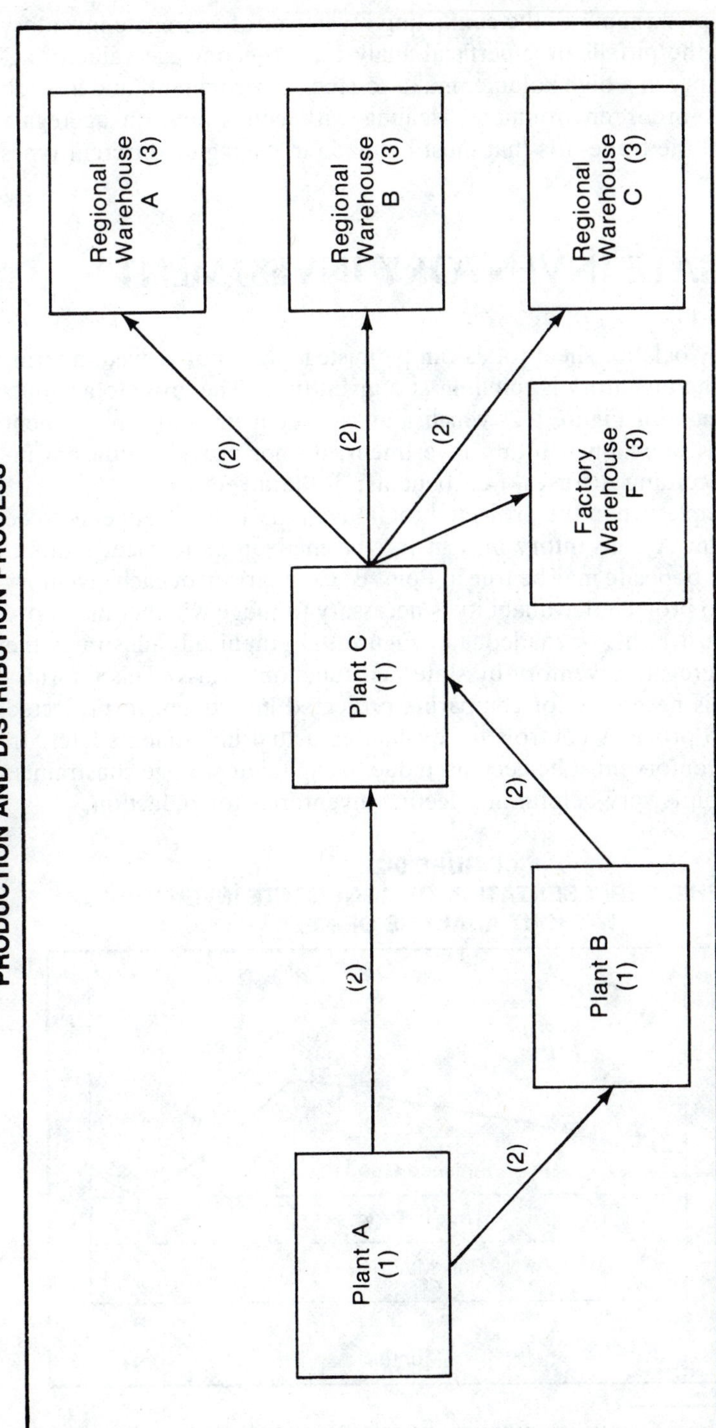


(1) Plants A, B, and C have raw materials, purchased parts, and work-in-process inventory. It may be cycle stock, demand and supply fluctuation (safety) stock, or anticipation stock.

(2) Transportation inventory exists between the plants and between Plant C and the regional warehouses.

(3) The warehouses have finished goods inventory including service parts. This inventory is cycle stock, fluctuation stock, and anticipation stock.

This chapter examines the conflicting objectives of aggregate inventory management; the pitfalls of superficial analyses; projecting the value of aggregate inventory in a high volume, make-to-stock environment, and in a job shop, make-to-order environment; dealing with constraints on aggregate inventory; and the trade-offs that must be made in managing different types of inventory.

# AGGREGATE INVENTORY INVESTMENT

Inventory balance sheet totals can be misleading if not viewed in terms of the needs the inventory is fulfilling at a given time. The gross totals illustrated graphically in Figure 9-2, which may represent inventory investment in past periods or planned future investment, do not provide sufficient information concerning the uses, i.e., benefits, of the inventory.

For example, when the projected total inventory balance appears to be excessive (Point A), inventory may in fact be inadequate to meet requirements; and the opposite may be true at Point B. Comparison of each inventory requirement to projected availability is necessary to judge whether inventory is excessive, just right, or inadequate. Figure 9-3 graphically illustrates the division of aggregate inventory by state and functional class. This information not only is necessary for comparing projected investment to projected needs but also provides controls for evaluating actual investments later. In addition, if inventory must be decreased due to capital or storage constraints, this information is very helpful in selecting inventories for reduction.

**FIGURE 9-2**
**GRAPHIC REPRESENTATION OF AGGREGATE INVENTORY WITHOUT ANALYSIS OF NEED[1]**

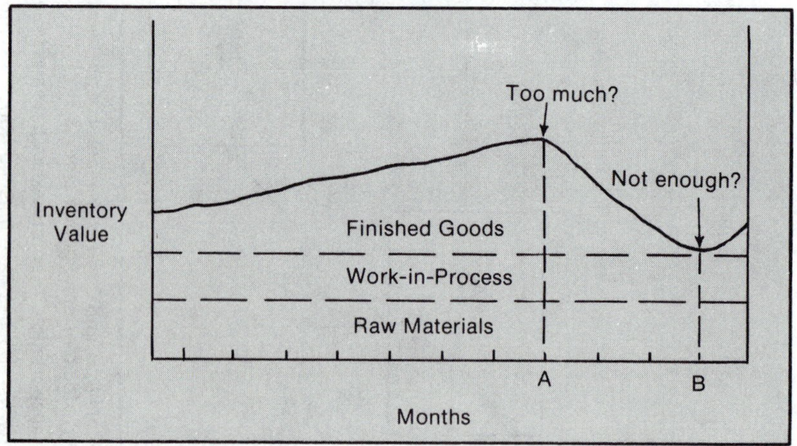


[1]Adopted from George Brandenburg's presentation "Master Planning" at the AIDS National Conference, Las Vegas, 1980.

**FIGURE 9-3**
**INVENTORY INVESTMENT VERSUS TIME**
**(BY STATE)[2]**

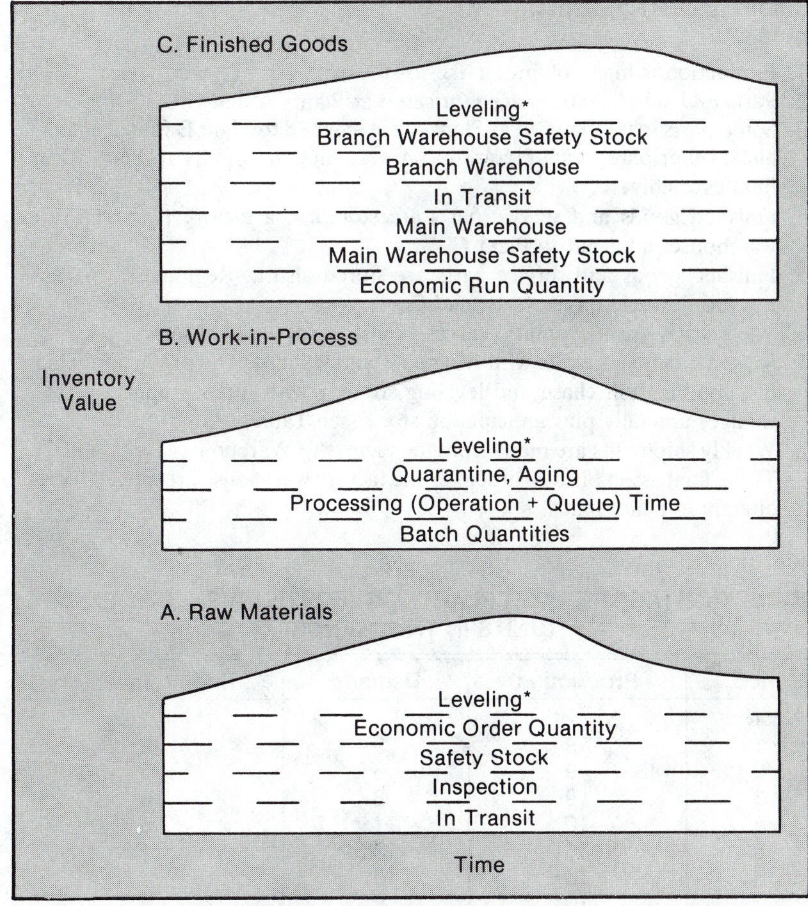


*Leveling may take place in each of the functional classifications.

Figures 9-1 and 9-3 indicate the determinants of aggregate inventory investment. Inventory fulfills anticipation (leveling), transportation (pipeline), cycle (lot size), and fluctuation (buffer) objectives; it exists as raw materials, purchase parts, work-in-process, and finished goods.

The production plan has a major impact on aggregate inventory investment in any environment. In the typical high volume, make-to-stock environment the production rate usually dominates all other factors in determining the aggregate inventory investment. In the typical job shop environment, the nature of specific orders is the dominating factor. We will use examples to demonstrate how projected aggregate inventory investment can be calculated in each of these situations.

[2]Ibid.

## Make-to-Stock Environment

Figure 9-1 illustrates a high volume, make-to-stock situation that has the following characteristics:

1. Production is high volume, make-to-stock.
2. Parts and subassemblies are fabricated at Plants A and B.
3. Some parts manufactured at Plant A are shipped to Plant B for subassemblies; other parts manufactured at *A* are shipped directly to Plant C for final assembly.
4. Finished goods and service parts are stored at a factory (i.e., central) warehouse, adjacent to Plant C.
5. Finished goods and service parts are stored also at Regional (i.e., Distribution) Warehouses A, B, and C.
6. The central warehouse also serves as a regional warehouse.
7. Seasonal demand exists with two peaks and troughs. The production plan is a combination chase and leveling strategy with three production rate changes annually plus anticipation stock (see Table 9-1).
8. Weekly shipments are made from the factory to Warehouses A, B, and C.
9. Those final assemblies destined for the factory warehouse are moved there directly in pallet loads.

**TABLE 9-1**
**PRODUCTION (AGGREGATE) PLAN; AGGREGATE INVENTORY EXAMPLE (UNITS IN THOUSANDS)**

| Period | Production | Demand | Ending Inventory* |
|---|---|---|---|
| −1 | | | 2 |
| 1 | 9 | 9 | 2 |
| 2 | 9 | 6 | 5 |
| 3 | 9 | 8 | 6 |
| 4 | 10 | 11 | 5 |
| 5 | 10 | 13.5 | 1.5 |
| 6 | 10 | 10 | 1.5 |
| 7 | 10 | 8 | 3.5 |
| 8 | 10 | 6 | 7.5 |
| 9 | 10 | 9.5 | 8 |
| 10 | 11 | 13 | 6 |
| 11 | 11 | 14 | 3 |
| 12 | 11 | 12 | 2 |

*Includes only anticipation and buffer stock.

The following elements constitute the inventory at any point in time:

1. Finished goods
   - Anticipation stock
   - Buffer stock
   - Transportation stock
   - Cycle stock

2. Work-in-Process
   Cycle stock
   Buffer stock
   Anticipation stock
   Transportation stock
3. Raw material
   Cycle stock
   Buffer stock
   Anticipation stock

The projected investment in finished goods each month is calculated as follows:

**Finished Goods Inventory.** Finished goods inventory consists of anticipation, buffer, cycle, and transportation stock. All except the latter are located in each of the warehouses; transportation stock exists between the factory and Warehouses A, B, and C. We will calculate average monthly investment for each type stock.

**Anticipation (Leveling) Stock.** The aggregate plan, contained in Table 9-1, determines the value of planned finished goods anticipation stock at the end of each period. Anticipation stock peaks first at 4.5 thousand units at the end of Period 3, descends to zero, and rises to 6.5 units at the end of Period 9 as illustrated in Figure 9-4.

Average finished goods anticipation stock during a given month equals one half the sum of the beginning and ending anticipation stock; and, of course, the beginning inventory equals the ending inventory of the previous period. Thus,

$$\overline{FG}(A)_i = .5[FG(A)_{i-1} + FG(A)_i]$$

Where:

$\overline{FG}(A)_i$ = the average anticipation stock in Period $i$
$FG(A)_i$ = the anticipation stock at the end of Period $i$

This model begs the question somewhat as it assumes $FG(A)_i$ is known. This assumption can be avoided by using the relationship described by the following model:

$$\overline{FG}(A)_i = \overline{FG}(A)_{i-1} + .5[(P_{i-1} - D_{i-1}) + (P_i - D_i)] + .5[\overline{FG}(B)_{i-1} - \overline{FG}(B)_i]$$

Where:

$P_i$ = production in Period $i$
$D_i$ = demand in Period $i$
$\overline{FG}(B)_i$ = average buffer stock in Period $i$

For example, since $\overline{FG}(A)_1 = .5$, and $\overline{FG}(B)_i$ is a constant 1.5, then

$$\begin{aligned}\overline{FG}(A)_2 &= .5 + .5[(9-9) + (9-6)] + .5(1.5-1.5)\\ &= 2, \text{ and}\\ \overline{FG}(A)_3 &= 2 + .5[(9-6) + (9-8)] + .5(1.5-1.5)\\ &= 4\end{aligned}$$

The average values of finished goods anticipation stock are listed in Table 9-2. The monetary value of anticipation stock is calculated by multiplying the number of units by the cost per unit, $80. The results of these calculations are listed in Table 9-2.

**TABLE 9-2**
**AVERAGE FINISHED GOODS INVENTORY BY FUNCTIONAL CLASS IN EACH PERIOD**

**A. Units (in thousands)**

| | Stock (Function) | | | | |
|---|---|---|---|---|---|
| **Period** | **Anticipation** | **Buffer** | **Transportation** | **Cycle** | **Total** |
| 1 | .5 | 1.5 | .66 | .83 | 3.49 |
| 2 | 2.0 | 1.5 | .66 | .83 | 4.99 |
| 3 | 4 | 1.5 | .66 | .83 | 6.99 |
| 4 | 4 | 1.5 | .74 | .92 | 7.16 |
| 5 | 1.75 | 1.5 | .74 | .92 | 4.91 |
| 6 | 0 | 1.5 | .74 | .92 | 3.16 |
| 7 | 1 | 1.5 | .74 | .92 | 4.16 |
| 8 | 4 | 1.5 | .74 | .92 | 7.16 |
| 9 | 6.25 | 1.5 | .74 | .92 | 9.41 |
| 10 | 5.5 | 1.5 | .81 | 1.02 | 8.83 |
| 11 | 3 | 1.5 | .81 | 1.02 | 6.33 |
| 12 | 1 | 1.5 | .81 | 1.02 | 4.33 |

**B. Value (in thousands of dollars)**

| | Stock (Function) | | | | |
|---|---|---|---|---|---|
| **Period** | **Anticipation** | **Buffer** | **Transportation** | **Cycle** | **Total** |
| 1 | 40 | 120 | 52.80 | 66.40 | 279.20 |
| 2 | 160 | 120 | 52.80 | 66.40 | 399.20 |
| 3 | 320 | 120 | 52.80 | 66.40 | 559.20 |
| 4 | 320 | 120 | 59.20 | 73.60 | 572.80 |
| 5 | 140 | 120 | 59.20 | 73.60 | 392.80 |
| 6 | 0 | 120 | 59.20 | 73.60 | 252.80 |
| 7 | 80 | 120 | 59.20 | 73.60 | 332.80 |
| 8 | 320 | 120 | 59.20 | 73.60 | 572.80 |
| 9 | 500 | 120 | 59.20 | 73.60 | 752.80 |
| 10 | 440 | 120 | 64.80 | 81.60 | 706.40 |
| 11 | 240 | 120 | 64.80 | 81.60 | 506.40 |
| 12 | 80 | 120 | 64.80 | 81.60 | 346.40 |

**FIGURE 9-4**
**FINISHED GOODS INVENTORY**
**(ANTICIPATION STOCK)**
**VERSUS TIME**

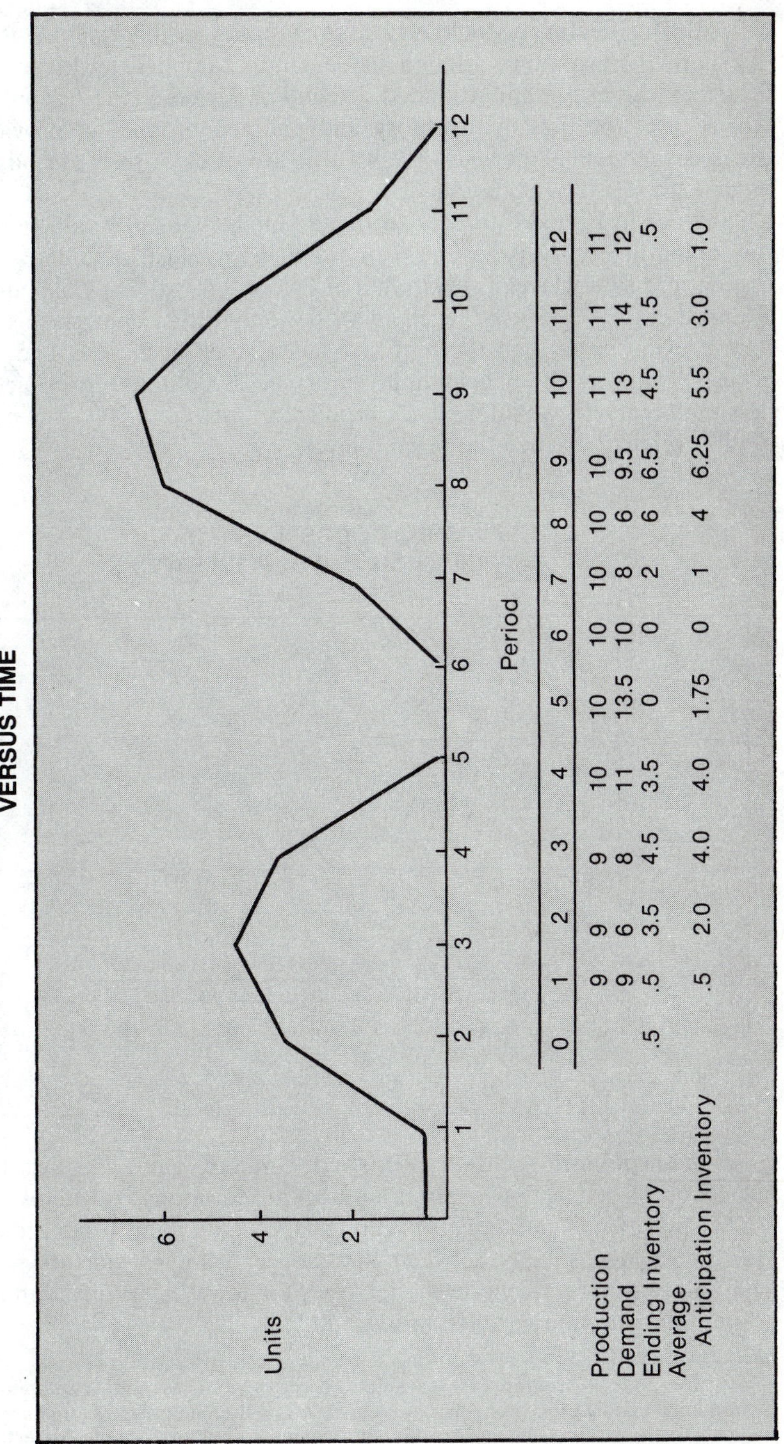


| | 0 | 1 | 2 | 3 | 4 | 5 | 6 | 7 | 8 | 9 | 10 | 11 | 12 |
|---|---|---|---|---|---|---|---|---|---|---|---|---|---|
| Production | | 9 | 9 | 9 | 10 | 10 | 10 | 10 | 10 | 10 | 11 | 11 | 11 |
| Demand | | 9 | 6 | 8 | 11 | 13.5 | 10 | 8 | 6 | 9.5 | 13 | 14 | 12 |
| Ending Inventory | .5 | .5 | 3.5 | 4.5 | 3.5 | 0 | 0 | 2 | 6 | 6.5 | 4.5 | 1.5 | .5 |
| Average Anticipation Inventory | | .5 | 2.0 | 4.0 | 4.0 | 1.75 | 0 | 1 | 4 | 6.25 | 5.5 | 3.0 | 1.0 |

**Buffer (Safety) Stock.** Safety stock policy in this example is to cover the normal maximum variation in demand, estimated as 15 percent. For example, the maximum estimated demand in Period 6 is 11.5 thousand units ($10 \times 1.15$). Beginning inventory and planned production provide safety stock coverage in all periods except 1, the last week or so of Period 5, Period 6, and the last half of Period 12.

Since in Period 6 forecast demand equals planned production and the beginning inventory is zero, 1.5 thousand units must be added to provide the desired safety level as illustrated in Figure 9-5. Adding 1,500 units to the planned ending inventory levels in all periods will accomplish this goal and also provide more than the required safety stock in Periods 1, 5, and 12.[3] Thus, we will let the beginning inventory be 2,000 units. If, in fact, it were less than that, we would hold the production rate at 11,000 units per month until inventory reached the desired level.

**FIGURE 9-5**
**FINISHED GOODS INVENTORY (ANTICIPATION AND BUFFER STOCK) VERSUS TIME**

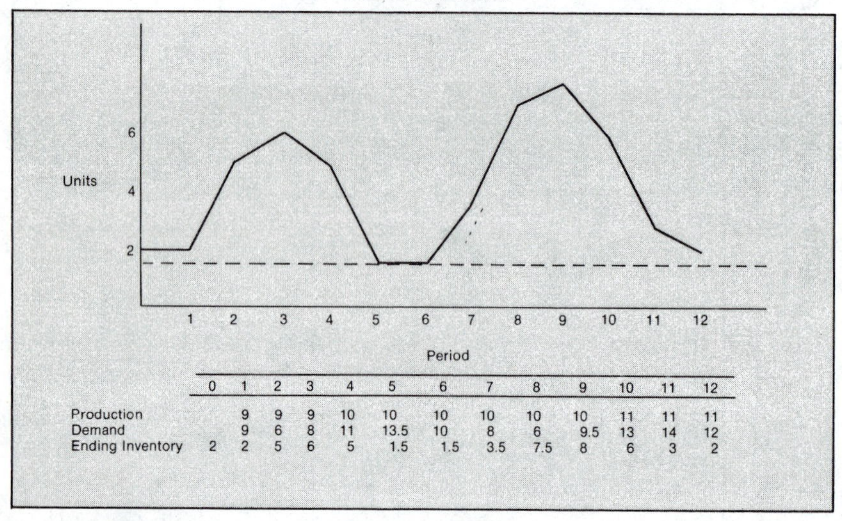


| | 0 | 1 | 2 | 3 | 4 | 5 | 6 | 7 | 8 | 9 | 10 | 11 | 12 |
|---|---|---|---|---|---|---|---|---|---|---|---|---|---|
| Production | | 9 | 9 | 9 | 10 | 10 | 10 | 10 | 10 | 10 | 11 | 11 | 11 |
| Demand | | 9 | 6 | 8 | 11 | 13.5 | 10 | 8 | 6 | 9.5 | 13 | 14 | 12 |
| Ending Inventory | 2 | 2 | 5 | 6 | 5 | 1.5 | 1.5 | 3.5 | 7.5 | 8 | 6 | 3 | 2 |

**Transportation Stock (Finished Goods).** Table 9-3 lists the daily allocation of production to the four stocking locations. All items produced on Monday, for example, go to Warehouse A, and items produced on Tuesday are divided equally between Warehouse B and the factory warehouse (F). Safety stock is stored in the factory warehouse; all production is moved to the four warehouses when produced.

[3]This policy is arbitrary in this example. Using overtime to produce safety stock in the period immediately preceeding its requirement is an alternate policy. Carrying costs, overtime costs, stock-out costs, and volatility of demand will influence policy selection.

**TABLE 9-3**
**DAILY ALLOCATION OF WEEKLY PRODUCTION TO WAREHOUSES AS A PERCENTAGE OF WEEKLY PRODUCTION**

| Warehouse | Monday | Tuesday | Wednesday | Thursday | Friday | Total |
|---|---|---|---|---|---|---|
| A | 20 | | | | | 20 |
| B | | 10 | 15 | | | 25 |
| C | | | | 5 | 20 | 25 |
| F | | 10 | 5 | 15 | | 30 |
| Total | 20 | 20 | 20 | 20 | 20 | 100 |

Those finished goods shipped to the factory warehouse move there directly from final inspection with virtually no transportation time. Transportation time, including loading and unloading, to Warehouses A, B, and C is 3, 2, and 2 days respectively. Table 9-4 reveals the percentage of weekly production in transport to each warehouse each day. For example, 20 percent of the weekly production is in transport to Warehouse A each Tuesday through Thursday and 25 percent is in transport to Warehouse B each Thursday and Friday. Thirty-two percent of weekly production is in transport on

**TABLE 9-4**
**PERCENTAGE OF WEEKLY PRODUCTION IN TRANSPORT BY DAY AND WAREHOUSE**

| Warehouse | Monday | Tuesday | Wednesday | Thursday | Friday | Average |
|---|---|---|---|---|---|---|
| A | | 20 | 20 | 20 | | 12 |
| B | | | | 25 | 25 | 10 |
| C | 25 | 25 | | | | 10 |
| Total | 25 | 45 | 20 | 45 | 25 | 32 |

the average. The average number of units in transportation inventory during any month equals the weekly production rate times the average percentage (expressed as a decimal) in shipment. For example, the average transportation inventory in Period 1 is 665 units ($.32 \times 9{,}000 \div 4.33$). The values of finished goods transportation stock are listed in Table 9-2.

It must be emphasized that this plan does not necessarily represent the most efficient allocation or transportation procedure. It does demonstrate how the investment in transportation stock can be calculated under a given set of conditions.

**Cycle Stock.** A shipment received at any of the three regional warehouses is not consumed the instant or day it arrives; it declines gradually until it reaches zero just as the next shipment arrives. This classical pattern of receipt and withdrawals for cycle stock is graphically represented for each of the three regional warehouses in Figure 9-6. Cycle stock in the factory warehouse increases in noninstantaneous fashion from Tuesday through

**FIGURE 9-6**
**DAILY CYCLE STOCK IN EACH WAREHOUSE AS A PERCENTAGE OF WEEKLY PRODUCTION**

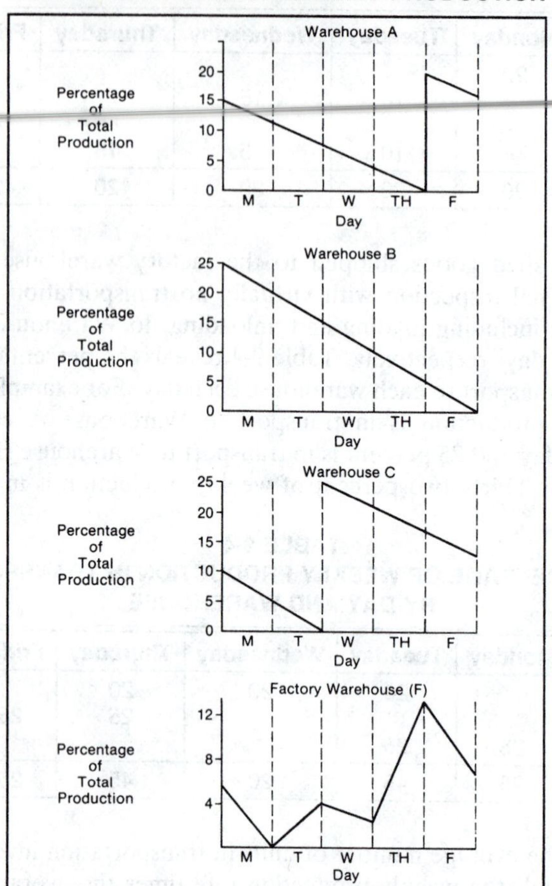


Thursday as receipts and withdrawals occur simultaneously. Since only withdrawals occur on Friday and Monday cycle stock bottoms out as the next lot begins to arrive. Figure 9-6 illustrates these relationships. Average cycle stock as a percentage of weekly production is determined by finding the average of the daily averages as illustrated in Table 9-5. This approach is a good illustration of how irregular situations can be measured. We will calculate the average cycle stock for each warehouse.

In the case of the regional warehouses (A, B, and C) the average value of cycle stock is one half the number of units received (see Table 9-5). In a given period and for a particular warehouse this equals the percentage of production shipped to the warehouse each week divided by two. Thus,

$$\overline{FG}(C)_{ij} = \frac{P_i p_j}{2 \times 4.33}$$

Where:

$\overline{FG}(C)_{ij}$ represents average finished goods cycle stock

$i$ represents the period (month)

$j$ represents the warehouse

$p_j$ represents the percentage, expressed as a decimal, of production shipped to Warehouse $j$

$P_i$ represents the total production for Month $i$, 4.33 weeks per month

**TABLE 9-5**
**AVERAGE CYCLE STOCK PER DAY PER WAREHOUSE AS A PERCENTAGE OF PRODUCTION**

| Warehouse | Day | | | | | |
|---|---|---|---|---|---|---|
| | Monday | Tuesday | Wednesday | Thursday | Friday | Average |
| A | 14.0 | 10.0 | 6.0 | 2.0 | 18.0 | 10.0 |
| B | 22.5 | 17.5 | 12.5 | 7.5 | 2.5 | 12.5 |
| C | 7.5 | 2.5 | 22.5 | 17.5 | 12.5 | 12.5 |
| F | 3.0 | 2.0 | 3.5 | 7.5 | 9.0 | 5.0 |
| Total | 47.0 | 32.0 | 44.5 | 34.5 | 42.0 | 40.0 |

Example: Cycle Stock, Warehouse A, Month 1

$$\overline{FG}(C)_{1A} = \frac{9{,}000 \times .20}{2 \times 4.33} = 207.7 \text{ units}$$

The average cycle stock by period in each warehouse is listed in Table 9-6. When production is greater than demand, average cycle stock in Warehouses A, B, and C still equals one half the number of units received. Those units not sold are transferred to anticipation stock at the steady rate required to have cycle stock equal zero when the next shipment arrives. (This is obviously not a physical transfer but a conceptual one consistent with the measurement of cycle and anticipation stock.) A similar transfer in the opposite direction—anticipation stock to cycle stock—occurs when demand exceeds production.

**TABLE 9-6**
**AVERAGE FINISHED GOODS CYCLE STOCK (UNITS) BY WAREHOUSE AND PERIOD**

| Warehouse | Period | | |
|---|---|---|---|
| | 1, 2, 3 | 4 through 9 | 10, 11, 12 |
| A | 207.7 | 230.8 | 253.8 |
| B | 259.6 | 288.4 | 317.3 |
| C | 259.6 | 288.4 | 317.3 |
| F | 103.8 | 115.4 | 126.9 |
| Total | 830.7 | 923.0 | 1,015.3 |

Stock arrives at the factory warehouse in pallet loads rather than in one large shipment each week. Thus, cycle stock is consumed as it arrives; and a noninstantaneous model for calculating average cycle stock is applicable as illustrated in Figure 9-6. The average cycle stock of Warehouse F is 5 percent of production as tabulated in Table 9-5.

The value of average finished goods inventory investment each period is tabulated in Table 9-2 and is graphically illustrated in Figure 9-7. It begins at a low of approximately $279,000 in Period 1, rises to about $573,000 in Period 4, drops to $253,000 in Period 6, and peaks at about $753,000 before falling again.

Table 9-2 and Figure 9-7 both reveal that over half the value is in anticipation stock ($IA$) during the peak inventory periods while safety stock ($IB$) comprises approximately 45 percent of the aggregate inventory value in the troughs. Substantial stock reductions in the peak periods require modification of the production plan. One possibility is to use anticipation stock as safety stock when possible. Safety stock then could be produced on overtime as required in the period preceding an inventory trough.

**FIGURE 9-7**
**AVERAGE FINISHED GOODS INVENTORY INVESTMENT, CUMULATIVE BY CLASS VERSUS PERIOD**

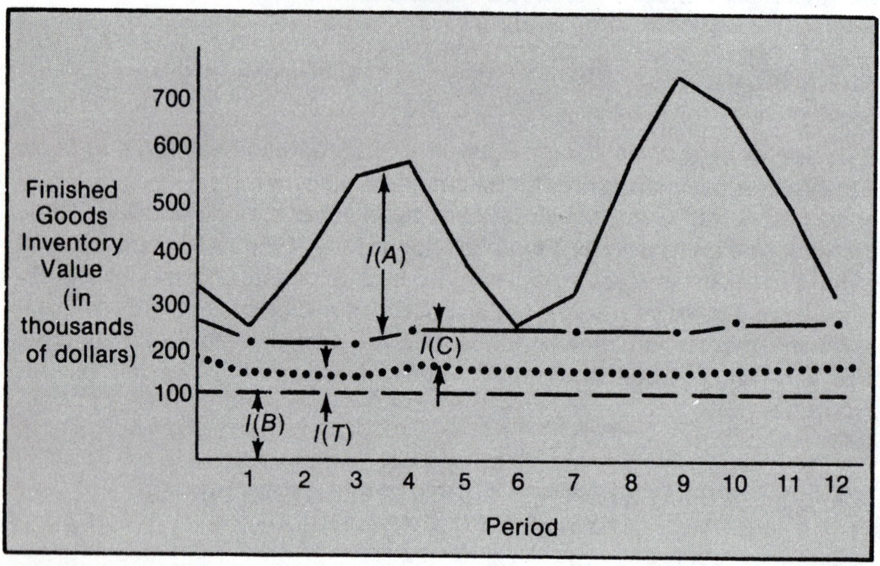


**Work-in-Process.** Processing methods, transportation requirements and schedules, order sizing and release decisions, and buffer stock policies affect the work-in-process inventory investment. Characteristics that affect the cycle stock, transportation stock, and buffer stock components of work-in-process in the example are listed next and illustrated in Figure 9-8.

1. Some manufactured parts are produced continuously and others are produced in lots (batch basis). The interval between runs of the latter type varies widely from item to item. The weighted (by value) average cycle time (manufacturing lead time) of all manufactured parts and subassemblies is 5.0 days, 1.0 week, at both Plants A and B.
2. Transportation time, including loading and unloading, from Plant A to Plant B, *A* to *C*, and *B* to *C* is one day in each case.
3. The weighted average of work-in-process safety stock at Plants B and C (items received from another plant) equals one day's output.
4. The weighted average cost of items fabricated at Plants A, B, and C is 40 percent of the unit cost of goods sold (*COS*), 60 percent of *COS*, and 95 percent of *COS* respectively.

**FIGURE 9-8**
**WORK-IN-PROCESS SCHEMATIC**

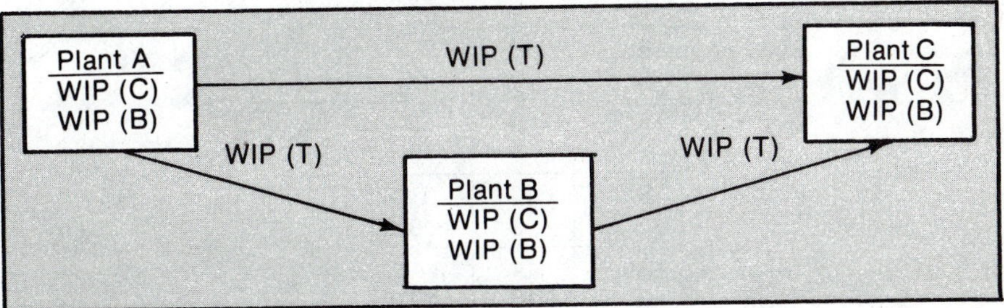


**WIP Cycle Stock.** In this example the monthly average WIP cycle stock depends on the planned finished goods production output of the current month and the following month ($P_i$ and $P_{i+1}$). Parts and subassemblies required in final assemblies shipped during the first week of a month are produced in Plants A and B during the preceding month (see Table 9-7). When the planned finished goods output of the following month equals that of the month under consideration,

$$\overline{\text{WIP}}(C)_{ij} = COSP_j \times P_i \times MLT_j$$

Where:

$\text{WIP}(C)_{ij}$ = the average WIP cycle stock in units at Plant $j$ during Month $i$
$P_i$ = finished goods output in Month $i$
$COSP_j$ = the average value of WIP cycle stock at Plant $j$ expressed as a decimal percentage of the unit cost of goods sold
$MLT_j$ = manufacturing lead time at Plant $j$, and
$P_i = P_{i+j}$

**TABLE 9-7**
**ALLOCATION OF PLANT PRODUCTION TO FINISHED GOODS OUTPUT BY PERIOD***

| Week | Plant A | Plant B | Plant C |
|---|---|---|---|
| 1 | 3<br>2 | 2 | 1 |
| 2 | 4<br>3 | 3 | 2 |
| 3 | 5<br>4 | 4 | 3 |
| 4 | 6<br>5 | 5 | 4 |
| 5 | 7<br>6 | 6 | 5 |
| 6 | 8<br>7 | 7 | 6 |
| 7 | 9<br>8 | 8 | 7 |
| 8 | 10<br>9 | 9 | 8 |
| 9 | 11<br>10 | 10 | 9 |

* The number in Cell *ij* is the week in which the items produced during Week *i* in Plant *j* will be included in finished goods shipments. For example, Cell 1B reveals that items produced during Week 1 in Plant B are shipped as finished goods in Week 2. Production in Plant A is divided equally between two weeks.

For example, the average WIP cycle stock at Plants A, B, and C in the first month is:

$$\overline{\text{WIP}}(C)_{1A} = .40 \times 9{,}000 \div 4\frac{1}{3}^{*} = 830.76 \text{ units}$$

$$\overline{\text{WIP}}(C)_{1B} = .60 \times 9{,}000 \div 4\frac{1}{3} = 1{,}246.15 \text{ units}$$

$$\overline{\text{WIP}}(C)_{1C} = .95 \times 9{,}000 \div 4\frac{1}{3} = 1{,}973.07 \text{ units}$$

*MLT = 1 week (1 ÷ 4⅓ months)

The cycle stock averages for all months except 3, 9, and 12 were calculated in this manner; they are recorded in Table 9-8. The values for Months 3, 9, and 12 are calculated using the following model:

$$\overline{\text{WIP}}(C)_{ij} = COSP_j \times MLT_j(p_{ij} \times P_i + p_{i+1,j} \times P_{i+1})$$

Where:[4] $COSP_j$, $MLT_j$, and $P_i$ are as defined earlier.

$p_{ij}$ = the percentage of WIP cycle stock at Plant $j$ during Period $i$ that will be used in finished goods shipped in Period $i$

$p_{i+1,j}$ = the percentage of WIP cycle stock at Plant $j$ during Period $i$ that will be used in finished goods shipped in Period $i + 1$, and

$p_{ij} + p_{i+1,j} = 1.0$

Since Plant C's entire cycle stock is consumed in the same period ($p_{iC} = 1.0$ and $p_{i+1,C} = 0$)

$$\overline{\text{WIP}}(C)_{ij} = COSP_C \times MLT_C \times P_i$$

The data in Table 9-7 reveal that:

$$\begin{aligned} p_{iB} &= 3.33 \div 4.33 \\ p_{i+1,B} &= 1.0 \div 4.33 \\ p_{iA} &= 2.83 \div 4.33, \text{ and} \\ p_{i+1,A} &= 1.5 \div 4.33 \end{aligned}$$

That is, Plant B's cycle stock is used in finished goods production one week later on the average and Plant A's cycle stock is used in finished goods production 1.5 weeks later on the average. Thus:

$$\overline{\text{WIP}}(C)_{iA} = COSP_A \times MLT_A \left( \frac{2.83}{4.33} P_i + \frac{1.5}{4.33} P_{i+1} \right)$$

$$\overline{\text{WIP}}(C)_{iB} = COSP_B \times MLT_B \left( \frac{3.33}{4.33} P_i + \frac{1.0}{4.33} P_{i+1} \right)$$

For example, calculating the $\overline{\text{WIP}}$ cycle stock during Month 3 at Plant A:

$$\overline{\text{WIP}}(C)_{3A} = .4 \times \frac{1.0}{4.33} \left( \frac{2.83}{4.33} \times 9{,}000 + \frac{1.5}{4.33} \times 10{,}000 \right)$$

$$= 862.6 \text{ units}$$

Using a model such as the previous one, which recognizes that WIP($C$) depends on finished goods output in the following month(s) as well as the present, requires additional calculations. Whether these added calculations are worth the trouble depends on the magnitude of the difference in production outputs ($|P_i - P_{i+1}|$) and the percentage of WIP($C$) dependent on the following month's output. The approach is presented here to illustrate how a model might be developed and used. The values of average WIP cycle stock are listed in Table 9-8.

[4]This is the general WIP cycle stock model for this example. It should aid in developing models for other situations.

**TABLE 9-8**
**AVERAGE WORK-IN-PROCESS (UNITS)***
**BY FUNCTIONAL CLASS AND MONTH**

**WIP Cycle Stock**

| | Month | | | | | |
|---|---|---|---|---|---|---|
| **Plant** | **1 & 2** | **3** | **4–8** | **9** | **10 & 11** | **12** |
| A | 831 | 863 | 923 | 955 | 1,015 | 951 |
| B | 1,246 | 1,278 | 1,385 | 1,417 | 1,523 | 1,458 |
| C | 1,973 | 1,973 | 2,192 | 2,192 | 2,411 | 2,411 |
| Total | 4,050 | 4,114 | 4,500 | 4,564 | 4,949 | 4,820 |

**WIP Buffer Stock**

| | Month | | |
|---|---|---|---|
| **Plant** | **1–3** | **4–9** | **10–12** |
| A | 171 | 190 | 210 |
| B | 257 | 286 | 314 |
| C | 407 | 452 | 498 |
| Total | 835 | 928 | 1,022 |

**WIP Transportation Stock**

| | Month | | |
|---|---|---|---|
| **From Plant** | **1–3** | **4–9** | **10–12** |
| A | 171 | 190 | 210 |
| B | 257 | 286 | 314 |
| Total | 428 | 476 | 524 |

**WIP Total**

| Month | | | | | |
|---|---|---|---|---|---|
| **1 & 2** | **3** | **4–8** | **9** | **10 & 11** | **12** |
| 5,313 | 5,377 | 5,904 | 5,968 | 6,495 | 6,366 |

*Rounded to the nearest integer

**WIP Buffer Stock.** The weighted average of WIP buffer stock $\overline{\text{WIP}}(B)$ at each plant equals one day's output. Thus,

$$\overline{\text{WIP}}(B)_{ij} = COSP_j \times P_i \div \text{working days per month}$$

Where:

$\overline{\text{WIP}}(B)_{ij}$ = the average WIP buffer stock during Period $i$ at Plant $j$, and $COSP_j$ and $P_i$ are as defined earlier

For example, if there are 21 working days in the first month,

$$\overline{\text{WIP}}(B)_{1\text{A}} = .4 \times 9{,}000 \div 21 = 171.42$$
$$\overline{\text{WIP}}(B)_{1\text{B}} = .6 \times 9{,}000 \div 21 = 257.14$$
$$\overline{\text{WIP}}(B)_{1\text{C}} = .95 \times 9{,}000 \div 21 = 407.14$$

The average WIP($B$)'s for the remaining months were calculated using 21 working days. The values are listed in Table 9-8. When a production rate change occurs these calculated values will be slightly inaccurate. An increased (decreased) finished goods production rate in one month can increase (decrease) WIP safety stock requirements the previous month in Plants A and B. We do not consider that here, since the effect is very small; and the modified calculations, if warranted, are similar to those for Periods 3, 9, and 12 when calculating WIP($C$).

This discussion of WIP($B$) began with the statement that the weighted average of buffer stock at each plant equalled one day's output. Such information is not always available and measuring the average buffer stock is seldom easy. When data and time are scarce, applying the principles of ABC analysis can help.[5] For example, determine the weighted average of *A* safety stock items (those relatively few items that have the major portion of total safety stock investment) and use that value as a basis for estimating the overall average.

**WIP Transportation Stock.** The average transportation stock WIP($T$) equals the average number of units in transit times the average transit time. Shipments are made daily from Plant A to Plant B, from Plant A to Plant C, and from Plant B to Plant C. One half of Plant A's output goes to Plant B and Plant C each. The general model for transportation inventory investment[6] is:

$$TII = TT \times SR$$

Where:

$TII$ = transportation inventory investment
$TT$ = transportation time
$SR$ = shipping rate

In our example $TT$ equals 1 day and $SR$ equals $COSP_j \times \frac{P_i}{21}$. Thus,

$$\overline{\text{WIP}}(T)_{ij} = COSP_j \times \frac{P_i}{21}$$

---

[5]See Chapter 6 for a discussion of ABC principles and techniques.

[6]See Chapter 6.

Where

> $\overline{\text{WIP}}(T)_{ij}$ is the value of WIP($T$) leaving Plant $j$ during Period $i$. This model applies only to Plants A and B, since materials shipped from Plant C are finished goods and were included in finished goods transportation stock.

For example, $\overline{\text{WIP}}(T)_{1A} = .40 \times 9{,}000 \div 21 = 171.42$, and
$\overline{\text{WIP}}(T)_{1B} = .60 \times 9{,}000 \div 21 = 257.14$

The WIP transportation stock for each month is calculated in the same manner. Table 9-8 contains these values.

**Raw Material and Purchase Parts.** The benefits and/or necessity of lot size order quantities (cycle stock), buffer stock, intransit (transportation) stock, and receiving inspection cause raw material and purchase parts inventories (*RM*). In the example these inventories exist at each plant. Estimating the projected investment in such inventory requires that order quantity sizes, safety stock levels, transit time, and inspection time be obtained.

The value of *RM* in-transit stock investment depends on the point at which title passes from the seller to the buyer. Since this may differ by supplier, determining the average value of *RM* transportation inventory can be a laborious task. And once determined, the value can change as new contracts are negotiated. However, the dynamic nature of the average value of all types of inventory—even with a constant production rate—is not uncommon. Costs may change; lot sizes may change; and safety stock levels may be raised or lowered. In our example the following information is available:

1. The weighted average of *RM* cycle stock equals a half month's supply.
2. The weighted average of *RM* safety stock equals one quarter of a month's supply.
3. On the average, incoming orders take 1.5 days, approximately 7.5 percent of a month, to clear inspection.
4. Title for most purchased items does not pass until they reach the receiving dock. However, a few items are purchased FOB (*free-on-board*, a designation of the point where title passes) at the supplier's loading dock. On average the company owns material in transit equal to .5 percent of the month's purchases.
5. The sum of the *RM* required at the three plant equals .40 *COS*.
6. Manufacturing lead time requirements cause the average *RM* investment for a month to be equally dependent on the planned *FG* outputs for that month and on the following month.

Analysis of the foregoing information gives the following models:

$$\overline{RM}(C)_i = .5 \times .4(.5 \times P_i + .5 \times P_{i+1})$$
$$\overline{RM}(B)_i = .25 \times .4(.5 \times P_i + .5 \times P_{i+1})$$
$$\overline{RM}(INSP)_i = .075 \times .4(.5 \times P_i + .5 \times P_{i+1})$$
$$\overline{RM}(T)_i = .005 \times .4(.5 \times P_i + .5 \times P_{i+1})$$

Thus:

$$\overline{RM}(TOT)_i = .83 \times .4(.5 \times P_i + .5P_{i+1})$$

Where:

$\overline{RM}(C)_i$ = the average *RM* cycle stock during Month *i*, expressed in *FG* units
$\overline{RM}(B)_i$ = the average *RM* buffer stock during Month *i*, expressed in *FG* units
$\overline{RM}(T)_i$ = the average *RM* in-transit stock during Month *i*, expressed in *FG* units
$\overline{RM}(TOT)_i$ = the average total *RM* during Month *i*
$\overline{RM}(INSP)_i$ = the average *RM* in-inspection stock during Month *i*, expressed in *FG* units

For example, during Month 9 of the example the investment in these different types of *FG* equivalent units is:

$$\begin{aligned}
\overline{RM}(C)_9 &= .5 \times .4(.5 \times 10{,}000 + .5 \times 11{,}000)\\
&= 2{,}100\\
\overline{RM}(B)_9 &= .25 \times .4(.5 \times 10{,}000 + .5 \times 11{,}000)\\
&= 1{,}050\\
\overline{RM}(INSP)_9 &= .075 \times .4(.5 \times 10{,}000 + .5 \times 11{,}000)\\
&= 315\\
\overline{RM}(T)_9 &= .005 \times .4(.5 \times 10{,}000 + .5 \times 11{,}000)\\
&= 21
\end{aligned}$$

These values and those for the other months are listed in Table 9-9. *FG* equivalent units are used so that the dollar value of *RM* can be obtained merely by multiplying by the unit *FG COS*.

**TABLE 9-9**
**AVERAGE RAW MATERIAL INVENTORY (*FGE* UNITS) BY FUNCTIONAL CLASS AND MONTH**

| | Class | | | | |
|---|---|---|---|---|---|
| **Month** | **Cycle** | **Buffer** | **In Inspection** | **In Transit** | **Total** |
| 1 & 2 | 1,800 | 900 | 270 | 18 | 2,988 |
| 3 | 1,900 | 950 | 285 | 19 | 3,154 |
| 4–8 | 2,000 | 1,000 | 300 | 20 | 3,320 |
| 9 | 2,100 | 1,050 | 315 | 21 | 3,486 |
| 10 & 11 | 2,200 | 1,100 | 330 | 22 | 3,652 |
| 12 | 2,000 | 1,000 | 300 | 20 | 3,320 |

Summing the totals of raw material, work-in-process, and finished goods each month gives the total average inventory investment in finished goods equivalent units (*FGE*'s). This is accomplished in Table 9-10. Multiplying the *FGE*'s by the unit cost of goods sold, $80, gives the projected dollar value investments listed in Table 9-11.

**TABLE 9-10**
**PROJECTED AVERAGE INVENTORY BY MONTH AND TYPE IN *FG* EQUIVALENT UNITS**

| Month | Class | | | Total |
|---|---|---|---|---|
| | *RM* | WIP | *FG* | |
| 1 | 2,988 | 5,313 | 3,490 | 11,791 |
| 2 | 2,988 | 5,313 | 4,990 | 13,291 |
| 3 | 3,154 | 5,377 | 6,990 | 15,521 |
| 4 | 3,320 | 5,904 | 7,160 | 16,384 |
| 5 | 3,320 | 5,904 | 4,910 | 14,134 |
| 6 | 3,320 | 5,904 | 3,160 | 12,384 |
| 7 | 3,320 | 5,904 | 4,160 | 13,384 |
| 8 | 3,320 | 5,904 | 7,160 | 16,384 |
| 9 | 3,486 | 5,968 | 9,410 | 18,864 |
| 10 | 3,652 | 6,495 | 8,830 | 18,977 |
| 11 | 3,652 | 6,495 | 6,330 | 16,477 |
| 12 | 3,320 | 6,366 | 4,330 | 14,016 |

**TABLE 9-11**
**PROJECTED AVERAGE INVENTORY INVESTMENT BY MONTH**

| Month | Inventory Investment* |
|---|---|
| 1 | $ 943 |
| 2 | 1,063 |
| 3 | 1,242 |
| 4 | 1,311 |
| 5 | 1,131 |
| 6 | 991 |
| 7 | 1,071 |
| 8 | 1,311 |
| 9 | 1,509 |
| 10 | 1,518 |
| 11 | 1,318 |
| 12 | 1,121 |

*In thousands of dollars.

The preceding calculations, tedious when performed with a desk calculator, can be programmed for computer processing. The difficult task is establishing the values of the parameters and their relation to inventory investment. For example, determining the average value of the cycle stocks, the value of the aggregate WIP cycle stock at a point in the manufacturing process, the average value of safety stock, and their relationship to monthly production output requires diligent analysis. When many items are involved, an ABC type approach is useful.

This example concerned a single product in a make-to-stock, continuous process—or mass production—environment. In a multiproduct environment, a similar process could be followed for each product.

## Job Shop Environment

In a continuous process or mass production environment the projected inventory investment depends primarily on the rate of flow and products being produced. Projecting inventory investment in a job shop environment requires an order-by-order and operation-by-operation—or operation group-by-group—analysis. The detailed procedures and calculations appropriate in a situation depend on the characteristics of that situation. However, the approach is the same.

Required prerequisite information includes purchasing and manufacturing lead time, a master production schedule (MPS), bills of materials, operation processes, and the value added at milestones in the production process of each item.

The following discussion explains and illustrates an approach for calculating projected WIP increases and decreases by period in the planning horizon.

Calculating changes in the WIP inventory consists of:

1. Calculating the time-phased increase in inventory for each item on the MPS
2. Summing by period these increases for all items on the MPS
3. Adding to these totals the funds allocated for anticipation type purchases
4. Decreasing period totals by an estimate of the purchases that have been made previously in anticipation (Step 3)

We will use Assembly 675000 to illustrate this approach. The MPS calls for 100 of these assemblies to be shipped in Week 30. Fabricating a 675000 assembly requires two subassemblies (first level), a purchased part, and paint. One of these subassemblies, Part 675200, is fabricated from three production parts; the other first level subassembly, 675100, is the assembly of two second level subassemblies, 675110 and 675120. Table 9-12 is a bill of materials describing the foregoing relationships and all other items required in the manufacture of 675000. It also lists the lead time of all items based on the manufacture of a lot of 100 assemblies; in addition, it lists the value added per 100 units for each item.

Figure 9-9 is a process chart indicating when material must be available and fabrication operations must be completed if the one hundred 675000 assemblies are to be transferred to finished goods in Week 30. The chart is based on normal manufacturing lead times. For example, Figure 9-9 reveals that the raw material, M3523, must be available by Week 17 and purchased part, P7472, must be available by Week 20.

**TABLE 9-12**
**ILLUSTRATION OF A BILL OF MATERIAL, ITEM LEAD TIMES, AND ITEM VALUE ADDED FOR AN MPS ITEM**

| Part No.[1] | Quantity[2] | Value Added | Item Lead Time (Weeks) | Cumulative Lead Time (Weeks) | Start[3] (Week) |
|---|---|---|---|---|---|
| 675000 | 1 | $ 4.60 | 2 | 2 | 28 |
| 675100 | 1 | 2.50 | 1 | 3 | 27 |
| 675110 | 1 | 4.80 | 2 | 5 | 25 |
| 675111 | 1 | 5.40 | 3 | 8 | 22 |
| M2787 | 2 lb. | .30 | 2 | 10 | 20 |
| 675112 | 1 | 14.40 | 8 | 13 | 17 |
| M3523 | 3 lb. | .30 | 2 | 15 | 15 |
| 675113 | 2 | 8.10 | 4 | 9 | 21 |
| M8619 | 3.5 lb. | 1.10 | 1 | 10 | 20 |
| 675120 | 1 | 8.40 | 3 | 6 | 24 |
| 675121 | 1 | 7.20 | 4 | 10 | 20 |
| P7472 | 1 | .25 | 3 | 13 | 17 |
| 675122 | 1 | 3.60 | 2 | 8 | 22 |
| M2786 | 6.5 lb. | 1.20 | 1 | 9 | 21 |
| P1314 | 2 | .84 | 2 | 8 | 22 |
| 675200 | 1 | 7.20 | 3 | 5 | 25 |
| 675210 | 1 | 3.60 | 2 | 7 | 23 |
| P4423 | 2 | 5.25 | 2 | 9 | 21 |
| 675220 | 1 | 1.80 | 1 | 6 | 24 |
| M3391 | 4 ft. | .40 | 1 | 7 | 23 |
| 675230 | 1 | 8.10 | 4 | 9 | 21 |
| M1851 | 2 lb. | .25 | 2 | 11 | 19 |
| P2783 | 1 | 6.70 | 4 | 6 | 24 |
| M1467 | 5 gal. | 13.00 | 1 | 3 | 27 |

[1]An *M* prefix indicates raw material and a *P* prefix indicates a purchased part.
[2]Raw material quantity requirements usually are specified in pounds, gallons, linear feet, or other bulk measure.
[3]See Figure 9-1.

Table 9-13 tabulates the increases in WIP as purchase items arrive, parts are manufactured, and assemblies completed. For example, plans are for M3523 to be available in Week 17, item 675121 completed by Week 24, and 675100 assembled by Week 28. The value added by completing these and similar activities for 100 items is recorded. The increases in WIP due to partial completion of an item's manufacture are not recorded in order to keep the example simple. For example, although labor is added to WIP during Weeks 25 and 26, no increase in WIP is recorded since no activities are completed. However, estimates of partial completion could be made and WIP increased accordingly.

Also, for the sake of simplicity, the value of purchased material was not transferred to manufactured items when they were completed. The value of these transfers can be calculated and the transfer programmed for computer processing.

**FIGURE 9-9**
**INVENTORY INVESTMENT VALUE ADDED**
**(TIME-PHASED WITH THE MPS)**

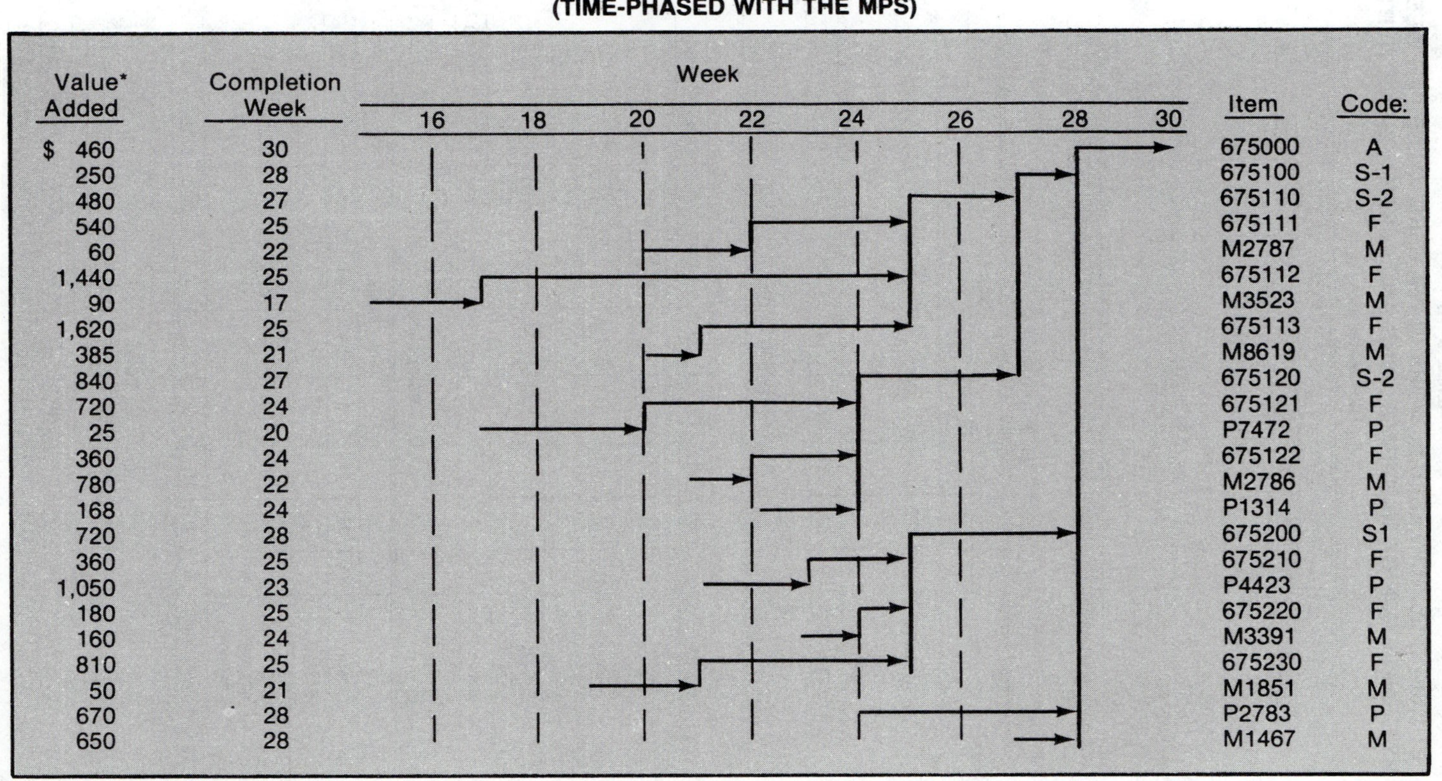


*Based on values in Table 9-12.

## TABLE 9-13
## CUMULATIVE INCREASES IN WORK-IN-PROCESS VALUE PER WEEK BY COMPLETION OF MANUFACTURING AND PURCHASING ACTIVITIES

### A. Raw Materials

| Item | Week 17 | 20 | 21 | 22 | 23 | 24 | 27 | 28 | 30 |
|---|---|---|---|---|---|---|---|---|---|
| M3523 | $90 | | | | | | | | |
| M8619 | | | $385 | | | | | | |
| M1851 | | | 50 | | | | | | |
| M2787 | | | | $ 60 | | | | | |
| M2786 | | | | 780 | | | | | |
| M3391 | | | | | | $ 160 | | | |
| M1467 | | | | | | | | $ 650 | |
| Cumulative Value | $90 | $90 | $525 | $1,365 | $1,365 | $1,525 | $1,525 | $2,175 | $2,175 |

### B. Purchase Parts

| Item | Week 17 | 20 | 21 | 22 | 23 | 24 | 27 | 28 | 30 |
|---|---|---|---|---|---|---|---|---|---|
| P7472 | | $25 | | | | | | | |
| P4423 | | | | | $1,050 | | | | |
| P1314 | | | | | | $ 168 | | | |
| P2783 | | | | | | | | $ 670 | |
| Cumulative Value | 0 | $25 | $25 | $25 | $1,075 | $1,243 | $1,243 | $1,913 | $1,913 |

### C. Fabricated Parts

| Item | Week 17 | 20 | 21 | 22 | 23 | 24 | 27 | 28 | 30 |
|---|---|---|---|---|---|---|---|---|---|
| 675121 | | | | | | $ 720 | | | |
| 675122 | | | | | | 360 | | | |
| 675111 | | | | | | | $ 540 | | |
| 675112 | | | | | | | 1,440 | | |
| 675113 | | | | | | | 1,620 | | |
| 675210 | | | | | | | 360 | | |
| 675220 | | | | | | | 180 | | |
| 675230 | | | | | | | 810 | | |
| Cumulative Value | 0 | 0 | 0 | 0 | 0 | $1,080 | $6,030 | $6,030 | $6,030 |

### D. Assemblies

| Item | Week 17 | 20 | 21 | 22 | 23 | 24 | 27 | 28 | 30 |
|---|---|---|---|---|---|---|---|---|---|
| 675110 | | | | | | | $ 480 | | |
| 675120 | | | | | | | 840 | | |
| 675100 | | | | | | | | $ 250 | |
| 675200 | | | | | | | | 720 | |
| 675000 | | | | | | | | | $ 460 |
| Cumulative Value | 0 | 0 | 0 | 0 | 0 | 0 | $1,320 | $2,290 | $2,750 |

### E. Total

| Week 17 | 20 | 21 | 22 | 23 | 24 | 27 | 28 | 30 |
|---|---|---|---|---|---|---|---|---|
| $90 | $115 | $550 | $1,390 | $2,440 | $3,448 | $10,118 | $12,408 | $12,868 |

Table 9-14 sums the investment for all items on the MPS. To keep the example relatively simple we have added only two other MPS items, assemblies 445000 and 925000. It also sums investment in raw material, purchase parts, fabricated parts, subassemblies, and assemblies. This is a laborious task when performed manually for a large number of MPS items. However, once the investment pattern of each MPS item is established and software obtained (developed), a computer can perform the summations by period with relative ease. For example, the totals are $610 for Week 16, $54,959 for Week 28, and $51,786 for Week 30. The $8,434 for Item 445000 is removed from the total in Week 30 since Item 445000 was shipped in Week 29.

**TABLE 9-14**
**AGGREGATE INVENTORY INVESTMENT FROM MPS, MULTIPLE ITEMS**

| | MPS Item | | | |
|---|---|---|---|---|
| | 675000 | 445000 | 925000 | |
| Quantity | 100 | 50 | 200 | Total |
| Week | | | | |
| 16 | $ — | $ — | $ 610 | $ 610 |
| 18 | 90 | 210 | 3,520 | 3,820 |
| 20 | 115 | 720 | 6,405 | 7,240 |
| 22 | 1,390 | 3,120 | 12,167 | 16,677 |
| 24 | 3,448 | 4,210 | 22,815 | 30,473 |
| 26 | 3,448 | 7,826 | 28,374 | 39,648 |
| 28 | 12,408 | 8,434 | 34,117 | 54,959 |
| 30 | 12,868 | —* | 38,918 | 51,786 |

*Assembly 445000 has been shipped to a customer.

# MANAGEMENT UNDER CONSTRAINTS

The shortage of financial resources frequently leads management to limit the capital available for inventory. When the projected inventory investment exceeds the limit, reductions in one or more of the functional types of stock can bring the investment within the acceptable bound. Since initial aggregate inventory plans usually are based on minimum cost strategies, reducing inventory investment often will increase total costs. Comparing the increased costs resulting from the reduced investment to the benefits gained will enable management to evaluate the constraint.

## Anticipation Inventory

Building inventory prior to vacation shutdowns or peak sales periods is a common practice in industry. An analysis comparing the costs of carrying anticipation inventory to the costs of changing production levels was included in Chapter 1.

## Cycle (Lot Size) Inventories

Finished goods with independent demand may be produced in Economic lot sizes to minimize the sum of carrying and setup costs. Purchased parts and raw material used in production at a relatively constant rate also may be purchased in economic order quantities.[7] Cycle stock inventory investment changes in direct proportion to purchase and production lot sizes as illustrated in Figure 9-10. Thus reducing lot sizes reduces inventory investment. However, the smaller lot sizes result in more orders per year and increased preparation (setup and ordering) costs. Figure 9-11 illustrates this relationship.

**FIGURE 9-10**
**LOT SIZE AND AVERAGE INVENTORY**
**(FINISHED GOODS AND PURCHASED ITEMS WITH INDEPENDENT DEMAND)**

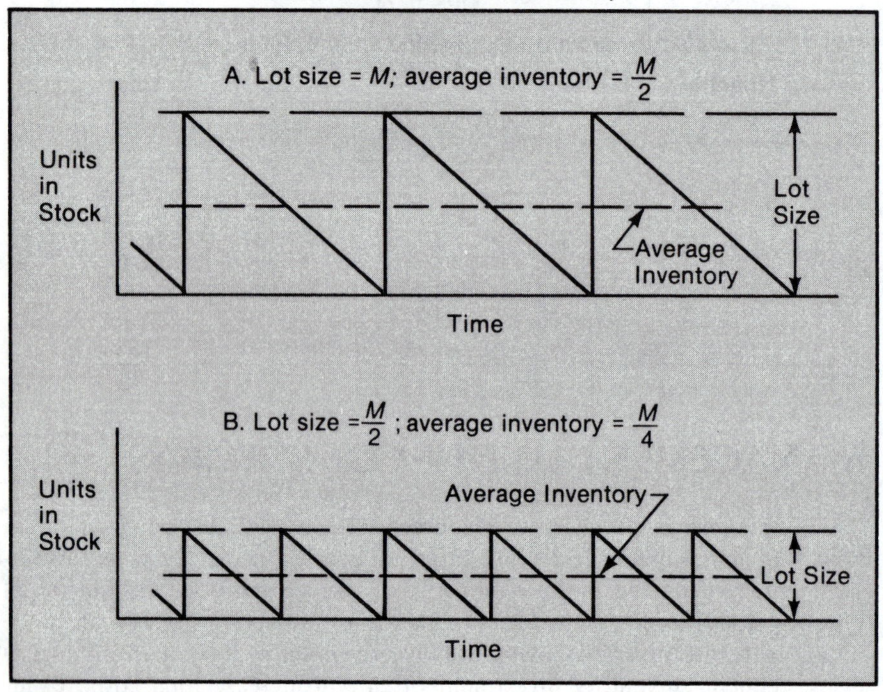


Three approaches to controlling cycle stock investment by modifying lot sizes are: (1) treating the carrying cost rate ($k$) as a policy variable, (2) the LIMIT procedure, and (3) the Lagrangian Multiplier approach. We will examine each.

[7]See Chapters 7 and 8 for a discussion of economic order quantities.

FIGURE 9-11
CYCLE STOCK INVESTMENT VERSUS ORDERING COSTS

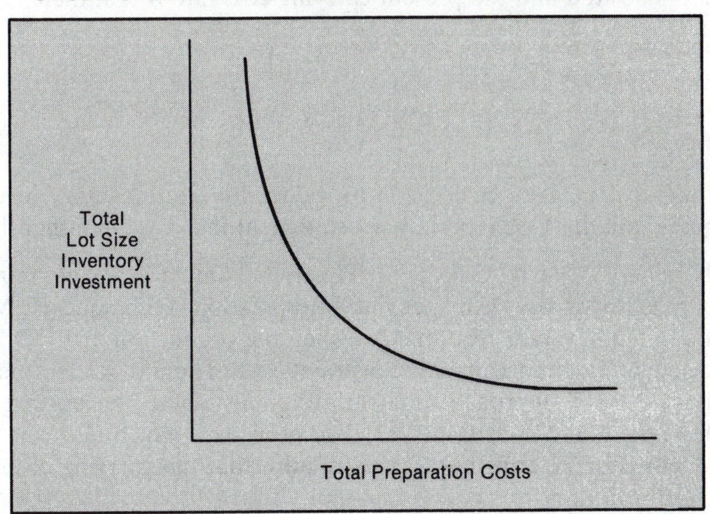


**The Carrying Cost Rate as a Policy Variable.** Robert G. Brown has pointed out that lot size adjustments can be made by treating the carrying cost rate ($k$) as a management policy variable. [1] Increasing $k$ will decrease the lot size in proportion to the square root of the ratio of the old to the new value of $k$ as proved in the following: designating the new values of $k$ and the EOQ as $k'$ and EOQ$'$ and recalling that the

$$\text{EOQ} = \sqrt{2SR \div (kC)}, \text{ then}$$
$$\text{EOQ}' = \sqrt{2\,SR \div (k'\,C)}$$

Thus

$$\text{EOQ}' \div \text{EOQ} = \sqrt{k} \div \sqrt{k'}, \text{ and}$$
$$\text{EOQ}' = \text{EOQ}\sqrt{k \div k'}$$

We can illustrate this with an example. Let the old EOQ be 20 units and the carrying cost rate be increased by 50 percent, then

$$\text{EOQ}' = 20\sqrt{.667} = 16.32, \text{ or } 17 \text{ units}$$

To reduce the average lot size stock investment by a percentage ($p$) one can calculate the ratio of the new carrying cost rate ($k'$) to the old carrying cost rate ($k$) using the following model

$$\frac{k'}{k} = \left(\frac{1}{1-p}\right)^2$$

For example, if a 25 percent reduction in the average cycle stock investment is desired and the present carrying cost rate is .20, then

$$\frac{k'}{.20} = \left(\frac{1}{1 - .25}\right)^2$$

$$k' = .2(1.78)$$

$$k' = .36$$

Thus, a management decision to reduce lot size inventory investment by 25 percent in this case is an implicit statement that $k$ is .36 rather than .20.

**LIMIT.** James D. Harty, George W. Plossl, and Oliver W. Wight introduced the Lot-Size Inventory Management Interpolation Technique (LIMIT) to calculate minimum total cost lot sizes when the production of EOQ lot sizes will exceed production capacity constraints. [2] Thomas R. Hoffmann extended the LIMIT approach to cover situations where the normal EOQ's exceeded investment constraints. [3] The procedure which also can be used to cope with storage constraints does require that the carrying cost rate be the same for all items.

**The Procedure.** This technique determines the relation of the aggregate EOQ requirements to the limited resource available and revises all the lot sizes by the same proportion to bring the aggregate EOQ resource requirements within the limit. When capital or storage space is insufficient, the EOQ's must be reduced; when production capacity is insufficient, the EOQ's must be increased. In the latter case production capacity requirements are lowered as a result of the decreased setup requirements. When both production capacity and either capital or storage space available are exceeded by the EOQ requirements, the manager must decide on the trade-off between added production capacity costs and added investment or storage costs. The procedure is described next and an example follows.

1. Group items on the basis of common carrying cost rates, common resource requirements, or common space requirements.
2. Determine the multiplier ($M$). The exact nature of the calculation depends on the constrained resource. The values described here relate to the group being analyzed and the applicable constraint.

   (a) Capital constraint

   $$M = \frac{\text{Limit on the cycle stock investment}}{\text{Aggregate EOQ investment required}}$$

   (b) Production capacity constraint

   $$M = \frac{\text{Aggregate EOQ setup hours required}}{\text{Limit on setup hours}}$$

   (c) Space constraint

   $$M = \frac{\text{Maximum space available for cycle stock}}{\text{Aggregate EOQ space requirements}}$$

3. Multiply the EOQ of each item in the group by $M$ to obtain the LIMIT Order Quantity (LOQ) for each item.
4. Calculate the aggregate capital (production or space capacity) required by the LOQ's and determine if the new requirements are within the limit.
5. Calculate the aggregate preparation (ordering and setup) and carrying costs of the LOQ's.
6. Decide if the benefits of operating within the constraint are greater than the added costs.

**An Example.** Table 9-15 contains data concering four independent demand items that have the same carrying cost rate, .3. The economic production lot size of these four final products is calculated using the basic model described in Chapter 7. For example, the EOQ for Item A is calculated as follows:

$$\text{EOQ} = \sqrt{\frac{2RS}{kC\,(1 - D \div P)}}$$

$R$ = 1,000 units  $k$ = .30
$C$ = \$10.00  $P$ = 50 units per day
$S$ = \$36.00  $D$ = 1,000 ÷ 250 = 4 units per day

$$\text{EOQ}(A) = \sqrt{\frac{2 \times 1{,}000 \times 36}{3 \times 10(1 - 4 \div 50)}} = 161.51$$

$$\text{EOQ}(A) \cong 162$$

The average lot size investment ($\bar{I}_{\$_i}$) for an item equals the product of the average quantity in inventory and the cost of an item. Thus,

$$\bar{I}_{\$A} = \frac{Q}{2}(1 - D \div P)C\text{; and}$$

$$\bar{I}_{\$A} = \frac{162}{2}(1 - 4 \div 50)\,10 = \$745.20$$

The annual carrying cost and annual preparation costs were calculated as described in Chapter 7. The aggregate average cycle stock investment for the four items ($A$, $B$, $C$, and $D$) is \$6,028.17 as recorded in Table 9-15. The limit for average cycle stock investment in this group of items is \$5,000. (Similar limits have been established for other groups to bring the aggregate investment for all cycle stock within a given constraint.) Therefore,

$$M = \$5{,}000 \div \$6{,}028.17 = .8294$$

The new order quantity, the LOQ, for each item equals .8294 times the EOQ. Thus,

$$\text{LOQ}(A) = .8294 \times 162 = 134.36$$
$$\text{LOQ}(A) \cong 134$$

**TABLE 9-15**
**AVERAGE CYCLE STOCK INVESTMENT[1]**
**ANNUAL CARRYING COSTS AND PREPARATION COSTS**

**A. With the EOQ**

| ($R$) Annual Requirements | Item | ($C$) Unit Cost | ($S$) Preparation (Setup and Ordering) Costs | ($P$) Daily Production Rate | EOQ | Average Inventory Investment | Annual Carrying Costs | Annual Preparation Costs | $(1 - D \div P)$ |
|---|---|---|---|---|---|---|---|---|---|
| 1,000 | *A* | $10.00 | $36 | 50 | 162 | $ 745.20 | $ 223.56 | $ 222.22 | .92 |
| 40,000 | *B* | 2.50 | 28 | 800 | 1,932 | 1,932.00 | 579.60 | 579.68 | .80 |
| 15,000 | *C* | 4.00 | 48 | 500 | 1,168 | 2,055.68 | 616.70 | 616.42 | .88 |
| 8,000 | *D* | 6.00 | 25 | 200 | 514 | 1,295.29 | 388.58 | 389.11 | .84 |
| | | | | | Total | $6,028.17 | $1,808.44 | $1,807.43 | |

Constraint: Maximum average investment = $5,000 ($I_K$).
Multiplier ($M$) = $I_K \div I$
= $5,000 ÷ $6,028.17
= .8294
LOQ = $M$ (EOQ)

**B. With the LOQ**

| Item | LOQ | Annual Inventory Investment | Annual Carrying Costs | Annual Preparation Costs |
|---|---|---|---|---|
| *A* | 134 | $ 616.40 | $ 184.92 | $ 268.65 |
| *B* | 1,602 | 1,602.00 | 480.60 | 699.12 |
| *C* | 969 | 1,705.44 | 511.63 | 743.03 |
| *D* | 426 | 1,073.52 | 322.06 | 469.48 |
| | Total | $4,997.36 | $1,499.21 | $2,180.28 |

[1] 250 operating days per year

The LOQ's for Items *B, C,* and *D* are obtained in the same manner; and average investment required by the LOQ is calculated in the usual manner.

$$\bar{I}_{\$} = \frac{\text{LOQ}}{2}(1 - D \div P)C\text{; thus}$$

$$\bar{I}_{\$}(A) = \frac{134}{2}(1 - 4 \div 50)\,10 = \$616.40$$

Table 9-15 includes the results of these calculations for all items.

The LOQ lot sizes require an aggregate average investment of approximately \$5,000, annual carrying costs of \$1,499.21, and preparation costs of \$2,180.30. Thus the trade-off is a \$373 (\$2,180 − \$1,807) increase in preparation costs for a decrease of approximately \$1,030 (\$6,028 − \$4,997) in inventory investment and a savings of \$309 (\$1,808 − \$1,499) in carrying costs. However, the actual increase in aggregate setup costs when the LOQ lot sizes are implemented depends on the utilization of equipment and personnel prior to the change.

If the affected workers and machines are operating on *undertime* (scheduled production is less than that normally obtained from available equipment and personnel), the added setups may be accomplished by otherwise idle personnel and machines, and the increased preparation costs will be substantially less than the straightforward calculations indicate. Conversely, if the affected workers and machines already are operating at capacity or on overtime, the increase in setup hours will exacerbate the capacity problem, and the costs of the added setups will be much greater than the standard calculations indicate. The inventory planner always should evaluate how well a model fits a given situation. The foregoing situations are good examples of cases in which the cost model should be altered.

**Lagrangian Multiplier.** The objective when constraints necessitate altering lot sizes is to minimize the sum of the aggregate carrying and preparation costs while meeting the constraint. Thus, the objective is:

1. For purchase items

$$\text{Minimize TC} = \sum_{i=1}^{n}\left(\frac{R_i S_i}{Q_i} + \frac{k_i C_i Q_i}{2}\right)$$

$$\text{subject to} \sum \frac{C_i Q_i}{2} \le L$$

2. For production items

$$\text{Minimize TC} = \sum_{i=1}^{n}\left(\frac{R_i S_i}{Q_i} + \frac{k_i C_i Q_i(1 - D_i \div P_i)}{2}\right)$$

$$\text{subject to} \sum \frac{C_i Q_i(1 - D_i \div P_i)}{2} \le L$$

When $k$ is the same for all items, the following Lagrangian expression can be developed for the previous minimization problem which is subject to a single constraint, capital invested.

$$h = \sum_{i=1}^{n} \frac{S_i R_i}{Q_i} + k \left[ \sum_{i=1}^{n} \frac{C_i Q_i (1 - D_i \div P_i)}{2} \right] + \lambda \left[ \sum_{i=1}^{n} \frac{C_i Q_i (1 - D_i \div P_i)}{2} \right] - \lambda L$$

Where:

$\lambda$ is the Lagrangian multiplier and $L$ is the limit on cycle stock investment

Setting the partial derivatives of the above expression, for production parts, with respect to $Q_i$ and $\lambda$ equal to zero and solving for $Q_i$ and $\lambda$ gives:

$$Q_i = \sqrt{\frac{2S_i R_i}{(k + \lambda) C_i (1 - D_i \div P_i)}}, \text{ and}$$

$$\lambda = \frac{\left[ \sum_{i=1}^{n} \sqrt{S_i C_i R_i (1 - D_i \div P_i)} \right]^2}{2L^2} - k \quad [4]$$

Using the data in Table 9-15A for example purposes gives

$$\lambda = \frac{(4{,}668.13)^2}{2 \times (5000)^2} - .30 = .1358$$

$$Q_A = \sqrt{\frac{2 \times 36 \times 1000}{(.30 + .1358) \times 10 \times .92}} = 134$$

$$Q_B = 1603; Q_C = 969; \text{ and } Q_D = 427$$

These are essentially the same results we obtained using the LIMIT approach. The differences are due to different rounding results.

Notice that this is the same result that the first approach, treating $k$ as a management policy variable, gives. For example, we must reduce an investment of \$6,028 to \$5,000, a 17.06 percent decrease. Using the model,

$$\frac{k'}{k} = \left(\frac{1}{1 - P}\right)^2$$

$$\frac{k'}{.30} = \left(\frac{1}{1 - .1706}\right)^2$$

$$k' = .4361$$

Thus, the value obtained for $k'$ equals $k + \lambda$ obtained by the Lagrangian approach. The two approaches are equivalent when all items have the same carrying cost. Under these circumstances it is difficult to justify using the

Lagrangian approach. However, when the carrying cost rates are not the same, the picture changes.

It is not unusual for different inventoried items to have different carrying cost rates. As discussed in Chapter 6, the carrying cost rate is affected by the costs of capital, storage, obsolescence, deterioration, taxes, and insurance. Although the cost of capital may be the same for all items, the other carrying cost rate factors may be different for different groups. For example, bulky low cost items will have a higher storage and handling cost per dollar value than do compact high cost items. When analyzing aggregate cycle stock investment, items should be grouped by common carrying cost rates. However this may not always be possible.

When all items in a group do not have the same carrying cost rate and lot sizes must be reduced to bring cycle stock investment within an upper bound, the LIMIT approach will give lot sizes whose sum of carrying costs and setup costs approaches the minimum possible; and the Lagrangian approach will give lot sizes with the minimum total costs. However, the Lagrangian model cannot be solved in a straightforward manner; the value of $\lambda$ must be found by trial and error. A numerical method such as Newton's is usually an efficient approach.[8]

For example, if the $k$'s of Items $A$, $B$, $C$, and $D$ of the previous example are .30, .25, .20 and .35 respectively, rather than .30, the EOQ's, LOQ's, and $\lambda$ OQ's are as listed in Table 9-16 on page 304.

The value of $\lambda$ in this situation is .18. It is found by attempting different values for $\lambda$ until the following condition is met.

$$L \geq \sum \sqrt{\frac{2R_iS_i}{(k_i + \lambda)C(1 - D_i \div P_i)}}$$

The values of the Lagrangian order quantities ($\lambda$OQ's) are included in Table 9-16 along with their carrying and setup costs. The total setup and carrying costs for the $\lambda$OQ's is approximately \$5 (\$3,477 − \$3,472) less than that of the LOQ's. If the carrying costs, setup costs, and other parameters of the items were different, the savings would not be the same. However, the difference in the costs of the LOQ's and the $\lambda$OQ's is usually relatively small due to the flatness of the total cost curve in the vicinity of the optimum order quantity.

**Insufficient Capacity.** Additional capacity may be gained by reducing the number of manufacturing orders per year for each item and thus the total number of setups. Some of the time previously devoted to setting up machines then can be used to produce output. When the preparation cost ($S$) is directly proportional to setup time and the cost per hour of setup time is

[8]Most introductory numerical analysis texts and many calculus texts include descriptions of Newton's method of numerically solving equations. Reference 4 also does.

**TABLE 9-16**
**AVERAGE CYCLE STOCK INVESTMENT**
**ANNUAL CARRYING COSTS AND PREPARATION COSTS**
**(WITH DIFFERENT $k$'S AND 250 OPERATING DAYS PER YEAR)**

**A. With the EOQ**

| Item | Annual Demand Units $R$ | Unit Cost $C$ | Preparation Costs $S$ | Carrying Cost Rate $k$ | Daily Production Rate $P$ | Finite Correction Factor $(1 - D_i \div P_i)$ | EOQ | I. Average Inventory Investment $C \frac{Q^*}{2}(1 - D_i \div P_i)$ | II. Annual Carrying Costs | III. Annual Preparation Costs |
|---|---|---|---|---|---|---|---|---|---|---|
| $A$ | 1,000 | $10.00 | 36 | .30 | 50 | .92 | 162 | $ 745.20 | $ 223.56 | $ 222.22 |
| $B$ | 40,000 | 2.50 | 28 | .25 | 800 | .80 | 2117 | 2,117.00 | 529.25 | 529.25 |
| $C$ | 15,000 | 4.00 | 48 | .20 | 500 | .88 | 1430 | 2,516.80 | 503.36 | 503.50 |
| $D$ | 8,000 | 6.00 | 25 | .35 | 200 | .84 | 476 | 1,199.52 | 419.83 | 420.17 |
| | | | | | | | | $6,578.52 | $1,676.00 | $1,675.14 |
| Totals | | | | | | | | | $3,351.14 | |

**B. With the LOQ**

| Item | LOQ | I | II | III |
|---|---|---|---|---|
| $A$ | 123 | $ 565.80 | $ 169.74 | $ 292.68 |
| $B$ | 1609 | 1,609.00 | 402.25 | 696.08 |
| $C$ | 1087 | 1,913.12 | 382.62 | 662.37 |
| $D$ | 362 | 912.24 | 319.28 | 552.49 |
| | | $5,000.16 | $1,273.89 | $2,203.62 |
| Totals | | | $3,477.51 | |

$$\text{LOQ's} = M \times \text{EOQ}$$

$$M = L \div \sum \frac{\text{EOQ}_i}{2}$$

$$= \$5{,}000 \div \$6{,}579$$

**C. With the λOQ**

| Item | $\lambda + k$ | λOQ | I | II | III |
|---|---|---|---|---|---|
| $A$ | .48 | 128 | $ 588.80 | $ 176.70 | $ 281.25 |
| $B$ | .43 | 1614 | 1,614.00 | 403.50 | 693.93 |
| $C$ | .38 | 1038 | 1,826.88 | 365.40 | 693.64 |
| $D$ | .53 | 387 | 975.24 | 341.25 | 516.80 |
| | | | $5,004.92 | $1,286.85 | $2,185.62 |
| Totals | | | | $3,472.47 | |

the same for all items in a group, the LIMIT approach will provide LOQ's that provide the added production capacity and that minimize the sum of carrying and setup costs under the constraint.

For example, if the EOQ's of a group of items require 2,000 hours of setup time in a work center and an additional 400 hours of production capacity are required in that work center, the LIMIT on setup hours is 1,600. Thus,

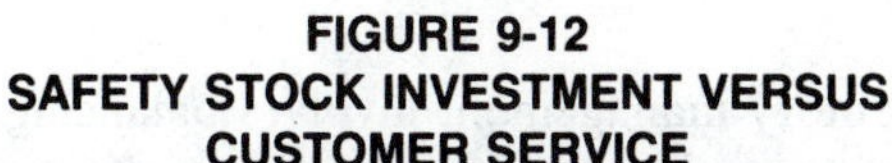

$$M = \frac{2{,}000}{1{,}600} = 1.25, \text{ and}$$

$$\text{LOQ's} = 1.25 \times \text{EOQ's}$$

# Buffer Stock

Customer service is related directly to safety stock investment as illustrated in Figure 9-12. An increase in safety stock increases customer service, all things being equal. Thus, management must evaluate the inventory investment-customer service trade-off when establishing safety stock policy and decision rules.

**FIGURE 9-12**
**SAFETY STOCK INVESTMENT VERSUS CUSTOMER SERVICE**

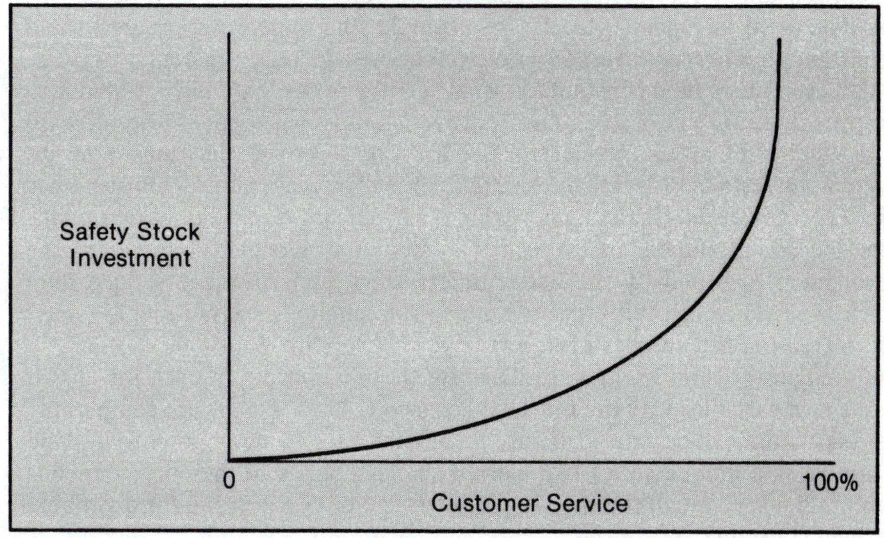


Factors such as the following must be considered when evaluating safety stock policy:

1. Each additional investment in safety stock gains a diminishing increase in customer service.

2. The exchange curve describing the trade-off between safety stock investment and customer service depends on the customer service objectives and the decision rule used to achieve these objectives. [5]
3. Customer service, safety stock, and lot size interact. Small lot sizes result in more orders per year and increased exposure to stock-outs. This relationship supports the application of the ABC principle to safety stock management. Concentrate control on those items with a relatively large number of exposures, long lead times, and high stock-out costs. Safety stock for slow moving, inexpensive items will be relatively high (a high safety factor), but require minimum investment.
4. Anticipation inventory can fill the safety stock function during periods when production exceeds demand.
5. The required customer service level for dependent demand items is 100 percent. The stock-out of a component for a subassembly can result in stock-outs at each of the remaining BOM levels in the manufacturing process. Safety stock is frequently replaced by safety time when ordering dependent demand items. This enables new orders to be released on an expedited basis in the event of scrap.

# THE TRADE-OFFS

Aggregate inventory management involves balancing inventory investment, customer service, and preparation (order and setup) cost objectives as illustrated in Figure 9-13. If, for example, the number of orders is held constant, increasing inventory investment will increase customer service. With cycle stock held constant (constant number of orders), increased investment will be in buffer stock and fewer stock-outs will occur. If we increase the number of orders, cycle stock will decrease[9]; if at the same time inventory investment is constant, safety stock will increase and so will customer service. As Gardner and Dannenbring point out, this is true only to a point; the increasing number of exposures to stock-out eventually outweighs the protection provided by the added safety stock and customer service then decreases. They call this point the edge of optimality since nothing is gained by increasing the number of orders beyond this point. [6]

Figures 9-14, -15, and -16 illustrate the relationship of each set of two exchange variables with the third held constant. These figures are comparable to taking three slices out of Figure 9-13, each slice being parallel to a plane formed by a unique set of two axes. The exact shape of the curve depends on the point at which the slice is taken (the point at which the third variable is held constant).

The foregoing discussion assumes a balanced inventory with the investment properly proportioned among items. If this is not the case, some items will have excessive inventory and others inadequate stock. None of the above relationships will be valid.

[9] See Figure 9-10.

**FIGURE 9-13**
**THE TRADE-OFFS: CUSTOMER SERVICE, INVENTORY INVESTMENT, AND NUMBER OF ORDERS**

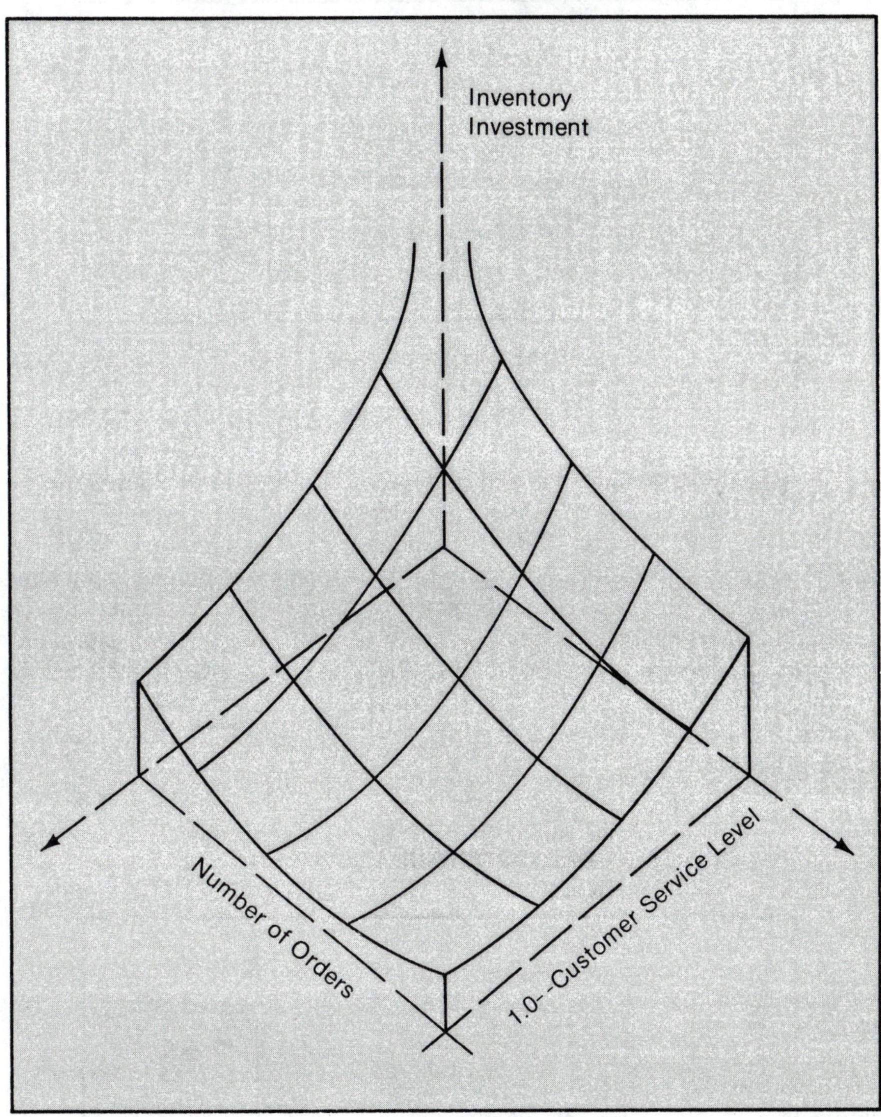


Production capacity usually constrains the number of production orders; setups require time that can be used for manufacturing items. In addition there is a limit to the number of orders that purchasing can process without sacrificing time required for activities such as vendor analysis, contract negotiations, and searches for alternate sources. The financial resources available for inventory investment also usually are limited.

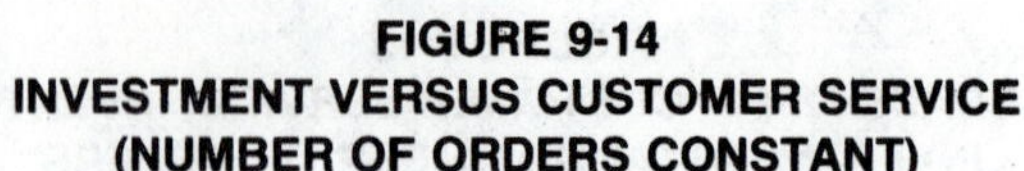

**FIGURE 9-14**
**INVESTMENT VERSUS CUSTOMER SERVICE**
**(NUMBER OF ORDERS CONSTANT)**

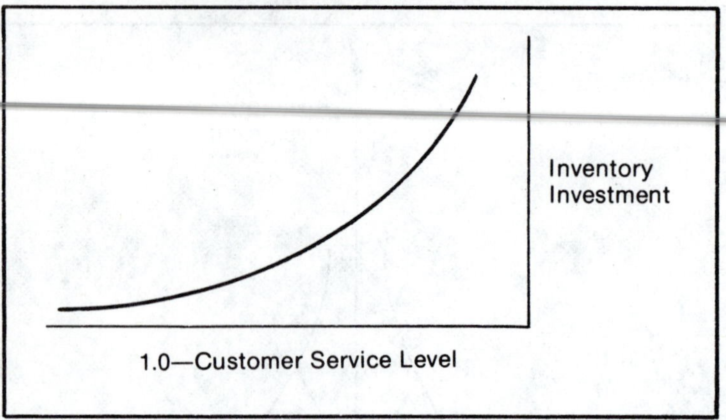


An analysis similar to that presented in Figure 9-13 enables management to evaluate available options, to determine if an aggregate plan is within constraints, and to select a reasonably good and feasible course of action. Gardner and Dannenbring present a Lagrangian approach for obtaining lot sizes and safety stock levels that provide maximum customer service for a given investment. [6] The approach is interesting and may provide valuable insight in some situations; however, it is laborious due to the numerical approximations required. It also assumes constant lead times and constant customer order sizes independent of the level of demand. Thus, its practical value is limited.

**FIGURE 9-15**
**NUMBER OF ORDERS VERSUS CUSTOMER SERVICE**
**(INVENTORY INVESTMENT CONSTANT)**

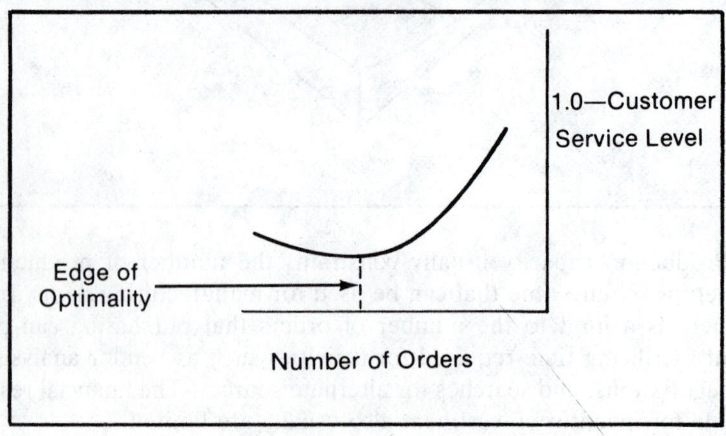

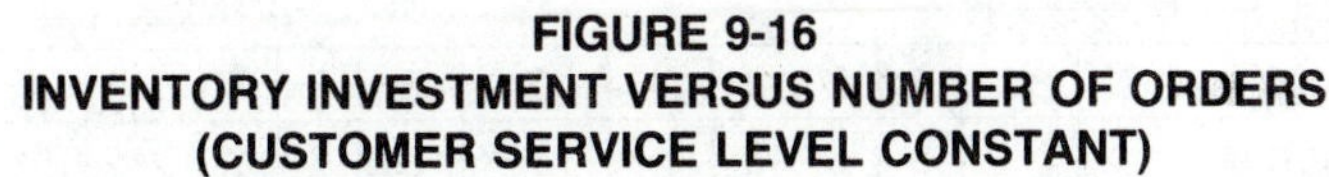

**FIGURE 9-16**
**INVENTORY INVESTMENT VERSUS NUMBER OF ORDERS (CUSTOMER SERVICE LEVEL CONSTANT)**

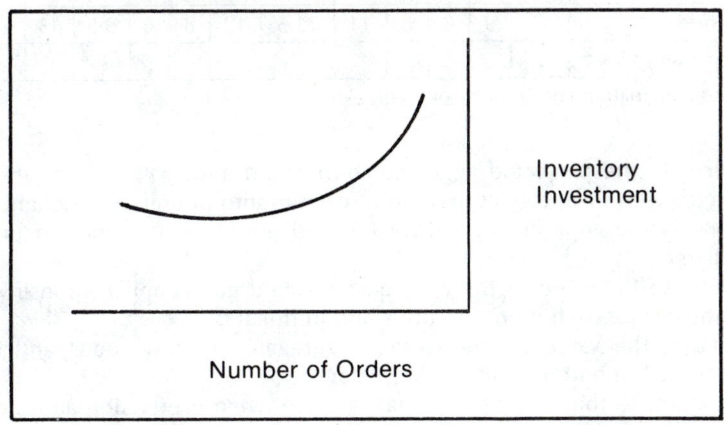


The difficult task is to estimate the relationships of customer service, inventory investment, and the number of orders. Determining the relationship of customer service and inventory investment with a constant number of orders was described in Chapter 7. The relationship of customer service to the number of orders with inventory investment held constant can be determined by adding the decrease in lot size investment to safety stock and calculating the effect of the increased safety stock on customer service. The effect on inventory investment of increasing the number of orders with constant customer service is calculated in a similar manner. As the number of orders increases, lot size inventory investments decrease by a greater amount than the increase required in safety stock to maintain a constant level of customer service. (This relationship is valid to the point of optimality.) Inventory investment increases by this difference.

Managing aggregate inventory is a complex and crucial challenge. It is intertwined with purchasing, transportation, and production scheduling. It usually involves decisions on trade-offs among customer service, inventory investment, and the number of production and purchase orders in an environment with investment and production capacity constraints.

## PROBLEMS

Use the following aggregate planning information in the first 10 problems.

The standard weighted average unit cost of finished goods is $40. The forecast demand and the planned aggregate production in thousands of units for the next 12 months is:

| Month | −1 | 1 | 2 | 3 | 4 | 5 | 6 | 7 | 8 | 9 | 10 | 11 | 12 |
|---|---|---|---|---|---|---|---|---|---|---|---|---|---|
| Production | | 8 | 8 | 8 | 12 | 12 | 12 | 7 | 7 | 7 | 13 | 13 | 13 |
| Demand | | 9 | 6 | 8 | 11 | 13.5 | 10 | 8 | 6 | 9.5 | 13 | 14 | 12 |
| Ending Inventory* | 2 | | | | | | | | | | | | |

*Includes anticipation and buffer stock only

1. Calculate the projected aggregate buffer and anticipation (combined) finished goods inventory at the end of each month in units and dollars.
2. What is the apparent aggregate finished goods buffer stock in units? in dollars?
3. Calculate the value of the aggregate finished goods anticipation inventory at the end of each month in units and in dollars.
4. What is the value of the average aggregate finished goods anticipation stock each month in units and dollars?
5. Shipment to the 5 warehouses takes place when production allocated to a given warehouse is complete. Thus, the shipment to Warehouse B is made at the end of Tuesday's production. Transportation time, including loading and unloading, to Warehouses A and B is 2 days each, to Warehouse C is 5 days, and to Warehouses D and E is 8 days each. The following lists the allocation of daily production to the 5 warehouses.

| Day | M | T | W | TH | F |
|---|---|---|---|---|---|
| Production % | 20 | 20 | 20 | 20 | 20 |
| Warehouse | | | Shipments | | |
| A | 15 | | | | |
| B | 5 | 20 | | | |
| C | | | 20 | | |
| D | | | | 20 | 10 |
| E | | | | | 10 |

Calculate the maximum and the average number of units and dollar value in transport to each warehouse. What is the average value of transportation inventory?

6. What is the average finished goods cycle stock in units and in dollars at each warehouse during each month?
7. What is the total average finished goods each month?
8. Components are manufactured at Plant A and shipped to Plant B for assembly. The weighted (by value) average cycle time of work-in-process is 2 weeks at Plant A and 1 week at Plant B. Transportation time between the 2 plants is 2 days; shipments are made daily. The weighted average cost of WIP when it leaves Plant A is 55% of the cost of goods sold. One day's buffer stock of incoming material is planned at Plant B.

a. Calculate the projected WIP cycle stock at Plant A each month and at Plant B each month.
b. Calculate the projected WIP safety stock at Plant B each month.
c. Calculate the projected average WIP transportation stock each month.
d. Calculate the projected total value of WIP each month.

**9.** The weighted average of RM cycle stock is .4 of a month's supply. The RM required at Plants A and B—primarily at A—equals 35% of the cost of goods sold. Incoming orders take an average (weighted by value) of 2 working days per month to clear inspection. (Use 20 working days per month.) On average, the company owned raw material in transit equals 1% of the month's purchases. Manufacturing lead time causes the RM expenditures for a given month to equal 40% of the RM required for the present month and 60% of the RM required for the following month's output. RM safety stock is approximately 1.5 days stock.

a. Calculate the average RM cyle stock during each month.
b. Calculate the average RM safety stock during each month.
c. Calculate the average RM in-transit stock during each month.
d. Calculate the total average RM stock during each month.

**10.** Calculate the average inventory investment for each month.

**11.** Eighty of Assembly 9800 are scheduled for completion in Week 20. Calculate the increase in WIP per week on the basis of the lead times and value added amounts shown in the table. An indented manufacturing BOM for Assembly 9800 is listed.

| Part No.* | Quantity | Value Added (Each) | Item Lead Time** |
|---|---|---|---|
| 9800 | 1 | $10.00 | 2 |
| M635 | 2 gal. | 9.00 | .5 |
| 9810 | 2 | 8.60 | 1 |
| 9811 | 1 | 15.00 | 2 |
| M3486 | 4 | 1.50 | 1 |
| P2715 | 1 | 6.00 | 3 |
| 9820 | 1 | 21.00 | 1.5 |
| 9821 | 3 | 8.40 | 1 |
| 9822 | 1 | 4.20 | 1 |
| M376 | 2 ft. | .75 | 1 |

**P* prefix on number indicates purchased component.
*M* prefix on number indicates material.
**In weeks.

**12.** Given the data in Table 9-15 and a maximum allowable average inventory investment of $5,500, calculate the LOQ's for Items *A*, *B*, *C*, and *D*. How does this affect annual carrying costs and annual preparation costs?

**13.** Given the data in Table 9-15 and a maximum allowable average investment $5,500, determine the Lagrangian multiplier (λ), and the λOQ's for Items *A*, *B*, *C*, and *D*.

**14.** Given the data in Table 9-15, calculate the new value of $k$ that will result in average inventory investments of \$5,500 and \$5,000.

**15.** Change the values of $k$ for Items $A$, $B$, $C$, and $D$ in Table 9-16 to .20, .30, .25, and .35 respectively and leave all other data the same. Then,

a. Calculate the LOQ's and the λOQ's.
b. Calculate the difference in the inventory related costs of the LOQ's and the λOQ's.
c. Repeat a. and b. for an inventory investment constraint of \$4,500.

**16.** Use the data in Table 9-15 plus the following information. The EOQ of the 4 items requires 200 hours of setup time in Work Center 28 during the next 6 months. Management has decided to gain 40 hours of additional capacity in Work Center 28 by changing the lot sizes of Items $A$, $B$, $C$, and $D$. Calculate the new lot sizes.

# SELECTED READINGS


**1.** Robert G. Brown, *Decision Rules for Inventory Management* (New York: Holt, Rinehart and Winston, 1967), p. 30.

**2.** James D. Harty, George W. Plossl, and Oliver W. Wight, *Management of Lot Size Inventories* (Washington, D.C.: American Production and Inventory Control Society, 1963), p. 21.

**3.** Thomas R. Hoffmann, "LIMIT Extended," *APICS Quarterly Bulletin* (January, 1964), pp. 65–70.

**4.** George Hadley and T. M. Whitin, *Analysis of Inventory Systems* (Englewood Cliffs, N.J.: Prentice-Hall, Inc., 1963), p. 55.

**5.** Robert G. Brown, *Materials Management Systems* (New York: John Wiley and Sons, Inc., 1977), p. 191.

**6.** Everette S. Gardner Jr. and David G. Dannenbring, "Analyzing Aggregate Inventory Trade-offs," *Management Science*, Vol. 25, No. 8 (August, 1979), pp. 709–720.

**7.** Elwood S. Buffa and Jeffrey G. Miller, *Production-Inventory Systems: Planning and Control*, 3d ed. (Homewood, Ill.: Richard D. Irwin, Inc., 1979).

**8.** N. Nicholas Edwards, "Target Level Inventories," *American Production and Inventory Control Conference Proceedings* (1975).

**9.** George W. Plossl, "How Much Inventory Is Enough?" *Production and Inventory Management*, Second Quarter (1971).

**10.** George W. Plossl and Oliver Wight, *Production and Inventory Control* (Englewood Cliffs, N.J.: Prentice-Hall, Inc., 1967).

**11.** Oliver Wight, *Production and Inventory Control in the Computer Age* (Boston, Mass.: BCI Publishing Co., Inc., 1974).

# —10—

# OTHER INVENTORY MODELS

Inventory decisions are made in many environments with different decision models appropriate in each. The models we have discussed in previous chapters have assumed that:

1. The cost of items is constant.
2. Demand is steady from period to period.
3. Preparation costs are constant.
4. Back orders are not permitted.
5. Demand is known with certainty.
6. The situation is dynamic; additional orders are placed over time as demand continues (lead time is shorter than the selling season).
7. Decisions affect only one level in the bill of materials (BOM).

The general models presented in this chapter provide a frame of reference for classifying situations, a basis for decision making in some situations, and insights helpful for developing more specialized models when necessary. These models concern situations in which:

1. Costs are not constant.
2. Back orders are possible.
3. Demand varies from period to period.
4. Demand is not certain.
5. The situation is static (lead time is longer than the selling season).

## DISCONTINUITIES IN THE COST STRUCTURE

The cost per unit, preparation costs per order, and the carrying cost rate may be a function of the lot size. Quantity discounts and the economies of large production runs affect item costs. Use of more expensive setups for large production runs is justified when the total run cost reduction is greater than any increase in carrying costs and setup costs. Increasing lot sizes for a relatively large number of items may increase capital and storage requirements to a point at which their carrying cost rate increases. We will examine some of these situations.

## Quantity Discounts

The cost of purchased items frequently is a function of the number of units purchased reflecting order entry, shipping, or manufacturing economies in the supplier's operation. For a three tier cost structure, illustrated graphically in Figure 10-1, this situation can be described as:

$$\begin{aligned}\text{Unit cost} &= C_1 \text{ when } Q > 0, \text{ but } < X_1\\ \text{Unit cost} &= C_2 \text{ when } Q \geq X_1, \text{ but } < X_2\\ \text{Unit cost} &= C_3 \text{ when } Q \geq X_2\end{aligned}$$

Where:

$C_3 < C_2 < C_1$
$X_1$ and $X_2$ are price break quantities, and
$Q$ is the order quantity (purchased lot size)

**FIGURE 10-1**
**TOTAL COSTS VERSUS LOT SIZE**
**BREAKS IN UNIT COST**

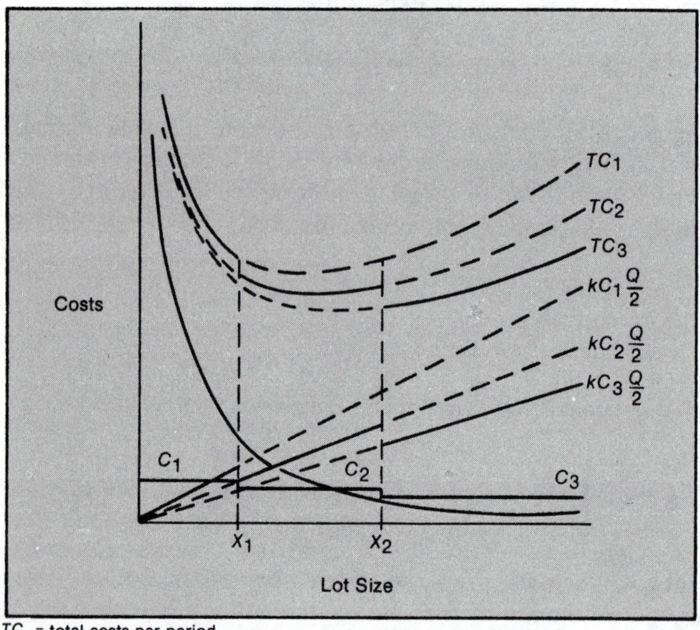


*TC* = total costs per period.
*k* = the cost rate of carrying one unit in inventory for the period.

The objective is to purchase the quantity that results in minimum total costs and violates no constraints. (One typical constraint, for example, is, Never purchase more than a year's supply, due to the probability of deterioration, product changes, etc.)

The following procedure gives the minimum total cost lot size:

1. Calculate the economic order quantity (EOQ) for each unit cost. If an EOQ is feasible, calculate its total lot size decision related costs. (A feasible EOQ is one that is greater than the quantity required to obtain the unit cost used in the EOQ calculation.)
2. Calculate the total lot size decision related costs of each of the minimum quantities that must be purchased to obtain the cost breaks.
3. The minimum cost order quantity is that quantity found in either Step 1 or 2 that has the lowest total costs and does not violate any constraints.

Let's look at an example. A company experiences a rather steady independent demand of 1,000 units annually for an item that it purchases. The item costs $50 when purchased in order quantities less than 100, $48 when purchased in order quantities greater than 99 and less than 250, and $47.50 when purchased in order quantities greater than 249. Ordering costs are $40 per order, and the carrying cost rate is .25.

Table 10-1 lists the EOQ calculated for each of the three costs. The EOQ's for $48 and $47.50 are not feasible since they are less than the quantity required to obtain the cost break. Table 10-2 lists the total lot size decision related costs of the feasible EOQ (80), and the two cost break quantities (100 and 250). In this case the minimum cost lot size is 100 units; it results in the lowest total costs. If the only constraint is that the order quantity must not exceed a year's supply, the order quantity would be 100 units. Chapter 13 deals with using return on investment (ROI) to evaluate quantity discounts.

**TABLE 10-1**
**EOQ'S FOR DIFFERENT UNIT COSTS**

| Unit Cost | Minimum Order Quantity | EOQ | EOQ Feasible? |
|---|---|---|---|
| $50.00 | — | 80 | Yes |
| 48.00 | 100 | 82 | No |
| 47.50 | 250 | 82 | No |

**TABLE 10-2**
**TOTAL LOT SIZE DECISION RELATED COSTS OF FEASIBLE EOQ'S AND COST BREAK QUANTITIES**

| Column 1 | Column 2 | Column 3 | Column 4 | Column 5 | Column 6 |
|---|---|---|---|---|---|
| Lot Size (*Q*) | Unit Cost (*C*) | Annual Item Costs (*CR*) | Annual Ordering Costs (*SR*/*Q*) | Annual Carrying Costs (*Ck Q*/2) | Total Costs (Columns 3 + 4 + 5) |
| 80 | $50.00 | $50,000 | $500 | $ 500.00 | $51,000.00 |
| 100 | 48.00 | 48,000 | 400 | 600.00 | 49,000.00 |
| 250 | 47.50 | 47,500 | 160 | 1,484.38 | 49,144.38 |

## Combined Cost Breaks

In some situations there are discontinuities in more than one cost factor. A discontinuity is a point (lot size) where the cost function changes abruptly (see points $X_1$ and $X_2$ in Figure 10-1). A decrease in the unit cost frequently is accompanied by an increase in the setup cost ($S$) when manufacturing an item. This situation is illustrated in Figure 10-2. The reduced unit costs typically are due to a more efficient process which requires a longer and more expensive setup.

**FIGURE 10-2**
**TOTAL COSTS VERSUS LOT SIZE**
**COMBINED SETUP AND UNIT COST BREAKS**

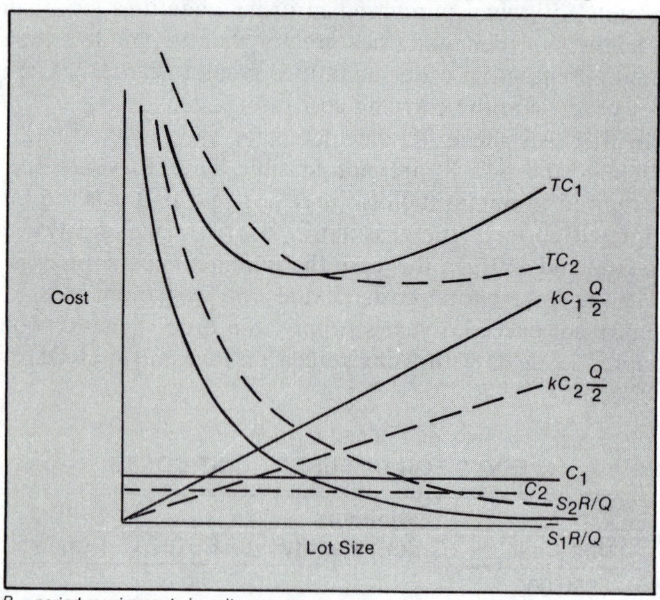


$R$ = period requirements in units.

## Simultaneous Cost Breaks

The procedure for determining the minimum total cost lot size when breaks in unit costs and setup costs occur at the same quantity follows:

1. Calculate the EOQ under each set of conditions.
2. Eliminate from consideration any EOQ that violates lot size constraints or that is infeasible.
3. Calculate the lot size decision related costs of the feasible EOQ's. If the EOQ associated with high cost setup is not feasible, calculate the total cost of the largest feasible lot size using the expensive setup and low item cost method. The lot size with the lowest total cost is the minimum cost order quantity.

Let us say, for example, that there is a rather steady demand of 200 units per year for a manufactured item. The company can use either of two methods to produce this item. The first method has a setup cost of $50 and a unit cost of $80; the second method costs $300 to set up and produces items for a variable unit cost of $70 (see Table 10-3). Management has assigned a carrying cost rate of .30. Competitive forces require that this independent demand item be made-to-stock. Production capacity with Method 1 is 500 units per year and 2,000 per year with Method 2. The production lot size for each method, then, is calculated in the usual manner[1]:

$$\text{EOQ}_i = \left[\frac{2RS_i}{kC_i(1 - D_i \div P_i)}\right]^{1/2}$$

$$\text{EOQ}_1 = \left[\frac{2 \times 200 \times 50}{.30 \times 80(1 - 200 \div 500)}\right]^{1/2} = 37^*$$

$$\text{EOQ}_2 = \left[\frac{2 \times 200 \times 300}{.30 \times 70(1 - 200 \div 2000)}\right]^{1/2} = 80^*$$

*Rounded to the nearest integer.

**TABLE 10-3**
**COMBINED BREAKS**
**TWO METHODS OF PRODUCTION**

| Method | Unit Cost (C) | Setup Cost (S) | EOQ (Q*)[1] | Feasible? |
|---|---|---|---|---|
| 1 | $80.00 | $ 50.00 | 37 | Yes |
| 2 | 70.00 | 300.00 | 80 | Yes |

[1]Optimum value lot size.

The total cost of each lot size is listed in Table 10-4. Here we can also see that the lowest total cost occurs using Method 2 and a production lot of 80 units.

For the purpose of further analysis, suppose management decrees that no more than a three months' supply of any item be produced at one time.

**TABLE 10-4**
**PRODUCTION LOT SIZE COSTS**
**BREAKS IN SETUP AND UNIT COSTS**

| Column 1 | Column 2 | Column 3 | Column 4 | Column 5 |
|---|---|---|---|---|
| EOQ (Q*) | Annual Item Costs (CR) | Annual Setup Costs $\left(\frac{SR}{Q}\right)$ | Annual Carrying Costs $kC\,Q\left(\frac{1 - D/P}{2}\right)$ | Total Costs (Columns 2 + 3 + 4) |
| 37 | $16,000 | $270.27 | $266.40 | $16,536.67 |
| 80 | 14,000 | 750.00 | 756.00 | 15,506.00 |

[1]See Chapter 7.

The largest possible lot size is now 50 units. Calculating the total costs with Method 2 using a lot size of 50 units gives:

$$
\begin{aligned}
CR &= \$14{,}000.00 \\
SR \div Q &= \phantom{\$}1{,}200.00 \\
kCQ(1 \div D \div P) \div 2 &= \underline{\phantom{\$1{,}2}472.50} \\
TC &= \underline{\$15{,}672.50}
\end{aligned}
$$

Thus, a lot size of 50 units using Method 2 is the most economical. The relationships of the parameter values substantially affect these decisions. Graphing the costs for both methods against possible lot sizes usually provides valuable insight.

# BACK ORDER MODELS

In many cases stock-outs can be handled by back ordering, i.e., by filling an order late after replenishment stocks arrive as illustrated in Figure 10-3.

**FIGURE 10-3**
**UNITS IN STOCK VERSUS TIME**
**(STOCK-OUTS PERMITTED)**

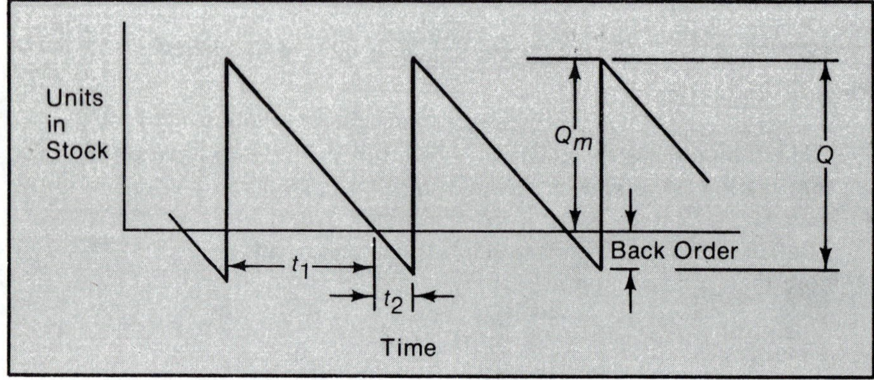


Back ordering frequently involves special handling (expediting) which is more expensive than routine order processing. It may require the use of alternative and more expensive routings or overtime for manufactured items; back ordered purchased items frequently must be obtained from alternative sources that charge higher prices for the shorter lead time. These costs frequently are directly proportional to the length of the time delay, and a rough estimate of back order costs can be based on that relationship.

On other occasions there is no penalty (costs) for a short delay in shipment. We will examine both of these situations.

## Time Delay Penalty

Items that are back ordered incur no carrying costs since they are shipped immediately. However, they do incur a cost proportional to the time they are back ordered. For example, order cancellations and returns may be related directly to the number of units back ordered and the time delay in shipment. When this situation exists, the following models give the minimum cost lot size, the maximum stock on hand, and the total costs. These models are derived in Appendix D.

$$Q = \sqrt{\frac{2RS}{kC}}\sqrt{\frac{(B + kC)}{B}}$$

$$Q_m = \sqrt{\frac{2RS}{kC}}\sqrt{\frac{B}{(B + kC)}}$$

$$TC = \frac{kCQ_m^2}{2Q} + \frac{SR}{Q} + \frac{B(Q - Q_m)^2}{2Q}$$

Where: $R$, $S$, $k$, $TC$, and $C$ are as defined earlier
$B$ = cost per year of each item back ordered
$Q_m$ = maximum units in inventory

The proportion of back ordered items cancelled or returned must be known as must the cost of returned and cancelled items. For example, let the unpacking, inspecting, returning to stores, return shipping damage, and foregone profits average \$5 per returned unit; and let the probability of an item being returned increase by 2 percent each working day an item is back ordered. Then the back order cost per unit-year (i.e., the cost of a returned item times the probability of return per day back ordered times the number of days per year) equals \$25 (\$5 × .02 × 250).

The preceding calculations assume that the probability of lost sales is related linearly to the number of days an item is back ordered. In most cases the probability of lost sales increases at an increasing rate each additional day. This factor usually is controlled by limiting the number of days a customer must wait. For example, a distributor sells an item with an annual demand of 60,000 units spread evenly throughout the year. It pays \$10 for each item; ordering and shipping costs total \$64 for each purchase; the carrying cost rate is .30 per year; and the cost of a back order is \$9 per unit-year. Let us, then, calculate the economic order quantity, the maximum quantity in stock, and the total costs per year.

$$Q = \sqrt{\frac{2RS}{kC}}\sqrt{\frac{(B + kC)}{B}} = \sqrt{\frac{2 \times 60{,}000 \times 64}{.3 \times 10}}\sqrt{\frac{(9 + 3)}{9}}$$

$$= 1{,}600 \times 1.154$$

$$= 1{,}846.4 \text{ or } 1{,}846$$

$$Q_m = \sqrt{\frac{2RS}{kC}}\sqrt{\frac{B}{(B + kC)}}$$

$$= \sqrt{\frac{2 \times 60{,}000 \times 64}{.3 \times 10}}\sqrt{\frac{9}{(.3 \times 10 + 9)}}$$

$$= 1{,}385.64 \text{ or } 1386$$

$$TC = \frac{kCQ_m^2}{2Q} + \frac{SR}{Q} + \frac{B(Q - Q_m)^2}{2Q}$$

$$= \frac{.3 \times 10 \times (1{,}386)^2}{2 \times 1{,}846} + \frac{64 \times 60{,}000}{1{,}846} + \frac{9 \times (1{,}846 - 1{,}386)^2}{2 \times 1{,}846}$$

$$= \$1{,}560.94 + \$2{,}080.17 + \$515.82$$

$$= \$4{,}156.93$$

Let us compare these total costs with those obtained if the opportunity to back order is ignored. Then,

$$Q = \sqrt{\frac{2RS}{kC}}, \text{ and}$$

$$TC = \frac{SR}{Q} + kC\frac{Q}{2}$$

$$Q = \sqrt{\frac{2 \times 60{,}000 \times 64}{.3 \times 10}} = 1{,}600$$

$$TC = \frac{64 \times 60{,}000}{1{,}600} + .3 \times 10 \times \frac{1{,}600}{2} = \$4{,}800$$

Considerable savings are lost by neglecting to back order.

When managers adopt a back ordering policy, they usually are interested in knowing the longest time a customer will have to wait for shipment. This is calculated easily, as is demonstrated by the following:

$$\begin{aligned} \text{Demand per day} &= \text{annual demand/operating days per year} \\ &= 60{,}000 \div 250 \\ &= 240 \text{ units} \\ \text{Longest delay} &= \text{back order quantity/demand per day} \\ &= (1{,}846 - 1{,}386) \div 240 \\ &= 1.92 \text{ days} \end{aligned}$$

A customer will wait 2 days at most. These calculations assume that no future sales will be lost with a 2 day maximum delay in shipping. If the longest delay possible is longer than desired, *B* can be increased until the longest delay is acceptable. (Increasing *B* decreases the longest delay.) Thus, *B* can be treated as a management policy variable in the same manner as *k* (the carrying cost rate) is.

## Back Orders without Penalty

Frequently orders can be shipped late without penalty for a given period. For example, customers may be willing to wait a day or two, or even a few weeks without cancelling their order or without the delay damaging the prospects of future orders. When a delay in delivery is possible without any added costs, the optimum lot size is larger than that calculated using the basic EOQ model. This situation is illustrated in Figure 10-4.

**FIGURE 10-4**
**INVENTORY ON HAND VERSUS TIME**
**(BACK ORDER WITHOUT PENALTY)**

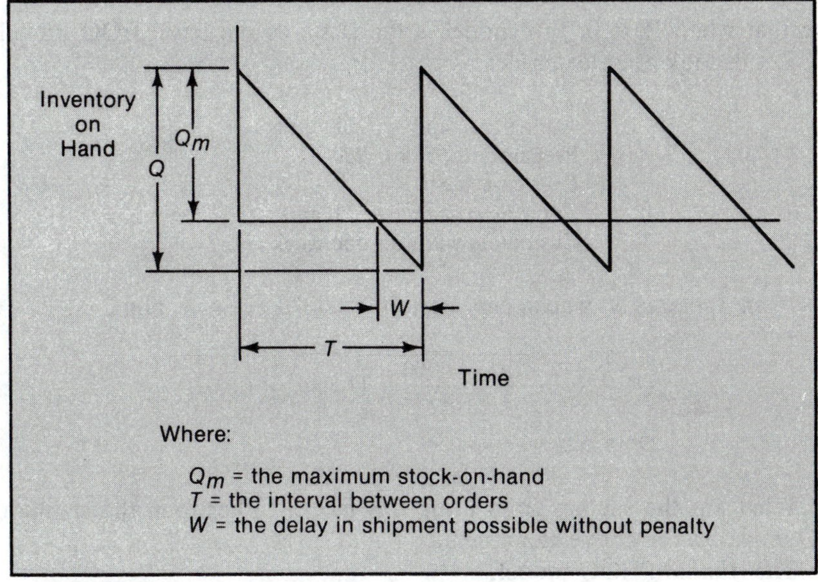


The conditions are:

1. Demand is independent, uniform, and known.
2. Customer does not expect or require immediate delivery. However, delay beyond a certain point can result in cancellation of either present or future orders.
3. Back orders can be included in the next order without any added costs due to expediting.

The minimum cost order quantity (EOQ, i.e., $Q^*$), can be calculated as follows (see Appendix E for the derivation of this model):

$$Q^* = \sqrt{\frac{2SR}{kC} + R^2W^2}$$

and the total annual costs are:

$$TC = SR/Q^* + kCQ^*/2 - kCRW + kCR^2W^2/2Q^*$$

Where:

$TC$ = total annual costs
$Q^*$ = the minimum cost lot size
$S$ = preparation (setup and ordering) cost per order
$R$ = annual demand
$k$ = cost rate of carrying an item in inventory one year
$C$ = unit cost
$W$ = time delay in delivery without back order penalty

Note that when $W = 0$, this model is the same as the basic EOQ model.

Let us look at an example:

Annual demand = 7,500 units
Preparation costs = \$50
Unit cost = \$10
Carrying cost rate = .30 and
Customers will wait one week

If the firm operates 50 weeks per year, $W = .02\left(\text{i.e., } \frac{1}{50}\right)$. Thus

$$Q^* = \sqrt{\frac{2 \times 50 \times 7{,}500}{.3 \times 10} + (7{,}500)^2 \times (.02)^2}$$

$$Q^* = 522$$

What are the savings from using this model rather than the standard EOQ model in the above example?

The standard EOQ model,

$$\text{EOQ} = \sqrt{\frac{2SR}{kC}},$$

gives an order quantity of 500. The total annual costs are:

$$\begin{aligned} TC &= SR/Q + kCQ/2 \\ &= (\$50 \times 7{,}500) \div 500 + (.3 \times \$10 \times 500) \div 2 \\ &= \$1{,}500 \end{aligned}$$

The revised model results in the following total annual costs:

$$\begin{aligned} TC &= SR/Q + kCQ/2 - kCRW + kCR^2W^2/2Q \\ &= \$50 \times 7{,}500 \div 522 + .3 \times \$10 \times 522 \div 2 - .3 \times \$10 \times 7{,}500 \times \\ &\quad .02 + .3 \times \$10 \times (7{,}500)^2 \times (.02)^2 \div (2 \times 522) \\ &= \$1{,}115.65 \end{aligned}$$

Savings = \$1,500 − 1,116.05 = \$383.95, slightly more than 25 percent! If comparable savings occur on a number of products, the total savings are substantial. D. Aucamp and D. Fogarty have shown that savings depend on the ratio of $W$ to the cycle time of the standard EOQ. When that ratio is relatively small, savings are neglible. Thus, actual savings depend on the parameters of the situation. [1]

# DISCRETE REQUIREMENTS MODELS

Continuous demand at a relatively constant rate is an assumption of the basic EOQ and periodic review models. However, demand often is discrete with lump quantities required by either customers or manufacturing. The quantity required also may vary considerably from period to period. Discrete lot size models are very useful in such situations. Discrete lot-sizing methods include the following techniques:

1. Lot-for-Lot (L4L)
2. The period order quantity (POQ)
3. Least total cost (LTC)
4. Part period balancing (PPB)
5. Dynamic programming
6. Heuristic methods

The L4L and LTC methods are described in Chapter 4. Descriptions of the other methods follow.

## The Period Order Quantity (POQ)

This method uses the standard EOQ in calculating a fixed number of period requirements to include in each order. Thus, the POQ avoids *remnants*, quantities carried in inventory until the next requirement, whereas using the EOQ for discrete demand frequently results in remnants. In many cases it results in lower inventory costs than the L4L method by combining the requirements for more than one period in a single order. The procedure follows:

1. Calculate the EOQ in the standard manner.
2. Use the EOQ to calculate $N$, the number of orders per year by dividing the annual requirements ($R$) by the EOQ.
3. Calculate the POQ by dividing the number of requirements planning time periods per year by $N$. Round off the result to obtain the POQ.
4. Begin with the first period's requirements and place an order to cover them plus those in the periods that follow until the number of periods specified by the POQ are covered.

This can be illustrated with an example. Let $R$ = 1,440 units annually, $S$ = \$60 per order, $k$ = .3 per year, $C$ = \$90 per unit, with 50 planning weeks per year. Following our procedure next we have:

1. $\text{EOQ} = \sqrt{\frac{2RS}{kC}} = \sqrt{\frac{2 \times 1{,}440 \times \$60}{.3 \times \$90}}$
   $= 80$

2. $N = \frac{R}{\text{EOQ}} = \frac{1{,}440}{80}$
   $= 18$

3. $\text{POQ} = \frac{\text{Planning periods per year}}{18}$
   $= \frac{50}{18} = 2.8 \text{ or } 3$

4. Applying this result to a given set of requirements when the lead time is two weeks results in the following planned order releases:

| Week | 1 | 2 | 3 | 4 | 5 | 6 | 7 | 8 | 9 | 10 | 11 | 12 |
|---|---|---|---|---|---|---|---|---|---|---|---|---|
| Net Requirements | * | * | 20 | 34 | 8 | 50 | 0 | 51 | 0 | 9 | 38 | 13 |
| Planned Receipts | | | 62 | | | 101 | | | | 60 | | |
| Planned Order Releases | 62 | | | 101 | | | | 60 | | | | |

*Covered by a previous order.

This approach does not minimize ordering and carrying costs, but it usually is less costly than ordering each period or arbitrarily selecting a fixed order period.

## Least Total Cost-Brute Force Method (LTC-BF)

There are two LTC methods. The one described in Chapter 4 is the technique most commonly identified as the LTC. It finds that initial order for which the difference between the carrying costs and the preparation costs is a minimum. It requires fewer calculations than the Least Total Cost-Brute Force method, but does not always give the minimum cost solution.

This method, (LTC-BF), on the other hand, considers all known requirements, examines all alternative ordering possibilities, and selects the one with the lowest total cost. The total costs of the lot sizing decision equal the sum of the preparation costs and the carrying costs. Thus,

$$TC_j = NS + kC\Sigma R_i W_i$$

Where:

$N$ = the number of preparations (orders)
$S$ = the cost per preparation
$k$ = carrying cost per period
$C$ = item cost per unit
$R_i$ = demand in Period $i$
$W_i$ = the number of weeks $R_i$ is in stock
$TC_j$ = total cost of alternative $j$

If, for example, requirements exist in Weeks 23, 26, 27, 31, and 32 and lead time is 1 week, then the L4L lot-sizing method calls for releasing orders in Weeks 22, 25, 26, 30, and 31. This approach will minimize carrying costs, but total costs will be high due to the number of orders. Table 10-5 lists all planned order release alternatives in this situation, and Table 10-6 lists the costs of each alternative. Alternative N (ordering the requirements for Period 23 in the first order, combining the requirements for Periods 26 and 27 in the second order, and combining the requirements for Periods 31 and 32 in the third) results in minimum costs.

**TABLE 10-5**
**EXAMPLE OF ALL PLANNED ORDER RELEASE ALTERNATIVES**

**A. Net Requirements per Week**

| Week | 22 | 23 | 24 | 25 | 26 | 27 | 28 | 29 | 30 | 31 | 32 |
|---|---|---|---|---|---|---|---|---|---|---|---|
| Net Requirements | | 15 | | | 35 | 5 | | | | 25 | 15 |

**B. Possible Lot Sizes and Order Releases***

| Alternative | Week | | | | | | | | | | |
|---|---|---|---|---|---|---|---|---|---|---|---|
| | **22** | **23** | **24** | **25** | **26** | **27** | **28** | **29** | **30** | **31** | **32** |
| A | 95 | | | | | | | | | | |
| B | 80 | | | | | | | | | 15 | |
| C | 55 | | | | | | | | 40 | | |
| D | 55 | | | | | | | | 25 | 15 | |
| E | 50 | | | | 45 | | | | | | |
| F | 50 | | | | 30 | | | | | 15 | |
| G | 50 | | | | 5 | | | | 40 | | |
| H | 50 | | | | 5 | | | | 25 | 15 | |
| I | 15 | | | 80 | | | | | | | |
| J | 15 | | | 35 | 45 | | | | | | |
| K | 15 | | | 35 | 30 | | | | | 15 | |
| L | 15 | | | 35 | 5 | | | | 40 | | |
| M | 15 | | | 35 | 5 | | | | 25 | 15 | |
| N | 15 | | | 40 | | | | | 40 | | |
| O | 15 | | | 40 | | | | | 25 | 15 | |

*Lead time = 1 week.

**TABLE 10-6**

**COSTS PER ALTERNATIVE**
**(LEAD TIME = 1 WEEK)**

| Alternative | Number of Orders ($N$) | Preparation Costs ($NS$*) | Carrying Costs** $kC\Sigma R_iW_i$ $.75\Sigma R_iW_i$ | Total Costs |
|---|---|---|---|---|
| A | 1 | $ 75 | .75(35×3+5×4+25×8+15×9) = $345.00 | $420.00 |
| B | 2 | 150 | .75(35×3+5×4+25×8) = 243.75 | 393.75 |
| C | 2 | 150 | .75(35×3+5×4+15×1) = 105.00 | 255.00 |
| D | 3 | 225 | .75(35×3+5×4) = 93.75 | 318.75 |
| E | 2 | 150 | .75(35×3+25×4+15×5) = 210.00 | 360.00 |
| F | 3 | 225 | .75(35×3+25×4) = 153.75 | 378.75 |
| G | 3 | 225 | .75(35×3+15×1) = 90.00 | 315.00 |
| H | 4 | 300 | .75(35×3) = 78.75 | 378.75 |
| I | 2 | 150 | .75(5×1+25×5+15×6) = 165.00 | 315.00 |
| J | 3 | 225 | .75(25×5+15×6) = 161.25 | 386.25 |
| K | 4 | 300 | .75(25×4) = 75.00 | 375.00 |
| L | 4 | 300 | .75(15×1) = 11.25 | 311.25 |
| M | 5 | 375 | ——— ——— | 375.00 |
| N | 3 | 225 | .75(5×1+15×1) = 15.00 | 240.00 |
| O | 4 | 300 | .75(5×1) = 3.75 | 303.75 |

*$S$ = $75 per preparation (order).
**$k$ = .006 per week; $C$ = $125 per unit.

The folly of this approach in most situations is immediately apparent. With thousands, perhaps hundreds of thousands, of items in inventory, the expense of the computer time required outweighs the benefits. Thus, methods requiring fewer calculations are used. They include the L4L and the short-cut LTC (see Chapter 4).

## Part Period Balancing

This method is relatively efficient in calculating lot sizes for discrete requirements. It uses the LTC order size as a starting point and incorporates *look ahead* and *look back* steps to calculate the effect of future requirements on the total lot size inventory costs of the next two orders—rather than only the next order. The economic part period factor (EPP) is frequently used in these calculations. The derived EPP is equal to the cost per preparation divided by the product of the inventory carrying cost rate for a period and the unit cost, letting,

$$S = \$75 \text{ per preparation}$$
$$C = \$125 \text{ per unit}$$
$$k = .006 \text{ per week}$$

The economic part period factor can then be calculated as follows:

$$\text{EPP} = \frac{\$75}{.006 \times 125} = 100$$

This reveals that in the situation described, carrying costs equal the preparation costs when an order results in 100 unit-weeks (part periods). Thus, 100 units in inventory for 1 week, or 50 units in inventory for 2 weeks, or 5 units in inventory for 10 weeks plus 10 units in inventory for 5 weeks result in carrying costs and preparation costs being equal.

The *generated EPP* is the number of part periods resulting from a given order. The EPP concept is useful in the LTC method. For example, Table 10-7 calculates and lists the generated EPP's as each requirement is added—in sequence—to the initial order using the data from the previous example.

Carrying costs and preparation costs are the closest to each other when the difference between the derived EPP and generated EPP is the closest to zero. Thus, the LTC method indicates that the lowest total cost solution exists when the requirements for Period 23, 15 units, and Period 26, 35 units, are combined in the first order.

After finding the LTC solution, part period balancing applies the look ahead test: If the total generated part periods of the first two orders (and thus the carrying costs) are decreased by adding the initial requirements of the second order to the first, add these requirements to the first order. If

**TABLE 10-7**
**EPP'S GENERATED**
**INITIAL ORDER ALTERNATIVES***

| Week | 22 | 23 | 24 | 25 | 26 | 27 | 28 | 29 | 30 | 31 | 32 |
|---|---|---|---|---|---|---|---|---|---|---|---|
| Net Requirements | | 15 | | | 35 | 5 | | | | 25 | 15 |

| Alternative | Order Quantity | Units × Weeks in Stock | Generated EPP | Derived EPP-Generated EPP |
|---|---|---|---|---|
| 1 | 15 | 15 × 0 | 0 | 100 |
| 2 | 50 | 15 × 0 + 35 × 3 | 105 | −5 |
| 3 | 55 | 15 × 0 + 35 × 3 + 5 × 4 | 125 | −25 |

*Lead time = 1 week.

not, leave the order as determined by the LTC approach. Repeat the test until it fails. Thus, if $N_1 R_{f+1} < N_2 R_{f+2}$, add $R_{f+1}$ to the initial order; and if $N_1 R_{f+1} > N_2 R_{f+2}$, then the tentative order becomes the planned order. Where:

$R_{f+1}$ = the first requirements following the final period of the first order
$N_1$ = the number of periods that the requirements in Period $f+1$ are carried if added to the initial order
$N_2$ = the number of periods that the second requirements in the second order are carried in the tentative solution

Returning to our example and the tentative solution with the second order solution included we have the following:

| Week | | 23 | 24 | 25 | 26 | 27 | 28 | 29 | 30 | 31 | 32 |
|---|---|---|---|---|---|---|---|---|---|---|---|
| Net Requirements | | 15 | | | 35 | 5[1] | | | | 25[2] | 5 |
| Generated Part Periods | Each Week | 0 | 0 | 0 | 35 × 3 | 0 | 0 | 0 | 0 | 100 | |
| | Cumulative | | | | 105 | | | | | 100 | |
| Planned Order Receipts | | 50 | | | | 30 | | | | | ? |

[1] $R_{f+1}$
[2] $R_{f+2}$

← $N_1$ → ← $N_2$ →

Which means that:

$$R_{f+1} = 5;\ R_{f+2} = 25;\ N_1 = 4;\ N_2 = 4;$$
$$N_1 R_{f+1} = 4 \times 5 = 20 < N_2 R_{f+2} = 4 \times 25 = 100$$

Therefore, the look ahead test indicates that the first order should be for 55 units covering the requirements in Periods 23, 26, and 27. The next order will be placed in Period 30 for requirements in Periods 31, 32, plus additional requirements as they arrive. Applying the look ahead test to determine if the Period 31 requirement should be added to the first order results in a negative answer.

The reduced costs of this approach can be verified by comparing the costs per period of the LTC initial order and the order recommended by the look ahead test.

The look back test is applied only if the look ahead test fails. It determines if total costs are decreased by adding the last requirements of the first order to the second order. The procedure is:

> Let $M$ equal the number of periods covered by the second order and $R_f$ and $N$ be as defined previously. Then if $NR_f > \sum_{i=1}^{M} R_{f+i}$, move $R_f$ to the second order. If not, the tentative orders are the planned orders.

The following example illustrates the look back test (preparation costs and the carrying cost rate are the same; only the requirements change):

| Week | | 23 | 24 | 25 | 26 | 27 | 28 | 29 | 30 |
|---|---|---|---|---|---|---|---|---|---|
| Net Requirements | | 15 | 25 | | 25 | 15 | 25 | | 25 |
| Generated Part Periods | Each Week | 0 | 25 | | 75 | 0 | 25 | | 75 |
| | Cumulative | 0 | 25 | | 100 | 0 | 25 | | 100 |
| Planned Order Receipts | | 65 | | | | 65 | | | |

The look ahead test fails. Applying the look back test gives:

$$NR_f = 3 \times 25 = 75 > \sum_{i=1}^{M} R_{f+i} = 15 + 25 + 25 = 65$$

Therefore, move the requirement for 25 units in Week 26 to the second order. This results in the following:

| Week | | 23 | 24 | 25 | 26 | 27 | 28 | 29 | 30 |
|---|---|---|---|---|---|---|---|---|---|
| Net Requirements | | 15 | 25 | | 25 | 15 | 25 | | 25 |
| Generated Part Periods | Each Week | 0 | 25 | | 0 | 15 | 50 | | 100 |
| | Cumulative | 0 | 25 | | 0 | 15 | 65 | | 165 |
| Planned Order Receipts | | 40 | | | 90 | | | | |

The revised planned order releases require the same number of orders as the tentative planned order releases but have lower carrying costs.

The savings of the part period balancing test can evaporate in a dynamic environment. Increased or shifting requirements can result in increased costs especially when an unusually small first order has been placed.

## Dynamic Programming

Wagner and Whitin applied the principles of dynamic programming to the following type situations:

1. Requirements are discrete and certain.
2. Demand may vary widely from period to period.
3. Orders cover the requirements for one or more whole periods.
4. The planning horizon contains a limited number of periods.
5. Complete orders arrive on schedule at the beginning of a period. (There are no partial order receipts and lead time is certain.)
6. There will be no inventory at the end of the planning horizon. [2]

These assumptions are not as detrimental to effective use of the technique as it may appear. Lead time can be controlled. Periods are added to planning horizon and new requirements develop before the time arrives to release the last order. New orders are calculated for periods not including the last. Thus, the no ending inventory constraint is rarely encountered. Requirements are discrete, known with certainty, and do vary widely from period to period in many dependent demand situations. In fact, the ability to handle wide variations in period requirements is a cardinal virtue of this approach.

A description of the procedure must include the many alternative paths a decision may follow in a particular situation. As a result, a complete description of the procedure makes it appear complex. The application, however, is not. Each step is simple and in any given situation only one path is followed.

**The Procedure.** There are 3 somewhat complex steps in the dynamic programming procedure for a planning horizon with requirements in 3 periods. These are given next and illustrated in Figures 10-5 and 10-6. (The reader may find it helpful to refer to the examples which follow while studying each step.)

1. Examine the first two requirements as an entity, and determine which of the following decisions has the least total cost. (Total costs equal preparation costs plus carrying costs.)
   (a) Combine requirements $R_1$ and $R_2$ in a single order for arrival when $R_1$ is required.
   (b) Order the requirements for each period separately with each to arrive in the period required.

   Thus,

$$TC(x) = nS + kC\Sigma R_i N_{ij}$$

**FIGURE 10-5**
**DYNAMIC ANALYSIS OF A PLANNING HORIZON WITH REQUIREMENTS IN 3 PERIODS**

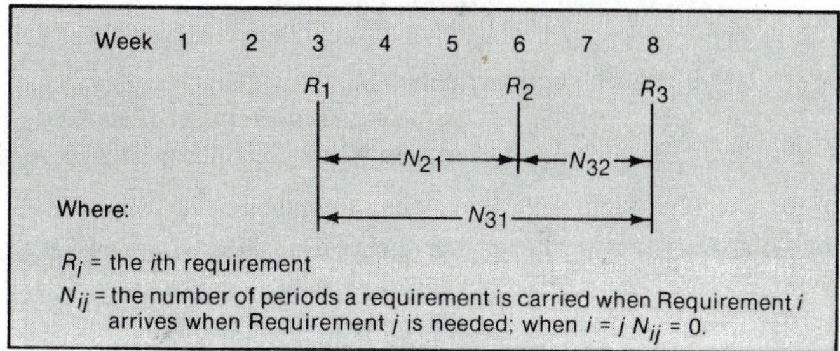


**FIGURE 10-6**
**SCHEMATIC OF DYNAMIC PROGRAMMING PROCEDURE THREE PERIODS WITH REQUIREMENTS**

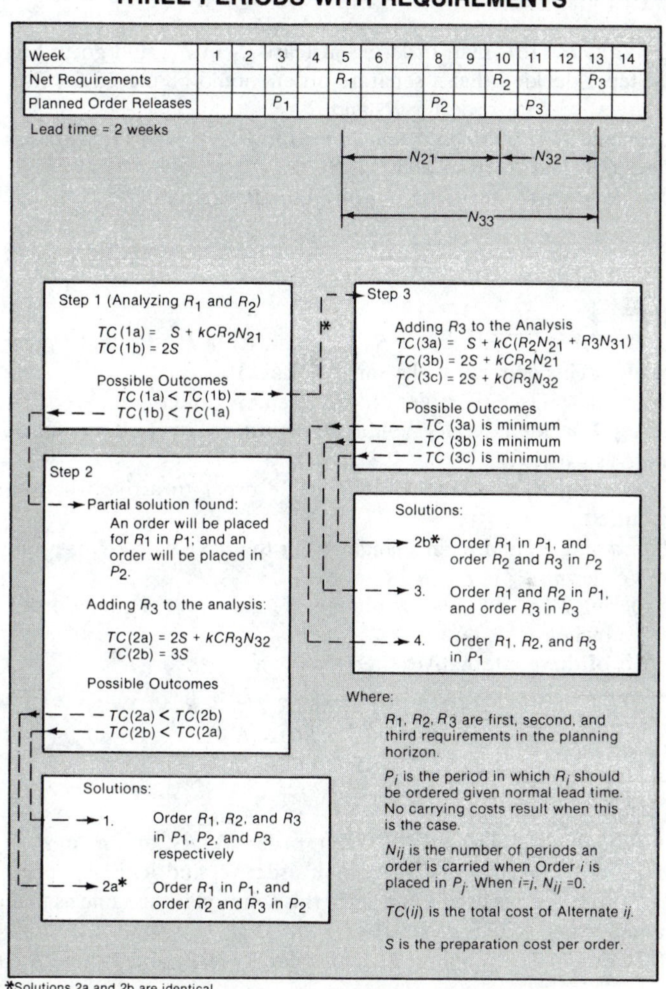

| Week | 1 | 2 | 3 | 4 | 5 | 6 | 7 | 8 | 9 | 10 | 11 | 12 | 13 | 14 |
|---|---|---|---|---|---|---|---|---|---|---|---|---|---|---|
| Net Requirements | | | | | $R_1$ | | | | | $R_2$ | | | $R_3$ | |
| Planned Order Releases | | | $P_1$ | | | | | $P_2$ | | | $P_3$ | | | |



*Solutions 2a and 2b are identical.

*Where:* $TC(x)$ = the total costs of Alternative $x$
$n$ = the number of orders
$S$ = the preparation cost per order
$k$ = the carrying cost rate per week
$C$ = unit cost
$R_i$ = the $i$th requirement
$N_{ij}$ = the number of periods a requirement is carried when Requirement $i$ arrives when Requirement $j$ is needed; when $i = j$, $N_{ij} = 0$.

The formulas for the two alternative decisions in Step 1, therefore, are as follows:

$$TC(1a) = S + kCR_2N_{21}$$
$$TC(1b) = 2S$$

If $TC(1b) < TC(1a)$, plan ordering $R_1$ in $P_1$ and at least $R_2$ in $P_2$. ($P_i$ is the period in which $R_i$ should be ordered given normal lead time.) Go to Step 2.
If $TC(1a) < TC(1b)$, plan ordering at least $R_1$ in $P_1$; and go to Step 3.

2. Since Step 1 decided that a separate order should be placed for $R_1$, two alternatives exist for ordering $R_2$ and $R_3$:
   (a) Combine $R_2$ and $R_3$ into one order for arrival when $R_2$ is required.
   (b) Order $R_2$ and $R_3$ in $P_2$ and $P_3$.
   The total costs, including $R_1$, of these alternatives are:

$$TC(2a) = 2S + kCR_3N_{32}$$
$$TC(2b) = 3S$$

Solutions:
(a) If $TC(2b) < TC(2a)$, order $R_1$, $R_2$, and $R_3$ in $P_1$, $P_2$, and $P_3$ respectively. (This decision is the same as L4L.)
(b) If $TC(2a) < TC(2b)$, order $R_1$ in $P_1$, and $R_2$ and $R_3$ in $P_2$.

3. Since Step 1 decided that $R_2$ should not be ordered by itself, the following alternatives exist:
   (a) Combining $R_1$, $R_2$, and $R_3$ in a single order to arrive when $R_1$, is required.
   (b) Combining $R_1$ and $R_2$ in a single order to arrive when $R_1$ is required, and ordering $R_3$ in $P_3$.
   (c) Ordering $R_1$ in $P_1$, and combining $R_2$ and $R_3$ in a single order for arrival when $R_2$ is due.
   The costs of these alternatives are:

$$TC(3a) = S + kC(R_2N_{21} + R_3N_{31})$$
$$TC(3b) = 2S + kC(R_2N_{21})$$
$$TC(3c) = 2S + kC(R_3N_{32})$$

Solutions:
(c) If $TC(3a) < TC(3b)$ and $< TC(3c)$, order $R_1$, $R_2$, and $R_3$ in $P_1$.
(b) If $TC(3b) < TC(3a)$ and $< TC(3c)$, order $R_1$ and $R_2$ in $P_1$ and $R_3$ in $P_3$, [the letter $b$ is used again since this solution is the same as that obtained when $TC(2a) < TC(2b)$].
(d) If $TC(3c) < TC(a)$ and $< TC(b)$, order $R_1$ in $P_1$ and $R_2$ and $R_3$ in $P_2$.

This exhausts all the possibilities for a situation in which only 3 periods have requirements. If requirements exist in 4 periods, the process is to determine the solution for the first three periods and use that as a base in analyzing the fourth requirement. This procedure is schematically illustrated in Figure 10-7 and in some examples that follow.

The advantage of dynamic programming is that the solution of any given step allows us to drop from further consideration all requirements prior to a decision to place an order. This is based on an *order cost* or *planning horizon theorem*, illustrated in the following examples.

**FIGURE 10-7**
**DYNAMIC PROGRAMMING PROCEDURE CONSIDERING FOURTH REQUIREMENT**

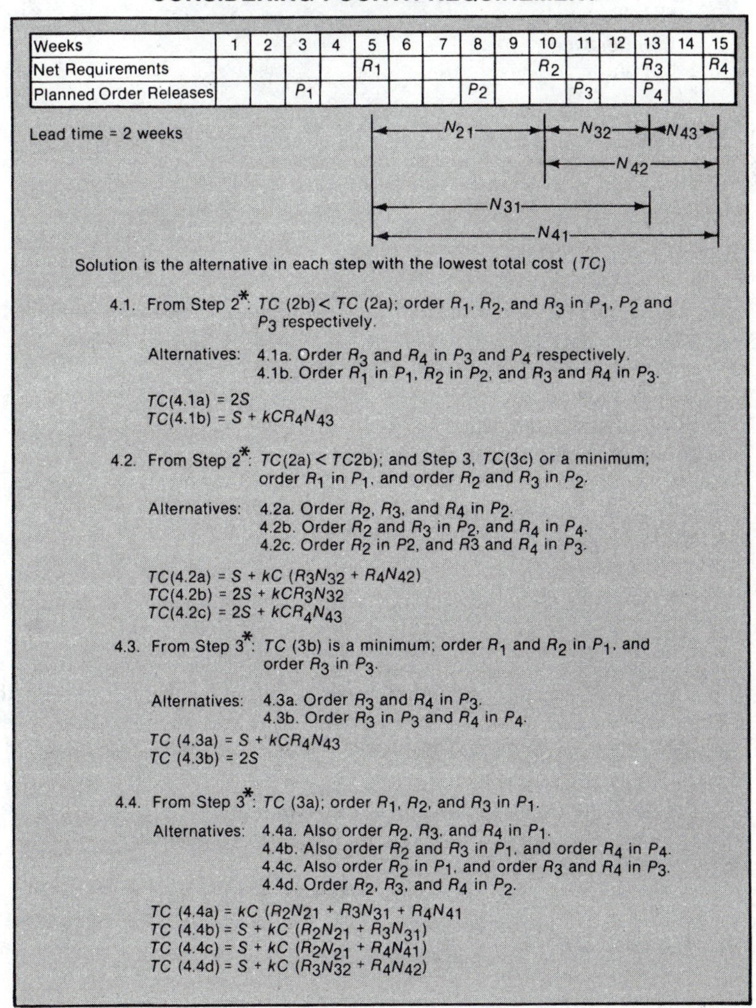

| Weeks | 1 | 2 | 3 | 4 | 5 | 6 | 7 | 8 | 9 | 10 | 11 | 12 | 13 | 14 | 15 |
|---|---|---|---|---|---|---|---|---|---|---|---|---|---|---|---|
| Net Requirements | | | | | $R_1$ | | | | | $R_2$ | | | $R_3$ | | $R_4$ |
| Planned Order Releases | | | $P_1$ | | | | | $P_2$ | | | $P_3$ | | $P_4$ | | |

Lead time = 2 weeks



Solution is the alternative in each step with the lowest total cost ($TC$)

4.1. From Step 2*: $TC$ (2b) < $TC$ (2a); order $R_1$, $R_2$, and $R_3$ in $P_1$, $P_2$ and $P_3$ respectively.

Alternatives: 4.1a. Order $R_3$ and $R_4$ in $P_3$ and $P_4$ respectively.
4.1b. Order $R_1$ in $P_1$, $R_2$ in $P_2$, and $R_3$ and $R_4$ in $P_3$.

$TC(4.1a) = 2S$
$TC(4.1b) = S + kCR_4N_{43}$

4.2. From Step 2*: $TC$(2a) < $TC$2b); and Step 3, $TC$(3c) or a minimum; order $R_1$ in $P_1$, and order $R_2$ and $R_3$ in $P_2$.

Alternatives: 4.2a. Order $R_2$, $R_3$, and $R_4$ in $P_2$.
4.2b. Order $R_2$ and $R_3$ in $P_2$, and $R_4$ in $P_4$.
4.2c. Order $R_2$ in P2, and R3 and $R_4$ in $P_3$.

$TC(4.2a) = S + kC\ (R_3N_{32} + R_4N_{42})$
$TC(4.2b) = 2S + kCR_3N_{32}$
$TC(4.2c) = 2S + kCR_4N_{43}$

4.3. From Step 3*: $TC$ (3b) is a minimum; order $R_1$ and $R_2$ in $P_1$, and order $R_3$ in $P_3$.

Alternatives: 4.3a. Order $R_3$ and $R_4$ in $P_3$.
4.3b. Order $R_3$ in $P_3$ and $R_4$ in $P_4$.

$TC\ (4.3a) = S + kCR_4N_{43}$
$TC\ (4.3b) = 2S$

4.4. From Step 3*: $TC$ (3a); order $R_1$, $R_2$, and $R_3$ in $P_1$.

Alternatives: 4.4a. Also order $R_2$, $R_3$, and $R_4$ in $P_1$.
4.4b. Also order $R_2$ and $R_3$ in $P_1$, and order $R_4$ in $P_4$.
4.4c. Also order $R_2$ in $P_1$, and order $R_3$ and $R_4$ in $P_3$.
4.4d. Order $R_2$, $R_3$, and $R_4$ in $P_2$.

$TC\ (4.4a) = kC\ (R_2N_{21} + R_3N_{31} + R_4N_{41}$
$TC\ (4.4b) = S + kC\ (R_2N_{21} + R_3N_{31})$
$TC\ (4.4c) = S + kC\ (R_2N_{21} + R_4N_{41})$
$TC\ (4.4d) = S + kC\ (R_3N_{32} + R_4N_{42})$

*See Figure 10-6.

**Planning Horizon Theorem.** If costs are minimized by having an order arrive at the beginning of Period $i$ when only $i$ periods are considered and there is no inventory at the end of Period $i$, the minimum costs will result by having an order arrive at the beginning of Period $i$ when requirements for periods beyond $i$ are considered. Thus, the least cost order sizes and planned order releases have been determined for periods preceding Period $i$. These points are shown in the following illustration:

| Week | 51 | 52 | 53 | 54 | 55 | 56 | 57 | 58 | 59 |
|---|---|---|---|---|---|---|---|---|---|
| Net Requirements | | | 35 | | 16 | | | 53 | 12 |

Lead time = 2 weeks
$C$ = \$83.33
$k$ = .006 per week
$S$ = \$60.00

1. $TC(1a) = S + kCR_2N_{21}$
$= \$60.00 + .006 \times \$83.33 \times 16 \times 2$
$= \$76.00$
$TC(1b) = 2S$
$= 2 \times \$60.00$
$= \$120.00$
$TC(1a) < TC(1b)$; therefore, go to Step 3 and add $R_3$ to the analysis.
3. $TC(3a) = S + kC(R_2N_{21} + R_3N_{31})$
$= \$60.00 + .006 \times \$83.33(16 \times 2 + 53 \times 5)$
$= \$208.50$
$TC(3b) = 2S + kCR_2N_{21}$
$= \$120.00 + .006 \times \$83.33(16 \times 2)$
$= \$136.00$
$TC(3c) = 2S + kCR_3N_{32}$
$= \$120.00 + .006 \times \$83.33 \times 53 \times 3$
$= \$199.50$
$TC(3b)$ is a minimum. We should order $R_1$ (35 units) and $R_2$ (16 units) in $P_1$ (Week 51), and order at least $R_3$ (53 units) in Week 56.

The planning horizon theorem tells us that there is no further need to consider $R_1$ and $R_2$; a minimum cost solution has been found for them. Thus, we proceed to Step 4.3 and examine the two possible alternatives for planning orders for $R_3$ and $R_4$.

4.3.[2] Alternatives are:
(a) A single order for $R_3$ and $R_4$ to arrive in $P_3$
(b) Order $R_3$ and $R_4$ to arrive in $P_3$ and $P_4$ respectively
$TC(4.3a) = S + kCR_4N_{43}$
$= \$60.00 + .006 \times \$83.33 \times 12 \times 1$
$= \$66.00$
$TC(4.3b) = 2 \times \$60.00 = \$120.00$

[2] From Figure 10-7.

$TC(4.3a) < TC(4.3b)$, therefore order $R_3$ and $R_4$ to arrive in $P_3$. The solution for the planning horizon is Order $R_1$ and $R_2$ in $P_1$, and $R_3$ and $R_4$ in $P_3$. The total cost is

$$\begin{aligned} TC &= nS + kC(R_2N_{21} + R_4N_{43}) \\ &= 2 \times \$60 + .006 \times \$83.33\ (16 \times 2 \times 12 + 1) \\ &= \$142.00 \end{aligned}$$

This is the same answer as we would obtain using the LTC-BF approach. However, when using the LTC-BF method, we had to calculate the cost of all options. Dynamic programming enables us to omit over 50 percent of the computations and obtain the same answer.

Another example would be good. Let us, therefore, consider the following. Let all factors except the requirements remain the same. The requirements now are:

| Week | 51 | 52 | 53 | 54 | 55 | 56 | 57 | 58 | 59 |
|---|---|---|---|---|---|---|---|---|---|
| Net Requirements | | | 16 | | 75 | | | 12 | 53 |

1. $$\begin{aligned} TC(1a) &= \$60.00 + .006 \times \$83.33 \times 75 \times 2 \\ &= \$135.00 \\ TC(1b) &= 2 \times \$60.00 \\ &= \$120.00 \end{aligned}$$

   $TC(1b) < TC(1a)$. Thus, the minimum cost decision includes releasing an order for $R_1$ (16 units) in $P_1$ (Week 51), and releasing an order in $P_2$ (Week 53) for at least $R_2$ (75 units). The planning horizon theorem reveals that we have found the minimum cost solution for $R_1$. We proceed to Step 2—since $TC(1b) < TC(1a)$—and analyze the alternatives for $R_2$ and $R_3$.

2. Alternatives are:
   (a) A single order for $R_2$ and $R_3$ in $P_2$
   (b) Order $R_2$ and $R_3$ in $P_2$ and $P_3$ respectively

   $$\begin{aligned} TC(2a) &= \$60.00 + .006 \times \$83.33 \times 12 \times 3 \\ &= \$78.00 \\ TC(2b) &= 2 \times \$60.00 \\ &= \$120.00 \end{aligned}$$

   Since $TC(2a) < TC(2b)$, we plan to combine $R_2$ and $R_3$ in an order in $P_2$. This solution is labeled Solution 2 in Figure 10-6 which leads us to evaluate the alternatives under Step 4.2 in Figure 10-7 when analyzing the addition of $R_4$. Go to Step 4.

4. The alternatives of 4.2 (see Figure 10-7) are:
   (a) Order $R_2$, $R_3$, and $R_4$ in $P_2$
   (b) Order $R_2$ and $R_3$ in $P_2$, and order $R_4$ in $P_4$
   (c) Order $R_2$ in $P_2$, and order $R_3$ and $R_4$ in $P_3$

   $$\begin{aligned} TC(4.2a) &= \$60.00 + .006 \times \$83.33(12 \times 3 + 53 \times 4) \\ &= \$184.00 \\ TC(4.2b) &= 2 \times \$60.00 + .006 \times \$83.33 \times 12 \times 3 \\ &= \$138.00 \\ TC(4.2c) &= 2 \times \$60.00 + .006 \times \$83.33 \times 53 \times 1 \\ &= \$146.50 \end{aligned}$$

Since $TC$(4.2b) is the minimum total cost, our complete solution is:
Order 16 units in Period 51
Order 87 units in Period 53
Order 53 units in Period 57

The total cost in this solution is:

$$TC = 3 \times \$60.00 + .006 \times \$83.33 \times 12 \times 3$$
$$= \$198.00$$

# Heuristic Models

The basic EOQ model ($Q^* = \sqrt{2RS/k}$) assumes a constant rate of demand. This assumption frequently is not valid; demand often varies substantially from period to period. When it does, lot sizes based on the basic model result in greater carrying and preparation costs than do lot sizes obtained by methods that consider variations in demand. Edward Silver and Harlan Meal have developed two lot-sizing methods for calculating order sizes when demand is known, deterministic, and varies from period to period. [3, 4] One allows orders to be placed at any time; the other requires that orders arrive at the beginning of the period. Their methods require more computer time than the EOQ, POQ, or L4L methods, and as Lowere points out, the resulting savings—compared with an EOQ approach—are less when the ordering cost and carrying cost are relatively low and demand is relatively high. [5]

**Nonrestricted Replenishment Timing.** This approach, which allows orders to be placed at any time in a period, requires perpetual inventory records (continuous review). Its iterative approach is described next and illustrated in the example which follows.

1. Begin with Period 1 and calculate the values of $T_i^2 D(T_i)$ and $\dfrac{2S}{Ck}$

Where:

$T_i$ = the time at the end of Period $i$
$D(T_i)$ = demand rate in Period $i$, expressed in units per period
$S$ = preparation (ordering and setup) cost
$C$ = unit cost
$k$ = carrying cost rate per period

2. Determine[3] if $T_i^2 D(T_i) \geq \dfrac{2S}{Ck}$. If it is, proceed to Step 3; if it is not, increase $i$ by one and repeat Steps 1 and 2.

[3]It is interesting to note that if demand is constant $[D(T_i) = D(T_2) = \cdots D(T_n)]$, the model $N = \dfrac{2S}{CkD(T)}$ is equivalent to $T = \dfrac{2S}{CkR}$ for determining the optimal order interval (see Chapter 7).

3. Calculate $N = \sqrt{\dfrac{2S}{CkD(T_i)}}$. If $T_i > N > T_{i-1}$, then $Q = \sum_{i=1}^{i=N} D(T_i)$; if not, round $N$ to whichever is closest, $i$ or $i-1$. For example let
$S$ = \$75
$C$ = \$30
$k$ = .30 per year, .006 per week
$D$ = the following:

| Time $T$ | 0 | 1 | 2 | 3 | 4 | 5 | 6 | 7 | 8 | 9 | 10 | 11 |
|---|---|---|---|---|---|---|---|---|---|---|---|---|
| Period (Week) ($i$) | 1 | 2 | 3 | 4 | 5 | 6 | 7 | 8 | 9 | 10 | 11 | |
| Demand | 10 | 12 | 14 | 12 | 22 | 25 | 15 | 20 | 36 | 35 | 31 | |

1. $\dfrac{2S}{Ck} = \dfrac{2 \times 75}{30 \times .006} = 833.33$

2.

| $i$ | $T_i^2 \, D(T_i)$ | $\overset{?}{>} 2S/Ck$ |
|---|---|---|
| 1 | $1 \times 10 = 10$ | $< 833.33$ |
| 2 | $4 \times 12 = 48$ | $< 833.33$ |
| 3 | $9 \times 14 = 126$ | $< 833.33$ |
| 4 | $16 \times 12 = 192$ | $< 833.33$ |
| 5 | $25 \times 22 = 550$ | $< 833.33$ |
| 6 | $36 \times 25 = 900$ | $> 833.33$ |

Therefore,the solution is between $T = 5$ and $T = 6$.

3. $N = \sqrt{\dfrac{2S}{CkD(T_6)}} = \sqrt{\dfrac{2 \times 75}{30 \times .006 \times 25}} = 5.77$

Since $6 > N > 5$,

$$Q = \sum_{i=1}^{5.77} D(T_i) = 10 + 12 + 14 + 12 + 22 + .77 \times 25$$
$$= 89$$

Thus, the first order is placed at $T = 0$ for 89 units, and the second order will be placed at $T = 5.77$.

The obvious next question is, What should the size of the second order be? Repeat the process after revising the values of $T_i$ to coincide with beginning and ending of periods. Thus,

| Time ($T$) | 0 | .23 | 1.23 | 2.23 | 3.23 | 4.23 | 5.23 |
|---|---|---|---|---|---|---|---|
| Period (i) | 1 | 2 | 3 | 4 | 5 | 6 | |
| Demand | 25 | 15 | 20 | 36 | 25 | 31 | |

1. $2S/Ck = 833.33$

2.

| $i$ | $T_i^2\, D(T_i)$ | $\overset{?}{>} 2S/Ck$ |
|---|---|---|
| 1 | $(.23)^2 \times 25 =$ | $1.32 < 833.33$ |
| 2 | $(1.23)^2 \times 15 =$ | $22.69 < 833.33$ |
| 3 | $(2.23)^2 \times 20 =$ | $99.46 < 833.33$ |
| 4 | $(3.23)^2 \times 36 =$ | $375.58 < 833.33$ |
| 5 | $(4.23)^2 \times 25 =$ | $447.32 < 833.33$ |
| 6 | $(5.23)^2 \times 31 =$ | $847.94 > 833.33$ |

Therefore, the solution is between $T = 4.23$ and $T = 5.23$.

3. $$N = \sqrt{\frac{2S}{CkT(D_6)}} = \sqrt{\frac{2 \times 75}{30 \times .006 \times 31}} = 5.18$$

Since $T_i > N$,

$$Q = \sum_{i=.23}^{5.18} D(T_i) = .23 \times 25 + 15 + 20 + 36 + 25 + .95 \times 31$$

$$= 131.20$$

The first order covered 5.77 periods; the second order covers from $T = 5.77$ to $T = 10.95$. Determination of the size of the second order will not take place until the time to release it. Many events, including scrap, additional orders, and order cancellations during the interval, can change demand in the remaining periods and the size of the second order prior to its release.

**Periodic Replenishment.** Frequently orders are placed only at one time during a period and an order must cover demand during one or more whole periods. Thus, the previous approach, which may order material for a fraction of a period, cannot be used. Silver and Meal have developed a method for calculating lot sizes that approach the minimum cost lot size under these conditions. [4] The method allows the demand rate to vary from period to period but requires the demand rate to be constant within each period. The procedure is given next and an example follows.

1. Begin with Period 1, $T = 1$.
2. Determine if

$$T^2 D_{T+1} > \frac{S}{Ck} + \sum_{j=1}^{T} (j - 1)\, D_j$$

If it is, go to Step 3.
If it is not, increase $T$ by 1 and repeat this step.

Where: $T$ = the period (i.e., 1, 2, . . . , $n$)
$D_j$ = demand rate in Period $j$, expressed in units per period
$S$ = cost of preparation (ordering and setup)
$C$ = unit cost
$k$ = carrying cost rate per period

3. A solution has been found and the order (replenishment) quantity is the sum of the demand from $T = 1$ through the last value of $T$ used in Step 2. This procedure is illustrated in the following example.

Demand for an item varies each week, and all items must be available at the beginning of the week. (The timing of the order release depends on the lead time.) Demand and other relevant data are given next:

$S$ = \$75
$C$ = \$30
$k$ = .30 per year, .006 per week
$D$ = the following:

| Week | 1 | 2 | 3 | 4 | 5 | 6 | 7 |
|---|---|---|---|---|---|---|---|
| Demand | 20 | 15 | 30 | 25 | 15 | 25 | 30 |

1. $T = 1$
$T^2 D_{T+1} = 1^2 \times 15$

$$\frac{S}{Ck} + \sum_{j=1}^{T} (j - 1)D_j = \frac{75}{30 \times .006} + (1 - 1) \times 20 = 416.66$$

2. Since $T^2 D_{T+1} < \frac{S}{Ck} + \sum_{j=1}^{T} (j - 1)D_j$, we increase $T$ by 1. We continue increasing $T$ until the condition required by Step 2 is obtained. The values are:

| Week ($T$) | $T^2 D_{T+1}$ | $\frac{S}{Ck} + \sum_{j=1}^{T} (j-1)D_j$ |
|---|---|---|
| 1 | 1 × 15 = 15 < | 416.66 + 0 = 416.66 |
| 2 | 4 × 30 = 120 < | 416.66 + 15 = 431.66 |
| 3 | 9 × 25 = 225 < | 416.66 + 75 = 491.66 |
| 4 | 16 × 15 = 240 < | 416.66 + 150 = 566.66 |
| 5 | 25 × 25 = 625 < | 416.66 + 210 = 626.66 |
| 6 | 36 × 30 = 1080 > | 416.66 + 335 = 751.66 |

A solution has been found: $T = 6$; place an order to cover the first six weeks.

3. $Q = \sum_{j=1}^{T} D_j = 20 + 15 + 30 + 25 + 15 + 25 = 130$

The size of the next order is determined when the order release point arrives. For example, if lead time is one week, the next order would be placed at the end of Week 4.

The objective of this method is to minimize inventory (preparation plus carrying) costs per time period. It accomplishes this by including the requirements of each successive period until the inventory costs per period increase. Table 10-8, which lists the costs per period of including 1, 2, 3, 4, 5, 6, or 7 periods in our example, illustrates this point. The inventory costs per period are lowest ($22.55) when six periods are included in the first order; thus, the algorithm gives an order quantity covering six periods.

**TABLE 10-8**
**INVENTORY COSTS PER PERIOD**
**ALL FIRST ORDER POSSIBILITIES**

| Period ($j$) | 1 | 2 | 3 | 4 | 5 | 6 | 7 |
|---|---|---|---|---|---|---|---|
| Demand ($D_j$) | 20 | 15 | 30 | 25 | 15 | 25 | 30 |

| Periods Included in First Order | Preparation Costs (s) | Carrying[1] Costs | Total Costs | Cost per Period |
|---|---|---|---|---|
| 1 | $75 | $ 0 | $ 75.00 | $75.00 |
| 1 and 2 | 75 | 2.70 | 77.70 | 38.85 |
| 1 through 3 | 75 | 13.50 | 88.50 | 29.50 |
| 1 through 4 | 75 | 27.00 | 102.00 | 25.50 |
| 1 through 5 | 75 | 37.80 | 112.80 | 22.56 |
| 1 through 6 | 75 | 60.30 | 135.30 | 22.55 |
| 1 through 7 | 75 | 97.80 | 172.80 | 24.68 |

[1] Carrying costs through Period $j = \sum_{j=1}^{T} (j - 1)CkD_j$

This procedure guarantees only a local minimum. If a relatively low demand occurs in Period $T + 2$ or beyond, further reduction in the inventory costs per period may be possible. For example, if demand is for only 5 units in Period 8, the lowest per period costs occur when ordering 165 units to cover Periods 1 through 8, as illustrated in Table 10-9. However, the algorithm still gives us a first order of 130 units for Periods 1 through 6. Thus, when the demand in any period beyond Period $T + 1$ is relatively low, a cost analysis of ordering through that period is advisable.

**TABLE 10-9**
**INVENTORY COSTS PER PERIOD**
**ALL FIRST ORDER POSSIBILITIES**
**REVISED DEMAND**

| Period ($j$) | 1 | 2 | 3 | 4 | 5 | 6 | 7 | 8 |
|---|---|---|---|---|---|---|---|---|
| Demand ($D_j$) | 20 | 15 | 30 | 25 | 15 | 25 | 30 | 5 |

| Periods Included in First Order | Preparation Costs (S) | Carrying[1] Costs | Total Costs | Cost per Period |
|---|---|---|---|---|
| 1 through 5 | $75 | $ 37.80 | $112.80 | $22.56 |
| 1 through 6 | 75 | 60.30 | 135.30 | 22.55 |
| 1 through 7 | 75 | 97.80 | 172.80 | 24.68 |
| 1 through 8 | 75 | 104.10 | 179.10 | 22.38 |

[1] Carrying costs through Period $j = Ck\sum_{j=1}^{T} (j - 1)D_j$

# STATIC INVENTORY SITUATIONS AND MODELS

Some inventory situations are static, that is, lead time is longer than the selling season. There is only one opportunity to order, and management must decide how many units to purchase or produce before demand is known. If demand exceeds the quantity purchased or produced, a stock-out occurs; if the quantity purchased or produced exceeds demand, a surplus results. The surplus usually is sold at a loss. There is no second chance; a second order will not arrive before the selling season ends.

Many organizations face this problem. For example, clothing manufacturers frequently produce seasonal clothing before knowing the exact quantity their sales representatives will sell. Christmas trees, cards, and decorations are produced under similar conditions. Unsold real Christmas trees have no value once the season ends. Leftover Christmas cards and decorations usually are sold at a heavy discount. Excess production of seasonal clothing is sold through outlet stores and to discount stores at a substantial discount. Long lead time items required in assembly frequently are ordered to forecast. If the sales rate is lower than the forecast, the added inventory costs are equivalent to selling at a discount; if sales exceed the forecast, sales and profits may be lost due to stock-outs or to back orders. Thus, some long lead time items ordered to a forecast also may be viewed as a static inventory problem.

If the demand is known with certainty, there is no problem. We order the amount required taking factors such as scrap and sample requirements into consideration. When demand is probabilistic, we must know or estimate the demand distribution and calculate the order quantity that maximizes the organization's objective.

A common objective in manufacturing and distribution is to maximize profit. The goal then is to order that number of units that maximizes expected profit $[E(Z)]$. To do this we must know the relevant income and costs in addition to the demand probability distribution. The probability of demand may be stated in a discrete or a continuous fashion. We will look at both cases.

## Discrete Probability Information

Examples of discrete demand probability distributions for three different static inventory decision situations are given in Table 10-10. In Case *C* the probabilities are listed for each possible demand from the .10 probability of selling none to the .10 probability of selling five units. There is no chance of a demand for six or more units. In Cases *A* and *B* the probabilities relate to a demand range, a common practice. For example, in Case *B* there is a .05 probability that demand will be between 51 and 150 units and a .20 probability that demand will be between 451 and 550 units. In such cases we solve for the most profitable order range.

**TABLE 10-10**
**EXAMPLES OF DISCRETE PROBABILITY DISTRIBUTIONS FOR THREE DIFFERENT STATIC INVENTORY DECISION SITUATIONS**

| Case A | | Case B | | Case C | |
|---|---|---|---|---|---|
| Probability of Demand $p(D)$ | Demand $D$ | Probability of Demand $p(D)$ | Demand $D$ | Probability of Demand $p(D)$ | Demand $D$ |
| .10 | 500,000 | .05 | 100 | .10 | 0 |
| .20 | 1,000,000 | .10 | 200 | .30 | 1 |
| .30 | 1,500,000 | .25 | 300 | .20 | 2 |
| .20 | 2,000,000 | .25 | 400 | .20 | 3 |
| .10 | 2,500,000 | .20 | 500 | .10 | 4 |
| .05 | 3,000,000 | .15 | 600 | .10 | 5 |
| .05 | 3,500,000 | 1.00 | | 1.00 | |
| 1.00 | | | | | |

Two methods of solving for the most profitable order quantity are:

1. Tabulate the expected profit of each order quantity and select the quantity that has the largest expected profit, and
2. Use marginal analysis to determine the most profitable order quantity

**Tabulation of Expected Profits.** We will use an example to illustrate this approach. An equipment dealer must special order an implement used only in the harvesting season. Reordering is not possible, and all unsold items are sold to a jobber at a loss. Carrying them until the following year would result in about the same loss and deprive the company of capital. The facts are:

$I$, income per unit (selling price) = \$200
$C$, cost per unit = \$150
$B$, stock-out cost per unit = \$30
$L$, unit salvage value (discounted selling price) = \$110
$Q$ = the number of units ordered
$p(D)$ = the probability of Demand ($D$), being $D$ units
$Z$ = total profit
$EZ(Q)$ = expected profit when quantity $Q$ is ordered
$p(D)$, the probability of demand for $D$ units, corresponds to Case $C$ in Table 10-10.

If $Q$ units are ordered and $Q \geq D$, the total profit equals the profit on the units sold minus the loss on the discounted units. If $Q \leq D$, the total profit equals the profit on the units ordered minus the stock-out costs on the units demanded but not available. Thus,

if $Q \geq D$, $Z = D(I - C) - (Q - D)(C - L)$, and
if $Q \leq D$, $Z = Q(I - C) - (D - Q)B$

From zero to five units may be ordered in this situation, and demand may be from zero to five units. Thus, 36 outcomes are possible. Each is listed in Table 10-11.

As shown in Table 10-12 the expected profit of ordering $Q$ units equals the sum of the products of each possible outcome (profit or loss) and its probability. Thus,

$$EZ(Q_j) = \sum_{i=1}^{n} p(D_i) \times Z(Q_j, D_i)$$

Where:

$EZ(Q_j)$ = the expected profit of Order Quantity $j$
$n$ = the number of different demands (or demand ranges)
$p(D_i)$ = the probability of Demand $i$
$Z(Q_j, D_i)$ = the profit that occurs when $Q_j$ is ordered and demand equals $D_i$

**TABLE 10-11**
**MATRIX OF POSSIBLE OUTCOMES (PROFITS)**
**STATIC INVENTORY PROBLEM**
**(IN DOLLARS)**

| Possible Demand ($D$) | Possible Order Quantities ($Q$) | | | | | |
|---|---|---|---|---|---|---|
| | 0 | 1 | 2 | 3 | 4 | 5 |
| 0 | 0 | −40 | −80 | −120 | −160 | −200 |
| 1 | −30 | 50 | 10 | −30 | −70 | −110 |
| 2 | −60 | 20 | 100 | 60 | 20 | −20 |
| 3 | −90 | −10 | 70 | 150 | 110 | 70 |
| 4 | −120 | −40 | 40 | 120 | 200 | 160 |
| 5 | −150 | −70 | 10 | 90 | 170 | 250 |

[1]Table 10-12 illustrates how the values are calculated.

Using the data from Table 10-11 and Case $C$ in Table 10-10, the expected profits of the different possible order quantities can be calculated as follows:

$$\begin{aligned} EZ(0) &= .10 \times 0 + .30 \times (-\$30) + .20 \times (-\$60) + .20 \times \\ &\quad (-\$90) + .10 \times (-\$120) + .10 \times (-\$150) \\ &= -\$9 - \$12 - \$18 - \$12 - \$15 \\ &= -\$66 \text{ (a loss)} \\ EZ(1) &= .10 \times (-\$40) + .30 \times \$50 + .20 \times \$20 + .20 \times \\ &\quad (-\$10) + .10 \times (-\$40) + .10 \times (-\$70) \\ &= -\$4 + \$15 + \$4 - \$2 - \$4 - \$7 \\ &= \$2 \end{aligned}$$

**TABLE 10-12**
**CALCULATION OF PROFIT WITH VARIOUS ORDER QUANTITY/DEMAND COMBINATIONS**

| | **Q = 0** | | |
|---|---|---|---|
| | **When Q ≥ D** | **When Q ≤ D** | |
| **D** | **Z = D(I − C) − (Q − D)(C − L)** | **Z = Q(I − C) − (D − Q)B** | **Z** |
| 0 | | 0($50) − (0 − 0) $30 = | $ 0 |
| 1 | | 0($50) − (1 − 0) $30 = | −$ 30 |
| 2 | | 0($50) − (2 − 0) $30 = | −$ 60 |
| 3 | | 0($50) − (3 − 0) $30 = | −$ 90 |
| 4 | | 0($50) − (4 − 0) $30 = | −$120 |
| 5 | | 0($50) − (5 − 0) $30 = | −$150 |
| | **Q = 1** | | |
| 0 | 0($50) − (1 − 0)($40) | = | −$ 40 |
| 1 | 1($50) − (1 − 1)($40) | = | $ 50 |
| 2 | | 1($50) − (2 − 1) $30 = | $ 20 |
| 3 | | 1($50) − (3 − 1) $30 = | −$ 10 |
| 4 | | 1($50) − (4 − 1) $30 = | −$ 40 |
| 5 | | 1($50) − (5 − 1) $30 = | −$ 70 |
| | **Q = 2** | | |
| 0 | 0($50) − (2 − 0) $40 | = | −$ 80 |
| 1 | 1($50) − (2 − 1) $40 | = | $ 10 |
| 2 | 2($50) − (2 − 2) $40 | = | $100 |
| 3 | | 2($50) − (3 − 2) $30 = | $ 70 |
| 4 | | 2($50) − (4 − 2) $30 = | $ 40 |
| 5 | | 2($50) − (5 − 2) $30 = | $ 10 |

$$\begin{aligned} EZ(2) &= .10 \times (-\$80) + .30 \times \$10 + .20 \times \$100 + .20 \times \\ &\quad \$70 + .10 \times \$40 + .10 \times \$10 \\ &= -\$8 + \$3 + \$20 + \$14 + \$4 + \$1 \\ &= \$34 \end{aligned}$$

And calculating the expected profit for $Q = 3$, 4, and 5 in the same manner gives:

$$EZ(3) = \$42;\ EZ(4) = \$26;\ \text{and } EZ(5) = -\$2.$$

Thus, the maximum expected profit ($42) occurs with an order quantity of 3 units.

**Marginal Analysis.** Profit maximization occurs at that point (quantity) at which the expected loss of ordering an additional unit equals the expected profit from that unit. In the example, the expected profit from ordering an additional unit equals the profit per unit times the probability of selling an additional unit plus the stock-out cost per unit times the probability of selling an additional unit. (Ordering an additional unit reduces the likelihood of a stock-out; thus it is a probable profit.) The expected loss from ordering an additional unit equals the probability of *not* selling an additional unit times the loss per unit not sold. Since we desire marginal profit to be greater than or equal to marginal loss, we set

$$\text{Marginal Profit} \geq \text{Marginal Loss}$$
$$P(D) \times (I - C) + P(D) \times B = [1.0 - P(D)] \times (C - L)$$

Where:

$P(D)$ = the probability of demand being $D$[4] or greater
$[1.0 - P(D)]$ = the probability of demand being for fewer units than $D$

Where:

$I$ = income per unit (selling price)
$C$ = cost per unit
$B$ = back order (or stock-out) cost per unit
$L$ = salvage value per unit

If we solve the above equation for $P(D)$ and determine the demand that corresponds to $P(D)$, setting the order quantity equal to that demand will maximize profit. Thus,

$$P(D) \times (I - C) + P(D) \times B - [1.0 - P(D)] \times (C - L) \geq 0$$
$$P(D) \geq \frac{C - L}{(I - C) + B + (C - L)}$$

Using the data from our earlier example where $I$ = \$200, $C$ = \$150, $L$ = \$110, and $B$ = \$30 we have the following:

$$P(D) \geq \frac{150 - 110}{(200 - 150) + 30 + (150 - 110)}$$
$$\geq .33$$

Since the probability of demand being 4 units or more is .2 and the probability of demand being 3 units or more is .4, $P(D) \geq .33$ corresponds to a demand of 3 units. The optimum order quantity is 3 units. This is the same solution that we obtained when tabulating expected profits of all possible order quantities.

What if there are no stock-out or back ordering costs? Then $B = 0$; and

$$P(D) = \frac{150 - 110}{(200 - 150) + 40} \geq .44$$

The optimum order quantity is now 2 units.

---

[4] P(D) is the cumulative probability complement represented in Figure 10-8.

FIGURE 10-8
PROBABILITY OF DEMAND ≥ $D_i$

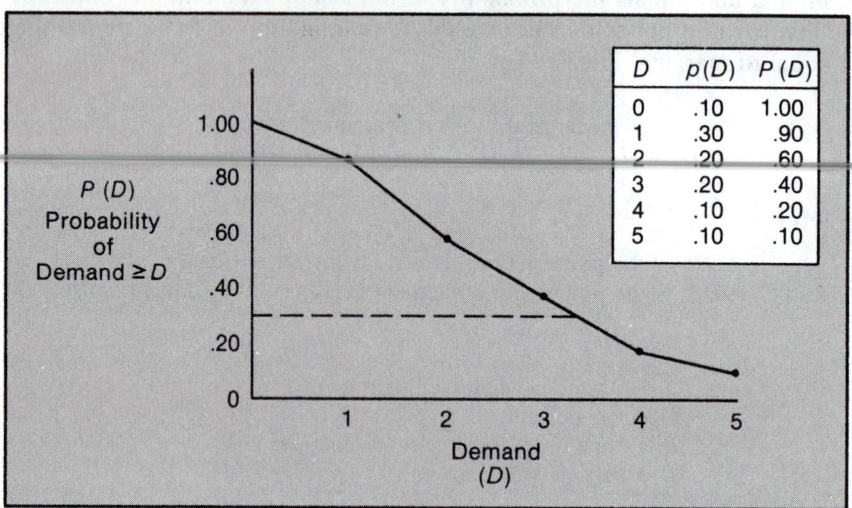


**Sensitivity Analysis.** Parameter values are usually estimates. Returning to the original data [$P(D) = .33$], the value of $P(D)$ must increase to .40 or decrease to .20 before the maximum profit order quantity changes. An analysis of the example situation will reveal that over a 10 percent change (error) in any single value is required to alter the optimum order quantity (see problems at the end of the chapter).

# Continuous Distribution

The probability of demand may be expressed as a continuous distribution as well as a discrete distribution. Two common continuous distributions are the equal probability and the normal distribution which are illustrated in Figures 10-9 and 10-10.

Marginal analysis can be used to solve a static inventory problem when a continuous distribution is used to describe the probability of demand. Let us examine an equal probability demand distribution first and then a normal probability demand distribution.

FIGURE 10-9
EQUAL PROBABILITY DISTRIBUTION

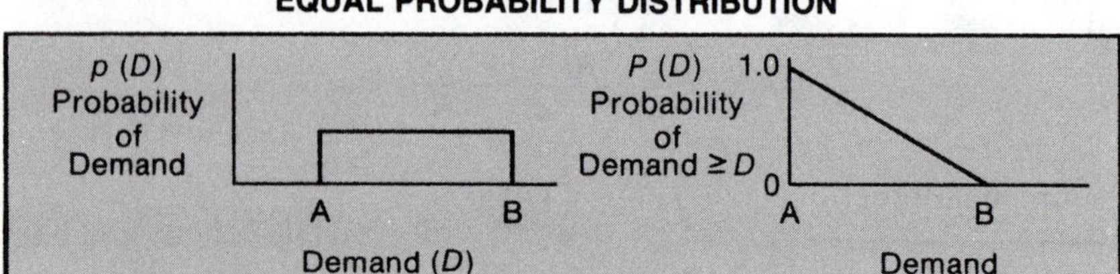

**FIGURE 10-10**
**NORMAL PROBABILITY DISTRIBUTION**

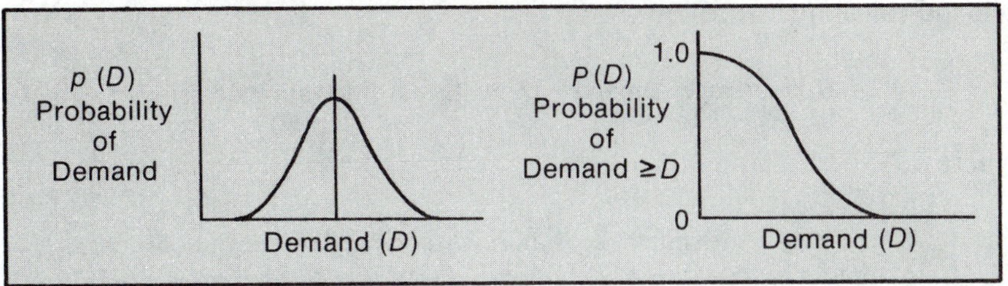


**Equal Probability Demand Distribution Example.** A company must decide how many spare parts to include in the last run for an item which is being discontinued. The parts cost \$20 each and are sold for \$40. Any not sold during the first year will be purchased by an odd lot jobber for \$10 each. If the company runs out of parts during the first year they must run additional units which will cost an estimated \$8 more. The cost of carrying an item in inventory is included in the \$20 cost. The company estimates that all quantities of spare parts from 1,001 to 2,000 have an equal probability of demand. Thus,

$$I = \$40;\ C = \$20;\ L = \$10;\ B = \$8;\ \text{and}$$

$$p(D) = \frac{1}{1,000}\Bigg|_{1,001}^{2,000};$$

$$P(D) = 1.0 - \sum_{D\,=\,1,001}^{D} p(D)$$

Where:

$p(D)$ = the probability of demand being $D$
$P(D)$ = the probability of demand being larger than $D$

From marginal analysis we obtain the following:

$$P(D) \geq \frac{C - L}{(I - C) + B + (C - L)} = \frac{20 - 10}{(40 - 20) + 8 + (20 - 10)}$$

$$\geq .263$$

Since each demand has a .001 (1 per 1,000) probability of occurring, it is easy to see that $P(D) \geq .263$ when $D = 1.738$. Thus, maximum profit is obtained by ordering 1,738.

**Normal Probability Demand Distribution Example.** Let's take the spare parts case again with all the factors the same except that the demand is normally distributed with a mean of 3,000 and standard deviation of 200. $P(D)$ was calculated earlier as .263. The optimum order quantity equals the demand calculated as follows:

$$Q^* = D = \text{average demand} + Z \times \text{standard deviation of demand}$$

Where:

$Z$ represents the number of normalized standard deviations corresponding to $(.5 - P(D)^*)$, and $P(D)^* < .50$ as represented in Figure 10-11.

$P(D)^*$ = the value of $P(D)$ when marginal profit equals marginal loss

If $P(D) > .50$,

$Q^*$ = average demand $-$ $Z \times$ standard deviation of demand.[5]

Thus, since $P(D) < .50$,

$$Q^* = 3{,}000 + .634 \times 200 = 3{,}127$$

**FIGURE 10-11**
**NORMAL PROBABILITY DEMAND DISTRIBUTION**

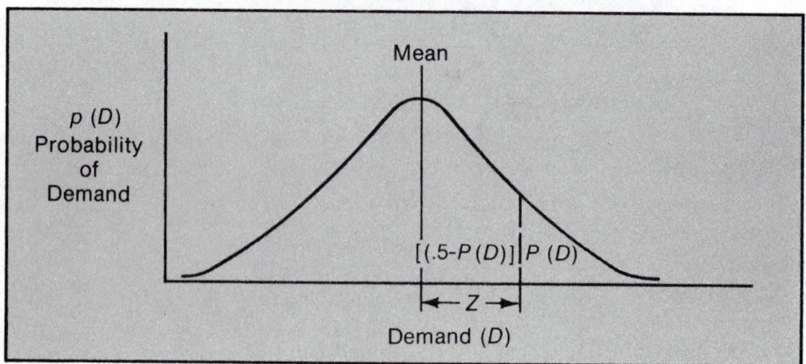


# MULTILEVEL (ECHELON) INVENTORY SITUATIONS

Many situations call for inventory decisions at different levels both in manufacturing and distribution. Multilevel distribution decisions are discussed in Chapter 11. Multilevel inventory situations in manufacturing can be rather involved in even a moderately complex interrelation of items as illustrated in Figure 10-12.

---

[5] The value of Z is obtained from Appendix H.

FIGURE 10-12
MULTILEVEL INVENTORY DECISION POINTS
THREE ASSEMBLIES WITH COMMON USAGE AT MANY LEVELS

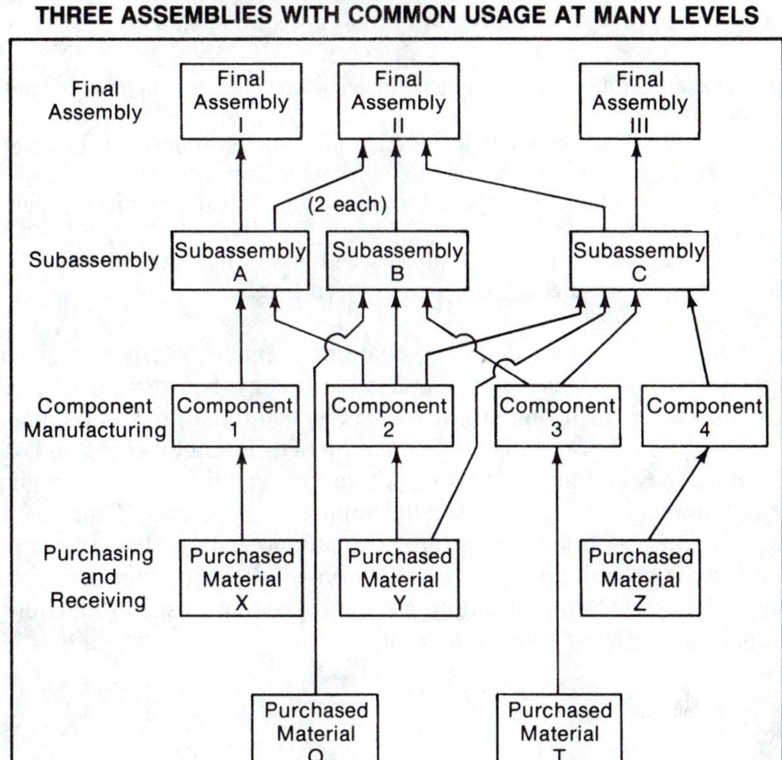


Material requirements planning determines the requirements per period of items at all levels. However, MRP in itself does not indicate when lot sizes should be combined to minimize costs, at what level safety stock should exist to achieve the desired customer service level at minimum costs, or if sufficient capacity is available when required.

Joseph R. Biggs et al simulated the use of various lot sizing rules and production order sequencing rules in a multilevel, multiproduct manufacturing environment. [6] In the situation studied, they found that different lot-sizing rules, dispatching rule combinations perform better with respect to different performance objectives, such as minimum late orders, minimum stock-outs, minimum number of setups, and minimum average inventory. They conclude that

1. Lot-sizing rules and order-prioritizing rules interact in the achieving of performance objectives.
2. Different product-process structures may result in different performance from the same lot-sizing rule and order-prioritizing rule combination.

Christopher New has pointed out the pitfalls of lot sizes based on traditional economic comparisons and computational efficiency. [7] He suggests that the best approach could be based on heuristics such as:

1. Set a target ratio for setup time to total machine involvement time (to limit nonmachining time).
2. Use a modified economic time cycle model to constrain the number of batches issued per time period to be within a given control band.
3. Decide on suitable time cycles for production of items and produce only to those cycles.
4. Fix lead time for planning purposes and always make the machine involvement time a given percentage of lead time.

Multilevel inventory decision situations require analysis of a given set of parameters and objectives to determine the best course of action. Generalized models recognizing inventory management and production management objectives are not available. Simulation of different lot-sizing and order-prioritizing rules in a given situation will aid in establishing decision guides.

In summary, there are literally hundreds of inventory management models; each appropriate for a different situation. This chapter examined only a few. Thorough analysis of a situation will help in determining which models, perhaps with modification, are appropriate to assist production and inventory management achieve its goal.

# PROBLEMS

**1.** The maintenance department in a relatively large organization purchases 1,200 light bulbs of a particular size for replacement each year. Bulbs are used throughout the year as electricians move from building to building replacing burnt out bulbs. Bulbs cost $1.50 in quantities less than 100, $1.30 for 100 to 499 bulbs, $1.20 for 500 to 999 bulbs, and $1.15 for 1000 or more bulbs. Ordering costs are $50 and the carrying cost rate is .40. How many bulbs should be purchased at one time?

**2.** A manufacturer of truck equipment for the utility industry purchases a motor for use in various subassemblies. They forecast a demand for 200 such motors at a steady rate throughout the coming year. The following is the price schedule for the motors:

| Order quantity | Price |
|---|---|
| 1 | $200 |
| 2–5 | 175 |
| 6–10 | 160 |
| 11–24 | 150 |
| 25–99 | 145 |
| 100 or more | 140 |

a. If the ordering cost is $60 and the carrying cost rate is .30, how many motors should the company order at one time?
b. The cost of capital increases, and management decides to change the carrying cost rate to .50. What effect should this have on the order quantity?
c. The carrying cost rate does not change, but the cost of processing a purchase order increases to $100. What effect should this have on the quantity ordered?

3. There is a steady demand of 500 units annually for an item assembled to stock. Two methods are available for fabricating this item. Method 1 results in a unit cost of $10 and a $50 setup cost per order. Method 2 has a setup cost of $160 and a unit cost of $9. Production capacity is 1,000 units per year with the first method and 2,000 per year with the second method. Let $k = .3$.

a. Which method should be used, and what should the lot size be?
b. It is discovered that $500 in tooling costs was not included in the cost of Method 2. Company policy is to absorb tooling over the first two years. What effect does this have on the decision?

4. Ajax Distributors experiences a rather steady annual demand of 40,000 units for an item. The item costs $25; ordering costs are $75 per order; and the carrying cost rate is .30. The company estimates that each unit back ordered costs 10 cents per day. The company operates 250 days each year.

a. What should the order quantity be?
b. What will be the maximum quantity in stock?
c. What is the total cost of this decision?
d. What is the longest a customer will have to wait?
e. If the company decides that no order shall be shipped more than a day late, how will the lot size be affected?

5. The Atlantic Office Products Company distributes Model 795 electric stapler. Experience indicates that a one-week delay in shipment does not affect sales. Model 795 costs $15. Ordering costs are $75; annual demand is 5,000 units; and carrying cost rate is .30.

a. What should the order size be?
b. What are the total costs of that lot size?
c. By how much do these costs differ from the costs of the basic lot size?

6. Weekly demand for an item is the following for the next ten weeks:

| Week | 1 | 2 | 3 | 4 | 5 | 6 | 7 | 8 | 9 | 10 |
|---|---|---|---|---|---|---|---|---|---|---|
| Demand | 30 | 30 | 30 | 30 | 20 | 20 | 15 | 25 | 30 | 20 |

The preparation cost is $250. The carrying cost rate is .30 per year, and the item costs $100. Orders can be placed anytime. Using Silver and Meal's algorithm (which does not require orders to arrive at the beginning of a period):

a. What should be the size of the first order?
b. How many weeks should it cover?
c. What are the inventory costs per period for the order?
d. What are the average inventory costs per period if orders are placed weekly? (There are no carrying costs for items carried a week or less).

7. Use Silver and Meal's second algorithm (material must be available at the beginning of the week) to determine how many periods the first order should cover under the following circumstances.

| Week | 1 | 2 | 3 | 4 | 5 | 6 |
|---|---|---|---|---|---|---|
| Demand | 80 | 100 | 125 | 75 | 50 | 110 |

$k = .006$
$C = \$100$
$S = \$320$

8. Use dynamic programming, Wagner and Whitin's model, to determine the following:

a. When should lot sizes be ordered under the following conditions?

| Week | 1 | 2 | 3 | 4 | 5 | 6 |
|---|---|---|---|---|---|---|
| Demand | 80 | 100 | 125 | 75 | 50 | 110 |

$k = .006$ Lead time = one week
$C = \$100$
$S = \$80$

b. When should lot sizes be ordered if all other factors remain the same, but $C = \$200$?
c. When should lot sizes be ordered if all factors remain the same as in a., except that $S = \$160$?
d. Calculate the total cost of each of the above solutions.

9. a. Calculate the cost of the following ordering rules for Situations a, b, and c in Problem 8.
(1) order each week
(2) order every 2 weeks
(3) order every 3 weeks
b. Compare these costs with those obtained in a. and comment.

10. Use dynamic programming (the Wagner-Whitin algorithm) to solve Problem 7.

11. The manufacturer of Mongoose clothing has decided to produce three new shirts for its spring and summer line. The shirts must be in production during January and February to fill early spring demand. Another production run will not take place until the following January. Distributors, some retailers, and large chains will place their orders after viewing the new shirts at the annual

clothing merchandisers' convention in late February. Relatively few orders are received during the remainder of the year. Sufficient capacity is available to produce any quantity of shirts. The shirts will sell at wholesale for $10 each; they cost $8 to produce. Shirts not sold by April 1 are sold to a distributor for $1 below cost; all orders received after April 1 are forwarded to him. The marketing department has submitted the following forecast of sales.

FORECAST SALES
(IN MILLIONS)

| Red | | Blue | | White | |
|---|---|---|---|---|---|
| Quantity | Probability | Quantity | Probability | Quantity | Probability |
| 1.0 | .10 | .5 | .10 | 1.8 | .10 |
| 1.1 | .10 | .6 | .20 | 1.9 | .10 |
| 1.2 | .10 | .7 | .30 | 2.0 | .20 |
| 1.3 | .10 | .8 | .20 | 2.1 | .20 |
| 1.4 | .10 | .9 | .15 | 2.2 | .20 |
| 1.5 | .10 | 1.0 | .05 | 2.3 | .10 |
| 1.6 | .10 | | | 2.4 | .10 |
| 1.7 | .10 | | | | |
| 1.8 | .10 | | | | |
| 1.9 | .10 | | | | |

a. How many of each should the manufacturer produce to maximize expected profits if there are no stock-out costs?
b. How many of each should be produced to maximize expected profit if there is a 50-cent stock-out cost for each shirt ordered, but not available?
c. How many of each should be produced to maximize expected profit if there is a 50-cent stock-out cost for each shirt and the leftover shirts are sold for $6 each?
d. How many of each should be produced if the stock-out cost is 50 cents, and there is a 50% chance of selling leftovers for $7 and a 50% chance of selling them for $6?

**12.** For a final assembly 100 units of a weldment (welded subassembly) are required. The subassembly operation has an ordering and setup cost of $150 and costs approximately $100. This subassembly is usually ordered only once a year due to the seasonal demand for the final product. Scrap on this type subassembly on a lot size of 100 units will run between 1 and 5 units with equal probability for any number. (Yield runs between approximately .9524 and 1.00.) The annual carrying cost rate is .30. If 100 acceptable units are not built, the job will be set up and run again.

a. How many units should the planner order to minimize expected costs?
b. How many units should the planner order to minimize expected costs if the cost of setup and ordering is $75?
c. If the item is usually manufactured twice a year and the cost of ordering and setup is $60, how many should the planner order?
d. How much will the costs of the order quantity obtained in b. differ from ordering 105?

13. A manufacturer of garden equipment is planning to produce a new sprinkler head for use in automatic lawn sprinklers. Sales are to builders of luxury homes and upper-middle and upper income individuals who install a sprinkler system. Eighty percent of all sales of such items usually take place in early spring.

Production is scheduled for February; production of fire extinguishing sprinklers and other water control system equipment is planned for the rest of the year. The new sprinklers cost $4 to produce and will be sold for $5. Those not sold in early spring will be sold for $3.75 to a distributor. Probable demand has a mean of 20,000 units with a standard deviation of 1,000 units.

If there is no stock-out cost, how many units should be produced to maximize profit?

14. The purpose of this problem is to illustrate each of the decision paths possible (see Figures 10-6 and 10-7) when using dynamic programming (the Wagner-Whitin algorithm) to determine the minimum cost order sizes and their planned releases. It is really 13 problems.

The following data concern a dependent demand item: $C$ = $83.33 per unit; $k$ = .006 per week; lead time = 2 weeks; and $S$ = $60.00 per order

a. Use dynamic programming to determine the planned order releases resulting in minimum total costs for each of the following sets of requirements.
b. Compare these costs with those of L4L planned order releases. What is the average savings per case? What percentage of the L4L costs is saved on the average?

| | Weeks | | | | | | | | |
|---|---|---|---|---|---|---|---|---|---|
| Case | 1 | 2 | 3 | 4 | 5 | 6 | 7 | 8 | 9 |
| A | | | 16 | | 75 | | | 53 | 130 |
| B | | | 16 | | 75 | | | 53 | 60 |
| C | | | 16 | | 75 | | | 12 | 10 |
| D | | | 16 | | 75 | | | 12 | 70 |
| E | | | 16 | | 75 | | | 12 | 30 |
| F | | | 35 | | 16 | | | 53 | 20 |
| G | | | 35 | | 16 | | | 53 | 130 |
| H | | | 35 | | 16 | | | 11 | 10 |
| I | | | 35 | | 16 | | | 11 | 70 |
| J | | | 35 | | 16 | | | 11 | 40 |
| K | | | 35 | | 20 | | | 20 | 2 |
| L | | | 35 | | 20 | | | 20 | 120 |
| M | | | 35 | | 20 | | | 20 | 30 |
| N | | | 35 | | 70 | | | 20 | 2 |

# SELECTED READINGS


1. Donald C. Aucamp and Donald W. Fogarty, "Minimum Cost Lot Size, Back Orders without Penalty," Working Paper (Edwardsville, Ill.: Southern Illinois University, June, 1981).
2. Harvey M. Wagner and Thomson M. Whitin, "Dynamic Version of the Economic Lot Size Model," *Management Science*, Vol. 5 (October, 1958), pp. 89–96.
3. Edward A. Silver and Harlan C. Meal, "A Simple Modification of the EOQ for the Case of the Varying Demand Rate," *Production and Inventory Management*, Vol. 10, No. 4, Fourth Quarter (1969), pp. 59–65.
4. ———, "A Hueristic for Selecting Lot Size Quantities for the Case of a Deterministic Time-Varying Demand Rate and Discrete Opportunities for Replenishment," *Production and Inventory Management*, Vol. 14, No. 2, Second Quarter (1973), pp. 64–74.
5. William M. Lowere, "Lot Size Rules—A One-Act Play," *Production and Inventory Management*, Vol. 16, No. 2, Second Quarter (1975), pp. 41–50.
6. Joseph R. Biggs, Stephen H. Goodman, and Stanley H. Hardy, "Lot-Sizing Rules in a Hierarchical Multistage Inventory System," *Production and Inventory Management*, Vol. 18, No. 1, First Quarter (1977), pp. 104–116.
7. Christopher C. New, "Lot Sizing in Multilevel Requirements Planning Systems," *Production and Inventory Management*, Vol. 15, No. 4, Fourth Quarter (1974), pp. 57–72.
8. Richard E. Bellman, *Dynamic Programming* (Princeton, N.J.: Princeton University Press, 1957).
9. George Hadley and Thomson M. Whitin, *Analysis of Inventory Systems* (Englewood Cliffs, N.J.: Prentice-Hall, Inc., 1963), pp. 336–345.
10. Rein Peterson and Edward A. Silver, *Decision Systems for Inventory Management and Production Planning* (New York: John Wiley & Sons, Inc., 1979), pp. 199–200.
11. Richard J. Tersine, *Materials Management and Inventory Systems* (New York: Elsevier North-Holland, Inc., 1976).

# —11—

# DISTRIBUTION AND INVENTORY CONTR

This chapter concerns the management of distribution inventory and the integration of administrative and physical controls.

Time and place have value. The objective of distribution inventory management is to have inventory in the right place at the right time at reasonable cost. In brief, the objective is to achieve a desired level of customer service at or below a specified cost; thus, establishing or maintaining a competitive advantage.

Distribution decisions affect:

1. Facilities
2. Transportation
3. Inventory investment
4. Stock-out frequency
5. Manufacturing
6. Communication and data processing

Distribution strategies and policies should be part of an integrated organization strategy encompassing all functional areas. Decisions made by marketing, engineering, finance, and manufacturing are linked systemically; i.e., decisions in one area also affect results in other areas.

The major distribution related questions include the following:

1. Should the company build to stock or build to order?
2. What part of the distribution function should the company perform, and what part should it subcontract?
3. What, if any, manufacturing or packaging should be performed at distribution facilities?
4. Where should distribution centers be located?
5. Should the company own and operate the transportation system?
6. Exactly what modes of transportation should be used?
7. How should distribution inventory be managed?

This chapter concentrates on the management of distribution inventory and addresses the other questions briefly.

Although most products made completely to order are shipped directly from the factory to the purchaser, many require that assistance be provided to the purchaser during installation and initial operations. Thus, distribution takes the form of field service technical assistance in bringing the equipment to an operating condition.

Purchasing distribution services of many types is possible. Warehouses can be leased; other firms with complementary product lines and existing distribution facilities may provide distribution services for a fee; and the primary purpose of some organizations is to provide distribution services. When the volume of sales is low in a particular area, it frequently costs less to purchase these services than to purchase and maintain wholly owned facilities.

Distribution centers often can perform some fabrication jobs more economically than the factory. For example, manufacturers of special truck bodies and related equipment such as derricks, aerial devices, and diggers frequently ship the equipment and truck body to the distributor for final assembly. The mounting of equipment and installation of hydraulic, pneumatic, and electrical lines frequently can be performed less expensively by the distributor, or fabricator. In addition, shipping costs usually are less as the truck chassis is shipped directly from the truck manufacturer to the distributor rather than through the truck body manufacturer. Performing final assembly, finishing, and packaging operations at distribution centers enables less expensive bulk shipments from the plant to the distribution point. Since the distance from the plant to the distribution point usually is substantially greater than the distance from the distribution center to the customer, considerable savings can result. A distribution center may purchase packaging materials locally and achieve additional transportation savings.

Selecting the lowest cost location for each of several warehouses in a distribution network is a complex problem. More than one plant may supply each warehouse, and shipments may be made between warehouses. It usually is best, however, to hold inventory at the central facility until the proper allocation to warehouses is clear. This avoids expensive movements between warehouses. Mathematical programming and simulation are useful for analyzing these problems. Arthur M. Goeffrion developed a trade-off curve of the sum of warehousing and transportation costs against the average level of response time to customer orders. Grouping the plant locations and customer demand by geographic area and product type, he used a computer model of this relationship to calculate the lowest cost network of warehouse locations. [1, 2]

The availability of company owned carriers can generate substantial savings. This is especially true when little competition exists among common (commercial) carriers.

The nature of the product, the distance, the cost, and time requirements determine the most appropriate mode of transportation. A pipeline is most economical for some liquids and gases sold in large volume at a low unit cost. Shipping very expensive, lightweight items long distances by air is frequently the least costly method because of reduced time and lower carrying costs.

Including the cost of carrying transportation inventory in the comparison of two transportation methods is straightforward. Find the difference between the transportation inventory costs of the two methods, and add it to the cost of the slower method. For example, let the weekly requirements ($A$) be \$100,000, the weekly carrying cost rate ($k$) be .006, the time ($t$) required for Shipping Method A be 1 week, and Shipping Method B require 2 weeks. Thus (from Chapter 6, and $A = R \times C$),

$$\begin{aligned} \text{TRIC(A)} &= t \times A \times k \\ &= 1 \times \$100{,}000 \times .006 \\ &= \$600 \\ \text{TRIC(B)} &= 2 \times \$100{,}000 \times .006 \\ &= \$1{,}200 \end{aligned}$$

The company can afford to pay up to \$600 more per year for shipping by Method A. The above analysis assumes that transit time is certain in both Methods A and B. However, if the variability (standard deviations) of the two delivery times were different, the added costs resulting from safety stock and expediting would need to be included in the analysis.

## DISTRIBUTION INVENTORY MANAGEMENT SYSTEMS

Distribution managers frequently encounter the classic transportation network problem described in Chapter 17, i.e., how to allocate resources from multiple sources to fill requirements at multiple locations. For example, the allocation of output from 3 plants to 4 distribution centers as illustrated in Figure 11-1.

The objective is to minimize the total transportation costs while providing the warehouses with their requirements ($D_j$) from available sources ($S_i$). The general model for this problem follows.[1]

$$\begin{aligned} &\Sigma X_{ij} \le S_i \qquad (1 \le i \le m) \\ &\Sigma X_{ij} = D_j \qquad (1 \le j \le n) \\ &X_{ij} \ge 0 \\ &\text{Minimum } TC = \Sigma\Sigma C_{ij} X_{ij} \end{aligned}$$

Where:

$X_{ij}$ = quantity shipped from Plant $i$ to Warehouse $j$
$m$ = number of plants
$n$ = number of warehouses
$C_{ij}$ = cost of shipping one unit from Plant $i$ to Warehouse $j$

[1]Chapter 17 describes its solution.

**FIGURE 11-1**
**ALLOCATION OF PRODUCTION TO WAREHOUSES**
**MULTIPLE PLANTS ($S_i$) AND MULTIPLE WAREHOUSES ($D_j$)**

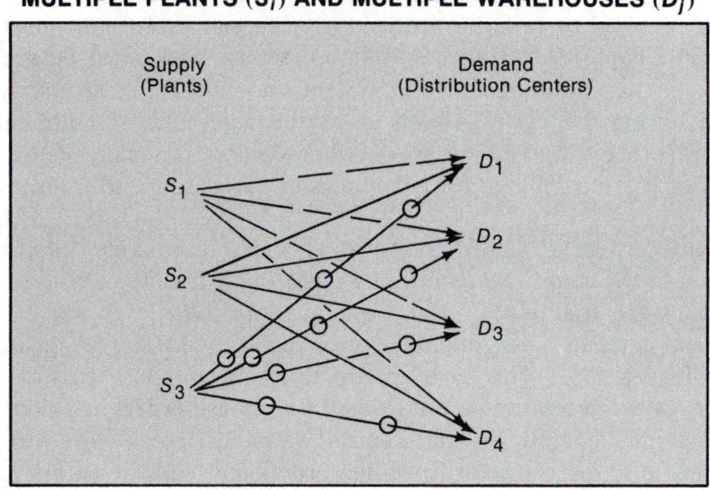


Distribution inventory management systems can be classified as pull or push systems. In a *Pull* system, the warehouse determines its requirements and orders from the factory; it "pulls" inventory into the warehouse. In a *Push* system, the forecast requirements for all warehouses are summed by period, and scheduled production and available inventory is allocated to the warehouses. The inventory is "pushed" into the warehouses. Actual systems frequently combine features of both push and pull systems.

## Pull Systems

The archtype pull system orders without regard for the needs of other warehouses, inventory available at the central warehouse, or the production schedule. The warehouse controls the ordering system. Traditional pull systems include the order point method, the periodic review method, the double order point method, and the sales replacement method. The base stock system is primarily a pull system but may exhibit some push system characteristics.

**The Order Point System.** The branch warehouse orders from the main warehouse whenever the quantity in stock at the branch reaches its order point. The order point is based on the normal demand during the average time required to obtain the order (*replenishment lead time*) from the central warehouse plus the safety stock. There is little interaction between the branch warehouse and the central warehouse (which receives the orders without any warning). This system can result in a very erratic demand on the central warehouse. It requires a relatively large safety stock at the central warehouse in addition to the safety stocks at the branch warehouses.

**The Periodic Review System.** With this system (sometimes called the fixed order interval or the cycle review system) branch warehouse inventory status is determined at a regular interval, and the warehouse orders the quantity required to bring inventory to the target level (maximum) as described in Chapter 7.[2] Branch warehouse safety stock must be greater in this system than in an order point system since it must cover variations in demand during the cycle as well as during lead time. Traditionally this method has been used in situations where orders for many items from a single source are combined for economies of purchasing and transportation.

**The Double Order Point System.** This method provides additional information to the central warehouse by reporting when the warehouse inventory equals the traditional order point quantity ($OP_1$ in Figure 11-2) plus the normal demand during manufacturing lead time ($MLT$) as illustrated by $OP_2$ in Figure 11-2. This enables the central warehouse to examine its inventory position relative to anticipated warehouse orders and take appropriate action. Theoretically the central warehouse need not carry safety stock since it is forewarned of pending orders and adds inventory required to meet those orders. See Robert W. Porter's treatment of the simulation of the performance of a distribution system with different inventory management systems. [3]

**FIGURE 11-2**
**DOUBLE ORDER POINT SYSTEM**

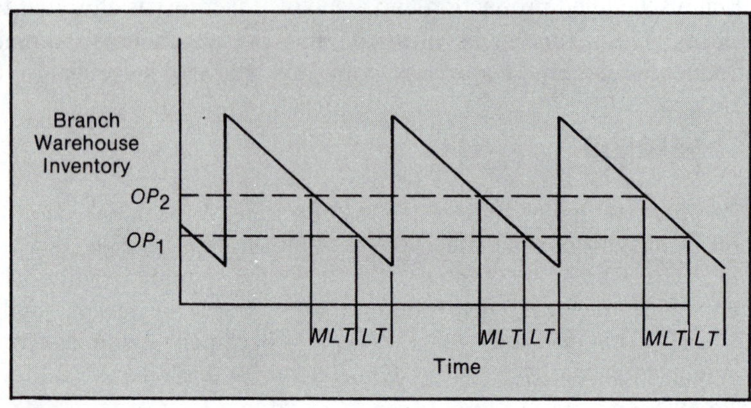


**The Sales Replacement System.** Each warehouse periodically (perhaps quarterly) establishes a stocking level for each item based on local demand. Sales at each warehouse are reported to the central warehouse at periods shorter than the normal order interval. Shipments replacing the quantities sold are sent to each warehouse at the end of the replenishment periods.

[2] Chapter 7 contains a description of the principles and basic techniques of the order point, periodic review, and combination order point-periodic review systems.

Periods usually are established to obtain economical shipments such as full truck loads. Increased warehouse reporting of sales to the central warehouse decreases the effect of erratic demand on the central warehouse. It enables manufacturing and purchasing to improve the coordination of planned orders with warehouse sales. [4]

**Advantages and Disadvantages of Pull Systems.** The advantages of a pull system are that it can operate autonomously and has lower data processing and communication expenses than a push system. Distributed data processing and minicomputers have decreased these costs substantially. However, pull systems have inherent disadvantages. In a strictly pull system, orders are placed on the central warehouse without any knowledge or consideration of the needs of other warehouses. The ordering warehouse usually is unaware of shipping plans that may include the combination of shipments to two or more warehouses or the use of a different size truck or railroad car. Orders also are submitted without regard to available inventory, production schedules, or irregular occurrences such as the addition of a new private label customer. As these deficiencies in pull systems have been recognized, communications between regional warehouses and the central supply have increased, and greater control of shipping quantities has been placed at the central supply. Thus, many actual systems with the basic characteristics of a pull system have taken on some characteristics of push systems.

**The Base Stock System.** Each retail outlet—if company owned—and each warehouse periodically (perhaps quarterly) establishes a stocking level for each item. Sales are reported on a weekly or, preferably, a daily basis to all inventory-holding facilities as illustrated in Figure 11-3 rather than only when ordering. Thus, the regional warehouse, the central warehouse, and the factory are aware of demand trends. This system usually is not subject to shock waves of unexpected demand. The primary advantage of this system is that it enables manufacturing, the central warehouse, and regional warehouses to plan and react on the basis of actual customer demand rather than the replenishment orders filled at secondary stock points such as regional warehouses. The system reduces the unpredictability of demand on the warehouses and the factory. The total demand for an item across the entire system is usually more stable than demand measured by individual stocking points in the system.

The base stock level at each stocking location equals the normal demand during replenishment lead time and the interval between sales reports plus the safety stock. The supplying operation—rather than the stocking location—initiates replenishment orders on the basis of customer demand and available stock. This system eliminates many of the inherent deficiencies of the classic pull systems by incorporating features now identified with push systems. [5]

**FIGURE 11-3**
**THE BASE STOCK SYSTEM**
**FLOW OF SALES DATA, ORDERS, AND INVENTORY**

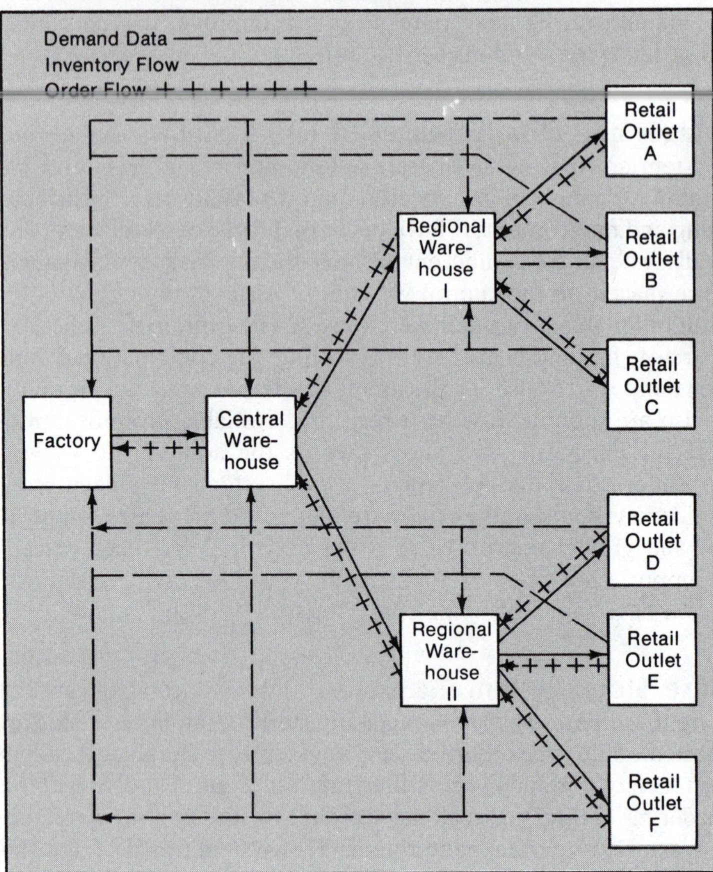


# Push Systems

Push systems consider total projected requirements (all warehouse and direct sales requirements), inventory available at the regional warehouses and the central warehouse, inventory in transit, and scheduled receipts from the source (plant or supplier) and determine the quantity available for each warehouse and direct factory sales. This allocation is controlled centrally on the basis of such criteria as equal days coverage, shipping schedules, and competitive factors. The central warehouse decides what to send, i.e., push, to the regional warehouses.

**Distribution Requirements Planning (DRP).** DRP ties production and distribution planning together by determining aggregate time-phased net requirements at the same point in the material flow as the Master Production

Schedule (MPS).[3] When the items on the MPS are not the final product and require finishing, packaging, or fabrication into a final assembly, these final operations can be viewed as the first stage in distribution. James Heskett points out that automobile assembly plants are distribution centers equipped to receive orders, fabricate individually designed final assembly configurations from standard components, and deliver them in a reasonable time. [6]

Figure 11-4 illustrates the application of DRP to a situation with three warehouses and sales direct from a central warehouse. Here the lead time, economic shipping quantity, forecast demand, projected orders, and projected on hand balance each week for each warehouse are given. The projected warehouse orders and the direct sales constitute the demand on the central supply source (warehouse). Subtracting these requirements from the on hand balance (950 units) at the central warehouse results in an order being planned for release in Week 1. This process is followed for all of the end items simultaneously. Consolidated shipments, therefore, on a regular basis are possible. Thus, distribution requirements are linked directly to the MPS.

**FIGURE 11-4**
**DISTRIBUTION REQUIREMENTS PLANNING (DRP)**

Warehouse A

| | Past Due | Week 1 | 2 | 3 | 4 | 5 | 6 | 7 | 8 |
|---|---|---|---|---|---|---|---|---|---|
| Gross Requirements* | | 80 | 80 | 80 | 70 | 80 | 90 | 90 | 90 |
| Scheduled Receipts | | | | 500 | | | | | |
| Projected On Hand | 204 | 124 | 44 | 464 | 394 | 314 | 224 | 134 | 44 |
| Planned Orders | | 500 | | | | | | | |

Warehouse B

| | Past Due | Week 1 | 2 | 3 | 4 | 5 | 6 | 7 | 8 |
|---|---|---|---|---|---|---|---|---|---|
| Gross Requirements* | | 30 | 30 | 30 | 20 | 30 | 35 | 35 | 35 |
| Scheduled Receipts | | | | | 200 | | | | |
| Projected On Hand | 100 | 70 | 40 | 10 | 190 | 160 | 125 | 90 | 65 |
| Planned Orders | | 200 | | | | | | | |

Warehouse C

| | Past Due | Week 1 | 2 | 3 | 4 | 5 | 6 | 7 | 8 |
|---|---|---|---|---|---|---|---|---|---|
| Gross Requirements* | | 120 | 120 | 120 | 100 | 120 | 140 | 140 | 140 |
| Scheduled Receipts | | | | | | | 700 | | |
| Projected On Hand | 600 | 480 | 360 | 240 | 140 | 20 | 580 | 440 | 300 |
| Planned Orders | | | | | 700 | | | | |

Direct Sales

| Past Due | Week 1 | 2 | 3 | 4 | 5 | 6 | 7 | 8 |
|---|---|---|---|---|---|---|---|---|
| | 50 | 50 | 50 | 50 | 50 | 50 | 50 | 50 |

Central Supply

| | Past Due | Week 1 | 2 | 3 | 4 | 5 | 6 | 7 | 8 |
|---|---|---|---|---|---|---|---|---|---|
| Gross Requirements* | | 750 | 50 | 50 | 750 | 50 | 50 | 50 | 50 |
| Scheduled Receipts | | | | | 1,000 | | | | |
| Projected On Hand | 950 | 200 | 150 | 100 | 1,150 | 1,100 | 1,050 | 1,000 | 950 |
| Planned Orders | | 1,000 | | | | | | | |

Order Quantities and Lead Time

| | Order Quantity | Lead Time (Weeks) |
|---|---|---|
| Warehouse A | 500 | 2 |
| Warehouse B | 200 | 3 |
| Warehouse C | 700 | 2 |
| Central Warehouse | 1,000 | 3 |

*Forecast

**Advantages of DRP Systems.** In a traditional order point system, an apparently excellent inventory position at the central warehouse can evaporate overnight if two or more warehouses reach their order point at the same time. [7] To illustrate this, let us calculate the order point for each warehouse and change the on hand quantities at Warehouses B, C, and Central as shown in Table 11-1.

[3]See Figure 11-4.

**TABLE 11-1**
**ORDER POINT EXAMPLE**

| Warehouse | A | B | C | Central |
|---|---|---|---|---|
| On Hand | 204 | 150 | 350 | 1150 |
| Forecast per Week | 80 | 30 | 120 | 280** |
| Order Point* | 240 | 120 | 360 | 1120 |
| Order Quantity | 500 | 200 | 700 | 1800 |
| Lead Time (weeks) | 2 | 3 | 2 | 3 |

*Equals demand during lead time plus 1 week's safety stock.
**Includes 50 units sold each week direct from central warehouse.

The stock in the central warehouse is above its order point and all appears well, but Warehouses A and C have just dropped below their order points. They then place orders for 500 and 700 units respectively (another 50 units required this week for direct sales). The central warehouse can make partial shipments to Warehouses A and C while holding stock for direct sales. (The central warehouse has not been informed of the forthcoming order from Warehouse B next week.) Warehouse B will be put on back order. Unless the central warehouse can expedite the production of its order and/or the shipment to Warehouse B, *B* will have a stock-out.

DRP avoids such problems by projecting branch warehouse requirements by period and generating planned orders on the central warehouse. The joint occurrence of two branch warehouse orders will be predicted and an order placed by the central warehouse with the factory to meet these requirements. DRP is especially beneficial when shipping cost factors make it advisable to ship in large quantities at relatively infrequent intervals.

Both the Double Order Point System and the Base Stock System will provide early warnings to the central warehouse of future orders and reduce these difficulties somewhat. Nonetheless, they can result in orders not necessarily aligned with true needs and relatively large safety stocks in regional warehouses. DRP is based on future time-phased requirements rather than on past sales and maintains most safety stock at the central warehouse.

In a strict pull system, branch warehouse orders are based on demand in one geographic area only. Filling such orders on a first come, first served basis leads to *suboptimization*, achieving one goal at the expense of other equally important goals. The branch warehouse lacks information concerning the needs of other warehouses, possible special shipping arrangements, central inventory, and manufacturing requirements. Also, in a pull system, branch warehouse managers usually are evaluated on the performance of their warehouse only. This frequently encourages decisions that hinder the accomplishment of organizational goals.

DRP enables distribution and manufacturing management to allocate inventory and production capacity, limited resources, and to meet total organizational requirements in a manner consistent with overall corporate goals such as aggregate customer service, inventory investment, and efficient manufacturing.

**Allocation and Push Systems.** The latest ship date is a common criteria for assigning priorities to warehouse shipments. The *latest ship date* is the day projected stock at a given warehouse will reach zero, minus the normal replenishment lead time of that warehouse. If, for example, the stock of Item 927 at Warehouse H is projected to reach zero on Day 85 and the replenishment lead time is 8 days, the latest ship date is Day 77.

Up to this point, we have addressed only the distribution of individual items, however, combining many items in one shipment (a joint shipment) is common. In a joint shipment, the major fixed cost of shipping is spread across many items with only a minor fixed shipping cost for each additional item. This is analogous to major and minor setups in production and to combined purchase orders. The economies result from full carloads and reduced paperwork per item.[4] The quantity of an item sent to a given warehouse may be limited by truck or train car capacities and the requirements for other items. In such cases, a good practice is to ship equal run out quantities of each item.

We also have assumed that the central warehouse has sufficient stock of an item to meet the requirements of all branch warehouses. When this is not the case, a reasonable approach is to send an equal run out quantity to each warehouse. These quantities, sometimes called fair shares, will provide each warehouse with coverage for the same number of days of projected sales.

Let, for example, the central warehouse have 140 units of Product A as the latest ship date for that product arrives in the Minneapolis branch warehouse. Additional receipts are not expected at the central warehouse for at least a week. The inventory and the requirements of the four warehouses are given in the following:

| Warehouse | On Hand | Requirements/Week | | | | | Daily Usage |
|---|---|---|---|---|---|---|---|
| | | 1 | 2 | 3 | 4 | 5 | |
| Minneapolis | 10 | 25 | 25 | 25 | 25 | 25 | 5 |
| Atlanta | 20 | 30 | 30 | 30 | 30 | 30 | 6 |
| Denver | 18 | 20 | 20 | 20 | 20 | 20 | 4 |
| Pittsburgh | 10 | 15 | 15 | 15 | 15 | 15 | 3 |
| Total | 58 | 90 | 90 | 90 | 90 | 90 | 18 |

The system has a total of 198 units; 140 units at the central warehouse plus 58 units at the four regional warehouses. Since 18 units are used each

[4]Calculation of economical joint lot sizes was treated in Chapter 8.

day, there are 11 days supply in the system. The objective is to ship each warehouse the quantity required to bring its stock to an 11 days supply. Thus,

$$Q_i = R_i - I_i$$

Where:

$Q_i$ = shipping quantity for Warehouse $i$
$R_i$ = requirements for Warehouse $i$ during run-out period
$I_i$ = inventory on hand in Warehouse $i$

Minneapolis, for example: $Q = 5 \times 11 - 10 = 45$. The quantities for the other warehouses are calculated in the same manner and are as follows:

| Warehouse | Quantity Allocated |
|---|---|
| Atlanta | 46 |
| Denver | 26 |
| Pittsburgh | 23 |
| Total | 95 |

Thus, the 140 units have been allocated to provide coverage for an equal time period in all warehouses. The central warehouse ships 45 units to the Minneapolis warehouse. If carriers are leaving shortly for the other warehouses, their respective fair shares may be sent to the other warehouses. The space available on a carrier is assigned on the basis of the relative priority of the items vying for shipment. This is similar to the technique Porter calls the Force-Balance method and to the allocation procedure described in American Software's *Inventory Management Systems*. [3,8] Thomas Newberry and Carl Bhame have pointed out the need to tie distribution to demand forecasting using forced concensus on a bottom up, top down basis. [9] A push allocation system works especially well when there are regular shipments to branch warehouses, say, every week or two, or when shipping costs do not require the shipment of relatively large quantities. Push allocation can combine the projection of branch warehouse and central supply requirements by period. Research and analyses of distribution systems have increased in the last few years and DRP and push allocation systems have resulted. We can look forward to further developments and refinements.

## INVENTORY ACCOUNTING AND PHYSICAL CONTROL

Successful inventory management requires adequate administrative, physical, and financial controls. These controls are achieved by inventory records and record-keeping practices, auditing practices, inventory evaluation methods, and storekeeping and security.

Inventory status may be recorded on a perpetual or periodic basis. *Perpetual recording* consists of recording each inventory transaction as or immediately after it occurs. Thus, a *perpetual inventory record* is an up-to-the-instant (real time) record of transactions and a statement of the current (1) quantity on order (and not received), (2) quantity in inventory, (3) quantity allocated (but still in inventory), and (4) quantity available for allocation. A perpetual recording system is required by the statistical order point inventory management and MRP systems.

In a strictly *periodic inventory recording system,* the inventory is counted or measured at a fixed interval; e.g., every two weeks, and the record of stock on hand is then updated. The quantity ordered, if any, is based on the quantity in stock and the expected usage. (See the description of periodic review inventory management systems in Chapter 7.)

Some data processing systems update inventory records daily or at even shorter intervals, say, every four hours. This is effectively a perpetual system if multiple transactions on any item during the interval period are unlikely, and the occasionally required remedial action is inexpensive.

Distributed computer systems with data entry from widely separated locations (hundreds or thousands of miles) are becoming relatively inexpensive. Communications and software, however, are not inexpensive. These cost conditions lead to maintaining real time inventory data on micro/mini computers at distribution centers and reporting periodically, for example, daily. This has increased the feasibility of perpetual inventory recording and DRP.

## The Inventory Record

An inventory record (see Figure 11-5[5]) contains permanent information and variable information. Each transaction changes variable information; permanent information changes only occasionally. Permanent information includes data such as the following:

1. The part number
2. The part name
3. A description
4. The storage location
5. The order point (independent demand items)
6. The lead time
7. The safety stock
8. Suppliers and their ratings

---

[5]See also Chapter 4, Figure 4-5, p. 113, for an illustration of an MRP format inventory record.

9. The cost
10. The yield
11. The group (if any) to which it belongs
12. Assemblies in which it is used
13. Shelf life
14. Batch control requirements
15. Substitutes
16. Item classification

This information is not truly permanent; it may change as the result of engineering changes, manufacturing process changes, or inventory management analysis, for example.

Variable information may include the following:

1. Quantities ordered, the dates, and the production or purchase order number
2. Quantities received, the dates, and the production or purchase order number
3. The balance on hand
4. Quantities issued, the date, and the manufacturing or shipping order number
5. Quantities allocated, the date, and the production or shipping order number
6. Quantities previously allocated that have been issued
7. The available balance
8. Batch identification

**FIGURE 11-5**
**INVENTORY RECORD EXAMPLE**

| | | |
|---|---|---|
| Part No. B281 | Order Quantity 400 | Suppliers |
| Name Bearing | Order Point[1] | |
| Location B-3 | Lead Time 1 wk. | |
| Class B | Yield 1.00 | |
| Group 12 | Shelf Life N/A | |
| Substitutes None | BCR[2] N/A | |
| Used on | Cost $3.75 | |
| Description Bearing | Safety Stock 50 | |

| Date | Ordered | | Received | | Issued | | Balance | Allocated | | Available |
|---|---|---|---|---|---|---|---|---|---|---|
| | Order No. | Quantity | Order No. | Quantity | Order No. | Quantity | | Order No. | Quantity | Quantity |
| 1/6 | | | | | | | 470 | | | 470 |
| 1/8 | | | | | | | | M-62 | 300 | 170 |
| 1/10 | | | | | | | | M-78 | 100 | 70 |
| 1/10 | P891 | 400 | | | | | | | | 470 |
| 1/15 | | | | | M84 | 300 | 170 | M-62 | -300 | |
| 1/17 | | | P891 | 400 | | | 570 | | | |

[1] Based on time-phased requirements.
[2] Batch control requirements.

The information required depends on the situation. For example, batch identification is not required in all circumstances. Shelf life, customer demands, trade practices, or statutes require it for some products especially in the food and pharmaceutical industries.

Sound inventory management requires accurate inventory records. Inaccurate records lead to situations such as the following:

1. Excess inventory of some items due to premature orders
2. Stock-outs, assembly and component fabrication department downtime
3. Increased overtime, extra setups, and increased expediting
4. Inaccurate monthly or quarterly profit and loss statements resulting in unexpected profits or losses when the annual physical inventory count occurs
5. Overplanning to guarantee enough, leading to excess inventories and high obsolescence

Six ingredients essential to obtain accurate inventory records are given next.

1. An appropriate attitude on the part of management
2. Clearly designating specific persons to be responsible for maintaining the accuracy of each recording activity
3. Providing adequate tools
4. Providing adequate instructions and training
5. Establishing accuracy goals and then measuring performance
6. Auditing records and reconciling inaccuracies

Management must lead by demanding accurate records. Bank tellers, bookkeepers, nurses' aids, and university admissions clerks all respond positively to an expectation of accurate records. Manufacturing, inventory, and purchasing personnel respond in the same manner when their supervisors demand accuracy. If an individual's job and increases in salary depend on accuracy, the accuracy of records increases substantially.

Counting and identification of items occurs in several places in the organization. Individuals performing these activities should be informed explicitly that their tasks require accuracy. For example, receiving clerks must count and identify incoming material accurately. The same holds for shipping clerks and outgoing items. Storekeepers must identify, count, and record material received and issued. In addition, they must record material locations accurately. The quantity of acceptable production and of scrap should be recorded after each operation by the operator.

Accurate records are difficult to maintain without adequate support. Containers holding a designated quantity, counting scales (the number of items is given by the weight), hand counters, and orderly storage facilitate accurate counts and records. Data describing issues, receipts, shipments, completions of operations, scrap, and allocation must be processed by the Production and Inventory Management (PIM) information system in a timely manner. The speed with which records must be updated depends on the frequency of transactions on an item. The availability of relatively inexpensive electronic data processing equipment makes slow reporting systems difficult to justify.

Adequate training of personnel is relatively inexpensive; inadequate training may be very expensive. Documentation of proper recording procedures with clear examples of the typical transactions can aid both the inexperienced and the new employee. Formal training is an excellent foundation for an understanding and appreciation of appropriate and accurate recording of transactions.

**Auditing Inventory Records.** Physically counting the quantity of each item in inventory is necessary to verify the accuracy of inventory records. The two basic methods are (1) periodic, usually annual, count of all items and (2) cyclic, continuous usually daily, counting of items with specified criteria determining the items that are counted during a given day.

An annual physical inventory does not support day-to-day inventory record accuracy. Validating the aggregate inventory values used for financial accounting statements is its primary purpose. Production usually is discontinued while the annual count is taken by a combination of line and staff personnel on temporary assignment. This relatively large group is not familiar with the appearance of most items, their location, and engineering changes that obsolete some items. Production downtime is expensive; time available for the count may be limited and, thus, accuracy may suffer.

Cycle counting involves the following:

1. Selecting and training a limited number of personnel to be (preferably) full-time counters
2. Establishing criteria for selecting items to count
3. Selecting items for counting each day
4. Counting those items, comparing counts to the inventory record, and determining the causes of any errors
5. Taking the action required to improve accuracy
6. Measuring the quality of records and changes in quality over time

**Initiating a Cycle-Counting Program.** Beginning the program by repetitively counting a small representative sample of items can spotlight problem areas very rapidly. Henry Jordan has pointed out that the sample should include purchased items, manufactured items, some difficult-to-count items, and some whose unit of measure changes as they are processed. [10] When any existing problems have been resolved and the count and records agree over a period with numerous transactions, begin the cycle counting program.

**Selecting Items to Count.** The frequency with which an item is counted should be related directly to the risk and importance of an error with the item. Inexpensive, low usage items that can be obtained from a local supplier in an hour or two are low risk items. They are *C* items in the typical ABC classification system that can be used to determine the frequency of counts. Selection of an item for counting frequently is based on activity criteria such as counting when:

1. An order is placed
2. An order is received
3. The inventory record balance is zero or negative
4. The last item is issued from stores
5. A specified number of transactions has been recorded

Each of these criteria usually results in an unbalanced work load for the counters. In such cases *A* items usually are counted first, *B* items next, and then *C* items. Counters may have other storekeeping tasks assigned on days when the workload is low.

The *Block System,* which counts items in the same storage area each day, may be used. It results in a balanced workload and is a more efficient process in terms of counts per man-hour. If, for the most part, different storage areas are used for *A, B,* and *C* items, the frequency of area counts can vary by classification.

All items should be counted at least once a year. Location audits also should take place to guarantee that all items physically in storage are counted.

Since operations continue during cycle counting, cutoff procedures must exist so that ongoing transactions do not alter the inventory record before a comparison is made. In an on-line system this problem is minimized since the count can be checked with the record immediately. Cycle counting may be performed at the end of the day or transactions may be suspended in the items to be counted during a given day. The practicality of any approach depends on the situation.

**Accuracy Goals and Performance Measurement.** Whenever the count and the record differ, the record must be adjusted. When that difference is beyond the specified tolerance, an analysis should be made to determine the cause, and the Accounting Department should be notified of the difference. Table 11-2 gives tolerances recommended by the APICS cycle-counting training aid. [10]

**TABLE 11-2**
**APICS RECOMMENDED TOLERANCES**

| Inventory Class | Percentage of Quantity | Dollar Value |
|---|---|---|
| *A* | ±0.2 | 100 |
| *B* | ±1 | 100 |
| *C* | ±5 | 100 |

Preparing a monthly cycle count cumulative variance report as illustrated in Table 11-3 enables management to track the progress of inventory accuracy.

**TABLE 11-3**
**CYCLE COUNT CUMULATIVE VARIANCE REPORT**
**(MONTH: MARCH)**

| | Previous Month | | Current Month | | Year-to-Date | |
|---|---|---|---|---|---|---|
| Inventory Class | Variance (Dollars) | Value (Percentage) | Variance (Dollars) | Value (Percentage) | Variance (Dollars) | Value* (Percentage) |
| *A* | −6,122 | 0.750 | −5,137 | 0.623 | −19,022 | 2.330 |
| *B* | 485 | 0.059 | −402 | 0.049 | 671 | .082 |
| *C* | −95 | 0.012 | 87 | 0.010 | −33 | .004 |

*Based on present inventory value.

## Inventory Evaluation Methods

There are four principal methods of costing inventory: FIFO (first in, first out); LIFO (last in, first out); the Moving Average Cost; and the Order (Specific) Cost. The value of inventory sold is included as an expense in calculating the cost of goods sold for a period and the value of items in stock at the end of the period is included as an asset on the balance sheet. Thus, the inventory costing procedure will affect the book value of inventory investment, profit, taxes, and cash flow.

**FIFO.** This method assumes that items are issued from stock in the same sequence that they are received. Oldest items leave first. The cost of sales is based on the cost of the oldest items in inventory and the asset value of the items remaining in stock is based on the cost of the newest items. During an inflationary period this procedure results in a lower cost of goods sold, increased earnings before taxes, increased taxes, and decreased cash flow when compared with other methods. The opposite results during a deflationary period. Table 11-4 is a simple example of the application of FIFO with an increasing item cost.

**LIFO.** This method assumes that the most recent arrivals in inventory are issued first. The newest items leave first. The cost of goods sold reflects the cost of the most recent arrivals in inventory and the asset value of the items remaining in inventory is based on the cost of the oldest items in inventory. During an inflationary period (newer items cost more than older items) this method results in a higher cost of goods sold, decreased earnings before taxes, decreased taxes, and increased cash flow when compared with other methods. The opposite results during a deflationary period. Table 11-5 is a simple example of LIFO with an increasing item cost.

**TABLE 11-4**
**FIFO COSTING OF INVENTORY**

| | Receipts | | | Issues | | | Balance[1] | | |
|---|---|---|---|---|---|---|---|---|---|
| Date | Units | Unit Cost | Total Cost | Units | Unit Cost | Total Cost | Units | Unit Cost | Total Cost |
| Jan. 1 | | | | | | | 400 | $3.00 | $1,200 |
| Jan. 10 | | | | 300 | $3.00 | $ 900 | 100 | 3.00 | 300 |
| Jan. 25 | 300 | $3.30 | $ 990 | | | | 100<br>300 | 3.00<br>3.30 | 1,290 |
| Feb. 3 | | | | 100 | 3.00 | 300 | 300 | 3.30 | 990 |
| Feb. 18 | | | | 200 | 3.30 | 660 | 100 | 3.30 | 330 |
| Mar. 1 | 400 | 3.35 | 1,340 | | | | 100<br>400 | 3.30<br>3.35 | 1,670 |
| Mar. 10 | | | | 100<br>200 | 3.30<br>3.35 | 1,000 | 200 | 3.35 | 670 |
| Mar. 25 | 400 | 3.40 | 1,360 | | | | 200<br>400 | 3.35<br>3.40 | 2,030 |

[1]Quarter cost of goods sold = $2,860; asset value = $2,030.

**TABLE 11-5**
**LIFO COSTING OF INVENTORY**

| | Receipts | | | Issues | | | Balance[1] | | |
|---|---|---|---|---|---|---|---|---|---|
| Date | Units | Unit Cost | Total Cost | Units | Unit Cost | Total Cost | Units | Unit Cost | Total Cost |
| Jan. 1 | | | | | | | 400 | $3.00 | $1,200 |
| Jan. 10 | | | | 300 | $3.00 | $ 900 | 100 | 3.00 | 300 |
| Jan. 25 | 300 | $3.30 | $ 990 | | | | 100<br>300 | 3.00<br>3.30 | 1,290 |
| Feb. 3 | | | | 100 | 3.30 | 330 | 100<br>200 | 3.00<br>3.30 | 960 |
| Feb. 18 | | | | 200 | 3.30 | 660 | 100 | 3.00 | 300 |
| Mar. 1 | 400 | 3.35 | 1,340 | | | | 100<br>400 | 3.00<br>3.35 | 1,640 |
| Mar. 10 | | | | 300 | 3.35 | 1,005 | 100<br>100 | 3.00<br>3.35 | 635 |
| Mar. 25 | 400 | 3.40 | 1,360 | | | | 100<br>100<br>400 | 3.00<br>3.35<br>3.40 | 1,995 |

[1]Quarter cost of goods sold = $2,895; asset value = $1,995.

**Weighted Moving Average.** This method calculates the value of items in inventory on the basis of their weighted average cost. The cost of items consumed by production equals the weighted average unit cost of inventory. This method smooths the effect of inflation and deflation on the valuation of inventory and the cost of goods sold. Table 11-6 is a simple example of this method with increasing item costs. Since Tables 11-4, 11-5, and 11-6 use the same data for the beginning balance, receipts, issues, and item costs,

**TABLE 11-6**
**WEIGHTED AVERAGE COSTING OF INVENTORY**

| | Receipts | | | Issues | | | Balance[1] | | |
|---|---|---|---|---|---|---|---|---|---|
| Date | Units | Unit Cost | Total Cost | Units | Unit Cost | Total Cost | Units | Unit Cost | Total Cost |
| Jan. 1 | | | | | | | 400 | $3.00 | $1,200.00 |
| Jan. 10 | | | | 300 | $3.00 | $900 | 100 | 3.00 | 300.00 |
| Jan. 25 | 300 | $3.30 | $ 990 | | | | 400 | 3.225 | 1,290.00 |
| Feb. 3 | | | | 100 | 3.225 | 322.50 | 300 | 3.225 | 961.50 |
| Feb. 18 | | | | 200 | 3.225 | 645 | 100 | 3.225 | 322.50 |
| Mar. 1 | 400 | 3.35 | 1,340 | | | | 500 | 3.325 | 1,662.50 |
| Mar. 10 | | | | 300 | 3.325 | 997.50 | 200 | 3.325 | 665.00 |
| Mar. 25 | 400 | 3.40 | 1,360 | | | | 600 | 3.375 | 2,025.00 |

[1]Quarter cost of goods sold = $2,865; asset value = $2,025.

they provide a comparison of the results of LIFO, FIFO, and the Weighted Moving Average.

**Order (Specific) Cost.** This method ties the cost of goods sold directly to the cost of the actual items used in production (or sold directly). The value assigned to items remaining in inventory also equals the actual costs of those items. This method is applicable to large expensive items with relatively low demand and whose cost may vary widely. It requires an information-processing system capable of tracing the flow of each purchase and each production lot through the entire production and distribution system.

**Selecting a Costing Procedure.** The Accounting or Finance Department usually selects the inventory costing procedure. The product process structure of an organization, the organization's objectives, and legal requirements influence the selection. The results of the different systems are very similar when costs are stable. United States companies must obtain approval from the Internal Revenue Service to use LIFO.

## Storekeeping and Security

Administrative control (records accuracy) and physical control are interdependent. Misplaced items, unrecorded issues, and pilferage can annul records accuracy. The principles of storekeeping and security (physical control) apply to all situations. The appropriate method of operationalizing these principles depends on the situation.

Storerooms should be "locked"; all material issues and movement should be authorized and recorded. Receipts must also be recorded. Although physically enclosing all items is not always possible—for example, bulk commodities such as coal and sand may have to be stored outdoors—all issues and receipts should be recorded. Other items may move directly from the receiving dock to the production line or from the final production work center to the shipping dock. In both cases, clearly defined control points must exist with the information system recording changes in inventory status when movement occurs. This situation is prevalent in continuous and repetitive production where containers of material may move from the receiving dock to the production line at regular intervals, e.g., every hour.

Fixed locations, random locations, and zoned random locations may be used to store inventory. The fixed location method permanently assigns a specific space to each item. This method minimizes problems in finding items. It is appropriate when item inventory levels are relatively stable, when receipt and withdrawal frequencies are stable, and when space is not a problem. Using this method when item inventory levels vary widely can lead to inefficient space utilization.

Storing items in part number sequence is possible in a fixed location system. This facilitates location but can be inefficient if handling and storage requirements vary widely for items in the same number range. Frequency of use and handling difficulty also is a sound basis for assigning locations. Convenient access should be provided for high volume items whose bulk or weight cause handling difficulties. The nature of certain items requires that they be segregated as a group and stored in temperature, humidity, or dust controlled facilities.

The random location approach assigns items to an available space. Different lots of the same item may be stored in different locations. Item location may become variable information—rather than permanent—on the inventory record. The locations of an item should be updated at each receipt and withdrawal. The method can utilize space efficiently when item inventory levels vary widely. However, it requires that storekeepers and material handlers frequently consult the inventory records before obtaining items or placing them in stores. Lax recording practices will lead to locating problems unless there are relatively few items or few location changes.

Zoned location combines some of the benefits of both the fixed and the random location system. Items are located in a space available basis within a designated zone. Grouping similar items in the same zone reduces the location problems that may result from the random location approach. Grouping may be based on storage requirements, nature of the item (for example, storing all hydraulic components in the same area), or on the basis of product line usage.

No single technique will necessarily meet all the needs of any one company. Many organizations, consequently, use a combination of these methods.

# PROBLEMS

The following information is relevant to Problems 1 through 9.

CENTRAL WAREHOUSE

| On Hand = 1,600 | Safety stock = 250 |
|---|---|

WAREHOUSE A

| | Past Due | Week 1 | 2 | 3 | 4 | 5 | 6 | 7 | 8 |
|---|---|---|---|---|---|---|---|---|---|
| Forecast Demand | 0 | 60 | 60 | 60 | 60 | 60 | 60 | 60 | 60 |
| On Hand | 300 | | | | | | | | |

WAREHOUSE B

| | Past Due | Week 1 | 2 | 3 | 4 | 5 | 6 | 7 | 8 |
|---|---|---|---|---|---|---|---|---|---|
| Forecast Demand | 0 | 150 | 150 | 150 | 150 | 200 | 200 | 200 | 200 |
| On Hand | 600 | | | | | | | | |

WAREHOUSE C

| | Past Due | Week 1 | 2 | 3 | 4 | 5 | 6 | 7 | 8 |
|---|---|---|---|---|---|---|---|---|---|
| Forecast Demand | 20 | 40 | 60 | 80 | 20 | 100 | 40 | 40 | 60 |
| Scheduled Receipts | 0 | 200 | | | | | | | |
| On Hand | 0 | | | | | | | | |

Replenishment lead times are three weeks for Warehouse A and two weeks for both Warehouses B and C. The economic shipping quantity is 240 units to Warehouse A, 600 units to Warehouse B, and 200 units to Warehouse C. Finished goods units cost $15. Manufacturing lead time is 3 weeks.

1. If all the warehouses use a basic order point system with safety stocks of 60, 100, and 50 units at Warehouses A, B, and C respectively, what is the order point of each warehouse? If actual demand is the same as forecast demand, in which periods will each warehouse place its next order?
2. Given the information in Problem 1, calculate the projected inventory each week in each warehouse and calculate the average inventory for each warehouse.
3. The central warehouse has 1,600 units at the beginning of Week 1; safety stock is 250 units; the production order quantity is 2,000 units; and the manufacturing lead time is 3 weeks. Calculate the order point for the stock at the central warehouse, the periods in which orders are released and received, and the quantity on hand at the end of each week.
4. Calculate the total inventory for each week in units and in dollars when the four warehouses are using the order point system.
5. If the *MLT* is 3 weeks, calculate the second order point for each warehouse. What are the implications of the results of the calculations in this case using the double order point system?
6. A sales replenishment system is used to manage the stock in Warehouses A, B, and C. The replenishment period is four weeks for each of the warehouses. Warehouse A's stock is replenished in Weeks 1, 3, and 7; Warehouse B is replenished in Weeks 2 and 6; and Warehouse C's stock is replenished in Weeks 1 and 5. Given the safety stocks for these warehouses in Problem 1 for an order point system,

a. Estimate the approximate safety stock for each warehouse in order to achieve the same level of service with the sales replenishment system.
b. Calculate the stocking level for each warehouse.
c. Assume that actual demand equals forecast demand. Calculate the order quantity each review period for each warehouse and the on hand balance at the end of each week at each warehouse. (Refer to the treatment in Chapter 7 of periodic review systems.)
d. Using an *OP* of 1,000 units and an order quantity of 2,000 units, calculate the inventory on hand each week at main warehouse.
e. Calculate the total inventory in the distribution system (the four warehouses) for each week in units and in dollars.

7. Using a DRP system, determine the planned orders for each warehouse and the projected inventory on hand at each warehouse each week. There is no safety stock at Warehouses A, B, and C. Calculate the order release timing, order receipt periods, and inventory on hand at the central warehouse each week. (Use a production order quantity of 2,000 and a safety stock of 250 at the central warehouse.)
8. Calculate the total inventory in the distribution system for each week in units and dollars when using a DRP system.
9. Compare the costs of carrying inventory in the order point, the sales replenishment, and the DRP systems for the eight-week period. Use a *k* of .30. Calculate the estimated differences in cost between the three methods for a year.
10. Design an inventory record for a dependent demand item used in ten to 15 different assemblies. The beginning balance and quantity available are both 650. Record the following events:

| Date | |
|---|---|
| 6/18 | 250 units allocated to order M93 |
| 6/21 | 300 units allocated to order M107 |
| 7/8 | 500 units ordered (M207) |
| 7/8 | 450 units allocated to order M123 |
| 7/16 | 300 units issued (M107) |

11. Prepare a cumulative cycle count variance report based on the following information. (Use these two months for year-to-date calculations.)

| Inventory Class | Previous Record Value | Month Actual Value | Current Record Value | Month Actual Value |
|---|---|---|---|---|
| A | $782,490 | $775,200 | $791,600 | $781,800 |
| B | 15,208 | 15,321 | 15,675 | 15,790 |
| C | 4,920 | 4,915 | 5,176 | 5,320 |

12. Based on the receipts and issues during the last two months (see top of page 378), determine the cost of goods sold for the two months and the asset value of the inventory at the end of the two months using (a) FIFO, (b) LIFO, and (c) the Weighted Average Costing.

| Date | Receipts | | Issues | Balance | |
|---|---|---|---|---|---|
| | Units | Unit Cost | Units | Units | Unit Cost |
| Mar. 1 | | | | 200 | $4.00 |
| Mar. 10 | 300 | $4.20 | | | |
| Mar. 15 | 200 | 4.25 | 100 | | |
| Mar. 30 | | | 200 | | |
| Apr. 5 | 300 | 4.40 | | | |
| Apr. 10 | | | 300 | | |
| Apr. 25 | | | | | |

# SELECTED READINGS


1. Arthur M. Geoffrion, "Better Distribution Planning with Computer Models," *Harvard Business Review* (July-August, 1976), p. 92.
2. ———, "Multicommodity Distribution System Design by Benders Decomposition," *Management Science* (January, 1974), p. 822.
3. Robert W. Porter, "Centralized Inventory Management in the Multilevel Distribution Network," *APICS 22d Annual International Conference Proceedings* (1979), pp. 81 and 82.
4. George W. Plossl and Oliver W. Wight, *Production and Inventory Control* (Englewood Cliffs, N.J.: Prentice-Hall, Inc., 1967), pp. 403–420.
5. John R. Magee and D. M. Boodman, *Production Planning and Inventory Control,* 2d ed. (New York: McGraw-Hill Book Company, 1967), p. 223.
6. James L. Heskett, "Logistics—Essential to Strategy," *Harvard Business Review* (November-December, 1977), pp. 85–96.
7. André J. Martin, "Distribution Resource Planning (DRP II)," *APICS 23d Annual International Conference Proceedings* (1980), pp. 161–165.
8. Thomas L. Newberry, ed., *Inventory Management Systems* (Atlanta, Ga.: American Software, October, 1978), pp. 8-1 and 8-2.
9. Thomas L. Newberry and Carl D. Bhame, "How Management Should Use and Interact with Sales Forecasts," *Inventories and Production Management,* Vol. 1, No. 3 (July-August, 1981), pp. 4–11.
10. Henry Jordan, *APICS Training Aid: Cycle Counting for Records Accuracy* (Washington, D.C.: APICS, 1980).
11. Robert G. Brown, *Materials Management Systems* (New York: John Wiley and Sons, Inc., 1977).
12. Quentin Ford, "Distribution Requirements Plannings—and MRP," *APICS 24th Annual International Conference Proceedings* (1981), pp. 275–278.
13. David P. Herron, "Managing Physical Distribution for Profit," *Harvard Business Review* (May-June, 1979), pp. 121–132.
14. Cary M. Root, André J. Martin, and Paul N. Lomas, "The ABC's of DRP," *APICS 22d Annual International Conference Proceedings* (1979), pp. 83 and 84.
15. Alan J. Stenger and Joseph L. Cavinato, "Adapting MRP to the Outbound Side—Distribution Requirements Planning," *Production and Inventory Management,* Vol. 20, No. 4 (1979), pp. 1–13.

# PART THREE

## IMPLEMENTATION AND CONTROL

Converting plans to reality requires systems and procedures for execution. Control closes the loop by measuring actual results, comparing them with planned results and deciding if objectives, decision processes, or methods of execution should be revised. After the planning, execution, and control systems have been developed, they must be implemented. The chapters in Part III concern (1) execution and control decision techniques and systems; (2) principles and techniques related to the design, development, and implementation of production and inventory management systems; and (3) the general management of production and inventory activities.

Order sequencing and release constitute the execution phase of production and inventory management. *Sequencing* is the determination of the order in which a plant or work center is to process a number of different jobs. *Dispatching* includes sequencing and the communication of sequencing and order release information to the plant. Since orders are released to manufacturing and to suppliers, order release principles and decision techniques are relevant to production (Chapter 12) and to purchasing (Chapter 13).

There is a fine line between the order release planning that is the basis for the short-range schedule (Chapter 5) and the actual order release. Factors such as scrap, late vendor delivery of a related item, and machine failure can change the order release decision right up to the scheduled release date. Work-in-process, queue lengths, work center utilization, and the completion status of related items should be considered. Input-output control, operation overlapping, operation splitting, order priority rules, mathematical programming, and simulation can be helpful in making sequencing (dispatching) and order release decisions.

Purchasing has many responsibilities. Those that relate directly to production and inventory management concern order quantities, order release, the cost of purchased items, vendor capacity, the lead time of purchased items, the vendor's flexibility in adjusting to engineering and schedule changes, and vendor delivery performance. Planning and control of vendor deliveries are as crucial to achieving production and inventory management objectives as planning and control of production. Techniques useful in controlling production also are useful in controlling vendor deliveries. Purchasing's role extends across the long-, medium-, and short-range planning horizons. New methods exist for extending capacity planning and control to encompass supplier's facilities and improve their delivery performance.

Control begins in the long range as anticipated, calculated, and simulated results of proposed plans are compared with desired results. Control continues with similar comparisons during medium- and short-range planning. Actual production and vendor deliveries should be recorded and compared with planned results and corrective action taken as required.

Information systems must be developed and implemented to operationalize the decision rules and guides developed for planning and control in each of the time horizons. The overall development and implementation usually are managed by two master plans. One is a plan of the information system configuration with perhaps different system configurations designated for different points in time as the organization moves from its present mode of operation to that desired in the future. The second contains the timing of activities and resource commitments required to achieve the planned information system configurations. This plan should specify the computer hardware, software, data, personnel, training, and funding required at each stage to achieve the plan.

Formal methodologies exist for designing information systems. These methods must be combined with an understanding of production and inventory management concepts and techniques to yield effective systems. Once designed and implemented, the performance of information systems must be monitored to determine if actual performance meets expectations. Even when a state-of-the-art Production Inventory Management (PIM) information system has been implemented successfully, the necessity of system maintenance and improvement exists.

The PIM function must be managed just as engineering, marketing, and accounting activities must. Managing the PIM function includes the basic activities of planning, organizing, staffing, executing, and controlling. Short- and long-term performance objectives are the basis for evaluating PIM management. Achieving inventory and production goals requires planning, execution, and control of departmental activities as well as adequate organization and staffing. Part III treats these subjects.

# —12—

# PRODUCTION ACTIVITY CONTROL

The time arrives when plans must be executed. The function of Production Activity Control (PAC) is to have operations conform to plans, to report on operating results, and to revise plans as required in order to achieve desired results. The principles, concepts and techniques of PAC have broad applicability. They are useful in manufacturing and nonmanufacturing environments such as an engineering design and drafting department, an insurance claims adjustment office, a data processing center, an advertising layout department, and a testing laboratory.

A PAC system in a job shop must be capable of the following:

1. Releasing orders to the production department on schedule (per the order release plan) having verified materials, information (blueprints and manufacturing processes), tooling, personnel, and equipment availability
2. Informing the production department of the scheduled start and completion dates of steps (individual operations) in the production process as well as the scheduled completion date of the order
3. Informing the production department of the relative priorities of the orders released
4. Recording actual performance of steps in the production process and comparing it to the schedule
5. Revising order priorities on the basis of performance and changing conditions
6. Monitoring and controling lead times, work center queues, and work-in-process (WIP)
7. Reporting work center efficiency, personnel attendance, operator times, and order quantity counts for planning, payroll, department efficiency, and labor distribution reports

In both repetitive discrete units production and continuous process type production, the PAC system has requirements slightly different from the job shop. The salient differences are that (1) daily run schedules are used to authorize and control production, not job orders; and (2) control is executed by counts at key points in the flow.[1]

[1]See the Introduction and Chapter 14 for a further discussion of these differences.

The PAC system closes the planning and control loop as illustrated in Figure 12-1. Although all PAC systems have the same functions, individual systems differ due to different outputs (products), production processes, facility layouts, multiplant or single production facility situations, and the available capacity of work force personnel and/or equipment.

This chapter begins by delineating PAC data requirements; then discusses principles, concepts, and techniques affecting PAC decisions; examines the decisions; and concludes with a coverage of PAC reports. Appendix F describes methods for sequencing orders and assigning tasks to resources.

**FIGURE 12-1**
**PRODUCTION ACTIVITY CONTROL**
**BLOCK DIAGRAM**

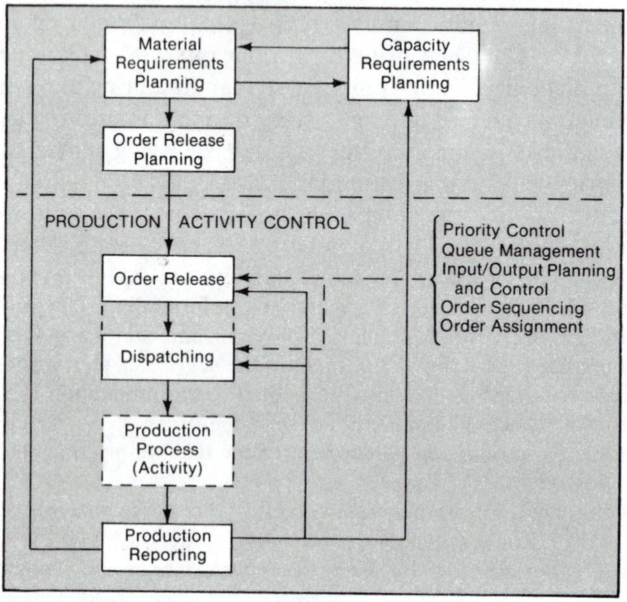

## DATA REQUIREMENTS

Certain data are required for a PAC System. In a manufacturing firm these usually are organized in the following files:

1. Planning files:
   a. Part (item) master file
   b. Routing file
   c. Work center file
2. Control files:
   a. Production order master file
   b. Production order detail file

# Planning Files

The part master file is required for many activities including Material Requirements Planning (MRP), inventory management, cost estimating, and PAC. In this file there is a record for each part. Each record is identified by a part number and contains relevant data such as inventory status and standard cost. In addition, the record for each item includes the following data required for PAC:

1. Part number—the unique item number assigned to the part
2. Part description—the name of the item
3. Manufacturing lead time—the normal time required to produce the item in the typical lot quantity (This information may be in the routing file also.)
4. On Hand quantity—the number of units of this part in stock
5. Allocated quantity—the number of units of this item that has been assigned to previously planned future orders
6. Available quantity—the difference between the on-hand quantity and the allocated quantity
7. On-Order quantity—the total number of units due on all outstanding orders for this part
8. Lot size quantity—the normal number of units of this item produced at one time (the order quantity).
9. Substitute Items—the part numbers of items (or materials) that may be used in place of this item

The routing file and the work center file are used for Capacity Requirements Planning (CRP) also and were described in Chapter 5, pages 128-130.

# Control Files

The production order master file contains a record of each active production order. The purpose of the file is to store summary data describing the nature, status, and priority of each order. It contains the following data required for PAC:

1. Production order number—the number assigned to uniquely identify each order or batch
2. Order Quantity—the number of units (e.g., pounds, gallons) to be produced on this order
3. Quantity completed—the number of units (or volume) reported through the last operation and final inspection
4. Quantity scrapped—the total number of units (or volume) scrapped at any point in the production of this order (Separate records of the quantity scrapped during setup and of the quantity scrapped when running the item at each work center may be kept.)

5. Material disbursed—the quantity of each item of materials or component parts released from stores for the production of this order
6. Due date (original)—the initial date on which this order was scheduled for completion
7. Due date (revised)—if rescheduled, the new date on which this order is scheduled for completion
8. Priority—a value used to rank this order relative to all other orders (Methods of establishing this value are treated later in this chapter.)
9. Balance Due—the order (or batch) quantity minus the sum of the quantities completed and scrapped (If some units are scrapped, the material requirements system will determine if another order is necessary to meet requirements.)

In a job shop environment there is a production order detail file for each order. The file for each order contains a record for each operation required by the production process for that order. The record for each operation typically contains the following data:

1. Operation Number—the number uniquely identifying the operation
2. Description—a brief description of the operation
3. Setup time reported—the number of hours reported for setting up the equipment for this operation on the given order
4. Run time reported—the number of hours reported for performing this operation on the given order
5. Quantity reported complete—the accounted number of units meeting quality requirements upon completion of this operation
6. Quantity reported scrapped—the number of units that were reported scrapped upon inspection during or immediately following this operation
7. Due date (revised)—if rescheduled, the new date on which this order is scheduled for completion

PAC procedures include other release, dispatching, and production reporting as illustrated in Figure 12-1. Queue length management, input/output (I/O) control, and priority control are interwoven and mutually supportive. Their principles and techniques are applied jointly in making order release and dispatching decisions. This chapter will treat other release and dispatching after examining queue length management, priority control, and I/O control.

# QUEUE LENGTH MANAGEMENT

The purpose of work center queues is to minimize work center idle time due to an uneven incoming flow of work. The objective of queue length management is to minimize the total of idle time and queue WIP costs. Material queues of only a half day or so may be planned in a continuous flow shop to avoid disruption of the process. In a repetitive flow shop where a specific process may be activated for a period of a few hours to a week, all material for a job may be scheduled to arrive a day or two in advance to assure its availability. Management frequently can achieve the desired balance of WIP and lead time objectives in a job shop by combining sufficient equipment and queues of two to four days. In an operating situation, determining the nature of queues at the critical work centers should be the first step. Meaningful queue level and material shortage goals then can be established. First, we will examine queue length distributions and then investigate operation overlapping and operation splitting, two methods of managing queues and lead times.

## Typical Queue Distributions

Figure 12-2 illustrates four different queue situations: (1) a controlled queue, (2) and excessive queue length, (3) an uncontrolled queue, and (4) substantial idle time due to an excessively short queue.

Figure 12-2 Part A illustrates a situation where the average queue length is 30 hours, the maximum length is 55 hours, and the work center never is idle because of lack of work and seldom is overloaded. On the other hand, the data in Figure 12-2 Part B exemplify a queue whose length is never less than 45 hours. It is obvious that the length of this queue can be reduced by 45 hours without affecting idle time. This reduction can be accomplished by releasing work to the work center at a reduced rate until the queue reduces. In short, the input of work must be reduced relative to work center output until a cumulative difference of 45 hours is achieved.

Queue length also can be measured statistically with planned average lengths based on the probability of a stock-out, a zero length queue. This approach calculates the planned average queue length by multiplying the standard deviation of the queue length observations by the number of standard deviations required to obtain the desired coverage. It assumes a queue length distribution on the basis of historical data and counts the item being machined as part of the queue. (Zero queue length corresponds to machine downtime.)

Let the queue in Figure 12-2 Part B have a normal distribution with a 70-hour average length and a standard deviation of 9.7 hours. If management's objective is to have a material shortage less than 1 percent of the time (a 99 percent service level), the planned average queue length should be approximately 22.6($2.33 \times 9.7$) standard hours. (The approximate number of standard deviations corresponding to 49 percent of the high side area under the normal curve is 2.33.)[2] Figure 12-3 illustrates the distribution of queue lengths.

The first approach in this example indicates that the average queue length can be reduced by up to 45 standard hours, and the statistical

[2]See Appendix H.

**FIGURE 12-2**
**TYPICAL QUEUE LENGTHS**
**(TIME SERIES AND FREQUENCY DISTRIBUTIONS)**

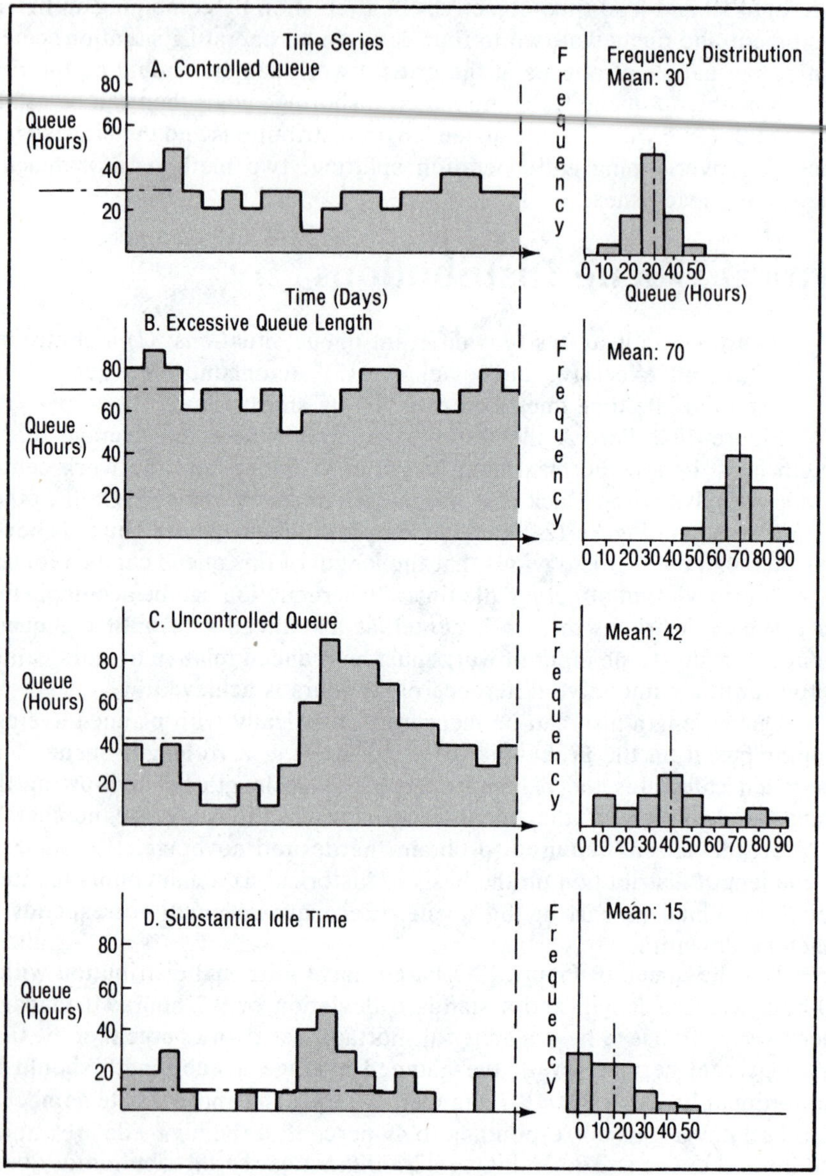

approach suggests that an average queue length of 22.6 standard hours (a 47.4-hour reduction in the average queue length) will meet idle time objectives. Neither approach is exact and both should be applied with caution. Queue length distributions seldom are perfectly normal and shortening

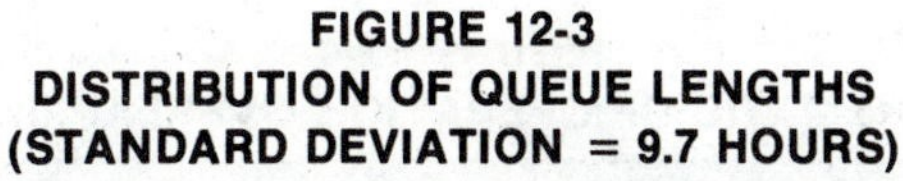

FIGURE 12-3
DISTRIBUTION OF QUEUE LENGTHS
(STANDARD DEVIATION = 9.7 HOURS)

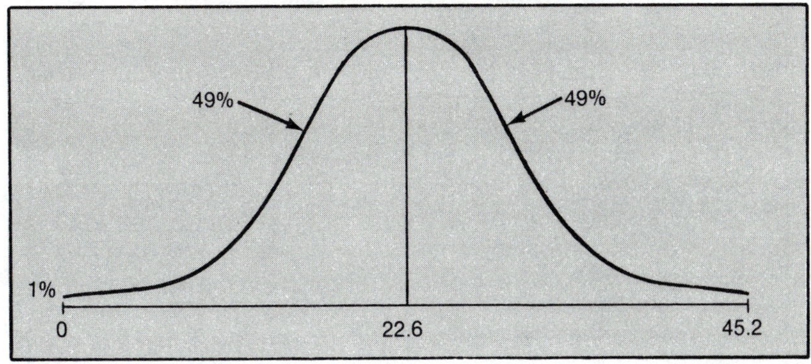


the length of a queue in itself will affect the distribution. In most cases, however, both approaches clearly indicate when a queue can be shortened. In most cases the change should be made gradually to minimize shop adjustment problems. A sudden decrease in queue length can motivate supervisors and operators to drag out available jobs. It should be made clear to shop personnel that the backlog still exists, but it has been moved from the plant to production planning and control.

Reductions in queue length at a gateway work center are achieved through I/O planning at that center. Selection of appropriate orders for processing in earlier work centers will result in the desired adjustments in downstream work center queues.

The conditions represented by Figure 12-2 Part D are typical of a work center with excessive available capacity. Jobs at overloaded work centers should be moved to work centers with excess capacity when possible (when the underloaded work center is a feasible route).

Figure 12-2 Part C illustrates a stickier situation, an uncontrolled queue. It is more likely to be found in downstream work centers with two or more operations having been completed in other work centers. A detailed analysis revealing the major source and processing patterns of incoming loads should provide clues for possible remedies. Analysis of order sequencing alternatives also may reveal options available for reducing the unusually long queues in this type situation.

# Operation Overlapping

Operation overlapping, schematically represented in Figure 12-4, is a technique used to reduce the total lead time of an order by eliminating the effect on lead time of the queue and transit time between two operations. It consists of the following:

**FIGURE 12-4**
**SCHEMATIC OF OPERATION OVERLAPPING**

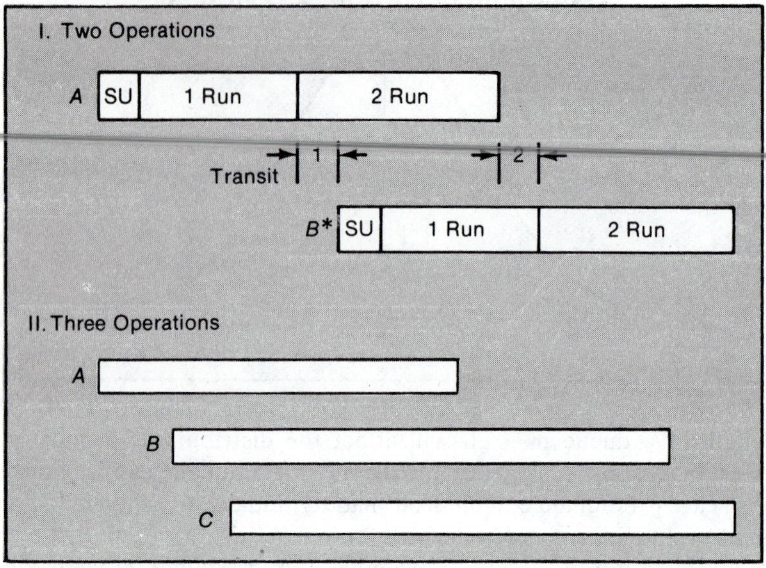

* Note: In some cases Operation B may be set up prior to arrival of the first batch.

1. A lot of parts is divided into at least two batches (sub-lots).
2. As soon as the first batch completes Operation A, it is moved to Operation B for immediate processing.
3. While operation A is being performed on the second batch, Operation B is performed on the first batch.
4. When Operation A has been completed on the second batch, it is moved immediately to Operation B.

If Operation B requires substantially shorter time per piece than Operation A, the first batch should be sufficiently large to avoid idle time at Operation B. Calculation of this minimum batch size is straightforward, where:

$Q$ = Total lot size
$Q_1$ = Minimum size of first batch
$Q_2$ = Maximum size of second batch
$SU_B$ = Setup time of Operation B
$P_A$ = Processing time per unit, Operation A
$P_B$ = Processing time per unit, Operation B
$T_{AB}$ = Transit time between Operations A and B

The necessary equations are given next.

$Q = Q_1 + Q_2$, and $Q_1P_B + T_{AB} + SU_B \geq Q_2P_A + T_{AB}$ (if $Q_2$ is to be at Operation B before Operation B is completed on $Q_1$).

Solving the above equations for $Q_1$ gives us the following:

$$Q_1 \geq \frac{QP_A - SU_B}{P_B + P_A}$$

For example, if

$$\begin{aligned}
Q &= 100 \text{ units} \\
P_A &= 10 \text{ minutes} \\
P_B &= 5 \text{ minutes} \\
SU_B &= 40 \text{ minutes, and} \\
T_{AB} &= 30 \text{ minutes, then} \\
Q_1 &\geq \frac{100 \times 10 - 40}{10 + 5} = \frac{960}{15} = 64
\end{aligned}$$

The result is checked easily. The time required to process 64 units in Operation B is 320 (64 × 5) minutes of run time plus 40 minutes for setup, a total of 360 minutes. This is exactly the time required to process the second batch of 36 units at Work Center A. Move time is the same for both. If fewer than 64 units were in the first batch, Work Center B would be idle awaiting arrival of Batch 2.

If Operation B can be set up prior to the arrival of parts, consideration of setup time drops out of the equation defining the minimum size of the first batch. For example,

$$Q_1 \geq \frac{100 \times 10}{10 + 5} = 66.7 \cong 67 \text{ units}$$

Reduction of total manufacturing lead time by the reduction of the total run time for Operations A and B is the benefit of operation overlapping, as illustrated in Figure 12-5. The disadvantages are the added cost of increased planning and control required by doubling the number of batches and material movements, plus the requirements that the first batch be moved immediately upon completion and that capacity be available at Work Center B when the first batch arrives. Time lost by not meeting these latter two requirements decreases the savings in lead time.

To calculate the difference between lead time without and with overlapping using the previous example, let:

$$\begin{aligned}
Q &= 100 \text{ units} \\
Q_1 &= 66 \text{ units} \\
Q_2 &= 34 \text{ units} \\
P_A &= 10 \text{ minutes} \\
P_B &= 5 \text{ minutes} \\
T_{AB} &= 30 \text{ minutes} \\
SU_A &= 80 \text{ minutes} \\
SU_B &= 40 \text{ minutes}
\end{aligned}$$

**FIGURE 12-5**
**COMPARISON OF LEAD TIME WITHOUT AND WITH OVERLAPPING**

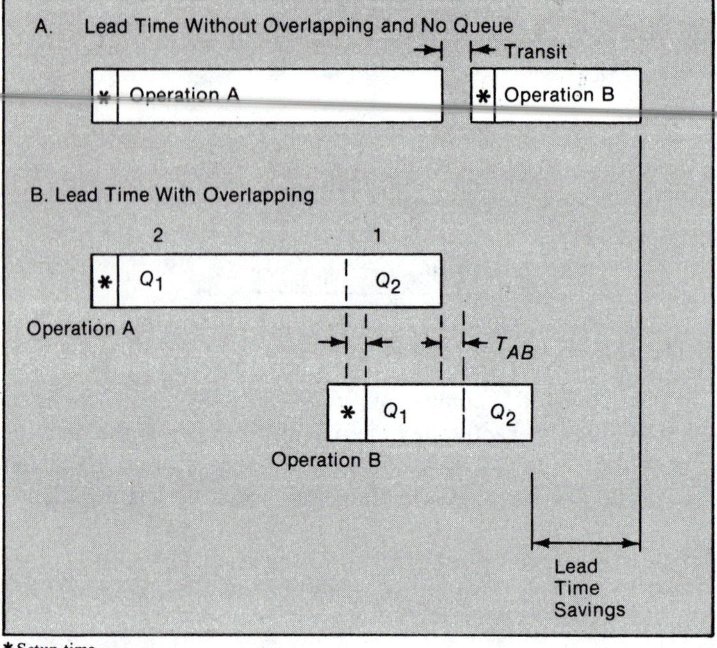


* Setup time

The total lead time without overlapping and no queue equals the total time for Operation A (setup and run) plus transit time plus the total time for Operation B (setup and run). Thus,

$$80 + 100 \times 10 + 30 + 40 + 100 \times 5 = 1{,}650 \text{ minutes}$$

The total lead time with overlapping and prior setup of Operation B equals the time for Operation A on Batch 1 (setup and run) plus transit time from Operation A to Operation B plus the total time for Operation B on Batches 1 and 2 (run only). Thus.

$$80 + 67 \times 10 + 30 + 100 \times 5 = 1{,}280 \text{ minutes}$$

The difference in lead times under the two conditions is 370 minutes (1,650 − 1,280). The actual savings depend on whether parts are required to set up the machine as well as the normal time an order would wait between processes. Usually the actual savings from overlapping come mainly from the elimination of queue time between operations.

When the processing time of Operation B is greater than that of Operation A, similar calculations can be performed to determine the batch sizes required to maximize lead time savings under the constraint of only one additional movement (dividing the lot into no more than two batches).

# Operation Splitting

Operation splitting, schematically represented in Figure 12-6, reduces total lead time by reducing the run time component. A production lot is divided into two or more batches and the same operation is then performed simultaneously on each of these sublots. Operation splitting reduces the processing (run time) component of manufacturing lead time at the cost of an additional setup. Conditions conducive to lot splitting include a relatively high ratio of total run time to setup time, idle duplicate equipment or work force personnel, and the feasibility of an operator running more than one machine. These conditions frequently exist. For example, in the cutting of large diameter ring gears the setup time is small in comparison with the run time of a lot of twenty or more.

Lots also may be split in a "setup offset" manner as illustrated in Figure 12-6 Part C. After the first machine is set up and running, the operator sets up the second machine. For this approach to be feasible, the time required to unload one part and load the following part must be shorter than the run time per part. In addition, shop practices (and the labor contract)

**FIGURE 12-6**
**OPERATION SPLITTING**
**IMPACT ON MANUFACTURING LEAD TIME**

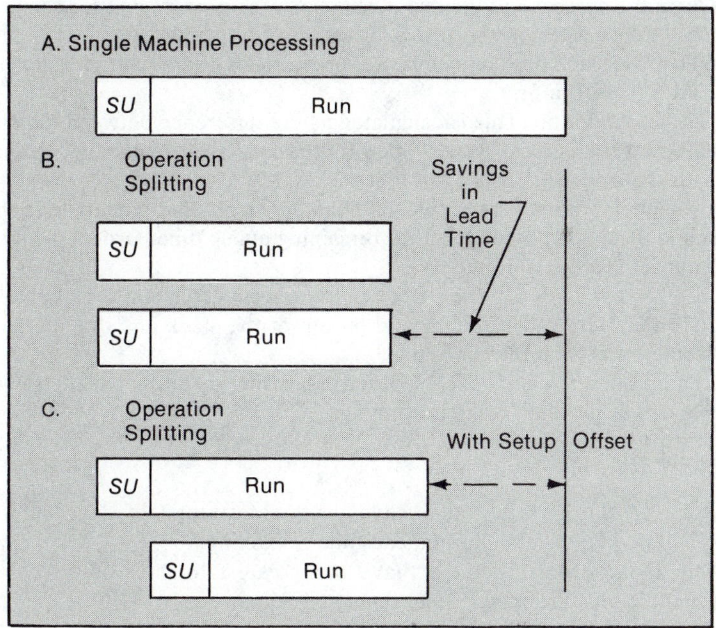

must allow an individual to run more than one machine. This approach reduces lead time and increases labor productivity. The appropriate mix of parts to equalize runout (see Chapter 8) or to meet cycle assembly requirements is committed as a group. Both overlapping and lot splitting are normal procedures in the work groups (work cells) of a group technology oriented shop as reported by Colin New. [1]

## PRIORITY CONTROL

The decision to release orders to the plant raises the questions, Which orders should be released? and, once released, In what sequence should they be processed? The latter question, arises at both gateway and downstream work centers. Many different priority rules are available for establishing the sequence in which orders are to be run. Some of the most common are as follows:

1. FCFS—first come, first served (Orders are run in the order they arrive in the department.)
2. SOT—shortest operation time (Orders are run in the inverse order of the time required to process them in the department.)
3. Due date—earliest due date first (Run the job with the earliest due date first.)
4. Start date—due date minus normal lead time (Orders with the earliest start date are run first.)
5. STR—slack time remaining (This is calculated as the difference between the current and the due dates minus the processing time remaining. Orders with the shortest STR are run first.)
6. STR/OP—slack time remaining per operation (Orders with the shortest STR/OP are run first.)
7. CR—critical ratio (This is calculated as the difference between the due date and the current date divided by the lead time remaining. Orders with the smallest CR are run first.)
8. QR—queue ratio (This is calculated as the slack time remaining in the schedule divided by the planned remaining queue time. Orders with the smallest QR are run first.)
9. LCFS—last come first served (This rule occurs frequently by default. As orders arrive they are placed on top of the stack and the operator usually runs the order on top.)
10. Random order—whim (The supervisors or the operators usually select whichever job they feel like running.)

For Overdue Orders:

11. Run those orders first that have the greatest total of days behind schedule plus manufacturing lead time remaining.
12. Run those orders first that have the greatest total of days behind schedule plus processing time remaining.

And another criterion:

13. Run orders first whose next operation is at a work center with little or no work.

Other methods of establishing order priorities are discussed in Appendix F.

A rule is considered static if the priority assigned to an order does not change as time and conditions change. A dynamic rule is one that revises order priorities as events (such as a change in inventory status, the passage of time, arrival of new orders, or the completion of operations) occur. In most cases, the PAC system should have the ability to report such events and revise order priorities in a dynamic fashion.

Interesting research providing valuable insights regarding the results of applying such rules in different situations has been conducted by many including Berry and Rao [2], Conway and Maxwell [3], Kanet [4], and Kettner and Bechte [5]. Most of this research involved simulating various plant situations and evaluating a constant priority rule over the long run on the basis of a constant set of criteria with arrivals following a specific statistical distribution.

However, observations of arrivals usually reveal that they vary widely and their distributions do not conform to established distributions. In addition, real world priority control systems are evaluated during relatively short periods since the relative importance of criteria shift. Criteria for evaluating a priority control system can include the following:

1. Percentage of orders delivered on time
   a. to customers
   b. to the assembly line
2. Lateness of late orders
3. WIP
4. Idle time
5. Minimizing setup time
6. Energy conservation

One or two of the foregoing may be dominant over a short period. The planner must be able to recognize shifting criteria, or even different criteria in different parts of the plant, and to organize dispatch lists accordingly. A *dispatch list* is a document which lists the jobs in a work center and indicates the priority of each. The frequency of revising the dispatch list depends on the environment. When orders are completed daily with new orders arriving and priorities also being revised frequently, a new dispatch list usually is delivered to the work center each day. The list also may include jobs at upstream work centers providing the supervisor with information concerning orders that will arrive shortly and an indication of their priority upon arrival. A computerized system may produce relative rankings on the basis of a criterion such as critical ratio, but review by a planner is required to determine if other considerations are overriding. Figure 12-7 illustrates the effects of different priorities on process flow. Figure 12-8 illustrates the results of different priorities on lead time distribution in a large job shop studied by Kettner and Bechte. [6]

**FIGURE 12-7**
**EFFECT OF ORDER PRIORITIES AND JOB SEQUENCING ON THE FLOW OF ORDERS AT A WORK CENTER, FUNNEL MODEL**

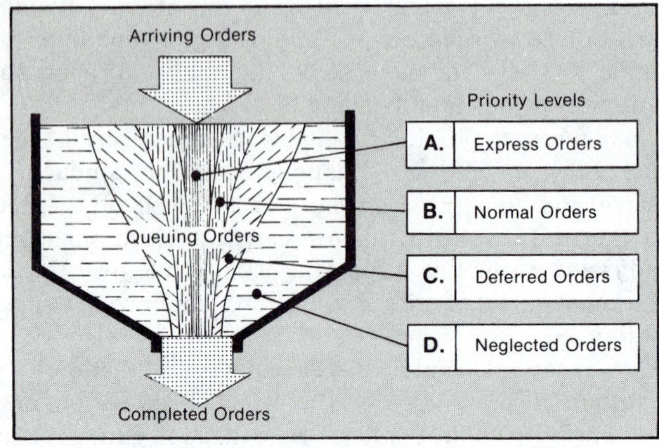


Courtesy of Wolfgang Bechte, Visiting Professor at Southern Illinois University, Edwardsville, Illinois.

The methods for establishing order priorities by the different rules are self-evident by definition in most cases. This is not true in the case of the critical ratio or queue ratio rules, two widely used techniques. Let's examine these techniques.

**FIGURE 12-8**
**DISTRIBUTION OF ACTUAL OPERATION LEAD TIMES IN A MACHINE SHOP QUANTIFYING THE EFFECT OF ORDER PRIORITIES AND JOB SEQUENCING**

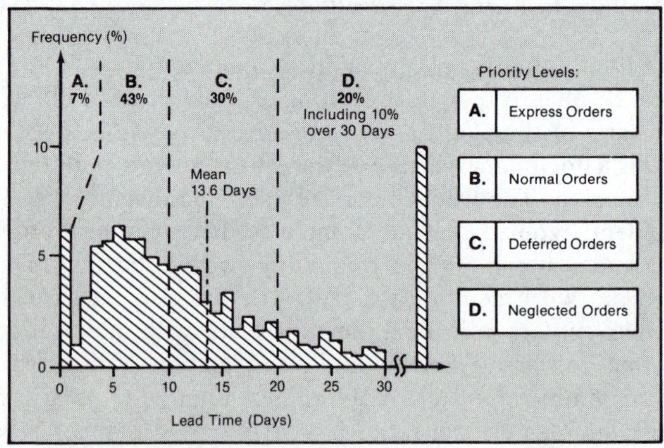


Courtesy of Wolfgang Bechte, Visiting Professor at Southern Illinois University, Edwardsville, Illinois.

# Critical Ratio Technique

The critical ratio (CR) is an index of the relative priority of an order. It is based on the dynamic ratio of the time remaining until the due date to the lead time remaining. It can be applied to the completion of the entire process or the completion of a specific operation. It is useful in either order point or time-phased requirements (due date) systems. The model used for computing the critical ratio in a due date environment follows:

$$\text{CR} = \frac{\text{current date due} - \text{present date}}{\text{lead time remaining}}$$

The critical ratios for three different situations are illustrated in Table 12-1. A CR of 1.0 indicates that the order is right on schedule; a CR greater than 1.0 indicates the order is ahead of schedule; and a CR smaller than 1.0 indicates the order is behind schedule. The smaller the CR, the higher the priority of the order. Later we will discuss priority indices for orders whose due dates have passed.

**TABLE 12-1**
**CRITICAL RATIOS, THREE CASES**
**(PRESENT DATE: DAY 164)**

| Order | Due Date* | Actual Time Remaining | Lead Time Remaining (Days) | CR |
|---|---|---|---|---|
| A | Day 197 | 33 | 22 | 33/22 = 1.5 |
| B | 186 | 22 | 22 | 22/22 = 1.0 |
| C | 175 | 11 | 22 | 11/22 = .5 |

*Numbered days include working days only

Let's examine CR's for specific operations. The data in Table 12-2 reveal the setup and run time, transit time, and queue time for a four-operation process. Let Operation 10 be complete, and let 16 working days

**TABLE 12-2**
**CRITICAL RATIO PER OPERATION**
**(16 DAYS REMAINING UNTIL DUE DATE)**

| Work Center | Operation Number | Setup and Run Time* | Transit Time | Queue Time | Total Time | CR |
|---|---|---|---|---|---|---|
| 1 | 10 | 1.8 | .5 | 1.5 | 3.8 | Complete |
| 2 | 20 | 3.0 | .5 | 4.0 | 7.5 | .71 |
| 3 | 30 | 2.3 | .5 | 2.5 | 5.3 | 2.19 |
| 4 | 40 | 1.9 | .5 | 3.0 | 5.4 | 2.96 |
| | Total | 9.0 | 2.0 | 11.0 | 22.0 | |

*All time is in days.

remain until the entire process is scheduled for completion. Our calculations, then, are as follows:

$$\text{CR of the total process} = \frac{\text{time remaining until due date}}{\text{normal lead time remaining}}$$

$$= \frac{16}{7.5 + 5.3 + 5.4} = \frac{16}{18.2} = .88$$

$$\text{The CR for each operation} = \frac{\text{time remaining to complete operation on schedule}}{\text{normal lead time for operation}}$$

$$\text{CR (Operation 20)} = \frac{16 - (5.3 + 5.4)}{7.5} = \frac{5.3}{7.5} = .71$$

$$\text{CR (Operation 30)} = \frac{16 - 5.4}{5.3} = \frac{11.6}{5.3} = 2.19$$

$$\text{CR (Operation 40)} = \frac{16}{5.4} = 2.96$$

Since most orders spend some time in queue prior to each operation, a CR less than 1.0 may be due to a normal wait before processing. A CR of .88 for this total process and a CR of .71 for Operation 20 both indicate a behind schedule condition; this is misleading. For example, an order being processed as planned in Table 12-2 would not enter Work Center 2 until 4.3 days had passed and then would spend 4.0 days in queue. Thus, Operation 20 is not planned to begin until 13.7 days (3.0 + 5.3 + 5.4) prior to scheduled completion of the order. Therefore, it is not alarming that Operation 20 has not begun when 16 days remain until the order is due.

## Queue Ratio

In their 1971 article Arnold Putnam and his colleagues report on refinements in the CR technique which address this problem. They describe the Queue Ratio (QR) dispatching rule that the Black and Decker Company developed. [6] It is calculated as follows:

$$\text{QR} = \frac{\text{slack time remaining in operation schedule}}{\text{planned queue time operation}}$$

$$\text{QR (Operation 20)} = \frac{\text{time remaining for Operation 20} - \text{Operation 20 run and setup time} - \text{transit time to Operation 20}}{\text{Operation 20 queue time}}$$

Thus, the QR for the previous situation is

$$\text{QR (Operation 20)} = \frac{(16 - 10.7) - 3.0 - .5}{4.0} = \frac{1.8}{4.0} = .45$$

An Operational QR greater than zero for an order waiting in that work center for processing reveals the proportion of queue time remaining. When QR equals zero, the process must be initiated or the order will be behind schedule. A QR greater than zero reveals that the order is still on schedule; as the QR approaches zero the priority of the order increases.[3]

# Overdue Jobs and Priority Indices

The CR technique should not be used to establish the priority of overdue orders. The data in Table 12-3 illustrate its failure in an overdue situation.

**TABLE 12-3**
**CRITICAL RATIO FOR OVERDUE ORDERS**
**(PRESENT DATE: DAY 35)**

| Order | Date Due | Actual Time Remaining | Manufacturing Lead Time Remaining | CR | Days Behind or Ahead of Schedule |
|---|---|---|---|---|---|
| A* | 40 | 5 | 2 | 2.5 | +3 |
| B | 35 | 0 | 10 | 0.0 | −10 |
| C | 35 | 0 | 8 | 0.0 | − 8 |
| D | 25 | −10 | 4 | −2.5 | −14 |
| E | 25 | −10 | 8 | −1.25 | −18 |

*Not overdue

Orders B and C both have a CR of 0.0 indicating identical priorities; but *B* is 10 days behind schedule and *C* is 8 days behind schedule. Clearly their priorities should not be the same. Order D has a CR of −2.5 which would indicate that it is in a poorer condition than Order E which has a CR of −1.25. This is not the case; Order E is further behind schedule than Order D.

The amount of time behind schedule can be used as a priority index to solve this problem. And as Putnam et al. have pointed out, ". . . when process time is a small but varying percentage of lead time and the slack and move time can be compressed by priority sequencing, ranking is improved using days overdue plus process time remaining rather than total lead time remaining." [6] This is illustrated in Table 12-4 which considers the processing time remaining.

The days behind schedule based on total manufacturing lead time in Table 12-3 indicates that Order B is further behind schedule than Order C and thus has a higher priority. A ranking based on processing time remaining rather than total manufacturing lead time gives Order C a higher priority as illustrated in Table 12-4.

[3] See Putnam et al. for descriptions of modified CR's used at Hughes Aircraft Co. and Stromberg-Carlson Corp. [6]

**TABLE 12-4**
**PRIORITY RANKING OF OVERDUE ORDERS BASED ON DAYS BEHIND SCHEDULE AND PROCESSING TIME REMAINING (PRESENT DATE: DAY 35)**

| Order | Date Due | Actual Time Remaining | Processing Time Remaining | Days Behind Schedule | Priority Rank |
|---|---|---|---|---|---|
| B | 35 | 0 | 4 | 4 | 4 |
| C | 35 | 0 | 5 | 5 | 3 |
| D | 25 | −10 | 1 | 11 | 2 |
| E | 25 | −10 | 3 | 13 | 1 |

## Due Date Criteria

Operation and order due dates are very popular for establishing order priorities (as illustrated in later dispatch list examples) due to their simplicity and ease of understanding. Planning (determining) the priorities of orders is the key to effective priority control. Priorities must reflect actual needs and be consistent among items going into the same assembly. As dealt with later in the dispatching section, continually changing order priorities will destroy their credibility.

# INPUT/OUTPUT CONTROL

I/O planning and control is an integrated process which includes (1) planning the acceptable input and output performance ranges per time period in each work center, (2) measuring and reporting actual inputs and outputs (feedback), and (3) correcting out-of-control situations. [7] Planning I/O and queues was examined in Chapter 5. Reporting systems are examined in a later section of this chapter and in Chapter 14. Typical out-of-control situations, possible causes, and corrective actions include the following:

1. Queues exceed upper limits. Possible causes include equipment failure, inefficient processing, and excessive input. Decreasing input or increasing process output is necessary to correct the situation (illustrated in Table 12-5).
2. Output is below the lower limit. Possible causes include equipment failure, inefficient processing, inadequate input or the wrong input at assembly work centers.
3. Inefficient equipment is utilized due to insufficient input and queues (illustrated in Table 12-6).

Equipment failure and inefficient processing are manufacturing engineering problems. Inadequate, excessive, or the wrong input are I/O prob-

**TABLE 12-5**
**INPUT/OUTPUT REPORT**
**(EXAMPLE OF OUT OF CONTROL QUEUE)**

| Work Center 7—Grinding | | | | | | | |
|---|---|---|---|---|---|---|---|
| Week Ending (Day) | Planned Input[1] | Actual Input[1] | Cum. Dev.[1] | Planned Output[1] | Actual Output[1] | Cum. Dev.[1] | WIP[1] (Beginning = 25)[2] |
| 110 | 70 | 68 | −2 | 70 | 62 | −8 | 31 |
| 117 | 70 | 75 | 3 | 70 | 58 | −20 | 48 |
| 124 | 70 | 72 | 5 | 70 | 63 | −27 | 57 |
| 131 | 70 | 64 | −1 | 70 | 57 | −40 | 64 |

[1] Hours.
[2] If the queue is viewed as including those units being serviced, WIP equals the queue.

lems which should be rectified by dispatching. I/O control is essential at critical (bottleneck) work centers whether they are gateway, intermediate, or the final work centers.

**TABLE 12-6**
**INPUT/OUTPUT REPORT**
**(EXAMPLE OF INADEQUATE INPUT AND QUEUE)**

| Work Center 8—Grinding | | | | | | | |
|---|---|---|---|---|---|---|---|
| Week Ending (Day) | Planned Input[1] | Actual Input[1] | Cum. Dev.[1] | Planned Output[1] | Actual Output[1] | Cum. Dev.[1] | WIP[1] (Beginning = 15) |
| 201 | 70 | 55 | −15 | 70 | 65 | −5 | 5 |
| 208 | 70 | 60 | −25 | 70 | 55 | −20 | 10 |
| 215 | 70 | 54 | −41 | 70 | 59 | −31 | 5 |
| 222 | 70 | 45 | −66 | 70 | 42 | −59 | 8 |

[1] Hours.

Figure 12-9 is a schematic representation of possible order flow patterns in a job shop with ten work centers. Figure 12-10 is a schematic of the

**FIGURE 12-9**
**ORDER FLOW PATTERNS IN A JOB SHOP**

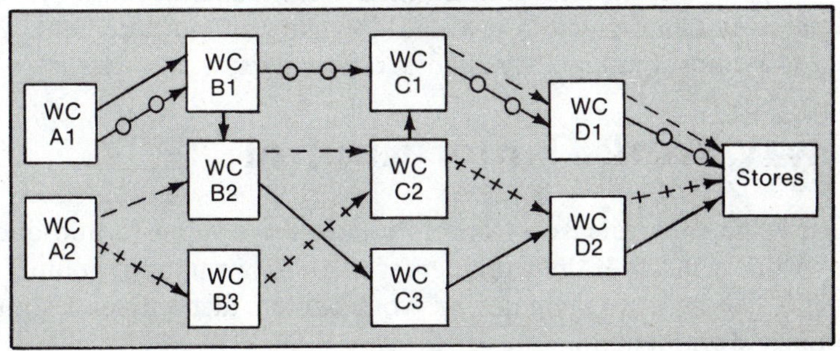

**FIGURE 12-10**
**FUNNEL MODEL OF A JOB SHOP**

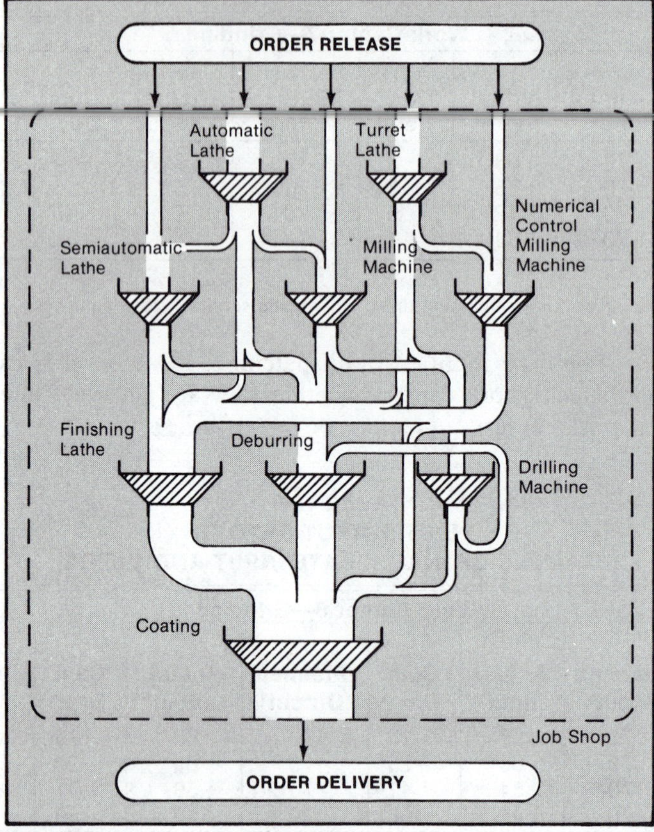


Courtesy of Wolfgang Bechte, Visiting Professor at Southern Illinois University, Edwardsville, Illinois.

flow patterns Von Hans Kettner and Wolfgang Bechte found in a large complex job shop. [5] Work Centers A1 and A2 in Figure 12-9 are gateway work centers. The first operation is performed in one of these two work centers. Work Centers B1, B2, B3, C1, C2, and C3 are intermediate centers and D1 and D2 are the finishing or final work centers. All work centers except gateway centers also are called downstream work centers. We will examine I/O control at each type work center.

## Gateway Work Center Control

Controlling the release of orders controls the input to and queues at gateway work centers. If the work center is running smoothly, output also is controlled. The input to the gateway work centers also influences inputs to downstream work centers.

There is little reason to have a long queue at the gateway work center. Keeping gateway queues at a minimum enables the dispatcher to use the latest available information when establishing order priorities. It also reduces WIP and expediting.

## Downstream Work Center Control

The input to and queues at downstream work centers are controlled by dispatching (order sequencing) at upstream work centers in the process flow. For example, if Work Center C3 in Figure 12-9 is running short of work, while there is a relatively large queue at Work Center C2, priority in Work Center B2 should be given to orders going to *C*3 next. This requires that order release decisions recognize the needs of downstream work centers as well as the gateway work centers, and of course, due dates.

## Final Work Center Control

Output of the final work centers influences shipments, billings, accounts receivable, and cash flow. Final output usually is one of the dominant measures of production management performance. Controlling final work center input is necessary to achieve the desired output. This involves coordinating the flow of parts, items, and subassemblies required in final assemblies. Dispatching is concerned with achieving control of the volume and specific items entering the final work centers. In some complex job shops, large-scale computer simulations are used to provide completion oriented priority control, extending backward from the final work center to gateway operations. [8]

# ORDER RELEASE

*Order release* initiates the execution phase of production; it authorizes production and/or purchasing. The planned order becomes a released order. Placement of a purchase order or the initiation of manufacturing follows shortly. Order release planning (see Chapter 5) may take place until the moment of order release. Authorization of order release is based on priority, the availability of materials and tooling, and the loads specified by I/O planning. Release of an order triggers the release of the following:

1. Requisitions for material and components required by the order (If some of these items are not required immediately and have not been allocated previously, they are allocated now.)
2. Production order documentation to the plant (This documentation usually includes: a set of both engineering drawings and manufacturing specifications, and a manufacturing routing sheet.)

3. Requisitions for tools required in the first week or so of production (Tooling, including tapes for numerically controlled machines, required in later operations is reserved—if not already reserved—for the appropriate period. Tooling can be included in the Master Production Schedule—MPS—item Bill of Materials—BOM—and its availability thus coordinated with material and equipment availability.)

The time required to deliver production order documentation, tooling and materials to the first operation is included in the normal planned lead time for the order. Once an order has been released, it may be added to the dispatch list.

# DISPATCHING

*Dispatching* informs first line supervision of the priority of available tasks, the sequence in which orders should be run. This information can be transmitted via a hardcopy (handwritten, typed, or computer printout) or via video output on a cathode ray tube (CRT); telephone and face-to-face conversation also can be used but do not document the decisions. A dispatch list should be prepared for each work center with the frequency of updating depending on the typical order-processing time. If orders take a day or less to process, dispatch lists usually are prepared daily. If they take a few days, lists may be prepared weekly with midweek revisions handled on an exception basis.

In a continuous process environment, a single list indicating which orders are to be started will control work on the entire line which may be viewed as a single work center. Table 12-7 is an example of simple dispatch list information. It identifies the date, the plant, and the work center; it includes the work center capacity; and lists the orders, their quantity, their capacity requirements, and their priority. Orders usually are listed in descending priority.

Figure 12-7 on page 394 designates order priority on the basis of a CR. The planner determines the final dispatch list ranking of orders on the basis

**TABLE 12-7**
**DISPATCH LIST INFORMATION**

**Plant 02 Department 27 Work Center M3 Capacity 85 hours**
**Date 7/1**

| Part Number | Order Number | Quantity | Standard Hours per Unit | Total Standard Hours | CR Priority |
|---|---|---|---|---|---|
| 9706 | S-4276 | 200 | .3 | 60 | .6 |
| B1319 | S-4518 | 100 | .8 | 80 | 1.0 |
| H4276 | S-4625 | 120 | 1.5 | 180 | 1.3 |

of multiple criteria including a formal priority index such as CR or scheduled start date, input control at downstream work centers, the availability of tooling, the status of other parts required in the same next assembly, energy consumption patterns, and sequencing and assignment criteria (treated in Appendix F). For example, if the next operations for Orders S-4276 and S-4518 were at work centers heavily loaded with high priority orders while the next operation for Orders S-4625 was at an idle work center, Order S-4625 would be listed first in spite of its CR or scheduled start date on this operation. In addition, environments in which the energy consumption costs of production are relatively high can foster scheduling rules incorporating constraints on energy consumption peaks. [9]

Few dispatching decisions can be made in a programmed automatic fashion. A computer can provide valuable assistance by keeping an accurate record of order status. It can provide an inquiry capability, responding to the requests of managers and planners concerning the status of any order. However, the dispatcher must exercise his judgment in balancing operating costs and customer service when determining the final priority of orders.

## Organization

Dispatching may be organized in a centralized or decentralized manner. Centralized dispatching exists when decisions are made in a single location and communicated to supervisors throughout the plant. It facilitates monitoring the progress of orders, coordinating the priority of orders required in the same assembly, and auditing the counts of lot quantities. Its advantage is that it can improve communications among dispatchers.

Decentralized dispatching exists when order sequencing decisions are made in the department. It has the advantage of decision making at the scene. The dispatcher may have a better grasp of the department's capabilities and efficient order sequencing. Wherever they are located, dispatchers must be aware of actual conditions in the work center and overall plant objectives and developments.

The development of computers, automatic counters, and electronic data collection devices has supported the adoption of centralized dispatching approaches while management's desire to give more responsibility to first line supervision has supported the adoption of decentralized dispatching. Such considerations often lead to the adoption of hybrid systems. Overall order status is kept in a central location which issues sequencing recommendations, and supervisors possess the authority to alter sequences within certain limits to achieve production efficiencies.

## Dispatch List Revisions

The due dates and priorities of orders may change due to developments such as forecast revisions, cancellation of orders, and the scrapping of another lot of the same item at a later stage in the production process. For example, let the following events occur after the dispatch list, shown in Table 12-8, is released on July 1.

1. The customer has cancelled his order, S-4276, for Part 9706.
2. The completion date for Order S-4609 Part M3563 has been moved back one week due to a delay in receiving other parts required in their common next assembly.
3. The due date of Order S-4625, Part H4276, has been advanced two weeks to fill requirements which were to be met by another order which was scrapped at a later operation.

The dispatcher must exercise judgment in informing shop supervision of revised priorities. If Order S-4276 is in process or finished, there is no point in revising its priority in Work Center M3. The priority can be changed in its next work center. Revising the priorities and listings of Orders S-4609 and S-4625 seems appropriate. However, continual revision of order priorities will destroy the credibility of dispatch lists. The dispatch list also may include orders that are due to arrive in the department shortly, as illustrated in Table 12-8. This enables supervisors to include these orders in their planning.

**TABLE 12-8**
**DISPATCH LIST INFORMATION WITH LOOK AHEAD**

Plant 02 Department 27 Work Center M3 Capacity 85 hours
Date 7/1

| Part Number | Order Number | Quantity | Standard Hours per Unit | Total Standard Hours | (Priority) Due Date |
|---|---|---|---|---|---|
| 9706 | S-4276 | 200 | .3 | 60 | 6/27 |
| B1319 | S-4518 | 100 | .8 | 80 | 7/1 |
| H4276 | S-4625 | 120 | 1.5 | 180 | 7/10 |
| | | **Orders Arriving Tomorrow** | | | |
| B7849 | S-4429 | 60 | .7 | 42 | 7/3 |
| M3563 | S-4609 | 50 | .4 | 20 | 7/2 |

# PRODUCTION REPORTING

Reports describing actual production status are necessary for control. Dynamic response to changing conditions is possible only if timely, accurate, and adequate information is available. The information must enable management to take meaningful corrective action concerning production schedules.

The production environment influences the design of the production reporting system. Reporting in a continuous process plant may take place on an exception basis with feedback occuring only when the output rate falls below an acceptable level. All reporting systems should have an exception reporting capability informing management whenever machine failure, material shortages, or similar events threaten planned output.

Parts fabrication in a job shop environment requires more data collection for control than continuous processes or repetitive manufacturing of discrete parts. Once a flow process is initiated, it will continue smoothly unless machine failure, employee absenteeism, scrap, a materials shortage, or production inefficiencies occur. Exception reporting usually works well in these circumstances. Flow in a job shop is more complex; order status estimates are less certain. Thus, the processing and movement of orders does not automatically follow their release into the production stream as do orders in a flow process. Control in a job shop usually requires information concerning the following:

1. The release of orders
2. The beginning and completion of operations
3. The movement of orders
4. The availability of processing information, tooling, and material
5. The queues in each work center.

Exception reporting is frequently adequate for controlling the availability of information required for processing, tooling, and material. Reporting both the beginning and completion of operations is appropriate when the total operation times are relatively long. For example, if the estimated completion time of processing a lot of parts through a particular operation was four days, reporting initiation of the operation makes sense. On the other hand, if an operation requires only an hour and one-half, reporting its completion should be sufficient.

## Data Collection

On-line reporting systems directly report events as they occur usually via a data terminal or other device capable of electronically transmitting the data to a centralized recording station. Such information is called *real time* since the records are updated instantaneously. Whether an organization requires real time information as provided by on-line processing or whether periodic reporting (by shift, day, or week) is sufficient for the desired control depends on the situation.

In some cases the operator reports the initiation or completion of an operation, order movement, etc., via a data terminal or by completing an operation reporting form included in the job packet. Figure 12-11 is an example of a reporting ticket. In other cases the supervisor or timekeeper is responsible for reporting this information.

**FIGURE 12-11**
**REPORTING TICKET**

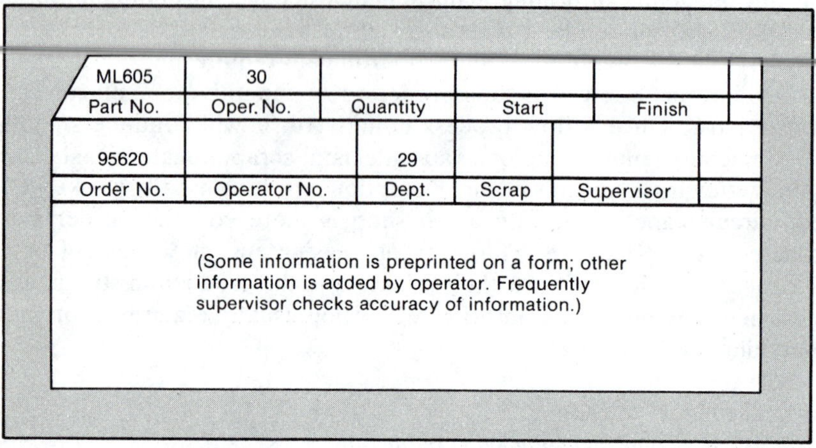

| ML605 | 30 | | | | |
|---|---|---|---|---|---|
| Part No. | Oper. No. | Quantity | Start | Finish | |
| 95620 | | 29 | | | |
| Order No. | Operator No. | Dept. | Scrap | Supervisor | |

(Some information is preprinted on a form; other information is added by operator. Frequently supervisor checks accuracy of information.)

# Typical Reports

The status of WIP, inventory availability, and work center queues and utilization influences dispatching and order release decisions. When an on-line, real time, reporting system exists with inquiry capability, management, dispatchers, and planners can obtain current status information virtually instantaneously. The response to their inquiry may be presented on a video output device and/or produced on a hard copy output. If on-line capability does not exist, daily status reports are required in most cases. In all cases, periodic summary reports are required to evaluate production performance.

The following information should be available to planners on either a real time or periodic basis.

1. Released order status (see Table 12-9) (This report gives the status of every order that has been released physically—dispatched—to the plant including part number, description, quantity, order release date, order due date, operations completed, order location, quantity scrapped, and quantity good.)
2. Unreleased order status (see Table 12-10) (This report lists all orders whose release is past due. The cause of their delayed release also is noted; for example, long queues of higher priority orders at gateway work centers, lack of required tooling, or lack of required material or parts.)
3. Dispatch list—priority scheduling report—(see Table 12-8 on page 404) (This report lists in priority sequence all orders in each department plus those expected to arrive shortly—perhaps in the next day. Standard hours required for processing also are listed.)

**TABLE 12-9**
**RELEASED ORDER STATUS REPORT**

| Date 5/24/83 (275) | | | | | Planned | | Actual | | | |
|---|---|---|---|---|---|---|---|---|---|---|
| Part Number | Description | Order Number | Quantity On Order | Quantity Completed | Release Date | Due Date | Release Date | Compl. Date | Location (Work Center) | MLTR* |
| P865 | pin | 952931 | 80 | —— | 270 | 290 | 270 | — | 17 | 15 |
| B6803 | bushing | 956735 | 160 | —— | 275 | 292 | 270 | — | 21 | 10 |
| R6027 | ring gear | 959063 | 40 | —— | 260 | 294 | 265 | — | 9 | 29 |

* MLTR—manufacturing lead time remaining (days).

**TABLE 12-10**
**UNRELEASED ORDER STATUS REPORT**

| Date 5/24/83 (275) | | | | | Planned[1] | | |
|---|---|---|---|---|---|---|---|
| Part Number | Description | Order Number | Order Type | Quantity | Release Date | Due Date | Cause[2] |
| SA9502 | value ass'y | 957021 | M | 100 | 270 | 280 | LOC |
| SA6807 | switch ass'y | 968052 | M | 250 | 265 | 275 | WCOL |
| ES3750 | gear | 968090 | P | 500 | 270 | 290 | VOL |
| B6750 | bracket | 970211 | M | 200 | 250 | 280 | TNA |

[1] Gregorian dates have been converted to shop calendar dates.
[2] Typical codes: LOC—lack of component; WCOL—work center overload; VOL—vendor overloaded; TNA—tooling not available.

4. Weekly I/O by department (see Tables 12-5 and 12-6 on page 399)
5. Exception reports (These should be designed to meet the needs of the organization. Possible exception reports include a scrap report, a rework report, and a late orders report as illustrated in Figure 12-12. A review of scrap reports will reveal if quality problems are recurrent with a particular item, operation, or operator. They also can trigger the release of new orders or a quantity increase on unreleased orders for the same item. The rework report also can alert management of quality problems and unplanned capacity requirements.)

   The purpose of the late orders report is to inform management of orders that require expediting and possibly of customers who should be informed of late delivery. If the late orders list is extensive, the possibility of a capacity problem or an unrealistic MPS should be investigated. The late orders report should focus on a number of orders that can be expedited efficiently and that have high priority.
6. Performance Summary Report (The performance summary report should state the number and percentage of orders completed on schedule during a specific period—week or month—and the lateness of late orders. A late orders aging report, similar to an accounts receivable aging report, will reveal the magnitude of any delivery problems. Performance also should be reported in terms of volume—tons, units, feet, etc.—or dollars. The causes of late orders also should be tabulated.)

**FIGURE 12-12**
**EXCEPTION REPORTS**
**(EXAMPLES)**

A. Scrap Report (weekly, daily, or by exception)

| Order Number | Part Number | Quantity | Operation | Cause |
|---|---|---|---|---|
| M7240 | 2784 | 12 | 30 | Operator error |
| M6843 | 6813 | 5 | 60 | Welding fixture out of alignment |

B. Rework Report (Items Requiring Rework)

| Order Number | Part Number | Quantity | Operation(s) | Cause |
|---|---|---|---|---|
| M6927 | B8315 | 30 | 40 & 50 | Eng. change |
| M7435 | B8316 | 40 | 40 & 50 | Eng. change |

C. Late Orders Report (or Delayed Orders Report)

Date 5/7

| Order Number | Part Number | Quantity | Due Date | Operation Time Remaining | Queue Time Remaining | Cause |
|---|---|---|---|---|---|---|
| 6895 | R7516 | 100 | 5/7 | 2 | 2 | Matl. late |
| 6743 | C8319 | 75 | 5/14 | 4 | 3 | Scrap |
| 7013 | 67059 | 120 | 5/17 | 6 | 6 | Machine down |
| 6985 | 28076 | 40 | 5/20 | 8 | 8 | Tool late |

The types of reports possible are many and varied. This chapter has included only some of them; the readings contain other examples. Too many reports diminish the value of each. Different situations require different information and different organization of that information.

PAC, to summarize, is concerned with converting plans into action, reporting the results achieved, and revising plans and actions as required to achieve desired results. Thus, PAC converts plans into action by providing the required direction. This requires the appropriate prior master planning of orders, work force personnel, materials, and capacity requirements.

Order release, dispatching, and progress reporting are the three primary functions of PAC. Dispatching is the activation of orders per original plans and those required to correct situations not conforming to plans. Order release and dispatching decisions are affected by queue management, I/O control, and priority control principles and techniques which are intertwined and mutually supportive. They are useful in the management of lead time, queue length, work center idle time, and scheduled order completion.

Reports on the status of orders, materials, queues, tooling, and work center utilization are essential for control. Many report types with various information are possible. Examining a given situation will reveal which reports and information are required.

# PROBLEMS

1. The planning department makes a work sampling study of queue lengths at six work centers over a four-week period of normal operation. The following data are obtained.

| Idle Time | Percentage of Time | | | | | |
|---|---|---|---|---|---|---|
| Consecutive Hours without Work (Hours) | Work Center | | | | | |
| | 101 | 102 | 103 | 104 | 105 | 106 |
| >40 | — | — | — | — | — | — |
| 32-40 | — | 2 | — | — | — | — |
| 24-32 | — | 2 | — | — | — | — |
| 16-24 | — | 4 | — | — | — | — |
| 8-16 | — | 2 | — | 3 | 6 | — |
| 0-8 | — | 14 | — | 5 | 4 | — |
| **Queue Length Hours** | | | | | | |
| 0-8 | — | 10 | 30 | 10 | 10 | 20 |
| 8-16 | — | 30 | 40 | 12 | 30 | 50 |
| 16-24 | — | 10 | 25 | 20 | 20 | 25 |
| 24-32 | 20 | 20 | 5 | 20 | 15 | 5 |
| 32-40 | 30 | 4 | — | 10 | 15 | — |
| 40-60 | 40 | 2 | — | 10 | — | — |
| >60 | 10 | — | — | 10 | — | — |

a. Draw a queue length frequency distribution chart for each work center.
b. In which work centers do the queues seem to be controlled?
c. Which work centers have uncontrolled queues?
d. In which work center can the queue be reduced substantially and by how many hours without affecting equipment utilization?

**2.** The planning department makes a work sampling study of four departments over a four-week period of normal operation. They obtain the following data concerning queue lengths:

| Work Center | Statistical Parameters of Queue Length |
|---|---|
| 201 | Normal distribution, mean = 42.1 hours, standard deviation = 8.6 hours |
| 202 | Normal distribution, mean = 20.7 hours, standard deviation = 6.5 hours |
| 203 | Rectangular distribution, approximately equal percentage in 0-8 hours idle; 0-8, 8-16, 16-24, 24-32, and 32-40 hours of queue |
| 204 | Normal distribution, mean = 12.2 hours, standard deviation = 7.5 hours |

a. Draw an approximate queue length frequency distribution for each work center.
b. Which work center(s) has (have) an excessive queue and/or idle time?

**3.** Planners have an order for which they are considering operation overlapping to reduce the manufacturing lead time (MLT). (The materials arrived late and the order is behind schedule.) The following data are available:

Lot size = 500 units
Processing time Operation A = 8 minutes
Processing time Operation B = 6 minutes
Minimum transit time, Operation A to Operation B = 40 minutes
Setup time Operation B = 1.5 hours
Assume parts will be processed immediately on Operation B.

a. If Operation B cannot be set up until the parts arrive, what is the minimum size of the sublot that should be run on Operation A before moving parts to B? The goal is that there be no idle time on Operation B.
b. What is the minimum size of the sublot if Operation B can be set up prior to the arrival of parts?
c. Disregarding queue time, how much time will be removed from the MLT in both of the above cases?
d. If the queue time at Operation B is normally 16 hours, how much total time will be removed from the MLT in *a* and in *b*?

**4.** A third operation, *C*, follows *A* and *B*. The following data concern it:

Processing time = 4 minutes
Setup time = .8 hours
Minimum transit time, Operation B to Operation C = 40 minutes

a. If Operation C cannot be set up until the parts arrive and there is to be no idle time at Operation C, what is the minimum size of the sublot that should be run on Operation B before moving parts to Operation C?

b. How much operation time will be removed from the MLT in this case?
c. If Operation C processing time is 12 minutes and the planners desire to have no more than 2 sublots, what is the minimum size of the sublot they should have run on Operation B before moving parts to Operation C?
d. If Operation C is 12 minutes and it is immediately adjacent to Operation B (no transit of parts is required), how many parts must be processed in *B* before Operation C can begin?

**5.** A planner also is considering operation splitting (parallel scheduling) for the item described in Problems 3 and 4. The data follow:

Lot size = 500 units

| Operation | A | B | C |
|---|---|---|---|
| Setup time (hours) | 1.0 | 1.5 | .8 |
| Operation time (minutes) | 8 | 6 | 4 |

a. By how much is MLT reduced if each operation is split between two machines with no setup offset?
b. By how much is MLT reduced if each operation is split between two machines if setups are offset?

**6.** The following orders are in queue at Work Center 112. The following data are available:

Present Date Day 50

| Order | Due Date | MLT Remaining (Days) |
|---|---|---|
| 129 | 65 | 12 |
| 133 | 78 | 32 |
| 137 | 59 | 10 |
| 138 | 85 | 30 |

a. Determine the relative priorities of these four orders on the basis of their CR.
b. Determine their relative priorities on the basis of their due dates.

**7.** The following data also are available for Order 137 (Problem 3).

Date Day 50 | Order 137

| Operation | Setup and Run Time (hours) | Transit* Time (days) | Queue* Time (days) | Total (days) | Due date |
|---|---|---|---|---|---|
| 20 | 8.8 | 1 | 2 | 4.1 | Day 53 |
| 30 | 15.2 | 1 | 3 | 5.9 | Day 59 |

* One eight-hour shift a day

a. What is the CR of Operation 20? of Operation 30?
b. What is the QR of Operation 20? of Operation 30?

8. The following data describe the status of the four orders in Department 795.

Present Date Day 75

| Order | Day due | MLT* Remaining | Processing Time* Remaining |
|---|---|---|---|
| 151 | 85 | 12 | 5 |
| 160 | 86 | 20 | 9 |
| 157 | 90 | 25 | 7 |
| 165 | 97 | 30 | 11 |

*In days

a. Calculate their CR.
b. Calculate the number of days each is behind schedule.
c. Calculate the days overdue plus processing time remaining for each order.
d. In what order would it be best to process these orders? Justify your answer.

9. Five items (A, B, C, D, and E) are run on a production line with minor adjustments in the line required for each. The plant is producing Item E and the supervisor asks which item to run next. There is no technological requirement to run the items in a particular sequence.

a. Which item should be run next given the ensuing information? Why?
b. Place the other items in priority order.

| Item | Present Inventory | Daily Demand |
|---|---|---|
| A | 1,600 | 80 |
| B | 1,000 | 50 |
| C | 200 | 10 |
| D | 1,200 | 75 |

10. A department has a normal capacity of 120 units of output a week. It is operating at full capacity and normal machine and worker utilization. Given the following data:

Beginning WIP = 240

| Week | Input | WIP | Output |
|---|---|---|---|
| 1 | 120 | 242 | 118 |
| 2 | 120 | 240 | 122 |
| 3 | 130 | | |

a. What do you expect the WIP and output in Week 3 to be?
b. What should the input be in Week 3 if you desire to decrease WIP by 20 units?

11. The following data concern two gateway work centers that perform similar operations:

| Week | Work Center A1 1 | 2 | 3 | 4 | Work Center A2 1 | 2 | 3 | 4 |
|---|---|---|---|---|---|---|---|---|
| Input | | | | | | | | |
| Planned | 80 | 80 | 80 | 80 | 80 | 80 | 80 | 80 |
| Actual | 75 | 85 | 80 | 82 | 82 | 76 | 80 | 82 |
| Output | | | | | | | | |
| Planned | 80 | 80 | 80 | 80 | 80 | 80 | 80 | 80 |
| Actual | 85 | 75 | 80 | 82 | 77 | 75 | 83 | 84 |
| WIP | | | | | | | | |
| Actual | 210 | 215 | 215 | 215 | 55 | 56 | 53 | 51 |
| | Beginning WIP = 200 | | | | Beginning WIP = 50 | | | |

a. If there is no idle time in either work center, what planned input do you recommend for each in Week 5?
b. If there is no idle time in Work Center A1, but about .5 hour idle time on one occasion due to material shortages in Work Center A2, what input do you recommend?
c. If there is no idle time in Work Center A1, but about .5 hour idle time on 6 different occasions in Work Center A2, what input do you recommend?

**12.** The following data are available concerning four orders in the Work Center A. All four require approximately the same processing time in Department A. *C* is the finishing department.

| Order | Processing Sequence |
|---|---|
| 128 | A-B1-C |
| 131 | A-B2-C |
| 133 | A-C |
| 141 | A-B1-B2-C |

| Present Queue in Hours — Work Center A | B1 | B2 | C |
|---|---|---|---|
| 20 | 40 | 10 | 5 |

a. If all the orders in Work Center A have the same priority, in what order will you schedule them? (Most of the orders presently in Work Center B1 go to *B*2 next.)
b. If the queue is 5 hours in Work Center B1 and 25 hours in both *B*2 and in *C*—and not what is given—how will you schedule the orders in Work Center A?

## SELECTED READINGS

**1.** C. Colin New, "MRP and GT: A New Strategy for Component Production," *Production and Inventory Management*, Vol. 18, No. 3 (1977), pp. 50-62.

**2.** William L. Berry and V. Rao, "Critical Ratio Scheduling: An Experimental Analysis," *Management Science*, Vol. 22, No. 2 (1975), pp. 192-201.

**3.** Robert W. Conway and W. L. Maxwell, "Network Scheduling by the Shortest Operation Discipline," *Operations Research*, Vo. 10, No. 1 (1962), pp. 51-73.

**4.** John J. Kanet, "On the Advisability of Operation Due Dates," *APICS 23d Annual Conference Proceedings* (1980), pp. 355-357.

**5.** Von Hans Kettner and Wolfgang Bechte, "Neue Wege der Fertigungssteurung durch belastungsorientierte Auftragsfreigabe," *VDI-Z* (*Society of German Engineers Journal*), Vol. 123, No. 11 (1981), pp. 459-466.

6. Arnold O. Putnam, R. Everdell, D. H. Dorman, R. R. Cronan, and L. H. Lindgren, "Updating Critical Ratio and Slack-Time Priority Scheduling Rules," *Production and Inventory Management*, Vol. 12, No. 4 (1971).
7. Oliver W. Wight, "Input/Output Control: A Real Handle on Lead Time," *Production and Inventory Management*, Vol 11, No. 3 (1970).
8. Raymond L. Lankford, "Short-Term Planning of Manufacturing Capacity," *APICS 21st Annual International Conference Proceedings* (1978), pp. 37-68.
9. Eugene F. Baker, "Flow Management the 'Take Charge' Shop Floor Control System," *APICS 22d Annual Conference Proceedings* (1979), pp. 169-174.
10. APICS, *APICS Shop Floor Control Reprints* (Washington, D.C.: The American Production and Inventory Control Society, 1973).
11. ———, *APICS Shop Floor Control Training Aid* (Washington, D.C.: The American Production and Inventory Control Society, 1979).
12. Kenneth R. Baker, *Introduction to Sequencing and Scheduling* (New York: John Wiley & Sons, Inc., 1974).
13. Wolfgang Bechte, *Steuerung Der Durchlaufzeit Durch Belastungsorientierte Auftragsfreigabe Bei Werkstattfertigung*, dissertation, Universitat Hannover (1980).
14. Frank S. Covaro and Stephen B. Oresman, "On-Time Deliveries Start with Centralized Dispatching," *Production and Inventory Management*, Vol. 8, No. 2 (1967).
15. Bill Edwards and Margaret O'Neill, "Checks and Balances in Job Shop Control," *Proceedings of the 21st Annual Conference of the American Production and Inventory Control Society* (1978), pp. 165-176.
16. Dave Garwood, "Delivery as Promised," *Production and Inventory Management*, Vol. 12, No. 3 (1971).
17. James H. Greene, *Production and Inventory Control*, rev. ed. (Homewood, Ill.: Richard D. Irwin, Inc., 1974).
18. Kenneth R. Griffin, "Job Shop Scheduling," *Production and Inventory Management*, Vol. 12, No. 3 (1971).
19. E. Ignall and L. E. Schrage, "Application of the Branch and Bound Technique to Some Flow-Shop Scheduling Problems," *Operations Research*, Vol. 13, No. 3 (1965).
20. William J. Jones, "The Integration of Shop Floor Control into the Materials System," *Proceedings of the American Production and Inventory Control Conference* (1978), pp. 133-141.
21. Raymond L. Lankford, "Scheduling the Job Shop," *APICS 16th Annual International Conference Proceedings* (1973), pp. 46-65.
22. Alphedor Perreault, "The Bottom Line of Shop Floor Control Begins with a Good Data System," *Proceedings of the American Production and Inventory Control Conference* (1978), pp. 103-111.
23. Arnold O. Putnam, "Scheduling Lot Production," *Proceedings of the 12th Annual International Conference of the American Production and Inventory Control Society* (1969).
24. Edward M. Stiles, "Controlling a Job Shop with EDP Techniques—A Case," *Production and Inventory Management*, Vol. 9, No. 3 (1968).
25. William R. Wassweiler, "Fundamentals of Shop Floor Control," *APICS 23d Annual Conference Proceedings* (1980), pp. 352-354.

# — 13 —

# PURCHASING

Purchased parts and materials constitute 30 to 60 percent of the cost of goods sold in most manufacturing firms. Thus, a small percentage decrease in the cost of purchased items can result in a much larger percentage increase in profits. For example, if the cost of purchased materials is 50 percent of sales and profit is 10 percent of sales, decreasing the cost of those same purchased materials to 48 percent of sales will increase profits by 20 percent (as illustrated in Figure 13-1). Sanford Volsky has reported how Lubriquip saved $140,000 in the cost of purchased items through a formal program focused on several high dollar product groups. [1] Since purchasing also is crucial in achieving product quality and delivery schedules, a study of purchasing policies, procedures, and decisions can be rewarding.

Purchasing usually has the task of obtaining all the goods and services required by the organization. This chapter focuses on the purchase of raw materials and components that are part of the final product. It does not concern other important activities, such as the purchase of new equipment, supplies, maintenance, and other support services.

Effective purchasing usually requires extensive groundwork prior to an order and control of the order upon receipt. As a result, the purchasing department frequently has responsibility for the receiving function; and all

**FIGURE 13-1**
**PURCHASING COSTS AND PROFITS AS A PERCENTAGE OF SALES INCOME: BASE AND REDUCED PURCHASING COSTS**

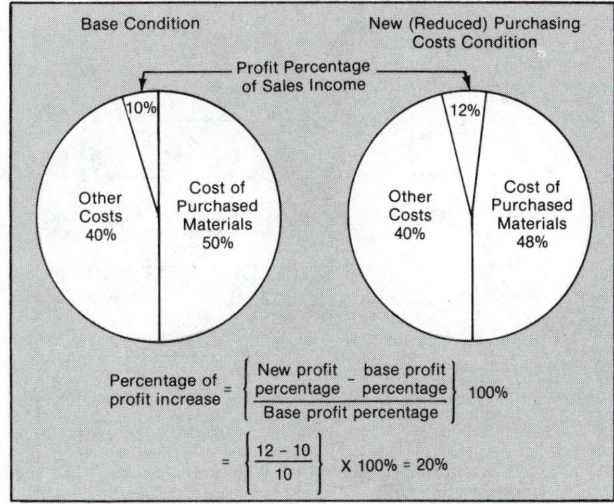

items may belong to purchasing until transferred from receiving to stores. Thus, this chapter also deals with receiving and its relationship to production and inventory management (PIM).

The objectives of purchasing materials and components are to (1) maintain a continuity of supply in keeping with a schedule, (2) provide material and components that meet or exceed a specified level of quality, and (3) obtain the required items at the lowest possible total cost consistent with delivery and quality requirements. These objectives are gained through activities such as the following:

1. Evaluating and approving vendors
2. Requesting quotations
3. Negotiating price and delivery
4. Preparing purchase orders
5. Determining purchase cash commitments
6. Tracking planned and open purchase orders
7. Determining order quantities and order release timing
8. Accurate processing of receipts
9. Handling receipts with discrepancies
10. Monitoring releases against blanket orders, systems, and other special contractual arrangements
11. Analyzing variances in item and vendor prices, deliveries, and quality

Purchasing's role in planning and controlling priorities and capacities is very similar to the role of production activity control (PAC). Purchasing closes the planning and control loop as illustrated in Figure 13-2.

**FIGURE 13-2**
**RELATIONSHIP OF PURCHASING TO OTHER PIM ACTIVITIES**

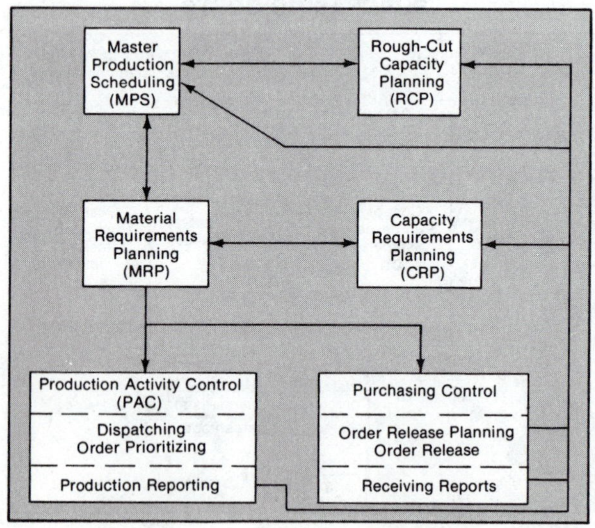

# THE PURCHASING CYCLE

The purchase of raw materials and components can be viewed as having three phases: one prior to the order, the order itself, and another after the order. The time prior to the order purchasing should be concerned with developing, evaluating, and selecting suppliers. Occasionally engineering will develop requirements for a material or component not available in the marketplace. Purchasing and engineering must work with suppliers, perhaps funding research, in developing such items. Purchasing also should be adding to the list of acceptable suppliers for specific materials and components. Strikes, fires, floods, other calamities, and changes in vendor pricing or manufacturing practices can disrupt a heretofore reliable supplier. The supply chain frequently has many links, and purchasing may have to develop suppliers of their suppliers.

Evaluation of potential suppliers is based on their manufacturing process, product quality, management, financial health, lead time, price, and capacity. The manufacturing process is a major determinant of product characteristics such as appearance, performance, reliability, and life expectancy. Poor management or inadequate financing can lead to a short life span for a supplier and to abrupt disruptions of deliveries. Unusually long or undependable delivery lead times decrease the competitive position of any supplier. An assessment of vendor capacity is necessary to determine what proportion of the requirements the vendor can handle and if additional suppliers are necessary. Supplier evaluations frequently involve a visit to the vendor's facility to examine the production and quality control management systems as well as the manufacturing process. Many organizations have a formal vendor qualification process that must be completed before a supplier's quotations will be accepted.

Supplier development and selection usually is a medium-range planning activity. During the same time period purchasing should participate in establishing the master production schedule (MPS). The buyer's role is similar to the production planner; he knows the production capacity of the vendors and their lead time. He should confirm that the MPS is realistic in terms of supplier lead time and capacity. An overstated MPS relative to purchase requirements will result in premium costs for overtime and transportation or late deliveries, disrupted production, other inventory sitting around, and perhaps idle work centers.

Whenever possible, purchasing should buy future capacity from vendors furnishing more than one item and release orders for specific items only when required by the vendor's short-range planning requirements. L. James Burlingame and R. A. Warren reported on such a relationship between Twin Disc Inc. and the Neenah Foundry Company. [2] Phillip Carter and Robert M. Monczka reported a similar relationship that Steelcase, Inc. has with its supplier of plywood seats and backs and its suppliers of fabric and yarn. [3]

A supplier's ability to adapt to engineering and schedule changes also is important; it is measured by monitoring the vendor's performance. The evaluation of suppliers continues through the control process. Purchasing is primarily an execution activity—as opposed to planning and control—with the dominant elements being order placement and receipt. Thus, we will examine the order placement and receiving phases in detail.

# ORDER PLACEMENT

A periodic review of inventory, an item reaching its order point, or the arrival of the planned order release date in a material requirements planning (MRP) system may reveal the need for additional purchased items and trigger a purchase requisition. A computerized system may generate a purchase requisition (see Figure 13-3) automatically on the planned order release date or when the inventory of an item decreases to or below its order point. The planner-buyer then may edit the requisition before placing the purchase

**FIGURE 13-3**
**SCHEMATIC OF PURCHASING PROCESS: ORDER PLACEMENT AND RECEIPT**

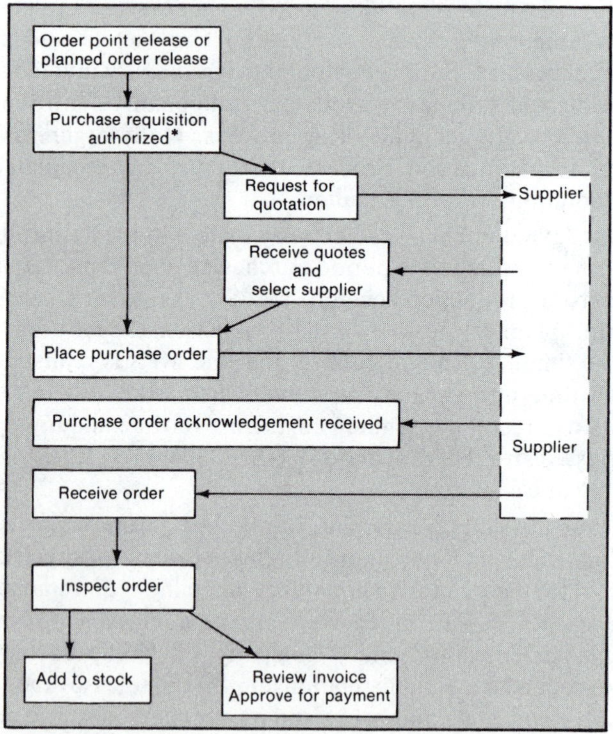


*In many cases, the organization has selected the primary and secondary suppliers in the order planning phase.

order. This is another situation where the ABC Principle may be applied with, for example, purchase orders for *A* and *B* items being reviewed. Each requisition is identified by number, and usually contains the item number, item name, date, quantity, buyer's name, due date, supplier number and name. Since there is not a standard requisition form suitable for all companies, this information may vary; for example, the purchase requisition also may include the price and the account to be charged. Requisition control may be acieved by a system capable of reporting purchase requisitions for which purchase orders have not been prepared and the reason.

Timing the release of a requisition requires that all segments of lead time be considered. These segments include the planner's time, the buyer's time, the time required by the vendor to process and ship the order, receiving and inspection, and movement to the required work center. If quotations are required prior to order placement, additional time is required. In most cases, however, the price of raw materials and components used repetitively is known prior to the required order release.

## Special Arrangements

The *blanket order* is probably the most common special arrangement between a purchaser and a supplier. It is a contract to purchase a minimum quantity over a period, usually a year. Purchasing negotiates the initial contract, which may involve a fixed price, a price range, or a price tied to another base such as the cost of labor or raw materials. The minimum and maximum quantities that may be ordered over a given subperiod, say every thirty days, may be specified also. Production and inventory control usually sends requisitions directly to the supplier requesting shipments of specified quantities by given dates; purchasing is involved only in establishing and renegotiating, if necessary, the contract.

A *standing order*, sometimes called a supply contract, is a blanket order for an indefinite period. It may specify a given quantity of an item to be shipped at fixed intervals or it may call for delivery only on receipt of a requisition with the quantity allowed to vary within a given range during specified intervals.

Blanket and standing orders are advantageous to both the buyer and the seller. The buyer receives a price discount because of the quantity commitment and eliminates the cost of repetitive purchase orders. The seller, in turn, receives a guarantee of sales for a relatively long period. If the seller's capacity planning suggests it, he can produce the same items early without the normal risk of building to stock. These contracts frequently contain provisions governing the notice required for revising or cancelling the contract as well as the costs of termination.

When more than one item produced on the same equipment is purchased from a supplier, the buyer may place an initial blanket order for a supplier's capacity only; later orders will specify which items are to be produced with this capacity. Both parties must agree to the lead time for the orders defining which items are to be produced.

Even when a blanket order does not exist, orders for *B* and *C* type items may be placed with the assumption that the catalog or last quoted price is still applicable. A purchase order acknowledgement sheet or ticket may be made part of the purchase order. The vendor then must use it to inform the purchaser if there have been any changes in price, delivery, or other specifications. The magnitude of the order and the probability of a change or misunderstanding determines if the purchaser will follow up with the supplier until an acknowledgement agreeing to the terms of the purchase order is received.

Rudy Friessnig of the National Semiconductor Corporation described system contracts and distributor contracts at the 1981 APICS International Conference as follows:

> *Systems/contracts* Under a systems contract, vendors maintain, at their facilities, backup supplies of materials, and periodically inventory and replenish materials at your facility. A special order form is completed by the supplier which replaces and serves the function of the purchase order, receiver, and the invoice. Hardware, stationery and operating supplies are typical commodities covered by a systems contract.
>
> *Distributor contracts* Under a distributor contract, vendors normally maintain, at their facilities, predetermined quantities of specific materials dedicated for your use. Purchase order releases are made against the master contract. [4]

Such contracts usually require shipment within a given time period, e.g., three days. If the supplier is unable to ship, the purchaser has the right to obtain the merchandise from a second supplier.

# Prerequisite Data

Purchasing activities require that certain data be available to the planner-buyer. This information may be kept on 3 × 5 cards, in notebooks, or, more typically today, in a computer file. A common organization is (1) the Item (part) Master File, (2) the Vendor File, (3) the Requisition File, (4) the Open Purchase Order File including a Master File and a Detail File, and (5) the Purchase History File.

The Item Master File is used in many activities including MRP, inventory management, and cost estimating. There is much similarity between the part master file of manufactured items (described in Chapter 12) and the master file for purchased items. The Item (part) Master File contains a record for each purchased item. The data in each record may be divided into general data and supplier data. Typical items in the general data portion include the item number, the item description, value classification, the on-hand quantity, the allocated quantity, available quantity, on-order quantity, lot size quantity, ordering rules, type of demand, and substitute items. The supplier data will include the supplier number, address, telephone number, supplier's item number, price, and lead time. The supplier information will be available for each approved supplier. Most item master files contain additional data to meet the needs of a given environment and for use in other activities.

The Vendor (supplier) File contains a record for each supplier; each record contains data describing the supplier performance, the location of the supplier, and the principal products obtained from the supplier. Typical data that might be included in such a file include:

1. A number uniquely identifying the supplier
2. The supplier's name
3. The supplier's address
4. The supplier's telephone number
5. The product or products sold by the supplier
6. The total units purchased this year to date—by item
7. The total dollars spent with the supplier this year
8. Information similar to Nos. 6 and 7 for one or more previous years
9. The percentage of units or lots that have not passed receiving inspection during the present year or last twelve months—perhaps by item
10. A measure of item performance in service
11. A measure of delivery performance, perhaps average lead time and standard deviation
12. Current price
13. Method of payment
14. Discount schedule
15. Payments due
16. Unfilled (outstanding) purchase orders

It would not be unusual to find additional information in the Vendor File; the data items listed, however, are most of those usually required for PIM.

The Open Purchase Order File contains a record of each released order. Since two or more items may be ordered on the same purchase order, the purchase order record frequently contains a master (or header) section and a detail section for each item. The master section of the file includes information such as the following:

1. The purchase order number—a unique number usually serially assigned to successive purchase orders
2. Order status—a code indicating whether partial shipments have been received, the total order has been received, the order has been cancelled, or the order has been closed
3. Purchase requisition number
4. Purchase requisition date

5. The supplier number
6. The buyer number
7. The number of shipments—a code indicating whether the order is for a single shipment, multiple shipments, a blanket order, a standing order, or any other special arrangement
8. Acknowledgement code—an indication of whether or not an acknowledgement is expected (If one is expected other data fields are required in the record to reveal the status of the acknowledgement.)
9. The total cost of the order
10. Special charges for transportation, special handling or packaging, insurance, expediting, etc.

The Purchase Order Detail File contains information such as the following:

1. The item number (with applicable engineering changes)
2. The item name
3. The item line number on the purchase order
4. The unit of measure
5. The unit price
6. The requisition number
7. The requisition date
8. The quantity ordered
9. Date required
10. Various other dates such as first and latest promised delivery dates, estimated delivery dates, shipping date, and date received
11. A location code revealing whether the item is at the supplier, in transit, in receiving, in inspection, in material review, or in stores
12. The receiving report number
13. The quantity received
14. The quantity accepted by inspection

Other data concerning the disposition of rejected items by the material review board also may be included.

A separate file, the Purchase History File, may exist for closed purchased orders since they are voluminous and the data they contain is not accessed as often as open order data. The records in this file may be identified by item (part) number, supplier number, and/or purchase order number. It typically includes quotation data, unit price, other costs, terms, relevant dates, quantities, the buyer, scheduled delivery date, delivery dates, scrap quantities, deviations from specifications, and rework.

The list of data included in the files just described is not exhaustive. Many other data may be required to achieve all the goals of purchasing in a given situation.

## Requisition Control

Release of a planned order should result in the preparation of the requisition. A computerized system may prepare a purchased order automatically for some inventory items (firm planned purchase orders, for example) on their planned order release date. Requisitions for selected items, say *A* items and emergency orders, may be edited and expedited or delayed by the buyer. The system should minimize the time buyer-planners spend on routine activities and allow them to concentrate on the *A* items, critical because of their cost, delivery problems, or quality problems.

The system must allow the planner-buyer to determine the status of all requisitions. The system should have the capability of listing requisitions of a given or higher priority for which purchase orders have not been prepared. Priority may be based on the age of the requisition, a critical ratio, the order receipt due date, or some combination.

Oliver Wight and Randall Benson both report on the combination of the traditionally separate roles of the planner and the buyer into one position, the planner-buyer. [5, 6] We have used the term *planner-buyer* in this text to represent either that situation or the traditional separation of the planner and the buyer. Combining the roles of the planner and buyer into a single position makes sense when a formal order release system generates valid due dates and when contact with each supplier can be maintained for the most part by a single planner-buyer.

## Vendor Lead Time and Delivery

MRP, capacity requirements planning (CRP), and input/output (I/O) planning and control aid in achieving desired supplier lead time and delivery. Providing suppliers with the planned requirements by period gives them valid priorities and reduces the surprises common when using order point systems. Using CRP and I/O planning to regulate the flow of orders to a supplier reduces the likelihood that orders will exceed the supplier's production capacity. Randall J. Benson has illustrated how open orders and firm planned orders can be used to inform a supplier of projected requirements by period and calculate the purchaser's cash commitments (see Figures 13-4 and 13-5 on pages 424 and 425). [6].

Supplier lead times are dynamic; they change as demand for the supplier's products vary, as the supplier increases or decreases capacity, and with the priority the supplier assigns to the purchaser's order. The planner-buyer should be sensitive to changes in the vendor's lead time and update the purchasing information system by revising the lead time in item and vendor records as these changes occur. Providing suppliers with long-term visibility of requirements and valid short-term priorities aids in controlling lead times. Richard R. Morency reported on the excellent results by Bausch and Lomb Inc. in controlling supplier lead time and managing supplier capacity through the development of an MPS, MRP, and contract purchasing. [7]

## The Purchase Order Quantity

Chapters 4, 7, 8, and 10 included detailed treatments of how to calculate order quantities. Those chapters dealt with, among other topics, the

**FIGURE 13-4**
**THE FIRM PLANNED ORDER WITH CASH COMMITMENTS**

Item = A20
Lead time = 3
Safety stock = 0
Cost = $5.00

Planner-Buyer = Garcia

6 Mo./Service Level = 87%
Inventory Turns = 5.0

| | Week | 19 | 20 | 21 | 22 | 23 | 24 | 25 | 26 | 27 | 28 | 29 | 30 | 31 | 32 |
|---|---|---|---|---|---|---|---|---|---|---|---|---|---|---|---|
| Gross Requirements | | | | 30 | | | 25 | | 50 | | 10 | | 40 | 35 | |
| Scheduled Receipts | | | | | | 40 | | | 40 | | | | | | |
| On-Hand | 35 | 35 | 35 | 5 | 5 | 45 | 20 | 20 | 10 | 10 | 0 | 0 | -40 | -75 | -75 |
| Planned Order Receipts | | | | | | | | | | | 35F | | 35F | 5 | |
| Planned Order Releases | | | | | | | | 35F | | 35F | 5 | | | | |
| Projected $ | | | | | | 200 | | | 200 | | 175 | | 175 | 25 | |

P1951 ACME 20 Week 23
P1957 BEST 20 Week 23
P1951 ACME 20 Week 26
P1957 BEST 20 Week 26

F ACME 20 Week 28
F BEST 15 Week 28
F ACME 20 Week 30
F BEST 15 Week 30

**FIGURE 13-5**
**TIME-PHASED VENDOR RECORD**

Vendor = ACME Planner-Buyer = Tanaka

| | Week | | | | | | | | | | | | | |
|---|---|---|---|---|---|---|---|---|---|---|---|---|---|---|
| Peg to | 19 | 20 | 21 | 22 | 23 | 24 | 25 | 26 | 27 | 28 | 29 | 30 | 31 | 32 |
| A20 | | | | | 200 | | | 200 | | 175 | | 175 | | |
| A51 | | 100 | | 100 | | 100 | | 100 | | 120 | | 120 | | 120 |
| D84 | | | 380 | | | | 290 | | | | 350 | | | |
| M02 | 350 | | | | | 350 | | | | | | | 350 | |
| Scheduled Receipts | 350 | 100 | 380 | 100 | 200 | 100 | | 300 | | | | | | |
| FPO Receipts | | | | | | 350 | 290 | | | 295 | 350 | 295 | 350 | 120 |
| Total Flow | 350 | 100 | 380 | 100 | 200 | 450 | 290 | 300 | | 295 | 350 | 295 | 350 | 120 |
| Vendor Capacity | 270 | 270 | 270 | 270 | 270 | 270 | 270 | 270 | 270 | 270 | 270 | 270 | 270 | 270 |
| Over/Under | +80 | -170 | +110 | -170 | -70 | +180 | +20 | +30 | -270 | +25 | +80 | +25 | +80 | -150 |
| Cumulative Deviation | +80 | -90 | +20 | -150 | -220 | -40 | -20 | +10 | -260 | -235 | -155 | -130 | -50 | -200 |

impact of dependent and independent demand, joint replenishment, and quantity discounts. This section is concerned with the transition order quantity and a ranking of quantity discount opportunities. The buyer-planner should ascertain the dominant factor when determining the quantity of an item to be purchased. Supplier packaging, transportation costs, quantity discounts, and production requirements can affect the purchase order quantity.

Let us analyze the following example. The MRP calls for 60 units of a purchased item for each of the next 12 weeks. Estimated requirements beyond that period are also 60 units per week. The company operates 50 weeks a year. The purchaser estimates that his cost of preparing a purchase order is $50. The supplier packages them in crates holding 150 units and charges an extra $20 for purchases of less than a full crate. The items cost $100 each at the supplier's dock. The supplier offers a 4 percent discount on orders for 600 or more units. The purchaser estimates it costs him $100 for his truck to pick up one partial or full crate and deliver it to his plant. Carrying additional crates on the same trip cost an estimated $10 per crate. (Alternate shipping methods are more expensive.) The purchaser uses a carrying cost rate of .30 per year. What is the most economical order quantity?

The lot-for-lot (L4L) order quantity approach results in a weekly order for 60 units. Applying the traditional economic order quantity (EOQ) model without consideration of the transportation costs, partial crate charges, or quantity discount gives an order quantity of 100 units. If we add the flat $100 transportation cost to the order preparation costs, the EOQ model gives an order quantity of 173 units. None of these approaches, however, considers the reduced transportation cost per unit when two or more crates are combined in one shipment; nor do they consider the quantity discount.

The total costs for the different likely order quantities are tabulated in Table 13-1. Total costs include the unit costs, carrying costs, ordering costs, partial crate costs, and transportation costs. These costs are calculated as follows:

Total Unit Cost = Cost per unit ($C$) times the annual requirements ($R$)
= $CR$

Carrying Cost = the product of the carrying cost rate ($k$), the cost per unit ($C$), the order interval ($t$—expressed in years by dividing the number of weeks by 50), the number of orders per year ($N$), and one half the order quantity ($Q/2$)
= $kCtNQ/2$

(Note: $tN$ equals 1.0 by definition when the period of analysis is one year.)

Ordering Cost = the number of orders per year ($N$) times the preparation cost per order ($S$)
= $NS$

Partial Crate Cost = the charge per partial crate ($Cp$) times the number of orders per year ($N$)
= $CpN$

Transportation Cost = the number of shipments per year ($N$) times the cost of transportation ($C_T$)
= $NC_T$
Where: $C_T = \$100 + \$10\,(M - 1)$
$M$ = number of crates per shipment

**TABLE 13-1**
**TABULATION OF TOTAL COSTS PER ORDER QUANTITY**

| | | |
|---|---|---|
| **A. Q = 60 units; N = 50** | | |
| Unit costs = \$100 × 3,000 | = | \$300,000 |
| Carrying costs = .3 × \$100 × .02 × 50 × 60/2 | = | 900 |
| Ordering costs = 50 × \$50 | = | 2,500 |
| Partial crate costs = \$20 × 50 | = | 1,000 |
| Transportation cost = \$100 × 50 | = | 5,000 |
| | | \$309,400 |
| **B. Q = 100 units; N = 30** | | |
| Unit costs = \$100 × 3,000 | = | \$300,000 |
| Carrying costs = .3 × \$100 × .03333 × 30 × 100/2 | = | 1,500 |
| Ordering costs = 30 × \$50 | = | 1,500 |
| Partial crate costs = \$20 × 30 | = | 600 |
| Transportation costs = \$100 × 30 | = | 3,000 |
| | | \$306,600 |
| **C. Q = 150 units (one crate); N = 20** | | |
| Unit costs = \$100 × 3,000 | = | \$300,000 |
| Carrying costs = .3 × \$100 × .05 × 20 × 150/2 | = | 2,250 |
| Ordering costs = 20 × \$50 | = | 1,000 |
| Partial crate costs = none | = | 0 |
| Transportation costs = \$100 × 20 | = | 2,000 |
| | | \$305,250 |
| **D. Q = 300 units (two crates); N = 10** | | |
| Unit costs = \$100 × 3,000 | = | \$300,000 |
| Carrying costs = .3 × \$100 × .10 × 10 × 300/2 | = | 4,500 |
| Ordering Costs = 10 × \$50 | = | 500 |
| Partial crate costs = none | = | 0 |
| Transportation costs = \$110 × 10 | = | 1,100 |
| | | \$306,100 |
| **E. Q = 600 units, C = \$96; N = 5** | | |
| Unit costs = \$96 × 3,000 | = | \$288,000 |
| Carrying costs = .3 × \$96 × .20 × 5 × 600/2 | = | 8,640 |
| Ordering costs = 5 × \$50 | = | 250 |
| Partial crate costs = none | = | 0 |
| Transportation costs = \$130 × 5 | = | 650 |
| | | \$297,540 |

The data in Table 13-1 reveal that the quantity discount is the dominant factor. Purchasing in order quantities of 600 units results in an annual savings of $7,710. Since average inventory investment increases from $7,500 to $30,000 when we purchase 600 units rather than 150 in one order, the rate of return on our investment equals $7,710 divided by the difference between $30,000 and $7,500 or approximately .34.

If the parameter values were different—as they are in many situations—the results would be different. Quite different results, for example, are obtained if the discount price break is at 1,200 rather than 600 units.

## The Transition or Special Opportunity Lot Size

Frequently a company will face one of the following situations: either the price of a purchased item will rise at some date in the near future, or an item becomes available at a lower than usual price for a short duration. Immediately it is apparent under these circumstances that one should order a larger than normal lot size before the price increase or while the lower price is in effect. The following model gives the one-time transition order quantity to obtain minimum total costs.[1]

$$Q^* = \frac{C_2}{C_1} Q_2^* + \frac{(C_2 - C_1)}{C_1} \frac{R}{k}$$

Where:

$Q^*$ = the minimum cost transition lot size
$C_1$ = the current unit cost or the short-term lower cost
$C_2$ = the future unit cost or the normal higher price
$C_2 > C_1$
$k$ = the carrying cost rate per unit time, usually a year
$R$ = requirements (demand) per unit time, usually a year
$Q^*_i$ = the minimum cost lot size with a unit cost of $C_i$
$S$ = the cost per preparation in dollars

Using the data from the example in Chapter 7, page 205, where:

$S$ = $45
$R$ = 60,000
$k$ = .3
$C$ = $2, and
$Q^*$ = 3,000

Let the new price be $2.10 for any orders placed one week from today. Then,

$$Q^* = \frac{C_2}{C_1} Q^*_2 + \frac{(C_2 - C_1)}{C_1} \frac{R}{k}$$

[1] See Appendix G for the derivation of this model.

$$= \frac{\$2.10}{\$2.00} \times 2{,}928 + \frac{(\$2.10 - \$2.00)}{\$2.00} \times \frac{60{,}000}{.3}$$
$$= 3{,}074 + 10{,}000$$
$$= 13{,}074$$

Let us examine another case. Using the same data, suppose that the supplier offers a special price of $1.95 per unit for the next week only. (He has a poor cash position and a surplus of inventory.) Then

$$Q^* = \frac{\$2.00}{\$1.95} \times 3{,}000 + \frac{(\$2.00 - \$1.95)}{\$1.95} \times \frac{60{,}000}{.3}$$
$$= 3{,}077 + 5{,}128$$
$$= 8{,}205$$

Both of these changes call for a substantial increase in the order size. The planner should consider other factors such as storage constraints, capital constraints, shelf life, possible engineering changes, and the possibility of abrupt changes in demand. In any event the orders probably would be rounded, for example, to an exact number of weeks of supply, 13,200 and 8,400 respectively.

The savings ($G$) obtained from using the transition lot size instead of the new minimum cost lot size are calculated using the following model which is derived in Appendix G:

$$G = \frac{(C_2 - C_1)}{C_1} \left[ \frac{(C_2 - C_1)\, R}{2k} + Q_2^* (C_2) + S \right]$$

In the first example, therefore,

$$G = \frac{(\$2.10 - \$2.00)}{\$2.00} \left[ \frac{(\$2.10 - \$2.00) \times 60{,}000}{2 \times .3} + 2{,}928 \times \$2.10 + \$45 \right]$$
$$= \$809.69$$

# Quantity Discounts

The unit price of many items varies with the quantity purchased; a lower unit cost exists for larger purchase quantities. Chapter 10 described the process for determining the minimum cost order quantity for individual items with a quantity discount schedule. However, analyzing quantity discounts on only an individual item basis can lead to excessive inventory. Purchasing larger than the basic order quantity frequently is economically justified for many items. Purchasing the larger quantity for all such items can result in overcrowded stockrooms and in an inventory investment exceeding financial resources. The buyer must be able to select the most advantageous discount opportunities given limited storage and financial capacity.

This selection can be based on a rate of return approach when opportunities concern items whose use is anticipated for the foreseeable future. When the opportunities concern items with different periods of anticipated usage, a present value approach is preferable. Let's examine the rate of return approach.

The rate of return approach ranks discount opportunities on the basis of their annual rate of return. Beginning with the highest rate of return opportunity and calculating the cumulative added inventory investment as the next highest rate opportunity is added in rank order sequence, the planner can determine the best selection of opportunities under a given investment constraint.

The annual rate of return (expressed as a percentage) earned by purchasing a discount quantity equals the annual net savings divided by the increased inventory investment. Annual net savings equal the annual decrease in total unit costs due to the price discount plus the annual ordering cost savings due to the reduced number of orders per year minus the increased inventory carrying costs. Let us calculate the rate of return obtained from the discount for Item 1 in Table 13-2.

Annual unit cost savings = .02 × \$54,800 = \$1,096
Annual ordering cost savings = Cost of ordering × decrease in the orders per year
Cost of ordering is given as \$32.
The decrease in orders per year = \$54,800 ÷ \$3,160 – (\$54,800 – \$1,096) ÷ \$5,000
Thus, annual ordering cost savings = \$32 × 6.6 = \$211

The annual increased inventory carrying costs equal the annual carrying cost rate (given as .35) times the increase in average inventory investment. Thus, the annual increase in inventory carrying costs = .35 × (\$5,000 ÷ 2 – \$3,160 ÷ 2) = \$322, and net savings = \$985.

$$\text{Rate of return percentage} = \frac{\text{Net savings}}{\text{Increased Inventory Investment}} \times 100$$

$$= \frac{\$985}{920} = 107.1\%$$

Similar data and the results of similar calculations are recorded in Table 13-2 for each of 9 items. Item 2 has two levels of discount. The increase in inventory investment due to the larger order size depends on the usage pattern. This example assumes a steady usage rate typical of independent demand, and the increase is estimated as one half the difference between the normal and discount order quantities. Thus, for Item 1 the increased inventory investment equals .5 times \$5,000 minus .5 times \$3,160 which equals

**TABLE 13-2**
**EVALUATION OF QUANTITY DISCOUNTS**
**RATE OF RETURN APPROACH**

**Ordering costs equal approximately $32. A carrying cost rate of .35 is used. Item 2 has a two-level discount schedule.**

| Item | Annual Requirements | EOQ | Discount Percent | Discount Order Quantity | Annual Discount | Ordering Cost Savings | Increase in Average Inventory | Increase in Carrying Costs | Net Savings | Rate of Return |
|---|---|---|---|---|---|---|---|---|---|---|
| 1 | $54,800 | $3,160 | 2.0 | $ 5,000 | $1,096 | $211 | $ 920 | $ 322 | $ 985 | 107.1% |
| 2-1 | 48,635 | 2,976 | 1.8 | 6,000 | 875 | 266 | 1,512 | 529 | 612 | 40.4 |
| 3 | 32,408 | 2,430 | 5.0 | 7,500 | 1,620 | 294 | 2,535 | 887 | 1,385 | 54.6 |
| 4 | 28,620 | 2,282 | 5.2 | 10,000 | 1,488 | 314 | 3,859 | 1,351 | 448 | 11.6 |
| 5 | 22,987 | 2,040 | 11.5 | 5,000 | 2,643 | 230 | 1,480 | 518 | 2,355 | 159.1 |
| 6 | 18,453 | 1,850 | 4.5 | 6,000 | 830 | 227 | 2,075 | 726 | 331 | 16.0 |
| 7 | 11,008 | 1,418 | 6.2 | 4,500 | 682 | 176 | 1,441 | 504 | 354 | 24.6 |
| 8 | 7,431 | 1,160 | 9.0 | 3,000 | 669 | 131 | 920 | 322 | 478 | 52.0 |
| 9 | 1,650 | 545 | 7.5 | 1,200 | 124 | 54 | 378 | 132 | 46 | 12.2 |
| 2-2 | 47,760 | 6,000 | 1.5 | 9,000 | 716 | 90 | 1,500 | 525 | 280 | 18.7 |

$920. When those units added to the order quantity to obtain a discount likely will be held for a relatively long period of little or no usage, estimate the increased investment as a higher proportion, say .75, of the difference between the order quantities.

The next step is to list all discount opportunities in rank order with ranks based on the rate of return as illustrated in Table 13-3. These calculations and tabulations aid management in answering questions such as: If a maximum of $5,000 can be added to inventory, which discounts should be taken? What additional investment is required to obtain all discounts with a rate of return greater than 30 percent? The rates of return, annual discount, and average increase in inventory listed in Table 13-3 in ranking order reveal that the discounts on Items 5, 1, 3, 8, and the first discount on Item 2 have a rate of return greater than 30 percent. The data in Table 13-3 also reveal that the discounts on Items 5, 1, and 3 are the best discount opportunities if there is a $5,000 limit on the added inventory investment for this group of items.

**TABLE 13-3**
**RANKING DISCOUNT OPPORTUNITIES BY RATE OF RETURN**

| Item | Rank | Return | Added Inventory | Cumulative Added Inventory |
|---|---|---|---|---|
| 5 | 1 | 159.1 | $1,480 | $ 1,480 |
| 1 | 2 | 107.1 | 920 | 2,400 |
| 3 | 3 | 54.6 | 2,535 | 4,935 |
| 8 | 4 | 52.0 | 920 | 5,855 |
| 2-1 | 5 | 40.4 | 1,512 | 7,367 |
| 7 | 6 | 24.6 | 1,441 | 8,808 |
| 2-2 | 7 | 18.7 | 1,500 | 10,308 |
| 6 | 8 | 16.0 | 2,075 | 12,383 |
| 9 | 9 | 12.2 | 378 | 12,761 |
| 4 | 10 | 11.6 | 3,859 | 16,620 |

# PURCHASING CONTROL

Purchasing should exercise control over individual purchase orders, purchase commitments, and vendor performances. Control of individual purchase orders begins with the control of the requisitions as described previously.

## Purchase Order Control

Purchasing should be able to determine the status of each order including whether it is currently a planned order, a firm planned order, placed, acknowledged, received, or closed. Acknowledgement may be required only if the supplier requests a change in the order price, quantity, or product specification. Purchasing can request acknowledgements also for orders to new suppliers, or for orders with an unusual quantity, product specification, or shipping instructions. The purchasing information system should provide the capability of monitoring acknowledgements and following up on those acknowledgements not received in the prescribed time.

# Purchase Commitments

Purchase orders call for deliveries that generate accounts payable and thus, negative cash flow. Controlling the cash commitments begins with the MPS, MRP, and the resulting planned purchase orders as illustrated in Figure 13-4, page 424. The planned order release dates, delivery lead times, and payment schedules determine when payment is due. Summing the cash commitments of the planned purchase orders from a given MPS enables management to evaluate the effect of purchases on projected cash requirements. Balancing projected cash requirements with budgeted available cash may require revisions in the MPS and planned purchase order releases. Working capital budgets may necessitate more frequent purchase orders for smaller quantities.

As purchase orders are released, actual cash commitments should be tabulated and compared to planned commitments. If significant variances exist, analysis can determine if they are due to price, quantity or delivery changes. Accounting and finance can use actual purchase order cash commitments in controlling short-term cash flow.

# Vendor Performance

Price, delivery, and quality are the primary criteria for measuring vendor performance. Although chance and uncontrollable facts affect vendor performance, they remain surrogate measures of purchasing's performance.

Dynamic economic conditions usually include opportunities for reduced cost purchases as well as inflationary pressures. Purchasing's aggregate cost goals should reflect these probable opportunities and pressures. [1, 6, 8] Controlling purchase item costs, total purchasing expenditures, and corporate profits requires that standard costs be established for purchased items, that actual costs be compared to standards, and that variances be analyzed. As Delbert L. Evans of the A. O. Smith Corporation noted:

> In the typical manufacturing company, purchased materials account for 40 percent to 60 percent of total product costs. In addition substantial sums are invested in expensed support materials. Obviously effective control of purchased material prices is important in controlling total product costs and maintaining company profitability. Further, accurate forecasts of purchased material price trends can be very useful, if not essential, to the company's business planning activities. [9]

Evans described how A. O. Smith Corporation was using three different reports to analyze the variances between standard and actual costs of individual items, individual buyers' purchases, and commodities. A report similar to that for commodities can be used for groups of items. The reports developed and used by a specific organization depend on the nature of the items purchased by that organization.

Typically suppliers have standard, bid, or contractual lead times in which they promise to deliver and actual delivery lead times. The latter can be measured in terms of their mean and standard deviation. Thus, purchasing can compare the supplier's actual lead times to the supplier's quoted or standard lead time; in addition, the actual lead times of different suppliers of the same item can be compared. Perhaps even more important than statistical measures of lead time is a supplier's ability to deliver the occasional rush order in an unusually short lead time.

Control of supplier quality requires the active cooperation of the quality control department, receiving, and purchasing. Supplier quality control begins with the vendor selection process. If a supplier has either inadequate manufacturing or poor quality control processes, receiving inspection will be bogged down with rejects; shipping will be returning merchandise; production stoppages will result from lack of material; and purchasing will be burdened with added administrative and clerical activities. In addition purchasing will have to select another supplier.

Purchasing must inform the supplier of the quality requirements, which may include physical shape, chemical composition, performance characteristics, labeling, and packaging requirements. Receiving inspection requirements can be established by quality control but purchasing should be sure that the receiving department has the proper inspection requirements. These requirements may call for 100 percent inspection or inspection of a sample. Selected items may be subjected to long run performance tests to obtain estimates of life expectancy and mean time between failures.

Reports summarizing the quality of an item, products from a specific supplier, or groups of items can be based on receiving inspection reports, warranty data, field service reports, and customer complaints. Quality control and purchasing frequently work together in developing these reports and quality standards for purchased items. This is another area in which the ABC Principle can be applied with inspection and reports focusing on critical items and attributes.

## ORDER RECEIPT AND RECEIVING

Receiving and purchasing activities are tied together by their very nature. Shipments from suppliers arrive at receiving. Receiving plays a crucial role in purchasing control. Shipments from suppliers arrive at receiving. Receiving must record the date of arrival; identify the supplier, the item, the quantity; inspect as required; forward the item to the proper location; and inform purchasing, inventory control, quality control, and accounting of these actions. All items may not require a detailed inspection of physical and performance characteristics. Purchasing, therefore, should ascertain that receiving knows the appropriate inspection procedures for all items. Sampling inspection procedures may be applicable in some cases; the entire shipment may be inspected in others; and a detailed inspection of physical and performance characteristics may not be required at all for some items. Receiving, however, should confirm that the items are labeled properly and correspond to the purchase order. Receiving then must decide whether to send items directly to a manufacturing work center or to a given storage location. This requires prior instructions from either purchasing or planning. Movement to the wrong location can result in production delays and lost items. Receiving may have a list of critical items that should be expedited through receiving and sent immediately to manufacturing. Also, receiving normally should notify the buyer-planner and manufacturing of their arrival.

Receiving should inform purchasing of partial shipments as well as quantities that exceed the overshipment tolerance. The buyer then can follow up on items still due and decide if the excess quantity should be returned to the supplier. Items that do not meet inspection requirements may be sent to a material review area. Representatives of quality control, engineering, purchasing, manufacturing, and sometimes the supplier then will decide on the disposition of the rejected item. Some may be reworked, others may be accepted as a usable variation, and others will be returned to the vendor.

Just-in-Time (JIT) purchasing requires suppliers to deliver components to the purchaser's receiving dock or sometimes directly to the production line as they are required. This approach is used widely in Japan and has been implemented at the Kawasaki Plant in Lincoln, Nebraska, as reported by Schonberger, Sutton, and Claunch. [10] Suppliers often are located near the purchaser, usually have a long term contract, for a year or the production season, and deliver once or twice daily. This approach reduces the purchaser's work-in-process.

Purchasing control is the final stage in the preorder, order, and post order purchasing cycle. Purchasing activities have a substantial impact on material costs, availability, and quality. Effective purchasing can decrease inventory investment, increase customer service, and improve profits dramatically.

## PROBLEMS

1. Distinguish between a blanket order, a systems contract, a distributor contract, and reserving vendor capacity.
2. A company's sales equalled $20,000,000 last year, profit was $4,000,000, and the cost of purchases was $11,000,000.

a. If the rate of inflation is zero, the sales volume remains the same, the engineering design is constant, and the same items are purchased and manufactured, how much must the cost of purchased items be reduced to increase profits by 20%.
b. If all things remain the same as in *a*, except that the inflation rate is 10%, what should the target cost of purchase items be to increase profits by 10% in last year's dollars?

**3.** The planned order receipts for an item follow; the item costs $42. Payment is required within four weeks of receipt. Calculate the time-phased planned cash commitments. (There are no planned receipts in weeks not shown.)

| Week | 2 | 10 | 18 |
|---|---|---|---|
| Planned Order Receipts | 250 | 300 | 275 |

**4.** The planned order receipts and the costs of four items follow. Payment is required within four weeks of receipt. Calculate the time-phased planned cash commitments during the next 12 weeks.

Planned Order Receipts
by Week

| Cost | Item | 1 | 2 | 3 | 4 | 5 | 6 | 7 | 8 |
|---|---|---|---|---|---|---|---|---|---|
| $18 | A | 10 | 10 | 10 | 10 | 10 | 10 | 10 | 10 |
| 31 | B | 0 | 17 | 0 | 17 | 0 | 17 | 0 | 17 |
| 7 | C | 33 | 0 | 46 | 18 | 0 | 25 | 30 | 25 |
| 77 | D | 8 | 7 | 21 | 16 | 0 | 12 | 18 | 12 |

**5.** The Wonarm Vending Machine company purchased five items from Sterling Products, Ltd. The projected demand for these items for the next six months follows.

Projected Requirements
by Month

| Stamping | 1 | 2 | 3 | 4 | 5 | 6 |
|---|---|---|---|---|---|---|
| A | 200 | 200 | 200 | 200 | 200 | 200 |
| B | 150 | 80 | 60 | 200 | 40 | 100 |
| C | 60 | 60 | 60 | 75 | 75 | 75 |
| D | 40 | 40 | 40 | 40 | 40 | 40 |
| E | 25 | 25 | 25 | 40 | 40 | 50 |

Sterling produces each of these items on the same line and estimates the capacity required for each to be:

| Item | Capacity (hours/unit) |
|---|---|
| A | .20 |
| B | .10 |
| C | .15 |
| D | .25 |
| E | .30 |

These estimates include setup time on the basis of running one lot per month.

If Wonarm purchases capacity, how many hours should they purchase in advance for each month?

**6.** The promised delivery lead times of four suppliers and their actual lead times on recent orders are as follows:

| Supplier | Promised Lead Time (days) |
|---|---|
| A | 10 |
| B | 15 |
| C | 5 |
| D | 20 |

Actual lead times of recent orders (oldest orders first) are:

Supplier A: 13, 12, 12, 11, 11, 11, 10, 10, 9, 8
Supplier B: 15, 14, 16, 13, 17, 12, 15, 14, 16, 15
Supplier C: 8, 9, 7, 6, 9, 5, 6, 8, 7, 8
Supplier D: 19, 18, 20, 20, 21, 22, 24, 26, 28, 30

a. What estimates of lead time should be used for planning order releases?
b. Evaluate the performance of each vendor. Use the percentage of late orders and days late per late order as a measure of performance.
c. Are any trends developing that require discussions or negotiations with a supplier?

**7.** The gross requirements and available inventory for the coming month for the five items discussed in Problem 5 follow:

| Item | | 1 | 2 | 3 | 4 | 5 |
|---|---|---|---|---|---|---|
| A | Gross Requirements | 50 | 0 | 100 | 100 | 0 |
| | Inventory | 60 | | | | |
| B | Gross Requirements | 20 | 40 | 40 | 0 | 0 |
| | Inventory | 25 | | | | |
| C | Gross Requirements | 30 | 30 | 0 | 0 | 0 |
| | Inventory | 10 | | | | |
| D | Gross Requirements | 0 | 0 | 0 | 20 | 20 |
| | Inventory | 5 | | | | |
| E | Gross Requirements | 25 | 25 | 0 | 25 | 0 |
| | Inventory | 50 | | | | |

In what order should they tell the supplier, Sterling Products, to run these items?

**8.** An item has a relatively steady demand of 250 units per month for the next year. The cost of placing a purchase order is $70, and company policy is to use an annual carrying cost rate of .40. Shipping costs are a flat $50 per shipment. The vendor has the following price schedule for the item.

| Quantity | Price (each) |
|---|---|
| 0-99 | $95 |
| 100-499 | 90 |
| ≥500 | 85 |

a. Calculate the total annual costs of an order quantity equal to:
   (1.) The monthly requirement
   (2.) The EOQ
   (3.) 500 units
b. What is the most economical order quantity?

**9.** All the facts of Problem 8 remain the same except that the supplier now offers free delivery. What is the most economical order quantity?

**10.** All the facts of Problem 9 remain the same except that the supplier now packs 100 items per crate and charges $100 for each partial crate. What is the most economical order quantity?

**11.** The following purchase discount opportunities are available to a company. (Ordering costs are not a factor.)

| | | | Discount | |
|---|---|---|---|---|
| Item | Annual Requirements | Order Quantity | Percentage | Order Quantity |
| 1 | $27,400 | $1,580 | 2.0 | $ 5,000 |
| 2 | 50,000 | 3,000 | 2.0 | 9,000 |
| 3 | 64,000 | 4,860 | 5.0 | 40,000 |
| 4 | 12,000 | 1,500 | 6.0 | 15,000 |
| 5 | 7,450 | 550 | 10.0 | 3,000 |
| 6 | 1,500 | 500 | 7.5 | 1,500 |

a. If the company takes advantage of only discounts with a rate of return greater than 20%, which ones will it not take?
b. Financial conditions prevent the company from investing more than $20,000 in purchase discount opportunities. Which opportunities should the company take?

**12.** The marginal out-of-pocket cost of placing, following up, and closing a purchase order is $100. Use the data from Problem 11 and this added information to calculate the revised rate of return for each purchase discount opportunity.

**13.** In the situation discussed in Problem 1, Chapter 7 ($R$ = 14,400, $C$ = 40 cents; $k$ = .25, and $s$ = $20), there is one change: an increase in price to 50 cents effective next Wednesday. The company is ready to order.

a. How many units should they order?
b. What will be the new lot size after the transition order?
c. How long will the transition order last?
d. What savings will be obtained with the transition order?
e. If the company has a general policy of not ordering more than a six months' supply, how many will they order? What will the savings be now?

**14.** The Near East Electronics Sales Company, Problem 2, Chapter 7 ($R$ = 16,000, $C$ = \$2, $k$ = .3, and $S$ = \$40) learns that the Model 19A meter will increase in price to \$2.18.

a. What should the transition order quantity be?
b. What will be the new lot size after the transition order quantity?
c. How much will they save with the transition order quantity?

# SELECTED READINGS


**1.** Sanford L. Volsky, "Purchasing's Inflation Fighter: The Computer," *APICS 24th Annual International Conference Proceedings* (1981), pp. 360-362.

**2.** L. James Burlingame and R. A. Warren, "Extended Capacity Planning," *APICS 17th Annual International Conference Proceedings* (1974), pp. 83-91.

**3.** Philip L. Carter and Robert M. Monczka, "Steelcase, Inc.: MRP in Purchasing," *Case Studies in Materials Requirements Planning* (Washington, D.C.: American Production and Inventory Control Society, 1978), pp. 105-129.

**4.** Rudy Friessnig, "In Line—Real Time Procurement," *APICS 24th Annual International Conference Proceedings* (1981), pp. 363-365.

**5.** Oliver W. Wight, *Production and Inventory Management in the Computer Age* (Boston, Mass.: Cahner Books, 1974), pp. 140-144.

**6.** Randall J. Benson, "Can Purchasing Supply Tomorrow's Factory?" *APICS 24th Annual International Conference Proceedings* (1981), pp. 355-359.

**7.** Richard R. Morency, "A Systems Approach to Vendor Scheduling under Contract Purchasing," *APICS 20th Annual Conference Proceedings* (1977), pp. 458-467.

**8.** Gilbert P. Trill, "PAYPUR: A Complete CRT, On-Line, Real Time Procurement," *Production and Inventory Management*, Third Quarter (1977).

**9.** Delbert L. Evans, "Measuring Purchasing Performance," *APICS 20th Annual Conference Proceedings* (1977), pp. 434-449.

**10.** Richard J. Schonberger, Doug Sutton, and Jerry Claunch, "KANBAN (Just-in-Time) Applications at Kawasaki USA," *APICS 24th Annual International Conference Proceedings* (1981), pp. 181-191.

**11.** IBM, *IBM COPICS*, Vol. 7 (White Plains, N.Y.: 1972).

**12.** Robert M. Monczka and Phillip L. Carter, "Productivity and Performance Measurement in Purchasing," *APICS 19th Annual Conference Proceedings* (1976), pp. 6-9.

**13.** Jinichiro Nakane and Robert W. Hall, "Transferring Production Control Methods Between Japan and the United States," *APICS 24th Annual International Conference Proceedings* (1981), pp. 192-194.

**14.** Richard J. Tersine and John H. Campbell, *Modern Materials Handling* (New York: Elsevier North-Holland, Inc., 1977), pp. 81-109.

**15.** Thomas F. Wallace, ed. *APICS Dictionary*, 4th ed. (Washington, D.C.: American Production and Inventory Control Society, 1980).

# —14—

# PRODUCTION AND INVENTORY MANAGEMENT SYSTEMS

A viable management information system is a requisite for successful production and inventory management (PIM). The term *system*, however, has been bantered about rather cavalierly in managerial circles. It has been combined and modified a thousand different ways in journal articles, texts, technical conferences, seminars, lectures, and everyday management conversations. The insights to the management process provided by system concepts caused this popularity. When technological innovations achieve early successes, enthusiasm tends to dominate prudence, caveats by the developers, and prescribed conditions for use. Systems were "in" and everyone—or nearly everyone—wanted to imbibe. In some cases the brewmaster had not prepared the ingredients properly and in others management overindulged. So, the innovations were overused, applied in inappropriate environments, and even misapplied. The usual sequence continued and hangovers from these experiences led to membership in the temperance union of those who swore off systems forever. The value of the technique was decried and a decline in the use of the innovation followed.

However, after a time of sobriety—dare we say proper aging—a reappraisal (of the applications which had been developed) and use with moderation in the appropriate circumstances can yield a more thoughtful outlook and appreciation of systems concepts. If so, pitfalls can be recognized and the concepts can be applied in a more rational manner to raise acceptance gradually to the level warranted by their actual value. We hope that this chapter provides the guidance to avoid management systems hangovers by the following:

1. Defining relevant terms
2. Describing basic systems concepts and their relationship with information systems
3. Describing information system development and design
4. Examining the essential ingredients of a PIM information system, its implementation concepts and techniques, and the importance of monitoring the system's performance

## DEFINITIONS

Definitions of dominant relevant terms follow; by their very nature these terms serve as an introduction to many of the concepts. A clear understanding of these terms usually is an excellent aid in problem solving and information system design activities.

## The Systems Approach

This is a group of concepts, methods and techniques used for problem solving, decision making, analyzing organizations, determining management processes, and evaluating organizational performance. It encompasses all the definitions, concepts, and techniques described in this chapter.

## System

This will be considered a group of elements which may be personnel, machines, and/or nonphysical entities such as energy and information, working in an interrelated fashion toward a set of objectives. This goal directed activity is viewed as inputs being processed, transformed into outputs.

## Systems Analysis

This is a somewhat formal methodology for the following:

1. Defining the problems of management as decision-making situations with constraints, resources, alternate courses of action available, and criteria by which to measure decision results
2. Analyzing the decision situation to determine the relationship of controlled and uncontrolled variables to the decision results, the outputs, and developing models which describe the relationships of inputs and processes, controlled variables, to outputs
3. Running the models by inserting different values for the variables controlled by management, calculating the results, evaluating the alternatives on the basis of these results, and identifying preferred courses of action under various sets of circumstances

The study of the relationships described by the models leads to decision rules and decision guidelines. The following are examples of simple rules and guidelines developed from models: (1) order 1,000 units of Final Assembly J9785 when the stock drops below 100 units; and (2) schedule 15 percent of capacity in Work Center A, Numerical Control (NC) Milling, as safety capacity.

## Management Systems

The decision rules adopted by an organization to plan, direct, and control its operation are its management systems. By its very nature a set of decision rules for a given situation implicitly declares that the organization has a model of that situation; it knows the relationship of the dominant controllable variables to the decision results. For example, before adopting lot sizing and order release rules, an organization should possess a good understanding of the effect of these rules on inventory costs and customer service in the given situation. Running a model will supply this information.

## Information Systems

Once the criteria, decision rules, and guides for making decisions have been selected, means of gathering, recording, processing, and communicating the required information to the proper decision makers at the right time must be developed. These methods of gathering, recording, processing, and communicating constitute the information system. Figure 14-1 is a flowchart representing the relationship of these stages in the development of an information system.

**FIGURE 14-1**
**SCHEMATIC OF MANAGEMENT INFORMATION SYSTEM DEVELOPMENT**

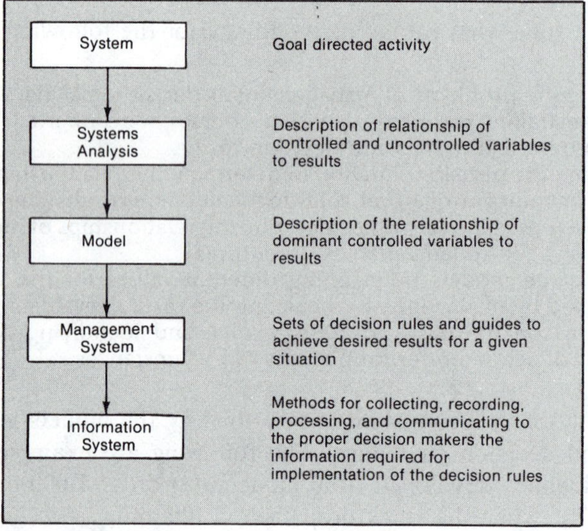


# SYSTEM CONCEPTS

This section contains an overview of rudimentary systems concepts necessary for a full understanding of management planning, directing, and control systems. It deals with the elements of a system, open and closed systems, and levels of analysis.

## System Elements

Figure 14-2 illustrates the concept that a system consists of five essential elements: inputs, processes, outputs, feedback, and a control unit. Inputs are all the resources consumed in the process, converted into outputs. For example, raw materials, labor, and purchase parts are inputs in a manufacturing system while information such as demand requirements, stock balances, lead times, unit costs, and the manufacturing processing sequence are inputs to a PIM system.

**FIGURE 14-2**
**BLOCK DIAGRAM OF SYSTEM ELEMENTS**

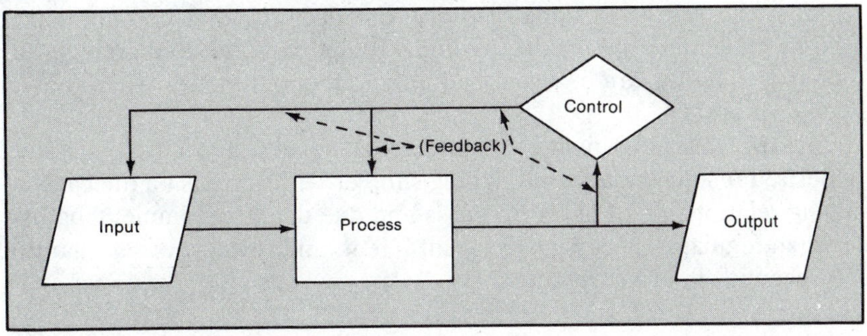

The process consists of all the activities that transform inputs into outputs. For example, machining of parts, heat treating, plating, painting, and packaging are all part of the process. In an information system the process is the changing of input data into information that can be used for decision making. It involves sorting, collating, tabulating, multiplying, etc.

Feedback includes the measuring of system performance, determining what the actual output of the system is, and transmitting that data to the control unit. Feedback also includes the transmission of regulation directives from the control unit where decisions are made, or recommended, to the individuals or mechanisms that control the inputs and processes.

The control unit is the decision-making unit. It receives the measurement of actual results through the feedback channels and then compares the actual results with the desired results. If actual results differ from desired results by more than an acceptable tolerance, the control unit directs that inputs and/or the process be changed to bring actual results into closer alignment with desired results. The ability to determine how inputs and processes should be changed in the event actual results differ from the desired results requires that the control unit know the relationship of inputs, processes, and outputs. In brief, the control unit, which may be a human such as the master scheduler, must have a model describing the relationship of inputs and processes (variables which management controls), and the results. Otherwise changes would be based on random guesses.

Systems that operate in this fashion immediately come to mind. When the thermostat in a home heating system senses that the temperature has dropped below a desired level it immediately activates the processing unit (the furnace) and delivers more fuel resulting in a warmer home. Physicians observe the progress of patients and continuously evaluate the efficacy of the therapy employed. In many cardiac care units, nurses have the authority (standing orders) to administer specific medications to patients exhibiting physiological characteristics requiring immediate action. The chef decides to add further seasoning on the basis of taste, and the machinist adjusts a machine tool if parts are beginning to exceed or approach a tolerance limit. Students are encouraged to devote more time to their studies when they are obtaining unsatisfactory grades. Few individuals go through a day without comparing the results of some activity and deciding that certain changes should be made if actual results are going to approach desired results. Such activities frequently can be described and understood better when they are viewed as a system.

In PIM, decisions made to bring actual results into closer alignment with desired results include reassigning shop order priorities on the basis of a changing relationship of order progress and due dates, recommending overtime when regular time capacity is insufficient, and revising order quantities due to changes in requirements.

## Open and Closed Systems

Traditional physical science terminology, and in particular engineering terminology, designated a system with feedback and control as a *closed system*. The input-process-output loop is closed when the feedback goes from output to control and back to the input and process. Systems without feedback were designated *open systems*. These are systems in which the input and process are not influenced by the results attained. In reality, there are very few systems in which results eventually do not influence input and process changes. Nonetheless, there are situations in which there is little feedback and control to modify results in a reasonable time; for practical purposes, such systems are open in a real time sense. Machining a lot of parts and not checking the dimensions of machined surfaces until the last part is run is an example.

In the social sciences, open and closed systems have a somewhat different meaning. A *closed system* is defined as one which either does not receive information concerning relevant developments in the environment, or one which does not use this information in reaching decisions concerning inputs and processes. The use of the word *closed* here is similar to its meaning when speaking of a closed mind. In this context an open system is one which not only receives but also seeks information from the environment and uses it in the decision-making process. This information flows to the control unit where it is used to evaluate the objectives themselves and to search for more efficient and effective methods of obtaining the results. This adds another level of analysis and increases the power of the concept.

Thus, two apparent contradictory definitions of open and closed systems exist. In one case, *open* describes a system without feedback while in the other it describes a system with feedback. The traditional *feedback-closed system* definition, however, refers to the internal level of analysis while the *feedback-open system* definition applies to the external level of analysis. Figure 14-3 illustrates this.

**FIGURE 14-3**
**SYSTEMS CONCEPT SCHEMATIC**
**INTERNAL AND EXTERNAL LEVELS OF ANALYSIS**

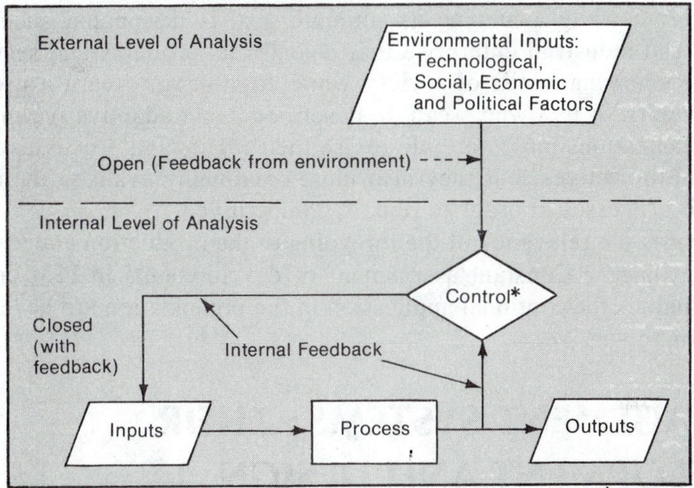


*External level of analysis: evaluation of environmental factors and decision to modify inputs, process, and/or desired outputs. Internal level of analysis: comparison of actual and desired output and decision to modify inputs or process.

Let's look at some examples differentiating internal and external levels of analysis using the systems concept. Take the case, circa 1907, of the general manager of a manufacturing organization which has just experienced its best annual sales and profit. As you might suspect, it is producing within desirable unit cost limits, achieving the desired quality, and shipping orders on schedule. It is in great shape at the internal level of analysis; it is achieving its objectives. Now let it be revealed that its business is horse-drawn carriages. Our hindsight view of the environment tells us that the outputs of this organization will fill the needs of society to a lesser degree each year. Some carriage manufacturers realized this; others did not. It all depended on how well their system functioned at the external level. History is replete with examples of governments, manufacturing organizations, service organizations, and academic institutions that either were ignoring information received from the environment or did not evaluate the information properly. The contrasting expansion policies of Sears and Montgomery Ward after

World War II are classic examples. The extraordinary expansion of Sears is history. Montgomery Ward, however, had plenty of company in its conservative approach, including literally hundreds of school boards which did not anticipate the burgeoning school populations—sometimes even after the children had been born. Today's world is no less dynamic than the immediate post-World War II period. In fact, it is difficult to disagree with Alvin Toffler's contention in *Future Shock* that the greatest challenge to individuals, organizations, and society itself will be the ability to cope with an ever increasing rate of change in technology and human behavior.[1]

An organization or group that has the ability to sense and measure the impact of developments in the environment on the organization and change its *modus operandi*—inputs, process, and output—so as not only to survive but to thrive while achieving its ultimate goal is designated an *adaptive system*. The industrial enterprise that changes its products and services to meet the changing needs of society while continuing to earn a profit and make a return to its owners can be described as an adaptive organization. Such organizations must not only revise their inputs and processes to meet immediate objectives, but they also must continually evaluate their objectives and processes in order to remain competitive.

What is the relevancy of the foregoing to the production and inventory control manager? Constant assessment of developments in PIM concepts and techniques for continual application in the organization are necessary if the firm is to survive.

## MANAGEMENT SYSTEMS: THEIR DEVELOPMENT AND DESIGN

Management information systems do not spring out of the blue; at least they should not if we expect them to contribute to PIM effectiveness and corporate productivity. There are rational approaches to developing an individual system and for planning the development of a group of related systems or systems modules. Examination of planning the development of a group of related systems or system modules is included in Chapter 15. Here we will make just a few further comments concerning the relation of systems analysis, models, decision rules, information systems, and the role of production-inventory managers.

### Individual System Development

The development, design, and implementation of the individual information system begins with systems analysis. As mentioned previously, the

[1] Alvin Toffler, *Future Shock* (New York: Bantam Books, Inc., 1971), pp. 19-35.

objective of systems analysis is to examine a decision situation and to determine how the controllable variables relate to the results obtained. Systems analysis usually begins with the recognition that a problem exists. The problem can be either of two types: (1) desired results are not being obtained, or (2) a decision must be made and no rules or guidelines have been established. An organization which continually misses due dates on many of its orders yet has an inventory investment well above the target level has the first type problem. The necessity of either building inventories or cutting back production and laying off employees in a downward trend market without any corporate policies or guides for selecting between such alternatives is an example of the second type problem. In the first case we assume that some system of decision making exists but is not working well; in the second no set of procedures for decision making exists. In both cases systems analysis is appropriate and consists of the following steps which are illustrated in Figure 14-4:

1. Defining the problem (Describe the nature of the situation as illustrated in the previous paragraph.)
2. Stating the objectives of the decision (For example, what service level, inventory investment level, and plant utilization are desired?)
3. Defining the available resources and the existing constraints (For example, what is capacity, what is the lead time, and what are present capacity requirements?)
4. Determining the uncontrollable and controllable variables and precisely how they relate to results

**FIGURE 14-4**
**INFORMATION SYSTEMS ANALYSIS SCHEMATIC**

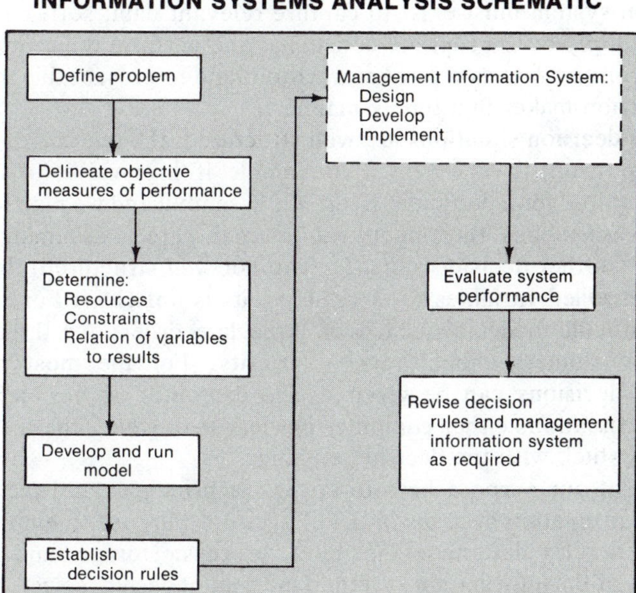

5. Developing a model of the relationship of these variables to the decision outcome by describing that relationship verbally, mathematically, or graphically
6. Determining the alternate courses of action which may be followed; i.e., the choices available to the decision maker
7. Using the model of the real world to evaluate the different decisions which can be made (In brief, run or operate the model to determine each outcome with different decisions. For example, mathematical and graphical descriptions of the relationship of demand, replenishment policies, and inventory status can be analyzed to determine the impact of different ordering systems on costs and customer service.)
8. Establishing decision rules or guides for making the decision on the basis of the results obtained by running the model
9. Evaluating the performance of the system in the real world and revising the model and decision rules as required

Systems analysis is not a one-shot affair. The results of actual operating systems must be reviewed after implementation to determine if the expected results are being obtained.

## Management Information Systems

Recurring types of decisions are most amenable to systems analysis and the development of decision rules which constitute a management system. The ordering of material and the scheduling of jobs are two examples of recurring PIM decisions. If decisions are to be made on the basis of a decision rule, which evaluates the facts in relation to management objectives, an information system must exist to capture relevant data; sort, collate, summarize, multiply by appropriate constants, and perform other processes required to convert raw data into information; and to present this information to the decision maker in a timely manner.

Some decision situations are well structured; the relation of controlled variables to results is very clear. For example, if three valves of a particular type are required for a particular hydraulic assembly and we plan to fabricate thirty such assemblies, then ninety valves are required—assuming no rejects or pilferage. Other decision situations are not well structured, the relationship of controlled variables to desired results is not clear. For example, it may be difficult to decide which of three late orders for three different preferred customers should receive priority. For the most part, well-structured decisions can be given to the computer or the clerk. In less structured situations either computer or clerk may gather the facts, but the manager is stuck with the decision making.

It is not our purpose here to cover the principles and techniques of designing information systems in detail; it is our purpose to emphasize that the decision rules determine the input, process, storage, and output requirements of the information system. One cannot design, select, or approve of an information system without at least implicitly agreeing that the model underlying the decision rules encompassed in that information system is applicable to the situation.

Management should strive to have recurring, well-structured decisions handled by an approved processing system whether it be manual, mechanical, or electronic. This allows management to devote its attention to the nonrecurring, less structured, and exception type situations. These activities include the planning and developing of management information systems, staffing and staff development, establishing performance goals, and measuring performance.

Information systems possess generic capabilities, can be designed with a data base or independent file structure, can incorporate minicomputers and thus decentralized data processing, and usually are developed in a modular fashion. These topics are examined before discussing the development of PIM systems.

# System's Management Capabilities

The objectives of a management system (decision-making process) dictate that an information system have certain capabilities. These capabilities can be classified as follows:

1. Reporting
   a. Historical
   b. Control (real time)—both alert and action
2. Inquiry
3. Search
4. Execution

**Reporting Capability.** Nearly all systems have some form of reporting capability—collecting data concerning an event and converting it to information describing that event in a summary form. A system capable of reporting sales per month of each stockkeeping unit (SKU) during the last five years has a *historical reporting capability*. Such information usually is required for forecasting capability.

A *real time reporting capability* usually implies that as events occur, data describing them are recorded immediately so that those events can be dealt with; i.e., controlled. The dominant characteristic of a real time information system is that the information be reported in sufficient time for management to take the necessary corrective action. (In computer terminology, real time is synonymous with *on-line*—the direct entry of data into computer memory as, or immediately after, an events occurs.) Thus, daily or weekly batch reporting of demand or production output may be real time in some cases while instantaneous reporting is required in others. Medical personnel, for example, require instantaneous reports if patients in a coronary care unit begin to experience irregular heart beats. In a similar fashion, some manufacturing processes that exceed certain limits must be reported immediately if the necessary corrective action is to be taken. Excessive temperatures or an improper chemical mix can be extremely dangerous unless corrected immediately. In repetitive manufacturing, malfunctioning equipment or defective material can result in substantial losses if not discovered and corrected immediately.

**Control Capability.** Control exists when reports (information) are available in sufficient time for management to bring deviant results (results which exceed predetermined limits) into alignment with planned results. The ability to report a situation that has exceeded predetermined limits is required in many systems. An alert capability exists when exceptions (situations exceeding defined limits) are reported to management for their review and decision concerning appropriate action. Examples of information systems with an alert control capability are ones that report the following:

1. Any item whose stock falls to or below its order point
2. Any production order that has a critical ratio below a certain value or is behind schedule at least a certain number of days
3. A purchase order requiring acknowledgement that has not been acknowledged after a certain time period
4. Back orders that have not been shipped in, say, three days
5. Vendor shipments more than, say, three days late

They inform management of an undesirable situation, and PIM personnel must decide what follow-up is appropriate.

An *action control capability* exists when the system itself takes action immediately to bring the situation under control or when management receives a report requiring immediate action. Some manufacturing processes, for example, have the built-in capacity to monitor temperatures, chemical properties, or physical dimensions and make the necessary adjustments when limits are exceeded. Equipment malfunction or material outage can shut down an entire production line and result in an expensive delay; a report of either usually requires immediate action.

**Inquiry Capability.** Some systems have the ability to determine the value of a characteristic of any item in a file, upon request. The ability of a system to report the quantity of an item in stock, the status of a production order, the cumulative year-to-date demand for a product, or the manufacturing lead time of an item are examples of inquiry capability. This information is obtained not by going through all records, but by a combined hardware and software capability to go directly to that place in the file where the desired data are held, retrieve, and report them.

**Search Capability.** Some systems have the capability to find upon request that item or items in a file that have a particular value for a specific characteristic. It is the inverse of the inquiry capability. Systems, for example, that have the capability of reporting the names of all PIM employees who are APICS Certified, that can provide a list of all the parts supplied by a given vendor, that can report all the parts requiring Magnaflux inspection, or that can report all items requiring processing in a given work center are examples of systems with search capability.

**Execution Capability.** Systems that automatically release some orders can be viewed as having execution capability. For example, purchase orders may be released against a blanket order, or a firm planned order may be released on a prespecified date unless the planner enters other instructions. This capability also may be viewed as an action control type capability with the lapse of time being the limit exceeded.

The importance of recognizing the different capabilities is that they require different software and hardware. Hardware and software complexity and cost usually increase progressively as system capability requirements go from simple historical reporting to exception reporting, to inquiry capability, and to search capability requirements. An exception system, for example, may require a simple, sequential access physical file structure; while search capability may require a direct access physical file structure and an indexing facility with the related additional software and storage capacity.

## The Modular Approach to Systems

A system module consists of a single set of inputs, processing, and outputs along with the necessary files as illustrated in Figure 14-5. A subsystem consists of one or more modules to carry out a particular function such

**FIGURE 14-5**
**A SYSTEMS MODULE**
**STOCK STATUS EXAMPLE**

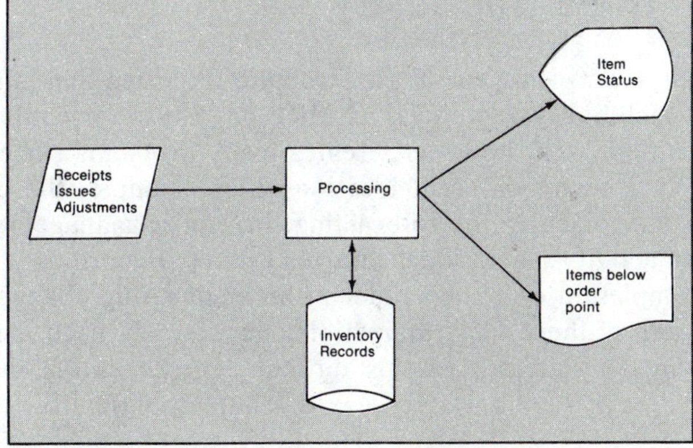

as forecasting, material requirements planning (MRP), or capacity requirements planning. The modular approach develops the subsystems in the sequence required by technological factors and existing conditions. The bill of materials (BOM) subsystem, for example, usually is developed prior to the MRP subsystem. Many of the modules that may belong in a PIM system are listed in Table 14-1. These titles in themselves, however, do not delineate exactly what the inputs, process, and output are, but give a general indication of the area of application. Some subsystems called purchasing, for example, may include a vendor performance module. Complete identification requires a description of the inputs, processes, files, and output of a system module.

**TABLE 14-1**
**SOME COMMON PIM SUBSYSTEMS OR MODULES**

| | |
|---|---|
| Production Planning | Order Release Planning |
| Resource Requirements Planning | Operation Scheduling |
| Forecasting | Shop Floor Control |
| Master Production Scheduling | Dispatching |
| Rough-Cut Capacity Planning | Work-in-Process Control |
| Order Entry | Purchasing |
| Bill of Materials Processing | Vendor Performance Analysis |
| Inventory Management | Receiving |
| Materials Requirements Planning | Distribution Requirements Planning |
| Tool Control | Product Costing |
| Capacity Requirements Planning | Job Costing |
| | Labor Reporting |

The modular approach enables system development and implementation to proceed at a rate consistent with the user's ability to absorb the system, as Gerald F. DeSantis has pointed out. [1] (Other characteristics of the modular approach are discussed later in the section discussing implementation.)

## Files and the Data Base

The simplest and least costly file structure to design and implement is one in which each subsystem, such as MRP or shop floor control, has its own files. This approach, however, creates many problems since the same data are stored in many different locations. For example, the part (item) master file may be used in the forecasting, inventory management, MRP, and production activity (shop floor) control systems. Recording of an event, such as the completion of a shop order or an engineering change, requires recording in each of these files. Maintaining accuracy in each file and consistency among the different files is difficult. Implementing inquiry and search capabilities in such a system also is relatively difficult.

A data base system combines all files—in a logical and operational sense—into one master file with many subdivisions. (Table 14-2 lists some of the files required by PIM information systems.) These subdivisions are

**TABLE 14-2**
**SOME COMMON PIM FILES**

| |
|---|
| Production Planning |
| Forecasts |
| Item Master |
| Inventory |
| Master Production Scheduling |
| Routing File |
| Work Center |
| Customer |
| Vendor |
| Production Order |
| Purchase Order |

combined temporarily as required to fit the application. This is accomplished by data base management software. Thus, files that are separated physically are joined logically. Several data base file systems may be developed with each serving two or more subsystems, or one data base file system may be developed to serve all PIM subsystems. In some cases, the PIM subsystems may be only one of the subsystems served by the data base. Figure 14-6 illustrates how some of these files might be handled by a data base management system.

**FIGURE 14-6**
**SIMPLIFIED ILLUSTRATION OF DATA BASE MANAGEMENT SYSTEM**

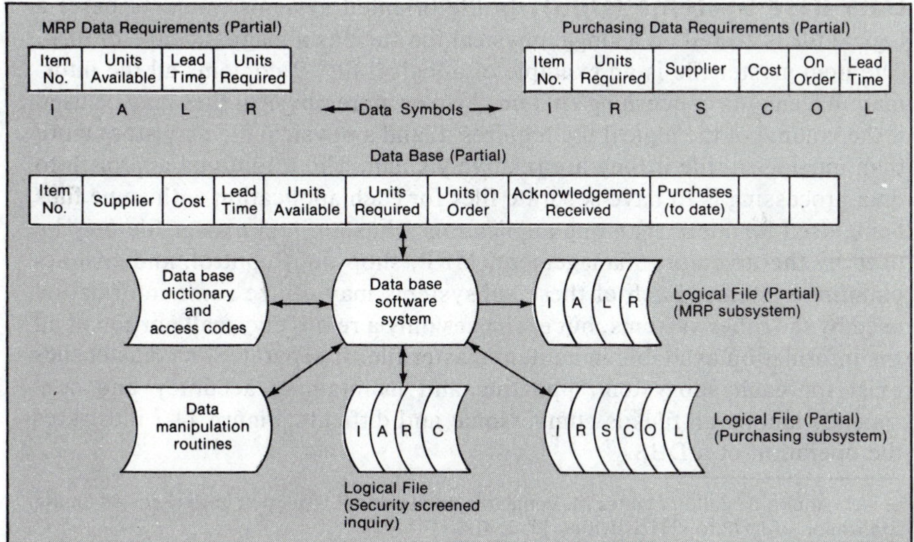

# Distributed Data Processing (DDP) and Minicomputers

Data processing can take place primarily at a central location with data entered and output received via remote terminals; or some of the processing, data storage, and control can take place at the remote terminal sites. The advent of powerful and relatively inexpensive minicomputers along with data base management techniques has made DDP feasible and appropriate in some cases.[2] Figure 14-7 illustrates a DDP system with a distributed data base.

FIGURE 14-7
DISTRIBUTED DATA PROCESSING
WITH DISTRIBUTED DATA BASE

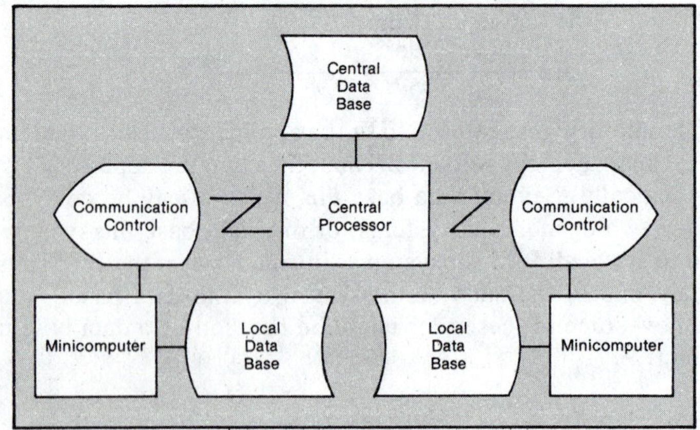


**Data Base Systems (DBS).** In file oriented systems (nondata base) a logical file is stored on a single physical file such as a magnetic tape or disk. The item master file is an example of a logical file; it contains all the information elements concerning an item. Two or more physical files may be used if the volume of the logical file requires it, and a physical file may store more than one logical file if they are relatively small. The traditional approach to data processing is to have separate files for each application with some files being used for more than one application. Thus an item master file may be used by the inventory management, MRP, shop floor control, and cost accounting systems. Each of these subsystems may utilize some information used by the other systems, but each uses only a relatively small portion of all the information available in an item master file. If separate item master files exist for each subsystem, updating and maintaining accuracy and consistency among all files is cumbersome and difficult. Figure 14-7 illustrates the operation of a DBS.

---

[2] Robert B. Vollum, James M. Venglarik, and Leland R. Kneppelt have reported on the application of DDP to PIM activities. [2, 3, 4]

The data base management approach integrates all information into a data base. Access to this information by any processing module (subsystem) is controlled by a data base management system (DBMS). This software permits the user to "see" only the logical file data for the process that is being executed. The system acts as though that data were a separate file. Subsystem module processing usually changes some of the data in the file; for example, the number of items in inventory or the customer orders received. These updated values are entered immediately into the data base upon completion of processing. The ability of the DBS to construct such files quickly and efficiently is a distinct advantage. The data base also is less likely to contain outdated information; all subsystems are processing the same data.

**Minicomputers.** Minicomputers with the power of second generation computers are available today at a small fraction of their cost. This enables an organization to perform systems processing at the plant, warehouse, or field service site without tying up or depending on the central computer. Data applicable to a given location and processing performed to manage their own daily activities can be handled by the local minicomputer.

**Distributed Processing.** The assignment of systems activities depends on the needs of the users, the computing and storage capability required, and the capability of the users and local equipment. Leland R. Kneppelt recommends that forecasting, production planning, resource requirements planning, master production scheduling (MPS), and rough-cut capacity planning be performed at the central site. [4] Since planning activities relate to overall management objectives and policies and since plans frequently are prepared monthly or quarterly, this makes sense. The MRP and capacity requirements plan also can be processed centrally due to computer capacity requirements and the need to integrate the effects of usage at all warehouses and production at all plants. Aggregate inventory reports also would be processed centrally.

Distributed processing (local minicomputer processing) would include shop floor control reports and scheduling, customer order processing, and local inventory management processes. Thus, in general, short-range priority and capacity planning and control are performed at the local site, and long- and medium-range planning and control activities are centralized.

Advantages of DDP and DBM systems using minicomputers include:

1. The failure of one processor (computer) does not shut down the entire system.
2. Greater throughput is possible since some tasks are allocated to local minicomputers.
3. Functions not economical for processing centrally can be added at local sites.
4. Greater cost-effectiveness due to the increasing power and low cost of minicomputers results.
5. Consistent data exist throughout the system.

Some disadvantages or problems are listed next:

1. Control of access to computers is more difficult.
2. Monitoring of local data entry and systems development activities to assure appropriate internal controls and systems integrity is more difficult.
3. Development of applications at local sites may be haphazard.

James M. Venglarik points out that the installation of distributed data processing should be based on all factors and not only on computer technology considerations. [3] The data processing system should be consistent with the systems objectives and capability of personnel.

# PIM INFORMATION SYSTEMS

Since there is no one set of decision techniques applicable to all organizations, it follows that there is no single PIM information system that is appropriate for all manufacturing firms. As Buffa and Miller have pointed out, the process technology, product positioning, product structure, organization structure and capability, organization goals, and the costs and benefits determine the nature of the appropriate information system. [5]

## Process Technology

Although basic PIM principles apply to both repetitive manufacturing and job shop manufacturing, their information system requirements usually differ somewhat. Scheduling of individal work centers usually is not required in repetitive manufacture. The rate of flow and line balancing allow the planner to schedule the entire line. In a job shop, however, priorities must be assigned to all orders in the work center. Capacity planning in job shop manufacturing also requires greater detail since orders flow between work centers in a variety of patterns as discussed in Chapters 5 and 12.

**Process Industries.** Sam Taylor has pointed out that process industries are capital intensive whereas fabrication and assembly industries are materials intensive. [6] As a result, MPS's in process industries schedule production runs on each line to use the expensive equipment fully. The required material then is calculated and obtained. The MPS is capacity oriented. Order releases frequently are not required, the MPS is authorization to produce. The BOM has fewer levels than it does in the typical fabrication plant and calculation of lot sizes is less complex.

In the common fabrication and assembly plant, MPS end item due dates determine time-phased material requirements and capacity requirements as discussed in Chapters 3 and 5. The MPS is based on the availability of material and then capacity availability is determined. If necessary, capacity definitely can be modified in many cases. The MPS is material oriented. The complex material flow, variations in shop efficiency and supplier deliveries, scrap, and changing order priorities require detailed order release planning and dispatching (shop floor control) as discussed in Chapters 5 and 12. Substantially different management information systems are required in process industries and in fabrication and assembly industries. R. Leonard Allen has reported on the application of standard manufacturing software to primary metals processing; and R. T. Rowan and J. A. Wellendorf have reported on the applicability and customization of commercial software packages in the process industry. [7, 8]

**Repetitive Manufacturing.** Production and inventory control systems for repetitive manufacturing have different requirements than project manufacturing, job shop, or flow manufacturing in the process industries. Repetitive manufacturing deals primarily with the mass production of discrete units and less with fluids, powders, and chemical change processes, as described in the Introduction. The following are some of the characteristics of repetitive manufacturing which create data collection, data processing, and information requirements different from the typical job shop:

1. The mass production configuration of the physical facilities plant requires MPS's that authorize runs for specific time periods.
2. Daily run schedules are used to authorize and control production, not job orders.
3. Production control is executed by counts at key points in the flow.
4. The status of raw material and purchased parts inventory is accomplished by *backflushing*, i.e., calculating the inventory withdrawn from stores by exploding the BOM applicable to the point of the count and multiplying each item by the count.
5. MPS's frequently are stated in cumulative values for the month or year. Cumulative values are used for control of incoming material, flow through key points, and finished production output.
6. The use of feeder plants supplying components often requires multiplant production planning.
7. Many items produced by repetitive manufacturing are produced to stock with national or international distribution systems. This requires a close linking of the MPS and the distribution plan. Lines of item flow can be long and control complex, when production and distribution both occur in different nations and perhaps on different continents.
8. Capacity planning resulting in the proper balance is especially challenging in multiplant, multiproduct environments. [32]

The foregoing covers many of the salient PIM problems of repetitive manufacturing, and documents the need for manufacturing control systems different from those found in the single plant job shop environment.

**Product Positioning.** The strategic decision to make-to-stock, make-to-order, or the common strategy of making components and subassemblies to stock and making final assemblies to order results in different systems requirements. Systems in companies producing to stock have a need for finished goods control and perhaps distribution management not required by the firm that builds only to order. Coordination of order entry, order related engineering activities, MPS, BOM variations, and shop scheduling frequently is crucial in the company that builds to order. Manufacturing of heavy equipment, large turbines and generators, and large pressure vessels frequently approaches one-of-a-kind project manufacturing and uses network models such as critical path management (CPM) and project evaluation and review technique (PERT) for planning and control.

**Organization and Organization Goals.** The assignment of tasks, duties, and decision-making authority within the organization defines who needs what information. The capabilities of users influence the complexity and sophistication of the system. In all cases the process and the output should be transparent to the user. The user needs to understand clearly how the data were obtained, the process they underwent, and what the output information means—what action, if any, should be taken.

W. Skinner has noted that different firms emphasize different strategies to maintain and improve their competitive positioning. [9] A firm may emphasize quality, delivery, price, flexibility—the willingness to modify the product or normal sales quantity requirement—or a combination of these. Emphasis on delivery requires a strong PIM system with emphasis on the availability of items and more than adequate capacity. An emphasis on price, on the other hand, demands minimum inventory and high resource utilization.

# System Design Specification

Developing the overall PIM system design specification begins with responses to a group of broad questions. Some concern such factors as process technology; others relate to factors covered in Chapter 15 concerning organization; and still others are related to concepts and principles examined in those chapters concerning PIM techniques. This group of questions includes but is not limited to the following:

1. What is the process technology of the company? Is it a continuous chemical type, repetitive discrete parts, job shop, or project manufacturing type organization? Perhaps it includes features of two or more of these types.
2. What is the product positioning strategy of the firm? Does it produce to stock, produce to order, both, or a little of each on various product lines?
3. What is the organizational structure of PIM activities? Should it be changed? If so, is an organizational change likely?

4. What data processing capability exists? If it is inadequate, are financial resources available to improve it?
5. How good are existing data resources? Is an accurate BOM available? Are past sales data available, by product, by SKU, or by period? Are operations process times, work center efficiency, and process yield data available? Do vendor capacity and lead time data exist?
6. What levels of aggregation are appropriate for end items, processes, time periods, work centers, or personnel?
7. How do present organizational personnel resources compare with the resources required by the systems development activity? Should additional individuals be hired? If so, when? Should outside resources be hired to assist in the design, development, education, and implementation phases on an ad hoc basis? If so, what should be the expertise of the outside resources?

Most of these questions concern the general nature and status of the business. Many other examples can be given. After answering such general questions, decisions concerning the overall design of the PIM information system must be made. These include the following:

1. What type management systems (planning and control techniques) are required? For example, should MPS be material oriented or capacity oriented?
2. What outputs (reports) are required? When?
3. What data need to be available to inquiry? to search?
4. What system module structures (subsystems) are feasible? What data base structure options are available? How do they relate? Which combination is preferable?
5. After the overall systems design is determined, in what order will the subsystems be developed?

The answers to these questions are used to develop a statement of system requirements in terms of specific output information, the time when it is needed, and by whom. Furthermore, the priority of the different requirements and the cost benefits of each should be documented. Successful system development and operation require the following:

1. Documentation
2. Forming a project team
3. Planning and controlling design and development
4. Software decisions
5. Planning and controlling the implementation
6. Monitoring and refining the system

(Chapter 15 discusses the formation of a project team and planning and controlling design and development.)

# Documentation

Max Gray and Keith R. London propose the following six classifications on the basis of application:

1. Analytical documentation
2. Management aids
3. System
4. Program
5. Operations (computer)
6. User aids [10]

Adequate documentation is important from the very beginning of the system development project. It leads to a better understanding of system objectives, methods, and status. It records top management's commitment to the system's objectives, budget, and schedule. It is necessary for adequate planning and control of system development, design, and implementation, and later is a requisite for system maintenance.

A systems design project begins with the recognition of a problem requiring systems analysis and data processing assistance. Analytical documentation records a description of the problem, the objectives of the project, possible solutions, and projected development time and costs. It is a proposal that should be approved in writing by management.

System documentation describes the objectives, input, processes (decision techniques), files, output (reports), controls and capability—for example, inquiry, exception reporting—of the system. It consists of such items as module block diagrams, system flow charts, input specifications, file specifications, output specifications, and a system test plan. It may combine narrative descriptions, charts, layouts, graphs, and mathematical models. The complexity of the system influences the detail of the systems documentation, which usually serves as the basis for PIM analysis of the system during all stages of development.

Program documentation includes the input, output, and files specification information contained in systems documentation, but in greater detail. It describes the program logic and methodology, equipment requirements, special programming techniques, subroutines used, and storage routines and requirements. It also includes a listing of the program and a description of the program test plan. PIM should verify that the test plan encompasses all operating conditions.

Operations documentation contains the instructions that data processing personnel follow in using a computer system to run the program. It may direct the operator to load certain tapes or disks or to enter certain data via the computer console.

User aids may be the most important documentation. They describe how data are prepared for entry into the system, when and how data should be collected and entered, and the content and nature of output reports. In keeping with one of the principles of information system design, users should be involved in the design of input and output content and format. Requiring users to approve this documentation in writing improves the likelihood that they will participate seriously in their development and share the responsibility for their success. Users frequently possess a knowledge of particular plant and office conditions that the systems designer is not aware of. Users include shop supervisors, storeroom personnel, purchasing and receiving personnel, and PIM personnel. When developing a new system, the implementation of MRP for example, a team consisting of representatives from each of the areas may be formed to participate with the systems and data processing representatives in the design, development, test, and implementation activities. Selecting one PIM individual who devotes time exclusively to systems development, design, implementation, and maintenance can avoid the problem of systems activities being neglected because of the press of daily planning and control activities. (This is discussed further in Chapter 15.)

Management aids are broad in scope. They are a composite of analytical documentation, systems and user aids providing management a view of the objectives, benefits, and the development-implementation plans, schedule, and cost. The written approval of these plans by top management is necessary in order to gain both commitment to and acceptance of shared responsibility for the system's success.

Systems, management aids, and user aids documentation are excellent sources of material for training personnel.

## Software

After deciding to automate the PIM information system, there are three alternatives: (1) rent (purchase) data processing services from a service bureau, (2) develop the software in-house, or (3) purchase (a license to use) a commercial software package. Treatment of these alternatives follows.

**Using a Service Bureau.** Service bureaus offer time-sharing systems either with on-site terminals or with off-site batch processing. In either case, the initial investment is less and the staffing requirements are lower than those required for in-house development or purchase of a commercial package. Measurable results usually can be obtained sooner, and the downside risk is lower. The results can be evaluated relatively quickly; and, if not satisfactory, the use of the service can be discontinued with minimum losses, as argued by Yost. [11] A disadvantage is that the company may have to adapt its operating policies to the existing software rather than vice versa. Initiating automatic data processing with service bureau time-sharing and later converting to an in-house system—sometimes developed with the assistance of the time-shared vendor—or to a purchased package is the route followed by some companies. [12] As a company increases the modules used in a service bureau system, the rental costs can increase to the point where they are greater over time than the savings in initial costs. Time-sharing processing through a service bureau is a viable option for the company without a computer, with little systems and programming expertise, limited capital, a good match between the service bureau system(s) and the company requirements, the availability of required data inputs, and the need to implement one or two modules rather quickly. The advent of minicomputers and the availability of packaged manufacturing software has decreased some of the initial cost advantages of service bureaus, however.

**In-House System.** The company can design, program, test, and implement a system using existing staff, added personnel, consultants, and available literature and training seminars. As the research of one of the authors revealed, this practice was common in the first half of the 70's. [13] The situation has changed dramatically as many commercial packages are available and are functioning successfully. Designing and programming the information system in-house can be somewhat like reinventing the wheel. This is a valid analogy if in-house requirements are similar to those provided by commercial packages. Mike Perski, a senior analyst for Abbot Laboratories, contends, however, that the benefits of package software in some circumstances are myths. He notes that modifications and unfamiliarity with system and program design, structures, and coding techniques can make installation more difficult than anticipated. He asserts that the initial savings in development and programming often are counterbalanced by increased testing, implementation, and maintenance costs. His experience based assertions support the need to examine thoroughly the match between systems requirements and the features of a commercial package including documentation, testing, and vendor support. [14] The many successful implementations of commercially available packages, however, indicate that they are a rational choice in many situations. Milton Cook states that the major advantages of software packages are as follows:

1. They take less time to implement.
2. They are, in general, tried and proven and as a result very reliable.
3. They are readily available, thereby drastically reducing design/programming time.
4. They are less expensive than internally developed systems.
5. Most importantly, they focus attention on using the system rather than distracting effort and attention to endless debate on the design of the system itself. [15]

Purchasing a commercially available software package typically gives the purchaser a license to use the software. (A contract also may be made with a software house for the development of a package that becomes the exclusive property of the buyer. This is less common and occurs most frequently when unique requirements, frequently engineering or research oriented programs, exist; this is not the type of purchased package discussed here.) The license may allow the purchaser to modify the program and use it in more than one location. These aspects, as well as others discussed later, of any prospective purchased package must be understood and documented. The cost of packages is substantial, typically running anywhere from $10,000 to $200,000. [16] Thus, we treat software evaluation in detail.

**Software Evaluation.** A description of the recommended steps in the software evaluation process follows. The first two steps, forming the project team and developing the systems requirements, are necessary prerequisites and usually precede the decision to computerize. For example,

1. If one does not exist already, form a project team consisting of members from data processing, systems analysis and design, and the system users. The latter usually include representatives from production planning and inventory management, and may include representatives from manufacturing (the shop), purchasing, engineering, and distribution. Too large a committee will hinder its progress, but users with a substantial stake in the project need to be involved. Frequently they can be added as their area enters into consideration. George Hoyt has reported how Sundstrand utilized a user department review board for developing the system specifications and a working committee of key department managers to review the systems specifications and system interfaces. [17]
2. Develop a narrative description of the objectives, requirements, and functions of the proposed system. Develop flow charts of the subsystems and a listing of the required inputs, procedures, and resulting reports. This information is required for developing the technical data processing features, such as audit trails, input/output (I/O) controls, and file maintenance reports. The cost benefit analysis (see Step 3) provides one basis for assigning priorities to the different requirements. At the preliminary stage the list of all possible requirements is usually comprehensive with priorities classified on a basis of (1) absolutely necessary, (2) highly desirable, and (3) useful but of limited value.
3. Perform a preliminary cost benefit analysis. Estimate projected savings from benefits such as reduced raw materials, work-in-process (WIP), and finished goods; improved delivery performance (customer service); improved flow of work through the plant, reduced lead time, and equipment and/or personnel utilization; and improved vendor performance including better deliveries and lower purchase item costs. Robert H. Murphy, Jr., suggests that a cost benefit analysis by activity be performed. He also notes that, similar to most capital improvement projects, costs are incurred months and years prior to the realization of savings and a discounted cash flow analysis is the appropriate approach. [18]

   The costs include system development and package evaluation manhours, travel to visit prospective software suppliers and present users of that software, the software package (usually 30 to 50 percent of the cost), computer hardware in some cases, the running of tests, pilot operations, and education and training. Other costs may result from changes in company practices; fencing, for example, may be required for the stockroom.

4. Review the information describing the features of available packages, hardware requirements, and the number of successful users. Criteria applied at this first pass typically include the necessary functional requirements and the data processing capability requirements, such as hardware compatibility and on-line inquiry features. Then verify that the package is operating successfully in a similar environment with comparable volume. This review usually will eliminate at least 50 percent of the candidates.
5. A detailed examination follows. This includes activities, such as reviewing the vendor's documentation of the system and programming code, attending vendor seminars at which their technical representatives make the presentations and are available for specific questions, visiting present users and questioning personnel who use the package, and obtaining a third party's (consultant's) evaluation. If not determined earlier, ascertain the availability and quality of a maintenance contract, the availability and cost of support programs including education and the flexibility of the program in interfacing with other functions, such as marketing, and in expanding as other features are added.
6. A rough quantitative evaluation is possible, then, by using the traditional weighted criteria approach; for example,
   a. List the criteria.
   b. Assign weighting coefficients, usually from zero to ten, to each criterion.
   c. Rate each vendor on each criterion and multiply the rating received by the weight assigned to the criterion.
   d. Sum the products (weighted ratings) for each candidate's package as illustrated in Figure 14-8. This process usually will eliminate all but two or three candidates.

**FIGURE 14-8**
**WEIGHTED CRITERIA PRELIMINARY EVALUATION OF PACKAGES**

| | | Package | | | |
|---|---|---|---|---|---|
| Criteria[1] | Weight | A | B | C | D |
| Costs | 10 | 4/40 | 5/50 | 8/80 | 6/60 |
| Support | 10 | 6/60 | 6/60 | 4/40 | 4/40 |
| Education and Training | 10 | 7/70 | 7/70 | 5/50 | 4/40 |
| Flexibility | 6 | 8/48 | 6/36 | 9/54 | 5/30 |
| Documentation | 7 | 7/49 | 8/56 | 2/14 | 6/42 |
| Evaluations | 5 | 8/40 | 9/45 | 1/5 | 5/25 |
| Conversion Problems | 4 | 8/32 | 7/28 | 2/8 | 9/36 |
| Modifications Required | 6 | 3/18 | 4/24 | 6/36 | 4/24 |
| Reliability | 7 | 9/63 | 6/42 | 4/28 | 9/63 |
| System Requirements Match[2] | 10 | 8/80 | 7/70 | 9/90 | 6/60 |
| TOTAL | | 500 | 481 | 405 | 420 |

[1]These criteria and weights are examples; the criteria and weights depend on a given situation. The list normally is much larger.
[2]Another entire evaluation chart may be developed for this criterion.[15]

The results of the evaluation illustrated in Figure 14-8 recommend that Packages C and D be eliminated from the competition and a final detailed proposal be requested from Suppliers A and B.

7. Request a formal proposal detailing costs, license fees and use permitted, modifications, support and training to be provided, an implementation timetable, and itemized costs.
8. Perform a final evaluation of the remaining candidates and include the implementation time requirements as one of the evaluation criterion.
9. Prepare an evaluation report with recommendations for management approval. Milton Cook recommends a table of contents similar to the following:

Executive summary
Present system capabilities
and deficiencies
Proposed system capabilities
Alternatives
Recommendation
Financial analysis
Implementation plan
Questions and answers
Appropriation request [15]

## Systems Implementation

Implementation involves more than conversion. Adequate documentation is a prerequisite; training and education are key elements; different types of testing are required; and equipment, procedures, inputs, files, output and performance measures all may change.

The need for documentation exists from the inception of the project, the development of functional requirements. Completely developing user and operations documentations prior to training and implementation is essential to adequate training and a reasonable expectation of success.

**Education.** The transition from one method of operation to another requires education and training of people in many different positions. This is especially true when a company is switching from a primarily informal system to a formal one. Top management, managers, staff personnel in production planning and materials management, and shop floor personnel—all require training. Education and training cover the *why* in addition to the *how*. Production planning and inventory management techniques may change; all involved personnel need to understand the objectives of these techniques and how they work.

Education may begin with top management; middle management personnel in related areas such as marketing, purchasing, engineering, and manufacturing; and key PIM personnel. Education of these individuals stresses the objectives, the rationale and approach of revised decision techniques, the benefits, costs, and the specific cooperation that is required from each area. The necessity of marketing's participation in the integration of the MPS and the distribution plan is an example of that last mentioned requirement—specific cooperation required from each area. A clear understanding of the role of the master scheduler and his interface with marketing, manufacturing, and distribution is crucial. Approval of a planned system calling for this integration through the master scheduler might be the time to select marketing, manufacturing, and distribution representatives to work with him.

Inventory planners-buyers, production planners, storeroom, receiving, purchasing personnel, shop supervisors, and shop floor control personnel (dispatchers) also must be trained. They do not need to know about the details of computer programs, file structures, or special formulas in most cases. The collection of data, data input, and information output, format and timing, are important to them. The education and training of these individuals, which encourages their critical evaluation of the planned system, has two benefits. First, it provides an opportunity for explaining why their criticisms are invalid or, if they are valid, it enables the system designers to revise the system prior to implementation. The daily users frequently spot detailed operating problems that systems design personnel and PIM management have overlooked. Second, and equally important, they appreciate the recognition of their competence and are more likely to be supportive of the system when it is implemented. The best of systems can fail in a nonsupportive user environment. George S. Hoyt discusses some very practical applications to training based on his experiences at Sundstrand. He points out the value of training that takes place after implementation, including returning errors to the originator for correction. [17] Education is expensive; it may involve preparing films, booklets, and instructions as well as many personnel hours spent in training sessions. Lack of adequate education and training is frequently more expensive than training, however. Knowledgeable, trained, and committed people are the key to successful implementation. User commitment means the assuming of responsibility for proper functioning of the system. Approval of the system by a written sign-off by all user departments is a good idea. The difference between involvement and commitment is illustrated well by the analogy of a ham-and-eggs breakfast in which the chicken is involved, but the pig is committed.

**Testing.** The management system, the computerized information system, programs, as well as I/O devices require testing. Testing of the management system occurs long before processing. The rationale of the new methods is reviewed; programs are run using either historical data, fabricated data representing all possible permutations of input data and processing runs; or live data are used to verify the functional results of the programs and systems. Systems modules, frequently developed in the required technological sequence, are tested to verify that they interface properly. Output from the BOM, for example, must be usable for the MRP module.

Data may be entered via an on-line terminal or via a recording form in the plant, a warehouse, or a field service and sales office. The method of input should minimize the possibility of error, minimize complexity, and recognize environmental factors such as conditions in the shop and the data available. Output needs to include not only the proper information, but it also should be clear and understandable, highlighting the critical items. Part of testing is to verify that these I/O objectives are achieved.

**Installation.** New systems may require changes in data processing equipment, functional systems, forms, data recorded, information provided, and, perhaps most importantly, the organization structure and the way the company does business. Thus, orientation, training, and testing are essential. Final responsibility for successful implementation belongs to the users; they are the crucial factor in a system's operation and must live with its results daily.

System installations (conversions) can take place in a number of ways, including:

1. Modular
2. Pilot
3. Parallel
4. Direct cut-over (cold turkey)

There are advantages and disadvantages to each of these methods with actual installations frequently combining two or more of them.

**Modular Approach.** This common approach consists of installing each functional module in the required technological sequence. The BOM Processor, for example, might be installed first; its installation then might be followed by the installation of an MPS, MRP, or inventory status module. The sequence in a given situation depends on the adequacy of existing MPS and inventory reporting systems. The modular approach allows data processing, systems, and user personnel to focus their efforts on the successful operation of one module at a time; it spreads the task over a longer period and usually requires fewer personnel. Since many functions depend on input data from other modules, this approach substantially reduces the probability of downstream modules malfunctioning because of faulty input or other failures of upstream modules.

**Pilot Approach.** A system or more frequently a system module is run using a representative set of the items which will be processed by the system when it is installed fully. An MRP module, for example, may be installed for a product or product line to determine if any bugs exist or if substantial improvements are required in the input, process, or output. The pilot product is representative in terms of levels in the BOM and other system processing characteristics of the products to be added later. Frequently the pilot model is run in parallel with the existing system. If, for example, a reasonably good inventory status reporting system exists, the new system may be run for selected representative items with the results of the new and the old systems compared. The cause of any differences, then, are analyzed. The pilot approach combines final testing and installation.

This approach can be used in both a micro and macro sense. The preceding describes the micro approach. In a multiplant or warehouse environment a complete system may be installed first in one plant or warehouse; and, after a satisfactory operation is achieved, it is installed in the remaining plants. This enables data processing, systems, and user personnel to work with one facility at a time during the installation in overcoming whatever problems may be unique to that facility.

**Parallel Approach.** Both the old system and the new are run simultaneously until the new system is operating successfully. This can be an expensive approach when different inputs and substantial manhours and computer time are required for both systems. It can lead to sloppiness in using the new system, a lack of commitment to the new system, and a continued dependence on the old system. It is not feasible when the new system uses a different management system—for example, when an MRP system replaces an order point system for component parts. It is normally most appropriate when used in conjunction with the pilot approach as described previously.

**Direct Cut-Over.** Discontinuing one system simultaneously with the installation of the new system is the direct cut-over (cold turkey) approach. This approach usually makes sense only when the existing system provides information of little value or after a pilot-parallel approach has demonstrated the effectiveness of the new system. It can stimulate commitment to the new system in all phases of design, testing, and implementation because it is a swim-or-sink situation. The disadvantages, however, are substantial. All problems may not be anticipated; the new system can fail, even temporarily; and manufacturing planning and control activities can be in disarray until the necessary changes are made. Building confidence in a system is difficult after such a debacle.

**Selecting an Installation Method.** The method of installing a new or revised information system can affect the system's performance substantially. Different methods are appropriate in different situations; a combination of methods frequently is proper. The following factors should influence the selection decision:

1. The adequacy of the present system
2. The functional similarities of the new and old system
   a. Decision techniques (e.g., MRP versus order point)
   b. Input requirements
   c. Output requirements

3. The availability of data processing, systems, and user representatives to aid in the transition
4. The magnitude of the change
   a. The number of items affected
   b. The number of work centers, warehouses, and personnel entering data
   c. The number of plants, warehouses, and offices affected
5. The attitude (receptiveness) of users to the new system

If, for example, the present system is totally inadequate, there is little justification for a parallel installation. If, however, the present system is relatively effective (but inefficient) and the new system is complex, a parallel—perhaps a pilot-parallel—approach may be best. Modular installations have achieved good results in multifacility (plants and warehouses) situations and in situations with limited installation support.

## Monitoring System Performance

Once a system is installed successfully, a new task arises; i.e., monitoring the system to assure that it is being used properly and is achieving the desired results. Even under the best conditions there is a tendency for the enthusiasm and attention to the necessary detail to wane once a system has been installed. Inventory withdrawals and receipts, scrap, changes in the BOM, and revised manufacturing processes may not be recorded properly. Cycle counting normally will catch some of these deficiencies in the system's integrity (data accuracy). A periodic check on the incorporation of other changes in other critical data such as lead times, engineering changes, and manufacturing processes will catch others. In addition, some users may make unilateral decisions to improve the system by changing the input data or the process at a local site. There is a need to verify that actual practice conforms to the documented, prescribed method. If it does not, determine why. Perhaps a bootlegged change is justified and should be formalized throughout the system.

Monitoring system performance involves not only checking that users and data processing personnel are following the proper procedures but also determining that the system is achieving management objectives. Has inventory, for example, been reduced to the amount expected? Has manufacturing lead time decreased? Has customer service improved? New systems do not achieve their objectives in a week or two; it usually takes six months or longer depending on the company's production, distribution, and sales cycle. Harvey N. Rose recommends an in-depth operational audit of the PIM systems at least every two years. [19]

The information system, MRP II (as defined in the *APICS Dictionary*), is itself a model of the physical items, processes, and flows in the factory. That is, the inventory records model the physical inventory; the BOM file models the production process; the updates to the inventory file model the physical receipt of material and the removal of items from inventory. A diagram of the relationship of the manufacturing information system modules closely parallels the diagram representing the physical flow of material through the plant. Since a model (the information system) is an approximation of reality, some of the problems in managing a firm arise because people forget this and behave as though the data and reality were the same. Since they are not, we must occasionally realign them through such techniques as a physical inventory, a periodic review of actual production processes, and/or studies of actual capacities.

# CURRENT DEVELOPMENTS

Computers have been a major factor in altering production management policies and practices during the last two decades. Computer related developments will continue to be a major cause of change in PIM. Two such developments already evident are microcomputers and the enhanced aid of computers in design and manufacturing. Ernest Pennente and Ted Levy reported that MRP is now possible on microcomputers due to the advent of 16-bit technology and high-capacity Winchester hard disks. Hardware in the $25,000 range and systems and MRP software estimated at less than $20,000 provide the small manufacturer ($1 million to $10 million annual sales) with data processing capability at an affordable price. [20] If history is any guide, these costs will decline in the next decade.

Computers are being used extensively in engineering design and manufacturing. Computer Aided Design (CAD) not only is used in design engineering analysis and product design, but also in calculating material layout and in specifying cutter location and tool paths for machining. Computer Aided Manufacturing International, a nonprofit association of computer hardware and software developers, has developed a software system called CAM-I Automated Process Planning (CAPP). CAPP generates standard routings on the basis of part characteristics determined according to a standard classification table. The process then is modified by the process engineer to match the requirements of a specific part. [21]

Computer Aided Manufacturing (CAM) usually refers to a broad range of techniques for discrete parts production including paper tape, numerically controlled (NC) machine tools; dedicated computer, numerically controlled machine tools (CNC); direct numerical control (DNC) of more than one machine by a single computer; and computer controlled robots. Computer aided inspection and automatic (computerized) storage and retrieval systems also exist. Computers also are used to control continuous manufacturing processes.

While some companies are beginning to explore the potential of CAD and CAM, others have a decade or more of experience. These experiences have been diverse, dealing with a variety of problems in design and manufacturing. Integration of different computerized systems has, at best, been partial in any organization. The challenge is to combine CAD, CAPP, CAM, computer aided inspection, production facility design, and PIM in an intergrated computer aided manufacturing system. [22]

Group Technology (GT) and cellular manufacturing are two approaches that partially integrate design and manufacturing systems. GT involves identifying items with either similar design or similar manufacturing process characteristics and grouping them into families of like items. Coding and classification schemes are used to record item attributes such as function, material, shape (internal and external dimensional relationships; e.g., length/diameter), surface finish, tolerances, weight, demand rate, function, processing operations, and their sequence in a computerized data base.

Analysis of the designs of items in the same group frequently leads to the discovery of some items with identical designs and others with very similar designs. Redundant designs can be eliminated and similar designs combined on a single drawing. Savings result in engineering and manufacturing. Analysis of similar designs and similar manufacturing processes can lead to the development of standardized processes and setups with minor modifications for each item. The development of such processes combined with the development of manufacturing cells usually generates larger cost reductions than parts coding alone.

*Cellular manufacturing*—frequently considered an integral part of group technology—is the organization of a small group of workers and machines in a repetitive production flow layout to manufacture a group of similar items. It achieves economies due to the modified equipment dedicated to the group, special tooling, reduced setup and run time, reduced material handling, shorter throughput time, and reduced WIP. Colin New, for example, reported a 70 percent average reduction in throughput time. [23] Figure 14-9 illustrates the differences between cellular manufacturing and job shop manufacturing flow patterns.

CAM and cellular manufacturing both can result in smaller lot sizes and, thus, reduced cycle stock. The production of a group of items on dedicated equipment presents problems in scheduling order releases and calculating lot sizes; multilevel requirements exacerbate these problems. Colin New reported on the success of combining MRP, GT, and Unicycle Period Batch Control (UPBC) to overcome these problems. Each cycle UPBC orders all components produced by a cell with a carefully planned loading sequence. MRP determines genuine requirements; GT achieves rapid throughput; and UPBC provides simple and reliable order sequencing, load planning, and order control. [23]

Clearly, the integration of CAD, CAPP, CAM, GT, MRP, and computer aided inspection is a major task facing manufacturing management. Increased computer capacity per dollar and continual improvements in software present manufacturing management with the task of developing manufacturing policies and strategies that recognize these developments.

**FIGURE 14-9**
**SCHEMATIC OF FUNCTIONAL LAYOUT AND GROUP TECHNOLOGY LAYOUT (PARTS FLOW)**

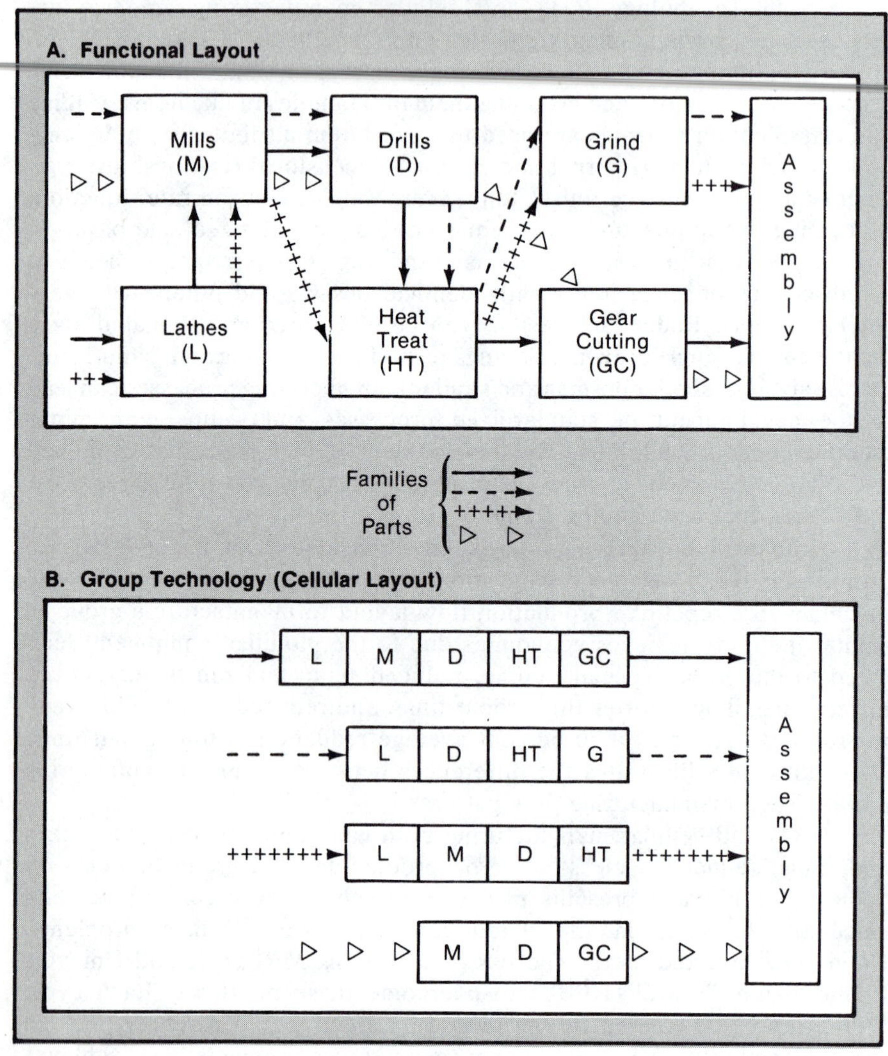


# PROBLEMS

1. Prepare a list of the key PIM system functions for the following types of firms. If you believe that critical information is lacking, make assumptions as consistent as possible with available information.

a. A small ($4,000,000 sales annually) high precision gear manufacturing company has a gear blanking department and five different gear cutting departments, each for a special type gear. Machinists are nonunion, highly paid, and each can operate most equipment. The company builds to order. The rank ordered priority of objectives is quality, delivery, and price. There are three supervisors who also serve as dispatchers, an operations manager who is the master scheduler, and the company president who is director of manufacturing, engineering, and marketing.

b. A medium-sized specialized truck body manufacturer.
   (1) Manufactures 20%—in dollars—of its final product, components, and subassemblies to stock.
   (2) Builds most final assemblies of major items to order. The competitive strength of the company lies in its ability to produce high quality final products with engineering modifications to the customer's specification.
   (3) Has approximately 400 shop employees, 15 departments, and 10 distributors where final mounting of truck bodies on chassis sometimes is performed.
   (4) Sells annually 25% to 50% of its product to the export market.
   (5) Experiences problems with delayed delivery from chassis manufacturer when truck bodies are mounted on the chassis at the plant.
   (6) Has wandering bottlenecks in the plant and in engineering as the mix of orders and order processing shifts.

c. A small process industry type company produces one item, a gel type soap for industrial use. It packs the soap in three different size containers and sells to one private label distributor, directly to local plants through its own three-agent sales force, and directly to tool and supply peddlers who contact gas stations and small plants in the area.

d. A medium-sized firm ($50,000,000 annual sales) specialty machine tool and replacement tooling manufacturer. The company produces to stock with emphasis on delivery and quality. Of all orders, 95% are shipped within 24 hours. It has two or three competitors, but estimates that it has 60 to 70% of the market. It sells its products from central warehouses, one on the West Coast, and one in Canada. It has a no-layoff policy; subcontracts some work in high demand years; has a labor agreement allowing personnel to be moved from department to department. Many components are manufactured as joint orders.

**2.** For each of the firms in Problem 1 complete the following:

a. List the logical files required.
b. Decide for what information, you recommend
   (1) An alert or action reporting capability
   (2) An inquiry capability
   (3) A search capability

**3.** Describe the difference between the concept of *real time* when referring to computer hardware and to information systems.

**4.** Develop a list of the modules, a flowchart for each, and a description of the input, processing steps, files, and outputs in an inventory management system for each company described in Problem 1.

**5.** What conditions require PIM personnel to have access to operations documentation?

6. A local truck equipment distributor and service center is not satisfied with its parts inventory management system. The local office of a national service bureau has proposed that the company use its services which include a package supposedly used successfully by truck equipment dealers in other cities. What are your recommendations? What steps should be taken to evaluate the proposal?
7. Which, if any, of the companies described in Problem 1 might economically use a service bureau? Justify your answers.
8. The company described in Problem 1b. is contemplating using a commercially available PIM package. Recommend a comprehensive evaluation program which it could follow.
9. The Ajax Manufacturing Company produces to stock and sells from a central warehouse and five regional distribution centers. Each of the distribution centers has three to six company owned warehouses which it serves. The company is planning to switch from its present pull system of distribution, which is based on weekly batched reports of sales and orders, to a push allocation type distribution system.
   a. Discuss the advantages and disadvantages of having minicomputers at the regional centers and at each warehouse.
   b. Develop an implementation plan including all the steps required.
   c. Indicate which type installation you would recommend and why.
10. Obtain the general PIM package specification from five firms with commercially available packages and perform a preliminary evaluation for each (or any number) of the firms in Problem 1.
11. Obtain the general PIM package specifications from five minicomputer manufacturers. Determine if any of them would be a feasible alternative for any of the companies in Problem 1.
12. Visit a local company which uses a PIM package and determine its strengths and weaknesses.
13. Which records probably are required in the item master file of the company in Problem 1d.?
14. The company described in Problem 1d. decides to use a data base system.
    a. Describe the data base down to the record level of detail.
    b. Illustrate how three different logical files might use the same items from the data base.
    c. What advantages does this company achieve from a data base? What, if any, disadvantages does it encounter?
15. The company described in Problem 1b. implements a file oriented system over a two-year period. List the steps it might follow in monitoring this system.
16. A local repetitive process manufacturing company provides original equipment parts for the automobile industry. It is interested in auditing the PIM system. Develop a plan listing the steps to be followed and measures to be applied in auditing its systems.
17. Another company, similar to that described in Problem 16, manufactures automotive parts for the replacement market only. How would a PIM systems audit for this company differ from that described in Problem 16?

# SELECTED READINGS


1. Gerald F. DeSantis, "Implementation Considerations in Systems Design," *APICS 20th Annual Conference Proceedings* (1977), pp. 210-216.
2. Robert B. Vollum, "Integrated Data Base: Solid Foundation or Deep Hole," *APICS 22d Annual Conference Proceedings* (1979), pp. 48-51.
3. James M. Venglarik, "Distributed Processing by Means of Minicomputer Networks," *APICS 22d Annual Conference Proceedings* (1979), pp. 58-60.
4. Leland R. Kneppelt, "Real Time, On-Line Distributed in the Manufacturing Systems Environment," *APICS 23d Annual Conference Proceedings* (1980), pp. 58-60.
5. Elwood S. Buffa and Jeffrey G. Miller, *Production-Inventory Systems: Planning and Control*, 3d ed. (Homewood, Illinois: Richard D. Irwin, Inc., 1979), pp. 700-703.
6. Sam G. Taylor, "Are Process Industries Different?" *APICS 23d Annual Conference Proceedings* (1980), pp. 94-98.
7. R. Leonard Allen, "The Applicability of Standard Manufacturing Software to Primary Metals Processing," *APICS 23d Annual Conference Proceedings* (1980), pp. 85-89.
8. R. T. Rowan and J. A. Wellendorf, "Implementing Manufacturing Control Software Package in a Process Industry," *APICS 23d Annual Conference Proceedings* (1980), pp. 81-84.
9. W. Skinner, "The Focused Factory," *Harvard Business Review* (May-June, 1974), pp. 113-121.
10. Max Gray and Keith R. London, *Documentation Standards* (New York: Brandon/Systems Press, Inc., 1969), pp. 14-16.
11. Gary S. Yost, "Inventory Through Timesharing," *ICP INTERFACE Manufacturing and Engineering* (Winter, 1981), pp. 14-16.
12. Paul Pinella and Eric Cheathan, "In-House Inventory Control," *ICP INTERFACE Manufacturing and Engineering* (Winter, 1981), pp. 18-21.
13. Donald W. Fogarty, "Change and the Materials Manager or Is Your System Open?" *APICS 15th Annual International Conference Proceedings* (1972), pp. 360-374.
14. Lois Paul, ed. "Benefits of Packaged Software Called Myths," *COMPUTERWORLD* (January 25, 1982).
15. Milton E. Cook, "How to Evaluate Software Packages," *APICS 24th Annual Conference Proceedings* (1981), pp. 126-130.
16. Richard Bourke, "Surveying the Software," *Datamation* (October, 1980), pp. 101-107.
17. George S. Hoyt, "Successes and Failure in MRP User Involvement," *APICS 20th Annual International Conference Proceedings* (1977), pp. 204-209.
18. Robert H. Murphy, Jr., "Assuring Cost-Effective Manufacturing Systems," *APICS 23d Annual Conference Proceedings* (1980), pp. 70-73.
19. Harvey N. Rose, "Auditing of P & IC Systems: The Necessary Ingredient," *APICS 21st Annual Conference Proceedings* (1978), pp. 436-454.
20. Ernest Pennente and Ted Levy, "MRP on Microcomputers," *Production and Inventory Management Review* (May, 1982), pp. 20-25.
21. Jan Johnson, "Pushing the State of the Art," *Datamation* (February, 1982), pp. 112-114.

**22.** John J. Len, "CAD/CAM—Productivity Tools for MRP Record Accuracy," *APICS 24th Annual International Conference Proceedings* (1981), pp. 374-377.

**23.** Colin New, "MRP & GT, A New Strategy for Component Production," *Production and Inventory Management*, 3d Quarter (1977), pp. 50-62.

**24.** Steven F. Bolander, Richard C. Heard, Samuel M. Seward, and Sam G. Taylor, *Manufacturing Planning and Control in Process Industries* (Washington, D.C.: American Production and Inventory Control Society, 1981), pp. 1-20.

**25.** Richard W. Bourke, "Selecting Software Smartly: The Early Steps," *Production and Inventory Management Review and APICS News* (May, 1981), pp. 13-16.

**26.** Milton E. Cook, "Developing a Successful P & IC Training Program," *APICS 23d Annual Conference Proceedings* (1980), pp. 6-8.

**27.** Gary W. Dickson, James A. Senn, and Normal L. Chervany, "Research in Management Information Systems, the Minnesota Experiments," *Management Science* (May, 1977).

**28.** Mikell P. Groover, *Automation, Production Systems, and Computer Aided Manufacturing* (Englewood Cliffs, New Jersey: Prentice-Hall, Inc., 1980).

**29.** Thomas G. Gunn, *Computer Applications in Manufacturing* (New York: Industrial Press, Inc., 1981).

**30.** Robert W. Hall, "Repetitive Manufacturing," *Production and Inventory Management*, 2d Quarter (1982), pp. 78-86.

**31.** George S. Hoyt, "The Art of Buying Software," *APICS 18th Annual Conference Proceedings* (1975), pp. 316-320.

**32.** Alvin Toffler, *Future Shock* (New York: Bantam Books, Inc., 1971), pp. 19-35.

# —15—

# MANAGING PIM

This chapter concerns the overall management of production and inventory planning and control activities, functions, and systems. Overall production and inventory management (PIM) begins with establishing a set of objectives which support the organizational goals; attaining these objectives requires the following basic management activities:

1. Planning all PIM activities
2. Developing an organizational structure consistent with the manufacturing process and corporate goals
3. Staffing the PIM organization
4. Executing the plan
5. Establishing policies and procedures for controlling PIM activities
6. Being cognizant of PIM technological developments and determining their relevancy to the firms objectives and situation
7. Coordinating PIM activities with those of marketing, manufacturing management, industrial engineering, and manufacturing engineering

This chapter examines the application of these basic management activities to PIM; and, since implementing innovation and change is a prevalent and substantial challenge, the chapter discusses the management of change.

## PERFORMANCE OBJECTIVES AND MEASURES

Management needs to establish performance objectives in measurable (quantitative) terms.[1] Manufacturing and marketing management establish customer service objectives (delivery lead time and desired achievement levels) to meet or surpass competition. PIM determines the aggregate inventory investment and production output required to support these objectives. PIM also establishes subsidiary objectives which are consistent with and support the general management goals. A possible set of PIM objectives for a company manufacturing to stock is listed in Table 15-1.[2] These objec-

[1] Possible measures have been discussed throughout the text and especially in Chapter 6.

[2] These objectives exist at a company with which one of the authors is familiar.

**TABLE 15-1**
**EXAMPLES OF PIM OBJECTIVES**

| **Customer Service** |
|---|
| Ship 95 percent of orders within 48 hours of receipt. |
| Ship 80 percent of back orders within 10 days. |
| Ship 100 percent of back orders within 4 weeks. |
| **Inventory Investment** |
| Aggregate inventory investment should be less than $15,000,000. |
| The historical inventory turnover rate should be equal to or greater than 4.0. |
| The aggregate inventory investment should be less than the projected cost of goods sold for the next three months. |
| **Work Force Personnel and Operating Efficiency** |
| There should be a policy of no layoffs. |
| Undertime should be less than 10 percent. |
| Overtime costs should not exceed $200,000 per quarter. |
| Lot sizes of 90 percent of all production runs should be within 10 percent of the economic order quantity. |

tives are based on corporate marketing, (product positioning and customer service); labor relations (retaining a highly skilled, well-compensated labor force with a productivity oriented attitude buttressed by profit sharing); and product cost objectives. They lead to subsidiary objectives which support their achievement. Some typical subsidiary objectives are:

1. A 100 percent accuracy on 90 percent of finished goods items in cycle counting (There is no annual physical inventory.)
2. A 100 percent accuracy and completeness in the bill of materials (BOM)
3. A 90 percent production of orders within the planned lead time
4. A 100 percent fulfillment of the master production schedule (MPS) in 10 out of every 13 weeks in the quarter
5. Target shipping dollar volume

Many other subsidiary objectives can be added to this list. Such additions might concern purchase commitments, the value of receipts, downtime due to material or tool shortages, and raw material and work-in-process (WIP) investment. The point is that establishing realistic objectives provides employees a target at which to aim and a measure of their performance. A set of overall PIM objectives and subsidiary objectives requires internal consistency, but objectives will differ depending on the nature of the organization. A company manufacturing to order, for example, will have objectives somewhat different from those contained in Table 15-1.

Sales volume, product lines, and manufacturing processes change; PIM objectives need to be reviewed periodically as suggested by Robert L. Janson. [1] Ernest Huge recommends that objectives be established for individuals such as planners with performance review and that merit raises be based on the results they achieve. He points out that this must be done with care, and the causes of deficient performances need to be attributed either to factors which the individual controls or to ones he does not control. His articles describe how designated objectives for one activity affect the achievement of the objectives of the next activity in the PIM loop. [2, 3]

PIM objectives include not only functional objectives such as customer service and inventory investment, but also planning, organization, staffing, training, and systems objectives the attainment of which will support the achievement of functional objectives. The implementation of a rough-cut capacity planning system, the development of a systems staff within the department, and the completion of shop floor control training sessions by all supervisors are examples.

# PLANNING

Although most firms have existing PIM organizations, personnel, policies, and procedures, developing ideal plans without regard to present constraints can provide a fresh look at a given situation. It frequently provides some surprises as to what can be achieved. Plans concern the design of the PIM organization, staffing, and the management system. (These plans are in addition to the operating plans concerning production and inventory.)

PIM needs to develop master plans of the organization structure, staffing, and management system it intends to have in order to achieve its performance objectives. The organization plan should define the departments, subgroups, and their functions; it needs to reveal the relationship of these units to other functions such as marketing, engineering, and the shop.

Staffing plans include a specification of the capabilities required to manage and carry out the various activities. A project manager, for example, with successful material requirements planning (MRP) system implementation experience may be required to manage the development and implementation of such a system. In some cases, more than one individual with the same capability may be required.

## The Management System Plan

This plan specifies all the information systems modules' requirements plus a description of each module's objectives, inputs, processes (design techniques), and outputs. This plan describes the data base, files, decision techniques such as forecasting methods and inventory management systems to be employed, and the reports and information included in each. The technological precedence of these modules is included, represented perhaps by a schematic. These plans constitute a blueprint of what is to be.

## Development and Implementation Plan

This is a schedule of the various steps required to achieve the desired organization, staffing, and management systems. These plans recognize the major tasks and their relationships, frequently describing them by a network model as illustrated in Figure 15-1. Such a plan clearly indicates priorities and can serve as the basis for determining required sources such as space, recruiting, training, equipment, systems, software, and the data required to accomplish the plan. Estimating the costs of these resources provides the necessary information for developing a time-phased budget for top management approval.

**FIGURE 15-1**
**SYSTEMS DEVELOPMENT PLAN**

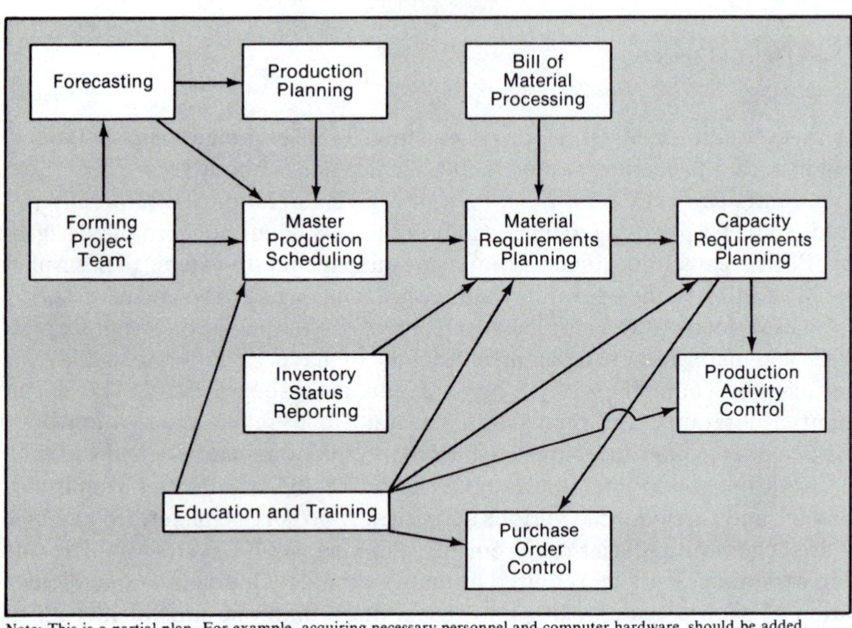


Note: This is a partial plan. For example, acquiring necessary personnel and computer hardware should be added.

Obtaining in writing top management approval of the plan and its development, including the budget, is an essential step. It greatly increases the probability that top management will understand the objectives, approaches, and requirements of the plan. As discussed in Chapter 14, management commitment is crucial because organization, staffing, and PIM systems affect most functional areas in the business; changes in operating procedures are required throughout the organization; substantial resources frequently are required to accomplish the changes; and key personnel must be transferred from daily operating decisions to detailed planning and implementation of any changes.

# ORGANIZATION

Organizing consists of grouping individuals to perform assigned tasks and establishing both the relationships among the groups and the flow of authority. Most groups (departments) have line duties which require the performance of specified tasks and they have staff duties which require providing information, advice, and support to other groups for the performance of their tasks. Basic principles of organization design include the following:

1. Form should fit function.
2. More than one PIM organization structure may work well in a given situation.
3. There must be a match between the capabilities and talents of individuals and the positions they occupy for the organization to operate at its full potential.
4. Reorganizing of itself rarely solves a problem.
5. Good morale, a team effort, realistic measurable objectives, and a good formal system can overcome a deficient organizational structure in many instances.
6. "The simpliest organization structure that will do the job is the best one." [3]

Peter Drucker states that organization design begins with the following type questions:

1. What are the truly important roles of the department? Which goal(s) is (are) dominant?
2. In which functions of PIM is excellence required to achieve these goals?
3. In which functions of PIM would inadequate performance jeopordize attainment of these goals? [4]

He asserts that " . . . the first concern must be those activities that are essential to the success of a business strategy and to the attainment of business objectives. They have to be identified, defined, organized, and centrally placed." [4]

The foregoing is an elaboration of the principle that the form of the organization should be consistent with its function. Oliver Wight recognizes this principle when he recommends that the traditional organization including a production control group and an inventory control group be replaced with one group responsible for priority and capacity planning and another group responsible for priority and capacity control. [5] Aman Motwane reports how this type organization was established at the Western Gear Corpo-

[3] Peter F. Drucker, *Management* (New York: Harper & Row, Publishers, Inc., 1974), p. 601.

[4] Ibid, p. 531.

ration. [6] Leland R. Kneppelt's recommendations concerning distributed data processing are consistent with this concept. [7]

There are many specific questions concerning PIM organization design that might be addressed. Some of these questions are:

1. What is the difference between the ideal organization structures for companies with a process manufacturing technology and those with a job shop manufacturing technology? Many similar questions concerning differences such as product positioning (making-to-stock versus making-to-order) also can be asked.
2. Under what conditions is the materials management approach appropriate?
3. What effect does multiplant manufacturing have on the organization design? What about international multiplant and/or distribution activities?
4. How should purchasing activities be integrated organizationally into planning and controlling materials? Should the roles of the planner and the buyer be combined?
5. When is the team approach appropriate?
6. Should PIM have a group of individuals exclusively devoted to system design, maintenance, and modification?
7. What is the role of the master scheduler?

# Organization Structure

The traditional organization of production and inventory planning and control activities is similar to the organization described in Figure 15-2. The inventory control department and production control departments are separate and distinct. The former works with a relatively formal system to plan and control inventories; one of its main tasks being to launch orders. The production control department is concerned primarily with getting these orders through the plant; it relies heavily on informal systems and expediting, as noted by Oliver Wight and Aman A. Motwane. [5, 6]

**FIGURE 15-2**
**TRADITIONAL PIM ORGANIZATION**

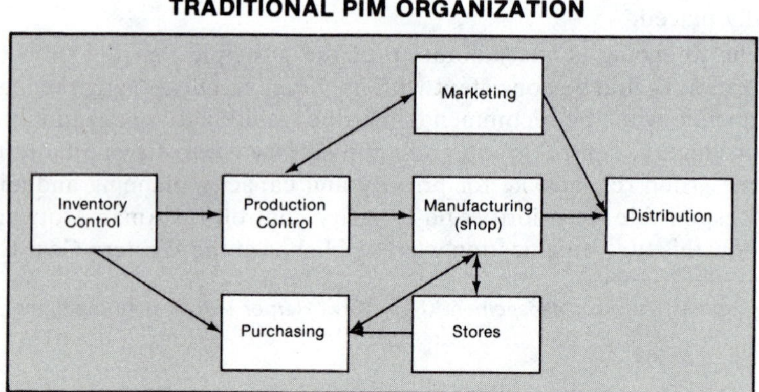

The deficiencies of the traditional organization are obvious. Inventory control and production control have inherent obstacles to control beginning with checking the feasibility of the production plan. If, for example, production control does not control the release of orders, it hardly controls production. Organizing PIM in a structure consistent with planning and controlling activities, as illustrated in Figure 15-3 and 15-4, is a more rational approach. (Many companies have overcome these deficiencies by developing systems that, in effect, reorganize production and inventory management without formally documenting the reorganization.)

The differences between job shops and flow production, either repetitive manufacturing of discrete parts or continuous processing of liquids and powders, have been discussed in the Introduction and other chapters of this text including Chapter 14. Relatively little has been written directly concerning any differences between PIM organization structures in process flow manufacturing and job shop manufacturing. Some points, however, can be made.

**FIGURE 15-3**
**FUNCTIONAL PIM ORGANIZATION ACTIVITY FLOW**

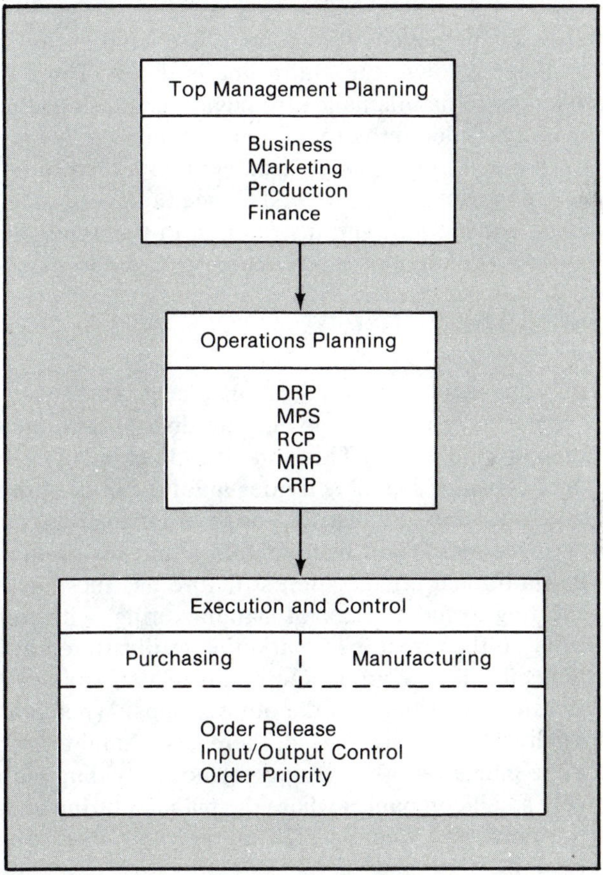

**FIGURE 15-4**
**FUNCTIONAL ORGANIZATIONAL STRUCTURE**

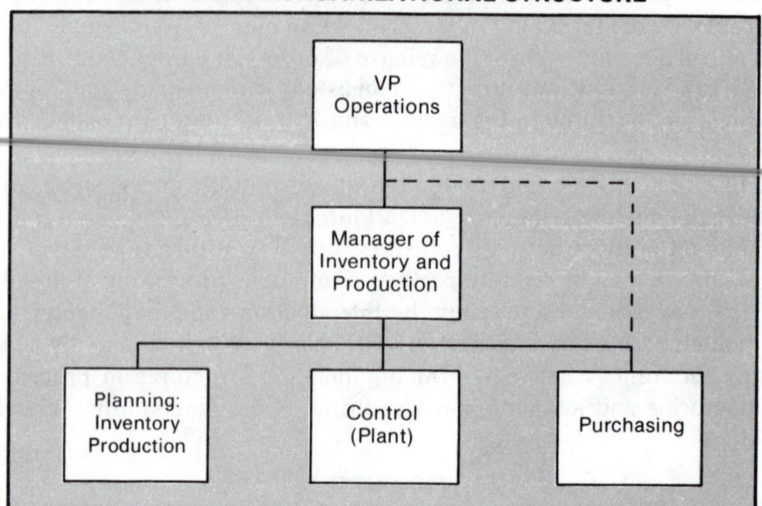


Preventative maintenance of equipment is crucial in flow manufacturing. If one machine is down, the entire line is down. Thus, planning and scheduling preventative maintainance frequently is a task of the production planning group and blended into production schedules. Flow manufacturing typically exists in a make-to-stock environment with distribution an important part in providing customer service. The need to coordinate purchasing, inventory control, production, and distribution in this type situation is apparent. The concept of materials management evolved to meet this need.

## Materials Management

A materials management organization places purchasing, inventory management, receiving, traffic, shipping, and distribution under one manager as illustrated in Figure 15-5. This organization explicitly gives one individual the task of coordinating all activities involved in providing the material required by production and distribution in order to attain customer service, inventory investment, and manufacturing and distribution efficiency objectives. The traditional organization structure has these activities along with others reporting to the director of manufacturing, with traffic and distribution reporting to the director of marketing as illustrated in Figure 15-6. This frequently results in each group attempting to attain its own goals which may not be consistent with those of the other groups. When parts shortages occur or when delivery dates are missed, there is a natural tendency for each group to place the blame on other groups for not providing the proper support. In relatively small companies where the manufacturing manager's span of control is not great and where marketing and manufacturing work well

FIGURE 15-5
A MATERIALS MANAGEMENT ORGANIZATION

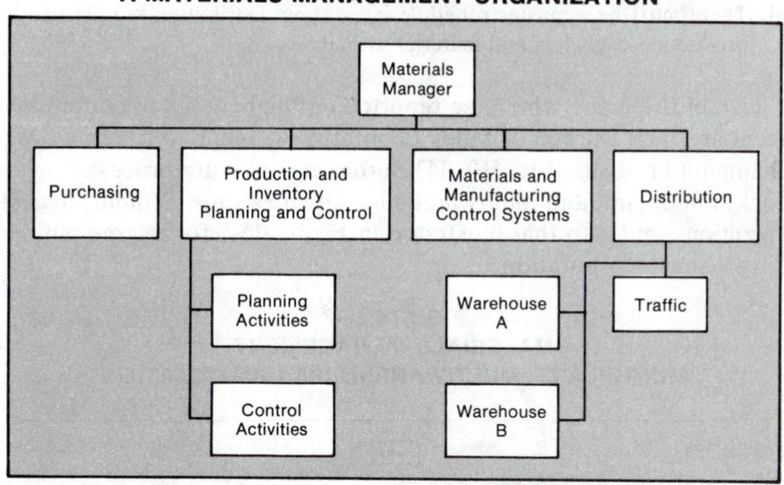


together, the difficulty of coordinating the goals and activities of the different groups managing materials can be overcome without adding another level of management usually associated with a materials management structure.

A materials management organization structure of itself will not solve any problems. Certain conditions must exist for its success as pointed out by Frank M. Zenobia, Jr., and Robert E. Fox. [8, 9] These include the following four conditions:

1. Top management must be committed to the system.
2. Users must understand the concept; accept it; be responsible for the system design; and must be trained to use the system.

FIGURE 15-6
TRADITIONAL ORGANIZATION OF MATERIALS MANAGEMENT ACTIVITIES

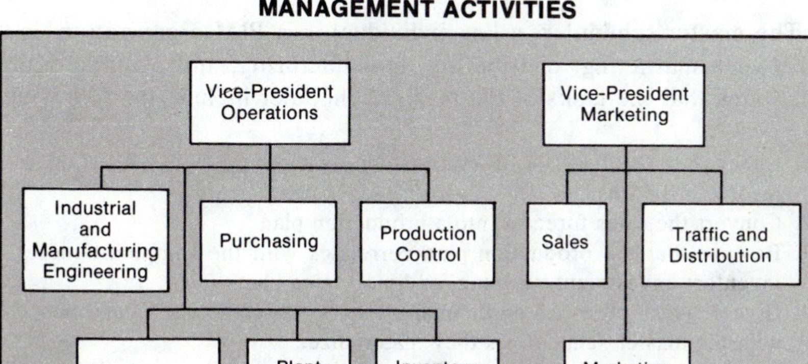

3. A formal materials management information system with data base integrity must exist.
4. There must be a master schedule integrating distribution requirements, production capacity, and material availability.

Two of the many who have reported on the benefits of materials management are Jack Durben of Miles Laboratories, Inc. and Albert L. Wolpin of Champion Products, Inc. [10, 11] Both companies are process flow, build to stock, multiplant, and multiwarehouse organizations. Wolpin suggests an organization similar to that illustrated in Figure 15-7 for a large multiplant, multiwarehouse corporation.[5]

**FIGURE 15-7**
**MATERIALS MANAGEMENT**
**MULTIPLANT, MULTIWAREHOUSE ORGANIZATION**

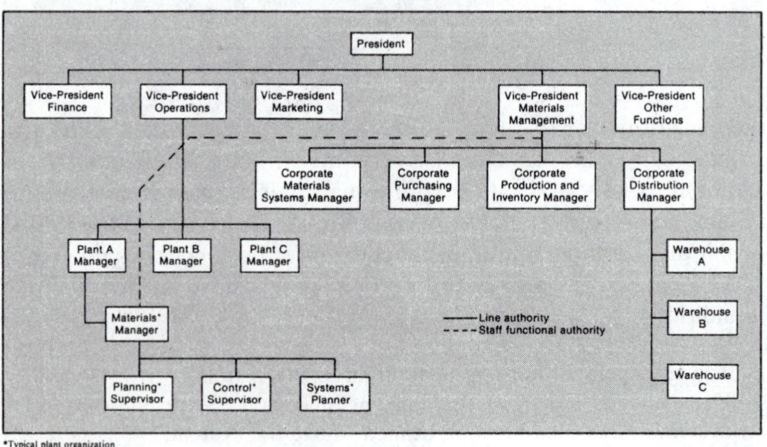


*Typical plant organization

# The Master Scheduler

The master scheduler, a key individual in a PIM organization, is the link between marketing, distribution, manufacturing, and planning. Oliver Wight states that the tasks of the master scheduler include the following:

1. Check the sales forecast for reasonableness and work with marketing to resolve questions.
2. Convert the sales forecast into a production plan.
3. Be sure that the production plan correlates with the shipping budget, inventory investment planning, and marketing plans.
4. Give delivery promises on incoming orders; match actual requirements with the master schedule as they materialize.

---

[5]See also Kenneth W. Tunnell and Gutram V. Stier's presentation for a treatment of organizing production and inventory control in a multinational company. [12]

5. Evaluate the impact of "top-down" inputs, such as a request for the introduction of a new product in much less than the normal delivery time.
6. Evaluate the impact of "bottom-up" inputs, such as anticipated delay reports from the shop or purchasing indicating that particular components will not be available as scheduled, or that planned production rates are not being attained.
7. Revise the master schedule when necessary for lack of material or capacity.
8. Call basic conflicts which the master schedule brings into focus to the attention of other members of management who need to face up to the problems in advance. [13]

Whether or not a firm has someone formally designated as the master scheduler, the tasks are essential. Combining them under the jurisdiction of one individual improves the likelihood that they will be coordinated and managed properly. Most importantly, it provides a focal point for the required coordination of marketing, manufacturing, distribution, and planning as well as a place to look when things are not going well. A review of the *APICS Conference Proceedings* of the last few years reveals that the position of master scheduler has been established in many different types of firms with beneficial results.

## The Manufacturing Control Systems Group

The design and implementation of a PIM information system is a major effort usually consuming months. System evaluation, maintenance, and refinement are also substantial tasks. Responsibility for system maintenance and refinement should be the user's, the same as design and development are. Managing the system and planning (or controlling) production and inventory are both full-time jobs in most organizations. Attempting to do both simultaneously will likely lead to neither task being performed well.

A major system development and implementation project usually requires the formation of a project team with full-time participation and usually management by PIM personnel. This is a natural launching point for a manufacturing control (materials management) systems group. In small organizations this may require only one or two individuals. In a large company the group may include systems designers and programmers. Corporate systems and data processing provide the policies and general procedures under which this group operates. Its tasks include those described as development, implementation, and training tasks in Chapter 14. Users are the primary source of systems improvements and refinements since they work with the system daily and, thus, are most familiar with its strengths and weaknesses.

Cash Powell, Jr., recommends that the PIM systems group have the task of evaluating requested refinements, controlling data, and training new personnel. [14] With the increasing cost-effectiveness of minicomputers and continued development in PIM concepts and techniques, a PIM systems group will be kept busy.

## Relationship with Purchasing

Planning and controlling supplier shipments is critical in planning and controlling fabrication, assembly, and distribution activities. When buyers are separate and distinct from planners (the traditional separation of purchase part inventory planners and inventory buyers) communication between the planner and the buyer is crucial. Time-phased requirements planning, part of MRP, can give the buyer valid priorities concerning purchased items. Combining the roles of the purchased items planner and buyer into a single planner-buyer position makes sense whenever a reliable formal priority planning system exists. Oliver Wight reports that this approach has worked well in many companies with the planner-buyer reporting to production inventory planning in some and to purchasing in others. [15] Cash Powell, Jr., reports that: "A planner-buyer releases MRP planning sheets for purchased material without a requisition from production control people and expedites delivery." [16] Whether this can happen gracefully only under a materials management organization, as Powell contends, is debatable. Nonmaterials management organizations where it is working well undoubtedly can be found. Many of the concepts, objectives, and management systems typical of a materials management organization likely will be found in those companies, but without an explicit formal materials management organization structure.

## Service Parts and New Products

Service parts sales contribute substantially to the profit and return on investment (ROI) of many firms. They typically are more profitable than finished goods sales. This is not surprising; availability and delivery of service parts is more important to the typical customer than the item's price. Service parts frequently are required for repair and maintenance of major equipment items; an hour or two of equipment downtime may be more costly than the service part. Thus, healthy prices on service parts frequently do not affect sales (sales are price inelastic over a considerable range); but availability and delivery are crucial.

Planning and controlling service parts delivery performance justifies assignment of this task to one or a group of individuals in many firms. This group needs to work closely with the master scheduler in planning for service parts and adjusting the schedule to meet unusual requirements. When service parts planning and the master scheduler do not work in concert, schedule disruption becomes common. Parts are bootlegged or removed from stores by "midnight requisitions" to meet service requirements. This usually is not discovered until the final assemblies are at the production line and parts shortages are discovered. Coordinating service parts requirements formally through the master scheduler will eliminate such costly experiences.

Products being developed, experimental models, and pilot models may be entirely revised final assemblies costing tens or hundreds of thousands of dollars or they may involve only a revised gasket design. Some firms have relatively stable product designs; other firms use an ability to develop new products and/or customized final assemblies as their competitive edge, as noted by Powell. [16] The latter situation warrants the existence of a new product manager to take care of the following:

1. Planning and control of engineering design activities (This may be done by engineering.)
2. Coordinating engineering design and the sales (product) specification (Production planning and manufacturing engineering personnel usually participate in the development of proposed cost and production schedules.)
3. Developing and releasing complete BOM's for new and/or modified products
4. Obtaining sources for new materials
5. Developing a realistic production schedule, working with engineering, marketing, and the master scheduler
6. Coordinating the implementation of engineering changes

This leads to an organization structure similar to that in Figure 15-8 for firms with a dynamic product design and substantial service parts sales.

**FIGURE 15-8**
**PIM ORGANIZATION STRUCTURE**
**DYNAMIC PRODUCT DESIGN AND**
**SUBSTANTIAL SERVICE PARTS SALES**

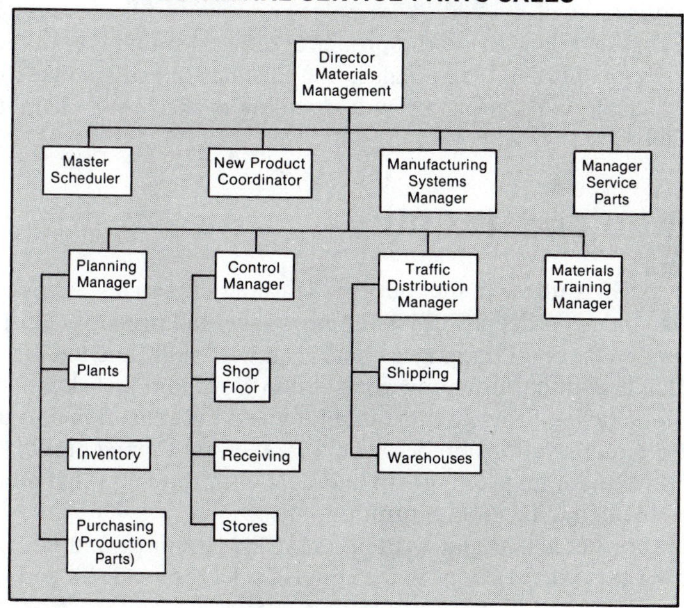

# STAFFING

Determining personnel requirements, recruiting and selecting personnel, and training the present staff and new personnel are all part of the staffing function. Few articles or papers presented recently have dealt explicitly with the task of determining the number and types of personnel required to run a PIM operation. Most companies back into a workable level of staffing through implicit trial and error. An assessment of staffing requirements is related directly to the functional requirements of the PIM information system (see Chapter 14) and the educational needs assessment described later in this chapter. These requirements reveal the knowledge and skills required by PIM personnel. The number of individuals required by a firm depends on its size, the manufacturing process, product positioning, number of plants, distribution system, and span of PIM activities in a given firm. Traditional industrial engineering techniques of job and workload analysis are useful in measuring personnel requirements.

Many of the references cited in this chapter note the shortage of available trained personnel relative to the demand. College texts and courses in production management, consequently, have changed substantially in the last five years and today are aligned more closely with the needs of industry. Master scheduling, independent and dependent demand, and MRP, for example, are part of nearly all texts and courses in production-operations management. This is due, to a large extent, to the pioneering work of Joe Orlickly and his successors on the APICS Academic Liaison Committee.

Peter Ryan's survey of companies in the Massachusetts high technology industry showed that about half the companies would hire an APICS certified college level graduate with no experience to fill openings in PIM. [17] They then would provide the proper additional training required. Raising the PIM capability of individuals in the firm has the advantage of present employees usually possessing an understanding of the firm's characteristics which affect PIM.

## Education and Training

Charles G. Andrew points out that learning objectives include knowledge, skills, and attitude. [18] Education is concerned primarily with knowledge and understanding; training is concerned with skills and understanding; and both have attitude formation goals. John Burnham's in-depth study of seven manufacturing firms documented the need for education and training. He found a direct relationship between a lack of continuing pragmatic education in PIM and a failure to grasp and deal with the major manufacturing control problems facing an organization. [19]

Much has been said and written about PIM training and education in the last few years. A review of this chapter's selected readings and the 1980 and 1981 APICS Conference Proceedings will verify this statement. These presentations and articles contain proposed basic education and training concepts, principles, and techniques as well as many experiential anecdotes. The latter, to their credit, include stories of failure as well as success. There is, fortunately, a general consensus on principles, concepts, and valuable techniques including the following:

1. Educational activities should encompass almost everyone in the firm. Changes in PIM technology change the way most firms do business. Successful implementation and continuing execution of this technology requires understanding, cooperation, and performance from a broad range of individuals.
2. Planning education and training programs requires a professional approach. This begins with an analysis of the needs of the organization.
3. Specific education and training goals should be established.
4. The results of education and training should be measured formally and explicitly.
5. Project teams headed by an overall manager or coordinator have worked well in achieving successful program designs and results.
6. Motivation for participant development and self-education is an important part of the program.
7. People are the key to successful PIM.
8. Management commitment is essential.
9. Education is expensive; but the benefits usually outweigh the costs.

## Needs Assessment

Planning requires objectives, and determination of objectives begins with an assessment of needs. Peter Grieco recommends using a competency model similar to that shown in Figure 15-9 for determining education and training needs. [20] The functional requirements of the management information systems (see Chapter 14) will provide a basis for determining the specific knowledge and skill required for successful operation and continued development of a company's PIM activities and systems. When specific capabilities are required depends on the plans for systems development and implementation. Knowledgeable users are a valuable aid in system development and design. Providing education after the system is designed can result in user dissatisfaction with approaches and techniques previously endorsed. Top management and key PIM managers certainly should be well versed in modern PIM technology prior to any major specific system design and development commitment. Training, on the other hand, is appropriate immediately prior to and during system installation.

In most firms educational needs will range from the broad and general principles of PIM (the relationship of major functions such as production planning, master production scheduling, resource planning, rough-cut capacity planning, and so on) to details concerning how and why shop order

**FIGURE 15-9**
**COMPETENCY MODEL FOR DETERMINING KNOWLEDGE AND SKILL REQUIREMENTS PER POSITION (ABRIDGED)**

| COMPETENCY AREAS | POSITION: Production Planner | Senior Planner | Planning Supervisor | Master Scheduler | Inventory Planner | Inventory Manager | Dispatcher | General Manager |
|---|---|---|---|---|---|---|---|---|
| Master schedule | 2 | 1 | 1 | 1 | 2 | 1 | 2 | 2 |
| BOM | 1 | 1 | 1 | 1 | 1 | 1 | 2 | 3 |
| MRP | 1 | 1 | 1 | 1 | 1 | 1 | 2 | 3 |
| CRP* | 1 | 1 | 1 | 1 | 1 | 1 | 2 | 3 |
| Lead time | 2 | 1 | 1 | 1 | 1 | 1 | 1 | 3 |
| Order release | 2 | 1 | 1 | 1 | 1 | 1 | 1 | 3 |
| Order quantities | 2 | 1 | 1 | 1 | 1 | 1 | 1 | 3 |

The competency required is defined by the following (these are illustrative and requirements will be different in different environments):

1. Requires knowledge of concepts, principles, and techniques plus the ability to apply them to routine and nonroutine decisions (expertise).
2. Requires knowledge of concepts, principles, techniques and the ability to apply them to routine decisions (a working knowledge of the field).
3. Requires knowledge of concepts, principles, and techniques to the extent necessary to understand how and why decisions are made by others and how they relate to other areas of the firm.

*Capacity Requirements Planning

priorities are determined. The broad overview knowledge required by corporate and production management is provided by many organizations with established performance records. Active participation in the APICS Certification Program is the best approach for PIM personnel to develop and solidify their knowledge of the principles, concepts, and basic decision techniques of the discipline, as noted by many including Charles Andrew, George Hoyt, Peter Ryan, and Robert Wheatley. [18, 21, 17, and 22] The intrinsic value of the program is the education and learning which occurs while preparing for the examination. Education concerning the specific environment, objectives, and system of a firm is built on a solid foundation when general principles, concepts, and techniques are understood. Training in the nitty-gritty details of managing and operating the firm's PIM system follows. Each step is crucial in a successful education and training program. The early educational programs provide the stimulus, attitudes, and management commitment required for success of the educational program and the system. Training is essential if the system is to work.

## Capability Assessment

The knowledge and capability of present personnel also need assessment. The numerous and wide range of individuals participating in PIM seminars, conferences, and training and the increasing number of Certified Practitioners and Fellows are evidence of the quantum leap in the knowledge level of the profession. It is still true, however, that the lack of knowledge of many people in the field is amazing, as E.M. Barnett notes. [23] The capability of personnel in the firm can be determined by reviewing personnel files and by individual interviews. Certification at the Practioner Level is *prima facie* evidence of an understanding of the basic concepts; certification at the Fellow Level generally indicates a deep and broad understanding of the principles, concepts, and techniques. One-on-one interviews can aid in determining individual experience, needs, and also in establishing individual professional growth objectives.

## Objectives and Performance Criteria

The true objective of education and training is improved PIM performance. Better customer service, decreased inventory turns, reduced lead times, lower work-in-process, etc., are the true objectives of the program. Attendance at seminars, participation in in-house training, certification, and demonstrated skill are important, but only to the extent that they are steps to improved operating performance. Thus, the education and training program must emphasize the objectives and operating details of an individual firm's system as well as the general principles and techniques of the field. The program also plays a role in developing a positive attitude toward the system and the opportunities it presents.

## Motivation

The value and importance of career oriented education would seem to be self-evident. Most participants, however, have attended other programs which they believe provided few tangible benefits. In addition, many believe that their years of experience, an occasional professional meeting, and browsing through a journal now and then have kept them current. These common obstacles can be overcome with the appropriate approach.

If the training is new systems oriented, having someone from a similar organization report on the benefits the system has provided his or her firm is a good beginning. Working with each member of the department to develop a personalized professional growth and career development path is appropriate in the management of any group of professionals but is especially necessary in a dynamic field and in a firm with increasing competency requirements. A self-graded evaluation examination frequently will point out personal deficiencies to an employee without embarrassment. Certification and successful completion of education and training courses are a valid basis for salary increments and promotions. Most successful programs have explicit learning objectives with testing to measure the achievement of those objectives. George Hoyt reports that Sundstrand uses learning contracts with some employees. Knowledge deficiencies, outside sources which the student may pursue on his or her own, and the obligations of both the company and the employee are documented in these contracts. [21] Broadly based user participation in establishing systems goals and competency requirements normally will lead to peer pressure to attain the objectives and to their acceptance.

## Managing Education

Education and training need to be more than occasional fireworks displays. Both need to be continuing activities with direction and leadership. In relatively large organizations a full-time director of training usually is needed. In small companies the director of the PIM training position may be combined with the manufacturing systems manager position. The point is that a specific person should have this task. This responsibility is best shared by a steering committee with representatives from top management, marketing, engineering, finance, data processing, manufacturing, and with project team members from PIM, data processing, and other areas such as distribution and engineering. The steering committee provides overall management guidance and support. The project team consists of users; many of these people will be on the project team guiding systems design and implementation activities. Different training project leaders may exist for different functional areas such as BOM processing and shop floor control. The project team needs to play an active role in planning the entire program, conducting the program, evaluating it, and making necessary changes. An education and training plan might be charted as illustrated in Figure 15-10.[6]

Education of PIM personnel alone will not do the job. Top management's understanding of the significance of production and inventory management to the firm's success provides a solid base for their commitment. New systems, closed loop manufacturing control, for example, frequently mean a new way of doing business. Engineering, marketing, and manufacturing are affected by the change. Their cooperation is essential to its success. Education must include management personnel from all functional areas.

---

[6]See Peter L. Grieco's presentation for further treatment. [20]

**FIGURE 15-10**
**EDUCATION AND TRAINING ACTIVITY PLAN**

| Activity | Time Periods 1 | 2 | 3 | 4 | 5 | 6 | 7 | 8 | 9 | 10 |
|---|---|---|---|---|---|---|---|---|---|---|
| Assess needs | X | | | | | | | | | |
| Evaluate competence | X | X | | | | | | | | |
| Develop preliminary plan | | X | | | | | | | | |
| Prepare budget | | X | | | | | | | | |
| Obtain management support | | X | | | | | | | | |
| Develop steering committee | X | | | | | | | | | |
| Develop project team | | X | X | | | | | | | |
| Outline course plan | | | X | | | | | | | |
| Develop program measurement techniques | | | X | | | | | | | |
| Train the trainers | | | X | | | | | | | |
| Hold pilot model courses | | | | X | | | | | | |
| Schedule education courses | | | | | X | | | | | |
| Schedule training courses | | | | | X | | | | | |
| Offer course* | | | | | X | X | X | X | X | X |
| Measure results (knowledge and skills) | | | | | X | X | X | X | X | X |
| Measure PIM performance results | | | | | | | X | X | X | X |
| Revise program as required | | | | | | | | X | X | X |

*Sequence course offerings consistent with time-phased requirements of competency requirements.

# EXECUTION

Execution of organization, systems, staffing, and education and training plans requires application of the principles and techniques of production activity (shop floor) control to these activities. The plans must be realistic in terms of the capacity, budget, and personnel available to attain them. Valid priorities for the activities must be established recognizing the sequential requirements of each. Implementing new information systems, for example, is not realistic prior to the required training and education. Release of directives (orders) to perform management tasks requires an estimate of lead time, input/output (I/O) planning and control, a measurement of capacity and load, and a control of priorities. This is accomplished through formal priorities and their control. Thus, just as a top executive such as the vice-president of sales or engineering may not change the priority of a shop order without working through the formal system, the same holds for revising the PIM organization structure or its information systems. Overloading the systems group with design projects or the department with a variety of training projects can have the same effect as overloading the shop with orders.

Priorities become confused, activities become inefficient, and many tasks are not completed on schedule. Proper execution requires adequate planning, control, and application of the basic concepts and techniques of order release and sequencing.

## CONTROL

Control closes the management loop of planning, execution, evaluation, and corrective action. Control of PIM is concerned with the following:

1. Assuring that PIM performance objectives, policies, and procedures support the organization's strategic objectives and are consistent with strategic plans
2. Evaluating planned organization and management system developments relative to state-of-the-art developments; to changes in the structure of the firm's market, products, or processes; and to changes in the availability of personnel and supporting services in education and counseling
3. Comparing actual organization and management system developments with planned developments
4. Comparing education and training results with planned results
5. Taking the corrective actions suggested by the evaluation performed in the preceding steps

Operational controls are discussed throughout this text; they include the many techniques for controlling forecasts, inventory, order releases, capacity, order sequencing, lead time, and so on. Management controls concern aggregate measures of performance such as inventory investment, production output, customer service, employment levels, personnel utilization, and overtime. Control should be an integral part of the management system. Limits may be established on the absolute value of inventory, the inventory turn ratio, overtime, or percentage of orders back ordered, for example, with exception reports to PIM whenever a limit is exceeded. Periodic meetings, perhaps biweekly, might be held to review performance against all major objectives.

Organization development and management system development also require control. The first step in control is a realistic plan specifying the different steps and milestones on the path to achieving a revised organization structure, better educated and trained employees, or a new or revised management system—as described in the planning section of this chapter. Actual organization changes, systems developments, staffing, and training accomplishments then are compared to plans on a periodic basis.

Management audits are an essential element of management control. The management audit provides an evaluation of the overall performance of PIM; it usually is performed by experts from outside the company. The use of external personnel is meant to increase the likelihood of an objective assessment and to provide some fresh inputs. The management audit may evaluate the following:

1. The contribution of the PIM organization to attaining the firm's objectives
2. The effectiveness and efficiency of PIM communications with other functional areas such as marketing, finance, and manufacturing
3. The department's performance objectives, their measurement, and degree of attainment
4. The department's research and development activities (Does the department have an organized approach to learning of and assessing new ideas and approaches?)
5. The capability of department managers (What is the contribution of each? Do they work together as a team?)
6. The efficiency of the present PIM systems
7. The department's organization structure, staff, and related plans (Are they consistent with the department's task and resources?)
8. The management information systems, their effectiveness relative to user needs and their efficiency in terms of hardware, software, and ease of user interaction
9. Top management's commitment to the PIM function in terms of interest, time, and resources

Management audits are not weekly or even quarterly routines, but they are appropriate every two to three years. It is not a bad idea to perform a partial audit each year using internal personnel.[7]

All elements of management are important; planning and control are particularly important. Without a plan or control, chances of attaining desirable goals decrease substantially. Firmness and consistency in monitoring progress toward goals convert plans into results.

# THE MANAGEMENT OF CHANGE

Kenneth Boulding asserts that the world of today is as different from the world of 1900 as the world of 1900 was different from the world of Julius Caesar. [25] Peter Drucker has noted that ". . . change is the order of things." [26] Rapid social and techonological change is the hallmark of modern society and production management. For example, MRP, distribution requirements planning (DRP), push-allocation distribution systems, I/O planning and control, and application of mathematical programming and simulation to production planning and scheduling problems along with the digital computer have arrived since 1950. Automated fabrication processes,

[7] See the articles by John Burnham and Harvey Rose for further treatment of PIM audits. [19, 24]

automated material handling and warehouse control, increased foreign competition, group technology and cellular manufacturing, the availability of mini and microcomputers and the increased cost of capital are examples of dramatic changes in operating conditions during the last ten years.

Many managers, pressed with short-term problems of performance and survival, become *fire fighters*, too busy coping with day-to-day operations to anticipate the challenges and opportunities of tomorrow. Their organization has only one mode of activity, the operational.

In order to provide some motivation and assistance for improved change management, we will next examine the types of change, the different phases of change management, and the organization structure and procedures suggested for improved change management. The practical steps that can be taken to establish and/or improve the management of change in PIM will be emphasized.

## Change Recognition

Planned change is always a reaction—either to events that have occurred or to anticipated events. The difference in timing between these two types of reactions is significant. Preparing for anticipated events is proactive rather than reactive. A consistent pattern of timely recognition of change possibilities takes place only in the organization that operates in the search mode as well as in the operational mode.

## The Search Mode

Formal acknowledgement of the search function, along with the operational planning and control function in the statement of departmental objectives, is the first step in achieving a search capability. Before establishing the direction and focus of departmental search activities, it is best to establish a framework for defining those areas in which a lack of sufficient operational knowledge exists in order to evaluate their operational merit.

**Management Inventories.** Organizing the departmental state of the art enables management to focus search activities rationally rather than haphazardly incorporating innovations on the basis of present fashions or the special interests of staff members or supervisors. A companion piece to the capability inventory is an inventory of techniques—inventory management systems, software packages, hardware development, and other tools available for use in PIM. Such an inventory reveals the techniques the department is aware of, those that have been evaluated, and those that seem relevant for its operation.

**Search Activities.** Capable personnel usually react favorably to expectations and demands that they participate in the search as well as the operational mode of the organization. Awareness of new developments reported in the literature, at technical conferences, and in the announcements of equipment manufacturers and software houses should be organized. Assigning different individuals to review specific journals, attend conferences, or review proceedings while others are reviewing hardware and software developments is one approach. Individuals also may volunteer for specific assignments.

These individuals can report periodically on their activities, the specific items reviewed, and their recommendations concerning the advisability of further study. Individual members of the department then may review the reports related to their special technical expertise. Organized search activities provide a stimulus for improvement and reinforce a group attitude supporting improvements and job security based on professional competence.

**Evaluation of Possible Changes.** Selecting specific capability areas for intensive investigation and study is the first phase of evaluation; the second is determining the advisability of implementing specific changes. Both evaluation phases occur continually and concurrently in most organizations, for different changes.

## Selection of Study Area

Evaluating present operations and defining areas of possible improvement precede selection of an area for intensive study. Candidate areas can be evaluated on a rational basis. For example, whether the department should assign priority to improving its procedures for preparing the MPS; for determining production and purchase lot sizes; for order release planning; for managing lead time and WIP inventory; or for warehousing and distribution can be based on the following criteria:

1. How vital is the system or area?
2. How effective is the present system?
3. What are the expected costs in terms of man-hours, equipment, and software to design and successfully implement any changes?
4. What are the expected benefits of the change?
5. How long will it take to complete the study and implementation phases?
6. Does the organization have the capability of making the study and carrying out likely change recommendations? This capability includes personnel capability, computer and other hardware devices, and data base requirements.

If the PIM system is failing in a vital area—all other things being equal—that problem should have highest priority. If, for example, shortages of raw materials and purchase parts are occurring frequently and stopping production for relatively long periods, this problem probably will have first priority. Expediting, rescheduling, and the usual fire-fighting type activities to solve a single occurrence are complemented by an investigation of the entire situation to find an approach eliminating a chronic problem.

Development of the required data base frequently receives top priority. Implementation of MRP, for example, requires an accurate and complete BOM; forecasting techniques require knowledge of past demand; and capacity planning needs the estimated times of the production processes for each item.

## Decision to Implement

A cost benefit analysis serves as a guide to the choice among the alternatives. The costs involved include both initial and operational. Initial costs include those of the study itself, training personnel in the new procedures, the development and debugging of the systems and programs, the design of forms, frequently the development of a data base, and electronic data processing equipment, as well as more mundane items such as file cabinets, card holders, and wall-mounted charts. Other initial costs are associated with the personnel time required to reduce the confusion possible with change implementation and to overcome the resistance to change. Operating costs include those associated with forms administration, data capturing expenses, computer processing, report preparation, report utilization, report storage, and system and software surveillance. The ability to estimate these costs grows exponentially with experience in change evaluation and implementation.

The ability to quantify the benefits depends to a large extent on the nature of the resulting improvement. For example, the benefit of a new inventory management system reducing inventory investment by 10 percent or the implementation of revised shop floor procedures reducing machine waiting time and WIP by specific percentages is less difficult to quantify than the benefits of a change improving customer service.

Methods for evaluating how effective a revised procedure will work can be divided into: (1) the rational approach, (2) simulation, (3) a pilot application, and (4) some combination of 1 through 3. The rational approach is the traditional one of examining the proposed method in terms of whether it makes sense. Using an MRP system to manage components and subassemblies in job shop manufacturing, for example, usually is appropriate. Simulation can be used to determine how well a proposed technique would have worked in the past year or two if the required data are available for those periods, or to project future performance on the basis of forecast data. The pilot approach involves the implementation of the technique in a limited manner for evaluation purposes. Thus, revised shop floor control procedures and priority rules may be implemented only in one division, one plant, or one department of a plant. After they have been in operation long enough to include all typical operating characteristics, the effect of the change can be determined. One of the difficulties of this approach is that both the old and the new procedures are existing concurrently in different parts of the organization, and both must interface with related systems. In addition, a procedure that is admittedly on trial may not receive the wholehearted support from operational personnel. Another type of pilot evaluation occurs when a technique has been implemented with successful results by another firm with similar operating conditions. Although frequently similar, conditions in any two organizations are seldom identical. The differences may be crucial. In addition, published reports of success may be embellished and may neglect the difficulties and bugs that are yet to be ironed out. The use of this type of pilot approach demands a close examination of the similarities and differences and an accurate evaluation of the impact of these differences on performance characteristics.

The evaluation phase of change management involves two different decisions. One is the decision to study an area and the other is the decision to implement a change.

## Implementation

Successful change implementation includes convincing those affected of the merits of the change, involving leaders in its selection and implementation, proper training, surveillance, occasional confrontation, and recognition of failure possibilities. Personnel who will be responsible for executing new procedures should be involved in the evaluation of those procedures. Their knowledge of operating conditions aids in evaluating prospective changes. Their involvement and knowledge of adopted changes usually reduce their resistance to the change. Including the leaders, both formal and informal, in the change selection and analysis activities is especially important. George Hoyt reported on the benefits of including a user representative, a user department review board, and a working committee with representatives from all interfacing departments when implementing an MRP system at the Sundstrand Corporation. [21]

All those involved in the use of the technique or equipment should be thoroughly trained in its application prior to its implementation. In addition, all departments whose cooperation is required in executing the change need to be included in orientation and training. This training is usually interlaced with the selling of the change. Many a good idea has gone down the drain because the precise method of application was not understood and not followed.

The effects of a change should be monitored and the results analyzed until all difficulties have been overcome and the change is clearly a profitable one. Audit the procedures to ascertain that the changes are being followed properly. Few changes generate an immediate payoff; many are costly to begin since things frequently get worse before they get better. For example, seldom does a revised inventory management system reduce inventory in the short run. The time required to reap the benefits of the change should be clear to all involved. Learning curve and other transitional effects should not be minimozed.

White and Taylor, Hills, and Davis recommend that the Lewin-Schein model of the change process be used as a basis for change implementation. [27, 28] The model is a stage process model of change within individuals. The three stages are unfreezing, changing, and freezing. The key to unfreezing present attitudes, norms, and behavior patterns (overcoming resistance to change) is a "felt need for change." Both of the foregoing references endorse management evaluating performance in terms of the new behavior objectives. This, of course, requires management commitment to the change, a factor whose importance is recognized by most writers on this topic.

Management of the PIM function, to summarize, requires planning, organizing, staffing, execution, and control. The goals of PIM must support the overall organization objectives and their attainment must be measurable in quantitative terms. Change pervades industry and PIM in particular. PIM needs to operate in both a search and an operational mode. Recognition of change and strategies for dealing with change are crucial in the management of PIM.

# QUESTIONS

1. Prepare a set of finished goods customer service goals that will be appropriate for a make-to-order, large equipment company.
2. Why does performance measurement itself affect motivation and behavior?
3. Identify at least two PIM management activities to which a network model (see Chapter 16) might be applied for planning and control purposes.
4. Visit a local firm and determine the hierarchy of objectives beginning with profit, ROI, and working down through various PIM goals.
5. Name at least two different organization strategies that directly affect PIM. Explain why.
6. How are the PIM organization structure, available staff, and management system related? Describe a situation in which the plans in these areas must be coordinated.
7. What is the value of a well-defined organization structure?
8. List the characteristics of an organization and its environment that should have a major influence on the design of an organization.

9. Some companies have different PIM organizations in different divisions. What is a rational explanation of this situation?
10. Name two companies which exemplify the types of firms that do not require a service parts department within PIM. Name two which exemplify types of firms that do.
11. A medium-sized manufacturer of specialty farm equipment builds components to stock and final assemblies to order. Its WIP inventories are high and customer service (meeting promised delivery dates) is poor. A proposal has been made to solve this problem by changing the present traditional organization to one that assigns the planning and control function to different groups. Comment.
12. In what type firm would you recommend that the scheduling of plant maintenance be part of the PIM planning task?
13. List the conditions under which a materials management organization is most likely to be cost-effective.
14. The vice-president of manufacturing at a local firm contends that the firm does not need a master scheduler. She says that the production control manager knows what is going on and adding a master scheduler would only increase the payroll. Comment.
15. The materials manager of an expanding multiplant firm that produces tools and equipment for the oil exploration and mining industries has proposed the addition of systems analyst and programmer positions as the nucleus of a systems group within PIM. The manager of corporate data processing objects to the change; he views it as redundant staffing. Comment.
16. How would you expect PIM staffing requirements to differ among the following types of firms:

    a. A manufacturer of components for the automobile industry
    b. A relatively small gear manufacturer
    c. A multiplant, multiwarehouse manufacturer of small tools
    d. A small chemical company that produces industrial strength hand soaps

17. The three individuals in a production and inventory-planning group contend that they are overloaded with work and require additional personnel. What procedure would you follow to evaluate their claim?
18. The director of manufacturing at a local plant whose inventory and shipping performances are below par contends that educational programs will be of little value to his PIM staff since the programs are too general and do not recognize the specific problems of his firm. Comment.
19. What is the difference between education and training in PIM?
20. How should education and training programs relate to management information systems plans?
21. Why are quantifiable performance objectives essential for control?
22. Give two examples of how exception management controls may be used in controlling PIM management activities.
23. Explain how the first stages of control take place long before any execution begins.
24. Materials management is convinced that a push allocation distribution system will be more effective than the present traditional order point system. Where do you believe the most resistance to this change will exist? Why? What steps do you recommend to overcome the resistance?

# SELECTED READINGS


1. Robert L. Janson, "Key Indicators for Production and Inventory Control," *APICS 24th Annual International Conference Proceedings* (1981), pp. 319-321.
2. Ernest C. Huge, "Materials Management by Objectives," *Production and Inventory Management*, Vol. 19, No. 1 (1978), pp. 25-35.
3. ———, "How to Attain Your Inventory Objective," *Production and Inventory Management*, Vol. 19, No. 4 (1978), pp. 1-15.
4. Peter F. Drucker, *Landmarks of Tomorrow* (New York: Harper & Row, Publishers, Inc., Colophon Books, Montclair, N.J., 1965).
5. Oliver W. Wight, *Production and Inventory Management in the Computer Age* (Boston, Mass.: Cahners Books, 1974), pp. 224-229.
6. Aman A. Motwane, "How to Organize a Production Planning Department," *APICS 24th Annual International Conference Proceedings* (1981), pp. 347-350.
7. Leland R. Kneppelt, "Real Time, On-Line, Distributed in the Manufacturing Systems Environment," *APICS 23d Annual Conference Proceedings* (1980), pp. 58-60.
8. Frank M. Zenobia, Jr., "Who and What Is Materials Management?" *APICS 21st Annual International Conference Proceedings* (1978), pp. 564-575.
9. Robert E. Fox, "Keep to Successful Materials Management Systems: A Contrast between Japan, Europe, and the U.S.," *APICS 23d Annual Conference Proceedings* (1980), pp. 440-444.
10. Jack N. Durban, "The Challenge of Managing Inventories," *APICS 21st Annual Conference Proceedings* (1978), pp. 879-895.
11. Albert L. Wolpin, "Materials Management," *APICS 21st Annual International Conference Proceedings* (1978), pp. 624-636.
12. Kenneth W. Tunnell and Gutram V. Stier, "Organizing for Production and Inventory Control in the Multinational Company," *APICS 17th Annual International Conference Proceedings* (1974) pp. 348-359.
13. Wight, op. cit., pp. 68 and 69.
14. Cash Powell, Jr., "Systems Planning/Systems Control," *Production and Inventory Management*, Vol. 18, No. 3 (1978), pp. 15-25.
15. Wight, op. cit., p. 142.
16. Powell, Jr., "MRP System—MRP Organization," *APICS 24th Annual International Conference Proceedings* (1981), pp. 339-343.

**17.** Peter F. Ryan, "Training and Education in Production/Material Control (Management's Survival Kit)," *APICS 23d Annual International Conference Proceedings* (1980), pp. 19-22.

**18.** Charles G. Andrew, "Certification—RX for Effective MRP II Education," *APICS 23d Annual International Conference Proceedings* (1980), pp. 1-5.

**19.** John M. Burnham, "The Operating Plant—Case Studies and Generalizations," *Production and Inventory Management*, Vol. 21, No. 4 (1980), pp. 63-94.

**20.** Peter L. Grieco, "The ABC's of Training," *APICS 24th Annual International Conference Proceedings* (1981), pp. 430-432.

**21.** George Hoyt, "Effective In-House MRP Training," *APICS 23d Annual International Conference Proceedings* (1980), pp. 26-30.

**22.** Robert W. Wheatley, "Materials Management Education—It Isn't Enough," *APICS 23d Annual International Conference Proceedings* (1980), pp. 9-12.

**23.** E. M. "Mac" Barnett, "Education—the Key to MRP Success," *APICS 24th Annual International Conference* (1981), pp. 135 and 136.

**24.** Harvey N. Rose, "Auditing of P & IC Systems—The Necessary Ingredient," *APICS 21st Annual Conference Proceedings* (1978), pp. 436-454.

**25.** Alvin Toffler, *Future Shock* (New York: Random House, Inc., 1970), p. 13.

**26.** Drucker, *Management* (New York: Harper & Row, Publishers, Inc., 1974), pp. 518-609.

**27.** Edna M. White, "Implementing an MRP System Using the Lewin-Schein Theory of Change," *Production and Inventory Management*, Vol. 21, No. 1 (1980), pp. 1-12.

**28.** Bernard Taylor III, Fredrick S. Hills, and K. Roscoe Davis, "The Effects of Change Factors on the Production Operation and the Production Manager," *Production and Inventory Management*, Vol. 20, No. 3 (1979), pp. 18-32.

**29.** Milton E. Cook, "Developing a Successful P & IC Training Program," *APICS 23d Annual International Conference Proceedings* (1980), pp. 6-8.

**30.** Jack N. Durben, "Material Management On-Line System," *APICS 24th Annual International Conference Proceedings* (1981), pp. 27-30.

**31.** Norris W. Edson, "Measuring MRP System Effectiveness," *APICS 24th Annual International Conference Proceedings* (1981), pp. 315-318.

**32.** J. Nicholas Edwards, "Measuring the Effectiveness of P & IC," *APICS 24th Annual International Conference Proceedings* (1981), pp. 311-314.

**33.** T. R. Fernie, "Control of Production," *Production and Inventory Management*, Vol. 18, No. 2 (1977), pp. 102-110.

**34.** Donald W. Fogarty, "Change and the Materials Manager or Is Your System Open?" *APICS 15th Annual International Conference Proceedings* (1972), pp. 360-374.

**35.** Gary A. Landis, "Promoting the PIC Function within the Organization through Effective Human Relations," *APICS 22d Annual Conference Proceedings* (1979), pp. 70 and 71.

**36.** Carl J. Poch, "In-House P & IC Training," *APICS 23d Annual International Conference Proceedings* (1980), pp. 13 and 14.

**37.** Carol Saunders and Steve McDonnell, "Education of the People, by the People, and for the People," *APICS 24th Annual International Conference Proceedings* (1981), pp. 131-134.

# PART FOUR

## OPERATIONS RESEARCH TECHNIQUES AND MODELS

While mathematical computations are common in many production and inventory control decisions, in practical settings complex mathematical models are not. However, a great deal of study has gone into logical and mathematical studies of inventory and production problems. In many cases, elegant mathematics have been used in analysis; but then the results have been implemented through simple approximations or heuristic rule of thumb procedures. In this section, some of those more complex techniques are explained and their applications illustrated.

The mathematical modeling of real world problems and subsequent analysis had its greatest growth period in the last 25 years. That growth paralleled the growth in computer capabilities, for many of the techniques were designed to handle complex problems having a large amount of data. Only with computers can some of the techniques be employed. Since many of the early efforts at mathematical modeling were in operational areas, this field of study became known as Operations Research (OR). Broadly construed, OR models mathematically or logically model real world situations in an effort to extract the significant features and allow formal mathematical and logical analysis to be performed.

Some mathematical models and decision rules—economic order quantity (EOQ), material requirements planning (MRP), lot sizing, reorder point (ROP), etc.—have been treated in earlier parts of this text. This section deals with three of the more general techniques that can be labeled OR; namely, Project Planning and Control, Mathematical Programming, and Simulation.

Project planning and its subsequent management and control have been a source of concern since the pyramids were built. In more recent times military and civilian construction of projects such as submarines and office buildings have focused attention on project planning techniques. Major plant moves or maintenance projects also lend themselves to this type of analysis as does the annual budget preparation and launching of a new product. In Chapter 16, formal techniques for dealing with these complex projects are described and explained.

Mathematical programming covers a variety of problems and techniques. Most fundamentally, a set of equations is used to represent the relationships between and among the variables of interest. This set can then be solved through rigorous mathematical techniques to yield optimal values for the variables. Additional information about the nature and sensitivity of the solution may also be available. Chapter 17 examines linear programming, the most common type of problem, and goal programming, a variation which may more clearly represent the real world in some instances. Representative problems are formulated to assist in understanding the application of these mathematical procedures.

Chapter 18 provides the most flexible technique for dealing with complex problems, particularly those involving risk and uncertainty, namely simulation. First, a logical model of a situation is constructed and then it is exercised by a process sometimes referred to as synthetic sampling; that is, we randomly select values for each of the probabalistic (stochastic) variables and compute the consequences on the system. By drawing many, perhaps thousands, of such samples, each obeying the appropriate probability distributions, we can get a picture of what is likely to happen in the real world if we install the system being analyzed and if future circumstances are as we hypothesize them to be. Since the logical models need not be capable of normal mathematical manipulation, this is a very flexible tool. However, since the relationships are often complex and the possible outcomes many, simulation almost invariably involves computers.

There are many other OR techniques, and new insights into problems are being made daily through mathematical research. These three areas, however, have been singled out because of their broad applicability and fundamental nature.

# —16—

# PROJECT MANAGEMENT

Project Evaluation and Review Technique (PERT) and Critical Path Method (CPM), have received acclaim and acceptance across the entire industrial spectrum. The primary reasons for this broad and enthusiastic reception are:

1. The principles underlying the procedure followed in applying these techniques are transparently clear.
2. The techniques provide an integrated approach to project planning, scheduling, and control that does work.
3. Plans and schedules can be developed in the detail warranted by the complexity of the project and by the degree of control desired.
4. The principles and procedures are applicable to projects of all types including such diverse activities as research, engineering design, construction, fabrication of an assembly line, preparation of a dinner, major surgery, the rebuilding of a blast furnace, installation of a new management information system such as material requirements planning (MRP), and the increase of production output by the addition of a second shift.

In manufacturing, these techniques are especially useful in planning and controlling the production of items that are custom designed around basic models to meet the special requirements of individual customers. The production cycle for such items usually includes design and production engineering activities as well as fabrication processes. This situation is common in the production of large equipment items such as material handling systems, truck bodies for utility companies, and industrial cleaning equipment.

Project management techniques are also helpful in the following types of production inventory management (PIM) activities:

1. Short-range planning—crew changes, equipment start-ups and teardowns
2. Increasing capacity—reducing planned maintenance time
3. Calculating manufacturing lead time—based on critical path of purchasing, fabrication, and assembly
4. Reducing work-in-process—reducing critical path of fabrication and assembly

# A PROJECT

Certain characteristics distinguish those tasks most suitable for the application of project management techniques. These characteristics include the following:

1. Projects have a definite beginning and end. The building of a new plant, the hiring and training of an additional labor crew, the design and fabrication of tooling for a new product, the installation of a new (substantially redesigned) PIM system—all possess this characteristic. Whereas installing a new assembly line and producing the first acceptable lot constitutes a project, running that assembly line for the next month or year is more appropriately viewed as an ongoing, repetitive nonproject activity.

2. Project activities are one-at-a-time activities for the most part, isolated by either time or space. The fabrication of a single large pressure vessel might be planned and controlled using project management techniques; planning and controlling the fabrication and assembly of ten such vessels at the same facility within the same time frame requires increased application of the principles and techniques discussed in the chapters concerning medium- and short-range planning.

3. Projects can be subdivided into activities which have definite beginnings and ends; that is, the nature of the process does not require that activities be initiated immediately upon completion of the preceding activity as is the case in certain refining processes where the next step must begin immediately due to the inability of the material to retain a chemical or physical property for any period without incurring substantial additional expense during a holding phase. Thus, the making of steel, the refining of gasoline, and the production of ice cream are not suited for the application of project management techniques; whereas, the launching of a space shot, the construction of a nuclear submarine, and the teardown, cleaning and restarting of a bottling line are.

4. The activities that must be performed to complete the project have a definite sequential relationship. There are known technological factors which require that certain activities be completed before (precede) others and which allow other activities to be performed simultaneously. Thus, each activity can be defined with respect to every other activity as preceding, succeeding or independent. Two activities which are independent may be performed in any order with respect to each other.

5. An estimate of the time required to complete each activity is available. These times are based on an assumed rate of the use of material, personnel and equipment. For example, a time estimate to "fabricate assembly fixture" is based on the use of personnel and equipment with certain capabilities and the availability of the material and information required for fabrication.

# BACKGROUND

PERT was developed jointly by members of Booz, Allen and Hamilton and the Navy's Special Project Office while planning the research, design, fabrication, and testing necessary for the production of the first nuclear submarine. They studied existing project management techniques and found none adequate for such a complex project. Application of PERT to the Polaris submarine project was one of the key factors for it being completed two years prior to the originally scheduled due date.

At about the same time, J. E. Kelley, Jr., of the Univac Division of Remington Rand, and Morgan Walker, of DuPont, working independently of the Polaris group, developed CPM as a result of a study concerning the planning and control of chemical plant maintenance. There are many similarities between PERT and CPM in their original form and some essential differences which we will discuss later. However, real world applications frequently incorporate features of both techniques in a hybrid fashion as desired by project management.

The forerunner of PERT and CPM was the Gantt chart developed by Henry Gantt around 1910. As illustrated in Figure 16-1 (which is based on activities listed in Table 16-1), the *Gantt chart*, or *bar graph* as it is sometimes called, is a graph with time on the horizontal axis and activities on the vertical axis. The following example used to illustrate these techniques has been taken from a real world situation with minor changes for the sake of simplicity. No changes have been made in essential characteristics.

**FIGURE 16-1**
**GANTT CHART**
**DESIGN, FABRICATION, AND ASSEMBLY**
**(MATERIAL HANDLING SYSTEM)**

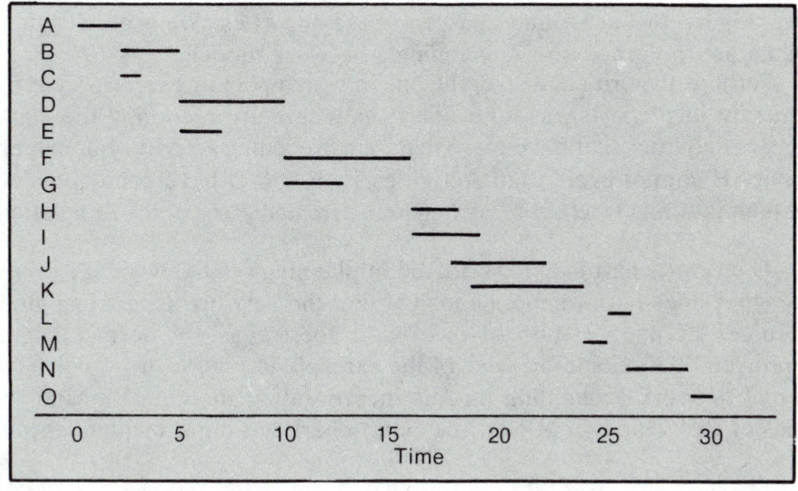

**TABLE 16-1**
**MATERIAL HANDLING SYSTEM**
**DESIGN, FABRICATION, AND ASSEMBLY**
**PLANNING DATA**

| Activity | | Activities | Activities | Activities | Requirements |
|---|---|---|---|---|---|
| **Symbol** | **Description** | **Preceding** | **Concurrent** | **Following** | **(Weeks)** |
| A | Mechanical Design (1) | None | None | B,C | 2 |
| B | Mechanical Design (2) | A | C | E,D | 3 |
| C | Electrical Design (1) | A | B,E | D | 1 |
| D | Electrical Design (2) | B,C | E | F,G | 5 |
| E | Mechanical Fabrication (1) | B | C,D,F,G | H,I | 2 |
| F | Mechanical Fabrication (2) | D | E,G | H,I | 6 |
| G | Electrical Fabrication (1) | D | E,F,I | H | 3 |
| H | Electrical Fabrication (2) | E,F,G | I | J,K | 2 |
| I | Mechanical Subassembly (1) | E,F | H,G,J | K | 3 |
| J | Mechanical Subassembly (2) | H | K,I | M | 4 |
| K | Electrical Installation (1) | H,I | J | M | 5 |
| L | Electrical Installation (2) | M | None | N | 1 |
| M | Piping Installation (1) | J,K | None | L | 1 |
| N | Piping Installation (2) | L | None | O | 3 |
| O | Start-up, Test, and Ship ( ) | N | None | None | 1 |

# DEVELOPING A NETWORK PLANNING MODEL

The firm whose activities are described in Table 16-1 and Figure 16-1 produces material handling systems. Some are standard assemblies fabricated to catalog specifications while others are custom designed and fabricated to meet customer requirements. The activities described in Table 16-1 are those required to complete the fabrication of a specific custom designed order. Figure 16-1 is a Gantt chart for these activities. We use this situation to illustrate the process of developing a network model.

Perhaps the critical phase, the one in which planning errors occur most frequently in preparing a Gantt chart, is accurately recording the starting points of activities that have more than one preceding activity. For example, Activity H cannot begin until Activities E, F and G have been completed. The temptation is to chart *H* as beginning immediately upon completion of *G*.

The Gantt chart is a powerful aid in planning relatively simple projects although it does not provide the insight that the network scheduling models such as PERT and CPM do. (However, it does reveal the normal length of the project: 30 weeks in the case of the example in Figure 16-1.) The advantages of network scheduling models incorporating the concepts and techniques of PERT and CPM over the Gantt chart and other techniques are as follows:

1. Explicit representation of the sequential relationship between the activities that must be performed to complete the project
2. Ease in determining the critical path; i.e., the longest path (connected sequence of activities) from the beginning to the end of the project
3. Ease in determining activities whose completion on schedule is not critical to completion of the project on schedule
4. Ability to determine the impact on project completion of the probability of different activities being completed in less, or in more, time than the most likely time estimate

First, we will develop a network with attributes common to both CPM and PERT, then we will describe those characteristics that differentiate these two techniques. As noted earlier, features of both can be combined in real world applications as long as the required data and information-processing capabilities are available. The steps in building a network planning model are to (1) obtain the necessary input data, (2) construct the network model, and (3) determine the critical path.

## Data Requirements

The necessary input data include a list of the activities that constitute the project, the time required to complete each activity, and the sequential relationships of the activities. Table 16-1 illustrates the input data required to construct a network model. The efficacy of the planning and control decisions based on the network model are directly affected by the accuracy and completeness of this data. (Grossly inaccurate or incomplete data lead to inadequate and unrealistic plans.)

It is not unusual to reorganize input data when developing the network. For example, the original data sheet for the material handling system included all mechanical design activities under one activity. Discussions between planning and engineering representatives working together on development of the network revealed that electrical design activities could begin at a point where mechanical design activities were only partially complete. This led to the decision to divide mechanical design into two activities: Mechanical Design (1) and Mechanical Design (2). Developing the network model frequently provides added understanding and improved planning and execution of the project.

## Constructing the Network

A network model is formed by connecting the symbols (arrows in this case) representing sequential activities in accordance with the input data. The arrows are connected to numbered nodes (junctions) which represent events, the completion of one activity and the beginning of another. Figure 16-2 includes the various symbols used in activity-on-the-arrow networks.

**FIGURE 16-2**
**NETWORK MODELING SYMBOLS AND CONVENTIONS**

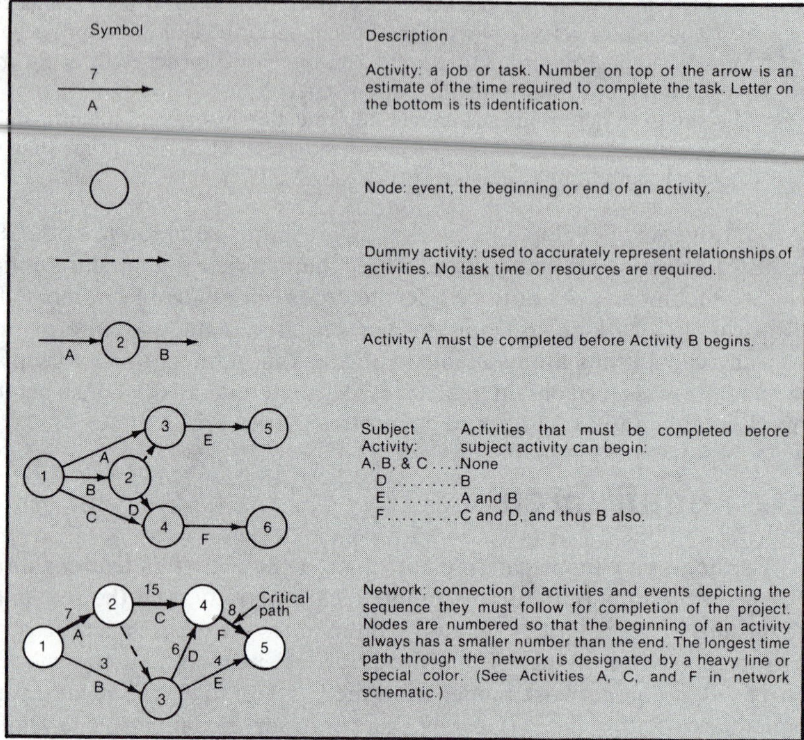

Symbol
Description
7
A
Activity: a job or task. Number on top of the arrow is an estimate of the time required to complete the task. Letter on the bottom is its identification.
Node: event, the beginning or end of an activity.
Dummy activity: used to accurately represent relationships of activities. No task time or resources are required.
A 2 B
Activity A must be completed before Activity B begins.
Subject Activity: Activities that must be completed before subject activity can begin:
A, B, & C ....None
D .........B
E..........A and B
F..........C and D, and thus B also.
Critical path
Network: connection of activities and events depicting the sequence they must follow for completion of the project. Nodes are numbered so that the beginning of an activity always has a smaller number than the end. The longest time path through the network is designated by a heavy line or special color. (See Activities A, C, and F in network schematic.)


Constructing the network begins with the proper connection of the activity (or activities) that has no predecessors, and connecting it to the activities that follow it immediately (as illustrated in Figure 16-3 on the basis of the data in Table 16-1). Activity A has no predecessors, and Activities B and C follow it immediately. The next step is to add the arrows for those activities that immediately follow the followers of the initial activity. Table 16-1 re-

**FIGURE 16-3**
**INITIATION OF A NETWORK**

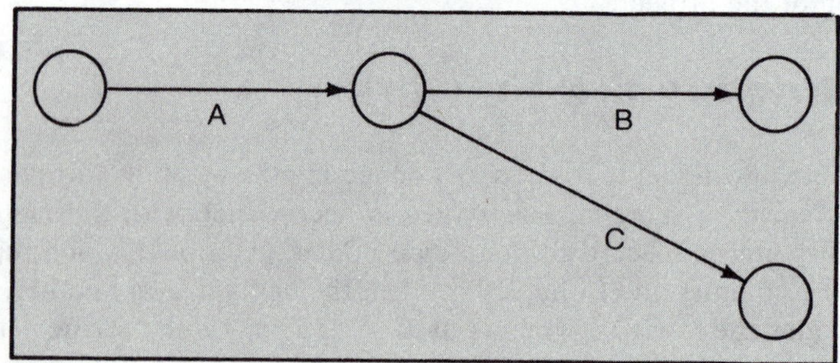

**FIGURE 16-4**
**NETWORK DEVELOPMENT CONTINUED**

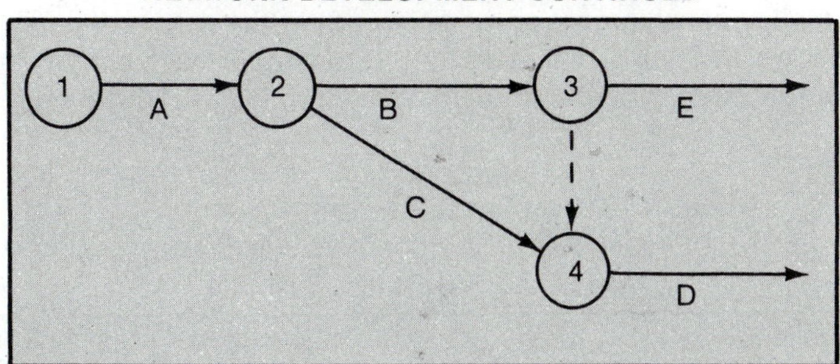


veals that *B* immediately precedes Activities D and E; and that Activity B is the immediate predecessor of *E*. These relationships require the use of an additional symbol, a dummy arrow, as illustrated in Figure 16-4.

Dummy activities do not represent a task; they require no time; nor do they use any resources. They are used to represent precedence requirements accurately, and uniquely identify activities. Without the dummy activity, for example, the network in Figure 16-5 would state that both Activities B and C must be completed before either *D* or *E* can begin. This is inaccurate.

**FIGURE 16-5**
**THE NETWORK WITHOUT A DUMMY ACTIVITY**
**(AN INACCURATE REPRESENTATION)**

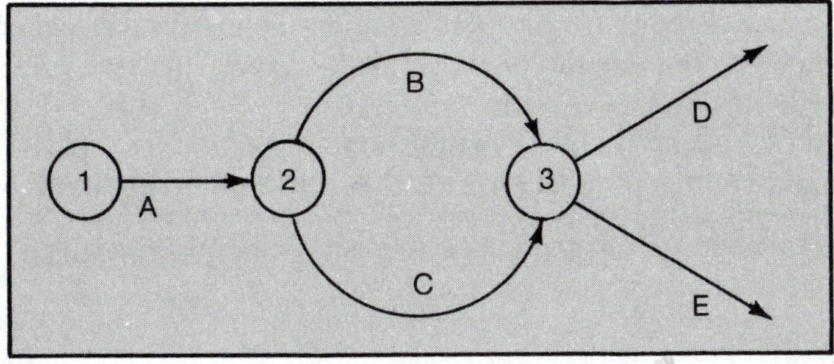


Construction of the network follows in this fashion until all activities are represented. A number is then assigned to each node so that the node at the beginning (tail) of each activity (arrow) has a smaller number than the node at the end (head). This rule is important in using computer programs that identify activities by their node numbers (*i*,*j*—where *i* represents the tail and *j* the head of each arrow), and whose logic is based on *i* being less than *j*. For example, *A* is denoted by (1,2). If one cannot assign the numbers in this manner, there is an inconsistency in the stated precedence relationships and they should be reviewed to determine the error. Note that the dummy activities have also been labeled.

## Determining the Critical Path

Complete development of the network per the data contained in Table 16-1 is shown in Figure 16-6. The time estimate for each activity has been added on top of each arrow to facilitate determination of the critical path.

**FIGURE 16-6**
**NETWORK MODEL**
**DESIGN, FABRICATION, AND ASSEMBLY**
**MATERIAL HANDLING SYSTEM**

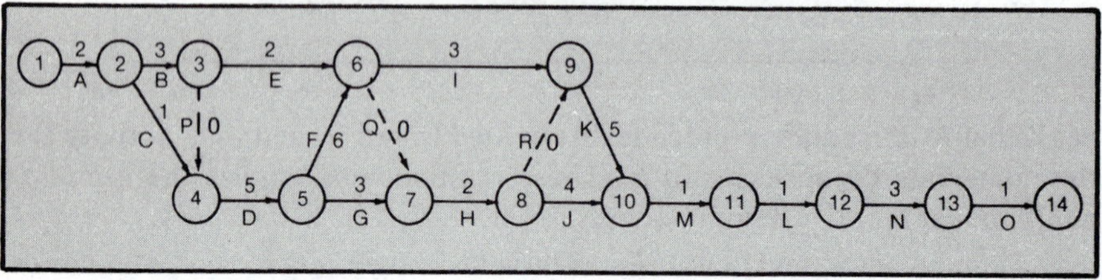


Determination of the critical path involves defining each possible path from the initiation of the project to its termination, then calculating the length of each path, and, finally, determining the longest path. The longest path is the *critical path* since it is the completion of activities on this path that determines whether or not the project is completed on schedule. On the other hand, activities not on the critical path may fall behind schedule and completion of the project within the schedule is still possible.

Table 16-2 lists the different paths that can be followed from the beginning to the end of the project as illustrated by the network model of Figure 16-6. Comparing the lengths of these paths reveals that the critical path

**TABLE 16-2**
**ACTIVITY PATHS IN FIGURE 16-6 AND THEIR LENGTHS**

| Number | Description (Activities) | Length (Weeks) |
|---|---|---|
| 1 | A,B,E,I,K,M,L,N,O | 21 |
| 2 | A,B,E,Q,H,R,K,M,L,N,O | 20 |
| 3 | A,B,E,Q,H,J,M,L,N,O | 20 |
| 4 | A,B,P,D,G,H,J,M,L,N,O | 25 |
| 5 | A,B,P,D,G,H,R,K,M,L,N,O | 26 |
| 6 | A,B,P,D,F,Q,H,J,M,L,N,O | 28 |
| 7 | A,B,P,D,F,Q,H,R,K,M,L,N,O | 29 |
| 8 | A,B,P,D,F,I,K,M,L,N,O | 30* |
| 9 | A,C,D,G,H,J,M,L,N,O | 26 |
| 10 | A,C,D,G,H,R,K,M,L,N,O | 23 |
| 11 | A,C,D,F,Q,H,J,M,L,N,O | 26 |
| 12 | A,C,D,F,Q,H,F,K,M,L,N,O | 27 |
| 13 | A,C,D,F,I,K,M,L,N,O | 28 |

*Critical Path

consists of Activities A,B,P,D,F,I,K,M,L,N, and O with a length of 30 weeks.

Two other things also are immediately apparent. Activities A, M, L, N, and O are on each path and thus, must be part of the critical path. If the path lengths were being calculated manually, these activities could be omitted until the longest length of the other segments was determined. They would then be added to determine the critical path length. The other obvious conclusion is that even in relatively simple situations, such as this example, there can be many possible paths. As the complexity of the project increases, the calculations required to determine the critical path increase at an even greater rate. Use of a computer program such as the one in Appendix K facilitates determination of the critical path and other attributes such as slack (float) time per activity.

## Latest and Earliest Start and Finish Times

The earliest and latest start and finish times can be calculated for each activity. The earliest start time (ES) of an activity is the sum of all the activities on the longest path to that activity. It is the earliest time an activity can begin, given that all preceding activities on this path begin as early as possible. Referring to the network in Figure 16-6, the ES for Activity I (6,9), is 16 weeks from the beginning of the project. This is based on the time to

**TABLE 16-3**
**ACTIVITY, ES,LS,EF,LF, AND SLACK TIMES**
**DESIGN FABRICATION AND ASSEMBLY**
**MATERIAL HANDLING SYSTEM**

| Activity | ES | LS | EF | LF | Total Slack | Free Slack |
|---|---|---|---|---|---|---|
| A | 0 | 0 | 2 | 2 | 0 | 0 |
| B | 2 | 2 | 5 | 5 | 0 | 0 |
| C | 2 | 4 | 3 | 5 | 2 | 2 |
| D | 5 | 5 | 10 | 10 | 0 | 0 |
| E | 5 | 14 | 7 | 16 | 9 | 9 |
| F | 10 | 10 | 16 | 16 | 0 | 0 |
| G | 10 | 14 | 13 | 17 | 4 | 3 |
| H | 16 | 17 | 18 | 19 | 1 | 0 |
| I | 16 | 16 | 19 | 19 | 0 | 0 |
| J | 18 | 20 | 22 | 24 | 2 | 2 |
| K | 19 | 19 | 24 | 24 | 0 | 0 |
| L | 25 | 25 | 26 | 26 | 0 | 0 |
| M | 24 | 24 | 25 | 25 | 0 | 0 |
| N | 26 | 26 | 29 | 29 | 0 | 0 |
| O | 29 | 29 | 30 | 30 | 0 | 0 |
| P | 5 | 5 | 5 | 5 | 0 | 0 |
| Q | 16 | 17 | 16 | 17 | 1 | 0 |
| R | 18 | 19 | 18 | 19 | 1 | 1 |

complete Activities A,B,P,D, and F, the longest path to I. The earliest finish time (EF) of an activity is equal to its earliest start time plus its activity time. For example, the earliest finish time for Activity I is 19 weeks. The latest finish time (LF) of an activity is equal to the scheduled project completion time minus the time requirements of the longest path from the end of that activity to the completion of the project. For example, the LF for Activity B is 5 (30 − 25) and the LF for Activity C is also 5. The latest start time (LS) for an activity is the latest time it can be started without delaying completion of the project. The LS of an activity is equal to the scheduled project completion time minus the time requirements of the longest path from the end of that activity to the completion of the project and the activity time. Or, more simply, it is the latest finish time minus activity time. Referring again to the network in Figure 16-6, the LS of Activity B is 2 (30 − 28), where 30 is the length of the critical path and 28 is the time required to complete Activities B,P,D,F,I,K,M,L,N, and O. The ES, EF, LS, and LF of all activities in Figure 16-6 are listed in Table 16-3.

## Slack (Float) Time

In general the term *slack* describes the amount of delay an activity can experience without affecting project completion. Whenever the desired project completion time is equal to the time requirements of the critical path, as is the case in the example illustrated in Figure 16-6, all activities on the critical path have zero slack.

There are two types of slack, total slack and free slack. *Total slack* is the amount of time that completion of an activity can slip and the project still be completed on schedule—given all the other activities are completed on schedule. It is equal to LS − ES, or to LF − EF. Total slack may include free slack and slack shared with another activity. *Free slack* is the amount of time the completion of an activity can slip and not delay the start of any subsequent activity.

For example, the total slack of Activity G in Figure 16-6 is 4 (17 − 13). Note that one week of Activity G's four weeks of slack is shared with Activity H. If the actual completion of *G* slips four weeks, *H* has no slack and must be completed without slippage to reach Node 9 in 19 weeks (the LS of Activity I). If, however, the completion of *G* slips three weeks or takes place on schedule, then Activity H has one week of slack. Thus, Activity G has four weeks of total slack and three weeks of free slack.

An alternative method of determining the critical path makes use of these concepts of ES and LS. By examining Figure 16-6, the ES for each activity can be computed by moving left to right through each node, assuming the project starts at time zero. Then the LS for each activity can be computed by moving right to left assuming the last event takes place at project completion time. The critical path is then noted as the sequence of activities for which the earliest and latest start times are equal; i.e., those that have zero slack. The following summarizes this:

Critical path = longest path through the network
Earliest start (ES) = longest path to an activity
Earliest finish (EF) = ES plus activity time
Latest finish (LF) = project completion time minus the time of the longest path to project completion
Latest start (LS) = LF minus activity time
Total slack = LS minus ES, or LF minus EF (LS minus ES = LF minus EF)
Free slack = ES of any subsequent activity minus EF

Calculation of each activity's free and total slack informs project management of those activities whose completion can be delayed (and how much each can be delayed) without affecting project completion and the amount of delay an activity can experience without affecting the ES of another activity. This information is valuable in scheduling project activities in a limited resource or time environment. In some cases, the time from the start of a project to its desired completion date may be greater than the length of the critical path. All activities have slack in such situations. Each activity on the critical path has total slack equal to the difference between the critical path length and the time from the beginning until the desired completion of the project. For example, if the desired completion of the example project was in Week 32 instead of Week 30 and the job was scheduled to begin in Week zero, then all activities would have an additional two weeks of slack. Part of the output for this problem from the computer program in Appendix K is given in Figure 16-7.

**FIGURE 16-7**
**SAMPLE COMPUTER OUTPUT**

NORMAL EVENT TIMES

| EVENT | EARLY OCCURRENCE | LATE OCCURRENCE | |
|---|---|---|---|
| 1 | 0 | 0 | CRITICAL |
| 2 | 2 | 2 | CRITICAL |
| 3 | 5 | 5 | CRITICAL |
| 4 | 5 | 5 | CRITICAL |
| 5 | 10 | 10 | CRITICAL |
| 6 | 16 | 16 | CRITICAL |
| 7 | 16 | 17 | |
| 8 | 18 | 19 | |
| 9 | 19 | 19 | CRITICAL |
| 10 | 24 | 24 | CRITICAL |
| 11 | 25 | 25 | CRITICAL |
| 12 | 26 | 26 | CRITICAL |
| 13 | 29 | 29 | CRITICAL |
| 14 | 30 | 30 | CRITICAL |

NORMAL ACTIVITY TIMES

| ACTIVITY | EVENT PRECEDENCE | ACTUAL | TOTAL SLACK | FREE SLACK |
|---|---|---|---|---|
| A | 1 - 2 | 2 | CRITICAL | 0 |
| B | 2 - 3 | 3 | CRITICAL | 0 |
| C | 2 - 4 | 1 | 2 | 2 |
| D | 4 - 5 | 5 | CRITICAL | 0 |
| E | 3 - 6 | 2 | 9 | 9 |
| F | 5 - 6 | 6 | CRITICAL | 0 |
| G | 5 - 7 | 3 | 4 | 3 |
| H | 7 - 8 | 2 | 1 | 0 |
| I | 6 - 9 | 3 | CRITICAL | 0 |
| J | 8 - 10 | 4 | 2 | 2 |
| K | 9 - 10 | 5 | CRITICAL | 0 |
| L | 11 - 12 | 1 | CRITICAL | 0 |
| M | 10 - 11 | 1 | CRITICAL | 0 |
| N | 12 - 13 | 3 | CRITICAL | 0 |
| O | 13 - 14 | 1 | CRITICAL | 0 |
| P | 3 - 4 | 0 | CRITICAL | 0 |
| Q | 6 - 7 | 0 | 1 | 0 |
| R | 8 - 9 | 0 | 1 | 1 |

EARLIEST POSSIBLE COMPLETION UNDER NORMAL CONDITIONS IS 30

# PERT

The distinguishing characteristic of PERT is its ability to encompass the inherent uncertainty of estimated activity completion times in certain types of projects. Although one may predict with relative certainty the time requirements of activities constituting a project with many similar predecessors, the time estimates of activities required to develop new technology or to perform a new and different task are inherently less certain. Thus, it is not surprising that a PERT approach frequently is adopted for research and design projects and that network models without provisions for measuring uncertainty are used in the management of many construction, equipment rebuilding, and assembly projects.

## Time Estimates

PERT achieves a probabilistic estimate of project completion by obtaining three estimates for each activity, describing the statistical distribution of possible times for each activity, and determining the standard deviation of each activity time and also of the project completion time. These three time estimates that are made for each activity when using PERT are given next.

1. The optimistic time (A) (the time required to complete the task if all goes especially well)
2. The pessimistic time (B) (the time required to complete the task if things go wrong)
3. The most likely time (M—the mode) (the time required to complete the task if all goes according to plan)

The *A* and *B* times are estimated on the basis that the probability of an actual time falling outside their range is about one in one hundred. The estimated average activity time and its variance calculation, shown on page 521, are based on the assumption that the distribution of activity times approaches that of a *beta* distribution.

Figure 16-8 illustrates the general shapes of two *beta* distributions. In one case it is skewed to the right and the *B* time is a greater distance from the *M* time than the *A* time estimate, and the mean time is greater than the *M* time. Figure 16-8 reflects the belief that delaying difficulties are most likely to occur. In the other case (the dotted line curve) just the opposite is true.[1]

The estimates of the average activity time ($t_e$) and measures of its variability ($\sigma_t^2$) are as follows:

[1] K. R. MacCrimmon and C. A. Ryavec, and A. R. Klingel, Jr., have published interesting reports of studies on the effects of the assumptions underlying PERT. [1,2]

FIGURE 16-8
PROFILES OF BETA DISTRIBUTIONS

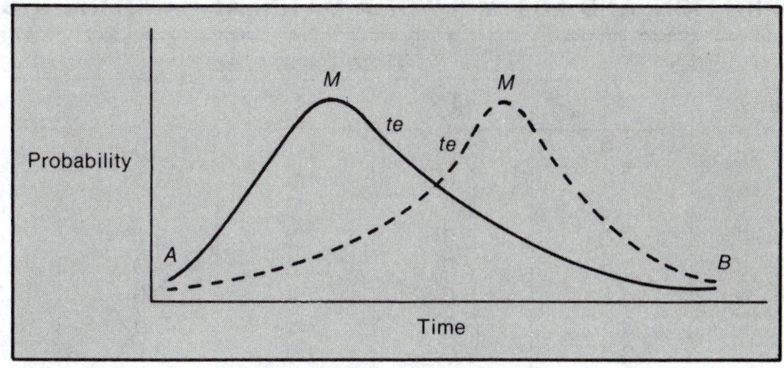


$$t_e = (A + 4M + B) \div 6$$
$$\sigma_t^2 = ([B\text{-}A] \div 6)^2$$

For example, let the three time estimates for Activity K from the earlier example be the following:

$$A = 4$$
$$M = 5$$
$$B = 8$$

Then,

$$t_e = (4 + 20 + 8) \div 6 = 5.33$$
$$\sigma_t^2 = ([8\text{-}4] \div 6)^2 = \frac{4}{9} \text{ or } .44 \qquad \sigma_t = \frac{2}{3} \text{ or } .67$$

These values indicate a distribution of activity times similar to that illustrated in Figure 16-9. Table 16-4 lists the optimistic, most likely, and pessimistic time estimates for the activities of the material handling system example discussed previously. These time estimates permit the calculation

FIGURE 16-9
DISTRIBUTION OF TIMES FOR ACTIVITY K

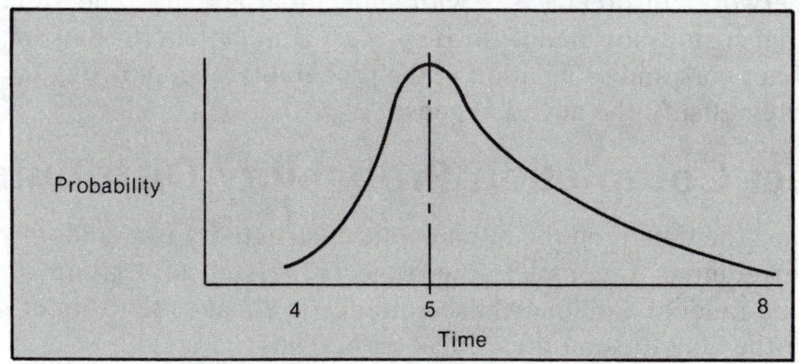

**TABLE 16-4**
**THREE TIME ESTIMATES, $t_e$, and $\sigma_t^2$ FOR ACTIVITIES IN THE DESIGN, FABRICATION, AND ASSEMBLY OF A MATERIAL HANDLING SYSTEM**

| Activity | Time Estimates* | | | | |
|---|---|---|---|---|---|
| | A | M | B | $t_e$ | $\sigma_t^2$ |
| A | 1.6 | 2.0 | 2.4 | 2.0 | .018 |
| B | 2.0 | 3.0 | 4.6 | 3.1 | .188 |
| C | .9 | 1.0 | 2.0 | 1.15 | .034 |
| D | 3.0 | 5.0 | 7.0 | 5.0 | .444 |
| E | .6 | 2.0 | 2.8 | 1.9 | .134 |
| F | 4.6 | 6.0 | 7.4 | 6.0 | .218 |
| G | 2.5 | 3.0 | 3.5 | 3.0 | .028 |
| H | 2.0 | 2.0 | 3.0 | 2.17 | .028 |
| I | 2.0 | 3.0 | 5.0 | 3.17 | .25 |
| J | 2.0 | 4.0 | 6.0 | 4.0 | .444 |
| K | 4.0 | 5.0 | 8.0 | 5.33 | .444 |
| L | 1.0 | 1.0 | 1.0 | 1.0 | 0 |
| M | .8 | 1.0 | 2.0 | 1.13 | .04 |
| N | 2.8 | 3.0 | 3.6 | 3.07 | .018 |
| O | 1.0 | 1.0 | 3.0 | 1.33 | .111 |

*Time estimates are in weeks.

of activity average time and variance estimates (also contained in Table 16-4).

The expected length of any path through a network is the sum of the expected lengths of the activities on the path. The longest such path is, of course, the critical path. Although the average time estimates of many activities differ slightly from the deterministic estimates given earlier, in this case the critical path is still that path consisting of Activities A,B,P,D,F,I,K,M, L,N, and O. However, the estimated project (critical path) length is now 31.13 weeks instead of 30 weeks due to the slightly longer average time estimates for Activities B,I,K,M,N, and O. This is not uncommon as deterministic point estimates of activity times tend to be the *M* time rather than the $t_e$ time, and activity time distributions tend to be skewed to the right. In many cases, differences between these two estimate types and the negligible variances of activity times do not justify the added costs of developing a PERT network. In other cases with substantial activity time variances or substantial costs associated with late project completion, the development of a PERT network and calculation of the probability of completing the project on schedule justify the added expense.

## Project Completion Probability Distribution

Since the time required to complete each activity is a random variable, the time required to complete the project (the sum of a group of activity times) is a random variable whose variance is equal to the sum of the variances of the activities on the critical path. Thus,

$$T_E = \sum_{i=1}^{k} t_{ei}, \qquad \sigma_T^2 = \sum_{i=1}^{k} \sigma_{t_i}^2$$

Where:

$T_E$ is the estimated average time required to complete the project
$\sigma_T^2$ is the variance of the distribution of estimated project completion time
$\sigma_{t_i}^2$ is the variance of estimated activity completion time
$t_{ei}$ is the estimated average element time
$i$ represents activities on the critical path
$k$ is the number of activities on the critical path

In our example, the critical path consists of Activities A,B,P,D, F,I,K,M,L,N, and O. Using the data contained in Table 16-4, $T_E$ and $\sigma_T^2$ can be calculated as follows:

$$\begin{aligned} T_E &= 2.0 + 3.1 + 0 + 5.0 + 6.0 + 3.17 + 5.33 + 1.13 + 1.0 + 3.07 + 1.33 \\ &= 31.13 \\ \sigma_T^2 &= .018 + .188 + 0 + .444 + .218 + .25 + .444 + 0.04 + 0 + 0.018 + .111 \\ &= 1.731 \end{aligned}$$

Since the standard deviation is equal to the square root of the variance, $\sigma_T = (1.731)^{1/2} = 1.316$.

Due to what is known in statistics as the central limit theorem, the distribution of a sum of random variables follows a normal, bell shaped distribution, regardless of the distribution of the components of the sum. This enables us to use the Table of Areas under the normal curve to calculate the probability of the project being completed within specific time frames.

To begin with, we know that there is a 50 percent probability that the project will be completed within 31.13 weeks, the average time, and a 50 percent chance that it will take longer; but what is the probability that it can be completed in 30.0 weeks, or in 35.0 weeks? To answer this type question we must calculate the number of standard deviations a desired completion time is from the average completion time. The following formula is used:

$$Z = \frac{T_D - T_E}{\sigma}$$

Where:

$T_D$ is the desired completion time
$Z$ is the number of standard deviations separating $T_D$ and $T_E$

Thus,

$$Z = \frac{30 - 31.13}{1.316} = -.86$$

Appendix H shows that the area of the curve from the mean to .86 standard deviations is equal to .3051. Figure 16-10 illustrates the relationship of $T_E$, $T_D$, and the probability of their occurrence. Since in this case $T_D$ is less than the average, the probability represented by the area between $T_E$ and $T_D$ is subtracted from .50 to determine the probability, $P(T_D)$, of completing the project on or before $T_D$. Thus,

$$P(T_D \geqslant 30) = .50 - .3051$$
$$= .1949$$

**FIGURE 16-10**
**RELATIONSHIP BETWEEN COMPLETION TIMES, STANDARD DEVIATIONS, AND PROBABILITIES**

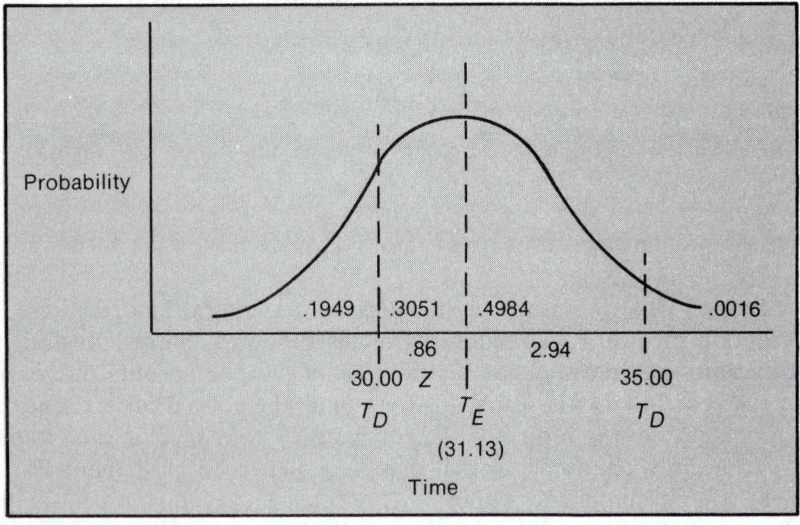


Performing the same calculations when $T_D$ equals 35.0 weeks gives the following:

$$Z = \frac{35 - 31.13}{1.316} = 2.94$$

Referring again to the Areas of a Standard Normal Distribution, we find that the area of the curve between the mean and the 2.94 standard deviations away is .4984. Since in this case the desired completion time is greater than the average, the probability represented by the area between $T_E$ and $T_D$ is added to .50 to obtain the probability of completing the project on or before $T_D$. Thus,

$$P(T_D \leqslant 35.0) = .50 + .4984$$
$$= .9984$$

Our calculations indicate that there is a 99.84 percent probability that the project will be completed within 35 weeks. This is misleading as it assumes a 100 percent probability of completing the activities on all other paths within 35 weeks. Calculating the exact probability of completing a project within a time period greater than $T_E$ is not straightforward. Subtracting the sum of the probabilities of the different paths requiring a time greater than $T_D$ from one; i.e., $1.0 - \Sigma P(T_{E_i} > T_D)$ will give a conservative probability estimate due to the interdependence of the paths. However, simulation (see Chapter 18) is an approach that can be used to estimate the probability of $T_D$ when $T_D > T_E$.

In summary, our time estimates and calculations indicate that it is almost certain that the project will be completed within 35 weeks and that there is slightly more than a 19 percent (19.49) probability that the project will be completed within 30 weeks.

# THE SCHEDULED ALLOCATION OF RESOURCES

Completion of the critical path network is a necessary planning step prior to scheduling. Decisions concerning which resources, workers, and machines will be assigned to tasks during a given period also are influenced by other factors such as the total resources available, other projects competing for the same resources, penalties for late completion, bonuses for early completion, and the relationship of the time available to the time required for completion of the project. The final schedule must be developed in concert with capacity requirements planning as discussed in Chapter 5.

Up to this point discussions of activity times were predicated on resources being allocated to activities at a normal rate (usually defined as the most efficient rate). However, in most cases management has the option of applying additional resources to decrease the duration of an activity by *crashing* the activity, or reducing the resources to a below normal rate and increasing the duration of the activity, or applying resources at the normal rate.

Recognition of the relationship of activity time durations to the allocation of resources was discussed first in literature concerning deterministic CPM models. However, the possibility of allocating resources to alter activity duration also exists in projects managed with the assistance of a PERT model; the distribution of possible activity times merely shifts. (In fact, other parameters in addition to the mean may change; but we will consider only changes in $t_e$).

Likely scheduling objectives include reduction of the project duration, cost minimization, and smoothing resource requirements over time. The typical real world project schedule usually requires that some balance be achieved between specific objectives in each of these areas. First, we will examine a case where resources are unlimited and the project duration must be shortened to a specific length with minimum additional costs.

Figure 16-11 illustrates the most typical relationship of activity times and resources allocation; this is the case in which an activity can be completed in normal time ($t_n$), at normal cost ($C_n$), or with the expenditure of additional resources in crash time ($t_c$), at a crash cost ($C_c$). It also may be completed in all times between $t_c$ and $t_n$ at costs between $C_c$ and $C_n$. Whether a single approximation of the slope is satisfactory or not depends on the degree of curvature.

**FIGURE 16-11**
**TOTAL COST VERSUS ACTIVITY DURATION**
**(A TYPICAL RELATIONSHIP)**

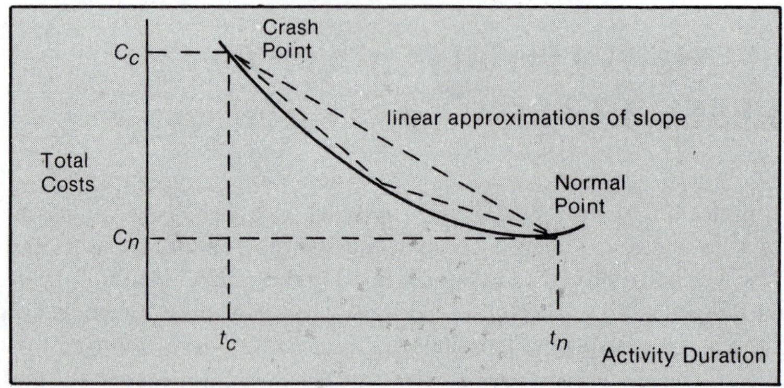


In real world situations, extending the time may either increase the total costs due to drawn-out inefficiencies or they may remain essentially the same. For example, if the normal procedure is to have four workers on an assembly, reducing the number to three will increase total costs only if some of the assembly operations are performed more efficiently by four persons working as a team. Increased costs associated with shortened activity times are the result of such things as overtime, additional setup and learning costs when the job is split among more workers, and the use of less skilled workers or less efficient machines.

## Cost Minimization

Project completion costs usually are a minimum when resources are expended at the normal, most efficient rate. If, however, the aggregate organizational demand for resources is unusually low at a particular time, surplus resources requiring no additional out-of-pocket expense may be applied to a project even when shortening its length is not a priority. In such a case the recorded costs of a particular project may increase due to inefficiencies, but total corporate expenditures will not increase and resources will be freed in a later period for which additional demand may materialize.

## Shortening Project Length

There are many occasions when it is desirable to complete a project in less than normal time. Bonuses for early completion, penalties for late completion, weather problems anticipated beyond a certain date, a combination of relatively light aggregate demand in proximate periods and heavy demand in later periods, and accelerated revenue generation are some of the possible justifications for attempting to complete a project early.

Resources must be available when required if a modified project schedule is to be implemented successfully. As illustrated shortly, analysis of project time-cost trade-offs will provide the information indicating when these resources are required. Thus, this analysis is initiated on the assumption that such resources are available. If there is competition for such resources, as frequently is the case, time-cost trade-off analysis results will be one of the inputs to the capacity allocation decision process described in Chapter 5.

The time-cost trade-off analysis begins with a determination of the approximate time-cost slope of each activity. This is a measure of the cost to shorten the duration of an activity. Table 16-5 lists the normal and the crash times and costs for each activity. All the times included in it approximate actual values while the cost figures are fictitious. Table 16-5 reveals, for example, that the cost of completing Activity F in six weeks, the normal time, is \$15,600 and the cost of completing it in three weeks, the crash time, is \$20,000. The cost slope is calculated as follows:

$$\text{Cost Slope} = \frac{C_c - C_n}{t_n - t_c}$$

Thus, the cost slope for Activity F equals \$1,467 per week ([20,000 − 15,600] ÷ [6 − 3]).

The following example illustrates how management can use cost slope and related information in resource allocation decisions required during project planning. If management desires to complete the design, fabrication, and assembly of the material handling system in 27 weeks rather than the normal 30 weeks, additional resources must be allocated to selected activities on the critical path. (Reduction of the duration of activities not on the critical path will not reduce the time required to complete the project.) In some cases it may be necessary to reallocate resources within the project, and in other cases it may be possible and desirable to obtain additional resources (external to the project).

If internal reallocation is required, additional resources should be sought from those activities where slack is greatest and applied to an activity or activities where they will have the greatest impact. For example, Activity E, Mechanical Fabrication 1, has nine weeks of slack. If some of the personnel and machines normally assigned to Activity E can be reallocated to Activity F, Mechanical Fabrication 2, the length of the critical path can be reduced.

**TABLE 16-5**
**NORMAL AND CRASH TIMES AND COSTS FOR ACTIVITIES IN THE DESIGN, FABRICATION, AND ASSEMBLY OF THE MATERIAL HANDLING SYSTEM**

| Activities[1] | Events | $t_n$[2] | $t_c$[3] | $C_n$ | $C_c$ | Cost Slope ($ per week) |
|---|---|---|---|---|---|---|
| A | 1-2 | 2.0 | 1.5 | $4,800 | $5,600 | $1,600 |
| B | 2-3 | 3.1 | 2.6 | 7,680 | 8,500 | 1,640 |
| C | 2-4 | 1.15 | .80 | 3,100 | 3,600 | 1,429 |
| D | 4-5 | 5.0 | 3.0 | 13,500 | 18,000 | 2,250 |
| E | 3-6 | 1.9 | .9 | 4,940 | 6,000 | 1,060 |
| F | 5-6 | 6.0 | 3.0 | 15,600 | 20,000 | 1,467 |
| G | 5-7 | 3.0 | 2.0 | 4,200 | 5,000 | 800 |
| H | 7-8 | 2.17 | 1.2 | 3,025 | 4,000 | 938 |
| I | 6-9 | 3.17 | 1.17 | 4,100 | 4,400 | 150 |
| J | 8-10 | 4.0 | 2.5 | 5,200 | 5,600 | 267 |
| K | 9-10 | 5.33 | 3.0 | 3,730 | 4,500 | 330 |
| L | 11-12 | 1.0 | .6 | 700 | 1,100 | 1,000 |
| M | 10-11 | 1.13 | .8 | 790 | 1,000 | 636 |
| N | 12-13 | 3.07 | 2.0 | 2,015 | 2,400 | 350 |
| O | 13-14 | 1.33 | 1.0 | 2,100 | 2,700 | 1,200 |
| P | 3-4 | 0 | 0 | 0 | 0 | 0 |
| Q | 6-7 | 0 | 0 | 0 | 0 | 0 |
| R | 8-9 | 0 | 0 | 0 | 0 | 0 |

[1]Critical path activities = A, B, D, F, I, K, L, M, N, and O.
[2]Normal time values are the same as average time in Table 16-4.
[3]Crash times are also averages from a distribution similar to that of $t_e$.

Guidelines for applying additional resources to the reduction of the critical path include the following:

1. Additional resources should be applied to activities with the smallest cost slope. This will minimize the costs of reducing the project length.
2. Additional resources should be applied to activities required relatively early in completion of the project. Once opportunities to reduce the project length are foregone, they cannot be regained. Should unplanned difficulties arise in early activities, later opportunities still will be available to compensate for unplanned delays.
3. Additional resources should be applied to critical path activities that also are on those noncritical paths whose lengths approach that of the critical path. Shortening the critical path by decreasing the time required to complete activities on the other near critical paths can result in a new critical path with some of the activity time reductions not reflected in a decreased project length.

Of the activities on the critical path, Activity I has the smallest cost slope, $150 per week. The project duration can be reduced two weeks (3.17 – 1.17) merely by investing an additional $300. Yet a total savings of three weeks is required to reduce the project to 27 weeks. Since a two-week reduction is achieved by applying additional resources to Activity I, another week reduction must be found. Candidate activities on the critical path, in ranking order of their cost slopes, are:

| Rank | Activity | Cost Slope | Possible Reduction (Weeks) |
|---|---|---|---|
| 1 | K | $330 | 2.33 |
| 2 | N | 350 | 1.07 |
| 3 | M | 636 | .33 |
| 4 | L | 1,000 | .4 |
| 5 | O | 1,200 | .33 |
| 6 | F | 1,467 | 3.0 |
| 7 | A | 1,600 | .5 |
| 8 | B | 1,640 | .5 |
| 9 | D | 2,250 | 2.0 |

Selecting Activity K for the planned application of an additional $330 will reduce the duration of Activity K by one week, but unless *H* or *J* (which go on in parallel) are reduced no reduction can be achieved. It is not uncommon for planned shortening of project length to increase the number or activities that are critical. It is also true that many possible options must be examined before selection of the one that best meets management's criteria is found. It is difficult to keep track of all the interactions in evaluating alternatives. However, this resource allocation problem can be formulated and solved as a linear programming problem as shown in Chapter 17 on pages 552 and 553.

## Other Cost Slopes

Not all activities possess one of the cost slopes illustrated in Figure 16-12. Many, however, do. Discontinuous cost slopes, for example, can exist in the case of purchase parts that may be delivered in, say, two weeks if shipped by truck or rail and in a day or two if shipped by air express. Nothing in between is possible for practical purposes. Some activities are inherently gestational and applying additional resources does not affect the time required to complete the activity. Physical growth, aging, fermentation, and some chemical processes cannot be shortened. Cerebral processes such as research and design also fall into this category on some occasions, as may product testing and evaluation. Decreasing the time requirements of some activities beyond a certain point may require an additional capital investment—as illustrated by a step increase in cost—to obtain the required additional personnel or machine capacity. Other cost slopes are also possible. The point is that the costs related to the possible durations of each activity must be analyzed to determine which cost slope adequately represents the cost-time relationship of each activity.

**FIGURE 16-12**
**OTHER COST SLOPES**

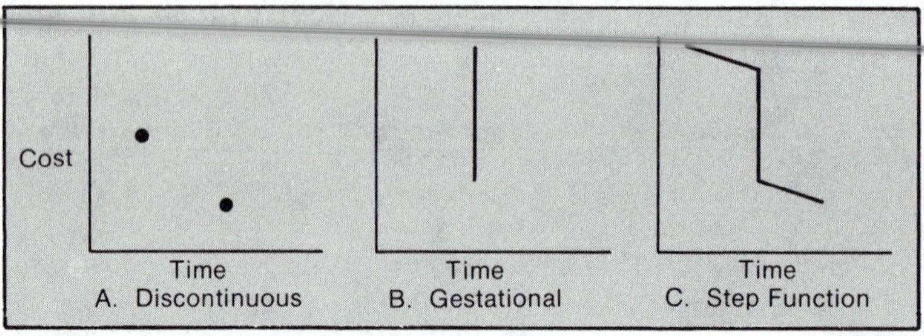

Cost

Time
A. Discontinuous

Time
B. Gestational

Time
C. Step Function

# PROJECT CONTROL

The greatest benefit of network models is the improved insight they provide concerning project completion status. For example, activities behind schedule, but with sufficient slack to still complete the project on schedule, do not require the corrective action that a behind schedule activity on the critical path with negative slack would demand.

Successful project completion requires timely monitoring of work completion and comparison to scheduled completion. Control of projects is based on the same principles that control ongoing, non-project type activities. Although these are covered in other chapters, it is worth repeating some of them here.

1. Plans should be realistic and not reflect an overstated estimate of capacity.
2. Control of the planning activity itself requires:
   a. Management commitment to the objectives of the plan and the availability of the resources and
   b. Agreement (preferably in writing) by the appropriate managers and supervisors that the precedence relationships, time estimates, and costs are realistic.
3. A performance reporting system with adequate, accurate, and timely information should exist. Most project completion situations are dynamic. Changing conditions and actual performance initiation and completion may change priorities.
4. Procedures should exist for evaluating performance on a regular basis, determining what, if any, corrective action is required, and revising schedules and operating plans accordingly.

Daily or at least weekly reports of performance to date listing revised, early, and late start and finish dates, activity slack, expected project completion, and activities to be initiated in the current period are necessary to implement control.

# ACTIVITY ON THE NODE

As mentioned earlier in this chapter, a project can be represented by a network with the activities on the node as well as by the activity-on-the-arrow approach which we have used to this point. Figure 16-13 is an example of an activity-on-the-node type network. It is based on the data contained in Table 16-1 and is the counterpart of the activity-on-the-arrow network in Figure 16-6.

Examination of Figure 16-13 reveals the advantages of the activity-on-the-node approach. Dummy activities are not required; manual network construction and modification are simpler. At one time there was a scarcity of available computer software packages for activity-on-the-node applications, but that is no longer the case. Either deterministic or probabilistic (PERT type) models can be used with either activity-on-the-arrow or activity-on-the-node representations. Selection between these two approaches depends primarily on local conditions and preferences.

**FIGURE 16-13**
**ACTIVITY-ON-THE-NODE NETWORK MODEL**
**DESIGN, FABRICATION, AND ASSEMBLY**
**MATERIAL HANDLING SYSTEM**

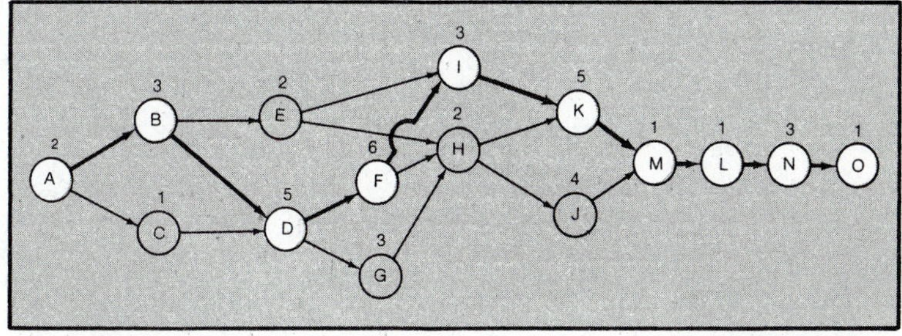


Let us point once again in summary that network models have been widely accepted as valuable aids in planning and controlling project type activities. They are especially useful in defining the relative priorities of the tasks that constitute the project, estimating the probability of completing the project within specified time periods, scheduling resources for specific tasks, and determining if task completion times require either a revision of the schedule or a reallocation of resources.

# PROBLEMS

1. What are the major differences between PERT and CPM?
2. Explain the difference between total and free slack.

**3.** What are dummy activities, and why are they used?

**4.** Solve the following CPM problem for both normal and full crash conditions.

| | Events | | Normal | | Crash | |
|---|---|---|---|---|---|---|
| Activity | Preceding | Following | Time | Cost | Time | Cost |
| A | 1 | 2 | 4 | 140 | 2 | 230 |
| B | 2 | 3 | 5 | 210 | 3 | 370 |
| C | 1 | 4 | 2 | 130 | 2 | 130 |
| D | 4 | 5 | 7 | 250 | 6 | 375 |
| E | 3 | 6 | 7 | 230 | 4 | 400 |
| F | 5 | 6 | 3 | 150 | 2 | 195 |

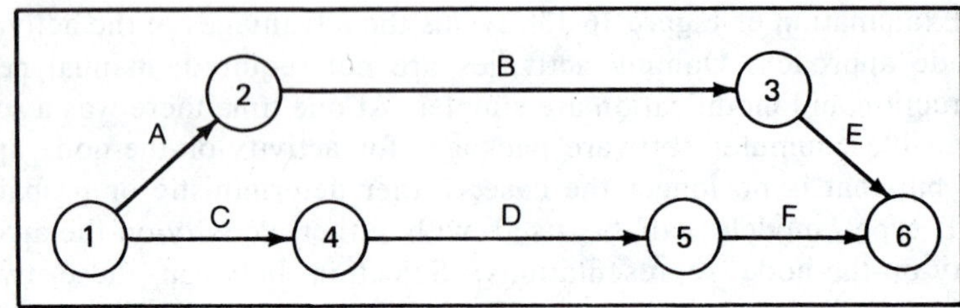


**5.** What is wrong with the following network?

| Activity | Preceding Activities | Following Activities |
|---|---|---|
| A | — | A |
| B | — | E |
| C | F,I | — |
| D | J,H | I,E |
| E | B,C | H |
| F | G | C |
| G | A | F,J |
| H | E | D |
| I | D | C |
| J | G | D |

**6.** Find the critical path, ES, LS, and slack for the following network.

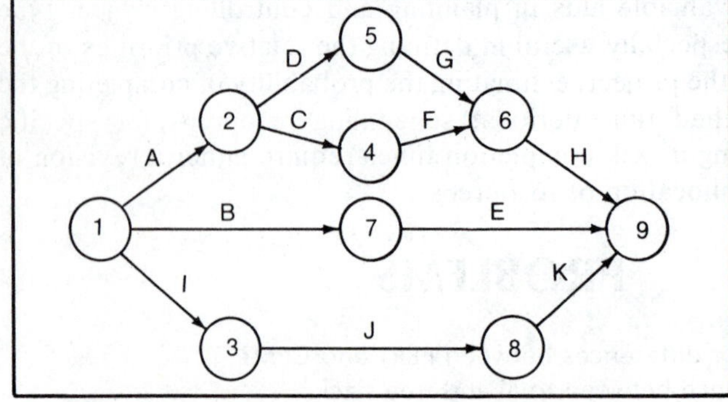


| Activity | $t_n$ |
|---|---|
| A | 3 |
| B | 5 |
| C | 4 |
| D | 2 |
| E | 6 |
| F | 4 |
| G | 3 |
| H | 5 |
| I | 4 |
| J | 3 |
| K | 5 |

7. In Problem 6, after one week (5 days) a progress report is made: Activities A,C,O, and I are finished, *B* is 60% completed, *J* will start on Day 6, as will *F*. The rest have not started nor are they scheduled. What has happened to the critical path and the slack for each activity?

8. Find the critical path of the following PERT network and determine the probability that the project will be completed in 28 days.

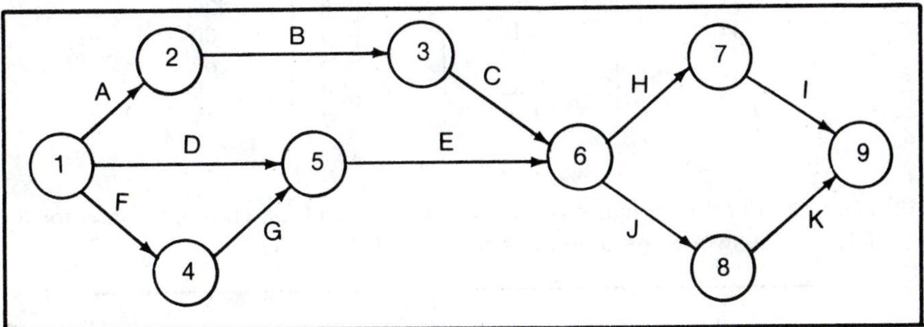


| Activity | Time Estimates A | B | M |
|---|---|---|---|
| A | 3 | 7 | 5 |
| B | 2 | 5 | 3 |
| C | 5 | 10 | 7 |
| D | 5 | 10 | 8 |
| E | 3 | 6 | 4 |
| F | 3 | 8 | 5 |
| G | 2 | 3 | 2 |
| H | 4 | 9 | 6 |
| I | 3 | 6 | 4 |
| J | 2 | 5 | 3 |
| K | 5 | 9 | 7 |

9. Find the critical path for both normal and full crash conditions. Assuming normal time operations cost $40 per day, what are the costs of each solution?

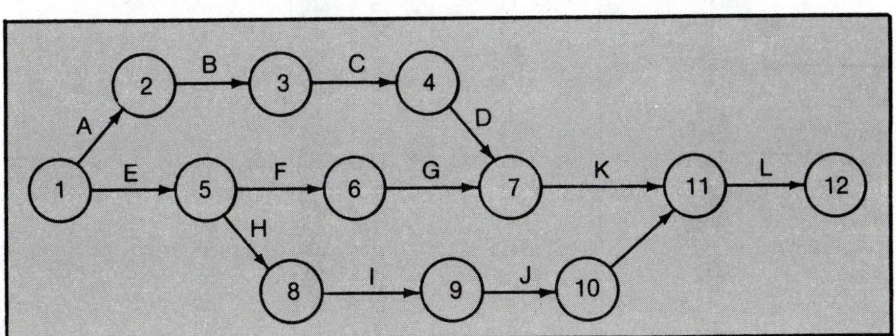

| Activity | Preceding Activities | $t_n$ | $t_c$ | $C_c$ per day |
|---|---|---|---|---|
| A | — | 4 | 3 | 60 |
| B | A | 6 | 4 | 100 |
| C | B | 5 | 4 | 50 |
| D | C | 3 | 3 | — |
| E | — | 7 | 4 | 85 |
| F | E | 6 | 3 | 55 |
| G | F | 6 | 4 | 65 |
| H | E | 7 | 6 | 120 |
| I | H | 3 | 3 | 00 |
| J | I | 4 | 3 | 80 |
| K | D,G | 5 | 4 | 90 |
| L | K,J | 3 | 2 | 45 |

**10.** Find the critical path and cost for both normal and full crash situations for the following networks. Assume normal cost of $40 per day.

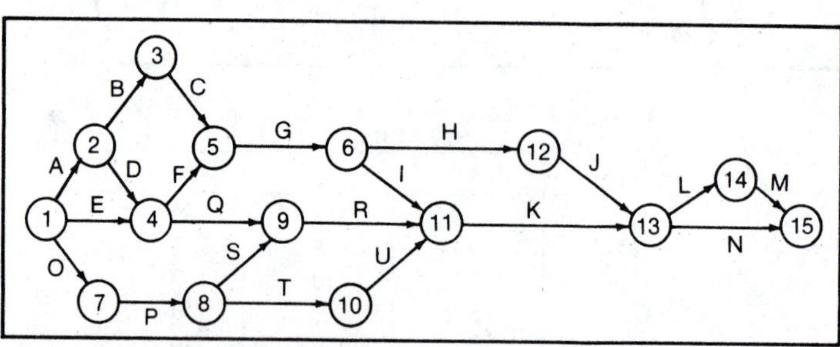


| Activity | Preceding Activities | $t_n$ | $t_c$ | $C_c$ per day |
|---|---|---|---|---|
| A | — | 3 | 2 | 65 |
| B | A | 5 | 3 | 105 |
| C | B | 4 | 3 | 120 |
| D | A | 7 | 5 | 65 |
| E | — | 11 | 7 | 90 |
| F | D,E | 4 | 3 | 45 |
| G | C,F | 3 | 3 | — |
| H | G | 6 | 5 | 40 |
| I | G | 5 | 2 | 65 |
| J | H | 5 | 3 | 105 |
| K | I,R,U | 7 | 4 | 45 |
| L | J,K | 3 | 3 | — |
| M | L | 2 | 1 | 110 |
| N | J,K | 3 | 2 | 60 |
| O | — | 9 | 7 | 75 |
| P | O | 2 | 2 | — |
| Q | D,E | 4 | 3 | 65 |
| R | Q,S | 6 | 5 | 95 |
| S | P | 3 | 2 | 55 |
| T | P | 5 | 3 | 80 |
| U | T | 3 | 1 | 60 |

**11.** Construct a precedence diagram for the following relationships.

| Activity | Preceding Activities | Succeeding Activities |
|---|---|---|
| A | None | C |
| B | None | C,D |
| C | A,B | E |
| D | B | E,F |
| E | C,D | G |
| F | D | H |
| G | E | None |
| H | F | None |

**12.** Referring to Problem 4, after doing the initial planning we find that an additional activity, *G*, must be done before *E* or *F* can proceed and must follow *A* and *C*. *G*'s normal time is 6 at a cost of $220, and it can be crashed to 5 at an additional cost of $100. Draw the revised network diagram and solve for the new critical path for both normal and crash conditions.

# SELECTED READINGS


**1.** Kenneth R. MacCrimmon and Charles A. Ryavec, "An Analytical Study of the PERT Assumptions," *Operations Research* (January-February, 1964), pp. 16-37.

**2.** A. R. Klingel, Jr., "Bias in PERT Project Completion Time Calculations for a Real Network," *Management Science*, Vol. 13, No. 4 (1966), pp. 194-201.

**3.** A. R. Burgess and James B. Killebrew, "Variation in Activity Level on a Cyclical Arrow Diagram," *Journal of Industrial Engineering*, Vol. 13, No. 2 (March-April, 1962), pp. 76-83.

**4.** C. T. Clingen, "A Modification of Fulkerson's PERT Algorithm," *Operations Research*, Vol. 12, No. 4 (July-August, 1964), pp. 629-631.

**5.** Salah E. Elmaghraby, "On Generalized Activity Networks," *Journal of Industrial Engineering*, Vol. 17, No. 11 (November, 1966), pp. 621-631.

**6.** ______, "On the Expected Duration of PERT Type Networks," *Management Science*, Vol. 13, No. 5 (January, 1967), pp. 299-306.

**7.** ______, "The Theory of Networks and Management Science, II," *Management Science*, Vol. 17, No. 2 (October, 1970), pp. 54-71.

**8.** D. R. Fulkerson, "Expected Critical Path Lengths in PERT Networks," *Operations Research*, Vol. 10, No. 6 (November-December, 1962), pp. 808-817.

**9.** James E. Kelley, "Critical Path Planning and Scheduling, Mathematical Basis," *Operations Research*, Vol. 9, No. 2 (May-June, 1961), pp. 296-320.

**10.** Richard I. Levin and Charles A. Kirkpatrick, *Planning and Control with PERT/CPM* (New York: McGraw-Hill Book Company, 1966).

**11.** Ferdinand K. Levy, Gerald L. Thompson, and Jerome D. Wiest, "The ABC's of the Critical Path Method," *Harvard Business Review* (September-October, 1963), pp. 98-108.

**12.** D. G. Malcolm, J. H. Roseboom, C. E. Clark, and W. Fazar, "Application of a Technique for Research and Development Program Evaluation," *Operations Research*, Vol. 7, No. 5 (September-October, 1959).

**13.** Joseph J. Moder and Cecil R. Phillips, *Project Management with CPM and PERT*, 2d ed. (New York: Litton Educational Publishing, Inc., Van Nostrand Reinhold Company, 1970).

**14.** L. R. Shaffer, J. B. Ritter, and W. L. Meyer, *The Critical Path Method* (New York: McGraw-Hill Book Company, 1965).

**15.** Richard M. Van Slyke, "Monte Carlo Methods and the PERT Problem," *Operations Research*, Vol. 11, No. 5 (September-October, 1963), pp. 839-860.

**16.** Jerome D. Weist, "Heuristic Programs for Decision Making," *Harvard Business Review* (September-October, 1966), pp. 129-143.

**17.** Jerome Wiest and Ferdinand Levy, *A Management Guide to PERT/CPM*, 2d ed. (Englewood Cliffs, N.J.: Prentice-Hall, Inc., 1977).

# —17—

# MATHEMATICAL PROGRAMMING

The techniques referred to as mathematical programming include methods to solve linear, nonlinear, integer, geometric, stochastic, goal, stochastic, 0-1, and mixed integer problems as well as the transportation problem, the assignment problem, and others. Each of these techniques and their associated solution procedures involve a model of some process or situation and the determination of a best or optimal (maximum or minimum) solution (in terms of profits, costs, or other measure or measures of merit) through the proper allocation of limited resources.

The fundamental concepts were developed in the 1940's and 1950's and have been elaborated upon ever since. Generally many practical problems involve prodigious amounts of computation; hence the rise in usefulness of mathematical programming has paralleled the growth in computers. Many texts are devoted exclusively to one or more of these techniques and lengthy users' manuals exist for standard computer packages. Our purpose here is only to acquaint or refresh the reader with the basic models and solution techniques, particularly as they are found in applications related to production and inventory control. Such applications include optimal blending of raw materials into final product, aggregate planning, optimal critical path method (CPM) schedules, capital budgeting, and other resource constrained, complex problems.

## LINEAR PROGRAMMING AND THE SIMPLEX SOLUTION TECHNIQUES

At the heart of linear programming (LP) is a model of the real world expressed in linear equations; i.e., all variables are to the first power (e.g., $X$, $Y$, etc., not $X^2$, nor products like $XY$). Furthermore, none of the variables can take on negative values and they must be continuously divisible; i.e., they can take on values like 0.5 or 3.167 as well as 4. Finally, there is no uncertainty in the coefficients or values in the model. (The various other mathematical programming techniques either relax these conditions to obtain more realistic models—e.g., nonlinear and stochastic programming—or impose additional conditions to handle real world situations more accurately, e.g., integer and goal programming. The solution procedures are generally more complex as a result.) While these conditions (linearity, nonnegativity, continuity, and certainty) may seem restrictive in developing models they have proved not to be a hindrance in many settings.

The general form of a linear programming problem is a set of linear relationships defining the trade-offs for each resource which is to be allocated and a single objective function which gives the contribution of each decision variable. Mathematically that might look like the following:

$$\text{Constraints or Requirements} \begin{cases} 5X + 6Y \leq 27.75 \\ 4X + 2Y \leq 13 \\ 3.6X + 8.1Y \geq 23 \end{cases}$$

$$\text{Objective} \quad \text{Maximize } 1.8X + 2Y$$

(Note: The nonnegativity constraint is usually not shown explicitly, nor is it required, since the solution procedure guarantees its existence.)

In a problem such as this (one having only two variables) the system of equations can be easily graphed and the solution obtained by inspection. Few real world problems are this simple, but the graph can illustrate the innate features of any mathematical programming problem so it is worthwhile examining briefly before going on to a purely mathematical procedure, the simplex technique.

## Graphical Representation and Solution

The first equation, $5X + 6Y \leq 27.75$, represents an area, technically a half plane, bounded by and including the line $5X + 6Y = 27.75$. Note that the inequality ($\leq$) is what distinguishes the line from the area bounded by the line. This is shown in Figure 17-1. Since both $X$ and $Y$ must be positive, the area is further confined to that bounded by the $X$ and $Y$ axes (the first quadrant). This is shown in Figure 17-2. We can now add the constraint $4X + 2Y \leq 13$, which, since any feasible solution must simultaneously satisfy both constraints, effectively chops off a corner of the first area (see Figure 17-3). Finally, the requirement that $3.6X + 8.1Y \geq 23$ confines the solution space to the area previously defined lying above $3.6X + 8.1Y = 23$ is illustrated in Figure 17-4.

The objective is to maximize the value of $1.8X + 2Y$. This equation defines a family of straight lines all parallel to each other and so having the same slope ($-1.8 \div 2.0$). Our task is to find the one positioned to have the largest sum and still intersect the solution space. In Figure 17-5 several have been drawn which intersect the feasible region at various places. Perhaps it is not obvious (but maybe it is after a little study) that the optimal solution will always lie on a corner (vertex) of the constrained space or on an edge connecting two corners and not on a line through the middle of the area. This

**FIGURE 17-1**
**HALF PLANE BOUNDED**
**BY 5X + 6Y = 27.75**

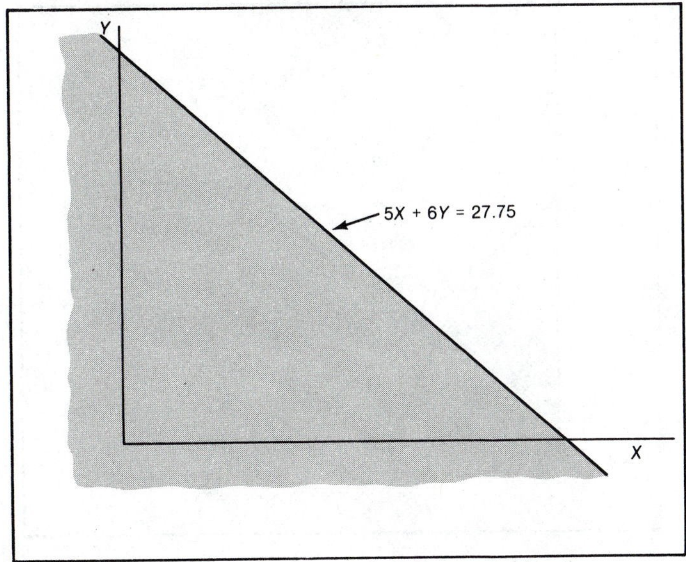


is one of the important discoveries of the theory of linear programming. It means that instead of having to search the entire area defined by the constraints we need only look at the corners in order to find the optimal solution. There are an infinite number of points in the area, but there is only a

**FIGURE 17-2**
**HALF PLANE FURTHER BOUNDED**
**BY THE *X* and *Y* AXES**

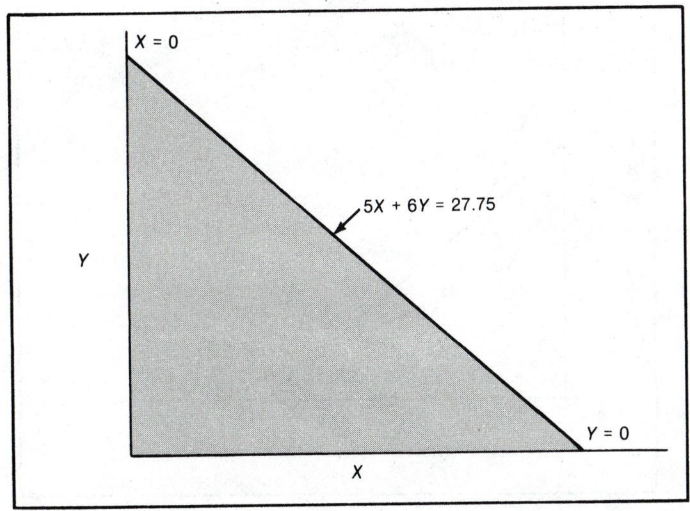

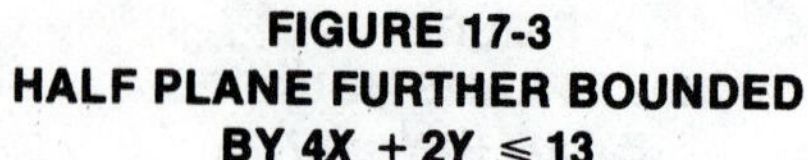

**FIGURE 17-3**
**HALF PLANE FURTHER BOUNDED**
**BY $4X + 2Y \leq 13$**

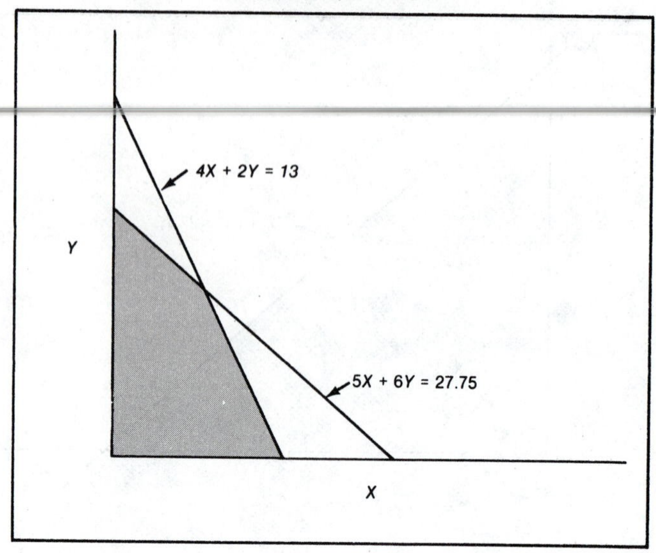


finite number of corners (four in our example). Purely mathematical techniques are simply organized methods of examining, either implicitly or explicitly, these corners.

**FIGURE 17-4**
**HALF PLANE WITH ALL CONSTRAINTS**
**IN PLACE**

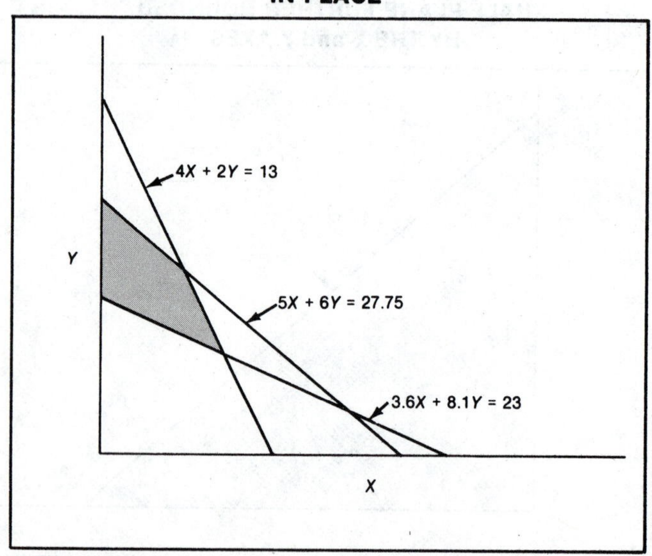

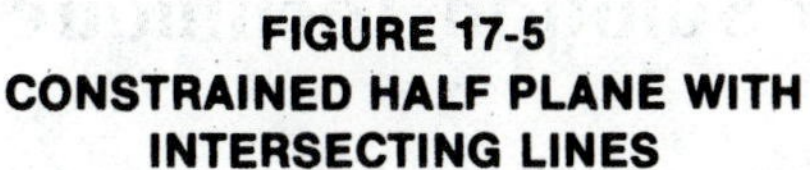

**FIGURE 17-5**
**CONSTRAINED HALF PLANE WITH INTERSECTING LINES**

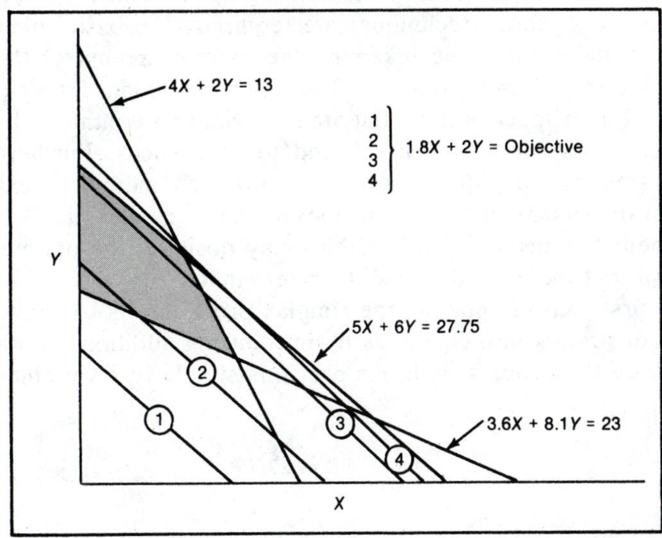


In our example the four candidates for possible optimal solutions are at:

| $X$ | $Y$ |
|---|---|
| 0 | 2.839 |
| 0 | 4.625 |
| 1.607 | 3.286 |
| 2.353 | 1.794 |

The value of the objective function at these points is 5.679, 9.25, 9.4643, and 7.823 respectively. Thus, the optimum occurs at $X = 1.607$ and $Y = 3.286$ as can be confirmed graphically as the most extreme point (from the origin) at which the line $1.8X + 2Y$ intersects the constrained area.

Perhaps it is worth noting that, if the coefficients of the objective function had a ratio of less than 5/6 (the coefficients of the first constraints), for example, $1.6 \div 2$, the optimum, then, would be at $X = 0, Y = 4.625$. If the ratio rose to greater than 4 to 2 (e.g., 1.8 to .8), then the optimum would be at $X = 2.353$, $Y = 1.794$. This sort of analysis of the structure of the problem and the impact of changes to the coefficients is referred to as postoptimality or sensitivity analysis and is commonly done when the real world coefficients have some uncertainty about them or when they could be altered.

# The Simplex Solution Technique

For problems having many variables, graphic solution procedures are inadequate, so algebraic techniques are required. The basic rule of action, however, remains the same: examine the extreme points of the solution space to find the optimum solution. The difference is that for simplex problems the solution space is not a flat area but rather a volume or hypercube; the corners, therefore, can be referred to as vertices. Furthermore, the algebraic simplex technique proceeds in an orderly manner to examine the vertices in such a way that each one does not have to be explicitly examined. The mathematics insures that variables stay positive, the optimum will be found, and that the procedure will then terminate.

The first step in applying the simplex procedure is to convert the inequality constraints into equalities by introducing additional variables. We can illustrate the process with our previous simple two variable example. Thus,

$$5X + 6Y \leqslant 27.75$$

becomes

$$5X + 6Y + S_1 = 27.75.$$

Where $\underline{S}_1$ takes on whatever slack value is necessary for given $X$ and $Y$ values in order that the sum will equal 27.75 exactly. Similarly,

$$4X + 2Y + S_2 = 13.$$

But, if we only included a slack variable in the third equation,

$$3.6X + 8.1Y \geqslant 23$$

to yield

$$3.6X + 8.1Y + S_3 = 23$$

then $S_3$ would have to be negative and that would violate the nonnegativity constraint. To take care of that we introduce an artificial variable with a positive coefficient and a slack variable with a negative coefficient; for example:

$$3.6X + 8.1Y + A_3 - S_3 = 23.$$

Now we must incorporate these additional variables into the objective function. Since the slack variables contribute nothing to the cost or profit, their coefficients are zero. The artificial variable, on the other hand, is just that, and while the simplex procedure needs it to get started, we do not want it in the final solution. To accomplish that we simply assign it a large negative profit coefficient, often referred to as "big $M$" where $M$ is a very large number. Thus the objective is to maximize

$$1.8X + 2Y + 0S_1 + 0S_2 - MA_3 + 0S_3$$

Subject to

$$\begin{aligned} 5X + 6Y + S_1 \qquad\qquad\qquad &= 27.75 \\ 4X + 2Y \qquad + S_2 \qquad\qquad &= 13 \\ 3.6X + 8.1Y \qquad\qquad + A_3 - S_3 &= 23 \end{aligned}$$

Now for convenience this can be converted to matrix form by just writing down the numeric values and remembering that those in the first column apply to $X$, the second column to $Y$, and so forth.

| | | | | | | | |
|---|---|---|---|---|---|---|---|
| Objective | 1.8 | 2 | 0 | 0 | $-M$ | 0 | |
| Subject to | 5 | 6 | 1 | 0 | 0 | 0 | 27.75 |
| | 4 | 2 | 0 | 1 | 0 | 0 | 13 |
| | 3.6 | 8.1 | 0 | 0 | 1 | $-1$ | 23 |

Now for an initial solution, we can assume both $X$ and $Y$ are zero and let $S_1 = 27.75$, $S_2 = 13$, $A_3 = 23$, and $S_3 = 0$. That choice for $X$ and $Y$ does not yield a good objective value, but the equations are satisfied and we have an initial feasible solution. In order to keep track of everything we will establish the following format or tableau (as it is sometimes called):

| $C_j$ | | 1.8 | 2 | 0 | 0 | $-M$ | 0 | |
|---|---|---|---|---|---|---|---|---|
| | | $X$ | $Y$ | $S_1$ | $S_2$ | $A_3$ | $S_3$ | Solution quantities |
| 0 | $S_1$ | 5 | 6 | 1 | 0 | 0 | 0 | 27.75 |
| 0 | $S_2$ | 4 | 2 | 0 | 1 | 0 | 0 | 13 |
| $-M$ | $A_3$ | 3.6 | 8.1 | 0 | 0 | 1 | $-1$ | 23 |
| $Z_j$ | | $-3.6M$ | $-8.1M$ | 0 | 0 | $-M$ | $M$ | $-23M$ |
| $C_j - Z_j$ | | $1.8 + 3.6M$ | $2 + 8.1M$ | 0 | 0 | 0 | $-M$ | |

The $C_j$ row ($j$ is the column number) at the top contains the coefficients of the objective function; the $C_j$ column at the left contains the objective coefficients of the variables in the solution (whose names appear in the second column). The values in the $Z_j$ row are the sum of the products of the $C_j$ column of coefficients with the $j$th column of coefficients in the body of the table; e.g., $Z_1 = 0 \times 5 + 0 \times 4 + 3.6(-M) = -3.6M$. The $C_j - Z_j$ row is used to determine which variable to next bring into the solution in order to get the greatest improvement in the objective function. To do this we look for the largest positive value $(2 + 8.1M)$ and find it under Column $Y$. This is referred to as the key column. Next we see which variable must go out when $Y$ comes in. To do this we compute the ratio of the solution quantities (in the right-hand column) to their respective coefficients in the key column and identify the smallest of these which is nonnegative. In our case the ratios are: $27.75 \div 6 = 4.625$, $13 \div 2 = 6.5$, and $8.1 \div 23 = 0.352$. The smallest of these is the last one and so row three is the key row. This means that we are going to bring into our solution $Y$ in place of $Z_3$. While the basic process is very similar to the usual Gaussian elimination procedure normally used in solving simultaneous equations, it is convenient here to compute the new table of coefficients with the following formula:

$$\text{New value} = \text{old value} - \frac{\begin{matrix}\text{corresponding value}\\ \text{in key row}\end{matrix} \times \begin{matrix}\text{corresponding value}\\ \text{in key column}\end{matrix}}{\text{key number}}$$

where the key number is the number at the intersection of the key row and key column (8.1 in our example). Thus, the new value in the $X$ column, first row (the one with $S_1$ in it) is computed as:

$$\text{New value} = 5 - \frac{3.6 \times 6}{8.1} = 2.333.$$

The new tableau is thus computed as follows:

| $C_j$ | | 1.8 | 2 | 0 | 0 | $-M$ | 0 | |
|---|---|---|---|---|---|---|---|---|
| | | $X$ | $Y$ | $X_1$ | $S_1$ | $A_3$ | $S_3$ | Solution quantities |
| 0 | $S_1$ | 2.333 | 0 | 1 | 0 | −.741 | .741 | 10.713 |
| 0 | $S_2$ | 3.111 | 0 | 0 | 1 | −.247 | .247 | 7.321 |
| 2 | $Y$ | .444 | 1 | 0 | 0 | .123 | −.123 | 2.840 |
| $Z_j$ | | .888 | 2 | 0 | 0 | .246 | −.246 | 5.680 |
| $C_j - Z_j$ | | .912 | 0 | 0 | 0 | $-.246-M$ | +.246 | |

Repeating this procedure, we find the largest value is .912 in the column headed by $X$ and the key row is the $S_2$ one with a ratio of $7.321 \div 3.111$. The new matrix is tabulated, then, as follows:

| $C_j$ | | 1.8 | 2.0 | 0 | 0 | $-M$ | 0 | |
|---|---|---|---|---|---|---|---|---|
| | | $X$ | $Y$ | $S_1$ | $S_2$ | $A_3$ | $S_3$ | Solution quantities |
| 0 | $S_1$ | 0 | 0 | 1 | −.750 | −.556 | .556 | 5.222 |
| 1.8 | $X$ | 1 | 0 | 0 | .321 | −.079 | .079 | 2.353 |
| 2 | $Y$ | 0 | 1 | 0 | −.143 | .159 | −.159 | 1.794 |
| $Z_j$ | | 1.8 | 2 | 0 | .292 | .176 | −.176 | 7.823 |
| $C_j - Z_j$ | | 0 | 0 | 0 | −.292 | $-.176-M$ | .176 | |

Repeating once again, the largest $C_j - Z_j$ is .176 under the column headed $S_3$ and the smallest ratio is 5.22 ÷ .556 for the row labeled $S_1$. The next matrix is thus:

| $C_j$ | | 1.8 | 2.0 | 0 | 0 | $-M$ | 0 | |
|---|---|---|---|---|---|---|---|---|
| | | $X$ | $Y$ | $S_1$ | $S_2$ | $A_3$ | $S_3$ | Solution quantities |
| 0 | $S_3$ | 0 | 0 | 1.800 | −1.350 | −1.00 | 1 | 9.400 |
| 1.8 | $X$ | 1 | 0 | −1.43 | .429 | 0 | 0 | 1.607 |
| 2 | $Y$ | 0 | 1 | .286 | −.357 | 0 | 0 | 3.286 |
| $Z_j$ | | 1.8 | 2 | .314 | .057 | 0 | 0 | 9.464 |
| $C_j - Z_j$ | | 0 | 0 | −.314 | −.057 | $-M$ | 0 | |

Examination of this $C_j - Z_j$ row shows that none of the values is positive and, therefore, no further improvement in the objective function can be made. The optimal solution is therefore $X = 1.607$ and $Y = 3.286$. This is, of course, the same solution we found earlier by graphical means. The advantage of the algebraic simplex technique is that a great deal more information can be obtained from this final matrix, and we are not limited to just two (or three) variables as we are for graphical presentations.

While extensive development of postoptimality or sensitivity analysis is beyond the scope of this text, an indication of some of the additional insights that can be gained from this technique is seen by looking at the meaning of the $C_j - Z_j$ row values. These are the so-called shadow costs (or shadow prices) and give the marginal change that would occur in the objective function for each unit of a variable that would enter the solution. For example, looking at the second solution matrix, page 544, we observed a shadow cost of .912 for Variable $X$. This means that the objective function will increase by .912 for each unit of $X$ we bring into the solution. Because of the constraints we could only bring in 7.321 ÷ 3.111 units and hence the objective function increased by .912 times 2.353, or 2.146. This is confirmed as 7.823 −5.680, the difference between the objective function values for the successive solutions (slight difference in last digit is due to rounding). Similar computations allow one to state the range of values for each constraint under which the solution will not change, or to predict the sensitivity of the solution to possible changes in the cost or price coefficients.

Obviously the amount of computation for this procedure is quite large; hence, computer programs have been developed to minimize the computational burden. Most medium to large computer installations have such programs, or they can be obtained from both computer manufacturers and independent software houses. Because of the ready availability of these programs, the difficulty in applying linear programming is not in solving such problems, it is in formulating—that is, stating—the problems in linear equations. The following section describes several such formulations.

# EXAMPLE FORMULATIONS OF PRACTICAL PROBLEMS

As pointed out earlier, the basic practicality of LP is in its ability to model complex real world situations. Problems, therefore, in operations management can be confronted by the decision maker using LP with greater confidence. The constant competitive conditions prevailing in business, industry, and government necessitate the use of tools that help in the decision-making process. Many have found LP to be such a tool.

## The Linear Programming Aggregate Planning Problem

The first example of the use of linear programming is found in the area of aggregate planning. The problem is to schedule varying levels of production over some set planning horizon so as to minimize costs. Simple to very complex formulations of the problem have been developed. The following will illustrate a possible formulation of this situation.

$D_i$ = predicted demand in Period $i$
$i$ = 1, 2, or 3 (model limited to 3-period time horizon)
$P_i$ = scheduled regular time production in Period $i$
$P_i^*$ = maximum regular time production that can be scheduled in Period $i$
$O_i$ = overtime scheduled in Period $i$
$O_i^*$ = maximum overtime that can be scheduled in Period $i$
$r$ = regular time cost per unit
$s$ = overtime cost per unit
$c$ = inventory carrying charge per unit per period
$h_i$ = cost of increasing production by one unit of output (hiring cost)
$f_i$ = cost of reducing production by one unit of output (firing cost)
$I_i$ = increase in production level in Period $i$
$R_i$ = reduction in production level in Period $i$

For each time period:

$$P_i \leq P_i^*, \text{ and}$$
$$O_i \leq O_i^*$$

The inventory constraints are as follows:

$$P_1 + O_1 \geq D_1$$

This assumes that the initial inventory is zero. The inventory at the end of Period 1 will be:

$$P_1 + O_1 - D_1$$

and so for Period 2 demand:

$$P_1 + O_1 - D_1 + P_2 + O_2 \geqslant D_2$$

Rearranging terms we next obtain:

$$P_1 + P_2 + O_1 + O_2 \geqslant D_1 + D_2, \textit{ or}$$

$$\sum_{k=1}^{2} P_i + \sum_{i=1}^{2} O_i \geqslant \sum_{i=1}^{2} D_1$$

This can be extended easily by analogy to Period 3 as:

$$\sum_{i=1}^{3} P_i + \sum_{i=1}^{3} O_i \geqslant \sum_{i=1}^{3} D_i$$

Next we examine the hiring and firing constraints. These, respectively, are simply:

$$I_i \geqslant P_i - P_{i-1}, \text{ and}$$
$$R_i \geqslant P_{i-1} - P_i$$

or by rearranging terms we have the following:

$$I_i - P_i + P_{i-1} \geqslant 0, \textit{ and}$$
$$R_i + P_i - P_{i-1} \geqslant 0$$

and, specifically for Period 1,

$$I_1 - P_1 \geqslant -P_O, \text{ and } R_1 + P_1 \geqslant P_O$$

So much for the constraints. Our objective is to minimize costs: costs of production, costs due to work force level changes, and inventory carrying costs. For the first period we have, respectively:

$$(rP_1 + sO_1) + (hI_1 + fR_1) + c(P_1 + O_1 - D_1)$$

For the second period we have similar production and change costs, and the inventory costs are:

$$c(P_1 + O_1 - D_1 + P_2 + O_2 - D_2)$$

The third period is a simple extension of these. The total cost can then be summarized as:

$$r \sum_{i=}^{3} P_i + s \sum_{i=1}^{3} O_i + h \sum_{i=1}^{3} I_i + f \sum_{i=1}^{3} R_i + c \sum_{i=1}^{3} \sum_{i=1}^{i} (P_j + O_j - D_j)$$

As an example consider the following case.

| Month | $D_i$ | $P_i^*$ | $O_i^*$ |
|---|---|---|---|
| 1 | 3,400 | 3,200 | 900 |
| 2 | 4,500 | 3,200 | 900 |
| 3 | 3,750 | 3,000 | 700 |

$r$ = \$17/unit  $f$ = \$12/unit
$s$ = \$25/unit  $c$ = \$4/unit
$h$ = \$30/unit  $P_O = 3{,}000$

The constraint equations are thus:

$$
\begin{aligned}
&P_1 \leqslant 3{,}200\\
&P_2 \leqslant 3{,}200\\
&P_3 \leqslant 3{,}000\\
&O_1 \leqslant 900\\
&O_2 \leqslant 900\\
&O_3 \leqslant 700\\
&P_1 + O_1 \geqslant 3{,}400\\
&P_1 + P_2 + O_1 + O_2 \geqslant 7{,}900\\
&P_1 + P_2 + P_3 + O_1 + O_2 + O_3 \geqslant 11{,}650\\
&I_1 - P_1 \geqslant -3{,}000, \text{ or } P_1 - I_1 \leqslant 3{,}000\\
&I_2 - P_2 + P_1 \geqslant 0\\
&I_3 - P_3 + P_2 \geqslant 0\\
&R_1 + P_1 \geqslant 3{,}000\\
&R_2 + P_2 - P_1 \geqslant 0\\
&R_3 + P_3 - P_2 \geqslant 0
\end{aligned}
$$

The objective function is:

$$17 \sum_{i=1}^{3} P_i + 25 \sum_{i=1}^{3} O_i + 30 \sum_{i=1}^{3} I_i + 12 \sum_{i=1}^{3} R_i + 4 \sum_{i=1}^{3} \sum_{i=1}^{i} (P_j + O_j - D_j)$$

The solution, obtained with a standard LP computer program, is:

| Month | $P_i$ | $O_i$ | $I_i$ | $R_i$ |
|---|---|---|---|---|
| 1 | 3,075 | 900 | 75 | 0 |
| 2 | 3,075 | 900 | 0 | 0 |
| 3 | 3,000 | 700 | 0 | 75 |

Examination of the solution shows that not all regular time capacity is used in the first two periods and yet overtime is used fully. At first glance this may seem wrong, but not when the cost of hiring is recognized. It is common for companies to resort to overtime or subcontracting when hiring costs are substantial.

This formulation of the aggregate planning problem is not very complex relatively. Other concepts such as subcontracting, underutilization of work force (without firing; i.e., insufficient utilization), and back orders or shortages might be included. [1]

# The Feed Mix Problem

Another classic linear programming problem is typified by the feed mix problem. (It could also arise in determining the optimal ingredients in grass seed manufacture, cereal making, or sausage formulation.)

Suppose the Super Chicken Production Company can purchase and mix one or more of three different grains, each containing different amounts of four nutritional elements. The production manager specifies that any feed mix for the chickens must meet certain minimal nutritional requirements and at the same time be as low in cost as possible. Grains can be bought and mixed on a weekly basis at known prices to meet known total nutritional requirements during that week.

The following table summarizes the production manager's requirements and options.

| | Contribution/Unit Weight | | | |
|---|---|---|---|---|
| Nutritional Ingredient | Grain 1 | Grain 2 | Grain 3 | Minimum Total Requirements |
| A | 1 | 0 | 1 | 1,200 |
| B | 3 | 2 | .5 | 4,000 |
| C | 5 | 7 | 9 | 5,500 |
| D | 0 | 3 | 4 | 750 |
| Cost/Unit Weight | $30 | $37 | $45 | |

Use the following symbols:

$X_1$ = amount of Grain 1 to include in mix
$X_2$ = amount of Grain 2 to include in mix
$X_3$ = amount of Grain 3 to include in mix

The requirements then are as follows.

For Nutritional Ingredient A:

$$X_1 + X_3 \geqslant 1{,}200$$

For Nutritional Ingredient B:

$$3X_1 + 2X_2 + .5X_3 \geqslant 4{,}000$$

For Nutritional Ingredient C:

$$5X_1 + 7X_2 + 9X_3 \geqslant 5{,}500$$

and for *D:*

$$3X_2 + 4X_3 \geqslant 750$$

These must be satisfied while minimizing:

$$30X_1 + 37X_2 + 45X_3$$

The solution to this problem is to use 1,180.64 units of Grain 1; 224.19 units of Grain 2; and 19.36 units of Grain 3 at a total cost of $44,385.48 for the entire feed mix.

## The Fluid Blending Problem

A variation on this problem is the fluid blending problem. This problem was one of the first ever formulated as a linear programming problem and variations of it are in wide use today in refineries, foundaries, and chemical plants. The problem is similar to the feed mix problem; however, in this problem a set of output blends are to be derived from a set of inputs. Let:

$X_{ij}$ = number of gallons of Input $i$ to be used in Output Blend $j$

The first constraints are then, assuming two inputs are to be blended into three outputs:

$$X_{11} + X_{12} + X_{13} \leq S_1 \text{ (the available supply of Input 1), and}$$
$$X_{21} + X_{22} + X_{23} \leq S_2.$$

The second set of constraints relates to the demand ($D_j$) for each output and is as follows:

$$X_{11} + X_{21} \geq D_1$$
$$X_{12} + X_{22} \geq D_2$$
$$X_{13} + X_{23} \geq D_3.$$

Suppose further that each Input Chemical $i$ contains a critical constituent (a), the proportion of which in each input is $a_i$. A constraint is that Output 1 must have at least a fraction of $r_{a1}$ of that constituent. These proportions can be related as:

$$\frac{a_1 X_{11} + a_2 X_{21}}{X_{11} + X_{21}} \geq r_{a1}.$$

This equation can be rewritten as:

$$a_1 X_{11} + a_2 X_{21} \geq r_a X_{11} + r_a X_{21}$$

and combining terms to get a simple linear equation we next have:

$$(a_1 - r_{a1}) X_{11} + (a_2 - r_{a1}) X_{21} \geq 0.$$

Similarly, Output 2 must have at least a proportion $r_{a2}$ of constituent $a$. The corresponding equation is formulated as follows:

$$\frac{a_1 X_{12} + a_2 X_{22}}{X_{12} + X_{22}} \geq r_{a2}, \text{ or}$$

$$(a_1 - r_{a2}) X_{12} + (a_2 - r_{a2}) X_{22} \geq 0.$$

Similarly, for output 3 we have the following:

$$(a_1 - r_{a3})\ X_{13} + (a_2 - r_{a3})\ X_{23} \geq 0.$$

A second critical constituent (b) might be constrained to be no more than proportions $r_{b1}$, $r_{b2}$, and $r_{b3}$ in their respective outputs. This results in similar equations which are given next.

$$\frac{b_1\ X_{11} + b_2\ X_{21}}{X_{11} + X_{21}} \leq r_{b1}, \text{ or}$$

$$(b_1 - r_{b1})\ X_{11} + (b_2 - r_{b1})\ X_{21} \leq 0$$

and, for the other two products,

$$(b_1 - r_{b2})\ X_{12} + (b_2 - r_{b2})\ X_{22} \leq 0$$
$$(b_1 - r_{b3})\ X_{13} + (b_2 - r_{b2})\ X_{13} \leq 0.$$

Assuming that Output 1 sells for $\$0_1$ per gallon, Output 2 for $\$0_2$ per gallon, and Output 3 for $\$0_3$ per gallon, and that Inputs 1 and 2 cost $\$I$, and $\$I_2$ respectively, the objective is to maximize profits; namely,

$$(0_1 - I_1)X_{11} + (0_1 - I_2)\ X_{21} + (0_2 - I_1)\ X_{12} + (0_2 - I_2)\ X_{22}$$
$$+ (0_3 - I_1)X_{13} + (0_3 - I_2)\ b_{23}.$$

As an example, suppose we have available 12,000 gallons of Input 1 and 8,000 of Input 2. Fluid 1 is 20 percent phosphorous and Fluid 2 is 15 percent phosphorous. Fluid 1 is also 75 percent inert ingredients and Fluid 2 is 80 percent inert ingredients. We wish to make 5,000 gallons of each of three outputs. The first is to be at least 17 percent phosphorous and not more than 77 percent inert ingredients. For the second the figures are 18 percent and 76 percent and for the third 19 percent and 78 percent. Output 1 sells for \$20 per gallon, Output 2 for \$17 per gallon, and Output 3 for \$22 per gallon. Inputs 1 and 2 cost 12 and 15 dollars per gallon respectively.

The set of equations would be as follows:

$$\begin{aligned}
X_{11} + X_{12} + X_{13} &\leq 12{,}000 \\
X_{21} + X_{22} + X_{23} &\leq 18{,}000 \\
X_{11} + X_{21} &\geq 5{,}000 \\
X_{12} + X_{22} &\geq 5{,}000 \\
X_{13} + X_{23} &\geq 5{,}000 \\
.03X_{11} - .02X_{21} &\geq 0 \\
.02X_{12} - .03X_{22} &\geq 0 \\
.01X_{13} - .04X_{23} &\geq 0 \\
-.02X_{11} - .03X_{21} &\leq 0 \\
-.01X_{12} + .04X_{22} &\leq 0 \\
-.03X_{13} + .02X_{23} &\leq 0
\end{aligned}$$

The objective is to maximize:

$$8X_{11} + 5X_{12} + 10X_{13} + 5X_{21} + 2X_{22} + 7X_{23}.$$

The optimal solution uses all Fluid 1 ($X_{11}$ + 3,000, $X_{12}$ = 4,000, and $X_{13}$ = 5,000) and 5,250 gallons of Fluid 2 ($X_{21}$ = 2,000, $X_{22}$ = 1,000, and $X_{23}$ = 1,250) and achieves a profit of $114,750. Note that only Output 3 is produced above its minimum requirement of 5,000 gallons.

## The Project Duration Reduction Problem

In Chapter 16 the problem of reducing project duration was introduced and examined. As was described, the analysis and determination of which activities to crash and by how much is quite complicated. It is difficult to enumerate all the possibilities; the number of them is quite large. If we assume, as we did in the example in Chapter 16, pages 527-529, that the cost slope is linear between normal and crash times then this problem can be formulated as a linear programming problem.

Consider Figure 17-6, a revision of Figure 16-11. The $i$ and $j$ refer to event numbers, and $C_{ij}$ would thus be the cost of the activity that lies between Event $i$ and $j$. The $t_{ij}$ are the activity times. $C^c_{ij}$ is the crash cost, $t^c_{ij}$ is the crash time, $C^n_{ij}$ is the normal cost, and $t^n_{ij}$ is the normal time.

**FIGURE 17-6**
**ACTIVITY COST VERSUS ACTIVITY DURATION**

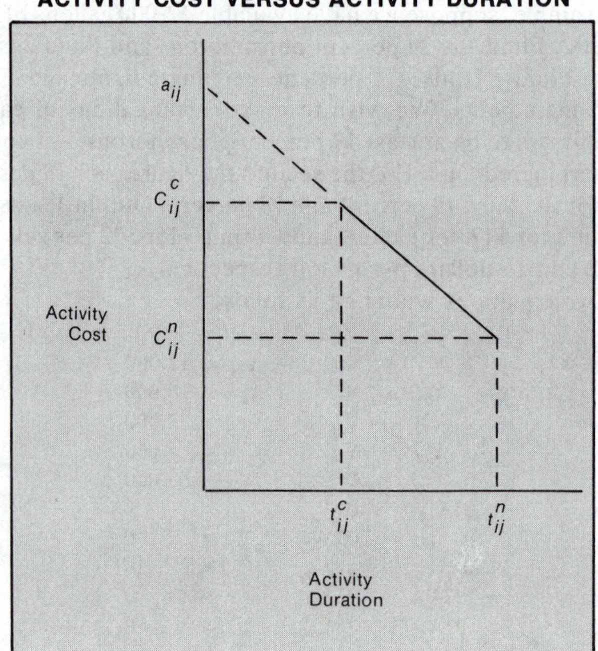

The slope ($b_{ij}$) of the cost trade-off line is:

$$b_{ij} = \frac{C^c_{ij} - C^n_{ij}}{t^n_{ij} - t^c_{ij}}$$

and hence the cost ($C_{ij}$) is as follows:

$$C_{ij} = a_{ij} - b_{ij}\, t_{ij}$$

The objective function is to minimize the sum of the $C_{ij}$'s within the constraints of not reducing the $t_{ij}$'s below their minimums (crash times) while remaining within the precedence relationships of the activities. This can be expressed as follows.

$$\text{minimize} \sum_{\text{all } ij} C_{ij} = \text{minimize} \sum_{\text{all } ij} (a_{ij} - b_{ij}\, t_{ij}), \text{ or}$$

$$\text{minimize} \sum_{\text{all } ij} - b_{ij}\, t_{ij}, \text{ or}$$

$$\text{maximize} \sum_{\text{all } ij} b_{ij}\, t_{ij}$$

subject to:

1. $t_{ij} \leqslant t^n_{ij}$
2. $t_{ij} \geqslant t^c_{ij}$
3. $x_i + t_{ij} - x_j \leqslant 0$
4. $x_e - x_1 \leqslant T$

Where:

$x_i$ = the time of occurrence of Event $i$
$x_e$ = the ending event and $T_c < T < T_n$
$T_c$ = the total time if all activities are crashed and $T_n$ is the total normal time

The first set of equations constrains the actual times not to exceed the normal times; the second set constrains the actual times not to be less than the crash times. The third set defines the precedence relationships, and the fourth equation sets the elapsed time goal. There is one equation of Types 1, 2, and 3 for each activity.

When the problem in Table 16-5, page 528, is thus formulated and solved, the optimal solution is to crash Activities I,J,K, and N to 2.17, 3.27, 3.27, and 2.0 weeks respectively at a cost of \$1,409.91.

If, instead of aiming for a particular date to finish on, a bonus is offered for each week ahead of normal that the project is completed, then a slight modification of the previous formulation will yield an optimum solution. To the objective function add $-Bx_e$ (where $B$ is the weekly bonus, and $x_e$ is the time of the last event). Also, replace Equation 4 with $x_1 = 0$. In this same example, if the bonus is \$500 a week, then it only pays to crash to Week 28 since the incremental cost of crashing one more week exceeds \$500. (Only Activities I, K, and N are crashed.)

# THE TRANSPORTATION ALGORITHM

Certain types of linear programming problems result in a set of equations that have a unique form. Because of this unique form a special algebraic technique is possible which both reduces and simplifies the computations necessary to solve the problem. One such class of problems arises when the problem is to find the assignment of quantities and routes by which to transport a commodity from a set of origins to a set of destinations in such a manner as to minimize transportation costs.

If we have a simple problem involving two origins ($A$ and $B$) and two destinations ($X$ and $Y$), we might have a shipping cost table like the following:

| | To | |
|---|---|---|
| From | $X$ | $Y$ |
| $A$ | 3 | 7 |
| $B$ | 8 | 9 |

Where, for example, this means that it costs $7.00 a unit to ship from $A$ to $Y$. If $A$ can supply 15 units and $B$, 12, and $X$ needs 17 and $Y$ needs 8, then the linear programming problem could be framed as follows.

Let $Q_1$ = quantity shipped from $A$ to $X$
$Q_2$ = quantity shipped from $A$ to $Y$
$Q_3$ = quantity shipped from $B$ to $X$
$Q_4$ = quantity shipped from $B$ to $Y$

Minimize $3Q_1 + 7Q_2 + 8Q_3 + 9Q_4$

Subject to
$$Q_1 + Q_2 \leq 15$$
$$Q_3 + Q_4 \leq 12$$
$$Q_1 + Q_3 + \geq 17$$
$$Q_2 + Q_4 \geq 8$$

Notice that in the constraints all the coefficients are one. Furthermore, there is a pattern of sets of ones (this would be more apparent if the problem had more sources and destinations). Notice also that the number of variables is $m$ times $n$ ($m$ = number of sources, and $n$ = number of destinations), while the number of constraints is $m + n$ (actually one of these is not needed because it is automatically satisfied if the others are). This problem formulation results in a very large linear programming problem for a relatively small transportation problem. Fortunately there is an alternative solution technique for this type of problem.

Consider the following situation:

| Source | Capacity |
|---|---|
| $S_1$ | 37 |
| $S_2$ | 75 |
| $S_3$ | 128 |

| Destination | Demand |
|---|---|
| $D_1$ | 18 |
| $D_2$ | 12 |
| $D_3$ | 30 |
| $D_4$ | 83 |
| $D_5$ | 97 |

Cost Table

| From \ To | $D_1$ | $D_2$ | $D_3$ | $D_4$ | $D_5$ |
|---|---|---|---|---|---|
| $S_1$ | 21 | 16 | 7 | 23 | 15 |
| $S_2$ | 15 | 8 | 12 | 9 | 21 |
| $S_3$ | 25 | 19 | 15 | 12 | 17 |

To get the transportation algorithm (procedure) started we need an initial, feasible solution. Later a good technique for doing so will be illustrated, but for now just assume we have the following:

Initial Solution

| From \ To | $D_1$ | $D_2$ | $D_3$ | $D_4$ | $D_5$ | Supply |
|---|---|---|---|---|---|---|
| $S_1$ | 18 | | 19 | | | 37 |
| $S_2$ | | 12 | | 63 | | 75 |
| $S_3$ | | | 11 | 20 | 97 | 128 |
| Demand | 18 | 12 | 30 | 83 | 97 | |

The cost of this solution is:

$$18 \times 21 + 12 \times 8 + 19 \times 7 + 11 \times 15 + 63 \times 9 + 20 \times 12 + 97 \times 17 = 3{,}228$$

Now consider how we might improve this solution. As an example, if we shipped from Supplier $S_1$ to Destination $D_5$ it would appear to save some cost ($15 per unit versus $17). If we did this we would not be able to ship as much to either $D_1$ or $D_3$ but we also would not have to ship as much from $S_3$ to $D_5$, and, therefore, could make up the shortfall for $D_3$ from $S_3$. To compute the impact we need only add 15, subtract 7, add 15, subtract 17, the respective unit shipping costs of each affected route, to get a result of 6. This means that it cost us $6 more for each unit shipped via this new route. A similar analysis can be done for each unused (empty square) route in the current solution. The problem with this is that it needs to be systematized so as to make sure the computations are done correctly. A common way of doing this is with the modified distribution (MODI) technique. While it does not on the surface appear to be the same as our what-if procedure, it is logically equivalent and results in the same values. Its advantage is that it is very orderly, and, if followed, guarantees obtaining the lowest cost solution.

To see how it works in our case we first construct a matrix containing the unit costs ($C_{ij}$) corresponding to the routes we have selected:

| From \ To | $D_1$ | $D_2$ | $D_3$ | $D_4$ | $D_5$ |
|---|---|---|---|---|---|
| $S_1$ | 21 | | 7 | | |
| $S_2$ | | 8 | | 9 | |
| $S_3$ | | | 15 | 12 | 17 |

Now we associate with each row a value $R_i$ ($i = 1, 2, 3$) and each column a $K_j$ ($j = 1, 2, 3, 4, 5$) chosen such that $R_i + K_j = C_{ij}$. Because of the nature of this type of problem, we can arbitrarily set any one of the $R$ or $K$ values to zero and then compute the rest. For example, if $R_3 = 0$, then $K_3$ must equal 15 so that $R_3 + K_3$ will equal $C_{33}$ which is 15. If $K_3$ is 15, then $R_1$ must be $7 - 15$, or $-8$. Thus $K_1$ must be $21 - (-8)$, or 29, etc. This can be shown in tabular form as follows:

| From \ To | $D_1$ | $D_2$ | $D_3$ | $D_4$ | $D_5$ | $R_i$ |
|---|---|---|---|---|---|---|
| $S_1$ | 21 | | 7 | | | −8 |
| $S_2$ | | 8 | | 9 | | −3 |
| $S_3$ | | | 15 | 12 | 17 | 0 |
| $K_j$ | 29 | 11 | 15 | 12 | 17 | |

The next step is to use these $R$ and $K$ values to compute the missing $C_{ij}$ values. For example, $C_{21} = R_2 + K_1 = -3 + 29 = 26$. Similarly, $C_{14} = -8 + 12 = 4$. The result of this is the following:

| From \ To | $D_1$ | $D_2$ | $D_3$ | $D_4$ | $D_5$ | $R_i$ |
|---|---|---|---|---|---|---|
| $S_1$ | 21 | 3 | 7 | 4 | 9 | −8 |
| $S_2$ | 26 | 8 | 12 | 9 | 14 | −3 |
| $S_3$ | 29 | 11 | 15 | 12 | 17 | 0 |
| $K_j$ | 29 | 11 | 15 | 12 | 17 | |

To complete the evaluation we now subtract these values from the original cost matrix, cell for cell. The result follows:

| From \ To | $D_1$ | $D_2$ | $D_3$ | $D_4$ | $D_5$ |
|---|---|---|---|---|---|
| $S_1$ | 0 | 13 | 0 | 19 | 6 |
| $S_2$ | −11 | 0 | 0 | 0 | 7 |
| $S_3$ | − 4 | 8 | 0 | 0 | 0 |

These are now the shadow costs just as in the corresponding simplex problem. Since we are minimizing cost, the meaning of these values is that the total cost would decrease by, for example, \$11 for each unit shipped from $S_2$ to $D_1$. Since this is the greatest per unit savings we can achieve, let's use it. What, however, is the maximum we can ship this way? If we put an $X$ in

Row 2, Column 1 of the shipping table, it will help us to visualize the needed changes.

| From \ To | $D_1$ | $D_2$ | $D_3$ | $D_4$ | $D_5$ |
|---|---|---|---|---|---|
| $S_1$ | 18 | | 19 | | |
| $S_2$ | X | 12 | | 63 | |
| $S_3$ | | | 11 | 20 | 97 |

If we ship $X$ units to $D_1$ from $S_2$, we will not need to ship $X$ units from $S_1$ to $D_1$; that means we will have $X$ more available from $S_1$ to $D_3$. Thus, we do not need the $X$ units at $S_3$ to $D_3$ since they are available at $D_4$. This means we can compensate at $D_4$ by not shipping $X$ units to $D_4$ from $S_2$. This just balances our original need for $X$ units from $S_2$ to $D_1$. On the shipping matrix this is shown as follows:

| From \ To | $D_1$ | $D_2$ | $D_3$ | $D_4$ | $D_5$ |
|---|---|---|---|---|---|
| $S_1$ | 7 | | 30 | | |
| $S_2$ | 11 | 12 | | 52 | |
| $S_3$ | | | | 31 | 97 |

This now is a new solution, having a cost of $11 \times (-11)$, or \$121 less than the previous solution. It must be evaluated in the same manner as the first one. If none of the shadow costs are negative, then it must be the optimal solution. If there are negatives then the improved solution must be developed and the process repeated until all the shadow costs are nonnegative.

In our case:

| From \ To | $D_1$ | $D_2$ | $D_3$ | $D_4$ | $D_5$ | $R_i$ |
|---|---|---|---|---|---|---|
| $S_1$ | 21 | | 7 | | | 21 |
| $S_2$ | 15 | 8 | | 9 | | 15 |
| $S_3$ | | | | 12 | 17 | 18 |
| $K_j$ | 0 | −7 | −14 | −6 | −1 | |

| From \ To | $D_1$ | $D_2$ | $D_3$ | $D_4$ | $D_5$ | $R_i$ |
|---|---|---|---|---|---|---|
| $S_1$ | 21 | 14 | 7 | 15 | 20 | 21 |
| $S_2$ | 15 | 8 | 1 | 9 | 14 | 15 |
| $S_3$ | 18 | 11 | 4 | 12 | 17 | 18 |
| $K_j$ | 0 | −7 | −14 | −6 | −1 | |

| From \ To | $D_1$ | $D_2$ | $D_3$ | $D_4$ | $D_5$ |
|---|---|---|---|---|---|
| $S_1$ | 0 | 2 | 0 | 8 | −5 |
| $S_2$ | 0 | 0 | 11 | 0 | 7 |
| $S_3$ | 7 | 8 | 11 | 0 | 0 |

| From \ To | $D_1$ | $D_2$ | $D_3$ | $D_4$ | $D_5$ |
|---|---|---|---|---|---|
| $S_1$ | $7-x$ | | 30 | | $X$ |
| $S_2$ | $11+x$ | 12 | | $52-x$ | |
| $S_3$ | | | | $31+x$ | $97-x$ |

| From \ To | $D_1$ | $D_2$ | $D_3$ | $D_4$ | $D_5$ |
|---|---|---|---|---|---|
| $S_1$ | | | 30 | | 7 |
| $S_2$ | 18 | 12 | | 45 | |
| $S_3$ | | | | 38 | 90 |

| From \ To | $D_1$ | $D_2$ | $D_3$ | $D_4$ | $D_5$ |
|---|---|---|---|---|---|
| $S_1$ | | | 7 | | 15 |
| $S_2$ | 15 | 8 | | 9 | |
| $S_3$ | | | | 12 | 17 |

| From \ To | $D_1$ | $D_2$ | $D_3$ | $D_4$ | $D_5$ | $R_i$ |
|---|---|---|---|---|---|---|
| $S_1$ | | | 7 | | 15 | 0 |
| $S_2$ | 15 | 8 | | 9 | | −1 |
| $S_3$ | | | | 12 | 17 | 2 |
| $K_j$ | 16 | 9 | 7 | 10 | 15 | |

| From \ To | $D_1$ | $D_2$ | $D_3$ | $D_4$ | $D_5$ | $R_i$ |
|---|---|---|---|---|---|---|
| $S_1$ | 16 | 9 | 7 | 10 | 15 | 0 |
| $S_2$ | 15 | 8 | 6 | 9 | 14 | −1 |
| $S_3$ | 18 | 11 | 9 | 12 | 17 | 2 |
| $K_j$ | 16 | 9 | 7 | 10 | 15 | |

| From \ To | $D_1$ | $D_2$ | $D_3$ | $D_4$ | $D_5$ |
|---|---|---|---|---|---|
| $S_1$ | 5 | 7 | 0 | 14 | 0 |
| $S_2$ | 0 | 0 | 6 | 0 | 7 |
| $S_3$ | 9 | 8 | 6 | 0 | 0 |

Since none of these shadow costs is negative the new solution is optimal.

Because the number of iterations for a problem such as this is related to how good the initial solution is, it is worthwhile considering how to obtain quickly a good solution. One of the best known and most reliable is known as Vogel's Approximation Method (VAM). The following is a somewhat simplified version that seems to give as good results. To illustrate it we will apply it to our sample problem.

Set up a matrix with only the marginal supply and demand figures (as shown next) and, then, referring to the original cost matrix for each column,

| From \ To | $D_1$ | $D_2$ | $D_3$ | $D_4$ | $D_5$ | Supply |
|---|---|---|---|---|---|---|
| $S_1$ | | | | | | 37 |
| $S_2$ | | | | | | 75 |
| $S_3$ | | | | | | 128 |
| Demand | 18 | 12 | 30 | 83 | 97 | |
| Cost difference | 6 | 8 | 5 | 3 | 2 | |

calculate the difference between the two lowest costs in that column. In the column having the largest difference select the lowest cost and enter a quantity to be shipped equal to the smaller of the demand or supply for that column and row; in this case Column 2, minimum cost in Row 2, the quantity assigned is 12 units. Cross off that column (or row if the supply is exhausted), reduce the available supply (or demand if not completely satisfied) by the assigned amount, and repeat this procedure until all the demands are satisfied. In our case the next two matrices would be as follows:

| From \ To | $D_1$ | $D_2$ | $D_3$ | $D_4$ | $D_5$ | Supply |
|---|---|---|---|---|---|---|
| $S_1$ | | | | | | 37 |
| $S_2$ | | 12 | | | | 63 |
| $S_3$ | | | | | | 128 |
| Demand | 18 | X | 30 | 83 | 97 | |
| Cost difference | 6 | X | 5 | 3 | 2 | |

| From \ To | $D_1$ | $D_2$ | $D_3$ | $D_4$ | $D_5$ | Supply |
|---|---|---|---|---|---|---|
| $S_1$ | | | | | | 37 |
| $S_2$ | 18 | 12 | | | | 45 |
| $S_3$ | | | | | | 128 |
| Demand | X | X | 30 | 83 | 97 | |
| Cost difference | X | X | 5 | 3 | 2 | |

Continuation of this process leads to an initial solution, which, when evaluated by the MODI technique, is found to be optimal. While this is not always the case, at least the solution will reduce the number of MODI iterations required compared with an arbitrary initial solution.

Several computational complexities—chiefly so-called degeneracy or a related phenomenon, e.g., alternate optimal solutions—may arise in these types of problems. Treatment of such issues is left to an operations research text.

# APPLICATION OF THE TRANSPORTATION FORMULATION TO AGGREGATE PLANNING

Besides the obvious application of the transportation technique to shipping problems, it can also be used to solve a simple aggregate planning problem. If the costs of changing levels of production from period to period are not significant; that is, there are no hiring and firing costs to be considered, then we can consider each period of regular and overtime production to be a source and each period of demand to be a destination in the transportation matrix. Thus, the rows are labeled $P_1$, $O_1$, $P_2$, $O_3$ (using the same symbols as in the earlier aggregate planning example in this chapter). The columns are demand in each period. The result follows:

| Production | Period 1 | Period 2 | Period 3 | Maximum Available |
|---|---|---|---|---|
| Regular Time 1 | | | | 3,200 |
| Overtime 1 | | | | 900 |
| Regular Time 2 | | | | 3,200 |
| Overtime 2 | | | | 900 |
| Regular Time 3 | | | | 3,000 |
| Overtime 3 | | | | 700 |
| Demand | 3,400 | 4,500 | 3,7 50 | |

Now the costs of producing and carrying inventory are used in arriving at the shipping costs. For Row 1, Column 1 that is just $r$ ($r = \$17$). For Row 1, Column 2 that is $r + c$ ($r + c = 17 + 4 = \$21$). The result follows:

| Production | Period 1 | Period 2 | Period 3 | Maximum Available |
|---|---|---|---|---|
| Regular Time 1 | 17 | 21 | 25 | 3,200 |
| Overtime 1 | 25 | 29 | 33 | 900 |
| Regular Time 2 | *X* | 17 | 21 | 3,200 |
| Overtime 2 | *X* | 25 | 29 | 900 |
| Regular Time 3 | *X* | *X* | 17 | 3,000 |
| Overtime 3 | *X* | *X* | 25 | 700 |
| Demand | 3,400 | 4,500 | 3,750 | |

The *X*'s indicate impossible activities; that is, production after demand. (A modified formulation would allow back orders, in which case the *X*'s would reflect production costs plus back order costs and a feasible activity.) In order to apply the solution procedure, simply assign an arbitrarily very high cost to these routes. Also, since the total maximum available exceeds total demand, we add a slack column to achieve balance and assign zero cost to using these routes.

An optimal solution is:

| | Period | | | | |
|---|---|---|---|---|---|
| Production | 1 | 2 | 3 | Slack | Maximum Available |
| Regular Time 1 | 2,750 | 450 | | | 3,200 |
| Overtime 1 | 650 | | | 250 | 900 |
| Regular Time 2 | | 3,150 | 50 | | 3,200 |
| Overtime 2 | | 900 | | | 900 |
| Regular Time 3 | | | 3,000 | | 3,000 |
| Overtime 3 | | | 700 | | 700 |
| Demand | 3,400 | 4,500 | 3,750 | 250 | 11,900 |

The weakness of this formulation is that the cost structure is not realistic enough. One result is that there are many alternate optimal solutions to this problem; that is, there are many other allocations of the productive capacity which are equally inexpensive.

# GOAL PROGRAMMING

One of the criticisms of linear programming is that there is room for only one objective function, and hence the several objectives that a decision maker may have, need to be expressible in a common measure (like dollars). Another difficulty arises because the constraints may not actually be as rigid as the solution procedure suggests. For example, a firm may wish to maximize profit, but it also wants to have stable employment, a diversified product line, and minimal pollution. These goals are not easily nor naturally transformed into dollar measures, nor are they easily set as constraints while the profit equation is maximized.

An alternative linear equation approach to this type of problem is goal programming (GP). To use this procedure, it is necessary to consider both the structural, or technological constraints (raw material and machine hour availability, for example), and objectives. For each constraint, possible deviations are stated, and for each objective, a target level is set. The objective is to minimize stated constraint deviations and variations from the target levels. The GP procedure provides a methodology for minimizing these deviations and for dealing with them in the rank order specified while not violating the technological constraints.

To see how this works, let's reconsider the LP problem stated earlier as:

$$5X + 6Y \leq 27.75$$
$$4X + 2Y \leq 13$$
$$3.6X + 8.1Y \geq 23$$

with the objective of maximizing:

$$1.8X + 2Y$$

Deviations below the goal are symbolized by:

$$d_n^-$$

and those above by:

$$d_n^+$$

Let's reconsider the problem as having the same constraints, but our goals are, first, to make just as much $X$ and $Y$ and, second, to maximize profit.

The constraints are restated as follows:

$$\begin{aligned} 5X + 6Y + d_1^- &= 27.75 \\ 4X + 2Y + d_2^- &= 13 \\ 3.6X + 8.1Y - d_3^+ &= 23 \end{aligned}$$

Note how these were constructed. Our less-than constraints allow a negative deviation (akin to the slack in an ordinary LP problem) and the greater-than constraint allows the subtraction of a positive deviation (a surplus). Our profit goal is added by setting some reasonably large value for the profit and allowing a negative deviation, e.g., the following:

$$1.8X + 2Y + d_4^- = 20$$

Now the equal production goal is constructed by allowing the difference between $X$ and $Y$ to be either positive or negative:

$$X - Y + d_5^- - d_5^+ = 0$$

Our objectives can then be stated as:

Priority 1: minimize $d_5^- + d_5^+$, and
Priority 2: minimize $d_4^-$

Before considering variations on this problem formulation, let us briefly look at the mechanics of the solution procedure. We begin by setting up a matrix similar to our original LP matrix (see Figure 17-7). The differences between Figure 17-7 and the matrix on page 543 are several. Across the top, in place of the costs ($C_j$'s) are the priority levels ($P_n$'s). Note particularly that for Equation 3, page 561, where an artificial variable is required in order to create a nonnegative basis (i.e., in a greater-than equation), a priority of $P_0$ is established instead of the big $M$ used in the LP simplex calcula-

**FIGURE 17-7**
**INITIAL GOAL PROGRAMMING MATRIX**

| | P = | 0 | 0 | 0 | 0 | 0 | $P_0$ | $P_2$ | $P_1$ | $P_1$ | |
|---|---|---|---|---|---|---|---|---|---|---|---|
| | Basis | $X$ | $Y$ | $d_1^-$ | $d_2^-$ | $d_3^+$ | $A_3$ | $d_4^-$ | $d_5^-$ | $d_5^+$ | RHS |
| 0 | $d_1^-$ | 5 | 6 | 1 | | | | | | | 27.75 |
| 0 | $d_2^-$ | 4 | 2 | | 1 | | | | | | 13.0 |
| $P_0$ | $A_3$ | 3.6 | 8.1 | | | -1 | 1 | | | | 23.0 ← |
| $P_2$ | $d_4^-$ | 1.8 | 2 | | | | | 1 | | | 20.0 |
| $P_1$ | $d_5^-$ | 1 | -1 | | | | | | 1 | -1 | 0.0 |
| | $P_2$ | -1.8 | -2 | | | | | | | | -20 |
| $C_j - Z_j$ | $P_1$ | -1 | 1 | | | | | | | 2 | 0 |
| | $P_0$ | -3.6 | -8.1 | | | | | | | | -23 |
| | | ↑ | | | | | | | | | |

tion. Below the matrix, in place of a single $C_j - Z_j$ row there are now several rows, one for each priority level and, by convention, they are ordered downward in increasing levels of importance. The entries are computed in a manner similar to the LP simplex. For the column head $X$:

$$C_j - Z_j = 0 - (5\times0 + 4\times0 + 3.6\times P_0 + 1.8\times P_2 + 1\times P_1) = -3.6P_0 - 1.8P_2 - P_1$$

These coefficients are then entered in their respective rows of the $C_j - Z_j$ priority levels.

Selecting a variable to enter the solution proceeds as in the LP simplex, but with a slight modification. We start with the highest priority and select the most negative element. We continue working with that level until all its entries are zero or positive and then move to the next lower level and examine its entries. We then select the most negative in that level, so long as no positive, non-zero $C_j - Z_j$ exists in that column for a priority level we have already dealt with. We continue in this stepwise manner through all levels of priority.

The criterion for which variable leaves the solution is the same as in the LP simplex; i.e., divide the RHS column entries by their respective positive coefficients in the selected entry variable column and choose the smallest. The remainder of the simplex computations are as illustrated previously.

Figure 17-8 shows the result of the first iteration. The entries in $C_j - Z_j$ for $P_0$ are all positive or zero so we move on to the $P_1$ row. The most negative of these is in the column headed $X$, and the smallest ratio is $2.840 \div 1.444$ in the row labeled $d_5^-$; so $X$ replaces $d_5^-$. Note that even if the $-.123$ in the column headed $A_3$ were the most negative it could not have been chosen because of the plus one in the row below it.

**FIGURE 17-8**
**FIRST ITERATION RESULT**

| | | 0 | 0 | 0 | 0 | 0 | $P_2$ | $P_2$ | $P_1$ | $P_1$ | |
|---|---|---|---|---|---|---|---|---|---|---|---|
| | | $X$ | $Y$ | $d_1^-$ | $d_2^-$ | $d_3^-$ | $A_3$ | $d_4^-$ | $d_5^-$ | $d_5^-$ | RHS |
| 0 | $d_1^-$ | 2.333 | | 1 | | .741 | -.741 | | | | 10.713 |
| 0 | $d_2^-$ | 3.111 | | | 1 | .247 | -.247 | | | | 7.321 |
| 0 | $Y$ | .444 | 1 | | | -.123 | .123 | | | | 2.840 |
| $P_2$ | $d_4^-$ | .911 | | | | .247 | -.247 | 1 | | | 14.321 |
| $P_1$ | $d_5^-$ | 1.444 | | | | -.123 | .123 | | 1 | -1 | 2.840 ← |
| | $P_2$ | -.911 | | | | -.247 | .247 | | | | -14.321 |
| $C_j - Z_j$ | $P_1$ | -1.444 | | | | .123 | -.123 | | | 2 | -2.84 |
| | $P_0$ | | | | | | 1 | | | | 0 |
| | | ↑ | | | | | | | | | |

Figure 17-9 shows the next iteration. Since all $P_1$ entries are zero or positive, we move to $P_2$ and find we can improve $P_2$ by bringing in $d_3^+$ in place of $d_2^-$ (as shown in Figure 17-10). Now the entry in the column headed $d_5^-$ cannot be brought into the solution because to do so would reduce achievement of Goal $P_1$. Since all other entries in Row $P_2$ are positive, this represents the optimal solution; that is:

$$X = Y = 2.167$$

and $P_2$ misses being achieved by 11.767 for a net profit of 20 − 11.767 or 8.233.

**FIGURE 17-9**
**SECOND GOAL PROGRAMMING ITERATION**

| | | $X$ | $Y$ | $d_1^-$ | $d_2^-$ | $d_3^+$ | $A_3$ | $d_4^-$ | $d_5^-$ | $d_5^+$ | RHS |
|---|---|---|---|---|---|---|---|---|---|---|---|
| 0 | $d_1^-$ | | | 1 | | .940 | -.940 | | -1.615 | 1.615 | 6.126 |
| 0 | $d_2^-$ | | | | 1 | .513 | -.513 | | -2.154 | 2.154 | 1.205 ← |
| 0 | $Y$ | | 1 | | | -.085 | .085 | | -.308 | .308 | 1.966 |
| $P_2$ | $d_4^-$ | | | | | .325 | -.325 | 1 | -.631 | .631 | 12.530 |
| 0 | $X$ | 1 | | | | -.085 | .085 | | .692 | -.692 | 1.966 |
| | $P_2$ | | | | | -.325 | .325 | | .631 | -.631 | -12.53 |
| $C_j - Z_j$ | $P_1$ | | | | | | | | 1 | 1 | 0 |
| | $P_0$ | | | | | | 1 | | | | 0 |
| | | | | | | ↑ | | | | | |

**FIGURE 17-10**
**FINAL SOLUTION MATRIX**

| | | $X$ | $Y$ | $d_1^-$ | $d_2^-$ | $d_3^+$ | $A_3$ | $d_4^-$ | $d_5^-$ | $d_5^+$ | RHS |
|---|---|---|---|---|---|---|---|---|---|---|---|
| 0 | $d_1^-$ | | | 1 | -1.833 | | | | 2.333 | 2.333 | 3.917 |
| 0 | $d_3^+$ | | | | 1.950 | 1 | -1 | | -4.200 | 4.200 | 2.350 |
| 0 | $Y$ | | 1 | | -.167 | | | | -.667 | .667 | 2.167 |
| $P_2$ | $d_4^-$ | | | | -.633 | | | 1 | .733 | -.733 | 11.767 |
| 0 | $X$ | 1 | | | .167 | | | | .333 | -.333 | 2.167 |
| | $P_2$ | | | | .633 | | | | -.733 | .733 | -11.767 |
| $C_j - Z_j$ | $P_1$ | | | | | | | | 1 | 1 | 0 |
| | $P_0$ | | | | | | 1 | | | | |

## Some Considerations and Limitations

It is well to note some of the considerations and limitations to GP. We still have linear equations and continuous variables. (Some research is being done on integer versions of GP.) Within any priority level the deviations must be commensurable; i.e., dollars or pounds or hours, but different levels may be in different dimensions. It is possible to give different weights to the various deviations within a level; that is, we could weight a negative deviation with a factor of two and a positive deviation with a one if we were more concerned with the former. Postoptimality analysis is more complicated for GP than for LP.

Because GP opens up a broader way of looking at problems, it lends itself to finding solutions to sets of problems in a sort of what-if mode. Interchanging the order of goals one and two in this previous example results in a quite different solution; namely the same solution as the plain LP formulation achieved. In more complex problems involving more goals it is likely that the decision maker will want to explore a variety of goal structures and to consider the sensitivity of the solutions to any structure changes as well.

## A Goal Programming Formulation of a Manufacturing Mix Problem

A standard linear programming illustration is the product mix problem, which is illustrated as follows. Among the many products a plant has, there are two that tend to cause a bottleneck in their conflicting use of manufacturing resources. They are motors and compressors. The motors require 2.25 hours of machining while the compressors require 1.5 hours each. The finishing operation requires 1.5 hours for each motor and 3 hours for each compressor. Storage is 1.5 cubic meters for each. Machining is limited to 13,500 hours, finishing is limited to 18,750 hours, and storage is confined to 11,250 cubic meters. The profit contribution of motors is $30 each, and for compressors it is $50 each. Determine how many motors and compressors to make in order to maximize profit.

Letting $X_M$ be the production quantity of motors and $X_C$ be the same for compressors, the problem can be formulated as follows:

$$\begin{aligned} \text{Maximize} \quad & 30X_M + 50X_C \\ \text{Subject to} \quad & 2.25X_M + 1.5X_C \leq 13{,}500 \\ & 1.5X_M + 3\;X_C \leq 18{,}750 \\ & 1.5X_M + 1.5X_C \leq 11{,}250 \end{aligned}$$

Calculation is straightforward and results in producing 2,500 motors and 5,000 compressors.

Suppose, however, we have some additional objectives; for example, to maximize sales, or to limit in-process inventory, or to allow limited overtime, or to restrict cash tied up in receivables. We can incorporate these if we change the preceding problem to allow a GP approach.

First, let's assume that we want to sell at least 3,000 of each product. In-process inventory in an amount of $200 is required for each motor and $375 for each compressor. The technological constraints of the linear programming formulation can be transformed as follows:

$$\begin{aligned} 2.25X_M + 1.5X_C + d_1^- - d_1^+ &= 13{,}500 \\ 1.5X_M + 3X_C + d_2^- - d_2^+ &= 18{,}750 \\ 1.5X_M + 1.5X_C + d_3^- - d_3^+ &= 11{,}250 \end{aligned}$$

If the limit on in-process inventory is $2 million, then

$$200X_M + 375X_C + d_4^- - d_4^+ = 2{,}000{,}000.$$

and for the sales goals:

$$\begin{aligned} X_M + d_5^- &= 3{,}000, \text{ and} \\ X_C + d_6^- - d_6^+ &= 3{,}000. \end{aligned}$$

The profit goal is contained in the following:

$$30X_M + 50X_C + d_7^- - d_7^+ = 300{,}000$$

Next, we must rank the conflicting goals. A possible ordering is listed here:

Priority 1: minimize $d_4^+$

Priority 2: minimize $d_5^- - d_6^-$

Priority 3: minimize $d_7^+$

Priority 4: minimize $d_1^- + d_2^- + d_3^-$

That is, in order, minimize the excess in-process inventory, make your sales goals, make your profit goal (if possible), and try not to exceed plant capacity.

The optimal solution is to make 4,375 motors and 3,000 compressors. Goals 1 and 2 are met, but profit is only $281,250 and capacity in both finishing and storage are exceeded.

If we interchange Goals 1 and 4, then the optimal solution is to make 3,000 motors and 4,750 compressors. This does not exceed plant capacity and it does meet sales goals. However, in-process inventory goes up to $2,381,250. In compensation for this 19 percent increase in inventory there is also a 16 percent increase in profits to $327,500. Whether this is acceptable or not depends upon financial constraints, but it certainly is worth exploring.

The other linear programming problems that were formulated could also be transformed into GP problems and conflicting goals considered.

The techniques of mathematical programming, to summarize, are varied. The essence of mathematical programming is the creation of a mathematical model and rigorous manipulation of the model to secure an optimum solution to a real world problem. Since mathematical programming is designed to deal with complex problems having many variables the models are often complex, albeit less complex than the real world. Since the modeling process always involves extraction of the important from the complex there is always some sort of simplification. In some problems this may involve too much simplification. But if the appropriate technique—linear programming, stochastic, or goal programming—is chosen the process and solution should at least shed light and provide information even though the solution is not optimal in the real world.

# PROBLEMS

1. Reformulate the linear programming aggregate planning problem, pages 556-548, to include limited subcontracting and constrain overtime production to be a proportion of regular time production. Also include beginning and ending inventory levels.
2. Solve the preceding problem assuming a modification of the example in the text to allow subcontracting at $27 per unit, not over 200 units per period, and overtime constrained to 25% of regular time production. Beginning and ending inventory is to be 300 units.
3. Reformulate and solve the transportation method aggregate planning problem, pages 554-559, assuming back orders are allowed. The added cost of a back order is $3 per unit.
4. Reformulate and solve the previous problem if demand increases 20% in each period, and subcontracting at $25 per unit is allowed.
5. Pacific Hoist and Crane makes two models of a jib crane. Since each has a profit of $250, they have been making equal quantities of each. Manufacturing limits are as follows:

| | Machining Hours/Unit | Welding Hours/Unit | Assembly Hours/Unit |
|---|---|---|---|
| Model 1051 | 5.25 | 1.75 | 5.25 |
| Model 1348 | 3.00 | 3.00 | 7.00 |
| Hours Available | 48,870 | 23,750 | 61,670 |

a. If they stay with their equal-quantity rule, how much should they make to maximize profit?
b. If they simply maximize profit, how many of each model do they produce?
c. Because of a machine failure, machining capacity is reduced to 37,125 hours. How does this affect the solutions to *a* and *b*?

**6.** Suppose that in the previous problem, in order to maintain a constant work force level, all the assembly capacity must be used exactly. At the same time, management wants to minimize overtime in machining and welding, maximizing profits and producing at least 9,000 Model 1051 and 3,000 Model 1348.

a. If the goals are ordered as stated here, what is the optimal solution?
b. If Goal 4 is placed above all the others, without changing their order, what is the solution?

**7.** Given the following aggregate planning data, what should be the production each month and how much inventory will be held each period? What will be the total cost?

| Month | Demand | Maximum Production Regular | Maximum Production Overtime |
|---|---|---|---|
| 1 | 4,275 | 3,700 | 900 |
| 2 | 4,760 | 4,000 | 1,000 |
| 3 | 5,545 | 4,500 | 1,100 |
| 4 | 4,438 | 4,000 | 1,000 |

$r$ = \$14/unit  $f$ = \$15/unit
$s$ = \$21/unit  $c$ = \$3/unit
$h$ = \$35/unit  $P_0$ = 3,500

**8.** Solve the following linear programming problem graphically.

Maximize $2X + Y$
Subject to
$3X + 2Y \geq 12$
$X + 1.4Y \leq 7$
$3X + 16Y \geq 24$
$X \geq 0, Y \geq 0$

**9.** Solve the following linear programming problem graphically.

Maximize $.6X + Y$
Subject to
$3X + 2Y \leq 45.0$
$.5X + Y \leq 62.5$
$X + Y \leq 75.0$

**10.** Solve Problem 9 by the simplex method.

# SELECTED READINGS

**1.** Barry Shore, *Operations Management* (New York: McGraw-Hill Book Company, 1973).

**2.** Frederick Hillier and Gerald Lieberman, *Introduction to Operations Research*, 2d ed. (San Francisco: Holden Day, Inc., 1974).

**3.** Sang M. Lee, *Goal Programming for Decision Analysis* (Pennsauken, N. J.: Auerbach Publishers Inc., 1972).

**4.** Donald Plane and Gary Kochenberger, *Operations Research for Managerial Decisions* (Homewood, Ill.: Richard D. Irwin, Inc., 1972).

**5.** Harvey Wagner, *Operations Research,* 2d ed. (Englewood Cliffs, N. J.: Prentice-Hall, Inc., 1974).

# —18—

# STOCHASTIC SIMULATION

Simulation is the process of designing a model of a decision situation and experimenting with the model to evaluate alternative decisions. The various mathematical, graphical, and tabular models discussed throughout this text are all simulation models in that they are representations of reality used to evaluate possible decisions. Stochastic (Monte Carlo) Simulation is different from analytic modeling approaches, such as economic order quantity (EOQ) and mathematical programming models, in that it does not solve for an optimal solution. Instead it runs a mathematical or logical model of the situation and determines by trial and error which settings of the decision variables result in satisfactory, if not the best, operating results.

In any situation there are certain variables that management controls. Order quantity, safety stock, the number of operators, the schedule, and order priority rules are examples of these variables. Stochastic simulation, based on the laws of probability, enables management to evaluate the possible settings, and combinations of settings, of these variables in terms of the results achieved. A simulation model enables management to answer what-if questions such as the following:

1. If a maintenance worker is added, will the savings due to decreased machine downtime be greater than the additional labor costs?
2. What effect will a 10 percent increase in safety stock have on stock-outs?
3. What effect will a planned 20 percent reduction in queue length have on work-in-process and idle time?

The exact values of some events such as demand, lead time, and machine failure in any period cannot be predicted with certainty, but the probability distribution of each can be known. In many situations the sequence of events may not be predictable. Periods of high demand, for example, may be bunched or intermingled with periods of low demand. Stochastic simulation is especially beneficial when events are nondeterministic, but probabilistic, or when the exact sequence of events cannot be predicted.

Descriptions of the stochastic simulation procedure and its rationale precede an example. Sensitivity analysis, building a simulation model, the use of computers in simulation, and some documented applications are discussed after the example.

## PROCEDURE AND RATIONALE

The procedure for creating a simulation is based upon building a logical representation of a system, recognizing the input variables and their statistical variations, exercising the model to make it behave like the real world it represents, and observing the consequences. The specific steps are as follows:

1. Describe the decision to be studied and its objective; for example, determining the level of safety stock that minimizes the sum of stock-out and inventory holding costs under stochastic demand conditions.
2. Construct a model that replicates reality and permits measurement of the objective function under different conditions.
3. Determine the frequency distribution of the uncontrollable events. Determination of more than one frequency distribution is necessary if more than one event is probabilistic.
4. Convert the frequency distribution(s) to cumulative probability distribution(s). The data may be fit to a theoretical distribution; for example, Poisson, or to an anticipated actual distribution.
5. Establish the initial conditions.
6. Generate (obtain) sets of random numbers (RN's), one set for each event to be simulated.
7. For each RN, determine the corresponding value of the event (input) of concern.
8. Insert these values in the model measuring the decision effectiveness and compute the results.
9. Repeat Steps 5, 6, and 7 many times, at least 100, for each of the alternatives. Determination of the exact number of repetitions required to achieve a statistical confidence in the results of the simulation is beyond the scope of this book.
10. Apply controls. Compare the parameters (mean and variance) of the simulated events to the actual distribution parameters.
11. Select the particular course of action that achieves the best results on the basis of the preselected criteria and which is within control limits.
12. Repeat Steps 6 through 11 using a new set of RN's and compare results.
13. Select the course of action that consistently produces the best results.

Two results of the procedure constitute its rationale: (1) the event values occur with the same relative frequency in the simulation as they do in reality and (2) the numerous repetitions of the procedure include the many possible sequential combinations and yield their measure of effectiveness. The probability of occurrence of each sequence is the same as it is in reality. For example, if in the real world there is a 5 percent probability that one machine will fail during an 8-hour period, simulated history will have one failure per 8-hour day approximately 5 percent of the time. If, in addition, an 8-hour period with only one failure can be followed by an 8-hour period with a small number of failures, or a relatively large number, or an average number of failures, simulation will include each possible sequential pattern in the proportion that it occurs in the real world. It is this combination of probabilistic events and a wide variety of possible sequential combinations with widely varying effects on outcomes that analytical solution approaches cannot represent adequately.

For example, consider the case of an organization, or a department within an organization, which receives a different number of orders each day, the orders varying in the time required for processing. The company is interested in determining how many machines it should have to minimize the combined cost of machine idle time and order waiting time. The company knows the cost of machine idle time, the cost of order waiting time, and the probability distributions of the number of orders each day and the number of hours required to process an order. The number of machines that will result in minimum total variable costs cannot be determined analytically because such approaches do not consider the sequential pattern of the hours required for processing. A stochastic simulation includes these sequential patterns.

This problem can be couched in a maintenance setting. Machine failure and repair time can be the probabilistic events rather than orders received and the time required for processing. Furthermore, our example can be expanded to include priority of processing rules such as first come, first served; a ratio of delivery time to lead time; and order profit. A first come, first served priority rule is used to keep the example simple.

The minimization of total variable costs—idle machine cost plus order-waiting cost—is the objective function. The company has calculated these costs as $3.00 an hour for idle machine time and $5.00 an hour for orders back ordered. Therefore, the measure of effectiveness is as follows:

Total variable costs =
$3 × idle machine hours +
$5 × hours for orders back ordered each day

(Note: The model oversimplifies reality for purposes of illustration. The cost figures are hypothetical.) The determination of such costs is a crucial step in any model-building procedure. The number of machines that minimizes these costs is the optimal number of machines (Steps 1 and 2).

The next step is to describe the frequency distribution of the probabilistic events. There are two such events: the number of orders per day and the number of machine hours required per order; therefore, two frequency distributions are required. The frequency distributions for these inputs, based on historical data, and their cumulative probability distributions are shown in Figure 18-1 (Steps 3 and 4).

The initial conditions (the backlog of orders and machine status in this case) must be set. The example has an arbitrary initial setting of no backlog and all machines idle. Considerable study is required in most situations to determine realistic initial conditions (Step 5).

**FIGURE 18-1**
**PROBABILITY DISTRIBUTION**

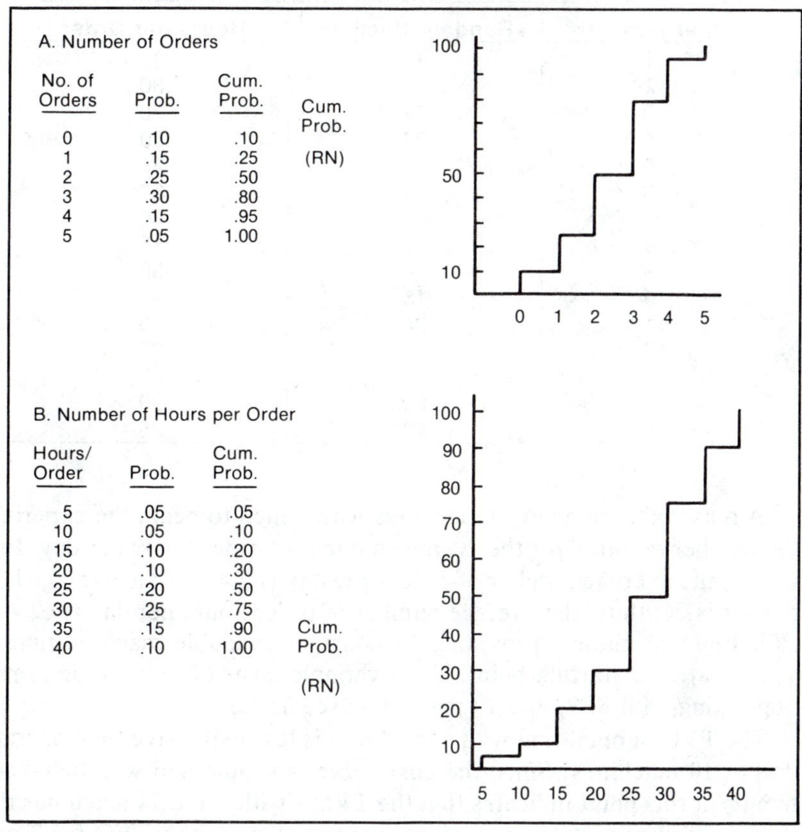


A. Number of Orders

| No. of Orders | Prob. | Cum. Prob. |
|---|---|---|
| 0 | .10 | .10 |
| 1 | .15 | .25 |
| 2 | .25 | .50 |
| 3 | .30 | .80 |
| 4 | .15 | .95 |
| 5 | .05 | 1.00 |

B. Number of Hours per Order

| Hours/ Order | Prob. | Cum. Prob. |
|---|---|---|
| 5 | .05 | .05 |
| 10 | .05 | .10 |
| 15 | .10 | .20 |
| 20 | .10 | .30 |
| 25 | .20 | .50 |
| 30 | .25 | .75 |
| 35 | .15 | .90 |
| 40 | .10 | 1.00 |

Tables 18-1 and 18-2 list the RN samples that determined the number of orders per day and the number of hours per order. These numbers were obtained by going to a random number table (see Appendix I), selecting an arbitrary starting point and taking that number and the next four two-digit numbers. Table 18-3 lists the summarized activity of the five days simulated in the one trial of this example. For the sake of brevity, only one trial of five days is made (Steps 6 and 7).

**TABLE 18-1**
**DETERMINATION OF THE NUMBER OF ORDERS**

| Day | Random Number | Number of Orders |
|---|---|---|
| 1 | 26 | 2 |
| 2 | 78 | 3 |
| 3 | 57 | 3 |
| 4 | 58 | 3 |
| 5 | 23 | 1 |

**TABLE 18-2**
**DETERMINATION OF THE NUMBER OF HOURS PER ORDER**

| Order Number | Random Number | Hours per Order |
|---|---|---|
| 1 | 85 | 35 |
| 2 | 75 | 30 |
| 3 | 74 | 30 |
| 4 | 28 | 20 |
| 5 | 40 | 25 |
| 6 | 69 | 30 |
| 7 | 60 | 30 |
| 8 | 11 | 15 |
| 9 | 74 | 30 |
| 10 | 15 | 15 |
| 11 | 04 | 5 |
| 12 | 21 | 20 |
| 13 | 97 | 40 |
| 14 | 66 | 30 |
| 15 | 42 | 25 |

A reasonable number of machines with which to begin the experiment is the number required for the average number of order hours per day. In the example, the average number of orders per day is 2.4 and the average hours per order is 26; thus, the average number of order hours per day is 62.4 (2.4 $\times$ 26). Eight machines, providing 64 hours of available machine time per day, is a rational starting point. Total variable costs (TVC) are determined for operating with 8, 9, and 10 machines (see Table 18-3).

The TVC of operating with 9 machines is less expensive than operating with 8 or 10 machines. Since the cost curve is simple and well behaved, a minimum at this point indicates that the TVC's with 7 and 11 machines must be higher. Therefore, it is not necessary to calculate the TVC for 7 or 11 machines (Step 8).

The following is a brief explanation of how the first few days' simulation was run using 8 machines. All others were performed in essentially the same manner.

1. The RN's listed in Tables 18-1 and 18-2 were obtained from a table of random numbers. The table was entered at two different points: one to obtain the RN's for the number of orders per day and another to obtain the RN's for the number of hours per order.
2. To determine the number of orders per day, the first RN, 26, is compared to the cumulative probability distribution (Figure 18-1) and found to correspond to 2 orders, since 26 is greater than 25 and less than 50. In the same manner 78 corresponds to 3 orders for the second day ($50 < 78 < 80$).
3. The number of hours per order are determined in the same manner using the second set of RN's and the cumulative distribution for the hours per order (Figure 18-1).

**TABLE 18-3**
**TRIAL ONE**
**FIVE DAYS SIMULATED ACTIVITY**

Where:
TVC = cost of idle time (CI) + cost of waiting time (CW)
CI = $3 an hour of machine idle time
CW = $5 an hour of orders held over each day

**A. Using 8 Machines—64 Hours of Available Machine Time/Day**

| Day | Order Hours Received | Total Order Hours to be Processed | Hours Idle | Hours Back Ordered | CI | CW |
|---|---|---|---|---|---|---|
| 1 | 65 | 65 | 0 | 1 | 0 | 5 |
| 2 | 75 | 76 | 0 | 12 | 0 | 60 |
| 3 | 75 | 87 | 0 | 23 | 0 | 115 |
| 4 | 50 | 73 | 0 | 9 | 0 | 45 |
| 5 | 20 | 29 | 35 | 0 | 105 | 0 |
| | | | | | $105 + | 225 = $330 TVC |

**B. Using 9 Machines—72 Hours of Available Machine Time/Day**

| Day | Order Hours Received | Total Order Hours to be Processed | Hours Idle | Hours Back Ordered | CI | CW |
|---|---|---|---|---|---|---|
| 1 | 65 | 65 | 7 | 0 | 21 | 0 |
| 2 | 75 | 75 | 0 | 3 | 0 | 15 |
| 3 | 75 | 78 | 0 | 6 | 0 | 30 |
| 4 | 50 | 56 | 16 | 0 | 48 | 0 |
| 5 | 20 | 20 | 52 | 0 | 156 | 0 |
| | | | | | $225 + | $ 45 = $270 TVC |

**C. Using 10 Machines—80 Hours of Available Machine Time/Day**

Similar calculations render TVC = $345

4. Thus, on the first day of simulation, two orders arrived and they require 35 and 30 machine hours respectively, a total of 65 hours which is one hour more than capacity. Thus, one order hour is back ordered at a cost of $5. The backlog initial condition was set at zero (Table 18-3).
5. Three orders arrive on the second day requiring 75 (30 + 20 + 25) machine hours. Adding these to the one-hour back order from Day 1 brings the total processing requirement to 76 hours, 12 more than capacity at a cost of $60 (Table 18-3).
6. The simulated inputs and costs for all other days are determined in the same manner.

As a further example of a simulation problem consider the following situation. A production process manufactures about 12 units per day; specifically, that is 12 units 80 percent of the time, 11 units 10 percent of the time, and 13 units 10 percent of the time. Orders are received according to the following distribution:

| Number of Orders/Day | Frequency |
|---|---|
| 5 | .10 |
| 6 | .15 |
| 7 | .25 |
| 8 | .35 |
| 9 | .15 |

Each order can be for one or more units. The distribution of order size is as follows:

| Units/Order | Frequency |
|---|---|
| 1 | .5 |
| 2 | .3 |
| 3 | .2 |

Some units not sold can be saved on a given day to satisfy demand the following day, but because of perishability we cannot save them a second day.

The company is considering expanding sales and wants to see what it has to do to production to handle various sales increases. The principal concern is with the service level. The new sales levels to be examined are for the following distributions:

| Number of Orders/Day | Frequency |
|---|---|
| 6 | .10 |
| 7 | .10 |
| 8 | .35 |
| 9 | .30 |
| 10 | .15 |

| Units/Order | Frequency |
|---|---|
| 1 | .2 |
| 2 | .5 |
| 3 | .3 |

The cases to be considered are (1) no increase in number of orders, but increased units per order; (2) increased orders, but no increase in size of orders; and (3) increase in both orders and size of orders. As a start, we will leave production as is or increase it by two units a day.

To facilitate analysis the computer program in Appendix L has been developed. Using it we first simulate our current situation to see whether the simulated results resemble current practice. This test of the accuracy or validity of the simulation model is sometimes termed *face validity*. After all, if we cannot simulate the current situation, how can we have any confidence in our simulation of predicted situations. This initial interaction with the computer is shown in Figure 18-2. Note also that another check on whether the simulation is working properly is to compare the theoretical means or averages of the distributions to the averages of the samples. Other tests may also be performed to verify that the simulation process is working properly. Since the service levels of the simulation are reasonably close to what we have observed, we can go on to explore the impact of increased sales.

**FIGURE 18-2**
**SAMPLE COMPUTER INTERACTION**

```
    CALL,ASIM

 TITLE       ? TEXT EXAMPLE BASE CASE
 SIMULATION LENGTH    ? 200
 PRINT EVERYTHING     ? NO
 WHAT IS THE PRODUCTION DISTRIBUTION
? 11,.1
? 12,.8
? 13,.1
?
 WHAT IS THE ORDER DISTRIBUTION
? 5,.1
? 6,.15
? 7,.25
? 8,.35
? 9,.15
?
 WHAT IS THE UNITS/ORDER DISTRIBUTION
? 1,.5
? 2,.3
? 3,.2
?
                                                          *****SERVICE*******
   DAY      ORDERS     DEMAND PRODUCTION AVAILABLE        EXCESS   UNSATISFIED
                                                          UNITS      ORDERS

 TOTALS
  200.     1476.      2504.     2394.                     598.       80.

            51 STOCKOUT DAYS
 SERVICE LEVEL (PER UNIT)      .948083
 SERVICE LEVEL (ORDERS)        .945799
 AVERAGE EXCESS       3.640000
 AVERAGE SHORTAGE      .650000

 AVERAGES            THEORETICAL      SAMPLE
 ORDERS                 7.300000     7.380000
 DEM./ORDER             1.700000     1.696477
 DEMAND/DAY            12.410000    12.520000
 PRODUCTION/DAY        12.000000    11.970000


 TITLE       ?
*END*
```

Table 18-4 summarizes some of our simulation runs. Note that with no change in production but increased orders service drops from 94 percent to 83 percent. To compensate for the increased orders we must raise production by two units each day to get a satisfactory 97 percent service level. But with increased units per order as well, we must further increase production to 17 units each day, on average, in order to have a 95 percent service level.

**TABLE 18-4**
**SERVICE LEVEL CHANGES AS A FUNCTION OF DEMAND AND PRODUCTION CHANGES**

| Demand Conditions | MPL* | Service Level |
|---|---|---|
| Current Level | 12 | 94% |
| Increased Orders | 12 | 83% |
| | 14 | 97% |
| Increased Order and Units/Order | 12 | 66% |
| | 14 | 78% |
| | 17 | 95% |

*Mean Production Level (Units per Day)

## Pitfalls and Safeguards

Most mathematical models of real world systems greatly oversimplify because, as the simple model is modified to achieve greater correspondence with reality, the mathematical complexities increase at a much greater rate than the model's correspondence to reality. For instance, note that the first example does not consider the possibility of machine failure. Inclusion of that factor could have been accomplished with the addition of a third probability distribution defining the probability of machine failures. Although it was omitted to keep the example simple, its inclusion would be desirable if machine failures were relatively common.

In addition, there is the slight possibility that nonrepresentative inputs might be generated by simulation. In one run of only 100 repetitions, there is always the possibility that the average RN, and therefore the average event value, may be considerably above or below the expected .50 value. Should this occur, the simulation results could be misleading.

A method exists for avoiding this pitfall. Running the simulation more than once, say four or five times, substantially reduces the possibility of nonrepresentative event values. Each run must be made with a unique set of RN's. The average measure of effectiveness value of these runs is used to evaluate the effect of the specific values of the controlled variables (number of machines in the example) being compared.

The values in Table 18-4 are the result of having replicated each run three times. Three was deemed sufficient because the service levels differed only slightly between runs.

## Sensitivity Analysis

After the initial solution of the problem is obtained, a sensitivity analysis is advisable. Such analysis evaluates the impact of changes in the parameters. For instance, would the optimum number of machines in the first example still be 9 if the cost of idle time were \$3.50 instead of \$3.00, or if the cost of back ordering were \$5.25 instead of \$5.00, or if processing time were reduced by 10 percent across the board because of increased operating efficiencies, or if the number of orders turned out to be 15 percent higher than anticipated? This analysis is performed by running the simulation with one or more of these factors changed to the alternate possibility and the resulting costs calculated.

Such an analysis enables us to evaluate how sensitive the decision is to variations in real world conditions. If changes similar to those described above have little or no effect on the decision, the situation is described as being *insensitive* relative to those factors. Each decision situation must be examined to determine its sensitivity to changes in specific parameters.

**Building a Simulation Model.** Each situation must be studied and a model developed for it. When a decision criterion, such as minimizing total costs or maximizing rate of return, has been selected, the designer of the simulation experiment must determine which variables influence the result and how they influence it. This requires that the designer possess adequate knowledge of and an insight into the real world situation. Without this capacity the odds are that the model will not tell it like it is. For example, he must decide whether to include the possibility of machine failure.

After the model has been developed, it must be validated. The model validation process begins with the usual questions: Does the model appear accurate? Does it provide reasonable answers? In short, does it have face validity? Do others familiar with the real world situation agree that the model is representative and the results reasonable? In addition, the model can be run using historical data and the results compared with actual results. For instance, does actual receipt of a specific number of orders and hours per order result in the same costs predicted by the model?

**Computers.** The digital computer's speed and accuracy has made the application of these concepts to industrial problems practical. A computer cannot construct a model of the real world, nor can it select the settings of controlled variables for the experiment. It cannot evaluate assumptions or estimate the extent the future will conform to the past unless given specific instruction how to do so. The designer still performs these vital functions.

Much of the early use of computers in simulation was performed using standard programming languages, such as FORTRAN and ALGOL. Though developing the FORTRAN program and running the simulation model on a digital computer was faster and more efficient than using a desk calculator, writing and debugging the program was a tedious and time-consuming task. The development of special simulation languages substantially reduced this task. Detailed descriptions and analyses of these languages are contained in the references listed in this chapter's selected readings.

## Benefits of Simulation

Simulation is relatively inexpensive; the cost of simulating a production system and using the model to experiment with different policies (for example, different scheduling priority systems) is much lower than experimenting with the system in reality. Simulation (building a model of the system, and manipulating that model, operating with different policies in effect) also provides those involved with a better understanding of the situation. It is an excellent training device, since the individuals involved get a feel for the interaction of the controlled variables and their impact on decision results.

## SOME APPLICATIONS

William Lee and Curtis McLaughlin reported on the development and implementation of a simulation model of the aggregate material management function in an $11 million firm. They evaluated decisions concerning work force size and stability, overtime, inventory fluctuations, and cash flow over given operating ranges of demand and capacity. [1]

David A. Collier studied the interaction of single stage lot size models (EOQ, lot-for-lot, period order quantity, etc.) in a material requirements planning system. He examined various combinations of these rules among the levels in a product structure. [2] This article is typical of the research going on in this area. An earlier paper on this same subject is one by Stephen H. Goodman, Stanley T. Hardy, and Joseph R. Biggs which uses a different, quite elaborate model. Their results examine these rules for various performance criteria. [3]

Frederick C. Weston, Jr., in his article, looked at EOQ, reorder point, and exponential smoothing interactions in an elementary setting. He demonstrated, among other things, that the results of this type of system may be quite contrary to generally accepted theory. [4]

Stochastic simulation, to summarize, is a synthetic method of dynamically representing a decision system over time and evaluating the alternate settings of controlled variables. It is quicker and less expensive than trial and error in the real world. It is especially useful when the complexity of a situation prevents application of an analytical model. Monte Carlo simulation works because (1) simulated event values occur with the same frequency they do in the real world and (2) sequential combinations of event values have the same probability of occurrence as they do in the real world. The advent of the digital computer with its capacity to handle a large quantity of data through many mathematical steps in a relatively short period of time with accuracy has been a boon to the utilization of Monte Carlo simulation. The development of special simulation programming languages has reduced the cost of Monte Carlo simulation; but, under certain conditions, languages such as FORTRAN and ALGOL more accurately and effectively portray realistic conditions.

The design of the simulation model and the experiment is the cornerstone of the process. Critical assumptions are always necessary: Will the future conform to the past? If historical data are not to be used, can a standard probability distribution be used to generate inputs? Inaccurate assumptions and sloppy experiments can generate misleading answers. Stochastic simulation is no panacea, but it is a valuable tool when applied properly.

# PROBLEMS

**1.** A common maintenance/inventory problem involves group replacement; for example, if one of several similar components fails in a given machine, should all be replaced in order to save subsequent downtime? The answer depends on service life (SL), repair time, and costs. The following table gives the service time distribution for an electronic tube in a machine. Each machine contains three tubes.

| SL | Probability of SL or less |
|---|---|
| 6,000 | .05 |
| 8,000 | .50 |
| 10,000 | .75 |
| 12,000 | .85 |
| 14,000 | .93 |
| 16,000 | .98 |
| 18,000 | 1.00 |

Cost of each tube is $50. The cost to replace 1, 2, or 3 tubes is $100 plus a variable cost of $10 a tube replaced.

Simulate the breakdown of the tubes in a machine for a period of 120,000 hours and determine which of the following policies is lowest cost:

1. Replace only the tube that fails.
2. Replace all tubes if any one fails.
3. Replace failed tube plus any that have been in service over 8,000 hours.

**2.** In some instances, the analytic approach to determining overall project completion discussed in Chapter 16 is not as desirable as using simulation to determine the distribution of a project completion date. For the following project assume triangular (rather than Beta) distribution of activity times and determine the approximate probability distribution for completion.

| | Time Estimates | | |
|---|---|---|---|
| Activity | Optimistic | Most Likely | Pessimistic |
| A | 1.6 | 2.8 | 4.3 |
| B | 3.4 | 4.6 | 6.0 |
| C | .8 | 2.0 | 2.8 |
| D | 1.4 | 2.5 | 3.5 |
| E | 2.1 | 2.9 | 4.2 |

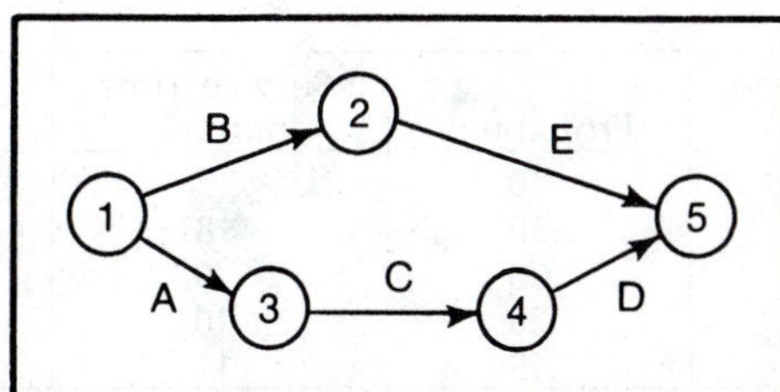

3. Some people advocate choosing the *a* value for exponential smoothing by simulating past experience using different *a* values and choosing that which minimizes the error. For the following set of data, what value of *a*, to the nearest tenth, minimizes the sum of the absolute errors.

| Period | Demand | Period | Demand | Period | Demand |
|---|---|---|---|---|---|
| 1 | 55 | 11 | 48 | 21 | 50 |
| 2 | 65 | 12 | 45 | 22 | 55 |
| 3 | 62 | 13 | 40 | 23 | 60 |
| 4 | 56 | 14 | 42 | 24 | 57 |
| 5 | 57 | 15 | 49 | 25 | 65 |
| 6 | 51 | 16 | 48 | 26 | 55 |
| 7 | 58 | 17 | 43 | 27 | 57 |
| 8 | 60 | 18 | 57 | 28 | 63 |
| 9 | 52 | 19 | 49 | 29 | 64 |
| 10 | 42 | 20 | 45 | 30 | 50 |

4. Use the computer program in Appendix L to determine the service level under the following circumstances.

| Numbers of Orders/Day | Frequency |
|---|---|
| 6 | .1 |
| 7 | .2 |
| 8 | .3 |
| 9 | .3 |
| 10 | .1 |

| Units/Order | Frequency |
|---|---|
| 1 | .5 |
| 2 | .3 |
| 3 | .1 |
| 4 | .1 |

Case 1. Produce 16 units each day.
Case 2. Produce an average of 16 units, but 10% of the time produce 15, and 10% of the time produce 17.

5. When equipment breaks down the repairman must go to a tool crib to get necessary tools and parts. An expansion in the number of machines is expected, and to minimize downtime the company is considering having two clerks on duty to serve 50% more repairmen. But first, it wants to simulate the situation to see how long repairmen wait under various assumptions. The distribution of time between arrivals at the tool crib is as follows:

| Interarrival Time (minutes) | Probability | Service Time (minutes) | Probability |
|---|---|---|---|
| 10 | .10 | 7 | .10 |
| 11 | .30 | 8 | .25 |
| 12 | .25 | 9 | .30 |
| 13 | .20 | 10 | .20 |
| 14 | .15 | 11 | .15 |

Perform a simulation for 50 arrivals, starting with no one at the crib and compute the average wait, average number waiting, and average service time. How does the latter compare with its theoretical time?

**6.** In Problem 5, if the changes in number of machines are made and the number of repairmen is increased so that interarrival times are as follows, what will happen (a) if there is no change in crib clerks, and (b) if there are 2 clerks present?

| Interarrival Time (minutes) | Probability |
|---|---|
| 7 | .10 |
| 8 | .25 |
| 9 | .30 |
| 10 | .20 |
| 11 | .15 |

**7.** In order to assemble the product it goes through three stations in sequence. Because of variability in the materials the time at each station is not constant. The following table gives the time distributions at each station.

| Station 1 | | Station 2 | | Station 3 | |
|---|---|---|---|---|---|
| Minutes | Probability | Minutes | Probability | Minutes | Probability |
| 3.2 | .1 | 3.2 | .05 | 3.0 | .05 |
| 3.3 | .2 | 3.3 | .2 | 3.2 | .15 |
| 3.4 | .4 | 3.4 | .5 | 3.4 | .60 |
| 3.5 | .2 | 3.5 | .2 | 3.6 | .15 |
| 3.6 | .1 | 3.6 | .05 | 3.8 | .05 |

a. Assume no buffer stock between stations and hence Worker 2 must wait for Worker 1 to finish before work at Station 2 can start; similarly for Worker 3. How long will it take to process 20 jobs?
b. Assume we start with 2 units partially assembled sitting between Stations 1 and 2 and between Stations 2 and 3. How long will it take to get 20 jobs processed?
c. Compare the worker idle time between *a* and *b*.

**8.** A company has one forklift that costs $100 a day regardless of whether it is used or not. Some days it has both incoming and outgoing orders that can keep 2 or 3 forklifts busy. They are rented at $150 a day as needed. The demand is as follows:

| Number Needed | Percentage of Days |
|---|---|
| 0 | 5 |
| 1 | 50 |
| 2 | 30 |
| 3 | 15 |

Simulate 30 days to estimate whether or not the company should buy a second forklift.

## SELECTED READINGS


**1.** William Lee and Curtis McLaughlin, "Corporate Simulation Models for Aggregate Materials Management," *Production and Inventory Management*, Vol. 15, No. 1 (1974), pp. 55-67.

**2.** David A. Collier, "The Interaction of Single-Stage Lot Size Models in a Material Requirements Planning System," *Production and Inventory Management*, Vol. 21, No. 4 (1980), pp. 11-20.

**3.** Stephen H. Goodman, Stanley T. Hardy, and Joseph R. Biggs, "Lot Sizing Rules in a Hierarchical Multistage Inventory System," *Production and Inventory Management*, Vol. 18, No. 1 (1977), pp. 104-116.

**4.** Frederick C. Weston, Jr., "A Simulation Approach to Examining Traditional EOQ/EOP and Single Order Exponential Smoothing Efficiency Adopting a Small Business Perspective," *Production and Inventory Management*, Vol. 21, No. 2 (1980), pp. 67-83.

**5.** D. N. Chorafas, *Systems and Simulation* (New York: Academic Press, Inc., 1965).

**6.** G. S. Fishman, "Estimating Sample Size in Computer Simulation Experiments," *Management Science*, Vol. 18, No. 1 (1971), pp. 21-38.

**7.** J. W. Forrester, *Industrial Dynamics* (Cambridge, Mass.: The M.I.T. Press, 1961).

**8.** Geoffrey Gordon, *System Simulation* (Englewood Cliffs, N.J.: Prentice-Hall, Inc., 1969).

**9.** ———, *The Application of GPSS V to Discrete System Simulation* (Englewood Cliffs, N.J.: Prentice-Hall, Inc., 1975).

**10.** IBM Corp., *Bibliography on Simulation Form 320-0924* (White Plains, N.Y.: 1966).

**11.** P. J. Kiviat, R. Villanueva, and H. M. Markowitz, *The SIMSCRIPT II Programming Language* (Englewood Cliffs, N.J.: Prentice-Hall, Inc., 1969).

**12.** ———, *The SIMSCRIPT II.5 Programming Language* (Los Angeles, Calif.: Consolidated Analysis Centers, Inc., 1973).

**13.** Herbert Maisel and Guiliano Gnugnoli, *Simulation of Discrete Stochastic Systems* (Chicago, Ill: Science Research Associates, 1972).

**14.** Claude McMillan, Jr. and Richard F. Gonzales, *Systems Analysis: A Computer Approach to Decision Models*, rev. ed. (Homewood, Ill.: Richard D. Irwin, Inc., 1968).

**15.** J. H. Mize and J. G. Cox, *Essentials of Simulation* (Englewood Cliffs, N. J.: Prentice-Hall, Inc., 1968).

**16.** T. J. Naylor, J. L. Balintfy, D. S. Burdick, and Kong Chu, *Computer Simulation Techniques* (New York: John Wiley & Sons, Inc., 1966).

**17.** A. A. B. Pritsker and P. J. Kiviat, *Simulation with GASP II: A FORTRAN Based Simulation Language* (Englewood Cliffs, N.J.: Prentice-Hall, Inc., 1969).

**18.** Michael S. Salvador et al., "Mathematical Modeling Optimization and Simulation Improve Large-Scale Finished Goods Inventory Management," *Production and Inventory Control Management*, 2d Quarter (1975).

**19.** Robert E. Shannon, *Systems Simulation–the Art and Science* (Englewood Cliffs, N. J.: Prentice-Hall, Inc., 1975).

**20.** F. P. Wyman, *Simulation Modeling: A Guide to Using SIMSCRIPT* (New York: John Wiley & Sons, Inc., 1970).

# PART FIVE

# APPENDIXES

The appendixes include a description of the Bill of Materials (BOM), the derivations of selected models used in the text, the Table of Areas of the Normal Curve, a Random Number Table, selected computer programs, and selected readings. Nearly all Production and Inventory Management (PIM) decisions require data contained in the BOM; thus, we include its description as an appendix rather than as part of a particular chapter.

The derivations are provided for those interested in the mathematical basis of the models and for those interested in developing models for similar situations. The Table of Areas of the Normal Curve is required in decision situations that include a probabilistic variable with a normal distribution; thus, it is used in many places in the text. The Random Number Table provides numerical values required for stochastic simulation without computer generated random numbers.

Three computer programs are available, one each for solving exponential smoothing, critical path, and simulation problems. Their objective is to introduce readers to the use of available software. Developing competency in the use of these programs should encourage students to use other software that is available at their organization and that is useful for solving PIM problems.

The selected articles illustrate the application of PIM principles, concepts, and techniques in real world situations representing a variety of problems and solutions. Some report on computerized systems in relatively complex situations while others report on manual systems in situations requiring minimal data processing.

The Stratton article emphasizes important practical aspects of forecasting including data accuracy, managing the vital few, balancing the forecast between levels, developing information system requirements, and measuring system performance. Both Brongiel and Civerolo examine relevant practical considerations related to master production scheduling and operations planning while the Schonberger article asks us (and argues) for an understanding of why and how outmoded techniques still may be used in some cases. The Edwards and O'Neill article reports in detail on a rather elaborate computerized shop floor control system in a complex manufacturing situation (many open orders in a large job shop). Their article contains excellent examples of system reports.

# SUPPLEMENTAL INFORMATION

# APPENDIX A
# THE BILL OF MATERIALS

An inclusive definition of a final product includes a list of the items, ingredients, and/or materials needed to assemble, mix, or produce that end product. This list is called a *bill of materials* (BOM). The BOM can take several forms and be used in many ways. It is created as part of the design process. It is then used by manufacturing engineers to determine which items should be purchased and which items should be manufactured. Production control uses it in conjunction with the master production schedule to determine the items for which purchase requisitions and production orders must be released (see Chapter 4). Accounting uses it to cost the product.

The simplest BOM is referred to as a *single level bill* (see Figure A-1). It consists of a list of all items needed to make the end item, including for each component (1) a unique part number, (2) a short verbal description, (3) the quantity needed for each single end item, and (4) the part's unit of measure.

**FIGURE A-1**
**BILL OF MATERIALS FOR ASSEMBLED LAMP**

| ABC LAMP COMPANY<br>Bill of Material<br>Part LA01—Lamp | | | |
|---|---|---|---|
| Part Number | Description | Quantity for Each Assembly | Unit of Measure |
| B100 | Base Assembly | 1 | Each |
| S100 | Shade | 1 | Each |
| A100 | Socket Assembly | 1 | Each |

While the single level BOM is sufficient when a product is assembled at one time from a set of purchased parts and raw materials it does not adequately describe a product that has subassemblies. If we decided to make the base and socket assemblies, then each of those would have sub items that were purchased. To illustrate the product structure we can draw a "tree" having several levels (see Figure A-2). Note that by convention the final product is at Level 0 and the level numbers increase as one looks down the tree.

**FIGURE A-2**
**MULTILEVEL TREE STRUCTURE AND LEVELS**

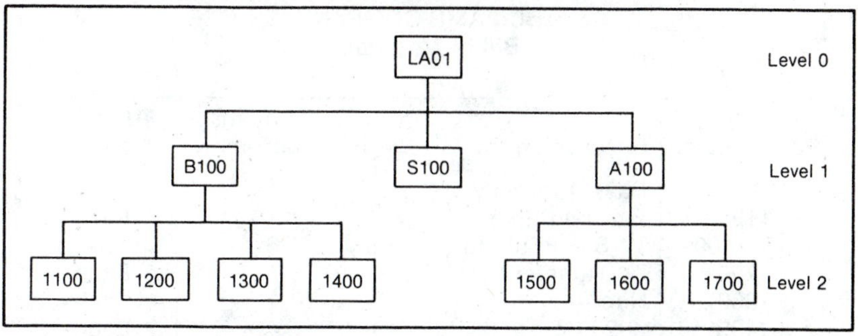

Corresponding to this tree structure is a multilevel BOM (see Figure A-3). Again each part or assembly is given a unique number, and (to aid in understanding the structure) the numbers for the components of a subassembly are indented under the respective subassembly numbers. When a component is used in more than one subassembly a *summary bill* may be produced for use by purchasing in which there is only one occurrence of the item along with its total quantity per final assembly. This type of bill is sometimes referred to as a *quick deck*.

**FIGURE A-3**
**INDENTED BILL OF MATERIALS**

| ABC LAMP COMPANY<br>Bill of Materials<br>Part LA01 | | | |
|---|---|---|---|
| Part Number | Description | Quantity for Each Assembly | Unit of Measure |
| B100 | Base Assembly | 1 | Each |
| 1100 | Finished Shaft | 1 | Each |
| 1200 | 7″ Diameter Steel Plate | 1 | Each |
| 1300 | Hub | 1 | Each |
| 1400 | ¼-20 Screws | 4 | Each |
| S100 | 14″ Black Shade | 1 | Each |
| A100 | Socket Assembly | 1 | Each |
| 1500 | Steel Holder | 1 | Each |
| 1600 | One-Way Socket | 1 | Each |
| 1700 | Wiring Assembly | 1 | Each |

If the wiring assembly were itself a subassembly then its components would be listed, and on the indented BOM the component part numbers would be further indented (see Figure A-4). As you may see the multilevel product structure is really made up of building blocks of single level product trees; that is, a BOM can be drawn up for each subassembly and only these single level bills need be retained. This is important when producing many different end items that have common subassemblies. We do not need to change every end item BOM when an engineering change takes place in a single common subassembly.

**FIGURE A-4**
**A LEVEL THREE BILL OF MATERIALS**

| ABC LAMP COMPANY Bill of Materials Part LA01 | | | |
|---|---|---|---|
| Part Number | Description | Quantity for Each Assembly | Unit of Measure |
| B100 | Base Assembly | 1 | Each |
| 1100 | Finished Shaft | 1 | Each |
| 7100 | ⅜" Steel Tubing | 26 | Inches |
| 1200 | 7" Diameter Steel Plate | 1 | Each |
| 1300 | Hub | 1 | Each |
| 1400 | ¼-20 Screws | 4 | Each |
| S100 | 14" Black Shade | 1 | Each |
| A100 | Socket Assembly | 1 | Each |
| 1500 | Steel Holder | 1 | Each |
| 1600 | One-Way Socket | 1 | Each |
| 1700 | Wiring Assembly | 1 | Each |
| 2200 | 16 Gauge Lamp Cord | 12 | Feet |
| 2300 | Std. Pkg. Terminal | 1 | Each |

To illustrate this and several other real life complexities let's assume that we now manufacture lamps with 3 different shades, 2 alternate base plates, and 2 types of sockets. Our original lamp was designated LA01. Working with the different components we now can have 12 different final products. To clarify this we can produce a matrix format of a summary BOM (see Figure A-5). An examination of the matrix shows that some parts are common to all models. In order to ease the planning task we could group together the wiring assembly and the finished shaft with a new part number, say 4000. These components are produced independently of one another and thus can be grouped as common parts. This part number is never stocked and so it is called a *phantom* part. Its only purpose is to reduce the number of items on the BOM. We can go further with the concept of restructuring our BOM's and, for some products, create new numbers to represent new subassemblies in order to shorten lead times; for example, subassemblies of plate, hub, and screws.

Another type of BOM is often useful in planning and handling engineering charges. It is referred to as a *planning bill*, a *pseudo bill*, a *phantom bill*, a *super bill*, or a *family bill*. If we look at the matrix form of the summary bill (Figure A-5) we can see that we could create a product structure diagram (see Figure A-6) for the family of lamps that consisted of pseudo subassemblies; namely base assemblies, shades, and socket assemblies. For each of these, in place of the quantity for each unit assembled, we state what the percentage split is for each type of component. Now, as we plan for a total of 10,000 lamps for each month, we can use this planning bill to derive the number of each type of component to build. Furthermore, if we decide to change to, say, a 16-inch green shade, only this single BOM, this modular bill, needs to be altered.

**FIGURE A-5**
**MATRIX FORMAT OF A SUMMARY BILL OF MATERIALS**
MODEL LA01 (QUANTITY FOR EACH ASSEMBLY)

| Component Number | Component Description | Unit of Measure | 01 | 02 | 03 | 04 | 05 | 06 | 07 | 08 | 09 | 10 | 11 | 12 |
|---|---|---|---|---|---|---|---|---|---|---|---|---|---|---|
| 1100 | Finished Shaft | Each | 1 | 1 | 1 | 1 | 1 | 1 | 1 | 1 | 1 | 1 | 1 | 1 |
| 2100 | ⅜″ Steel Tube | Inches | 26 | 26 | 26 | 26 | 26 | 26 | 26 | 26 | 26 | 26 | 26 | 26 |
| 1200 | 7″ Dia. Steel Plate | Each | 1 | | 1 | 1 | 1 | | 1 | 1 | | | | |
| 1201 | 8″ Dia. Steel Plate | Each | | 1 | | | | 1 | | | 1 | 1 | 1 | 1 |
| 1300 | Hub | Each | 1 | 1 | 1 | 1 | 1 | 1 | 1 | 1 | 1 | 1 | 1 | 1 |
| 1400 | ¼-20 Screws | Each | 4 | 4 | 4 | 4 | 4 | 4 | 4 | 4 | 4 | 4 | 4 | 4 |
| S100 | 14″ Black Shade | Each | 1 | 1 | | | 1 | 1 | | | | | | |
| S101 | 15″ White Shade | Each | | | 1 | | | | 1 | | 1 | 1 | | |
| S102 | 15″ Cream Shade | Each | | | | 1 | | | | 1 | | | 1 | 1 |
| 1500 | Steel Holder | Each | 1 | 1 | 1 | 1 | 1 | 1 | 1 | 1 | | | | |
| 1600 | One-way Socket | Each | 1 | 1 | 1 | 1 | | | | | 1 | | 1 | |
| 1601 | Three-way Socket | Each | | | | | 1 | 1 | 1 | 1 | | 1 | | 1 |
| 1700 | Wiring Assembly | Each | 1 | 1 | 1 | 1 | 1 | 1 | 1 | 1 | 1 | 1 | 1 | 1 |
| 2200 | 16 Gauge Lamp Cord | Feet | 1 | 1 | 1 | 1 | 1 | 1 | 1 | 1 | 1 | 1 | 1 | 1 |
| 2300 | Std. Plug Terminal | Each | 1 | 1 | 1 | 1 | 1 | 1 | 1 | 1 | 1 | 1 | 1 | 1 |
| B100 | Base Assembly—7″ | Each | 1 | | 1 | 1 | 1 | | 1 | 1 | | | | |
| B101 | Base Assembly—8″ | Each | | 1 | | | | 1 | | | 1 | 1 | 1 | 1 |
| A100 | Socket Assembly—One-way | Each | 1 | 1 | 1 | 1 | | | | | 1 | | 1 | |
| A101 | Socket Assembly—Three-way | Each | | | | | 1 | 1 | 1 | 1 | | 1 | | 1 |

**FIGURE A-6**
**A PLANNING BILL TREE STRUCTURE**

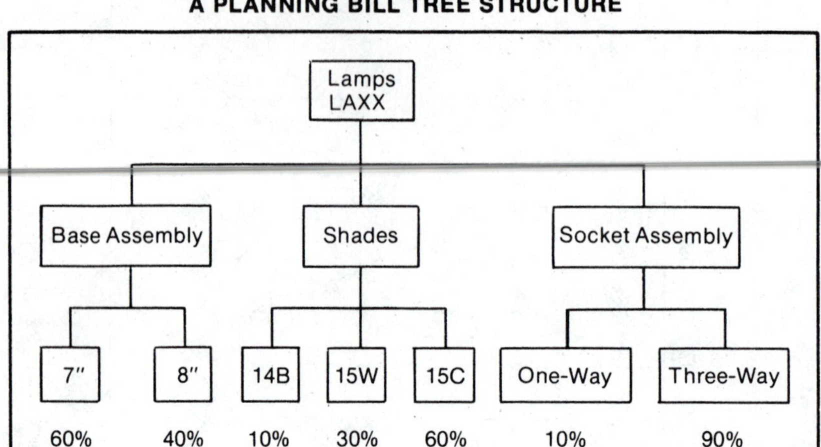


# SELECTED READINGS

1. Robert Gessner, "A Family BOM Fairy Tale," *APICS News* (February, 1980), p. 4.
2. Larry C. Jackson, *Bills of Materials, APICS Training Aid* (Washington, D.C.: American Production and Inventory Control Society).

# APPENDIX B
# DERIVATION OF OPTIMUM CYCLE MODEL

Each item in a joint replenishment group need not be included in each joint replenishment order. The model to determine the number ($n_i$) of joint order cycles between orders for Item $i$ is developed in the following manner.[1] The total period cost model in terms of order intervals ($T$'s) and all items ordered each cycle is:

$$TC = (S + \Sigma s_i) \div T + TAk \div 2$$

If all items are not ordered each cycle, annual preparation costs become $[S + \Sigma(s_i \div n_i)] \div T$ and annual carrying costs become $kT\Sigma n_i a_i \div 2$

Where:

$TC$ = total costs
$S$ = the major preparation costs of an order independent of the number of items
$s_i$ = the minor (incremental) preparation costs incurred by the inclusion of an item
$T$ = the interval between orders, usually expressed as a decimal fraction of a year
$A$ = the aggregate requirement for the period in dollars
$k$ = the carrying cost rate per year
$n_i$ = joint order cycles between orders for Item $i$
$a_i$ = the period requirement for Item $i$ in dollars

Verification of these modifications is straightforward. For example, let $S$ = \$50.00, $s_1$ = \$10.00, $s_2$ = \$12.00, $s_3$ = \$16.00, $s_4$ = \$20.00, and $T$ = .25 (4 orders each year). Then annual preparation costs, if each item is ordered each cycle, equals (\$50.00 + \$58.00) ÷ .25 (i.e., \$432.00). However, if items 3 and 4 are ordered each alternate cycle ($n_1$ and $n_2 = 1$; $n_3$ and $n_4 = 2$), then annual preparation costs are as follows:

$$= [\$50.00 + \$10.00 + \$12.00 + (\$16.00 \div 2) + (\$20.00 \div 2)] \div .25 = \$360.00$$

The difference (\$72.00) between the cost of ordering each item every cycle and not ordering Items 3 and 4 twice a year is exactly the savings obtained by multiplying the sum of $s_3$ and $s_4$ by 2. The average inventory of an item is now $Tn_i a_i \div 2$ since the product $Tn_i$ is the fraction of period inventory obtained when Item $i$ is

[1] Robert G. Brown, *Decision Rules for Inventory Management* (New York: Holt, Rinehart & Winston, 1967), pp. 48-52.

added. Thus, the total cost model including the possibility of different intervals for individual items is as follows:

$$TC = [S + \Sigma(s_i \div n_i)] \div T + kT\Sigma n_i a_i \div 2$$

Proceed in the normal manner to obtain the optimum value of $T$ with the following first derivative of TC (with respect to $T$):

$$TC' = -[S + \Sigma(s_i \div n_i)] \div T^2 + k\Sigma n_i a_i \div 2$$

Setting $TC'$ equal to zero and solving for $T$ gives the following:

$$T = \left\{\frac{2[S + \Sigma(s_i \div n_i)]}{k\Sigma n_i a_i}\right\}^{1/2}$$

And since all the terms in the second derivative ($TC''$) are positive, the above expression defines a minimum total cost. However, our problem is not solved: the values of $n_i$ have not been determined. Robert Brown suggested the following approach for determining the cycle lengths of individual items. The total costs of Item $i$ as a function of $n_i$ are defined by the following equation:

$$c(n_i) = s_i \div (n_i T) + kTn_i a_i \div 2$$

Taking the first derivative of $c(n_i)$,

$$c'(n_i) = -s_i \div (n_i^2 T) + kTa_i \div 2,$$

setting $c'(n_i)$ equal to zero and solving for $n_i$ gives

$$n_i = \frac{1}{T}\left(\frac{2s_i}{ka_i}\right)^{1/2}$$

Again, all the terms in the second derivative are positive; thus the foregoing model for $n_i$ will generate a minimum value for $c(n_i)$. However, the above model usually does not produce an integer solution for $n_i$. Brown gives the values in Table 8-4 (see page 248) for determining how to round off $n_i$'s.

# APPENDIX C DERIVATION OF MAXIMUM PRODUCTION RUN QUANTITY

Some equipment is used exclusively for the production of a group of items. There are occasions in such situations when production of an item (say, Item A) reaches its optimum lot size before any other item reaches its order point. In such a case, management must decide whether to continue producing Item A or to switch to another item. Switching immediately to another item with ample inventory makes little sense. If forecast demand justifies maintaining the present item production rates, production of Item A should continue until the item inventories are balanced. This approach provides equal run out times ($T_i$'s) as did the process described previously (pages 251-253) for calculating equal run-out lot sizes when an item's order point is reached earlier than forecast.

Under ideal conditions (when demand for each item equals its forecast), the average group inventory ($\Sigma\bar{I}_i$) is defined by the following:[1]

$$\Sigma\bar{I}_i = \Sigma Q^*_i\,(1 - D_i \div P_i) \div 2$$

Since the production lot for any item must last until its next run, a time labeled $T$, the following holds true:

$$Q^*_i = TD_i$$

Therefore, the following also defines the average group inventory:

$$\Sigma\bar{I}_i = T\Sigma D_i\,(1 - D_i \div P_i) \div 2$$

The maximum inventory for an item occurs at the end of its production run and is twice the average inventory. This can be illustrated numerically using the data in Table 8-2 (see page 246). Thus, the following obtains:

$$I^*_i = TD_i\,(1 - D_i \div P_i)$$

And since

$$T = \frac{2\Sigma\bar{I}_i}{\Sigma D_i\,(1 - D_i \div P_i)}$$

---

[1] Robert G. Brown, *Management Decisions for Production Operations* (Hinsdale Ill.: Dryden Press, 1971), p. 206.

Then

$$I^*_i = \frac{2\Sigma \bar{I}_i D_i (1 - D_i \div P_i)}{\Sigma D_i (1 - D_i \div P_i)}$$

In the ideal case (when actual demand equals forecast demand), $I^*_i$ is reached when $Q^*_i$ is produced. (Note that the data in Table 8-2 will not verify this relationship since that data concern production on equipment shared by different groups. However, this relationship can be verified using the example data in Tables 8-9 and 8-10 on pages 261 and 262.) When actual demand does not equal forecast demand, the actual group inventory ($\Sigma I_i$) must be determined and used in the foregoing model. Thus,

$$I^*_i = \frac{2(\Sigma I_i) D_i (1 - D_i \div P_i)}{\Sigma[D_i (1 - D_i \div P_i)]}$$

# APPENDIX D
# DERIVATION OF OPTIMUM ORDER QUANTITY
# BACK ORDER WITH PENALTY

In this situation, total costs equal preparation costs plus carrying costs plus back order costs, and are formulated as follows:

$$TC = \frac{SR}{Q} + kC\,\frac{Q_m}{2}\,t_1\,\frac{R}{Q} + \frac{B\,(Q - Q_m)}{2}\,t_2\,\frac{R}{Q}$$

Where:

$Q^*$ = optimum order quantity
$TC$ = total annual costs
$R$ = annual demand
$S$ = preparation (ordering + setup) costs for each setup
$Q$ = lot size
$k$ = the cost rate of carrying an item in inventory one year
$C$ = unit cost
$Q_m$ = maximum inventory on hand
$B$ = cost of back ordering one unit for a year
$t_1$ = length of time during a cycle when stock is available; in years
$t_2$ = length of time during a cycle when stock is not available
$T$ = $t_1 + t_2$

The following is obtained from Figure 10-3 (see page 318) and from the laws of geometry:

$$\frac{t_1}{Q_m} = \frac{t_2}{Q - Q_m} = \frac{T}{Q}$$

Thus, $t_1$ equals $\frac{Q_m T}{Q}$; and $t_2$ equals $\frac{(Q - Q_m)\,T}{Q}$

And, since the number of cycles for each year ($N$) equals $\frac{R}{Q}$, the following relationships exist:

$$T = \frac{1.0}{N}$$

$$\text{and } T = \frac{Q}{R}, \text{ then}$$

$$t_1 = \frac{Q_m}{Q} \times \frac{Q}{R} = \frac{Q_m}{R}$$

$$t_2 = \frac{(Q - Q_m)}{Q} \times \frac{Q}{R} = \frac{(Q - Q_m)}{R}$$

Substituting the foregoing equivalents of $t_1$ and $t_2$ in the total cost equation gives the following:

$$TC = \frac{SR}{Q} + kCQ_m^2 \div 2Q + B(Q - Q_m)^2 \div 2Q$$

Since there are two unknowns ($Q$ and $Q_m$), we must partially differentiate with respect to $Q$ and $Q_m$ and solve for both as follows:

$$\frac{\delta TC}{\delta Q_m} = 2kCQ_m \div (2Q) - 2B\ (Q - Q_m) \div (2Q) = 0$$

$$= kCQ_m \div Q - B\ (Q - Q_m) \div Q = 0$$

$$kCQ_m = BQ - BQ_m$$

$$Q_m\ (kC + B) = BQ$$

$$Q_m = \left(\frac{B}{kC + B}\right) Q$$

$$\frac{\delta TC}{\delta Q} = -\frac{SR}{Q^2} - \frac{kCQ_m^2}{2Q^2} + \frac{B[4Q\ (Q - Q_m) - 2\ (Q - Q_m)^2]}{4Q^2} = 0$$

$$= -4SR - 2kCQ_m^2 + B(2Q^2 - 2Q_m^2)$$

$$= -2SR - Q_m^2\ (kC + B) + BQ^2 = 0$$

Inserting the value of $Q_m$ obtained earlier into the previous equation gives:

$$-2SR - \frac{B^2}{(kC + B)^2} Q^2\ (kC + B) + BQ^2 = 0$$

$$-2SR + Q^2\left(B - \frac{B^2}{kC + B}\right) = 0$$

$$-2SR + Q^2\left(\frac{BkC + B^2 - B^2}{kC + B}\right) = 0$$

$$Q^2 = \frac{2SR(kC + B)}{BkC}$$

$$Q = \sqrt{\frac{2SR}{kC} \times \frac{(kC + B)}{B}}$$

# APPENDIX E
# DERIVATION OF OPTIMUM ORDER QUANTITY BACK ORDER WITHOUT PENALTY

In this situation, now, total costs equal preparation costs plus setup costs, and are formulated as follows:

$$TC = \frac{SR}{Q} + kC \times (\overline{IOH})$$

Where:

$Q^*$ = optimum order quantity
$TC$ = total annual costs
$S$ = preparation (ordering + setup) costs for each setup
$R$ = annual demand
$Q$ = order quantity
$k$ = the cost rate of carrying an item in inventory one year
$C$ = unit cost
$\overline{IOH}$ = average inventory on hand

From Figure 10-4 (see page 321), it can be seen that:

$$\overline{IOH} = Q_m \times (T - W) \div 2T$$

Where:

$Q_m$ = maximum inventory on hand
$T$ = cycle time in years

By definition, and examining Figure 10-4, we see the following:

$$T = \frac{Q}{R} \text{ and } Q_m = Q - RW$$

Substituting the last three equations in the total cost equation yields the following:

$$TC = \frac{SR}{Q} + kC\,(Q - RW)\,(\frac{Q}{R} - W) \div (\frac{2Q}{R})$$

$$TC = \frac{SR}{Q} + \frac{kCR}{2Q}\left(\frac{Q^2}{R} - QW - QW + RW^2\right)$$

$$TC = \frac{SR}{Q} + \frac{kCQ}{2} - kCRW + kCR^2W^2 \div (2Q)$$

Taking the first derivative of $TC$ with respect to $Q$, setting it equal to zero, and solving for the optimal value of $Q$ ($Q^*$), gives us the following:

$$\frac{\delta(TC)}{\delta Q} = 0 = \frac{-SR}{Q^2} + \frac{kC}{2} - \frac{kCR^2W^2}{2Q^2}$$

$$Q^2\ kC = 2SR + kCR^2W^2$$

$$Q^* = \sqrt{\frac{2SR}{kC} + R^2W^2}$$

Applying the second derivative test for a minimum yields the following:

$$\frac{\delta\ (TC)}{\delta\ Q^2} = \frac{2SR}{Q^3} + \frac{kCR^2W^2}{Q^3}$$

Since all terms are positive, the second derivative evaluated at $Q^*$ will be positive, and $Q^*$ gives a minimum $TC$.

# APPENDIX F
# SEQUENCING

Frequently a scheduler or supervisor must decide the sequence in which orders should be run through two or more work centers when all orders have essentially the same priority. This appendix describes techniques for sequencing orders to minimize the total processing time in the case of the following:

1. Two or more orders having the same operation sequence through two work centers
2. Two or more orders having different operation sequences through two work centers

## TWO MACHINES, MANY ORDERS (JOHNSON'S ALGORITHM)

Here the situation is that there are two work centers (*A* and *B*), and there are many orders (*n*'s) each having the same operation sequence—Operation A followed by Operation B. The objective is to sequence the orders to minimize the time from the beginning of the first order to the completion of the last order. [1] The procedure for this is as follows:

1. List the jobs and their operation-processing times for each work center.
2. Select the shortest processing time. If it is in the first work center, schedule that order first. If it is in the second work center, schedule it last. In case of a tie, pick either.
3. Repeat Step 2 for the remaining orders until all are scheduled.

Illustrating this with the following will be beneficial:

Step 1: The jobs and their operation-processing times for the work centers.

| | Operation Times (Hours) | |
|---|---|---|
| Order No. | Work Center A | Work Center B |
| 1 | 10 | 11 |
| 2 | 5 | 10 |
| 3 | 8 | 6 |
| 4 | 4 | 6 |
| 5 | 2 | 8 |
| 6 | 4 | 3 |

Step 2: The shortest time is 2 hours for Order 5 in Work Center A. Schedule it first.

Step 3: The shortest time of the remaining orders is 3 hours for Order 6 in Work Center B. Schedule Order 6 last.
The shortest time of the remaining orders is 4 hours for Order 4 in Work Center A. Schedule it second.
The shortest time of the remaining orders is 5 hours for Order 2 in Work Center A. Schedule it third.
The shortest time of the remaining orders is 6 hours for Order 3 in Work Center B. Schedule it fifth. This leaves Job 1 scheduled fourth.

This results in the following sequence:

| | | Operation Times (Hours) | |
|---|---|---|---|
| Sequence | Order No. | Work Center A | Work Center B |
| 1 | 5 | 2 | 8 |
| 2 | 4 | 4 | 6 |
| 3 | 2 | 5 | 10 |
| 4 | 1 | 10 | 11 |
| 5 | 3 | 8 | 6 |
| 6 | 6 | 4 | 3 |

The times for these orders are plotted in sequence in Figure F-1 which reveals the results and rationale of this approach.

**FIGURE F-1**
**SCHEMATIC OF ORDER SEQUENCE**
**(PROCESS SEQUENCE A-B)**

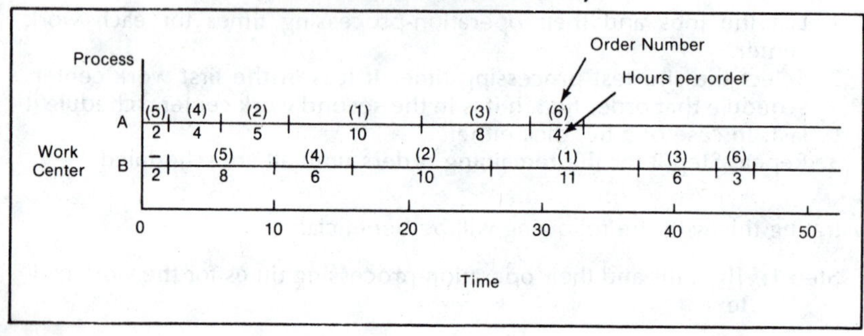


Examination of Figure F-1 reveals that this approach accomplishes its objective (minimum total processing time from beginning to end) by means of the following:

1. Starting orders on the second process as soon as possible
2. Running orders continuously on the first process
3. Minimizing the time required for processing on the second operation after all processing is finished on the first

The reader's natural tendency is to suspect that the preceding example has been stacked to present the technique in a favorable light. In fact, it has, by having the aggregate of times for Process A (33 hours) be substantially less than the aggregate time for Process B (46 hours). However, if we reverse the situation and let Operation B be first, then the solution may not appear as favorable; but it is. In the new situation it minimizes total processing time. The reverse operational sequence (*B-A*) and resulting sequence of orders is listed next. Figure F-2 reveals that again, minimum time passes before the second process (*A* in this case) is activated; and minimum time is required to complete the second operation once the first operation has been completed on all orders.

| | | Operation Times (Hours) | |
|---|---|---|---|
| Sequence | Order No. | Work Center B | Work Center A |
| 1 | 6 | 3 | 4 |
| 2 | 3 | 6 | 8 |
| 3 | 1 | 11 | 10 |
| 4 | 2 | 10 | 5 |
| 5 | 4 | 6 | 4 |
| 6 | 5 | 8 | 2 |

**FIGURE F-2**
**SCHEMATIC OF ORDER SEQUENCE**
**(PROCESS SEQUENCE B-A)**

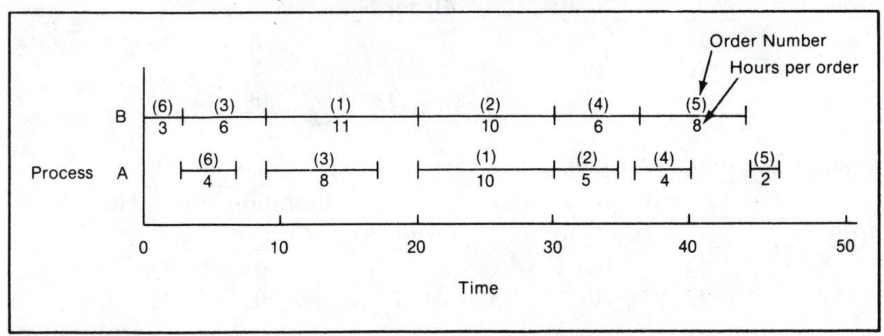


# TWO WORK CENTERS, NONUNIFORM OPERATIONAL SEQUENCE, MANY ORDERS

The logic of the preceding approach can be applied to the scheduling of many orders with different operational sequences in two work centers. The situation this time is that there are two work centers (*A* and *B*). There are many orders (*n*'s); some are processed in the sequence A-B; others are processed in the sequence B-A; and others are processed only in one work center, A or B. For example, the following orders have been received for processing in a given planning period. They will be processed prior to any orders that arrived later. The objective is to sequence the orders to minimize the time from the beginning of the first order(s) to the completion of the last order. The procedure is as follows:

| Sequence | Order No. | Operation Times (Hours) Work Center A | Work Center B |
|---|---|---|---|
| 1 | A only | 12 | 0 |
| 2 | A-B | 16 | 8 |
| 3 | B-A | 8 | 15 |
| 4 | B only | 0 | 12 |
| 5 | A-B | 10 | 30 |
| 6 | A-B | 25 | 12 |
| 7 | B only | 0 | 16 |
| 8 | B-A | 7 | 25 |
| 9 | B-A | 18 | 4 |
| 10 | A only | 13 | 0 |

1. List the orders and their operation-processing times for each work center, grouping them on the basis of their operation sequence.

Applying Step 1 to our example and grouping orders by their operation sequence results in the following lists:

Operation Sequence: A-B

| Order No. | Operation Times (Hours) WC A | WC B |
|---|---|---|
| 2 | 16 | 8 |
| 5 | 10 | 30 |
| 6 | 25 | 12 |

Operation Sequence: B-A

| Order No. | Operation Times (Hours) WC A | WC B |
|---|---|---|
| 3 | 8 | 15 |
| 8 | 7 | 25 |
| 9 | 18 | 4 |

Operation Sequence: A only

| Order No. | Operation Times (Hours) WC A | WC B |
|---|---|---|
| 1 | 12 | 0 |
| 10 | 13 | 0 |

Operation Sequence: B only

| Order No. | Operation Times (Hours) WC A | WC B |
|---|---|---|
| 4 | 0 | 12 |
| 7 | 0 | 16 |

2. In both work centers, schedule first those orders which have their first operation in that work center. Use Johnson's approach to establish their sequence.

Returning to the example, the first three orders scheduled in proper sequence for processing in Work Center A should be 5, 6, and 2. Per Johnson's approach, Order 5 is first because it requires the smallest processing time in Work Center A and Order 2 is last because it has the smallest processing time in Work Center B. Following the same procedure, the first three orders scheduled for Work Center B are, in proper sequence, 8, 3, 9.

3. In each work center schedule next those orders processed only in that department. They may be scheduled in any sequence.

Thus, the next orders scheduled in Work Center A are Orders 1 and 10, and the next orders scheduled in Work Center B are Orders 4 and 7.

4. Complete the schedule in each work center by adding those orders scheduled first in the other department and sequence them in the same order as they were in the first Work Center.

The next orders in proper sequence, run in Work Center A, are Orders 8, 3, and 9. Thus, the complete schedule of orders in Work Center A is 5,6,2,1,10,8,3,9 or 5,6,2,10,1,8,3,9. The final three orders in Work Center B should be scheduled for processing in a 5, 6, 2 sequence. The complete schedule of orders in Work Center B is 8,3,9,4,7,5,6,2 or 8,3,9,7,4,5,6,2.

Figure F-3 schematically represents the sequence and time requirements of these orders in Work Centers A and B based on the option of running Order 1 prior to Order 10 in Work Center A. It reveals the continuous use of Work Center A and B which guarantees that the total process time is a minimum.

**FIGURE F-3**
**SCHEMATIC OF ORDER SEQUENCE**

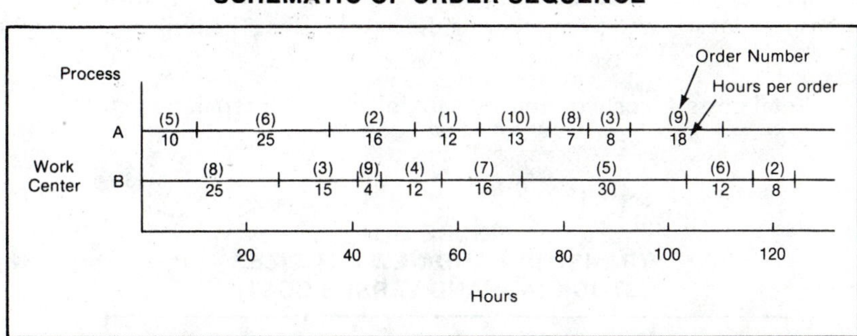


# MANY JOBS AND MANY WORK CENTERS

Situations requiring processing in three or more work centers are more common than those requiring processing in only two work centers. To date, a straightforward process for solving these complex real world problems has not been found. Ignall and Schrage have developed a branch and bound technique for solving this problem. [2] Description of these and related techniques are beyond the scope of this book. See *Introduction to Sequencing and Scheduling* by Kenneth R. Baker for a more complete discussion of this topic. [3]

# SELECTED READINGS


**1.** S.M. Johnson, "Optimal Two-End Three-Stage Production Schedules with Setup Times Included," *Naval Research Logistics Quarterly*, Vol. 1, No. 1 (March, 1954).

**2.** E. Ignall and L. E. Schrage, "Application of the Branch and Bound Technique to Some Floor Shop Scheduling Problems," *Operations Research*, Vol. 13, No. 3 (1965).

**3.** Eugene F. Baker, "Flow Management the 'Take Charge' Shop Floor Control System," *APICS 22d Annual Conference Proceedings* (1979), pp. 169-174.

# APPENDIX G
# DERIVATION OF THE TRANSITION LOT SIZE MODEL

When a price increase is imminent the objective is to purchase a transition order quantity that maximizes the savings achieved by ordering at the present price. Figure G-1 illustrates the different inventory status over time from ordering the transition lot size and from ordering the new lot size. The basic lot size model is as follows:

$$\text{Total costs} = \text{costs of units} + \text{carrying costs} + \text{preparation costs}$$
$$= CR + \frac{kCQT}{2} + \frac{SR}{Q}$$

**FIGURE G-1**
**TRANSITION AND NEW LOT SIZES**
**(STOCK-ON-HAND VERSUS COST)**

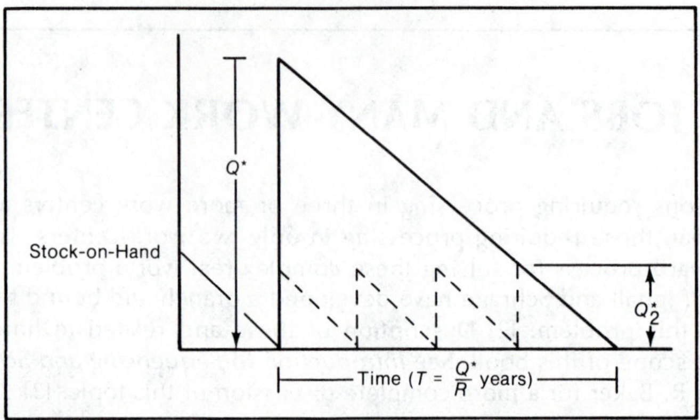


The objective in this situation is to order a lot size that maximizes the savings (the cost reduction) by ordering the transition lot size ($Q^*$) rather than the new lot size ($Q^*_2$). Since the carrying cost rate ($k$) is expressed in annual terms it must be multiplied by $T$ (the transition order interval expressed as a decimal percentage of a year). The transition lot size model must include the cost of the item since it is not a constant as it is in the basic model. If $Q^*_2$ is the order quantity, the number of orders during the transition period is $Q^*$ divided by $Q^*_2$; whereas if $Q^*$ is the order quantity, one order is placed during the transition period. The following model results:

$$\text{Maximize } TC_2 - TC^*$$

Where:

$$TC_2 = Q^*C_2 + \frac{Q^*_2}{2} C_2k \frac{Q^*}{R} + \frac{SQ^*}{Q^*_2}$$

And where:

$Q^*$ = the minimum cost transition lot size
$C_1$ = the current unit cost or the short-term lower cost
$C_2$ = the future unit cost or the normal higher price
$C_2 > C_1$
$k$ = the carrying cost rate per unit time, usually a year
$R$ = requirements (demand) per unit time, usually a year
$Q^*_2$ = the minimum cost lot size with a unit cost of $C_2$
$S$ = the cost per preparation in dollars

Substituting $Q^*_2 = \sqrt{\dfrac{2RS}{kC_2}}$ in the foregoing equation yields the following:

$$TC_2 = Q^*C_2 + Q^*\left(\sqrt{\frac{kSC_2}{2R}} + \sqrt{\frac{kSC_2}{2R}}\right)$$

$$= Q^*C_2 + Q^* \sqrt{\frac{2kSC_2}{R}}$$

$$TC^* = C_1Q^* + \frac{Q^*}{2} C_1k \frac{Q^*}{R} + \frac{SQ^*}{Q^*}$$

$$TC_2 - TC^* = (C_2 - C_1)Q^* + Q^* \sqrt{\frac{2kSC_2}{R}} - \frac{C_1kQ^{*2}}{2R} - S$$

Taking the first partial derivative of $TC_2 - TC^*$ with respect to $Q^*$ and setting it equal to zero gives us the following:

$$\frac{\delta\,(TC_2 - TC^*)}{\delta Q^*} = C_2 - C_1 + \sqrt{\frac{2kSC_2}{R}} - \frac{C_1kQ^*}{R} = 0$$

$$Q^* = \frac{R}{C_1k}(C_2 - C_1) + \frac{R}{C_1k}\sqrt{\frac{2kSC_2}{R}}$$

$$= \frac{R}{C_1k}(C_2 - C_1) + \frac{C_2}{C_1}\sqrt{\frac{2RS}{kC_2}}$$

$$Q^* = \frac{R}{C_1k}(C_2 - C_1) + \frac{C_2Q^*_2}{C_1}$$

Applying the second derivative test we next obtain:

$$\frac{\delta^2\,(TC_2 - TC^*)}{\delta Q} = -\frac{C_1k}{R}$$

Since $C_1$, $k$, and $R$ are always positive, the second derivative is negative and the first provides the value of $Q^*$ that maximizes the savings.

# APPENDIX H
# AREAS OF THE NORMAL CURVE

0 +Z or -Z 0

| Z | .00 | .01 | .02 | .03 | .04 | .05 | .06 | .07 | .08 | .09 |
|---|---|---|---|---|---|---|---|---|---|---|
| 0.0 | .0000 | .0040 | .0080 | .0120 | .0160 | .0199 | .0239 | .0279 | .0319 | .0359 |
| 0.1 | .0398 | .0438 | .0478 | .0517 | .0557 | .0596 | .0636 | .0675 | .0714 | .0753 |
| 0.2 | .0793 | .0832 | .0871 | .0910 | .0948 | .0987 | .1026 | .1064 | .1103 | .1141 |
| 0.3 | .1179 | .1217 | .1255 | .1293 | .1331 | .1368 | .1406 | .1443 | .1480 | .1517 |
| 0.4 | .1554 | .1591 | .1628 | .1664 | .1700 | .1736 | .1772 | .1808 | .1844 | .1879 |
| 0.5 | .1915 | .1950 | .1985 | .2019 | .2054 | .2088 | .2123 | .2157 | .2190 | .2224 |
| 0.6 | .2257 | .2291 | .2324 | .2357 | .2389 | .2422 | .2454 | .2486 | .2517 | .2549 |
| 0.7 | .2580 | .2611 | .2642 | .2673 | .2704 | .2734 | .2764 | .2794 | .2823 | .2852 |
| 0.8 | .2881 | .2910 | .2939 | .2967 | .2995 | .3023 | .3051 | .3078 | .3106 | .3233 |
| 0.9 | .3159 | .3186 | .3212 | .3238 | .3264 | .3289 | .3315 | .3340 | .3365 | .3389 |
| 1.0 | .3413 | .3438 | .3461 | .3485 | .3508 | .3531 | .3554 | .3577 | .3599 | .3621 |
| 1.1 | .3643 | .3665 | .3686 | .3708 | .3729 | .3749 | .3770 | .3790 | .3810 | .3830 |
| 1.2 | .3849 | .3869 | .3888 | .3907 | .3925 | .3944 | .3962 | .3980 | .3997 | .4015 |
| 1.3 | .4032 | .4049 | .4066 | .4082 | .4099 | .4115 | .4131 | .4147 | .4162 | .4177 |
| 1.4 | .4192 | .4207 | .4222 | .4236 | .4251 | .4265 | .4279 | .4292 | .4306 | .4319 |
| 1.5 | .4332 | .4345 | .4357 | .4370 | .4382 | .4394 | .4406 | .4418 | .4429 | .4441 |
| 1.6 | .4452 | .4463 | .4474 | .4484 | .4495 | .4505 | .4515 | .4525 | .4535 | .4545 |
| 1.7 | .4554 | .4564 | .4573 | .4582 | .4591 | .4599 | .4608 | .4616 | .4625 | .4633 |
| 1.8 | .4641 | .4649 | .4656 | .4664 | .4671 | .4678 | .4686 | .4693 | .4699 | .4706 |
| 1.9 | .4713 | .4719 | .4726 | .4732 | .4738 | .4744 | .4750 | .4758 | .4761 | .4767 |
| 2.0 | .4772 | .4778 | .4783 | .4788 | .4793 | .4798 | .4803 | .4808 | .4812 | .4817 |
| 2.1 | .4821 | .4826 | .4830 | .4834 | .4838 | .4842 | .4846 | .4850 | .4854 | .4857 |
| 2.2 | .4861 | .4864 | .4868 | .4871 | .4875 | .4878 | .4881 | .4884 | .4887 | .4890 |
| 2.3 | .4893 | .4896 | .4898 | .4901 | .4904 | .4906 | 4909 | .4911 | .4913 | .4916 |
| 2.4 | .4918 | .4920 | .4922 | .4925 | .4927 | .4929 | .4931 | .4932 | .4934 | .4936 |
| 2.5 | .4938 | .4940 | .4941 | .4943 | .4945 | .4946 | .4948 | .4949 | .4951 | .4952 |
| 2.6 | .4953 | .4955 | .4956 | .4957 | .4959 | .4960 | .4961 | .4962 | .4963 | .4964 |
| 2.7 | .4965 | 4966 | .4967 | .4968 | .4969 | .4970 | .4971 | .4972 | .4973 | .4974 |
| 2.8 | .4974 | .4975 | .4976 | .4977 | .4977 | .4978 | .4979 | .4979 | .4980 | .4881 |
| 2.9 | .4981 | .4982 | .4982 | .4983 | .4984 | .4984 | .4985 | .4985 | .4986 | .4986 |
| 3.0 | .4986 | .4987 | .4987 | .4988 | .4988 | .4988 | .4989 | .4989 | .4989 | .4990 |

# APPENDIX I
# RANDOM NUMBER TABLE*

| | | | | | | | | | |
|---|---|---|---|---|---|---|---|---|---|
| 6663 | 696 | 6964 | 6935 | 3077 | 6821 | 8774 | 1951 | 9228 | 9856 |
| 8558 | 8714 | 9132 | 3207 | 6221 | 8776 | 9366 | 5563 | 6306 | 2010 |
| 8666 | 5692 | 397 | 7806 | 3527 | 5242 | 3519 | 8278 | 9806 | 9540 |
| 4535 | 3457 | 319 | 6396 | 550 | 8496 | 8441 | 2896 | 5307 | 2865 |
| 7709 | 209 | 1590 | 1558 | 7418 | 6382 | 7624 | 8286 | 4225 | 7145 |
| | | | | | | | | | |
| 7472 | 681 | 9746 | 4704 | 5439 | 7495 | 4156 | 4548 | 4468 | 7801 |
| 5792 | 245 | 8544 | 2190 | 6749 | 6243 | 9089 | 5974 | 4484 | 8669 |
| 5370 | 4385 | 9413 | 4132 | 8888 | 9775 | 8511 | 6520 | 1789 | 816 |
| 4914 | 1801 | 9257 | 3701 | 3520 | 823 | 5915 | 5341 | 2583 | 113 |
| 6227 | 8568 | 1319 | 681 | 8898 | 9335 | 3506 | 4813 | 5271 | 5912 |
| | | | | | | | | | |
| 7077 | 878 | 1730 | 93 | 9731 | 6123 | 6100 | 389 | 522 | 7478 |
| 8044 | 7232 | 7466 | 349 | 3467 | 174 | 1140 | 5425 | 2912 | 7088 |
| 4280 | 3474 | 3963 | 5364 | 7381 | 8144 | 7645 | 5116 | 300 | 6762 |
| 8821 | 4375 | 9853 | 9138 | 596 | 6294 | 3415 | 4358 | 2713 | 8343 |
| 8523 | 5591 | 3956 | 3516 | 8472 | 2884 | 8550 | 3524 | 3919 | 3967 |
| | | | | | | | | | |
| 6558 | 3999 | 480 | 3046 | 8285 | 1693 | 2330 | 7610 | 2674 | 3679 |
| 1806 | 3227 | 9710 | 8548 | 5003 | 6345 | 6815 | 9612 | 3378 | 5091 |
| 9256 | 103 | 1347 | 8074 | 4534 | 373 | 9885 | 1182 | 795 | 7094 |
| 6128 | 2383 | 9223 | 4459 | 8974 | 4525 | 441 | 7379 | 677 | 6135 |
| 4913 | 6686 | 4453 | 223 | 7344 | 6333 | 8080 | 1075 | 5077 | 2590 |
| | | | | | | | | | |
| 3491 | 9060 | 496 | 5251 | 2385 | 3425 | 7426 | 827 | 7816 | 3100 |
| 1530 | 7750 | 1800 | 5491 | 4713 | 3572 | 8914 | 3287 | 3518 | 4166 |
| 5894 | 9256 | 1529 | 4922 | 7235 | 9046 | 5771 | 3954 | 6794 | 1984 |
| 7107 | 7293 | 5387 | 9880 | 4642 | 6092 | 4389 | 3820 | 4119 | 5821 |
| 5337 | 8973 | 322 | 7474 | 5526 | 7386 | 3476 | 762 | 9613 | 8789 |
| | | | | | | | | | |
| 9644 | 9317 | 7214 | 9388 | 5131 | 7891 | 6504 | 8672 | 4880 | 1557 |
| 3820 | 4209 | 4876 | 6906 | 9257 | 4447 | 8541 | 5250 | 8272 | 9513 |
| 7142 | 7821 | 9281 | 16 | 4180 | 2971 | 7259 | 3844 | 3801 | 5372 |
| 3342 | 965 | 3189 | 7217 | 428 | 6227 | 8967 | 1417 | 4771 | 157 |
| 7599 | 6804 | 3587 | 7765 | 9790 | 5331 | 8654 | 5337 | 8883 | 1268 |
| | | | | | | | | | |
| 5905 | 5242 | 3262 | 2409 | 1039 | 8727 | 2752 | 3265 | 1110 | 6722 |
| 9016 | 268 | 2134 | 8633 | 9959 | 8970 | 2688 | 9149 | 8124 | 3244 |
| 3508 | 3038 | 3095 | 6480 | 3089 | 7948 | 7897 | 4792 | 9288 | 5206 |
| 9393 | 2211 | 6921 | 8622 | 2688 | 7890 | 1363 | 1282 | 9525 | 5299 |
| 8151 | 355 | 688 | 3432 | 8580 | 9888 | 2402 | 0 | 1307 | 1611 |
| | | | | | | | | | |
| 6730 | 6635 | 9948 | 3730 | 5977 | 6089 | 6678 | 7734 | 1086 | 1435 |
| 1834 | 3191 | 4042 | 7264 | 9511 | 549 | 4267 | 2888 | 9166 | 1935 |
| 9028 | 7539 | 3215 | 9958 | 7826 | 7569 | 633 | 4506 | 807 | 5650 |
| 6556 | 7547 | 1155 | 1975 | 7882 | 5929 | 1493 | 7455 | 4865 | 2179 |
| 4285 | 8922 | 8721 | 3307 | 6236 | 6329 | 5228 | 7599 | 6689 | 1946 |

*From _Production: Management and Manufacturing Systems_, Second Edition, by Thomas R. Hoffmann. © 1971 by Wadsworth Publishing Company, Inc. Reprinted by permission of Wadsworth Publishing Company, Belmont, California 94002.

# COMPUTER PROGRAMS

# APPENDIX J
# PROGRAM ILLUSTRATING EXPONENTIAL SMOOTHING

```
      PROGRAM EXPO(INPUT,OUTPUT,TAPE2,TAPE5=INPUT)
*
*           THIS PROGRAM ILLUSTRATES EXPONENTIAL SMOOTHING
*           AND COMPARES SIMPLE SMOOTHING, SMOOTHING WITH TREND
*           CORRECTION AND TRIPLE EXPONENTIAL SMOOTHING.
*            DATA MAY BE SAVED ON TAPE2 AND REUSED.
*
      COMMON Y(100),FORE(3,100,2),N
*
*           BLOCK 0001  INITIALIZATION
*
      PRINT*, TITLE',
      READ(5,8,END=519) ANS
 8    FORMAT(5A6)
*           ZERO OUT ARRAYS
 13   DO 15 I=1,100
        Y(I) = 0.
        DO 15 J = 1,2
          DO 15 K = 1,3
 15   FORE(K,I,J)=0 0
*
*           BLOCK 0100  DATA INPUT
*
      PRINT*,'INPUT DATA FILE NAME;IF ON-LINE, ENTER "ORIGIN"',
      READ 8 ,ANS
      IF(ANS .EQ. 'ORIGIN') GOTO 104
      CALL GETPF(5HTAPE2,ANS,0,0)
      ITP=1
      K=0
 105  K=K+1
      READ(2,*,END=114)Y(K)
      GOTO 105
 104  PRINT*,'YOU MUST  ENTER  AT  LEAST FOUR DATA VALUES.  '
      PRINT* 'INPUT ACTUAL DATA, ONE VALUE PER LINE.'
      PRINT*,'TERMINATE DATA ENTRY WITH CARRIAGE RETURN.'
      K=0
 107  K=K+1
      READ(5,*,END=114) Y(K)
      GOTO 107
 114  IF(K .LT. 5) GOTO 104
      Y(K)=0.0
      KNT=K
 116  PRINT*,'ENTER ONE ALPHA VALUE',
      READ,A
      IF(A .LT. 1.) GOTO 110
      PRINT*,'ALPHA SHOULD BE LESS THAN ONE- TRY AGAIN'
      GO TO 116
 110  IF(A .GT. 0.) GOTO 230
      PRINT*,'ALPHA SHOULD BE GREATER THAN ZERO- TRY AGAIN'
      GO TO 116
*
```

```
*             BLOCK 0200  INITIALIZE FORECAST CONSTANTS
*
*             COMPUTE INITIAL FORECAST ESTIMATE
  230   YSUMK= 0.
        DO 221  I = 1 3
  221   YSUMK=YSUMK+Y(I)
        YSUMK = YSUMK/3.0
        A1 = 1. - A
        AA12 = A/(A1*A1*2.)
        AR2 = (A/A1)**2
        CO1 = AA12*(6. - 5.*A)
        CO2 = AA12*2.*(5. - 4.*A)
        CO3 = AA12*(4. - 3.*A)
        S1 = YSUMK
        S2 = S1
        S3 = S1
        AC =S1
        BC = 0.
        CC = 0.
        N = 4
*
*             BLOCK 0300  COMPUTE FORECASTS
*
*               THIRD ORDER SMOOTHING
  325   FORE(3,N,1)=AC + BC + CC/2.
        S1 = A*Y(N) + A1*S1
        S2 = A*S1 + A1*S2
        S3 = A*S2 + A1*S3
        AC = 3.*(S1-S2) + S3
        BC = CO1*S1 - CO2*S2 + CO3*S3
        CC = AR2*(S1+S3-2.*S2)
        N = N + 1
        IF (Y(N-1) .NE. 0.0) GOTO 325
        CALL EVAL(3)
*             SIMPLE EXPONENTIAL SMOOTHING
        FORE(1,4,1) = YSUMK
        N = 4
  332   N=N+1
        FORE(1,N,1) = A*Y(N-1) + A1*FORE(1 N-1,1)
        IF (Y(N) .NE. 0.0) GOTO 332
        N=N+ 1
        CALL EVAL(1)
*             EXPONENTIAL SMOOTHING WITH TREND CORRECTION
        T = 0.
        N = 4
  341   FORE(2,N,1)=FORE(1,N,1) + T/A
        N=N+1
        D = FORE(1,N,1) - FORE(1,N-1,1)
        T    = A*D + A1*T
        IF (Y(N-1) .NE. 0.0) GOTO 341
        CALL EVAL(2)
*
*             BLOCK 0400  PRINT OUTPUT
*
        PRINT 411, A
  411   FORMAT(1X,70('*')//' SMOOTHING COEFFICIENT  'F4.3//
+             2X,'PERIOD',3X,'ACTUAL',4X,'FIRST',4X,'ERROR',3X,
+             'SECOND',4X,'ERROR',4X 'THIRD',4X,'ERROR'/)
        DO 415 I=4,KNT
          PRINT 414  I,Y(I),FORE(1,I,1),FORE(1,I,2),FORE(2,I,1),
+         FORE(2,I,2),FORE(3,I,1),FORE(3,I,2)
  415   CONTINUE
  414   FORMAT(I8,7(F9.2))
        PRINT 493, FORE(1,1,2),FORE(2,1,2),FORE(3,1,2)
  493   FORMAT(//'AVE. ABS. ERROR ',1X,3(11X,F7 2)/71('*')/)
*
*             BLOCK 0500 STOP OR RECYCLE
*
        PRINT*,'DO YOU HAVE MORE ALPHA VALUES ',
```

```
      READ 523,AFN
523   FORMAT(A3)
      IF(AFN .EQ. 'YES') GOTO 116
      IF(ITP.EQ.1) GOTO 501
      PRINT*,'DO YOU WANT TO SAVE THIS DATA',
      READ 523,BFN
      IF(BFN .NE. 'YES') GOTO 501
      PRINT*,'ON WHICH FILE',
      READ 8,ANS
      REWIND 2
      KNT=KNT-1
      DO 503 I=1,KNT
503   WRITE(2,*) Y(I)
      ENDFILE 2
      REWIND 2
      CALL SAVE(5HTAPE2,ANS,0,0,0)
501   PRINT*,'DO YOU HAVE ANOTHER SET OF DATA'
      READ 523,BFN
      IF(BFN .EQ. 'YES') GOTO 13
519   STOP
      END
*
*             END OF MAIN PROGRAM
*
      SUBROUTINE EVAL(IA)
*
*             COMPUTE FORECAST ERRORS
*
      COMMON Y(100),FORE(3,100,2),N
      YSUM=0.
      M = N - 2
      DO 218 I=4,M
        FORE(IA,I,2) = ABS(FORE(IA,I,1) - Y(I))
        YSUM=YSUM+ FORE(IA,I,2)
218   CONTINUE
      SN = N - 5
      FORE(IA,1,2) = YSUM/SN
      RETURN
      END
*
*             END OF PROGRAM EXPO
:
```

# APPENDIX K
# CRITICAL PATH PROGRAMMING

```
00100 PRINT " ","CRITICAL PATH PROGRAM"
00110 PRINT " ","---------------------"
00120 PRINT
00130 PRINT "FILE INPUT";
00140 INPUT A$
00150 IF A$ = "YES" THEN 00180
00160 LET A9 = 1
00170 GO TO 00400
00180 LET A9 = -1
00190 RESTOREFILE(CPMIN)
00200 DIM N(201), E(201), L(201), P(501), S(501), T(501), R(501)
00210 DIM U(501), W(501), X(501), Y(201), Z(201), D(501), C(501)
00220 DIM B$(501)
00230 REMARK -- B$(I) ARE THE NAMES OF THE ACTIVITIES
00240 REMARK -- N(I) IS THE NUMBER OF EVENT I
00250 REMARK -- E(I) IS THE EARLIEST TIME FOR EVENT I
00260 REMARK -- L(I) IS THE LATEST TIME FOR EVENT I
00270 REMARK -- P(I) IS THE EVENT PRECEDING ACTIVITY I
00280 REMARK -- S(I) IS THE EVENT SUCCEEDING ACTIVITY I
00290 REMARK -- T(I) IS THE NORMAL TIME TO COMPLETE ACTIVITY I
00300 REMARK -- R(I) IS THE NUMBER OF THE I"TH-RANKED ACTIVITY
00310 REMARK -- U(I) IS THE NORMAL COST FOR ACTIVITY I
00320 REMARK -- W(I) IS THE CRASH TIME TO COMPLETE ACTIVITY I
00330 REMARK -- X(I) IS THE CRASH COST FOR ACTIVITY I
00340 REMARK -- Y(I) IS THE EARLIEST CRASH TIME FOR EVENT I
00350 REMARK -- Z(I) IS THE LATEST CRASH TIME FOR EVENT I
00360 REMARK -- N1 IS THE NUMBER OF EVENTS
00370 REMARK -- N2 IS THE NUMBER OF ACTIVITIES
00380 REMARK -- C1 IS THE MINIMUM TIME TO COMPLETE THE PROJECT
00390 REMARK -- C2 IS THE MINIMUM CRASH TIME FOR THE PROJECT
00400 FOR I = 1 TO 201
00410 LET E(I) = Y(I) = 0
00420 LET L(I) = Z(I) = 0
00430 LET N(I) = I
00440 NEXT I
00450 REMARK -- READ IN ACTIVITY DATA
00460 GOSUB 00650
00470 GOSUB 03000
00480 LET J1 = 0
00490 REMARK -- FIND EARLY EVENT TIMES
00500 GOSUB 01340
00510 REMARK -- FIND LATE EVENT TIMES
00520 GOSUB 01580
00530 REMARK -- PRINT EVENT TIMES
00540 GOSUB 01890
00550 REMARK -- PRINT ACTIVITY TIMES
00560 GOSUB 02170
00570 REMARK -- PRINT COMPLETION TIME AND COST
00580 GOSUB 02660
00590 IF P5 = 1 THEN 00610
00600 GO TO 02940
00610 IF J1 = 1 THEN 02940
00620 LET J1 = 1
00630 GO TO 00490
00640 REMARK -- SUBROUTINE TO READ EVENT NUMBERS
00650 REMARK -- SUBROUTINE TO READ ACTIVITIES
00660 LET N2 = -1
00670 LET N1 = 0
00680 PRINT
00690 PRINT "DO YOU WISH TO INCLUDE A CRASH TIME AND COST ANALYSIS";
```

```
00700 INPUT A$
00710 IF A$ = "YES" THEN 00740
00720 LET P5 = 0
00730 GO TO 00750
00740 LET P5 = 1
00750 IF A9 < 0 THEN 01040
00760 PRINT "IN RESPONSE TO EACH '?', INPUT ACTIVITY DATA"
00770 PRINT "IN THE FOLLOWING FORMAT:"
00780 PRINT "AC,PE,SE,NT,NC,";
00790 IF P5 = 1 THEN 00810
00800 GO TO 00820
00810 PRINT "CT,CC"
00820 PRINT "FOLLOWED BY A CARRIAGE RETURN."
00830 PRINT "AC = ACTIVITY NAME"
00840 PRINT "PE = PRECEEDING EVENT"
00850 PRINT "SE = SUCCEEDING EVENT"
00860 PRINT "NT = NORMAL TIME"
00870 PRINT "NC = NORMAL COST"
00880 IF P5 = 0 THEN 00910
00890 PRINT "CT = CRASH TIME"
00900 PRINT "CC = CRASH COST"
00910 PRINT "TO TERMINATE DATA ENTRY, TYPE A SET OF -1'S"
00920 FOR I = 1 TO 501
00930 LET N2 = N2 + 1
00940 IF P5 = 1 THEN 00970
00950 INPUT  B$(I), P(I), S(I), T(I), U(I)
00960 GO TO 00980
00970 INPUT B$(I), P(I), S(I), T(I), U(I), W(I), X(I)
00980 IF P(I) < 0 THEN 01120
00990 IF N1 > S(I) THEN 01010
01000 LET N1 = S(I)
01010 NEXT I
01020 PRINT "TOO MANY ACTIVITIES. REDIMENSION ARRAYS."
01030 STOP
01040 FOR I = 1 TO 501
01050 LET N2 = N2 + 1
01060 INPUTFILE(CPMIN) B$(I), P(I),S(I),T(I),U(I),W(I),X(I)
01070 IF P(I) < 0 THEN 01120
01080 IF N1 > S(I) THEN 01100
01090 LET N1 = S(I)
01100 NEXT I
01110 GOTO 01020
01120 RETURN
01130 REMARK -- SUBROUTINE TO ASSIGN RANK TO ACTIVITIES
01140 REMARK -- IF N5 = 0, RANK ON ASCENDING ORDER OF PREDECESSOR
01150 REMARK -- IF N5 = 1, RANK ON DECENDING ORDER OF SUCCESSOR
01160 FOR I = 1 TO N2
01170 LET R(I) = I
01180 NEXT I
01190 LET N9 = N2
01200 LET N9 = N9 - 1
01210 LET N8 = 0
01220 FOR I = 1 TO N9
01230 IF N5 = 1 THEN 01260
01240 IF P(R(I)) <= P(R(I+1)) THEN 01310
01250 GO TO 01270
01260 IF S(R(I)) >= S(R(I+1)) THEN 01310
01270 LET R1 = R(I)
01280 LET R(I) = R(I+1)
01290 LET R(I+1) = R1
01300 LET N8 = 1
01310 NEXT I
01320 IF N8 = 1 THEN 01200
01330 RETURN
01340 REMARK -- SUBROUTINE TO FIND EARLY EVENT TIMES
01350 REMARK -- RANK ACTIVITIES ON ASCENDING ORDER OF PREDECESSOR
01360 LET N5 = 0
01370 GOSUB 01130
01380 FOR I = 1 TO N2
01390 LET N3 = P(R(I))
01400 GOSUB 01530
```

```
01410 LET I1 = K
01420 LET N3 = S(R(I))
01430 GOSUB 01530
01440 LET I2 = K
01450 IF J1 = 1 THEN 01490
01460 IF E(I2) >= E(I1) + T(R(I)) THEN 01510
01470 LET E(I2) = E(I1) + T(R(I))
01480 GO TO 01510
01490 IF Y(I2) >= Y(I1) + W(R(I)) THEN 01510
01500 LET Y(I2) = Y(I1) + W(R(I))
01510 NEXT I
01520 RETURN
01530 REMARK -- SUBROUTINE TO FIND INTERNAL NUMBER (K) OF EVENT N3
01540 FOR K = 1 TO N1
01550 IF N(K) = N3 THEN 01570
01560 NEXT K
01570 RETURN
01580 REMARK -- SUBROUTINE TO FIND LATE EVENT TIMES
01590 REMARK -- RANK ACTIVITIES IN DECENDING ORDER OF SUCCESSORS
01600 LET N5 = 1
01610 GOSUB 01130
01620 FOR I = 1 TO N2
01630 LET N3 = S(R(I))
01640 GOSUB 01530
01650 LET I1 = K
01660 LET N3 = P(R(I))
01670 GOSUB 01530
01680 LET I2 = K
01690 IF J1 = 1 THEN 01730
01700 IF L(I2) >= L(I1) + T(R(I)) THEN 01750
01710 LET L(I2) = L(I1) + T(R(I))
01720 GO TO 01750
01730 IF Z(I2) >= Z(I1) + W(R(I)) THEN 01750
01740 LET Z(I2) = Z(I1) + W(R(I))
01750 NEXT I
01760 LET N3 = S(R(1))
01770 GOSUB 01530
01780 IF J1 = 1 THEN 01840
01790 LET C1 = E(K)
01800 FOR I = 1 TO N1
01810 LET L(I) = C1 - L(I)
01820 NEXT I
01830 GO TO 01880
01840 LET C2 = Y(K)
01850 FOR I = 1 TO N1
01860 LET Z(I) = C2 - Z(I)
01870 NEXT I
01880 RETURN
01890 REMARK -- SUBROUTINE TO PRINT EVENT TIMES
01900 PRINT
01910 IF J1 = 1 THEN 01940
01920 PRINT " ","NORMAL EVENT TIMES"
01930 GO TO 01950
01940 PRINT " "," CRASH EVENT TIMES"
01950 PRINT
01960 PRINT "EVENT","EARLY","LATE"
01970 PRINT " ","OCCURENCE","OCCURENCE"
01980 PRINT
01990 IF J1 = 1 THEN 02100
02000 FOR I = 1 TO N1
02010 IF L(I) < 0.01 THEN 02080
02020 IF ABS(E(I) - L(I)) <= .001 THEN 02050
02030 PRINT N(I), E(I), L(I)
02040 GO TO 02060
02050 PRINT N(I), E(I), L(I), "CRITICAL"
02060 NEXT I
02070 GO TO 02160
02080 LET L(I) = 0
02090 GO TO 02020
02100 FOR I = 1 TO N1
02110 IF ABS(Y(I) - Z(I)) <= .001 THEN 02140
```

```
02120 PRINT N(I), Y(I), Z(I)
02130 GO TO 02150
02140 PRINT N(I), Y(I), Z(I), "CRITICAL"
02150 NEXT I
02160 RETURN
02170 REMARK -- SUBROUTINE TO PRINT ACTIVITY TIMES
02180 LET J9 = 0
02190 PRINT
02200 IF J1 = 1 THEN 02230
02210 PRINT " ","NORMAL ACTIVITY TIMES"
02220 GO TO 02240
02230 PRINT " "," CRASH ACTIVITY TIMES"
02240 PRINT
02250 PRINT "ACTIVITY","EVENT","ACTUAL","TOTAL","FREE"
02260 PRINT " ","PRECEDENCE"," ","SLACK","SLACK"
02270 PRINT
02280 FOR I = 1 TO N2
02290 LET S1 = L(S(I)) - E(S(I)) - T(I)
02300 GOSUB 02560
02310 IF J1 = 1 THEN 02420
02320 LET S1 = L(I2) - E(I1) - T(I)
02330 IF ABS(S1) <= .001 THEN 02350
02340 GO TO 02360
02350 LET J9 = 1
02360 LET D(I) = E(I2) - (E(I1) + T(I))
02370 IF J9 = 1 THEN 02400
02380 PRINT B$(I), P(I); " - "; S(I), T(I), S1, D(I)
02390 GO TO 02530
02400 PRINT B$(I), P(I); " - "; S(I), T(I), "CRITICAL", D(I)
02410 GO TO 02530
02420 LET C = Z(I2) - Y(I1) - W(I)
02430 IF ABS(C) <= .001 THEN 02450
02440 GO TO 02460
02450 LET J9 = 1
02460 LET C(I) = Y(I2) - (Y(I1) + W(I))
02470 IF T(I) >= W(I) + C(I) THEN 02490
02480 LET C(I) = T(I) - W(I)
02490 IF J9 = 1 THEN 02520
02500 PRINT B$(I), P(I);" - "; S(I), W(I), C, C(I)
02510 GO TO 02530
02520 PRINT B$(I), P(I);" - "; S(I), W(I), "CRITICAL", C(I)
02530 LET J9 = 0
02540 NEXT I
02550 RETURN
02560 REMARK -- SUBROUTINE TO FIND INTERNAL NUMBERS
02570 REMARK --    (MEMORY LOCATIONS) OF PREDECESSOR AND
02580 REMARK --    SUCCESSOR EVENTS OF ACTIVITY I
02590 LET N3 = P(I)
02600 GOSUB 01530
02610 LET I1 = K
02620 LET N3 = S(I)
02630 GOSUB 01530
02640 LET I2 = K
02650 RETURN
02660 REMARK -- SUBROUTINE TO CALC & PRINT TIME & COST FIGURES
02670 LET J2 = J6 = 0
02680 FOR I = 1 TO N1
02690 IF J2 >= N(I) THEN 02720
02700 LET J2 = N(I)
02710 LET J6 = I
02720 NEXT I
02730 PRINT
02740 IF J1 = 1 THEN 02780
02750 PRINT "EARLIEST POSSIBLE COMPLETION UNDER NORMAL CONDITIONS";
02760 PRINT " IS"; L(J6)
02770 GO TO 02790
02780 PRINT "EARLIEST POSSIBLE COMPLETION IF CRASH IS"; Z(J6)
02790 PRINT
02800 LET J3 = J4 = J5 = 0
02810 FOR I = 1 TO N2
02820 IF J1 = 1 THEN 02850
```

```
02830 LET J3 = J3 + U(I)
02840 GO TO 02860
02850 LET J4 = J4 + X(I)
02860 NEXT I
02870 IF J1 = 1 THEN 02910
02880 PRINT "NORMAL COMPLETION COST IS $"; J3;
02890 LET R9=J3
02900 GO TO 02920
02910 PRINT "COST FOR FULL CRASH OF ALL ACTIVITIES IS $"; J4;
02920 PRINT
02930 RETURN
02940 PRINT
02950 PRINT "TO SAVE YOUR INPUT DATA, REMEMBER TO"
02960 PRINT  "SAVE,CPMIN=MYFILE"
02970 RESTOREFILE(CPMIN)
02980 STOP
02990 REMARK - SUBROUTINE TO SAVE AND EDIT DATA
03000 PRINT "DO YOU WISH TO CHANGE ANY DATA";
03010 INPUT A$
03020 IF A$ = "NO" THEN 03170
03030 PRINT "WHAT IS THE ACTIVITY'S NAME";
03040 INPUT A$
03050 FOR I=1 TO N2
03060 IF B$(I) = A$ THEN 03080
03070 GO TO 03140
03080 PRINT "ENTER ENTIRE NEW DATA LINE"
03090 IF P5 = 1 THEN 03120
03100 INPUT B$(I),P(I),S(I),T(I),U(I)
03110 GO TO 03000
03120 INPUT B$(I),P(I),S(I),T(I),U(I),W(I),X(I)
03130 GO TO 03000
03140 NEXT I
03150 PRINT "NO SUCH ACTIVITY"
03160 GO TO 03030
03170 RESTOREFILE(CPMIN)
03180 FOR I = 1 TO N2
03190 PRINTFILE(CPMIN) B$(I);",";P(I);S(I);T(I);U(I);W(I);X(I)
03200 NEXT I
03210 LET A2 = -1
03220 PRINTFILE(CPMIN) "END,";A2;A2;A2;A2;A2;A2
03230 RETURN
03240 END
:
```

# APPENDIX L
# SAMPLE SIMULATION PROGRAM

```
 TITLE      ? SAMPLE SIMULATION
 SIMULATION LENGTH    ? 200
 PRINT EVERYTHING     ? NO
 WHAT IS THE PRODUCTION DISTRIBUTION
? 11,.1
? 12,.8
? 13,.1
?
 WHAT IS THE ORDER DISTRIBUTION
? 5,.1
? 6,.15
? 7,.25
? 8,.35
? 9,.15
?
 WHAT IS THE UNITS/ORDER DISTRIBUTION
? 1,.5
? 2,.3
? 3,.2
?
                                                              ******SERVICE*******
   DAY       ORDERS    DEMAND PRODUCTION AVAILABLE     EXCESS   UNSATISFIED
                                                       UNITS       ORDERS

 TOTALS
  200.      1476.     2504.     2394.                  598.       80.

             51 STOCKOUT DAYS
 SERVICE LEVEL (PER UNIT)      .948083
 SERVICE LEVEL (ORDERS)        .945799
 AVERAGE EXCESS     3.640000
 AVERAGE SHORTAGE    .650000

 AVERAGES          THEORETICAL      SAMPLE
 ORDERS               7.300000     7.380000
 DEM./ORDER           1.700000     1.696477
 DEMAND/DAY          12.410000    12.520000
 PRODUCTION/DAY      12.000000    11.970000


 TITLE      ?
:

      PROGRAM SIMSIM (INPUT,OUTPUT,TAPE5=INPUT,TAPE6=OUTPUT)
**********            PROGRAM IDENTIFICATION                    **********
*                                                                        *
*        SIMPLE INVENTORY SIMULATION PROGRAM                             *
*        WRITTEN BY T. HOFFMANN  10/06/81                                *
*                                                                        *
**************************************************************************
*                                                                        *
**********            VARIABLE IDENTIFICATION                   **********
*                                                                        *
*        ALEFT    = AVERAGE LEFT OVER                                    *
*        ALFT     = LEFT OVERS AVAILABLE FOR NEXT DAY                    *
*        ANS      = ANSWERS TO INPUT QUESTIONS                           *
*        ASHORT   = AVERAGE SHORTAGE                                     *
*        AVAIL    = AVERAGE UNITS EACH DAY                               *
*        AXCESS   = AVERAGE EXCESS                                       *
*        CD       = COUNTER OF DAYS                                      *
*        DAY      = NUMBER OF DAYS TO SIMULATE                           *
```

```
*          DORDR   = DAILY NUMBER OF ORDERS                              *
*          DEM     = DEMAND OF EACH ORDER                                *
*          DUSO    = DAILY COUNT OF UNSATISFIED ORDERS                   *
*          FIFO    = LEFTOVERS TO BE USED FIRST                          *
*          LNSAT   = UNSATISFIED ORDERS PREVIOUS DAY                     *
*          LPR     = DETAIL PRINT SWITCH                                 *
*          NORDR   = NUMBER OF ORDERS IN A DAY                           *
*          NSTOUT  = NUMBER OF STOCKOUT DAYS                             *
*          SDDEM   = SAMPLE AVERAGE DAILY DEMAND                         *
*          SLO     = SERVICE LEVEL IN ORDERS                             *
*          SLU     = SERVICE LEVEL IN UNITS                              *
*          PRO     = SAMPLE DAILY PRODUCTION                             *
*          TDDEM   = THEORETICAL AVERAGE DAILY DEMAND                    *
*          TDEM    = TOTAL DEMAND                                        *
*          TOTO    = TOTAL ORDERS                                        *
*          TOTDEM  = TOTAL DEMAND                                        *
*          TOTPRO  = TOTAL PRODUCTION                                    *
*          TUSO    = TOTAL UNSATISFIED ORDERS                            *
*          TUSHRT  = TOTAL UNITS SHORT                                   *
*          TUXCES  = TOTAL UNITS EXCESS                                  *
*          XS      = DAILY EXCESS                                        *
*                                                                        *
*****                ARRAY IDENTIFICATION                            *****
*                                                                        *
*          AMEAN   = MEAN OF EACH DISTRIBUTION                           *
*          CDF     = CUMMULATIVE DENSITY FUNCTION                        *
*          FD      = FREQUENCY DISTRIBUTION                              *
*          XD      = QUANTITY DISTRIBUTION                               *
*                                                                        *
*****                SUBROUTINE AND FUNCTION NAMES                   *****
*                                                                        *
*          RANDOM  = RANDOM NUMBER GENERATOR                             *
*          READER  = READS DISTRIBUTION DATA                             *
*          SAMPLE  = SAMPLES FROM THE DISTRIBUTIONS                      *
*                                                                        *
**************************************************************************
*                                                                        *
**********           STORAGE ALLOCATION                         **********
*                                                                        *
      COMMON XD(3,10),FD(3,10),CDF(3,10)
      DIMENSION AMEAN(3)
*                                                                        *
**************************************************************************
*                                                                        *
**********           READ PARAMETERS AND INITIALIZE             BLOCK 0100
*                                                                        *
  101 LOP = 0
      LPR = 0
      WRITE(6,*) 'TITLE',
      READ(5,102,END=599) ANS
  102 FORMAT(A5)
      WRITE(6,*) 'SIMULATION LENGTH',
      READ(5,*) DAY
      WRITE(6,*) 'PRINT EVERYTHING',
      READ(5,102,END=103) ANS
      IF(ANS .EQ. 'YES') LPR = 1
  103 ALFT = 0.0
      XS = 0.0
      TOTO = 0.0
      TOTDEM = 0.0
      TOTPRO = 0.0
      LNSAT=0
      TUXCES = 0.0
      TUSHRT = 0.0
      AVAIL = 0.0
      DUSO=0.0
      NSTOUT=0
      TUSO=0
      CD = 0.0
*                                                                        *
**************************************************************************
```

```
*                                                                            *
**********           READ DISTRIBUTIONS AND SET ARRAYS               BLOCK Ø2ØØ
*                                                                            *
      WRITE(6,*) 'WHAT IS THE PRODUCTION DISTRIBUTION'
      CALL READER(1)
  2Ø2 WRITE(6,*) 'WHAT IS THE ORDER DISTRIBUTION'
      CALL READER(2)
      WRITE(6,*) 'WHAT IS THE UNITS/ORDER DISTRIBUTION'
      CALL READER(3)
      DO 2Ø6 I = 1,3
          AMEAN(I) = Ø.Ø
          DO 2Ø7 J = 1,1Ø
              AMEAN(I) = XD(I,J)*FD(I,J) + AMEAN(I)
  2Ø7     CONTINUE
  2Ø6 CONTINUE
      DO 2Ø8 I = 1,3
          CDF(I,1)=FD(I,1)
          DO 215 J = 2,1Ø
              CDF(I,J) = CDF(I,J - 1) + FD(I,J)
  215     CONTINUE
  2Ø8 CONTINUE
      WRITE(6,2Ø9)
  2Ø9 FORMAT(52X,'******SERVICE*******'/3X,'DAY',6X,
     1'ORDERS',4X,'DEMAND PRODUCTION AVAILABLE',3X,'EXCESS',
     23X,'UNSATISFIED'/52X,'UNITS',6X,'ORDERS'/)
*                                                                            *
******************************************************************************
*                                                                            *
**********           SAMPLE DISTRIBUTIONS                            BLOCK Ø3ØØ
*                                                                            *
*          DETERMINE PRODUCTION FOR THIS DAY                                 *
*                                                                            *
  31Ø CD = CD + 1.Ø
      PRO = SAMPLE(1)
      AVAIL=AVAIL+PRO
*                                                                            *
*           DETERMINE NUMBER OF ORDERS THIS DAY                              *
*                                                                            *
      NORDR = SAMPLE(2)
      DEM=Ø.Ø
*                                                                            *
*           DETERMINE DEMAND FOR EACH ORDER                                  *
*                                                                            *
      DO 313 K=1,NORDR
          DEM = DEM + SAMPLE(3)
          IF(DEM .LE. AVAIL) GOTO 313
          TUSO=TUSO+1.Ø
          DUSO=DUSO+1.Ø
  313 CONTINUE
      FIFO=DEM-ALFT
      XS=PRO-FIFO
      IF(XS .LT. Ø.Ø) THEN
              TUSHRT = TUSHRT + XS
              NSTOUT=NSTOUT+1
          ELSE
              TUXCES = TUXCES + XS
      ENDIF
      ASHORT =-TUSHRT/CD
      AXCESS = TUXCES/CD
      DORDR = FLOAT(NORDR)
      TOTO = TOTO + DORDR
      TOTDEM = TOTDEM + DEM
      TOTPRO = TOTPRO + PRO
*                                                                            *
*           TEST WHETHER OR NOT TO PRINT DETAIL                              *
*                                                                            *
      IF(LPR .EQ. Ø) GOTO 33Ø
      WRITE(6,322) CD,DORDR,DEM,PRO,AVAIL,XS,DUSO
  322 FORMAT(1X,F5.Ø,6F1Ø.Ø)
  33Ø AVAIL = Ø.Ø
      LNSAT = INT(DUSO)
```

```
      DUSO=0.0
*                                                                        *
*         COMPUTE LEFT OVERS FOR TOMORROW                                *
*                                                                        *
      IF(XS .LT. 0.0) GOTO 326
      IF(FIFO .GE. 0.0) GOTO 340
      ALFT = PRO
      GO TO 341
  340 ALFT = XS
      GO TO 341
  326 ALFT = 0.0
  341 AVAIL = ALFT
*                                                                        *
*         IF NUMBER OF DAYS SIMULATED SO FAR IS LESS THAN DESIRED,       *
*         GO BACK TO SIMULATE NEXT DAY.  ELSE PRINT SUMMARY DATA.        *
*                                                                        *
      IF(CD .LT. DAY) GOTO 310
*                                                                        *
**************************************************************************
*                                                                        *
**********        COMPUTE AVERAGES AND PRINT THEM            BLOCK 0400
*                                                                        *
      TDEM=TOTDEM
      ALFT=TUXCES+TUSHRT
      WRITE(6,443)
  443 FORMAT(1X,'TOTALS')
      WRITE(6,442) CD,TOTO,TDEM,TOTPRO,ALFT,TUSO
  442 FORMAT(1X,F5.0,3F10.0,10X,2F10.0/)
      TOTPRO = TOTPRO/CD
      SLU=(TDEM+TUSHRT)/TDEM
      SLO=(TOTO-TUSO)/TOTO
      TOTDEM = TOTDEM/TOTO
      TOTO = TOTO/CD
      WRITE(6,*) NSTOUT,' STOCKOUT DAYS'
      WRITE(6,402) SLU
  402 FORMAT(' SERVICE LEVEL (PER UNIT)',F11.6)
      WRITE(6,403) SLO
  403 FORMAT(' SERVICE LEVEL (ORDERS)',F13.6)
      WRITE(6,404) AXCESS
  404 FORMAT(' AVERAGE EXCESS',F12.6)
      WRITE(6,405) ASHORT
  405 FORMAT(' AVERAGE SHORTAGE',F10.6)
      WRITE(6,410)
  410 FORMAT(/' AVERAGES',8X,'THEORETICAL',4X,'SAMPLE')
      WRITE(6,406) AMEAN(2),TOTO
  406 FORMAT(' ORDERS ',8X,2F12.6)
      WRITE(6,407) AMEAN(3),TOTDEM
  407 FORMAT(' DEM./ORDER',5X,2F12.6)
      SDDEM=TOTO*TOTDEM
      TDDEM=AMEAN(2)*AMEAN(3)
      WRITE(6,408) TDDEM,SDDEM
  408 FORMAT(' DEMAND/DAY',5X,2F12.6)
      WRITE(6,409) AMEAN(1),TOTPRO
  409 FORMAT(' PRODUCTION/DAY',1X,2F12.6///)
*                                                                        *
*         GO BACK TO READ ANOTHER PROBLEM                                *
*                                                                        *
      GOTO 101
*                                                                        *
**************************************************************************
*                                                                        *
**********        TERMINATION BLOCK                          BLOCK 0500
*                                                                        *
  599 STOP
      END
*                                                                        *
**************************************************** END OF MAIN PROGRAM
*                                                                        *
      FUNCTION SAMPLE(NTYPE)
*                                                                        *
**********        PROGRAM IDENTIFICATION                      **********
```

```
*                                                                      *
*       THIS SUBROUTINE SAMPLES FROM THE CUMULATIVE                    *
*       DISTRIBUTIONS OF EACH TYPE.                                    *
*                                                                      *
************************************************************************
*                                                                      *
**********          VARIABLE IDENTIFICATION                  **********
*                                                                      *
*       NTYPE   = IDENTIFIES WHICH DISTRIBUTION BEING SAMPLED          *
*       RNO     = RANDOM NUMBER FOR SAMPLING                           *
*                                                                      *
*****               ARRAY IDENTIFICATION                          *****
*                                                                      *
*       CDF     = CUMMULATIVE DENSITY FUNCTION                         *
*       FD      = FREQUENCY DISTRIBUTION                               *
*       XD      = QUANTITY DISTRIBUTION                                *
*                                                                      *
*****               SUBROUTINE AND FUNCTION NAMES                 *****
*                                                                      *
*       RANDOM  = RANDOM NUMBER GENERATOR                              *
*                                                                      *
************************************************************************
*                                                                      *
**********          STORAGE ALLOCATION                       **********
*                                                                      *
      COMMON XD(3,10),FD(3,10),CDF(3,10)
*                                                                      *
************************************************************************
*                                                                      *
**********          SAMPLING BLOCK                          BLOCK 0100
*                                                                      *
      RNO = RANDOM(0.0)
      DO 102 I = 1,10
         IF(RNO .LE. CDF(NTYPE,I)) GOTO 103
  102 CONTINUE
  103 SAMPLE = XD(NTYPE,I)
      RETURN
      END
*                                                                      *
********************************************      END OF FUNCTION SAMPLE
*
      SUBROUTINE READER(INDEXI)
*                                                                      *
**********          PROGRAM IDENTIFICATION                   **********
*                                                                      *
*       DATA IS READ INTO THE APPROPRIATE ARRAY                        *
*                                                                      *
************************************************************************
*                                                                      *
**********          VARIABLE IDENTIFICATION                  **********
*                                                                      *
*       DX      = QUANTITY                                             *
*       FX      = FREQUENCY                                            *
*       INDEXI  = ARRAY INDEX 1                                        *
*       INDEXJ  = ARRAY INDEX 2                                        *
*       SUMF    = SUM OF FREQUENCIES                                   *
*                                                                      *
*****               ARRAY IDENTIFICATION                          *****
*                                                                      *
*       FD      = FREQUENCY DISTRIBUTION                               *
*       XD      = QUANTITY DISTRIBUTION                                *
*                                                                      *
************************************************************************
*                                                                      *
**********          STORAGE ALLOCATION                       **********
*                                                                      *
      COMMON XD(3,10),FD(3,10),CDF(3,10)
*                                                                      *
**********          COMPUTATION BLOCK                       BLOCK 0100
*                                                                      *
  100 SUMF = 0.0
```

```
      INDEXJ = Ø
  1Ø1 READ(5,*,END=1Ø2) DX,FX
      INDEXJ=INDEXJ+1
      XD(INDEXI,INDEXJ)=DX
*                                                                      *
*          DATA MUST BE IN ASCENDING ORDER                             *
*                                                                      *
      IF(DX .LT. XD(INDEXI,INDEXJ-1)) GOTO 9Ø1
      FD(INDEXI,INDEXJ)=FX
      SUMF = SUMF + FX
*                                                                      *
*          GO BACK TO READ MORE DATA                                   *
*                                                                      *
      GOTO 1Ø1
*                                                                      *
  1Ø2 IF(INDEXJ .EQ. Ø) GOTO 1Ø4
*                                                                      *
*          TEST FOR DATA INPUT ERROR - SUM NOT EQUAL TO ONE            *
*                                                                      *
      IF(SUMF .GT. 1.Ø15 .OR. SUMF .LT. .985) GOTO 9Ø5
*                                                                      *
*          ZERO OUT REST OF ARRAY                                      *
*                                                                      *
      INDEXJ=INDEXJ+1
      DO 1Ø6 K=INDEXJ,1Ø
          XD(INDEXI,K)=Ø.Ø
          FD(INDEXI,K)=Ø.Ø
  1Ø6 CONTINUE
  1Ø4 RETURN
*                                                                      *
************************************************************************
*                                                                      *
**********            ERROR MESSAGE BLOCK                    BLOCK Ø9ØØ
*                                                                      *
  9Ø1 WRITE(6,9Ø2)
      WRITE(6,9Ø3)
      WRITE(6,9Ø4)
  9Ø2 FORMAT(//' ERROR IN DATA ENTRY.')
  9Ø3 FORMAT(' VALUES MUST BE IN ASCENDING ORDER.')
  9Ø4 FORMAT(' RE-ENTER THIS ENTIRE DATA SET.'/)
      GOTO 1ØØ
  9Ø5 WRITE(6,9Ø2)
      WRITE(6,9Ø6)
      WRITE(6,9Ø4)
  9Ø6 FORMAT(' FREQUENCIES MUST TOTAL ONE')
      GOTO 1ØØ
      END
*                                                                      *
********************************************* END OF SUBROUTINE READER
*                                                                      *
      FUNCTION RANDOM(DUM)
*                                                                      *
**********            PROGRAM IDENTIFICATION                  **********
*                                                                      *
*          RANDOM NUMBER GENERATOR                                     *
*          CALLED FROM SAMPLE                                          *
*                                                                      *
************************************************************************
*                                                                      *
**********            VARIABLE IDENTIFICATION                 **********
*                                                                      *
*          B       = CONSTANT MULTIPLIER = 3213.Ø                      *
*          C       = HIGH ORDER DIGITS OF PRODUCT                      *
*          D       = LOW ORDER DIGITS OF PRODUCT                       *
*          F       = CONSTANT SCALE FACTOR = 1.ØE7                     *
*          S       = CONSTANT SCALE FACTOR = 1ØØØØ.Ø                   *
*          DUM     = DUMMY ARGUMENT OR BIAS FACTOR                     *
*          R       = RANDOM DIGITS                                     *
*                                                                      *
************************************************************************
*                                                                      *
```

```
**********          STORAGE ALLOCATION                        **********
*                                                                      *
      DATA S/10000./F/1.0E7/B/3213.0/C/1230000./D/4567./
*                                                                      *
**********          GENERATE RANDOM NUMBER                    BLOCK 0100
*                                                                      *
      R = AMOD((AMOD(B*C,F) + AMOD(B*D,F)),F)
      D = AMOD(R,S)
      C = R - D
      RANDOM = R/F + DUM
      RETURN
      END
*                                                                      *
***********************************************   END OF FUNCTION RANDOM
************************************************   END OF PROGRAM SIMSIM
```

# SELECTED READING EXCERPTS

# APPENDIX M
# HOW TO DESIGN A VIABLE FORECASTING SYSTEM*

Management's concern about realistic forecasts is centered around the growth in the materials management area, where the forecast becomes the basic input in determining future requirements for finished goods, goods in process, and raw materials. Today's financial accountant also promotes this concern through inventory planning and funds flow analysis in developing pro forma financial statements.

In most companies, the single individual who ultimately receives the responsibility for forecasting is the Marketing Product Manager. [1] The concept of product management has promulgated the establishment of this prophetic man in almost all modern marketing organizations. Being a recipient of the forecasting responsibility he usually tries to establish broad brush sales dollar projections for those major products or product groups under his control. In submitting these forecasts to the manufacturing organization, he normally feels his job is complete and presumes manufacturing will satisfy the customer demand. However, the manufacturing manager does not deal in sales dollars and unless he has a firm fix on the average expected selling price for each product or product group, he cannot convert the forecast into meaningful production units. What the production manager can do is initiate a suggestion that improvements in the forecasting system be made to allow for forecasting in meaningful production units, and maybe even in finished goods stockkeeping units. If this sounds familiar and you want to help your marketing product managers improve their forecasting ability, perhaps you can try this approach.

## WHAT PRODUCTS AND ITEMS NEED FORECASTING

If you ask a marketing manager which products he needs to forecast on a regular monthly basis, he will most likely say none and suggest you use the company-wide inventory levels, or an order point technique for replenishing the

* William B. Stratton, *Production and Inventory Management*, Vol. 20, No. 1 (1979), pp. 17-27. (Reprinted by permission of the American Production and Inventory Control Society.)

branch inventories. Ask the manufacturing production scheduling manager the same question and he will likely say, "Why everything, of course. Why forecast any unless you include them all; we have to prepare schedules for everything, don't we?" Such a situational standoff will not answer the question nor improve the communications necessary for establishing better production and inventory control methods.

Management should carefully review with marketing and manufacturing which stockkeeping items, or product groups of items, need forecasts. The selection process can use some specific standard criteria that will meet and satisfy the needs of both organizations. The simplest and usually most convenient criterion is an estimate of expected annual dollar sales volume. Use of historical accounting sales reports that show the items or product groups in descending sequence can provide a good starting point (see Table 1). A review of the report and the adoption of some arbitrary cutoff point in annual sales dollar volume can generate a first cut list of items to forecast.

**TABLE 1**
**ANALYSIS OF SALES REPORT**
**MARKET 5**
**DESCENDING SEQUENCE**

| Catalog Number | Description | YTD Sales | Accum. Sales | Line Count | Accum. Sales % | |
|---|---|---|---|---|---|---|
| 1500109 | X-Ray | $117,247 | $117,247 | 1 | 24.91 | A Items |
| " 104 | " | 77,213 | 194,460 | 2 | 41.32 | " " |
| " 199 | " | 59,196 | 253,656 | 3 | 53.90 | " " |
| " 106 | " | 52,161 | 305,817 | 4 | 64.99 | " " |
| " 107 | " | 30,341 | 336,157 | 5 | 71.43 | " " |
| 1500253 | X-Ray | $ 20,990 | $357,148 | 6 | 75.89 | Non A |
| " 142 | " | 15,128 | 372,275 | 7 | 79.11 | Items |
| " 256 | " | 14,658 | 386,933 | 8 | 82.22 | " " |
| " 089 | " | 11,658 | 398,592 | 9 | 84.70 | " " |
| " 097 | " | 10,121 | 408,713 | 10 | 86.85 | " " |
| " — | " | — | — | — | — | " " |
| " 197 | " | 2,163 | 464,704 | 23 | 98.75 | " " |
| " 087 | " | 2,031 | 466,735 | 24 | 99.18 | " " |
| " 183 | " | 1,503 | 468,238 | 25 | 99.50 | " " |
| " 252 | " | 1,280 | 469,526 | 26 | 99.70 | " " |
| " 045 | " | 1,122 | 470,648 | 27 | 100.00 | " " |

A combination of information provided from descending sales reports, plus the introductory application of the ABC Technique, prompted our marketing product managers to examine their product lines more closely. Within a short time, recommended lists were being prepared regarding stock codes, inventory levels, and possible discontinuance of low sales, low profit items. Needless to say, this review and analysis period on the part of marketing provided an excellent introductory level training program for inventory management concepts.

Having established the groundwork in employing the above techniques, a further analysis was undertaken to examine the overall product lines of the entire division. In developing this analysis three major criteria were used—sales, factory costs, and net return. A composite summary of the overall picture for the division is shown in Table 2.

**TABLE 2**
**A, B, C ANALYSIS APPROACH**
**SALES DOLLARS, FACTORY COST, AND NET RETURN**

| Percent of Value | Sales Dollars No. Items | Factory Cost No. Items | Net Return No. Items |
|---|---|---|---|
| 50 | 45 | 50 | 22 |
| 60 | 75 | 82 | 43 |
| 70 | 125 | 132 | 70 |
| 80 | 215 | 240 | 110 |
| 90 | 385 | 450 | 185 |
| 100 | 2,000 | 2,000 | 2,000 |

An examination of Table 2 illustrates that if management puts its major efforts on those items that comprised 90 percent of the sales dollar volume (385 items out of 2,000), it could manage things more intelligently. A quarterly or semiannual review of the remaining 1,615 items could be handled when time permits.

The marketing product managers who had some experience working with a computerized forecasting system on a product group basis quickly realized the potential of forecasting in units other than sales dollars. In fact, they suggested the inclusion of two levels of forecasting, via product group (family) and by finished goods stockkeeping units. The unit forecast would be used to direct the final stages of manufacturing requirements, while the product group forecast would be used to determine longer term sales, profit, and capacity planning requirements.

The product group forecast was selected based upon an expected sales volume where agreement was reached to forecast products with sales equal to or greater than $100,000. The basis of the forecast for the product groups was also changed from dollars to production units of thousands of square feet.

Now that everyone was satisfied with the published list of what items/products needed forecasting at each level, our next step was to obtain a good demand data base.

## BOOKING DEMAND REPORTS

The establishment of a good demand data base is critical for determining better estimates of future customer demand. The use of sales history (orders shipped), compared with actual demand (orders booked), has high impact on the variability of the historical data, especially if back orders are occurring frequently.

The focal point of customer demand is the order department, and the creation of an order entry bookings demand report with several levels of detail is desirable in building an accurate demand data base.

The level of demand detail required depends upon the distribution network, the market structure, and the manufacturing operating process. Those companies fortunate enough to rely on a single manufacturing plant, a master warehouse, and several branch warehouses can simplify their demand reporting. The simplification occurs if one summarizes company-wide demand by market and by product group.

From the previous discussion on which levels of demand detail were required in building a historical base for forecasting, the decision was made to request several select demand report formats. These report formats were reviewed, revised,, and finalized in the preparation of electronic data processing (EDP) systems project requests. The actual production of the reports in the desired format required approximately one full year of programmer/analyst support. The task was lengthy due to revisions and restructure of two master files used for developing the reports.

The sketching of a forecast triangle was used to help describe the necessary levels of demand and forecast more clearly. [2] Figure 1 is a sample of GAF's forecast triangle for its photographic products. The triangle consists of three distinct levels.

Stockkeeping units (385 A Items)
Product Group 000's sq. ft. (75 families)
Film/paper Type 000's sq. ft. (50 master roll types)

The third level is simply an accumulation of the product group forecast expressed in a more condensed plant oriented nomenclature.

**FIGURE 1**
**GAF PHOTO PLANT FORECASTING TRIANGLE**
**ITEM, PRODUCT GROUP, AND FILM TYPE**

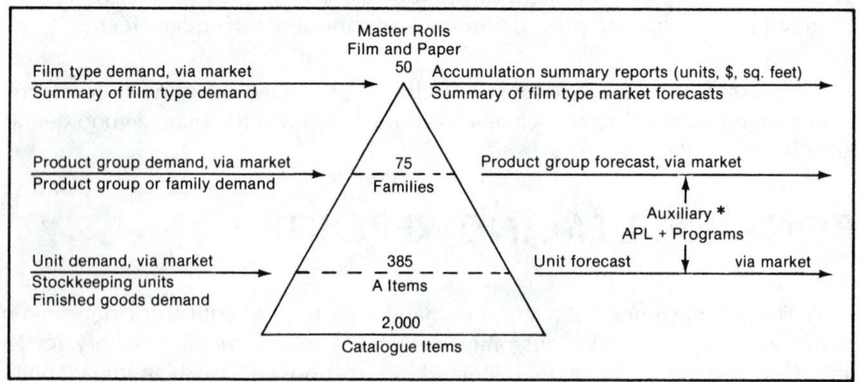


*These auxiliary APL + programs provide the balancing or forcing of unit and product group forecast.

## OBTAINING A MARKETING/MANUFACTURING COMMITMENT

The process of getting into the business of forecasting customer demand is not an easy task. There must be an upper level management commitment to select and apply the manpower required for the project to succeed.

With our company the commitment was made on a project basis by both the Director of Manufacturing and the Director of Marketing. The manpower assigned to the project was essentially three persons—a marketing, manufacturing, and systems analyst representative. The three representatives were given the opportunity to develop a formal "action plan" management-by-objectives project write-up for review and approval by corporate management. [3] The techniques used in evaluating the alternate software forecasting packages involved application of the Kepner-Tregoe decision analysis worksheets. [4] The work sheets provided an ideal mechanism for listing the *musts* and *wants* of all parties concerned. Use of this work sheet helped to eliminate certain individual desires which did not provide tangible benefits to the total project.

## SELECTING A FORECASTING SOFTWARE PACKAGE

The evaluation and selection of a good forecasting software package that can be easily modified to serve both marketing and manufacturing needs is a compromising project. To insure the best interests of both organizations, it is important that the members selected for the implementation team consist of objective individuals who can easily resolve the likes and dislikes of each vendor's software package.

The consolidation of a wish list submitted by each group and a review meeting to classify each wish into a must or want using the guidelines of a typical Kepner-Tregoe decision analysis works well. This K-T technique helps eliminate certain hang-ups on special format output reports and preferred built-in user simulations to evaluate the optimum alpha factor for each item forecast.

An appraisal of several systems was undertaken in our selection process where we examined three alternatives.

1. Keep the current software package we had on lease and expand the system with more nonrecurring analyst-programmer costs.
2. Lease a terminal and hook into a time-sharing forecasting system and write auxiliary APL programs to provide specific reports not available from the time-sharing system directly.
3. Bring in an alternate software package to run in-house and cancel the lease on the current system.

The results of the decision analysis we conducted showed the best alternative was to use the time-sharing forecasting system. The major reasons for selecting this system were the feasibility of getting the system up and the state of the art quality it possessed. However, the justification for selecting an outside time-sharing system versus use of a leased software package run on the company's own computer was a problem.

In order to convince management that the time-sharing forecasting system was superior, an economic analysis was prepared to illustrate the benefits. Table 3 shows the comparison.

**TABLE 3**
**ECONOMIC COMPARISON OF TIME-SHARING VERSUS AN IN-HOUSE SYSTEM**
**($/Month)**

| Cost Category | In-House | Time-Sharing |
|---|---|---|
| 1. EDP charges* | $ 480 | $ 90 |
| 2. Connect time charges | — | 135 |
| 3. Storage charges | — | 75 |
| 4. Software package use or lease | 350 | 125 |
| 5. Printing and handling charges | — | 10 |
| 6. Clerical support | 250 | 90 |
| 7. Programmer maintenance | 50 | — |
| 8. Terminal lease | — | 200 |
| Total charges | $1,130 | $725 |

*Use of an in-house system would result in the allocation of EDP expenses to the appropriate department using the system. The time-sharing cost in this category was for the expected computer usage in CRU's.

Additional in-house nonrecurring cost for programmer support amounting to $20,000 was also involved in bringing up a competitive system.

# A BALANCED SYSTEM

An interesting situation occurred during development of our two-level forecasting system that illustrates the need for a procedure of balancing or forcing close control of the item forecasts and their corresponding product group forecast. The marketing product manager for the domestic graphic film market was submitting both unit and product group forecasts to manufacturing on a monthly basis. The marketing product manager for the export graphic film market was submitting only a product group forecast. Suddenly a base supply problem created a shortage of a major product and a joint marketing/manufacturing meeting was called to review requirements using the product group forecast and to allocate the product accordingly. A decision was made to not ship any product against certain export orders, but instead to try to meet domestic demand. Basically a good decision was made based on limited information; however, a quick and dirty analysis of the domestic market unit forecast compared with the product group forecast showed an imbalance. The domestic market product group forecast was approximately 30 percent higher than was needed to meet the item forecasts. A demonstration of this imbalance, a reduction in the product group forecast, and a reallocation program prevented shorting the export requirements.

The lesson learned by the graphic film example caused us to further check other items versus product group forecast. Eventually we structured two very useful auxiliary APL programs to link the two forecast files to provide a review of the historical item/product demand compared with the expected future item/ product forecast demand.

This mechanism for balancing the item (SKU) forecast with the product group (family) forecast became a very powerful part of the overall system. The development of two reports—(1) a historical picture of the last 12 months, and (2) a projection of the next 12 months—forced a balancing between requirements in the scheduling production operations.

Other improvements in the system were made with relative programming ease. There are, however, two significant alterations that greatly improved the turnaround time from the product managers and relieved their dread of reviewing the monthly forecast.

## MARKETING (MANAGEMENT) OVERRIDES

The marketing managers found the process of providing changes, either positive or negative to the statistical model forecast a monumental task. If there was a new model generated due to a change in the pattern of demand, this problem was magnified in their minds tenfold. What the marketing managers desired and what we provided was an absolute market forecast number that was kept on the files until they changed it. This meant additional file storage, but the cost outweighted the complaints. For planning purposes, the marketing managers asked for printouts of the forecast in units, dollars, and square feet. Since the forecasting system uses a master file with user defined fields, the conversions were quite easy to provide on several reports.

## SLIDING INSTEAD OF ROLLING FORECAST REPORT

Use of a monthly rolling forecast that moved ahead, each time covering a new added month and lopping off the oldest month, was another stumbling block. Again we reevaluated the needs and modified the report format. The new format, Table 4, is referred to as a sliding forecast. It shows one complete year of history, the current year actual and projection, plus the next year's projection. This format allows a shift upward in time once a year, after the January demand is posted. The format also adds the current year actual plus forecast to give a year-to-date and year-end projection. The particular figure illustrated shows the square feet, dollars, and pounds of base conversions for planning purposes.

## TABLE 4
## SAMPLE FORECAST FORMAT PRODUCT GROUP X-RAY FILM

Component name is: 1500 Index No. 04 Dollar conversion value is: 0.5250
Description: X-Ray Film Base conversion value is: 50.500

| | Jan. | Feb. | March | April | May | June | July | Aug. | Sept. | Oct. | Nov. | Dec. | Total |
|---|---|---|---|---|---|---|---|---|---|---|---|---|---|
| Prior hist. (sq ft/mo): | 3,270 | 3,478 | 7,380 | 2,227 | 3,663 | 3,885 | 3,121 | 2,863 | 5,334 | 3,924 | 3,346 | 3,463 | 45,954 |
| Prior hist. (ytd sq ft): | 3,270 | 6,748 | 14,128 | 16,355 | 20,018 | 23,903 | 27,024 | 29,887 | 35,221 | 39,145 | 42,491 | 45,954 | |
| Curr. hist. (sq ft/mo): | 3,219 | 3,600 | 4,420 | 2,575 | 2,975 | 5,100 | 2,675 | 2,975 | 5,300 | 2,875 | 2,975 | 5,400 | 44,089* |
| Curr. hist. (ytd sq ft): | 3,219 | 6,819 | 11,239 | 13,814 | 16,789 | 21,889 | 24,564 | 27,539 | 32,839 | 35,714 | 38,689 | 44,089 | |
| Current year: 1978 | | | | | | | | | | | | | |
| Model forecast (sq ft): | | 3,375 | 4,212 | 3,365 | 3,360 | 4,193 | 3,350 | 3,345 | 4,174 | 3,334 | 3,329 | 4,155 | 40,192 |
| Market forecast (sq ft): | | 3,600 | 4,420 | 2,575 | 2,975 | 5,100 | 2,675 | 2,975 | 5,300 | 2,875 | 2,975 | 5,400 | 40,870 |
| Market dollars forecast: | | 1,890 | 2,320 | 1,352 | 1,562 | 2,677 | 1,404 | 1,562 | 2,782 | 1,509 | 1,562 | 2,835 | 21,457 |
| Mkt forecast (lbs base): | | 181,800 | 223,210 | 130,038 | 150,238 | 257,550 | 135,088 | 150,238 | 267,650 | 145,188 | 150,238 | 272,700 | 2,063,935 |
| Future year: 1979 | | | | | | | | | | | | | |
| Model forecast (sq ft): | 3,319 | 3,314 | 4,137 | 3,304 | 3,299 | 4,118 | 3,289 | 3,284 | 4,099 | 3,274 | 3,269 | 4,080 | 42,786 |
| Market forecast (sq ft): | 3,790 | 3,784 | 4,724 | 3,770 | 3,763 | 4,698 | 3,749 | 3,742 | 4,672 | 3,729 | 3,722 | 4,657 | 48,800 |
| Market dollars forecast: | 1,990 | 1,987 | 2,480 | 1,979 | 1,976 | 2,466 | 1,968 | 1,965 | 2,453 | 1,958 | 1,954 | 2,445 | 25,620 |
| Mkt forecast (lbs base): | 191,395 | 191,092 | 238,562 | 190,385 | 190,032 | 237,249 | 189,325 | 188,971 | 235,936 | 188,315 | 187,961 | 235,179 | 2,464,400 |

Note: *Actual demand + forecast demand is combined to give year end projection as though it were current history. Forecast is expressed in 000's square feet, 000's dollars, and pounds of polyester base. History is expressed in 000's square feet only. Report was generated after posting January 1978 demand.

# MEASURE OF FORECAST PERFORMANCE

The evaluation, selection, and implementation of a workable "marketing oriented" forecasting system as described in this article is incomplete without some measure of forecast performance. Many software packages include a technique for measuring forecast performance. [5] However, the measurements are usually too complicated for most marketing managers to understand. An example is application of measuring errors in standard deviations. It is a lot simpler to compare absolute marketing forecast numbers with the statistical model, or actual demand numbers, and illustrate percentage errors in monthly forecast performance reports.

A catch in designing forecast performance reports is deciding which forecast we compare with which actual month's demand. Since the lead times may vary for a unit forecast, compared with a product group forecast, we designed a forecast performance report that showed the last four forecasts submitted compared with the actual demand. This type of report illustrated the capability of the product manager and the model to respond to new input as time progressed. The literature on measuring forecast performance tells us that forecasts are more accurate for aggregates (product groups) and shorter planning horizons. This concept allowed us to structure only product group forecast performance reports with guidelines on expected accuracy. Table 5 illustrates the product group forecast performance report for several medical X-ray items sold in the civilian, federal, and export markets. This type of forecast performance report shows the improvements (if there are any) in the market or model forecast over time. Since a

**TABLE 5**
**X-RAY**
**NOVEMBER FORECAST PERFORMANCE REPORT**
**(IN THOUSANDS OF SQUARE FEET)**

| Product Group | Market | Description | Past Projections | | | | Nov. Actual |
|---|---|---|---|---|---|---|---|
| | | | Aug. | Sept. | Oct. | Nov. | |
| 1500 | Civilian | X-Ray Med. | 3,307 | 2,982 | 3,738 | 4,398 | 3,346 |
| | | | 4,315 | 3,515 | 3,515 | 3,515 | |
| 1500 | Federal | X-Ray Med. | 562 | 406 | 532 | 517 | 552 |
| | | | 1,304 | 1,304 | 1,304 | 1,304 | |
| 1500 | Canada | X-Ray Med. | 236 | 236 | 360 | 360 | 320 |
| | | | 420 | 420 | 1,000 | 1,000 | |
| 1500 | Export | X-Ray Med. | 484 | 484 | 596 | 596 | 400 |
| | | | 250 | 300 | 325 | 350 | |

| Product Group | Market | Description | % Error of Past Projections* | | | | |
|---|---|---|---|---|---|---|---|
| | | | Aug. | Sept. | Oct. | Nov. | |
| 1500 | Civilian | X-Ray Med. | − 1 | − 10 | 11 | 31 | Model |
| | | | 28 | 5 | 5 | 5 | Market |
| 1500 | Federal | X-Ray Med. | 1 | − 26 | − 3 | − 6 | Model |
| | | | 136 | 136 | 136 | 136 | Market |
| 1500 | Canada | X-Ray Med. | − 26 | − 26 | 13 | 13 | Model |
| | | | 31 | 31 | 213 | 213 | Market |
| 1500 | Export | X-Ray Med. | 21 | 21 | 49 | 49 | Model |
| | | | − 38 | − 25 | − 19 | − 13 | Market |

*Percentage error is expressed as a deviation ± from the actual demand.

90-day lead time is required for planning purposes, only the August projection of November demand might be used as the standard of performance in measuring marketing's accuracy.

# CONCLUSION

The reliability of any marketing forecast is dependant upon the emphasis upper management puts on the marketing product managers to improve their estimates, and the emphasis the forecasting analyst puts on improving the forecasting system as a workable management tool. The importance of a good forecasting sytem as the front end of a materials management system is critical to product and inventory control.

The benefits of the forecasting system discussed in this article have impacted the performance of the division. The system provides positive input to support monthly business meetings where the effects of the latest forecasting information is used to review and discuss operational objectives for future time periods.

## SELECTED READINGS

1. Philip Kotler, *Marketing Management Analysis, Planning and Control* (Englewood Cliffs, N.J.: Prentice-Hall, Inc., 1976), pp. 405-417.
2. Thomas L. Newberry, "System Highlights," *American Software* (1977), pp. 4-7.
3. George L. Morrisey, *Management by Objective and Results* (Reading, Mass.: Addison-Wesley Publishing Co., Inc., 1970), pp. 75-80.
4. Charles H. Kepner and Benjamin B. Tregoe, *The Rational Manager* (New York: McGraw-Hill Book Company, 1965), pp. 173-206.
5. Robert Goodell Brown, *Materials Management Systems* (New York: John Wiley & Sons, Inc., 1977), pp. 49-52.

# APPENDIX N
# A MANUAL/MECHANICAL APPROACH TO MASTER SCHEDULING AND OPERATIONS PLANNING*

Master scheduling has become the focus of much of the current literature in our field—and for good reason. It is the master schedule that supplies the link between the high, and sometimes illusory, expectations of the marketing group of a company with the practical realities of the manufacturing environment. It is the filter through which the forecast flows, siphoning external irregularity into internal consistency. The master schedule drives the MRP which, in turn, drives most of the manufacturing systems in the company.

Yet, most articles on the subject tend to imply that the master schedule should be manually prepared. Isn't that an irony? That something manually prepared—in some cases tediously, in others hurriedly, yet always prone to human error—be used as a source for a sophisticated network of computerized inventory control, capacity planning and shop floor control systems. Master schedulers, planning analysts, basic planners—or whatever term your company calls them—must be the most underpaid professionals in the business. The responsibility that falls on their shoulders could be compared to the responsibility of the younger Wallenda brothers—the ones who support the rest of their family on the tightrope.

The master schedule should be a real schedule—one that can be met, rather than an ideal which can never be attained. Yet, by the very fact that an ideal plan becomes tempered by reality (or even by just starting out with an attainable modified plan) upper management has already lost many of its key indicators to an awareness of troubles brewing in the company. Attainable plans are plans that have already been modified for capacity, for machine limitations, for late vendor deliveries, for late manufacturing schedules, and a miscellaneous collection of additional limiting factors. Yet those are the very things that should be brought to upper management's attention, since upper management might very well be the only one that has power to do anything about removing them as limiting factors. Other decisions made by the master planner should, in some cases, be made by the marketing function, by the financial function, or even in some small companies, by the president of the company.

---

*Bob Brongiel, *Production and Inventory Management*, Vol. 20, No. 1 (1979), pp. 66-74. (Reprinted by permission of the American Production and Inventory Control Society.)

# SCOPE

The intent of this article is to put upper management, or possibly the president of a small company, back in the driver's seat. A system is outlined that could be set up on either a time-sharing or an in-house computer which, basically, aids the master scheduler in preparing a master plan. Utilizing a simple data file (consisting of a part number, lot size, safety stock, and beginning inventory) the computer arrives at an ideal plan of finished goods production to meet a marketing forecast. This plan is then summarized in dollars to express an ideal operating plan. The ideal finished goods production is then modified to reflect reality. Reasons for modifications are summarized, categorized and reviewed by upper management for approval, and as an indication of anticipated late deliveries and bottlenecks. Any changes to the modified plan by upper management are made to it and the revised modified plan is then entered in the computer. The new plan then becomes the master plan and is summarized by dollars (projected back orders are also indicated). This becomes the official operating plan of the company.

# GENERAL COMMENTS ABOUT TYPE OF COMPANY

The type of company that currently uses this approach is a low-volume, make-to-stock pharmaceutical manufacturing company. There are approximately 500 finished goods part numbers divided unevenly among 15 varied product groups. The organization is functionally organized with the conventional marketing, finance, and manufacturing groups reporting directly to the president of the company.

The master plan is prepared for a two-year horizon. However, it is broken down into a six-month (short- to medium-range) forecast period by month and a six-quarter (medium- to long-range) forecast period by quarters.

# THE SYSTEM

The system which I will describe was developed, on and off, within the course of one year's time. However, the basic files and programming (utilizing an extended form of the BASIC programming language) were set up on a time-sharing computer in less than one month's time. No in-house computer support was required. However, since running the system on a time-sharing system is slow and involves duplicating much of a standard data base, attempts are now being undertaken to set up the entire system on an in-house computer. Testing of the system and refinements to it were done throughout the course of the year and are still being investigated. An interesting point to note concerning the entire system is that it was developed entirely (to include programming) by users; i.e., production planning and inventory control personnel and upper-level managers (as opposed to systems personnel).

The ideal master plan is illustrated in Figure 1.* It is *ideal* in the sense that it is generated entirely by the computer program designed to keep the inventory level for each item above a predetermined minimum safety stock. Three basic elements are involved in the computation of the master plan: (1) Forecast Elements, (2) Inventory Elements, and (3) Production Elements.

## Forecast Elements

These elements include the safety stock determination, the forecast itself, and the class of the item. The safety stock is calculated, based on the class of the item, utilizing standard service level methodology. A one-year history of actual versus forecast demand is evaluated and a safety stock in units is computed by multiplying the adjusted MAD times the respective service level factor. This is all done on an in-house program. The safety stock is then compared to projected demand and converted to a weekly figure (i.e., one week's supply, two weeks' supply, etc.). Contrary to theoretical and popular literature, a different safety stock is calculated for each item for each period in the future based on the forecast for that period. We find that this approach tends to adjust more for significant upward or downward trends in the forecast than a conventional static reorder point approach. Manual intervention to arrive at a number of weeks of safety stock is the means by which the theoretical computation is modified to reflect reality. Problem items get additional safety stock.

The forecast itself is given to production planning as eight quarterly figures by areas; i.e., domestic sales and international sales. When used in the computation of the master plan, the first two quarterly figures are each divided by three to arrive at monthly sales figures for short- to medium-range planning. The remaining forecast figures are left in quarterly periods and used to project the medium- to long-range plan. Demand itself is entirely independent.

Class assignments are a direct result of upper-level management's attempt to indicate in which direction the company wishes to move, rather than a simple ABC analysis of annual usage. An *X* class was assigned to items that were deemed non-stockers or items that are pending deletion.

## Inventory Elements

A beginning quarter inventory figure (B INV) for each item is used to begin the computation of the plan. Adjustments to this inventory include back orders and negative adjustments (−ADJ). Negative adjustments may be peculiar to the pharmaceutical business, since most chemical products are subject to dating restraints. Any lots still remaining in finished goods inventory which become short dated or out-of-date must be subtracted from the beginning available inventory figure to arrive at a more accurate beginning inventory. The resulting inventory (E INV) is used as the starting point to compute future required production quantities and resulting month and quarter-ending inventories. The ideal plan will always maintain the inventory level above the safety stock number of weeks (POS) quantity for each respective future period.

*All figures are found on pages 637-639.

# Production Elements

The production quantity is determined from a predetermined computation of an Economical Production Quantity (EPQ). These orders are determined through standard EOQ logic overridden by manual adjustments based on machine limitations, dating restrictions and for any additional limiting factors. Production is scheduled in lots, or multiples of standard lots, and is rigidly regulated for traceability by the Food and Drug Administration. Future consideration in regard to EPQ's is to have the subroutine to calculate an EPQ within the production plan program itself. In this manner, a new EPQ could be calculated for any significant variation in forecast usage.

The ideal plan is generated both, as in Figure 1, with a column below the production quantities for adjustments; and, as in Figure 2, in terms of dollars of production, sales and period-ending inventories all at standard cost dollars. The production file, by finished goods number, is maintained as a data file in the computer.

# THE ADJUSTMENTS

The master planner(s) utilizes the ideal plan as a worksheet to begin an in-depth determination of the feasibility of the plan. Any production that cannot be met is indicated, as in Figure 3, below the ideal production quantity. Adjustments are made only to the short- to medium-range forecast period and every attempt is made to get back on schedule within the shortest possible time. Adjustments are also made with every intention to keep the production quantities similar to those computed. Total production units before the adjustments and after the adjustments should basically remain constant; the only difference being in the periods in which production occurs.

# THE REAL

The adjustments are then inputted as changes to the production data file in the computer and the "real" plan is calculated. A new month and quarter-end inventory is calculated for each period forecast (see Figure 4) and a summary of standard cost dollars is again computed utilizing the new production and ending inventories (see Figure 5). Both master schedules and dollar summaries are then received by upper management to determine the dollar impact of missed production on forecast sales. Any significant missed production is evaluated as to causes and remedies. Reasons for not being able to meet the ideal plan are summarized and ranked in order of significance by potential missed sales dollars. Trade-offs are determined by collective bargaining in the hopes of maximizing profit margins and synergistic effects. Marketing, finance, and manufacturing approach all significant potential projected back orders as to their effects on profit and what would be in the best interest of the company as a whole.

All changes made by upper management are reflected in the new production plan which is used as the company game plan.

# CONCLUSION

The simplicity of this entire procedure masks its potential to be an important tool for the manager who wants to know what is ailing his business. Knowing the real reasons why things aren't as they should be could make the difference between managements who act and those who react.

The aforementioned system is not complicated. In fact, it is entirely the opposite. On-line systems to compute EOQ's and safety stocks aren't necessary for the essence of the concept. The system can be as simple or as complicated as a company would like to make it. The guts of the system lie in the forced interrelationships among the decision makers of the company. This alone can sometimes work miracles.

# REFERENCES


1. Green, J. H. *Production and Inventory Control Handbook*. New York: McGraw-Hill, Inc., 1970.
2. Orlicky, Joseph A. *Material Requirements Planning*. New York: McGraw-Hill, Inc., 1975.
3. Plossl, G. W., and Wright, O. W. *Production and Inventory Control*. New Jersey: Prentice Hall, Inc., 1967.
4. APICS, "Master Production Scheduling Reprints" (1977).


**FIGURE 1**
**FINISHED GOODS PLAN FOR 300 PRODUCT GROUP**

| | | | MONTHS | | | | | | QUARTERS | | | | | |
|---|---|---|---|---|---|---|---|---|---|---|---|---|---|---|
| | | | JAN | FEB | MAR | APR | MAY | JUN | J-A-S | O-N-D | J-F-M | A-M-J | J-A-S | O-N-D |
| 300-010 | SS | 2.0 WKS | | | | | | | | | | | | |
| A | | FRCST | 1967 | 1967 | 1967 | 1983 | 1983 | 1983 | 6050 | 6100 | 6200 | 6250 | 6350 | 6400 |
| EPQ | 2,400 | PROD | 2400 | 2400 | 2400 | 0 | 2400 | 2400 | 7200 | 4800 | 7200 | 4800 | 7200 | 7200 |
| B INV | 2083 | ADJ'D | ----- | ----- | ----- | ----- | ----- | ----- | ----- | ----- | ----- | ----- | ----- | ----- |
| -ADJ | 383 | | | | | | | | | | | | | |
| E INV | 1700 | INV | 2133 | 2567 | 3000 | 1017 | 1433 | 1850 | 3000 | 1700 | 2700 | 1250 | 2100 | 2900 |
| | | POS | 4 | 5 | 6 | 2 | 3 | 4 | 6 | 3 | 5 | 2 | 4 | 5 |
| 300-020 | SS | 1.0 WKS | BACKORDERS | | 5439 | | | | | | | | | |
| B | | FRCST | 3908 | 3908 | 3908 | 3693 | 3693 | 3693 | 10434 | 9789 | 9144 | 8499 | 7854 | 7209 |
| EPQ | 3,500 | PROD | 10500 | 7000 | 3500 | 3500 | 3500 | 3500 | 10500 | 10500 | 7000 | 10500 | 7000 | 7000 |
| B INV | 0 | ADJ'D | ----- | ----- | ----- | ----- | ----- | ----- | ----- | ----- | ----- | ----- | ----- | ----- |
| -ADJ | 0 | | | | | | | | | | | | | |
| E INV | -5439 | INV | 1153 | 4245 | 3837 | 3644 | 3451 | 3258 | 3324 | 4035 | 1891 | 3892 | 3038 | 2829 |
| | | POS | 1 | 4 | 4 | 4 | 4 | 4 | 4 | 5 | 2 | 5 | 5 | 5 |
| 300-030 | SS | 1.0 WKS | | | | | | | | | | | | |
| C | | FRCST | 167 | 167 | 167 | 167 | 167 | 167 | 500 | 500 | 500 | 500 | 500 | 500 |
| EPQ | 100 | PROD | 300 | 100 | 200 | 200 | 100 | 200 | 500 | 500 | 500 | 500 | 500 | 500 |
| B INV | 30 | ADJ'D | ----- | ----- | ----- | ----- | ----- | ----- | ----- | ----- | ----- | ----- | ----- | ----- |
| -ADJ | 30 | | | | | | | | | | | | | |
| E INV | 0 | INV | 133 | 67 | 100 | 133 | 67 | 100 | 100 | 100 | 100 | 100 | 100 | 100 |
| | | POS | 3 | 2 | 2 | 3 | 2 | 2 | 2 | 2 | 2 | 2 | 2 | 2 |
| 300-040 | SS | 0.0 WKS | | | | | | | | | | | | |
| X | | FRCST | 0 | 0 | 0 | 250 | 250 | 250 | 0 | 750 | 0 | 750 | 0 | 750 |
| EPQ | 250 | PROD | 0 | 0 | 0 | 250 | 250 | 250 | 0 | 750 | 0 | 750 | 0 | 750 |
| B INV | 0 | ADJ'D | ----- | ----- | ----- | ----- | ----- | ----- | ----- | ----- | ----- | ----- | ----- | ----- |
| -ADJ | 0 | | | | | | | | | | | | | |
| E INV | 0 | INV | 0 | 0 | 0 | 0 | 0 | 0 | 0 | 0 | 0 | 0 | 0 | 0 |
| | | POS | 0 | 0 | 0 | 0 | 0 | 0 | 0 | 0 | 0 | 0 | 0 | 0 |

## FIGURE 2
## DOLLAR SUMMARY FOR SPECIAL PRODUCT GROUP

BEG INV $ 25,445
S/D INV $ -6,133
END INV $ 19,312
BACKORDERS $ 28,446

| | FORECAST DOLLARS | | | PRODUCTION | INVENTORY DOLLARS | | |
|---|---|---|---|---|---|---|---|
| PERIOD | DOMESTIC | INT'L | TOTAL | | SFTY STK | SS + LS/2 | END INV |
| JAN | 44,727 | 7,952 | 52,679 | 99,996 | 18,755 | 46,920 | 38,184 |
| FEB | 44,727 | 7,952 | 52,679 | 69,813 | 18,755 | 46,920 | 55,318 |
| MAR | 44,727 | 7,952 | 52,679 | 57,447 | 18,755 | 46,920 | 60,087 |
| APR | 48,425 | 8,141 | 56,566 | 35,006 | 18,569 | 46,734 | 38,526 |
| MAY | 48,425 | 8,141 | 56,566 | 56,331 | 18,569 | 46,734 | 38,291 |
| JUN | 48,425 | 8,141 | 56,566 | 62,270 | 18,569 | 46,734 | 43,994 |
| J-A-S | 128,001 | 24,992 | 152,993 | 166,402 | 18,477 | 46,642 | 57,404 |
| O-N-D | 139,095 | 25,560 | 164,655 | 153,606 | 18,290 | 46,456 | 46,354 |
| J-F-M | 121,822 | 26,128 | 147,950 | 148,097 | 18,199 | 46,364 | 46,501 |
| A-M-J | 132,916 | 26,696 | 159,612 | 153,606 | 18,012 | 46,177 | 40,494 |
| J-A-S | 115,643 | 27,264 | 142,907 | 148,097 | 17,920 | 46,086 | 45,684 |
| O-N-D | 126,738 | 27,832 | 154,570 | 162,565 | 17,734 | 45,899 | 53,679 |

## FIGURE 3
## FINISHED GOODS PLAN FOR 300 PRODUCT GROUP

| | | | MONTHS | | | | | | QUARTERS | | | | | |
|---|---|---|---|---|---|---|---|---|---|---|---|---|---|---|
| | | | JAN | FEB | MAR | APR | MAY | JUN | J-A-S | O-N-D | J-F-M | A-M-J | J-A-S | O-N-D |
| 300-010 | SS | 2.0 WKS | | | | | | | | | | | | |
| A | | FRCST | 1967 | 1967 | 1967 | 1983 | 1983 | 1983 | 6050 | 6100 | 6200 | 6250 | 6350 | 6400 |
| EPQ | 2,400 | PROD | 2400 | 2400 | 2400 | 0 | 2400 | 2400 | 7200 | 4800 | 7200 | 4800 | 7200 | 7200 |
| B INV | 2083 | ADJ'D | ----- | ----- | ----- | ----- | ----- | ----- | ----- | ------ | ------ | ------ | ------ | ------ |
| -ADJ | 383 | | | | | | | | | | | | | |
| E INV | 1700 | INV | 2133 | 2567 | 3000 | 1017 | 1433 | 1850 | 3000 | 1700 | 2700 | 1250 | 2100 | 2900 |
| | | POS | 4 | 5 | 6 | 2 | 3 | 4 | 6 | 3 | 5 | 2 | 4 | 5 |
| 300-020 | SS | 1.0 WKS | BACKORDERS | | 5439 | | | | | | | | | |
| B | | FRCST | 3908 | 3908 | 3908 | 3693 | 3693 | 3693 | 0434 | 9789 | 9144 | 8499 | 7854 | 7209 |
| EPQ | 3,500 | PROD | ~~10500~~ | 7000 | ~~3500~~ | 3500 | 3500 | 3500 | 10500 | 10500 | 7000 | 10500 | 7000 | 7000 |
| B INV | 0 | ADJ'D | 3500 | ----- | 10500 | ----- | ----- | ----- | ----- | ------ | ------ | ------ | ------ | ------ |
| -ADJ | 0 | | | | | | | | | | | | | |
| E INV | -5439 | INV | 1153 | 4245 | 3837 | 3644 | 3451 | 3258 | 3324 | 4035 | 1891 | 3892 | 3038 | 2829 |
| | | POS | 1 | 4 | 4 | 4 | 4 | 4 | 4 | 5 | 2 | 5 | 5 | 5 |
| 300-030 | SS | 1.0 WKS | | | | | | | | | | | | |
| C | | FRCST | 167 | 167 | 167 | 167 | 167 | 167 | 500 | 500 | 500 | 500 | 500 | 500 |
| EPQ | 100 | PROD | ~~300~~ | ~~100~~ | 200 | 200 | 100 | 200 | 500 | 500 | 500 | 500 | 500 | 500 |
| B INV | 30 | ADJ'D | ----- | 400 | ----- | ----- | ----- | ----- | ----- | ------ | ------ | ------ | ------ | ------ |
| -ADJ | 30 | | | | | | | | | | | | | |
| E INV | 0 | INV | 133 | 67 | 100 | 133 | 67 | 100 | 100 | 100 | 100 | 100 | 100 | 100 |
| | | POS | 3 | 2 | 2 | 3 | 2 | 2 | 2 | 2 | 2 | 2 | 2 | 2 |
| 300-040 | SS | 0.0 WKS | | | | | | | | | | | | |
| X | | FRCST | 0 | 0 | 0 | 250 | 250 | 250 | 0 | 750 | 0 | 750 | 0 | 750 |
| EPQ | 250 | PROD | 0 | 0 | 0 | 250 | 250 | 250 | 0 | 750 | 0 | 750 | 0 | 750 |
| B INV | 0 | ADJ'D | ----- | ----- | ----- | ----- | ----- | ----- | ----- | ------ | ------ | ------ | ------ | ------ |
| -ADJ | 0 | | | | | | | | | | | | | |
| E INV | 0 | INV | 0 | 0 | 0 | 0 | 0 | 0 | 0 | 0 | 0 | 0 | 0 | 0 |
| | | POS | 0 | 0 | 0 | 0 | 0 | 0 | 0 | 0 | 0 | 0 | 0 | 0 |

## FIGURE 4
## FINISHED GOODS PLAN FOR SPECIAL PRODUCT GROUP

| | | | MONTHS | | | | | | QUARTERS | | | | | |
|---|---|---|---|---|---|---|---|---|---|---|---|---|---|---|
| | | | JAN | FEB | MAR | APR | MAY | JUN | J-A-S | O-N-D | J-F-M | A-M-J | J-A-S | O-N-D |
| 300-010 | 8S 2.0 WKS | | | | | | | | | | | | | |
| A | | FRCST | 1967 | 1967 | 1967 | 1983 | 1983 | 1983 | 6050 | 6100 | 6200 | 6250 | 6350 | 6400 |
| EPQ | 2,400 | PROD | 2400 | 2400 | 2400 | 0 | 2400 | 2400 | 7200 | 4800 | 7200 | 4800 | 7200 | 7200 |
| B INV | 2083 | INV | 2133 | 2567 | 3000 | 1017 | 1433 | 1850 | 3000 | 1700 | 2700 | 1250 | 2100 | 2900 |
| -ADJ | 383 | POS | 4 | 5 | 6 | 2 | 3 | 4 | 6 | 3 | 5 | 2 | 4 | 5 |
| E INV | 1700 | | | | | | | | | | | | | |
| | | INV $ | 24235 | 29157 | 34080 | 11549 | 16283 | 21016 | 34080 | 19312 | 30672 | 14200 | 23856 | 32944 |
| 300-020 | SS 1.0 WKS | BACKORDERS 5439 | | | | | | | | | | | | |
| B | | FRCST | 3908 | 3908 | 3908 | 3693 | 3693 | 3693 | 10434 | 9789 | 9144 | 8499 | 7854 | 7209 |
| EPQ | 3,500 | PROD | 3500 | 7000 | 10500 | 3500 | 3500 | 3500 | 10500 | 10500 | 7000 | 10500 | 7000 | 7000 |
| B INV | 0 | INV | -5847 | -2755 | 3837 | 3644 | 3451 | 3258 | 3324 | 4035 | 1891 | 3892 | 3038 | 2829 |
| -ADJ | 0 | POS | -6 | -3 | 4 | 4 | 4 | 4 | 4 | 5 | 2 | 5 | 5 | 5 |
| E INV | -5439 | | | | | | | | | | | | | |
| | | INV $ | 0 | 0 | 20068 | 19058 | 18049 | 17039 | 17385 | [illegible]1103 | 9890 | 20355 | 15889 | 14796 |
| 300-030 | SS 1.0 WKS | | | | | | | | | | | | | |
| C | | FRCST | 167 | 167 | 167 | 167 | 167 | 167 | 500 | 500 | 500 | 500 | 500 | 500 |
| EPQ | 100 | PROD | 0 | 400 | 200 | 200 | 100 | 200 | 500 | 500 | 500 | 500 | 500 | 500 |
| B INV | 30 | INV | -167 | 67 | 100 | 133 | 67 | 100 | 100 | 100 | 100 | 100 | 100 | 100 |
| -ADJ | 30 | POS | -4 | 2 | 2 | 3 | 2 | 2 | 2 | 2 | 2 | 2 | 2 | 2 |
| E INV | 0 | | | | | | | | | | | | | |
| | | INV $ | 0 | 3959 | 5939 | 7919 | 3959 | 5939 | 5939 | 5939 | 5939 | 5939 | 5939 | 5939 |
| 300-040 | SS 0.0 WKS | | | | | | | | | | | | | |
| X | | FRCST | 0 | 0 | 0 | 250 | 250 | 250 | 0 | 750 | 0 | 750 | 0 | 750 |
| EPQ | 250 | PROD | 0 | 0 | 0 | 250 | 250 | 250 | 0 | 750 | 0 | 750 | 0 | 750 |
| B INV | 0 | INV | 0 | 0 | 0 | 0 | 0 | 0 | 0 | 0 | 0 | 0 | 0 | 0 |
| -ADJ | 0 | POS | 0 | 0 | 0 | 0 | 0 | 0 | 0 | 0 | 0 | 0 | 0 | 0 |
| E INV | 0 | | | | | | | | | | | | | |
| | | INV $ | 0 | 0 | 0 | 0 | 0 | 0 | 0 | 0 | 0 | 0 | 0 | 0 |

## FIGURE 5
## DOLLAR SUMMARY FOR SPECIAL PRODUCT GROUP

BEG INV $ 25,445 END INV $ 19,312

S/D INV $ -6,133 BACKORDERS $ 28,446

| | FORECAST DOLLARS | | | PRODUCTION | INVENTORY DOLLARS | | |
|---|---|---|---|---|---|---|---|
| PERIOD | DOMESTIC | INT'L | TOTAL | | SFTY STK | SS + LS/2 | END INV |
| JAN | 44,727 | 7,952 | 52,679 | 45,569 | 18,755 | 46,920 | 24,235 |
| FEB | 44,727 | 7,952 | 52,679 | 87,630 | 18,755 | 46,920 | 33,117 |
| MAR | 44,727 | 7,952 | 52,679 | 94,057 | 18,755 | 46,920 | 60,087 |
| APR | 48,425 | 8,141 | 56,566 | 35,006 | 18,569 | 46,734 | 38,526 |
| MAY | 48,425 | 8,141 | 56,566 | 56,331 | 18,569 | 46,734 | 38,291 |
| JUN | 48,425 | 8,141 | 56,566 | 62,270 | 18,569 | 46,734 | 43,994 |
| J-A-S | 128,001 | 24,992 | 152,993 | 166,402 | 18,477 | 46,642 | 57,404 |
| O-N-D | 139,095 | 25,560 | 164,655 | 153,606 | 18,290 | 46,456 | 46,354 |
| J-F-M | 121,822 | 26,128 | 147,950 | 148,097 | 18,199 | 46,364 | 46,501 |
| A-M-J | 132,916 | 26,696 | 159,612 | 153,606 | 18,012 | 46,177 | 40,494 |
| J-A-S | 115,643 | 27,264 | 142,907 | 148,097 | 17,920 | 46,086 | 45,684 |
| O-N-D | 126,738 | 27,832 | 154,570 | 162,565 | 17,734 | 45,899 | 53,679 |

# APPENDIX O
# UNLOADING THE OVERLOADED MASTER PRODUCTION SCHEDULE*

Can a master scheduler unload a front-end loaded master production schedule (MPS) and keep his/her job? Even if one's job is not in jeopardy, such a problem can cause headaches, frustrations, and missed customer deliveries. Sunbell Corporation in Albuquerque, New Mexico, was confronted with an overloaded master production schedule. Through careful analysis and planning, a way was found to unload the MPS; eliminate the headaches and frustrations; and create a realistic schedule that people trusted and executed.

## PROFILE OF SUNBELL PRODUCTS

Sunbell has three divisions—a moccasin and doll division on the Ogalala Sioux Indian Reservation in Pine Ridge, South Dakota; a jewlery division; and a decorative copper division, Gregorian Copper. The jewelry and copper divisions are located in Albuquerque.

Since Gregorian Copper was subject to the overload problem which will be discussed, a little background on the production process of this division follows. Gregorian copper is manufactured from a roll of heavy gauge, solid copper. After five or six press operations, i.e., blanking, chopping, trimming, deep drawing, and spinning on a lathe, the raw material is turned into a component part. Some component parts are soldered to form stock numbers. After forming, soldering, and assembling the component parts and subassemblies, the finished product is sent through four more operations before it is complete. First, a chemical treatment process called oxidizing darkens the finish. Next, the item goes to the polishing area where it is given a bright, polished finish to produce a soft, warm color contrast. Then it is lacquered and baked under intense heat to produce a protective finish. Finally, the item is ready to be wrapped and sent to the finished goods area. Following this procedure, such products as kettles, mugs, trays, bases, candelabra, bowls, serving pieces, and other decorative items for the living room, den, kitchen, and patio are produced. Total manufacturing lead time from

---

*John J. Civerolo, *Production and Inventory Management*, Vol. 21, No. 4 (1980), pp. 1-10. (Reprinted by permission of the American Production and Inventory Control Society.)

raw material to finished product is 16 weeks. This time is broken down into five weeks for raw materials, three weeks for component parts, and eight weeks for assembly into a finished product. Customers expect delivery in two weeks.

# Overloaded Master Production Schedule

It became clear that Gregorian had an overload problem for two reasons. First, Marketing had originally made a forecast based on sales estimates for the coming fiscal year. As actual sales were tracked and compared to the forecast, the forecast error showed that the actual forecast, recalculated monthly for the complete year, was running 25 percent over the original projections made by Marketing (Figure 1; all figures are shown on pages 644-647).

Second, the Summary MPS Report by groups of items showed that the scheduled receipts amount past due or due in the month of May exceeded the company's current production capabilities. Gregorian Copper was producing between 14,000 -16,000 pieces per month. However, Figure 2, under the scheduled receipts column, clearly indicated that the past due receipts plus the May scheduled receipts equaled 25,000 pieces. This total clearly outstripped the company's capacity.

Certain activities were hampering production efforts. Handwritten priority "hot lists" were being generated by shipping personnel and sent to the foremen on the shop floor, causing confusion as to what was really needed and conflicting with the shop floor information provided daily to the foremen. (This daily information will be explained later in the article.)

There were hurried calls from Marketing to Production Control to find out when an item would be finished or how long it would take to have the item assembled and expedited. Expeditors were running from department to department chasing jobs and telling foremen to hurry up. Everything in the division was past due—component parts, subassemblies, and finished items. Manufacturing personnel had become accustomed to these informal procedures. Productivity was dropping, and inventory was building as more pieces were being expedited than were needed to satisfy an order. This was evident in a certain group of items—the expeditors would push 200 pieces of an item through the plant, but would really only need 25. The rest would remain in inventory. These informal activities were becoming very expensive and time consuming. As a result, headaches and frustrations mounted. A solution had to be found!

Sunbell had already determined that the forecast (bookings) plus backlog (orders in the house) exceeded the current capacity. Production capability had to be determined. The master scheduler met with marketing representatives to determine how to schedule in-house orders for shipment. Marketing provided specific customer service objectives to follow in order to meet order shipping dates. They were:

1. Ship to preferential customers first. (Marketing provided a list of these customers.)
2. Ship orders requesting a specific shipping date.
3. Maintain a service level of 85 percent or greater.
4. Process back orders within three weeks.
5. Process immediate orders, i.e., those without specific shipping dates, within a week and a half.

After receiving Marketing's input, the plant manager, production supervisor, and master scheduler decided on a production plan for the next ten weeks. However, the production plan required to meet customer service objectives proved unrealistic because it exceeded a current capacity. The bottleneck appeared to be in one area—polishing. Capacity had to be increased.

## Unloading the Overloaded Schedule

The following alternatives to increase polishing capacity were considered:

1. Overtime
2. Additional personnel
3. Additional shifts
4. Purchase of additional machinery for polishing
5. A combination of the foregoing

Each of these solutions were considered in great depth. Financial constraints made it impossible to procure additional machine capacity. Overtime of one hour per day and a four-hour shift on Saturday was not enough to meet the production plan. Adding a shift and more personnel presented another problem—training. Twelve additional people would have been required in the polishing area immediately to increase capacity to meet the plan. Since the polishing area required trained personnel to polish the different types of complex items, the necessary training could not be accomplished in a short period.

Subsequently, an alternative production plan was proposed that required a revision of customer objectives set by Marketing. The new objectives allowed:

1. A service level of 80 percent
2. Four weeks, instead of three, to process back orders
3. Immediate orders, i.e., those without specific shipping dates, to be processed within 2 to 2½ weeks.
4. Customers with specific shipping dates within the next ten weeks to be contacted to see if a partial shipment could be made or if the original date could be moved back.

In some cases, Marketing adjusted the priority of orders daily. With one hour of overtime per day and four hours on Saturday, plus two additional people added to the polishing area every two weeks over a three-month time period, the revised production plan, Figure 3, was challenging but possible.

At last, Gregorian Copper had a production plan that everyone in the company found agreeable. Now came the arduous task of revising the MPS to correspond to the production plan. The revised customer service objectives had to be specifically translated into individual MPS stock number adjustments. The master scheduler and a production planner started by looking at the bookings (forecast), gross requirements, and backlog for each stock number in the Gregorian line (Figure 4).

Each stock number had to be analyzed to see the amount of change necessary and which weeks had to have their gross requirements reduced or increased. The scheduled receipts then had to be rescheduled. A total of 168 stock numbers had to be adjusted. This process took the master scheduler and production planner twelve hours each to accomplish. The revised MPS was fed into MRP and the production planners rescheduled the subassemblies, component parts, and raw materials to conform to the new MPS.

Once all the changes had been made on the MPS and scheduled receipts had their work order due dates rescheduled, it was necessary to make sure the foremen understood and worked to the department due dates on their daily work report (Figure 5). This report is generated from the shop floor control system.

This shop floor control system was not included in the original MPS and MRP system design. What we failed to do originally was close the loop. This failure proved a serious mistake. As a result of the exclusion of this reporting system, work order due dates were constantly missed. The implementation of this system completed all the necessary ties required for a closed-loop MRP system.

The shop floor control system takes the order due dates assigned by MRP and, using the routing file, assigns department due dates.

It was initially important that the foremen start to use and believe in the schedule. No deviations were allowed. This meant that the generation of all hot lists and priority lists from Shipping and Marketing were stopped. If an item was required sooner than its current due date, the master scheduler or a production planner was asked to change the date. The plant manager and the production supervisor monitored the schedule daily to make sure that the foremen met the schedule.

It was equally important that all data fed the foremen's daily report was accurate and valid. Educational classes were held by the master scheduler and production supervisor for the foremen. The foremen's reports were reviewed to ensure that they understood the information contained in this report and communicated any problems to the correct personnel. The production schedule was tracked daily. Should any conditions arise that would cause the schedule to be missed—such as scrap, rework, data keying errors, or due dates not being followed—these conditions were corrected as soon as possible to keep the schedule valid.

# RESULTS

The results were exceptional. The overload problem was corrected with the following improvements:

1. A 93 percent service level was achieved and maintained.
2. All existing back orders were filled.
3. The back order level dropped to zero for three weeks and then rose to a mere 7 percent.
4. Immediate orders, orders without specific shipping dates, were shipped in five working days or less.
5. The orders with specific shipping dates were meeting scheduled shipping dates.

The sales volume continued to run 25 percent above the original forecast.

The same results can be achieved by any company with an overloaded MPS if these steps are followed:

1. Marketing must be involved and must make a realistic commitment as to how the orders are to be shipped.

2. Manufacturing must do all it can to meet Marketing's needs. If this is impossible, then negotiate with Marketing. Once a compromise is reached, it must be expressed in the production plan.
3. Translate the production plan into the Master Production Schedule.
4. The foremen must understand what is expected of them and their daily reports must be accurate and valid.
5. The schedule must be tracked daily, or at least weekly, to make sure that the plan is being executed.

When these commitments are made and followed, it is easy to see how a company can unload an overloaded master production schedule. Following this plan will enable the master scheduler to keep his/her job, shipping dates and minimize frustration by meeting on time.

**FIGURE 1**
**MARKETING FORECAST VERSUS ACTUAL FORECAST**

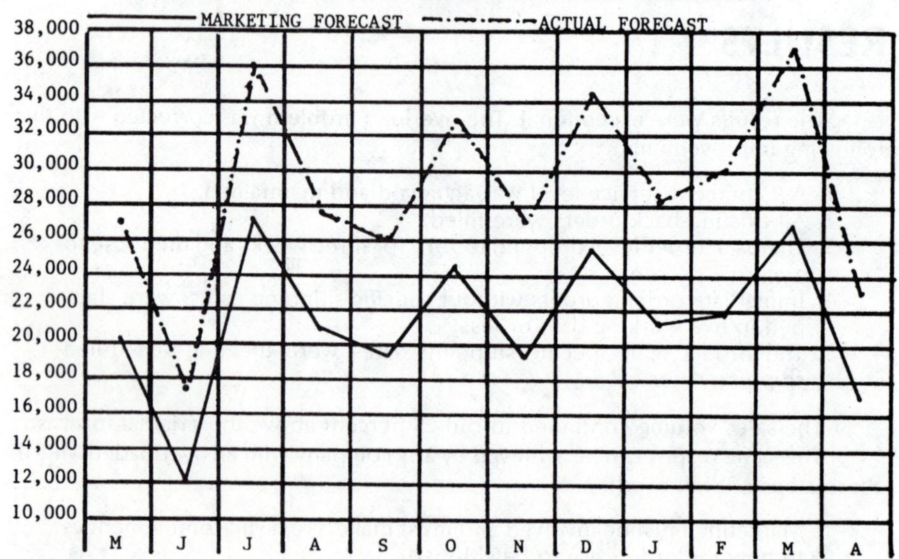

## FIGURE 2
## GRAND TOTAL OF MPS SUMMARY

Date 5/07/79 GRAND TOTAL OF MPS SUMMARY FOR ALL METAL/CATEGORY - GREG- Page 25
BEGINNING 1OH 23,429

| | BOOKINGS | BACKLOG | GROSS REQUIREMENTS | PROJECTED ON-HAND | SCHEDULED RECEIPTS | PLANNED ORDER RECEIPTS |
|---|---|---|---|---|---|---|
| PAST DUE (4/30/79) | $ 0 | $ 3,743 | $ 3,743 | $ 5,253 | $ 5,348 | $ 0 |
| MAY | $ 22,420 | $13,355 | $ 22,958 | $21,868 | $19,792 | $ 0 |
| JUNE | $ 25,480 | $ 361 | $ 16,552 | $25,422 | $20,006 | $ 100 |
| JULY | $ 29,665 | $ 1,174 | $ 36,029 | $23,548 | $33,055 | $ 1,100 |
| AUGUST | $ 33,244 | $ 217 | $ 27,301 | $16,646 | $ 2,299 | $ 18,100 |
| SEPTEMBER | $ 29,172 | $ 25 | $ 26,149 | $16,180 | $ 462 | $ 25,221 |
| OCTOBER | $ 25,995 | $ 0 | $ 32,665 | $17,512 | $ 707 | $ 33,290 |
| NOVEMBER | $ 23,568 | $ 0 | $ 26,503 | $19,181 | $ 298 | $ 27,879 |
| DECEMBER | $ 19,160 | $ 0 | $ 34,545 | $17,941 | $ 30 | $ 33,275 |
| JANUARY | $ 35,376 | $ 0 | $ 27,636 | $13,425 | $ 0 | $ 23,120 |
| FEBRUARY | $ 37,356 | $ 30 | $ 23,160 | $12,625 | $ 0 | $ 27,360 |
| MARCH | $ 36,530 | $ 0 | $ 37,015 | $12,110 | $ 0 | $ 36,500 |
| APRIL | $ 20,742 | $ 0 | $ 22,209 | $12,355 | $ 104 | $ 22,350 |
| GRAND TOTALS | $343,728 | $19,401 | $341,470 | | $82,101 | $248,295 |

## FIGURE 3
## MARKETING FORECAST VERSUS ACTUAL FORECAST (REVISED PLAN)

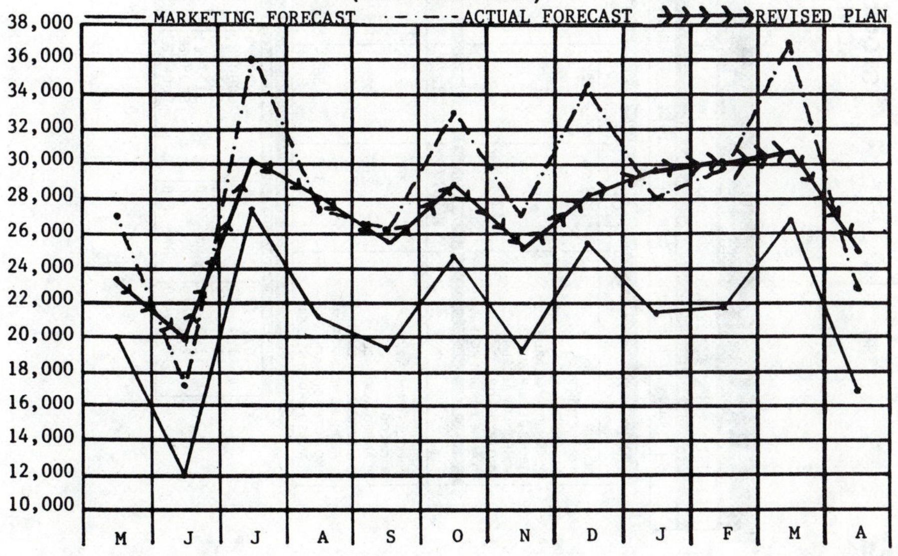

# FIGURE 4
## STOCK NUMBER EXAMINED BY MASTER SCHEDULER PRODUCTION PLANNER

| PART NUMBER | DESCRIPTION | U/M | TYPE | A.B.C. | UNIT PRICE | METAL CODE | CAT. CODE | DIV. CODE | L.T. CODE | MFG. L.T. | PUR. L.T. | ORDER QTY. | MIN. QTY. | MUL. QTY. |
|---|---|---|---|---|---|---|---|---|---|---|---|---|---|---|
| 421C | CANDELABRA | EA | 5 | B | | 05 | 70 | G | M | 40 | | 0 | 500 | 0 |

| MAX. QTY. | SHRINKAGE | PEG? | HORIZON | L.T. FENCE | JOB LOT SIZE | | | | |
|---|---|---|---|---|---|---|---|---|---|
| 0 | 000 | N | 000 | 080 | 15 | 1 EXPEDITE. 06 | 2 | 3 | 4 |

| | | PAST DUE | CURRENT WEEK | WEEK OF | WEEK OF | WEEK OF | WEEK OF | WEEK OF | WEEK OF | WEEK OF | WEEK OF | WEEK OF |
|---|---|---|---|---|---|---|---|---|---|---|---|---|
| | | 9/10/79 | 9/17/79 | 9/24/79 | 10/01/79 | 10/08/79 | 10/15/79 | 10/22/79 | 10/29/79 | 11/05/79 | 11/12/79 | 11/19/79 |
| BOOKINGS | | | 210 | 210 | 164 | 164 | 164 | 164 | 164 | 210 | 210 | 210 |
| PRODUCTION PLAN | | | | | | | | | | 127 | 150 | 150 |
| **BACKLOG** | | | 86 | | 4 | | | 19 | 4 | 20 | | |
| PLANNED AVAILABLE | | | | | | | | 33 | 29 | 9 | 9 | 289 |
| GROSS REQUIREMENTS | | | 86 | | 4 | | | 19 | 4 | 147 | 150 | 150 |
| SCHEDULED RECEIPTS | | | | | | | | 45 | | | | 280 |
| **PROJECTED ON HAND** | 81 | 81 | 5- | 5- | 9- | 9- | 9- | 17 | 13 | 134- | 284- | 154- |
| PLANNED ORDER RELEASE | | | | | | | 500 | | 500 | | 500 | |

| | WEEK OF | WEEK OF | WEEK OF | WEEK OF | WEEK OF | WEEK OF | WEEK OF | WEEK OF | WEEK OF | WEEK OF | WEEK OF |
|---|---|---|---|---|---|---|---|---|---|---|---|
| | 11/26/79 | 12/03/79 | 12/10/79 | 12/17/79 | 12/24/79 | 12/31/79 | 1/07/80 | 1/14/80 | 1/21/80 | 1/28/80 | 2/04/80 |
| BOOKINGS | 210 | 99 | 99 | 99 | 99 | 99 | 236 | 236 | 236 | 236 | 276 |
| PRODUCTION PLAN | 205 | 205 | 205 | 205 | 223 | 223 | 223 | 223 | 223 | 223 | 223 |
| **BACKLOG** | | 3 | | | | | | | | | |
| PLANNED AVAILABLE | 289 | 286 | 486 | 486 | 986 | 1186 | 1686 | 1686 | 2186 | 2186 | 2686 |
| GROSS REQUIREMENTS | 205 | 208 | 205 | 205 | 223 | 223 | 223 | 223 | 223 | 223 | 223 |
| SCHEDULED RECEIPTS | | | 200 | | | 200 | | | | | |
| **PROJECTED ON HAND** | 359- | 567- | 72- | 277- | 0 | 23- | 254 | 31 | 192- | 85 | 138- |
| PLANNED ORDER RELEASE | | 500 | | 500 | | 500 | | 500 | | | 500 |

| SCHEDULED RECEIPTS | | | | | | | | | | | | | | |
|---|---|---|---|---|---|---|---|---|---|---|---|---|---|---|
| DUE DATE | QUANTITY | SCRAP | ORDER NUMBER | S | DUE DATE | QUANTITY | SCRAP | ORDER NUMBER | S | DUE DATE | QUANTITY | SCRAP | ORDER NUMBER | S |
| 10/22/79 | 45 | | S000281 | A | 12/31/79 | 100 | | S000285 | A | | | | | |
| 11/19/79 | 80 | | S000283 | A | 12/31/79 | 100 | | S000286 | A | | | | | |
| 11/19/79 | 100 | | S000284 | A | 2/11/80 | 100 | | S177120 | A | | | | | |
| 11/19/79 | 100 | | S177121 | A | 2/11/80 | 95 | | S178149 | A | | | | | |
| 12/10/79 | 100 | | S000282 | A | | | | | | | | | | |
| 12/10/79 | 100 | | S000287 | A | | | | | | | | | | |

PLANNER CODE **F**

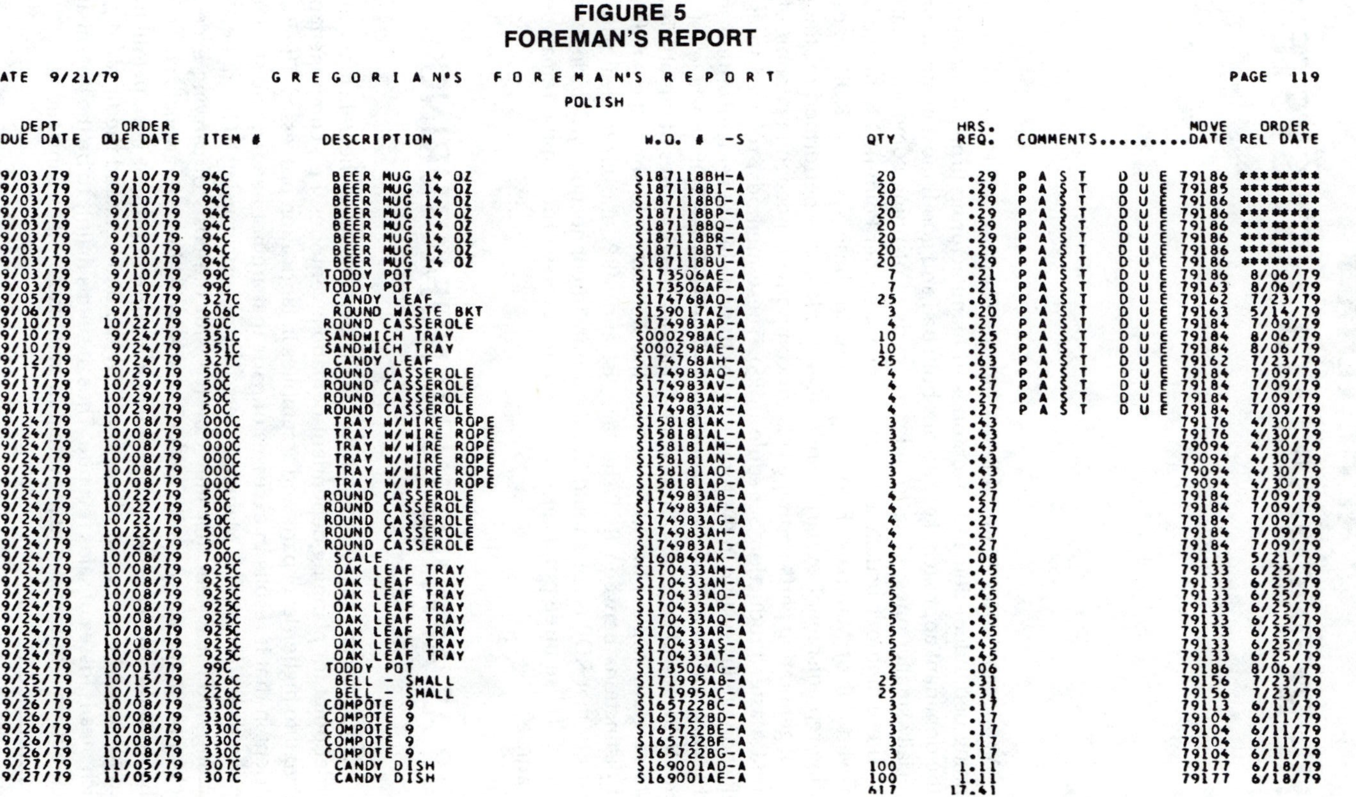

**FIGURE 5**
**FOREMAN'S REPORT**

DATE 9/21/79     G R E G O R I A N'S   F O R E M A N'S   R E P O R T     PAGE 119

POLISH

| DEPT DUE DATE | ORDER DUE DATE | ITEM # | DESCRIPTION | W.O. # -S | QTY | HRS. REQ. | COMMENTS.......... | MOVE DATE | ORDER REL DATE |
|---|---|---|---|---|---|---|---|---|---|
| 9/03/79 | 9/10/79 | 94C | BEER MUG 14 OZ | S187118BH-A | 20 | .29 | P A S T D U E | 79186 | ******** |
| 9/03/79 | 9/10/79 | 94C | BEER MUG 14 OZ | S187118BI-A | 20 | .29 | P A S T D U E | 79185 | ******** |
| 9/03/79 | 9/10/79 | 94C | BEER MUG 14 OZ | S187118BO-A | 20 | .29 | P A S T D U E | 79186 | ******** |
| 9/03/79 | 9/10/79 | 94C | BEER MUG 14 OZ | S187118BP-A | 20 | .29 | P A S T D U E | 79186 | ******** |
| 9/03/79 | 9/10/79 | 94C | BEER MUG 14 OZ | S187118BQ-A | 20 | .29 | P A S T D U E | 79186 | ******** |
| 9/03/79 | 9/10/79 | 94C | BEER MUG 14 OZ | S187118BR-A | 20 | .29 | P A S T D U E | 79186 | ******** |
| 9/03/79 | 9/10/79 | 94C | BEER MUG 14 OZ | S187118BT-A | 20 | .29 | P A S T D U E | 79186 | ******** |
| 9/03/79 | 9/10/79 | 94C | BEER MUG 14 OZ | S187118BU-A | 20 | .29 | P A S T D U E | 79186 | ******** |
| 9/03/79 | 9/10/79 | 99C | TODDY POT | S173506AE-A | 7 | .21 | P A S T D U E | 79186 | 8/06/79 |
| 9/03/79 | 9/10/79 | 99C | TODDY POT | S173506AF-A | 7 | .21 | P A S T D U E | 79163 | 8/06/79 |
| 9/05/79 | 9/17/79 | 327C | CANDY LEAF | S174768AO-A | 25 | .63 | P A S T D U E | 79162 | 7/23/79 |
| 9/06/79 | 9/17/79 | 606C | ROUND WASTE BKT | S159017AZ-A | 3 | .20 | P A S T D U E | 79163 | 5/14/79 |
| 9/10/79 | 10/22/79 | 50C | ROUND CASSEROLE | S174983AP-A | 4 | .27 | P A S T D U E | 79184 | 7/09/79 |
| 9/10/79 | 9/24/79 | 351C | SANDWICH TRAY | S000298AC-A | 10 | .25 | P A S T D U E | 79184 | 8/06/79 |
| 9/10/79 | 9/24/79 | 351C | SANDWICH TRAY | S000298AE-A | 10 | .25 | P A S T D U E | 79184 | 8/06/79 |
| 9/12/79 | 9/24/79 | 327C | CANDY LEAF | S174768AH-A | 25 | .63 | P A S T D U E | 79162 | 7/23/79 |
| 9/17/79 | 10/29/79 | 50C | ROUND CASSEROLE | S174983AQ-A | 4 | .27 | P A S T D U E | 79184 | 7/09/79 |
| 9/17/79 | 10/29/79 | 50C | ROUND CASSEROLE | S174983AV-A | 4 | .27 | P A S T D U E | 79184 | 7/09/79 |
| 9/17/79 | 10/29/79 | 50C | ROUND CASSEROLE | S174983AW-A | 4 | .27 | P A S T D U E | 79184 | 7/09/79 |
| 9/17/79 | 10/29/79 | 50C | ROUND CASSEROLE | S174983AX-A | 4 | .27 | P A S T D U E | 79184 | 7/09/79 |
| 9/24/79 | 10/08/79 | 000C | TRAY W/WIRE ROPE | S158181AK-A | 3 | .43 | | 79176 | 4/30/79 |
| 9/24/79 | 10/08/79 | 000C | TRAY W/WIRE ROPE | S158181AL-A | 3 | .43 | | 79176 | 4/30/79 |
| 9/24/79 | 10/08/79 | 000C | TRAY W/WIRE ROPE | S158181AM-A | 3 | .43 | | 79094 | 4/30/79 |
| 9/24/79 | 10/08/79 | 000C | TRAY W/WIRE ROPE | S158181AN-A | 3 | .43 | | 79094 | 4/30/79 |
| 9/24/79 | 10/08/79 | 000C | TRAY W/WIRE ROPE | S158181AO-A | 3 | .43 | | 79094 | 4/30/79 |
| 9/24/79 | 10/08/79 | 000C | TRAY W/WIRE ROPE | S158181AP-A | 3 | .43 | | 79094 | 4/30/79 |
| 9/24/79 | 10/22/79 | 50C | ROUND CASSEROLE | S174983AB-A | 4 | .27 | | 79184 | 7/09/79 |
| 9/24/79 | 10/22/79 | 50C | ROUND CASSEROLE | S174983AF-A | 4 | .27 | | 79184 | 7/09/79 |
| 9/24/79 | 10/22/79 | 50C | ROUND CASSEROLE | S174983AG-A | 4 | .27 | | 79184 | 7/09/79 |
| 9/24/79 | 10/22/79 | 50C | ROUND CASSEROLE | S174983AH-A | 4 | .27 | | 79184 | 7/09/79 |
| 9/24/79 | 10/22/79 | 50C | ROUND CASSEROLE | S174983AI-A | 4 | .27 | | 79184 | 7/09/79 |
| 9/24/79 | 10/08/79 | 700C | SCALE | S160849AK-A | 5 | .08 | | 79113 | 5/21/79 |
| 9/24/79 | 10/08/79 | 925C | OAK LEAF TRAY | S170433AM-A | 5 | .45 | | 79133 | 6/25/79 |
| 9/24/79 | 10/08/79 | 925C | OAK LEAF TRAY | S170433AN-A | 5 | .45 | | 79133 | 6/25/79 |
| 9/24/79 | 10/08/79 | 925C | OAK LEAF TRAY | S170433AO-A | 5 | .45 | | 79133 | 6/25/79 |
| 9/24/79 | 10/08/79 | 925C | OAK LEAF TRAY | S170433AP-A | 5 | .45 | | 79133 | 6/25/79 |
| 9/24/79 | 10/08/79 | 925C | OAK LEAF TRAY | S170433AQ-A | 5 | .45 | | 79133 | 6/25/79 |
| 9/24/79 | 10/08/79 | 925C | OAK LEAF TRAY | S170433AR-A | 5 | .45 | | 79133 | 6/25/79 |
| 9/24/79 | 10/08/79 | 925C | OAK LEAF TRAY | S170433AS-A | 5 | .45 | | 79133 | 6/25/79 |
| 9/24/79 | 10/08/79 | 925C | OAK LEAF TRAY | S170433AT-A | 5 | .45 | | 79133 | 6/25/79 |
| 9/24/79 | 10/01/79 | 99C | TODDY POT | S173506AG-A | 2 | .06 | | 79186 | 8/06/79 |
| 9/25/79 | 10/15/79 | 226C | BELL - SMALL | S171995AB-A | 25 | .31 | | 79156 | 7/23/79 |
| 9/25/79 | 10/15/79 | 226C | BELL - SMALL | S171995AC-A | 25 | .31 | | 79156 | 7/23/79 |
| 9/26/79 | 10/08/79 | 330C | COMPOTE 9 | S165722BC-A | 3 | .17 | | 79113 | 6/11/79 |
| 9/26/79 | 10/08/79 | 330C | COMPOTE 9 | S165722BD-A | 3 | .17 | | 79104 | 6/11/79 |
| 9/26/79 | 10/08/79 | 330C | COMPOTE 9 | S165722BE-A | 3 | .17 | | 79104 | 6/11/79 |
| 9/26/79 | 10/08/79 | 330C | COMPOTE 9 | S165722BF-A | 3 | .17 | | 79104 | 6/11/79 |
| 9/26/79 | 10/08/79 | 330C | COMPOTE 9 | S165722BG-A | 3 | .17 | | 79104 | 6/11/79 |
| 9/27/79 | 11/05/79 | 307C | CANDY DISH | S169001AD-A | 100 | 1.11 | | 79177 | 6/18/79 |
| 9/27/79 | 11/05/79 | 307C | CANDY DISH | S169001AE-A | 100 | 1.11 | | 79177 | 6/18/79 |
| | | | | | 617 | 17.41 | | | |

# APPENDIX P
# THE ROP/SHORTAGE LIST SYSTEM*

As widespread as Material Requirements Planning (MRP) has become for planning dependent-demand inventories in manufacturing firms, it may not yet be the dominant approach. For reasons both bad and good, most manufacturers, especially smaller ones, cling to older methods of planning component-part orders. These methods usually are some form of Reorder Point (ROP), in combination with Bill of Materials (BOM) explosion. In these systems, ROP plans for routine replenishment of parts, while BOM explosion is performed for the purpose of generating parts-shortage lists for components needed in support of the current Master Production Schedule (MPS). These methods, referred to as the ROP/shortage list system in the remainder of this article, are seldom written about and seem poorly understood (except by old-timers). Since ROP/shortage list continues to be in wide use, it warrants our attention. The purposes of this article are: (1) to carefully explain the ROP/shortage list system, (2) to show the similarities and distinctions between ROP/shortage list and MRP, and (3) to deal with the half-truth that ROP is, or should be, used only in connection with independent demand. These three points are discussed, in reverse order, in the remainder of the article.

## ROP AS APPLIED IN MANUFACTURING

Orlicky [1] and many others have clearly demonstrated the deficiency of the reorder point for planning dependent-demand inventories, i.e., component parts that go into higher-level parts and assemblies in fabrication processes. The ROP is deficient in that it results in excesses of parts that are not needed and stock-outs of parts that are needed. Manufacturers that persist in using ROP (rather than adopting MRP) may feel that they can live with the costs of carrying excesses. Stock-outs, on the other hand, may not be so easily ignored, rationalized or lived with. Stock-outs of parts not only result in idle work-in-process (i.e., parent items idled for lack of a part), but ultimately delay the end item and the finished good which means losses of sales revenue. Thus, it seems mainly to be the potential for stock-outs that indicts the ROP system in manufacturing organizations.

---

*Richard J. Schonberger, *Production and Inventory Management*, Vol. 21, No. 4 (1980), pp. 106-117. (Reprinted by permission of the American Production and Inventory Control Society.)

## Shortage Lists

But the many manufacturers who use ROP rarely use it alone (as a retailer, or wholesaler, or office storeroom will). In manufacturing, the ROP system generally is linked to BOM explosion for the purpose of producing a parts-shortage list. In the ROP/shortage list system, ROP provides for routine replenishment of parts, and shortage lists try to compensate for the ROP failures. That is, shortage lists state what parts are in short supply—and in what quantities—relative to the next time bucket on the MPS.

The means of producing shortage lists is BOM explosion of MPS end items into a parts-needed listing, followed by subtraction of parts on hand, (as indicated in the item master file) from parts needed. The method is identical with MRP processing. (Old-timers would refer to the ROP/shortage list approach simply as Bill of Materials explosion. Since MRP also includes BOM explosion, that term is no longer precise enough.) In fact, net requirements in MRP are equivalent to parts shortages in shortage-list generation. The key difference is that MRP generates net requirement based on MPS quantities extending out into the future by the maximum cumulative lead time, while parts shortage lists are produced at the last minute in support of the current MPS. Last-minute notice of parts shortages, of course, requires expediting or parts chasing which the advance-planning feature of MRP is able to minimize.

## Late Orders

MRP would seem to be more effective than ROP/shortage list in assuring that the right parts are there to meet order due dates, because expediting to chase down parts on a shortage or hot list will fail relatively often. The superiority of MRP to provide needed parts is most pronounced where the number of parts per end item is large and where BOMs are deep. In such cases of complex end products, shortages of only a few parts can shut down large blocks of capacity and perhaps result in losses of a good deal of sales revenue.

In the case of simpler end products the advantage of MRP over ROP/ shortage list is not so clear. In such cases, when expediters fail to obtain a shortage-list item, only a small number of other parts in the related BOM are delayed. A part that is in the BOM's for numerous products (like polyethelene powder used in plastics molding/extrusion) would rarely appear on a shortage list, because the ROP for such an item would include a large safety stock. (Also, the purchasing department would go to great lengths to assure reliable suppliers.)

Thus, it seems that the ROP/shortage list system may usually protect against serious failures to deliver end items on time—if the company products are not complex.

## Excess Inventories

ROP/shortage list may also be compared with MRP on the basis of inventory excess when ROP/shortage list system inevitably results in too much inventory, since ROP routinely replenishes component parts stocks regardless of whether or not there are parts requirements derived from master production schedules. Such excess inventory is avoidable through proper or full use of MRP. But many operating MRP systems are inadequately supported. Weaknesses in demand forecasting, master scheduling, BOM structuring, integrity of inventory records, and so forth, can cause the MRP system also to result in excess inventories. Developing an MRP system requires a large commitment of funds and attention, a commitment that smaller manufacturers especially may feel is unwarranted, in view of the number of MRP systems that have failed to live up to expectations. Thus, the ROP/shortage list system, which for many manufacturers has been in operation for many years, survives.

# THE MODERN COMPUTER-BASED ROP/SHORTAGE LIST SYSTEM

In the preceding discussion, the term ROP/shortage list was introduced; the approach was briefly described and contrasted with MRP; and reasons why many manufacturers continue to use the ROP/shortage list were suggested. A more detailed look at ROP/shortage list—as it is applied in the modern firm with computer processing—seems warranted. There are several reasons why the full story about the ROP/shortage list deserves to be told, including:

1. ROP/shortage list plants may still be in the majority and perhaps will be for years to come.
2. Many companies that have an MRP system use it for some plants or divisions or product lines but not others; and perhaps for job-lot production but not flow-shop, custom orders; and perhaps for job-lot production but not flow-shop, custom orders, or service-part business. There is a need to promote understanding of the hybrid system: part MRP and part ROP/shortage list.
3. Full appreciation for and deep understanding of MRP-based production and inventory control may be possible only by also having full understanding of important alternative systems, especially ROP/shortage list.

The following discussion begins with a summary of similarities and distinctive differences between computer-based ROP/shortage list and MRP. The summary is followed by a detailed illustration of computer processing steps under each approach, as applied to a particular hypothetical assembly and its component parts.

## Summary of Similarities and Differences

ROP/shortage list was in wide use before the computer era; it was an early and common application on unit-record equipment (which uses punched cards, tabulators, and printers), circa 1950. With the introduction of business computers in the 1960s, ROP/shortage list was among the first major applications (along with payroll and bookkeeping) to be converted to computers—well before computer-based MRP was introduced.

Computer-based inventory planning in factories includes several common steps regardless of whether MRP or ROP/shortage list is used:

1. An MPS is set up manually and loaded into the computer.
2. A computer file containing BOM's is referred to for each end item on the MPS.
3. A computer program explodes BOMs into gross parts requirements.
4. On hand balances in the computerized item master file are subtracted from gross requirements.
5. The result is called *net requirements* in MRP and a *shortage list* in the ROP/shortage list system.

There are major differences in how the above steps are used in MRP and ROP/shortage list. Key differences are:

1. In MRP, five steps are used to plan virtually all parts for fabrication. But the five steps comprise only the shortage list element of the MRP/shortage list system—an element used only to plan exceptions. The other element, ROP, "plans" the vast majority of parts orders, and exceptions—parts badly needed for the current time bucket—appear on the latest shortage list.
2. In MRP the five steps are used for planning net requirements for (usually) 52 weeks into the future. In ROP/shortage list the five steps are used to plan a shortage list for only the current time bucket (e.g., next week).

An example of component parts planning for a pencil sharpener module serves to illustrate these points.

# Example

Figures 1 and 2 show two methods of planning orders for parts to go into a pencil sharpener module. Figure 1 shows an assembly diagram for the module, a shavings receptacle, and it includes a step-by-step example of how many parts might be ordered for the module using the ROP/shortage list system. Figure 2 is a contrasting step-by-step discussion of the same planning situation, except using MRP.

A major difference is made apparent in point number 1 of the two figures: Each calls for an MPS and exploding the BOM. But in Figure 1 the result is a parts shortage list for the next week only, and in Figure 2 it is planned order releases for 52 weeks.

Next compare Step 2. On Monday morning the shortage list becomes a hot list, which is turned over to expeditors. But on Monday morning in the MRP case, planned order releases that are in the current time bucket (number 1) are calmly turned over to scheduling (for made parts) or purchasing (for bought parts).

Steps 3 through 6 are the same in the two figures. Parts are made or bought (Step 3). Parts made or bought are counted, and the count is entered as an addition to the on hand balance in the item master file (Step 4). Parts needed to go into a parent (the shavings module in this case) are withdrawn from storage and delivered to the proper work center (Step 5). Parts issued are deducted from the on-hand balance in the item master file (Step 6). With these steps, all inventory records are updated for next week's run.

**FIGURE 1**
**INVENTORY PLANNING VIA ROP AND SHORTAGE LISTS, PENCIL SHARPENER MODULE**

ROP/Shortage-List Steps

1. Over the weekend, the computer explodes the bill of materials for each end item appearing next week on the master production schedule. The result is a parts shortage list. A portion of the explosion process is shown below for a module that goes into a pencil sharpener.

| | Parts Needed - | | Parts Available = | | Parts Short |
|---|---|---|---|---|---|
| | | | In Stock | On Order | |
| Subassembly | 600 | Shavings modules | | 600 | |
| Component Parts | 600 | Molded plastic shavings receptacle | 500 | | 100 |
| | 600 | Stamped metal end plate | 1500 | | |
| | 1200 | Screw | 1400 | | |

Assembly diagram for shavings module

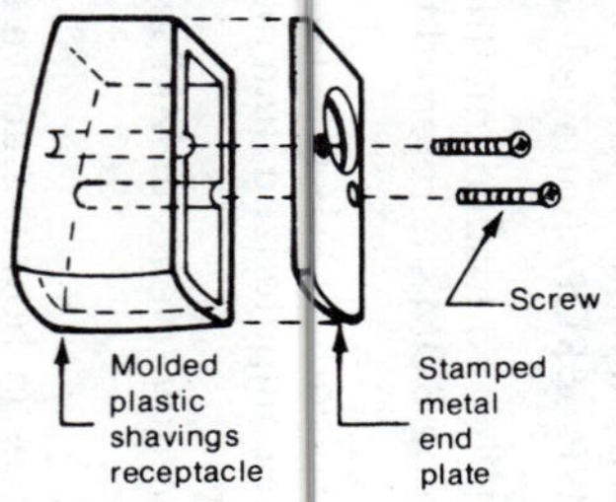

2. On Monday morning parts-shortage list becomes a hot list. Expeditors rush through a make order (or buy order) for hot items--the receptacle in this case.

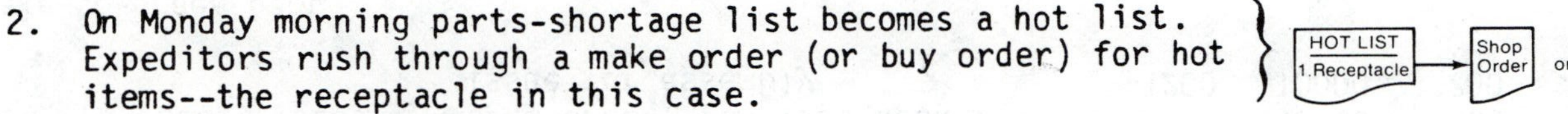


3. The receptacle is made (or bought) in a lot of 200 units.

4. Production counts (or purchased-part counts) are recorded as receipts in computer inventory records, thus increasing the balance in stock by 1200 receptacles and 600 shavings modules (less any that are scrapped).

5. All parts are withdrawn from storage and delivered to the work center where they are assembled.

6. Parts issued are recorded in inventory records, thus decreasing the balance in stock by 600 receptacles, 600 end plates and 1200 screws (plus any extras needed).

7. Stock record balances are compared with ROPs and:
   End plates are down to 300, which is below the ROP of 400, and therefore put on order in the lot size of 1200 (a normal order, not a special).
   Screws are already on order, in the lot size of 10000, as a result of reaching the ROP of 2000 last week.
   Shavings receptacle is above ROP of 400 and is not ordered.
   Shavings module is a make-to-order part and therefore is not replenished by ROP.

*(Continued on next page)*

Summary of Transactions Processed

| Part | ROP | Lot Size | Transaction | Receipts | Issues | On Order | On Hand | Balance |
|---|---|---|---|---|---|---|---|---|
| Shavings Module | * | * | Beginning balance | | | | 0 | 0 |
| | | | Assembly order | | | 600 | 0 | 600 |
| | | | Production count | +600 | | | 600 | 600 |
| Shavings Receptacle | 400 | 1200 | Beginning balance | | | | 500 | 500 |
| | | | Hot-List order | | | 1200 | 500 | 1700 |
| | | | Production (buy) count | +1200 | | | 1700 | 1700 |
| | | | Issue for assembly | | -600 | | 1100 | 1100 |
| End Plate | 400 | 1200 | Beginning balance | | | | 900 | 900 |
| | | | Issue for assembly | | -600 | | 300 | 300 |
| | | | Below ROP; place order | | | 1200 | 300 | 1500 |
| Screw | 2000 | 10000 | Open order from last week | | | 10000 | 1400 | 11400 |
| | | | Issue for assembly | | -1200 | 10000 | 200 | 10200 |

*A make-to-order part

In summary...

Parts are reordered in two ways:

1. The ROP way. This is the normal way for perhaps thousands of component parts. It is based on stock depletion and perpetual comparison with ROP.

2. The hot-list way. This is for the special exceptions--parts that the ROP process didn't provide on time or in the right amount. The hot list is revealed by the process of exploding the BOM.

NOTE: The hot list may also include parts that have reached their ROP and are on order but that need speeding up (which shows up via BOM explosion). For example, the screw for the shavings moduled reached its ROP last week. The order is in process, but the stock on hand is getting very low; the order could end up on the next hot list.

Step 7 is very different in the two figures. In ROP/shortage list, stock record balances are used for comparison with reorder points for every part in the item master file. (This may be done every day.) The usual ROP rule is followed: If the balance is below the ROP, order it. The ROP order is not based on the parent-item needs but on past usage. In MRP, stock record balances are used in next week's computer run to compute net requirements for parts to go into parents at a future date. Stock record balances serve a reference file purpose in both MRP and ROP/shortage list, but in ROP the reference data may trigger a current reaction but not future planning.

ROP/shortage list transactions are summarized after the seven steps in Figure 1, and samples of MRP outputs are shown to the right in Figure 2. The ROP/shortage list summary shows a beginning balance for the parent and each component. Orders, receipts, and issues are the transactions that change the status of the item in inventory records. Three types of orders are noted: (1) The shavings receptable appears on a shortage list and becomes a hot list order. (2) The end-plate balance falls below its ROP in the current period and becomes an ROP order. (3) The screw balance fell below its ROP last week, and it is an open order this week.

The samples of MRP outputs show a planned order release for 600 of the parent (module) in a future time bucket, Week 4 in the example. That quantity becomes the requirement for each of the three parts.

The summary at the bottom of Figure 1 shows why some writers have referred to this parts ordering system as a push-pull system: Orders for parts that have hit their ROPs are formally pushed out to the shop and to vendors, and hot orders for parts appearing on shortage lists are informally pulled through by expeditors [2]. But in smaller firms without data-processing power, expeditors do

## FIGURE 2
## INVENTORY PLANNING VIA MPS-MRP, PENCIL SHARPENER MODE

MRP Steps

1. Over the weekend, the computer explodes the bill of materials for each end item on the master production schedule for the next 52 weeks. MRP processing results in planned order releases. A portion of the MRP process is shown at the right for a module that goes into a pencil sharpener.

2. When the planned order release--for the shavings receptacle in this case--becomes current, the order is rescheduled and released to production (or purchasing).

3.
4. Steps 3-6 are the same
5. as in Figure 8-10.
6.

7. Stock record balances are used in next week's MRP run in computing net requirements.

In summary...

All parts orders are planned in the needed quantities and offset for lead time, via MRP.

*Sample MRP Outputs*

| Shavings module | | Week | | | | | | | |
|---|---|---|---|---|---|---|---|---|---|
| LT = 1 week | | 1 | 2 | 3 | 4 | 5 | 6 | 7 | 8 |
| Gross requirements | | 0 | 0 | 0 | 0 | 600 | 0 | 0 | 0 |
| Scheduled receipts | | | | | | | | | |
| On hand | 0 | 0 | 0 | 0 | 0 | 600 | 0 | 0 | 0 |
| Planned order release | | | | | 600 | | | | |

From POR, shavings module

| Shavings receptacle LT= 2 week; Q = 1200 | | | | | | | | | |
|---|---|---|---|---|---|---|---|---|---|
| Gross requirements | | 0 | 0 | 0 | 600 | 0 | 0 | 0 | 0 |
| Scheduled receipts | | | | | | | | | |
| On hand | 500 | 500 | 500 | 500 | 1100 | 1100 | 1100 | 1100 | 1100 |
| Planned order release | | | 1200 | | | | | | |

From POR, shavings module

| End plate LT = 2 weeks; Q = 1200 | | | | | | | | | |
|---|---|---|---|---|---|---|---|---|---|
| Gross requirements | | 0 | 0 | 0 | 600 | 0 | 0 | 0 | 0 |
| Scheduled receipts | | | | | | | | | |
| On hand | 900 | 900 | 900 | 900 | 300 | 300 | 300 | 300 | 300 |
| Planned order release | | | | | | | | | |

From POR, shavings module

| Screw LT = 3 weeks; Q = 10,000 | | | | | | | | | |
|---|---|---|---|---|---|---|---|---|---|
| Gross requirements | | 0 | 0 | 0 | 600 | 0 | 0 | 0 | 0 |
| Scheduled receipts | | | | | | | | | |
| On hand | 1400 | 1400 | 1400 | 1400 | 800 | 800 | 800 | 800 | 800 |
| Planned order release | | | | | | | | | |

not have benefit of a shortage list. They discover shortages in the stockroom when they try to assemble parts—referred to as staging—to meet a due date.

Figure 2 shows that in MRP a planned order matures (Step 2); that is, it moves toward the current week—instead of being pushed out to production on short notice. In MRP, orders are formally pushed onto production, but gently and with advance planning. A few orders may still have to be pulled by informal expediting. But the more common way of handling urgent orders is by formally rescheduling them—via MRP weekly updating—thereby avoiding expediting.

# CONCLUSION

In all of the diversity of the manufacturing sector there is room for more than one production and inventory control system. MRP-based systems can be effective for job-lot production in many industries. But MRP requires an investment in talent, equipment, training and time that many firms have not seen fit to expend. (There are always many other demands for investment.)

MRP may be hard to implement in an industry or firm without a history of technological innovation and advanced information systems development. (The fastest and smoothest MRP adoption by manufacturers in the author's geographical area was at Instrument Specialties Company which has a large staff of electronic engineers and computer scientists and a history of technological innovation. But in the same area several metals, plastics, woods, and pharmaceutical firms—which are not so accustomed to handling changes—had considerable difficulty in implementing MRP.) MRP is less necessary in firms that are regulated, are in oligopolistic positions, are highly protected by patents or otherwise free of heavy competition in the cost and customer service areas. In such cases ROP/shortage list may be justifiable—or if not justifiable, likely. It is too early for the practitioner, student, or teacher to turn his back on this older approach. Instead, perhaps there is justification and room for refining and promoting understanding of traditional systems, such as ROP/shortage list.

# REFERENCES

1. Joseph Orlicky, *Material Requirements Planning* (New York: McGraw-Hill Book Company, 1975), p. 37.
2. For example: Oliver Wight, *Production and Inventory Management in the Computer Age* (Boston, Mass.: Cahner Books, 1974).

# APPENDIX Q
# CHECKS AND BALANCES IN JOB SHOP CONTROL (OR WELCOME TO THE REAL WORLD)*

Otis Engineering Corporation is an approximately 300 million dollar company. There are 2,500 employees at the Dallas plant and 2,100 field employees throughout the world. We produce oilfield products and services. Otis operates in a job shop mode where the manufacturing function is oriented toward fast response and frequent production plan changes. We utilize an automated, fully integrated, manufacturing control system. Because Otis is oriented toward fast response and frequent production plan changes, we do not use a Master Production Schedule to drive our manufacturing operation. A statistical type forecast plus customer orders are used in place of a Master Production Schedule to drive the manufacturing operation. The total system is people oriented and relies heavily on everyone working efficiently within the strict conforms of a formal system.

Our plant produces items both for stock and to order. About half of the productive time is devoted to standard stock items for inventory replenishment and about half to non-standard items made to customer order. We have approximately 3,000 customer orders in house at any given time. These sales orders are for both customer orders and inventory. Part of our daily routine for our materials system is to gather all the transactions, update the various files, and perform MRP. After MRP, the files are again updated with the information generated by MRP. During the MRP process, the need to either purchase or manufacture merchandise is recognized. This results in shop orders being produced for those items to be manufactured and a buy list is produced for outside purchases.

The purpose of the Otis scheduling system is to commit manufacturing and purchasing resources to those orders that are most important to Otis and its customers. It serves as a shop model for predicting and maintaining timely delivery of customer orders. The degree of an order's importance is measured by a priority or sequence number. This number is based on customer required dates and ranges from 0 to 98,000 (see Figure 1; all figures are shown on pages 661-667). Line items on an order have the same priority as the order (see Figure 2). Second

---

*Bill Edwards and Margaret O'Neill, *Proceedings of the 21st Annual Conference of the American Production and Inventory Control Society* (1978), pp. 165-176. (Reprinted by permission of the American Production and Inventory Control Society.)

level bills of material items have a priority one greater than the order; third level items have a priority two greater than the order, and so on. Due to frequent changes in customer requirements, orders can be resequenced manually by assigning new priority numbers between two existing numbers (see Figure 3). It is common for an order to be resequenced up and down many times before it is shipped.

Currently, the Otis production scheduling system is processing approximately 21,000 manufacturing jobs with an average of 6 operations per job. Every night 126,000 operations are scheduled on Otis' 70 work centers for a period of twenty weeks. Rescheduling nightly gives the daily effect of changing manufacturing plant conditions and changing purchase part and raw material due in dates.

The manufacturing start or capacity search date is determined by the material availability date, or the required date minus the calculated lead time, whichever is later. The calculated lead time is equal to the sum of the set up times plus the sum of the run times plus the sum of the transit times plus work center queue times. Queue times are historical values for each work center.

Capacity tables are constructed for every work center, representing each day of the twenty week planning horizon(see Figure 4).

A great amount of effort is usually involved in the design and implementation of a computerized scheduling system, but often overlooked is the formidable effort required to measure and maintain the results. It must not be thought that a utopia exists and that every job can be run as scheduled with infallible accuracy because many dislocations do occur. The system should be used to assist in identifying the problems and delays and respond with the necessary action to correct. This can be accomplished through the use of simple (and reliable) daily reports and programs. The following text includes descriptions of reports generated by the computer for use in checking, auditing, and controlling the job shop with brief explanations of each.

An accurate scheduling system cannot be maintained without a basic, reliable shop work list. The list produced for the Otis shop (see Figure 5) is printed daily and reflects job status for a three (3) day period. The work list not only indicates which jobs are actually on the machine, but which jobs are ready to be worked next. Since priorities are unique for each job, it is a simple matter to determine which one should be run next. If for some reason the job with the highest priority has not arrived at the work center, the previous work center is also listed on the work list for location purposes.

Jobs will appear on a "Days On" list (see Figure 6) when they are not worked as scheduled. Production Control receives the list daily and a planner is assigned to audit jobs listed. Again, this is a basic list that will indicate the job and work center involved. After identifying the job it is usually a simple matter to determine and solve the problem. Occasionally, the problem is not that simple, but in any case the job has been identified and the planner will pursue it until appropriate action is taken. This list also assists in identifying queue problems especially at work centers that have a large number of jobs that are scheduled and have not been worked.

If a problem is known to exist on a job and cannot be solved immediately, it is necessary to code the job so that the appropriate department can take action. For example, it is discovered that a job scheduled to be worked on a N/C tape lathe does not have the tape ready. It is necessary to flag this job by inserting a simple letter code on a SRT problem. The codes generate a list that is received by the department responsible. In this case, it is the N/C Programming Department. Other problems might include engineering changes, tooling problems, or lost material.

As jobs are worked during the day, data collection transactions are made via terminals throughout the plant indicating job step completions and rejections. The transactions are updated three (3) times each day and a list is derived after each update indicating error type transactions (see Figure 7). A planner is assigned to correct these errors, which include wrong steps and quantity discrepancies. It is important that the errors are identified and corrected before the next update so that scheduling can be as accurate as possible.

So far, we have noted how Production Control uses a few simple reports to insure that the jobs keep moving as scheduled. But what about shop decisions and the attempt to balance the load? The Schedule Load/Capacity Report (see Figure 8) is received daily and is the main tool used in this process.

The report includes each work center group and indicates the capacity and finite load on a weekly basis. Also illustrated are current and future work plans. A section of this report (Figure 9) includes work available to be machined (in hours and days), total load, efficiency, utilization, and priority queue which indicates the number of jobs and hours in each priority segment. Using this report, load balancing, manpower, and overtime decisions can be made to insure a smooth flow of jobs through each work center.

When overloads or bottlenecks are discovered at any particular work center it may be necessary to select jobs for an alternate routing. A work center queue file list can be requested for this purpose (see Figure 10). This is a list of every job that is scheduled at a work center in priority sequence with alternates listed that have already been established. Other attractive jobs may be selected from this list that do not have established alternates and sent to N/C Programming or Manufacturing Engineering to be reviewed.

It has been discussed that through the use of a few key reports, the system can be monitored, checked, and balanced. There are CRT programs available to further monitor the system and also for information input and output.

If a particular work center requires work, a display is available that indicates jobs whose raw material or parts are available in inventory and has not been issued (see Figure 11). This is used primarily for gateway work centers whose available workload has been depleted.

During the course of each day it is necessary to change, add, or delete machine operations of jobs being worked in the shop. This may be due to more desirable or efficient alternates, workload balance, rework or data collection error corrections. The program used for this is called Job Detail Display (see Figure 12). If a job number is known, it can be called up and displayed at any time during the day and checked for location or status.

In some cases it may be desirable to list parts or raw material due in for a specified job. This is especially true when one is trying to search for the controlling or critical item on a final assembly. The Job Component Explosion display (see Figure 13) lists all items and due dates of items not on hand, including the item with the longest date. Again, all that is necessary to know is the job number.

The individual work center's basic work plan can also be updated and overridden using a program called Capacity Planning and Override Update (see Figure

14). This program is used primarily to change manpower or hours due to load requirements in order that scheduling reflect what is actually happening.

Otis is no different than most manufacturing concerns in that a "hot list" is used to expedite jobs (see Figure 15). This list is called the Critical Order Analysis and includes the top one hundred fifty (150) sales orders. The list illustrates the sales order number, the jobs needed to complete the order, the routing of each of the jobs, and the sequence number (priority number). This is just another simple tool used to keep the jobs moving and to insure that sales order dates are met.

The Otis scheduling system is only as good as the information available to it. The input of information and action in solving problems is essential in maintaining the customer requirement date. Any delay to a job can disrupt the original schedule date and cause customer dissatisfaction which results in lost sales orders.This is why it is not necessary to create output difficult to read and understand. Sophistication is necessary only in creating the system and maintaining the related programs. Identify the problems, but keep it simple. Welcome to the real world.

**FIGURE 1**

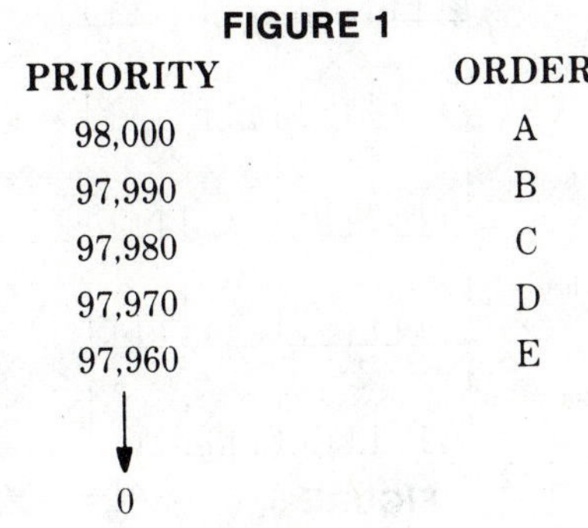

PRIORITY
ORDER
98,000
A
97,990
B
97,980
C
97,970
D
97,960
E
0


**FIGURE 2**

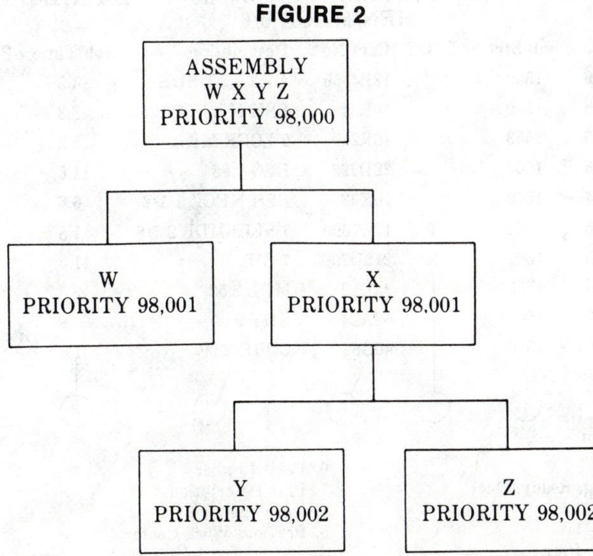

## FIGURE 3

| PRIORITY | ORDER | RESEQUENCED ORDER |
|---|---|---|
| 98,000 | A | |
| 97,995 | | Z |
| 97,990 | B | |
| 97,986 | | P |
| 97,984 | | Q |
| 97,980 | C | |
| 97,970 | D | |
| 97,960 | E | |
| ↓ | | |
| 0 | | |

## FIGURE 4

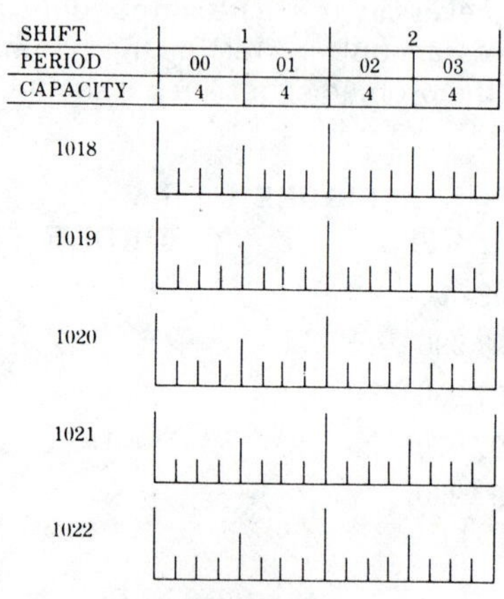


## FIGURE 5

### SHOP DATE 1559 3/7/77 WORK LIST FOR WC 30 N.C. LATHE-L & S MOD MEN/MACH 6/6

| Pty | ST | Job No | Sch Strt | TTQE | Part No | Description | Job Time | Prev WC |
|---|---|---|---|---|---|---|---|---|
| 690 | W | 634859 | 1559 | | 12P4556 | 4 1/2 RET SUB | 4.5 | 78 |
| 952 | W | 635215 | 1559 | | 10R34 | FSH NECK 2.125 | 3.3 | 30 |
| 876 | W | 635916 | 1559 | | 10R240 | 2 LOCK MDL | 15.2 | 78 |
| 774 | R | 634106 | 1560 | | 22D222 | HSG 1.88 | 11.5 | 53 |
| 786 | | 634494 | 1560 | | 10X33 | FSH NECK 1 1/2 | 6.8 | 78 |
| 754 | | 634530 | 1561 | T | 12R7090 | 7 SLIP MDL 2 7/8 | 1.8 | 78 |
| 750 | R | 635475 | 1561 | R | 212D7065 | 7 GID | 11.3 | 82 |
| 889 | R | 636634 | 1559 | | 33D12 | MDL 2.50 | 2.3 | 78 |
| 761 | | 773376 | 1561 | | 62A24 | BDY 2.50 | .9 | 78 |
| 762 | | 773586 | 1560 | | 40G83 | CORE 2.00 | 1.6 | 78 |
| (1) | (2) | (3) | (4) | (5) | (6) | (7) | (8) | (9) |

**Detail Description**

1. Priority
2. Status (Working, Ready, Due)
3. Job Number
4. Schedule Start Date
5. Tape or Tooling Flag
6. Part Number
7. Part Description
8. Job Time
9. Previous Work Center

## FIGURE 6

### SHOP DATE 1560 3/8/77 JOBS ON WORK LIST OVER 2 DAYS

| WC | Pty | Days On | ST | Job No | TTQE | Part No | Description |
|---|---|---|---|---|---|---|---|
| 16 | 848 | 3 | R | 634358 | | 41X275 | MN MDL 4.56 |
| 18 | 891 | 4 | R | 138605 | | 78D214 | HSG |
| 23 | 814 | 3 | R | 769479 | L | 521K112 | LWR BYP SHT |
| 25 | 878 | 3 | R | 634669 | | 31T509 | CPL |
| 28 | 932 | 3 | R | 772337 | N | 80P84 | WELD RING |
| 31 | 798 | 4 | R | 769762 | | 11X44 | 2.313 9CR LN |
| 33 | 893 | 3 | R | 769607 | | 44A98 | CAGE |
| 44 | 968 | 3 | R | 853599 | K | 47A90 | CENTRALIZER |
| (1) | (2) | (3) | (4) | (5) | (6) | (7) | (8) |

**Detail Description**

1. Work Center
2. Priority
3. Days on List Without Activity
4. Status
5. Job Number
6. Tape or Tooling Flag
7. Part Number
8. Part Description

## FIGURE 7

### 3/5/77 PRODUCTION ERROR AND ASSUMPTION REPORT

| Sta | Job No | TR | Stp | Qty | Badge | Time | WK-CCU | HM-CCU | Name | Error Message |
|---|---|---|---|---|---|---|---|---|---|---|
| 213 | 768528 | 11 | 070 | 0 | 3513 | 10.51 | 74 | 74 | VanZandt | BadQty = 1 Assum = 0 |
| 124 | 768630 | 12 | 035 | 7 | 6819 | 14.50 | 00 | 10 | Clark | BadStep = 030 Assum = 035 |
| 131 | 769397 | 11 | 030 | 24 | 5611 | 12.98 | 10 | 10 | Killion | BadQty = 28 Assum = 24 |
| 221 | 769879 | 12 | 030 | 0 | 6441 | 14.51 | 52 | 29 | Meeker | BadQty = 21 Assum = 0<br>BadStep = 030 Assum = 030 |
| 221 | 770376 | 11 | 070 | 14 | 6074 | 14.01 | 29 | 29 | Barrett | BadQty = 17 Assum = 14 |
| 124 | 771289 | 12 | 030 | 0 | 3678 | 14.51 | 27 | 27 | Bell | BadQty = 1 Assum = 0 |
| 124 | 771388 | 12 | 010 | 0 | 0979 | 14.51 | 00 | 25 | Johns | BadStep = 100 Assum = 010 |
| 131 | 772003 | 12 | 030 | 5 | 4495 | 14.50 | 13 | 13 | Box | BadStep = 030 Assum = 030 |
| (1) | (2) | (3) | (4) | (5) | (6) | (7) | (8) | (9) | (10) | (11) |

**Detail Description**

1. Terminal Number
2. Job Number
3. Transaction Type
4. Step Number
5. Quantity
6. Employee Badge Number
7. Time Transaction
8. Work Center Transacted
9. Work Center Empl. Making Transaction
10. Employee Name
11. Error Message

## FIGURE 8

### REPORT DATE 3/8/77 SCHEDULE LOAD/CAPACITY REPORT
### SHOP DATE 1560
### WORK CENTER 30 N.C. LATHE-L & S MODEL MAX UNITS 6

| Week | Start | Work-Plan S | D | H | Units 1 | 2 | 3 | Cap | Load | L/C % | Load-To-Capacity-Ratio 0% 100% | Over (Under) |
|---|---|---|---|---|---|---|---|---|---|---|---|---|
| 1 | 1560 | 2 | 4 | 9 | 5 | 4 | 0 | 204 | 203 | 99% | .xxxxxxxxx | |
| 2 | 1564 | 2 | 5 | 9 | 6 | 6 | 0 | 340 | 334 | 98% | .xxxxxxxxx | -5 |
| 3 | 1569 | 2 | 5 | 9 | 6 | 6 | 0 | 340 | 269 | 79% | .xxxxxxxx | -70 |
| 4 | 1574 | 2 | 5 | 9 | 6 | 6 | 0 | 340 | 237 | 69% | .xxxxxxx | -102 |
| 5 | 1579 | 2 | 4 | 9 | 6 | 6 | 0 | 272 | 67 | 24% | .xx | -204 |
| 6 | 1583 | 2 | 5 | 9 | 6 | 6 | 0 | 340 | 55 | 16% | .xx | -284 |
| . | | | | | | | | | | | | |
| . | | | | | | | | | | | | |
| . | | | | | | | | | | | | |
| 20 | 1651 | 2 | 5 | 9 | 6 | 6 | 0 | 340 | 0 | | | -340 |
| (1) | (2) | (3) | (4) | (5) | (6) | (7) | | (8) | (9) | (10) | (11) | (12) |

**Detail Description**

1. Week (Current to 20)
2. Week Start Date (M-Day)
3. Shifts
4. Days
5. Hours (Per Shift)
6. Units (First Shift)
7. Units (Second Shift)
8. Capacity (Hours)
9. Load (Hours)
10. Percent Load
11. Load Profile
12. Over (Under) Load (Hours)

## FIGURE 9

### SCHEDULE LOAD CAPACITY REPORT
### WORK CENTER 30 N.C. LATHE-L & S MODEL

(1)-READY LOAD 3 DAYS AVAILABLE FOR WORK 163 HOURS AVAILABLE FOR WORK

(2)-CURRENT LOAD 1339 HOURS TODAY .70 UTILIZATION —(4)

(3)-AVERAGE LOAD 1281 HOURS PAST YEAR .90 EFFICIENCY —(5)

| PRIORITY | 0-99 | 100 | 200 | 300 | 400 | 500 | 600 | 700 | 800 | 900 | |
|---|---|---|---|---|---|---|---|---|---|---|---|
| NR JOBS | 5 | 66 | 13 | | | | 26 | 55 | 15 | 4 | |
| QUEUE | | 2 | 2 | | | | | 1 | | | (6) |
| JOB HRS | 86 | 676 | 57 | | | | 143 | 227 | 66 | 82 | |

SHORT TERM QUEUE - 2 WEEKS

| PRIORITY | 0-99 | 100 | 200 | 300 | 400 | 500 | 600 | 700 | 800 | 900 | |
|---|---|---|---|---|---|---|---|---|---|---|---|
| NR JOBS | | 30 | 12 | | | | 8 | 50 | 10 | | |
| QUEUE | | 4 | 2 | | | | 1 | 1 | | | (7) |
| JOB HRS | | 275 | 51 | | | | 29 | 195 | 31 | | |

**Detail Description**

1. Work Available (Days and Hours)
2. Total Load
3. Average Load (Moving Average)
4. Utilization
5. Efficiency
6. Queue (No. of Jobs and Hours in Pty Segments)
7. Short Term Queue

## FIGURE 10

### MANUFACTURING SCHEDULING - QUEUE FILE LIST

| Part Number | Job Number | Opr | W/C | Job Time | Sch/St | Alternate | Pty | Search |
|---|---|---|---|---|---|---|---|---|
| 12P2014 | 635676 | 030 | 29 | 4.57 | 1571 | | 773 | 1571 |
| 40G365 | 769579 | 040 | 29 | 1.76 | 1570 | | 771 | 1563 |
| 22A843 | 770161 | 040 | 29 | 3.25 | 1570 | 39 | 770 | 1564 |
| 131L579 | 635879 | 060 | 29 | 1.19 | 1571 | 20 | 769 | 1561 |
| 33L12 | 773584 | 030 | 29 | 3.88 | 1571 | | 767 | 1560 |
| 12R7224 | 770142 | 030 | 29 | 12.27 | 1571 | | 766 | 1560 |
| 211C378 | 772752 | 030 | 29 | 1.18 | 1571 | 30 | 760 | 1560 |
| 12P4641 | 636183 | 030 | 29 | 19.98 | 1587 | | 758 | 1561 |
| (1) | (2) | (3) | (4) | (5) | (6) | (7) | (8) | (9) |

**Detail Description**

1. Part Number
2. Job Number
3. Step Number
4. Work Center
5. Job Time
6. Schedule Start Date
7. Alternate Work Center
8. Priority
9. Search for Capacity Date

## FIGURE 11

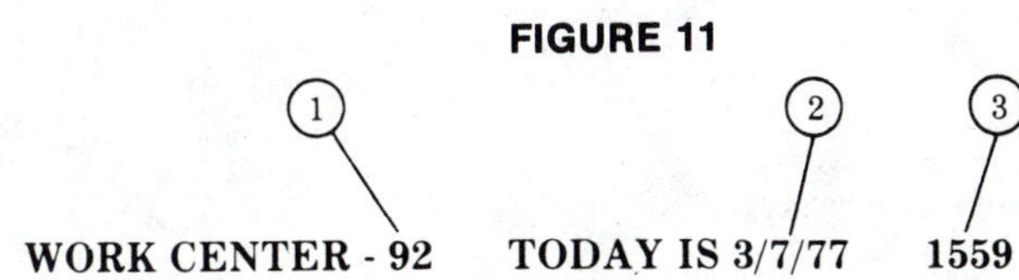


**WORK CENTER - 92 TODAY IS 3/7/77 1559**

| Job Number | Operation | Date Scheduled | | Job Time | Job Time Accumulated |
|---|---|---|---|---|---|
| 565010 | 010 | 3/7/77 | 1559 | .68 | .68 |
| 564895 | 020 | 3/8/77 | 1560 | .22 | .90 |
| 565022 | 020 | 3/8/77 | 1560 | 5.82 | 6.72 |
| 564837 | 020 | 3/9/77 | 1561 | 12.99 | 19.71 |
| 564965 | 020 | 3/10/77 | 1562 | .34 | 20.05 |
| 564823 | 010 | 3/10/77 | 1562 | 2.34 | 22.39 |
| 564898 | 020 | 3/17/77 | 1567 | 3.53 | 25.92 |
| 564899 | 020 | 3/18/77 | 1568 | 3.36 | 29.28 |
| 565030 | 020 | 3/18/77 | 1568 | .34 | 29.62 |
| (4) | (5) | (6) | (7) | (8) | (9) |

**Detail Description**

1. Work Center
2. Today's Calendar Date
3. Today's Shop or Manufacturing Date
4. Job Number
5. Operation or Step Number
6. Calendar Date Job is Scheduled To Start on Above Work Center
7. Shop or Manufacturing Date Job is Scheduled to Start on Above Work Center
8. Operation or Step Time on Above Work Center
9. Accumulated Hours

**LIST JOBS WHOSE RAW MATERIAL OR PARTS ARE IN INVENTORY FOR THE SPECIFIED WORK CENTER**

**<u>WOP</u> - WORK CENTER JOB PULL-AHEAD**

## FIGURE 12

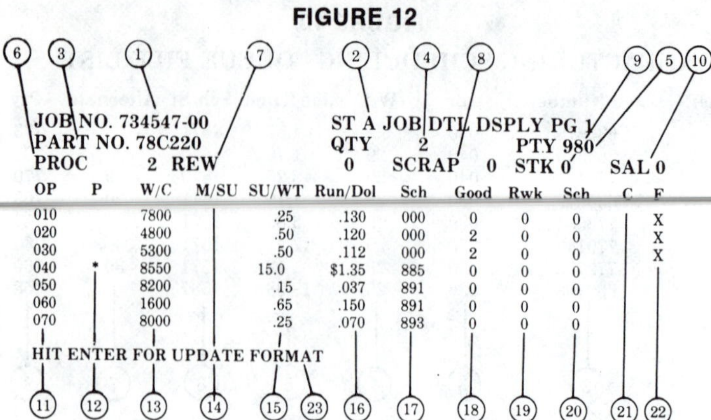

JOB NO. 734547-00 ST A JOB DTL DSPLY PG 1
PART NO. 78C220 QTY 2 PTY 980
PROC 2 REW 0 SCRAP 0 STK 0 SAL 0

| OP | P | W/C | M/SU | SU/WT | Run/Dol | Sch | Good | Rwk | Sch | C | F |
|---|---|---|---|---|---|---|---|---|---|---|---|
| 010 | | 7800 | | .25 | .130 | 000 | 0 | 0 | 0 | | X |
| 020 | | 4800 | | .50 | .120 | 000 | 2 | 0 | 0 | | X |
| 030 | | 5300 | | .50 | .112 | 000 | 2 | 0 | 0 | | X |
| 040 | * | 8550 | | 15.0 | $1.35 | 885 | 0 | 0 | 0 | | |
| 050 | | 8200 | | .15 | .037 | 891 | 0 | 0 | 0 | | |
| 060 | | 1600 | | .65 | .150 | 891 | 0 | 0 | 0 | | |
| 070 | | 8000 | | .25 | .070 | 893 | 0 | 0 | 0 | | |

HIT ENTER FOR UPDATE FORMAT

**Detail Description**

1. Job Number
2. Job Status: A = Active E = Engr. Hold Etc.
3. Part Number
4. Original Quantity
5. Priority
6. In Process Quantity
7. Rework Quantity
8. Scrap Quantity
9. Quantity Received in Inventory
10. Salvage Quantity
11. Operation or Step No.
12. Pointer-Job Loc.
13. Work Center
14. Multiple Setup-More Than One Man or Machine Working on Job at Same Time
15. Set-up Time/Weight for Heat Treat Sendout
16. Run Time/Dollars for Sendout
17. Schedule Start Date for Each Step
18. Quantity OK After Completion of Each Step
19. Rework Quantity Per Step
20. Scrap Quantity Per Step
21. Certification Flag (Test or Material)
22. Data Collection Activity Flag (X)
23. Use to Revise Job Detail See JJD Update Format

**JJD - JOB DETAIL DISPLAY (PLANT JOB)**

## FIGURE 13

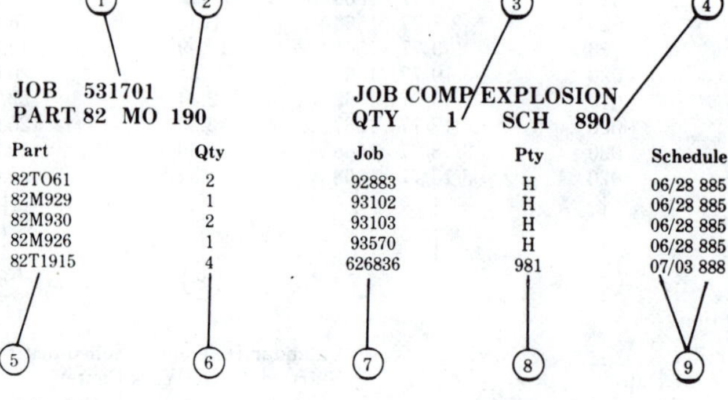

JOB 531701 JOB COMP EXPLOSION
PART 82 MO 190 QTY 1 SCH 890

| Part | Qty | Job | Pty | Schedule |
|---|---|---|---|---|
| 82TO61 | 2 | 92883 | H | 06/28 885 |
| 82M929 | 1 | 93102 | H | 06/28 885 |
| 82M930 | 2 | 93103 | H | 06/28 885 |
| 82M926 | 1 | 93570 | H | 06/28 885 |
| 82T1915 | 4 | 626836 | 981 | 07/03 888 |

**Detail Description**

1. Job Number
2. Part Number
3. Job Quantity
4. Schedule Start Date
5. Part Number of Part, Subassembly or Raw Material Due In for Above Job
6. Quantity of Sub-Part or Raw Material Required
7. Due-In Reference of Sub-Part or Raw Material. Purchase Contracts Have Five Digits. Jobs Have Six Digits.
8. Priority of Due-In Jobs or Purchase Contract Due-In Date Hardness
9. Calendar and Shop Date or Due-In Part or Raw Material

**LISTS PART(S) OR RAW MATERIAL DUE IN FOR SPECIFIED JOB. LISTS ONLY ITEMS NOT ON HAND?**

**JCD - JOB COMPONENT EXPLOSION**

## FIGURE 14

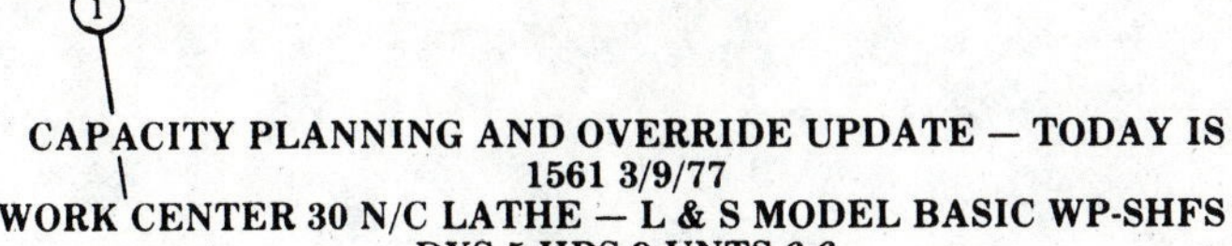

**CAPACITY PLANNING AND OVERRIDE UPDATE — TODAY IS 1561 3/9/77**

**WORK CENTER 30 N/C LATHE — L & S MODEL BASIC WP-SHFS 2 DYS 5 HRS 9 UNTS 6-6**

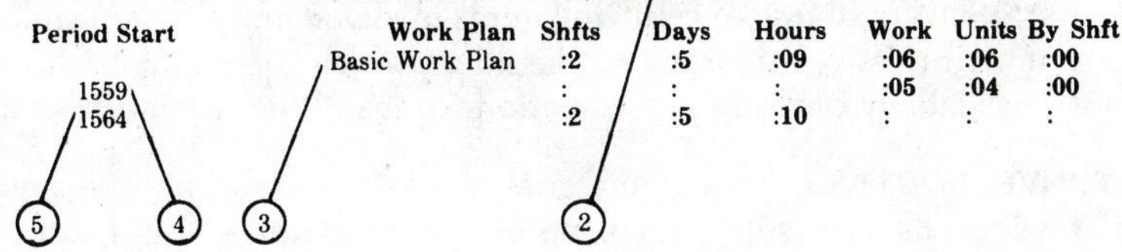

| Period Start | Work Plan | Shfts | Days | Hours | Work | Units By Shft | |
|---|---|---|---|---|---|---|---|
| | Basic Work Plan | :2 | :5 | :09 | :06 | :06 | :00 |
| 1559 | | : | : | : | :05 | :04 | :00 |
| 1564 | | :2 | :5 | :10 | : | : | : |

**Detail Description:**

1. Work Center Number and Description
2. Basic Work Plan - Shifts, Days per Week, Hours Per Day and Units Per Shift
3. Update Line for Basic Work Plan
4. Override Work Units on Shop Date 1559
5. Override Days Per Week. Shifts and Hours Must be Filled in. Shifts and Hours May be Overridden in a Like Manner.

**USED TO UPDATE BASIC WORK PLAN AND OVERRIDE BASIC WORK PLAN FOR WEEKLY AND DAILY VARIATIONS**

**ORU - CAPACITY PLANNING AND OVERRIDE UPDATE**

## FIGURE 15

### JOB ORDER ANALYSIS

| SO No | Req | Job | Seq | Qty | Part No | Last Act | Route |
|---|---|---|---|---|---|---|---|
| 14332 | 1/13 | 556726 | 97670 | 1 | 82MO606 | 12/15 | 99 |
| 14369 | 12/3 | 240893 | 96690 | 2 | 212EB9006 | 12/17 | 94 99 |
| 14508 | 12/9 | 180018 | 97990 | 1 | 111LO27 | | 82 87 81 80 |
| | | 138111 | | 1 | 111L125 | 12/15 | 82 71 80 |
| | | 630790 | | 1 | 111L122 | 12/16 | 19 82 71 80 |
| | | 759772 | | 1 | 111L235 | 12/16 | 85 82 |
| 14516 | 11/17 | 180771 | 97850 | 3 | 99CO1 | 12/16 | 80 |
| 14536 | 11/24 | 890108 | 97430 | 10 | 11RQ1002 | 12/16 | 44 71 80 |
| 14636 | 11/30 | 180060 | 97390 | 5 | 212EB5016 | | 72 74 80 |
| | | 88905 | | 15 | 212B5322 | 12/17 | Qty Ordered 25 |
| | | 760923 | | 5 | 212B5221 | 12/15 | 16 29 44 71 80 |
| 14713 | 12/20 | 180632 | 96840 | 2 | 34PO1505 | | 70 81 80 |
| | | 180640 | | 2 | 34PO1506 | | 70 81 80 |
| | | 180652 | | 2 | 34P1515 | 12/17 | 75 82 81 80 74 80 |

**Detail Description**

1. Sales Order Number
2. Customer Required Date
3. Source
4. Sequence Number
5. Quantity
6. Part Number
7. Last Data Collection Activity
8. Routing

# GLOSSARY*

**ABC ANALYSIS** A method of classifying items involved in a decision situation on the basis of their relative importance. Classification may be on the basis of monetary value, availability of resources, variations in lead time, shelf life, etc.

**ACTIVE INVENTORY** Covers raw material, work-in-process, and finished products that will be used or sold within the budgeted period without extra cost or loss.

**ACTUAL COSTS** Those labor and material costs that are charged against a job as it moves through the production process (cf. Standard costs).

**ACTUAL COST SYSTEM** A cost system that historically collects costs as they are applied to production, and allocates indirect costs based upon their specific costs and achieved volume.

**ADAPTIVE SMOOTHING** An extension of exponential smoothing that includes the use of transcendental fitting functions (e.g. exponential and trigonometric functions). Alternatively, adaptive smoothing is a term applied to a form of exponential smoothing in which the smoothing constant is automatically adjusted as some function of forecast error measurement.

**AGGREGATE INVENTORY** All the inventory including anticipation, fluctuation, cycle, and transportation stock.

**ALGORITHM** A prescribed set of well defined rules or processes for the solution of a problem in a finite number of steps; for example, the full statement of the arithmetic procedure for calculating the lot size for one item.

**ALLOCATION** **1.** Material allocated to an order but not withdrawn from stock. **2.** In an MRP system, an allocated item is one for which a picking order has been released to the stockroom, but not yet sent out of the stockroom. It is an "uncashed" stockroom requisition. **3.** A process used to distribute material in short supply.

**ANTICIPATION INVENTORIES** Additional inventory above basic pipeline stock to cover projected trends of increasing sales, planned sales promotion programs, seasonal fluctuations, plant shutdowns and vacations.

**ASSEMBLY** A group of subassemblies and/or parts that are put together; the total unit constitutes a major subdivision of the final product. When two or more components or subassemblies are put together by the application of labor or machine hours, it is called an assembly. An assembly may be an end item or a component of a higher level assembly (cf. Component, Subassembly).

---

*Adapted with permission from the *APICS Dictionary*, 4th ed. (Washington, D.C.: American Production and Inventory Control Society, 1980).

**ASSEMBLY LEAD TIME** The time that normally elapses between the time a work order is issued to the assembly floor and receipt of the assembly into stock or shipping.

**AUTOMATIC RESCHEDULING** Allowing the computer to automatically change due dates on scheduled receipts when it detects that due dates and required dates are out of phase.

**AVAILABLE MATERIAL** A term usually interpreted to mean *material available for planning* and thus including not only the on hand inventory but also inventory on order. Material *available for use* would, of course, be only the material on hand which has not been assigned (cf. Reserved material).

**AVAILABLE STOCK** *See* Available material.

**AVAILABLE TO PROMISE** The uncommitted portion of a company's inventory or planned production. This figure is frequently calculated from the Master Production Schedule and is maintained as a tool for order promising.

**BACKLOG** All of the customer orders booked, i.e. received but not yet shipped. Sometimes referred to as *open orders* or the *order board*.

**BACK ORDER** An unfilled customer order or commitment. It is an immediate (or past due) demand against an item whose inventory is insufficient to satisfy the demand (cf. Stock-out).

**BACKWARD SCHEDULING** A scheduling technique where the schedule is computed starting with the due date for the order and working backward to determine the required start date. This can generate negative times, thereby identifying where time must be made up (cf. Forward scheduling).

**BILL OF CAPACITY** *See* Product load profile.

**BILL OF LABOR** *See* Product load profile.

**BILL OF MATERIAL** A listing of all the subassemblies, parts, and raw materials that go into a parent assembly showing the quantity of each required to make an assembly.

**BILL OF MATERIAL PROCESSOR** Refers to the computer programs supplied by many manufacturers for maintaining, updating, and retrieving bill of material information on direct access files.

**BILL OF MATERIAL STRUCTURING** The process of organizing bills of material to perform specific functions (cf. Bill of material, Planning bill, Transient bill).

**BILL OF RESOURCES** *See* Product load profile.

**BIN LOCATION FILE** A file that specifically identifies the physical location where each item in inventory is stored.

**BLANKET ORDER** A long-term commitment to a vendor for material against which short-term releases will be generated to satisfy requirements.

**BLOCK CONTROL** Control of the production progress groups or *blocks* of shop orders for products undergoing the same basic processes (cf. Flow control).

**BOTTLENECK** A facility, function, department, etc., that impedes production—for example, a machine or work center where jobs arrive at a faster rate than they leave.

**BOX-JENKINS TECHNIQUE** A forecasting approach based on regression and moving average models, where the model is based not on regression of independent variables, but on past observations of the item to be forecast, at varying time lags, and on previous error values from forecasting.

**BRANCH WAREHOUSE** A separate stocking location removed from the main manufacturing plant typically carrying finished goods inventory or service parts (cf. Stockkeeping unit).

**BREAK-EVEN CHART** A graphical tool showing the total variable cost and fixed cost curve along with the total revenue (gross income) curve, both at all possible outputs. The point of intersection is defined as the break-even point, i.e., the point where revenues just equal costs (cf. Variable costs).

**BREAK-EVEN POINT** The level of production or the volume of sales at which operations are neither profitable nor unprofitable (cf. Break-even chart).

**BUCKETED SYSTEM** An MRP system under which all time-phased data is displayed in accumulated time periods, or *buckets*. If the period of accumulation would be one week, then the system would be said to have weekly buckets (cf. Bucketless system, Time bucket).

**BUCKETLESS SYSTEM** An MRP system which in all time-phased data is received, stored, processed and reported by specific dates and not in weekly (or larger) time buckets (cf. Bucketed system, Time bucket).

**BUDGET** A plan that includes an estimate of future costs and revenues related to expected activities. The budget serves as a pattern for and a control over future operations.

**BUFFER STOCK** *See* Safety stock.

**BULK STORAGE** Large scale storage vessels for raw materials, intermediates, or finished products in the process industries. Each vessel normally contains a mixture of lots. Materials may be replenished and withdrawn for use or pack-out simultaneously.

**BUSINESS CYCLE** A seemingly recurring change in general business activity going from a low point (depression) to a high point (prosperity). While called a *cycle* it is doubtful that extreme conditions recur with clocklike regularity. Understanding of cycles is important to forecasting (cf. Random variation, Seasonal).

**BUSINESS PLAN** A statement of income projections, costs and profits usually accompanied by budgets and a projected balance sheet as well as a cash flow (source and application of funds) statement. It is usually stated in terms of dollars only. The business plan and the production plan although frequently stated in different terms, should be in agreement with each other (cf. Manufacturing resource planning).

**BUYER** An individual whose functions may include vendor selection, negotiation, order placement, vendor follow-up, measurement and control of vendor performance, value analysis, evaluation of new materials and processes, etc. In some companies, the functions of order placement and vendor follow-up are handled by the vendor scheduler (cf. Vendor scheduler).

**BY-PRODUCT** A material of value produced as a sideline of a production process. Ratio of by-product to primary product is usually fixed. By-products may be recycled, sold as is, or used for other purposes such as cleaning solvents (*syn.*: coproduct).

**CAD/CAM** Computer Aided Design/Computer Aided Manufacturing. Two highly specialized technical applications of a computer to improve productivity.

**CAPACITY** **1.** In a general sense, refers to an aggregated volume of workload. It is a separate concept from priority (cf. Load, Priority). **2.** The highest sustainable output rate that can be achieved with the current product specifications, product mix, work force, plant, and equipment (cf. Efficiency).

**CAPACITY CONTROL** The process of measuring production output and comparing it with the capacity requirements plan, determining if the variance exceeds preestablished limits, and taking corrective action to get back on plan if the limits are exceeded (cf. Input/output control).

**CAPACITY PLANNING** *See* Capacity requirements planning.

**CAPACITY REQUIREMENTS PLANNING (CRP)** The function of establishing, measuring, and adjusting limits or levels of capacity that are consistent with a production plan. The term capacity requirements planning in this context is the process of determining how much labor and machine resources are required to accomplish the tasks of production. Open shop orders (and planned orders in the MRP system) are input to CRP which "translates" these orders into hours of work by work center by time period (cf. Infinite loading, Resource requirements planning).

**CARRYING COST** Cost of carrying inventory usually defined as a percentage of the dollar value of inventory per unit of time (generally one year). This depends mainly on the cost of capital invested as well as the costs of maintaining the inventory, such as taxes and insurance, obsolescence, spoilage, and space occupied. Such costs usually vary from 20 to 40 percent annually, depending on the environment (cf. Cost of capital, Economic order quantity).

**CENTRALIZED DISPATCHING** Organization of the dispatching function into one central location. This often involves the use of data collection devices for communication between the centralized dispatching function, which usually reports to the Production Control Department, and the shop manufacturing departments (cf. Decentralized dispatching).

**CHANGEOVER COST** The sum of the setup cost and the teardown cost for a manufacturing operation (cf. Idle time).

**COMMODITY BUYING** Grouping like parts or materials under one buyer's control for the procurement of all requirements to support production releases.

**COMMON PARTS BILL (OF MATERIAL)** A type of planning bill that groups all common components for a product or family of products into one bill of material (cf. Modular bill, Planning bill, Super bill).

**COMPONENT** An inclusive term used to identify a raw material, ingredient, part, or subassembly that goes into a higher level assembly, compound, or other item. May also include packaging materials for finished items (cf. Assembly).

**CONSIGNED STOCKS** Are inventories generally of finished products that are in the possession of customers, dealers, agents, etc., but remain the property of the manufacturer by agreement with those in possession.

**CONSTANT** A quantity that has a fixed value (cf. Variable).

**CONSTRAINT** A limitation placed on the maximization or minimization of an objective function. These usually result from scarcity of the resources necessary for attaining some objective (cf. Linear programming, Nonlinear programming, Objective function).

**CONTINUOUS PRODUCTION** A production system in which the productive units are organized and sequenced according to the steps to produce the product. The routing of the jobs is fixed and setups are seldom changed (cf. Intermittent production).

**CORRECTIVE ACTION** Action that must be taken to get actual inventories, production, or quality back on plan such as altering the number of people assigned to a particular department, changing overtime schedules, adjusting subcontract volume, or instructing employees in appropriate procedures.

**COST CENTER** The smallest segment of an organization for which costs are collected, such as the lathe department. The criteria in defining cost centers are that the cost be significant and the area of responsibility be clearly defined. A cost center may not be identical to a work center. Normally, it would encompass more than one work center (cf. Work center).

**COSTED BILL OF MATERIAL** A form of bill of material that (besides providing the normal information such as components, quantity per, effectivity data etc.) also extends the quantity per of every component in the bill by the cost of the components.

**COST FACTORS** The units of input that represent costs to the manufacturing system; for example: labor hours, purchased material.

**COST OF CAPITAL** Refers to the imputed cost of maintaining a dollar of capital invested for a certain period, normally one year. This cost is normally expressed as a percentage and may be based upon factors such as the average expected return on alternative investments and the current bank interest rate for borrowing (cf. Economic order quantity).

**CRITICAL PATH METHOD (CPM)** A network planning technique used for planning and controlling the activities in a project. By showing each of these activities and their associated times, the critical path can be determined. The critical path identifies those elements that actually constrain the total time for the project (cf. Project evaluation and review technique).

**CRITICAL RATIO** A dispatching rule that calculates a priority index number by dividing the time to due date remaining by the expected elapsed time to finish the job as in the following example:

$$\frac{\text{Time Remaining}}{\text{Work Remaining}} = \frac{30}{40} \times .75.$$

Typically ratios of less than 1.0 are behind, ratios greater than 1.0 are ahead, and a ratio of 1.0 is on schedule (cf. Dispatching rules).

**CUMULATIVE LEAD TIME** The longest length of time involved to accomplish the activity in question (*syn.*: Stacked lead time).

**CUMULATIVE MANUFACTURING LEAD TIME** The composite lead time when all purchased items are assumed to be in stock.

**CURVE FITTING** An approach to forecasting based upon a straight line, polynomial or other curve that describes some historical time series data.

**CUSTOMER ORDER** An order for a particular product or a number of products from a customer. Often referred to as an *actual demand* to distinguish it from a *forecast demand*.

**CUSTOMER SERVICE** The availability of items when promised to the customer (many measures are available).

**CYCLE** **1.** The interval of time during which a system or process (such as seasonal demand or a manufacturing operation) periodically returns to similar initial conditions. In inventory control, a cycle is often taken to be the length of time between two replenishment shipments. **2.** The interval of time during which an event or set of events is completed. In production control, a cycle is often taken to be the length of time between the release of a manufacturing order and shipment to the customer or inventory (*syn.*: Manufacturing lead time).

**CYCLE COUNTING** A physical inventory-taking technique where inventory is counted on a periodic schedule rather than once a year.

**CYCLE STOCK** One of the two main components of any item inventory, the cycle stock is the most active part; i.e., that which depletes gradually and is replenished cyclically when orders are received. Another part of the item inventory is the safety stock which is a cushion of protection against uncertainty in the demand or in the replenishment lead time (cf. Lot size, Safety stock).

**DATA** Any representation such as numeric characters to which meaning can be assigned.

**DATA BASE** A data file philosophy designed to establish the independence of computer programs from data files. Redundancy is minimized and data elements can be added to, or deleted from, the file designs without necessitating changes to existing computer programs.

**DATA BASE MANAGEMENT** A set of rules about file organization and processing (generally contained in complex software) that controls the definition and access to complex, interrelated files which are shared by numerous application systems.

**DATA COLLECTION** The method of recording a transaction at its source and transmitting it to a central storage device or computer.

**DATA FILE** A collection of related data records organized in a specific manner (one record for each inventory item showing product code, unit of measure, production costs, transactions, selling price, production lead time, etc.)

**DECENTRALIZED DISPATCHING** The organization of the dispatching function into individual departmental dispatchers (cf. Centralized dispatching).

**DECISION THEORY** Analysis of alternative actions where the consequences of the actions depend upon uncertain states of the world.

**DELINQUENT ORDER** A line item on the customer open order that has an original schedule ship date prior to the current date (*syn.:* Past due order; cf. Back order).

**DELIVERY POLICY** The company's goal for the time to ship product after receipt of a customer's order. The policy is sometimes stated as *our quoted delivery time*.

**DELIVERY SCHEDULE** The required or agreed time or rate of delivery of goods or services purchased by a customer for a future period.

**DELPHI METHOD** A forecasting approach where the opinions of experts are combined in a series of questionnaires. The results of each questionnaire are used to design the next questionnaire so that a convergence of the experts' opinions is obtained.

**DEMAND** A need for a particular product or component. The demand could come from any number of sources, e.g., customer order, forecast, interplant, branch warehouse, service part, or from manufacturing at the next higher level.

**DEMAND MANAGEMENT** The function of recognizing and managing all of the demands for products to insure that the master scheduler is aware of them. It encompasses the activities of forecasting, order entry, order promising, branch warehouse requirements, inter-plant orders, and service parts requirements (cf. Master production schedule).

**DEPARTMENT OVERHEAD RATE** The overhead rate applied to jobs passing through a department (cf. Overhead).

**DEPRECIATION** An allocation of the original value of an asset against current income to represent the declining value of the asset as a cost of that time period. Depreciation does not involve a cash payment; it acts as a tax shield and thereby reduces the tax payment.

**DETAILED SCHEDULING** The actual assignment of target starting and/or completion dates to operations or groups of operations to show when these must be done if the manufacturing order is to be completed on time. These dates are used in the dispatching operation (cf. Dispatching; *syn.:* Operations scheduling).

**DETAIL FILE** A temporary reference file, usually containing current data to be processed against a master file at a later date (cf. Master file).

**DETERIORATION** Product spoilage, damage to the package, etc. One of the considerations in inventory carrying cost (cf. Obsolescence).

**DETERMINISTIC MODELS** Models where uncertainty is not included. Examples include inventory models and those that assume demand and delivery time is known (cf. Stochastic models).

**DIRECT LABOR** Labor that is specifically applied to the product being manufactured or utilized in the performance of the service.

**DIRECT MATERIAL** Materials that become a part of the final product in measurable quantities.

**DISCOUNT** An allowance or deduction granted by the seller to the buyer (usually when certain stipulated conditions are met by the buyer) which reduces the cost of the goods purchased. A *quantity discount* is an allowance determined by the quantity or value of purchase. A *cash discount* is an allowance extended to encourage payment of invoice on or before a stated date which is earlier than the net date. A *trade discount* is a deduction from an established price for items or services, often varying in percentage with volume of transactions, made by the seller to those engaged in certain businesses and allowed irrespective of the time when payment is made.

**DISCRETE REQUIREMENTS** Requirements that vary substantially from period to period.

**DISPATCHER** A production control person whose primary function is dispatching.

**DISPATCHING** The selecting and sequencing of available jobs to be run at individual work stations and the assignment of these jobs to workers (cf. Centralized dispatching, Decentralized dispatching, Detailed scheduling, Expediting).

**DISPATCHING RULES** The logic used to assign priorities to jobs at a work center (cf. Critical ratio, Due data rule).

**DISTRIBUTED PROCESSING** A data processing organizational concept under which computer resources of a company are installed at more than one location with appropriate communication links. Processing is performed at the user's location (generally on a minicomputer) and is under the user's control and scheduling, as opposed to processing for all users being done on a large, centralized computer system.

**DISTRIBUTED SYSTEMS** Computer systems in multiple locations throughout an organization working in a cooperative fashion, with the system at each location primarily serving the needs of that location but also able to receive from and supply information to other systems within the network.

**DISTRIBUTION** *See* Physical distribution.

**DISTRIBUTION COST** This represents those items of cost for which the marketing or distribution organization is responsible.

**DISTRIBUTION OF FORECAST ERRORS** Tabulation of the forecast errors according to the frequency of occurrence of each error value. The errors in forecasting are, in many cases, normally distributed even when the observed data do not come from a normal distribution (cf. Normal distribution).

**DISTRIBUTION REQUIREMENTS PLANNING (DRP)** Determining the needs to replenish inventory at branch warehouses. Frequently a time-phased order point approach is used where the planned orders at the branch warehouse level are exploded via MRP logic to become gross requirements on the supplying source. In the case of multilevel distribution networks, this explosion process can continue down through the various levels of master warehouse, factory warehouse, etc., and become input to the master production schedule. Demand on the supplying source(s) is recognized as dependent, and standard MRP logic applies (cf. Physical distribution, Push distribution system, Time-phased order point).

**DISTRIBUTION RESOURCE PLANNING** The extension of Distribution Requirements Planning into the planning of the key resources contained in a distribution system: warehouse space, work force personnel, money, trucks and freight cars, etc. (cf. Distribution requirements planning).

**DOCUMENTATION** The process of collecting and organizing documents or the information recorded in documents. It usually refers to the development of material specifying inputs, operations, and outputs of a computer system.

**DOWNTIME** Time when the machines in the plant are not producing because they are down for repairs or other reasons (*syn.:* Idle time).

**DRP** Abbreviation for Distribution Requirements Planning.

**DUE DATE** The date at which purchased material or production on order is due to be available for use.

**DUE DATE RULE** A dispatching rule that directs the sequencing of jobs by the earliest due date.

**DYNAMIC PROGRAMMING** A method of sequential decision making in which the result of the decision in each stage affords the best possible exploitation of the expected range of likely (yet unpredictable) outcomes in the ensuing decision making stages (cf. Linear programming).

**ECONOMIC ORDER QUANTITY (EOQ)** A fixed order quantity that minimizes the total of carrying and preparation costs under conditions of certainty and independent demand.

**EFFICIENCY** The relationship between the planned resource requirements, such as labor or machine time, for a task(s) and the actual resource time charged to the task(s). (cf. Capacity **2**).

**END ITEM** A product sold as a completed item or repair part; any item subject to a customer order or sales forecast.

**END PRODUCT** *See* End item.

**ENGINEERING CHANGE** A revision to a parts list, bill of materials, or drawings, authorized by the engineering department. Changes are usually identified by a control number and are made for safety, cost reduction, or functionality reasons. In order to effectively implement engineering changes, all affected functions such as materials, quality assurance, assembly engineering, etc., should review and agree to the changes.

**ENGINEERING DRAWINGS** A blue print or white print that visually presents the dimensional characteristics of a part or assembly at some stage of manufacture.

**EOQ** Abbreviation for Economic order quantity.

**EOQ TABLES** Tables listing several ranges of monthly usages in dollars and the appropriate order size in dollars or months usage for each usage range.

**EXCEPTION REPORTS** Reports that list or flag only those items that deviate from plan.

**EXPECTED VALUE** The average value that would be observed in taking an action an infinite number of times. The expected value of an action is calculated by multiplying the outcome of the action by the probability of achieving that outcome (cf. Decision theory).

**EXPEDITER** A production control person whose primary duties are expediting.

**EXPEDITING** The "rushing" or "chasing" of production or purchase orders that are needed in less than the normal lead time.

**EXPLOSION** An extension of a bill of material into the total of each of the components required to manufacture a given quantity of upper-level assemblies or subassemblies.

**EXPONENTIAL SMOOTHING** A type of weighted moving average forecasting technique in which past observations are geometrically discounted according to their age.

**EXPOSURES** The number of times in an order point/order quantity system that the system risks a stock-out. This number of exposures is arrived at by dividing the lot size into the annual usage.

**EXTRINSIC FORECAST** A forecast based on a correlated leading indicator such as estimating furniture sales based on housing starts.

**FAMILY CONTRACTS** Grouping families of similar parts together on one purchase order to obtain pricing advantages and a continuous supply of material.

**FAS** Abbreviation for Final assembly schedule.

**FIFO** First in, first out method of inventory evaluation. The assumption is that the oldest inventory (first in) is the first to be used (first out); cf. LIFO.

**FILE** An organized collection of records or the storage device for keeping these records.

**FINAL ASSEMBLY SCHEDULE (FAS)** Also referred to as the *finishing schedule* as it may include other operations than simply the final operation. It is a schedule of end items either to replenish finished goods inventory or to finish the product for a make-to-order product.

**FINITE LOADING** Putting an amount of work into a department equal to or less than its capacity in any period.

**FIRM PLANNED ORDER (FPO)** An order that only a planner may change; it is coded to prevent automatic revision by the computer.

**FIRST-COME-FIRST-SERVED RULE** A dispatching rule under which jobs are sequenced by their arrival times (cf. Dispatching rules).

**FIRST ORDER SMOOTHING** This phrase refers to single exponential smoothing (does not include trend correction). Cf. Second order smoothing.

**FIXED INTERVAL REORDER SYSTEM** A periodic reordering system where the time interval between orders is fixed, such as weekly, monthly, or quarterly, but the size of the order is not fixed and orders vary according to usage since the last review.

**FIXED ORDER QUANTITY** A lot sizing technique in MRP that will always cause a planned order to be generated for a predetermined fixed quantity (or multiples thereof if net requirements for the period exceed the fixed order quantity). (Cf. Economic order quantity, Lot-for-lot, Period order quantity.)

**FIXED ORDER QUANTITY SYSTEM** An inventory control where the size of the order is fixed but the time interval between orders depends on actual demand.

**FIXED PERIOD ORDER** *See* Period order quantity.

**FLOAT** **1.** Refers to *work-in-process*; an extra quantity due to batch production; is sometimes used to indicate *cycle stock*. **2.** In CPM, the extra time before an activity becomes critical.

**FLOATING ORDER POINT** An order point that is responsive to changes in demand and/or to changes in lead time.

**FLOOR STOCKS** Stocks of inexpensive production parts held in the factory from which production workers can draw without requisitions.

**FLOW CONTROL** A term used to describe a specific production control system that is based primarily on setting production rates, feeding work into production to meet these planned rates, and then, following it through production to make sure that it is moving. Flow Control has its most successful application in repetitive production (cf. Order control).

**FLUCTUATION INVENTORY** Inventories that are carried as a cushion to protect against forecast error (cf. Safety stock).

**FORECAST ERROR** The difference between actual demand and forecast demand; typically stated as an absolute value.

**FORECAST PERIOD** The time unit for which forecasts are prepared, such as monthly, weekly, or quarterly.

**FORWARD SCHEDULING** A scheduling technique where the scheduler proceeds from a known start date and computes the completion date for an order usually from the first operation to the last (cf. Backward scheduling).

**FPO** Abbreviation for Firm planned order.

**FREE ON BOARD (F.O.B.)** Without cost to the buyer, the seller is required to place the goods aboard the transporting carrier at a specified place—such as shipping point, destination, name of a city, mill, warehouse, etc.

**FREE SLACK** The amount of time the completion of an activity can slip and not delay the start of any subsequent activity.

**FREQUENCY DISTRIBUTION** A table that indicates the frequency with which data fall into each of any number of subdivisions of the variable. The subdivisions are usually called classes (cf. Histogram).

**FROZEN MASTER SCHEDULE** *See* Planning fence.

**FUNCTION** **1.** In business, it is a job, task, or possibly a process. **2.** In mathematics, it is an algebraic expression describing the relation between two or more variables, the function taking on a definite value, or values, when special values are assigned to the argument(s), i.e., independent variable(s), of the function.

**GANTT CHART** An early type of control chart especially designed to show graphically the relationship between planned performance and actual performance (named after its originator, Henry L. Gantt). It is used for: machine loading, where one horizontal line is used to represent capacity and another to represent load against that capacity; following job progress where one horizontal line represents the actual progress of the job against the schedule in time.

**GAPPED SCHEDULE** The finishing of every piece in a lot at one work center before any piece in the lot can be processed at the succeeding work center, the movement of material in complete lots causing time gaps, thus, between the end of one operation and the beginning of the next (cf. Overlapped schedule).

**GATEWAY WORK CENTER** A work center in which work begins.

**GROSS REQUIREMENTS** The total of independent and dependent demand for a part or an assembly prior to the netting of on hand inventory and scheduled receipts.

**GROUP TECHNOLOGY** An engineering and manufacturing philosophy that identifies the sameness of parts, equipment, or processes. It provides for rapid retrieval of existing designs and anticipates a cellular type production equipment layout.

**HANDLING COST** The cost involved in handling inventory.

**HARD COPY** A printed computer report, message, or special listing such as transaction list, memory dump, etc.

**HARDWARE** The actual computer system machine units (cf. Software).

**HARMONIC SMOOTHING** An approach to forecasting based on fitting some set of sine and cosine functions to the historical pattern of a time series.

**HASH TOTAL** An arithmetic total of data that would not normally be added together, such as part of job numbers, for checking to see that all transactions have been processed.

**HEDGE** **1.** In Purchasing, it is any purchase or sale transaction having as its purpose the elimination of the negative aspects of price fluctuations. **2.** In master production scheduling, it is a quantity of stock used to protect against uncertainty in demand.

**HEURISTIC** A form of decision making where the decisions are made by rule of thumb or intuition instead of by optimization.

**HISTORGRAM** A graph of contiguous vertical bars representing a frequency distribution in which the groups or classes of items are marked on the X axis, and the number of items in each class is indicated by a horizontal line segment drawn above the X axis at a height equal to the number of items in the class.

**HOLD POINTS** Stock points for semifinished inventory.

**IDLE TIME** Time when operators or machines are not producing because of problems with setup, maintenance, lack of material, tooling (cf. Machine utilization). *Syn.:* Downtime.

**IMPLEMENTATION** The act of installing a system into operation. It concludes the system project with the exception of appropriate follow-up or post installation review.

**IMPLODE** Compression of detailed data into a summary-level record or report.

**INACTIVE INVENTORY** Designates the stocks that are in excess of contemplated consumption within the planning period.

**INDENTED BILL OF MATERIAL** A form of multilevel bill of material. It exhibits the highest level subassemblies closest to the left side margin and all the components going into these subassemblies are shown indented to the right of the margin; all subsequent levels of components are indented farther to the right. If a component is used in more than one subassembly within a given product structure, it will appear more than once, under every subassembly in which it is used.

**INDEPENDENT DEMAND** Demand for an item is considered independent when such demand is unrelated to the demand for other items. Demand for finished goods, parts required for destructive testing, and service parts requirements are some examples of independent demand.

**INDIRECT COST** Cost that is not directly incurred by a particular job or operation. Certain utility costs, such as plant heating, are often indirect. An indirect cost can be either a fixed or a variable cost and is distributed to the product through the overhead rates.

**INDIRECT LABOR** Work required to support production in general without being related to a specific product; e.g., floor sweeping.

**INFINITE LOADING** Showing the work in a work center by time period required regardless of the capacity available to perform this work. Infinite loading can be used to perform the technique called *capacity requirements planning*.

**IN-PROCESS INVENTORY** *See* Work-in-Process.

**INPUT** **1.** Work entering a production facility. **2.** Data to be processed.

**INPUT/OUTPUT (I/O) CONTROL** A technique for capacity control where actual output from a work center is compared with the planned output developed by CRP. The input is also monitored to see if it corresponds with plans so that work centers will not be expected to generate output when jobs are not available (cf. Capacity control).

**INPUT/OUTPUT (I/O) PLANNING** A capacity planning technique that plans input and output to a plant or department with differences between input and output affecting work-in-process and lead time.

**INSTANTANEOUS RECEIPT** The receipt of an entire lot size quantity in a very short period of time (cf. Noninstantaneous receipt).

**INTERACTIVE** Refers to those applications where a user communicates with a computer program via a terminal, entering data and receiving responses from the computer.

**INTERMITTENT PRODUCTION** A production system in which the productive units are organized according to function. The jobs pass through the functional departments in lots and each lot may have a different routing.

**INTERPLANT DEMAND** Material to be shipped to another plant or division within the corporation. Although it is not a customer order, it is usually handled by the master production scheduling system in a similar manner (cf. Demand management).

**INTERPOLATION** The process of finding a value of a function between two known values. Interpolation may be performed numerically or graphically.

**INTERROGATE** Retrieve information from computer files by use of predefined inquiries or unstructured queries handled by a high-level retrieval language.

**INTRANSIT LEAD TIME** The time lag between the date of shipment at supplier shipping point and the date of receipt at the customer's dock.

**INVENTORY INVESTMENT** The number of dollars that are tied up in all levels of inventory.

**INVENTORY MANAGEMENT** The branch of business management concerned with the planning and control of inventories.

**INVENTORY TURNOVER** A relative measure of inventory investment; frequently the ratio of an annualized cost of sales to inventory investment at a particular time or an average.

**INVENTORY USAGE** The value or the number of units of an inventory item consumed over a period of time.

**INVENTORY WRITE-OFF** A deduction of inventory dollars from the financial statement because the inventory is no longer saleable or because of *shrinkage*, i.e. the value of the physical inventory is less than its book value.

**ITEM** Any unique manufactured or purchased part or assembly (that is, end product, assembly, subassembly, component, or raw material).

**ITEM MASTER FILE** Typically this computer file contains identifying and descriptive data, control values (lead times, lot sizes, etc.), and can contain data on inventory status, requirements and planned orders. There is normally one record in this file for each stockkeeping unit.

**JOB LOT** A relatively small number of specific parts or products that is produced at one time.

**JOB ORDER** *See* Manufacturing order.

**JOB ORDER COSTING** A costing system in which costs are collected to specific jobs. This system can be used with either actual or standard costs in the manufacturing of distinguishable units or lots of products (cf. Process cost system).

**JOB SHOP** A functional organization whose departments or work centers are organized around particular types of equipment or operations, such as drilling, forging, spinning, or assembly. Products flow through departments in batches corresponding to individual orders (*syn.:* Intermittent production).

**JOB SHOP LAYOUT** The arrangement of equipment in functional areas.

**JOB STATUS** A periodic report showing the plan for completing a job (usually the requirements and completion date) and the progress of the job against that plan (cf. Stock status).

**JOINT ORDER** An order on which several items are combined for the purpose of obtaining volume or transportation economies.

**KIT** The components of an assembly that have been pulled from stock and readied for movement to the assembly area.

**KITTING** The process of removing components of an assembly from the stock room and sending them to the assembly floor as a kit of parts.

**LABOR LOADING** The process of applying expected labor requirements against the capacity for that labor (cf. Finite loading, Infinite loading).

**LABOR PRODUCTIVITY** The rate of output of a worker or group of workers, per unit of time, compared to an established standard or rate of output.

**LABOR TICKET** A form used to record the application of labor to specific jobs or production operations.

**LAP-PHASING** *See* Overlapped schedule.

**LCL** Less than a carload lot shipment.

**LEAD TIME** A span of time required to perform an activity. In a production and inventory control context, the activity in question is normally the procurement of materials and/or products either from an outside supplier or from one's own manufacturing facility.

**LEAD TIME INVENTORY** This is inventory that is carried on hand during the lead time period in simple inventory systems. The lead time inventory will be equal to forecast usage during the replenishment lead time (*syn.*: Active inventory).

**LEAD TIME OFFSET** A term used in MRP where a planned order receipt in one time period will require the release of that order in some earlier time period based on the lead time for the item. The difference between the due date and the release date is the lead time offset.

**LEAST SQUARES METHOD** A method of curve fitting that selects a line of best fit through a plot of data so as to minimize the sum of squares of the deviations of the given points from the line.

**LEAST TOTAL COST** A dynamic lot sizing technique that calculates the order quantity by comparing the carrying cost and the setup (or ordering) costs for various lot sizes and selects the lot where these are most nearly equal.

**LEVEL** Every part or assembly in a product structure is assigned a level code signifying the relative level in which that part or assembly is used within that product structure. Normally the end items are assigned Level 0, the components/subassemblies going into it Level 1, and so on.

**LIFO** Last in, first out method of inventory evaluation. The assumption is that the most recently received (last in) is the first to be used or sold (first out) (cf. FIFO).

**LIMIT (LOT SIZE INVENTORY MANAGEMENT INTERPOLATION TECHNIQUE)** A technique for looking at the lot size for groups of products to determine what effect economic lot size will have on the total inventory investment and production.

**LIMITING OPERATION** In a series of operations with no alternative routings, the capacity of the total system can be no greater than the operation with the least capacity. As long as this limiting condition exists, the total system can be effectively scheduled by simply scheduling the limiting operation (*syn.:* Bottleneck).

**LINEAR DECISION RULES** A modeling approach for the establishment of aggregate work force levels, based upon minimizing the total cost of hiring, firing, holding inventory, back orders, payroll, overtime, and undertime.

**LINEAR PROGRAMMING** Mathematical models for solving linear optimization problems through minimization (or maximization) of a linear function subject to linear constraints.

**LINE BALANCING** A flow process that can be divided into elemental tasks, each with a specified time requirement per unit of product and a sequence relationship with the other tasks. Line balancing is the assignment of these tasks to work stations so as to minimize the number of work stations and to minimize the total amount of unassigned time at all stations. Line balancing can also mean a technique for determining the product mix that can be run down an assembly line to provide a fairly consistent flow of work through that assembly line at the planned line rate.

**LINE ITEM** One item on an order, regardless of quantity.

**LOAD** This is the amount of scheduled work ahead of a manufacturing facility, usually expressed in terms of hours of work or units of production.

**LOAD CENTER** *See* Work center.

**LOAD PROFILE** A display of future capacity requirements based on planned and released orders over a given span of time (*syn.*: Load projection).

**LOAD PROJECTION** *See* Load profile.

**LOCATOR FILE** A file used in the stockroom or storeroom indicating where each item is to be stored.

**LOGISTICS** In an industrial context, this term refers to the art and science of obtaining and distributing material and product. (In a military sense where it has greater usage its meaning can also include the transportation of personnel.)

**LOG NORMAL DISTRIBUTION** A continuous probability distribution where the logarithms of the variable are normally distributed.

**LONG-RANGE RESOURCE PLANNING** A planning activity for long term capacity decisions, based on the production plan and perhaps on even more gross data (e.g., sales per year) beyond the time horizon for the production plan. This activity is to plan long term capacity needs out to the time period necessary to acquire gross capacity additions such as a major factory expansion.

**LOT-FOR-LOT (L4L)** A lot-sizing technique in MRP that generates planned orders in quantities equal to the net requirements in each period.

**LOT SIZE** The amount of a particular item that is ordered from the plant or a vendor (*syn.:* Order quantity).

**LOT SIZE CODE** A code that indicates the lot-sizing technique selected for a given item.

**LOT SIZE INVENTORY** Inventories that are maintained whenever quantity price discounts, shipping costs, or setup costs, etc., make it more economical to purchase or produce in larger lots than are needed for immediate purposes.

**LOT-SIZING** The process of, or techniques used in, determining lot size.

**LOT-SPLITTING** Dividing a lot into two or more batches and simultaneously performing the same operation on each batch using two or more machines (or lines).

**LOW-LEVEL CODE** Identifies the lowest level in any bill of material at which a particular component can appear. Net requirements for a given component are not calculated until all the gross requirements have been calculated down to that level. Low-level codes are normally calculated and maintained automatically by the computer software (cf. Level).

**MACHINE CENTER** *See* Work center.

**MACHINE LOADING** The accumulation by work station(s), machine, or machine group of the hours generated from the scheduling of operations for released orders by time period.

**MACHINE UTILIZATION** The percent of time that a machine is running production as opposed to idle time. (cf. Idle time, Running time).

**MAD** *See* Mean absolute deviation.

**MAJOR SETUP** The machine setup and other activities (clerical and administrative) required when one or more items in a group of items is ordered.

**MAKE-OR-BUY DECISION** The act of deciding whether to produce an item in-house or buy it from an outside vendor.

**MAKE-TO-ORDER PRODUCT** The end item is finished after receipt of a customer order. Frequently long lead time components are planned prior to the order to reduce the delivery time to the customer. Where options or other subassemblies are stocked prior to customer orders arriving, the term *assemble-to-order* is frequently used.

**MAKE-TO-STOCK PRODUCT** The end item is shipped from finished goods "off the shelf" and therefore is finished prior to a customer order arriving.

**MANUFACTURING CALENDAR (M-DAY CALENDAR)** A calendar, used in Inventory and Production Planning functions, that numbers only the working days so that the component and work order scheduling may be done based on the actual number of work days available.

**MANUFACTURING LEAD TIME** The total time required to manufacture an item. Included here are order preparation time, queue time, setup time, run time, move time, inspection, and put-away time.

**MANUFACTURING ORDER** A document or group of documents conveying authority for the manufacture of specified parts or products in specified quantities.

**MANUFACTURING PROCESS** The series of activities performed upon material to convert it from the raw or semifinished state to a state of further completion and greater value.

**MANUFACTURING RELEASE** *See* Manufacturing order.

**MANUFACTURING RESOURCE PLANNING** A method for the effective planning of all the resources of a manufacturing company. Ideally it addresses operational planning in units, financial planning in dollars, and has a simulation capability to answer what-if questions. It is made up of a variety of functions, each linked together: business planning, production planning, master production scheduling, material requirements planning, capacity requirements planning, and the execution systems for capacity and priority. Outputs from these systems would be integrated with financial reports such as the business plan, purchase commitment report, shipping budget, inventory projections in dollars, etc. Manufacturing resource planning is a direct outgrowth and extension of MRP (often referred to as MRP II).

**MARGINAL COST** The additional out of pocket costs incurred when the level of output of some operation is increased by one unit (cf. Marginal revenue).

**MARGINAL REVENUE** The additional income received when the level of output of some operation is increased by one unit (cf. Marginal cost).

**MASS PRODUCTION** High quantity production characterized by detailed planning of every operation and specialization of equipment and labor.

**MASTER FILE** A main reference file of information such as bills of material or routing files (cf. Detail file).

**MASTER PRODUCTION SCHEDULE (MPS)** For selected items, it is a statement of what the company expects to manufacture. It is the anticipated build schedule for those selected items assigned to the master scheduler. The master scheduler maintains this schedule and, in turn, it becomes a set of planning numbers that drives MRP.

**MASTER SCHEDULE** *See* Master production schedule.

**MASTER SCHEDULE ITEM** A part number selected to be planned by the master scheduler. The item is deemed critical in terms of its impact on lower level components and/or resources such as skilled labor, key machines, dollars, etc.

Therefore, the master scheduler, not the computer, would maintain the plan for these items. A master schedule item may be an end item, a component, a pseudo number, or a planning bill of material.

**MASTER SCHEDULER** The job title of the person who manages the Master Production Schedule.

**MATERIAL** Any commodity used directly or indirectly in producing a product, viz., raw materials, component parts, subassemblies, and supplies (cf. Reserved material, Available material).

**MATERIAL REQUIREMENTS PLANNING** A system that uses bills of material, inventory and open order data, and master production schedule information to calculate requirements for materials. It makes recommendations to release replenishment orders for material. Further, since it is time-phased, it makes recommendations to reschedule open orders when due dates and need dates are not inphase. It is primarily a scheduling technique, i.e., a method for establishing and maintaining valid due dates on orders (cf. Manufacturing resource planning).

**MATERIALS MANAGEMENT** A term to describe the grouping of management functions related to the complete cycle of material flow, from the purchase and internal control of production materials to the planning and control of work-in-process to the warehousing, shipping and distribution of the finished product. It differs from *materials control* in that the latter term, traditionally, is limited to the internal control of production materials.

**MATRIX** A mathematical array having height, width,and, sometimes, depth, into which collections of data may be stored and processed.

**MATRIX BILL OF MATERIAL** A chart made up from the bills of material for a number of products in the same or similar families. It is arranged in a matrix with parts in columns and assemblies in rows (or vice versa) so that requirements for common components can be summarized conveniently.

**MAXIMUM INVENTORY** The maximum allowable inventory for an independent demand item. Example would be the sum of the economic lot size plus two times the reserve stock (cf. Min-max system).

**MAXIMUM ORDER QUANTITY** An order quantity modifier, applied after the lot size has been calculated, that limits the order quantity to a preestablished maximum.

**M-DAY CALENDAR** *See* Manufacturing calendar.

**MEAN** The arithmetic average of a group of values (cf. Median,Mode).

**MEAN ABSOLUTE DEVIATION (MAD)** The average of the absolute values of the deviations of observed values from the expected value. MAD can be calculated based on observations and the arithmetic mean of those observations. An alternative is to calculate absolute deviations of actual sales data minus forecast data. These data can be averaged in the usual arithmetic way or with exponential smoothing.

**MEDIAN** The middle value in a set of measured values when the items are arranged in order of magnitude. If there is no single middle value, the median is the average of the two middle values (cf. Mode, Mean).

**MINIMUM COST ORDER QUANTITY** *See* Economic order quantity.

**MINIMUM INVENTORY** The minimum allowable inventory for an independent demand item.

**MINIMUM ORDER QUANTITY** An order quantity modifier, applied after the lot size has been calculated, that increases the order quantity to a preestablished minimum.

**MIN-MAX SYSTEM** An inventory management technique. A replenishment order is placed when the available stock falls to the minimum level or below it. The quantity is the difference between the available quantity and the maximum (target) level.

**MINOR SETUP** The incremental preparation activities required when processing the second, third, and ensuing items in a group of items. These are the clerical, receiving, expediting, and minor machine adjustments associated with each item in the group.

**MODE** The most common or frequent value in a group of values (cf. Mean, Median).

**MODEL** A representation of a process or system that attempts to relate the most important variables in the system in such a way that analysis of the model leads to insights into the system. Frequently the model is used to anticipate the result of some particular decision in the real system (cf. Simulation).

**MODULAR BILL (OF MATERIAL)** A type of planning bill that is arranged in product modules or options. It is often used in companies where the product has many optional features; e.g. automobiles (cf. Common parts bill, Planning bill).

**MODULE** A program unit that is discrete and identifiable with respect to design, compilation, and testing; eventually combines with other units to form a complete program.

**MONTE CARLO SIMULATION** A subset of digital simulation models based on random or stochastic processes (cf. Simulation).

**MOVEMENT INVENTORY** A type of in-process inventory that arises because of the time required to move goods from one place to another (cf. Transportation inventory).

**MOVE ORDER** The authorization to move a particular item from one location to another.

**MOVE TICKET** A document used in dispatching to authorize and/or record movement of a job from one work center to another. It also may be used to report other information such as the active quantity or the material storage location.

**MOVE TIME** The actual time that a job spends in transit from one operation to another in the shop (cf. Transit time).

**MOVING AVERAGE** An arithmetic average of the *n* most recent observations. As each new observation is added, the oldest one is dropped. The value of *n*, the number of periods to use for the average, reflects responsiveness versus stability in the same way that the choice of a smoothing constant does in exponential smoothing.

**MPS** Abbreviation for Master production schedule.

**MRP** Abbreviation for Material requirements planning.

**MULTILEVEL BILL OF MATERIAL** A multilevel bill shows all the components that are directly or indirectly used in an assembly together with the quantity required of every component. If a component is a subassembly, all the components of the subassembly will also be exhibited in the multilevel bill.

**MULTILEVEL WHERE USED** Lists all the assemblies in which that component is directly used and the next higher level assemblies in which the parent assembly is used.

**MULTIPLE REGRESSION MODELS** A form of regression analysis where the model involves more than one independent variable such as sales being forecast based upon housing starts, GNP, and disposable income.

**NET CHANGE MRP** An approach by which the Material Requirements Plan is continually retained in the computer. Whenever there is a change in requirements (open order or inventory status) or engineering usage, a partial explosion is made only for those parts affected by the change. Net changes systems may be continuous and totally transaction oriented or done in a periodic—often daily—batch (cf. Regeneration MRP).

**NET REQUIREMENTS** In MRP, the net requirements for a part or an assembly are derived as a result of netting gross requirements against inventory on hand and the scheduled receipts. Net requirements, lot sized and offset for lead time, become planned orders.

**NETTING** The process of calculating net requirements.

**NETWORK PLANNING** A generic term for techniques that are used to plan complex projects. Two of the best known network planning techniques are the Critical Path Method and PERT.

**NONINSTANTANEOUS RECEIPT** The receipt of a lot quantity over a period of time because of a relatively slow process.

**NONLINEAR PROGRAMMING** Similar to linear programming but incorporating a nonlinear objective function and linear constraints, or a linear objective function and nonlinear constraints, or both a nonlinear objective function and nonlinear constraints.

**NONSIGNIFICANT PART NUMBERS** Part numbers that are assigned to each part but do not convey any information about the part. They are identifiers, not descriptors (cf. Significant part numbers).

**NORMAL DISTRIBUTION** A particular statistical distribution. For a distribution to be classified as a *normal distribution*, it must be unimodal and symmetrical; that is to say, a deviation from the mean is as likely to be minus. When graphed the normal distribution takes the form of a bell-shaped curve (cf. Frequency distribution).

**OBJECTIVE FUNCTION** The goal or function that is to be optimized in a model. Most often it is a cost function that we are attempting to minimize subject to some restrictions or a profit function which we are trying to maximize subject to some restriction (cf. Constraint).

**OBLIGATED MATERIAL** *See* Reserved material.

**OBSOLESCENCE** Loss of product value resulting from a model or style change, or technological development (cf. Deterioration).

**OFFSETTING** *See* Lead time offset.

**ON HAND** The balance shown in perpetual inventory records as being physically present at the stocking locations.

**ON ORDER** The stock on order is the quantity represented by the total of all outstanding replenishment orders. The on order balance increases when a new order is released, and it decreases when material is received to fill an order, or when an order is cancelled (cf. On hand, Open order).

**OPEN ORDER** **1.** An active manufacturing order or purchase order. **2.** An unfilled customer order.

**OPERATION SPLITTING** *See* Lot splitting.

**OPERATIONS SCHEDULING** *See* Detailed scheduling.

**OPERATIONS SEQUENCE** The sequential steps that manufacturing engineering recommends that a given assembly or part follow in its flow through the plant.

**OPERATION START DATE** The date when an operation should be started based on the work remaining and the time remaining to complete the job.

**OPERATION TICKET** *See* Work order.

**OPPORTUNITY COST** The return on capital that could have resulted had the capital been used for some purpose other than its present use. It usually refers to the best alternative use of the capital; at other times, however, to the average return from feasible alternatives.

**OPTIMIZATION** Achieving the best possible solution to a problem in terms of a specified objective function.

**ORDER** A catchall term which may refer to such diverse items as a purchase order, shop order, customer order, planned order.

**ORDER CONTROL** Control of the progress of each customer order or stock order through the successive operations in its production cycle.

**ORDER ENTRY** The process of accepting and translating what a customer wants into terms used by the manufacturer. This can be as simple as creating shipping documents for a finished goods product line or a more complicated series of activities including engineering effort for make-to-order products.

**ORDERING COST** When calculating economic order quantities, it refers to the costs that increase as the number of orders placed increases. Includes costs related to the clerical work of preparing, issuing, following and receiving orders, the physical handling of goods, inspections, and machine setup costs if the order is being manufactured (cf. Carrying cost).

**ORDER INTERVAL** The time period between the placement of two successive orders.

**ORDER POINT** The inventory level such that if the total stock on hand plus on order falls to or below the order point, action is taken to replenish the stock. The order point is normally calculated as: forecast usage during the replenishment lead time plus safety stock. *Syn.*: reorder point. Cf. Time-phased order point.

**ORDER PREPARATION LEADTIME** The time required to analyze requirements and open order status, and to create the paperwork necessary to release a purchase requisition or a work order.

**ORDER PROMISING** The process of making a delivery commitment, i.e., answering the question when can you ship. For make-to-order products this usually involves a check of uncommitted material and availability of capacity.

**ORDER QUANTITY** In a fixed order system of inventory control, the fixed quantity that should be ordered each time the available stock (on hand plus on order) falls below the order point. However, in a variable reorder quantity system the amount ordered from time period to time period will vary (cf. Economic order quantity, Lot size; *syn.*: Replenishment order quantity).

**ORDER QUANTITY MODIFIERS** Order quantity calculations based upon one of the lot-sizing rules. However it may be necessary to adjust the calculated lot size due to some special considerations. These adjustments are called order quantity modifiers. *See* Maximum order quantity, Minimum order quantity.

**ORDER SCHEDULING** *See* Detailed scheduling.

**ORDER-UP-TO-LEVEL** *See* Target inventory level.

**OUT-OF-POCKET COSTS** Costs that involve cash payments such as direct labor as opposed to depreciation which does not (cf. Marginal cost).

**OUTLIER** A datum that falls significantly away from other data for a similar phenomenon.

**OUTPUT** **1.** Work being completed by a production facility. **2.** The result of a computer program.

**OUTPUT CONTROL** *See* Input/Output control.

**OUTPUT STANDARD** *See* Performance standard.

**OVERHEAD** Costs incurred in the operation of a business that can not be directly related to the individual products or services produced. These costs (such as light, heat, supervision, maintenance) are grouped in several pools (department overhead, factory overhead, general overhead) and distributed to units of products, or service, by some standard method such as direct labor hours, direct labor dollars, direct materials dollars.

**OVERHEAD PERCENTAGE** The percentage applied to a labor cost (machine hours or material) to calculate the overhead cost of performing work in that work center. It is used to distribute those costs that cannot be directly related to specific products or services.

**OVERLAPPED SCHEDULE** The overlapping of successive operations, whereby the completed portion of a job lot at one work center is processed at one or more succeeding work centers before the pieces left behind are finished at the preceding work center(s). *Syn.*: Lap-phasing, Telescoping. (Cf. Gapped schedule)

**OVERRUN** The quantity received from manufacturing or a vendor that is in excess of the quantity ordered.

**OVERTIME** Work beyond normal established working hours that usually requires a premium be paid to the workers.

**PARALLEL CONVERSION** A method of system implementation that overlaps with the operation of the system being replaced. It minimizes the risk consequences of a poor system.

**PARALLEL SCHEDULE** Use of two or more machines or job centers to perform identical operations on a lot of material. Duplicate tooling and setup is required (*syn.:* Lot splitting).

**PARAMETER** A coefficient appearing in a mathematical expression, each value of which determines the specific form of the expression. Parameters define or determine the characteristics or behavior of something, as when the mean and standard deviation are used to describe a set of data.

**PARETO'S LAW** A concept developed by Vilfredo Pareto, an Italian economist, that simply says that a small percentage of a group accounts for the largest fraction of the effort, value, etc. (cf. ABC analysis).

**PARKINSON'S LAW** A tongue-in-cheek observation that work expands so as to fill the time available for its completion.

**PART** Normally refers to a material item that is used as a component and is not an assembly or subassembly.

**PARTIAL ORDER** Any shipment received or shipped that is less than the amount ordered.

**PART NUMBER** A number that serves to uniquely identify a component, product, or raw material (cf. Significant part numbers).

**PART PERIOD BALANCING (PPB)** A dynamic lot-sizing technique that uses the same logic as the Least Total Cost method. The difference is that PPB employs the routine called *Look Ahead/Look Back*.

**PARTS REQUISITION** An authorization either in the form of a slip of paper or a punched card that identifies the type and quantity of parts required to be withdrawn from an inventory.

**PART TYPE** A part within a bill of material may be defined, among others, as regular, phantom, or reference.

**PAST DUE** An order that has not been completed on time (*syn.*: Delinquent; cf. Back order).

**PEGGED REQUIREMENT** A requirement at a component level that shows the next level parent item and the source of the demand that actually created the requirement (cf. Pegging).

**PEGGING** In MRP, pegging displays for a given item the details of the sources of its gross requirement and/or allocations. Pegging can be thought of as "live" where-used information.

**PERCENT OF FILL** A measure of the effectiveness with which the inventory management system responds to actual demand. The percent of customer orders filled off the shelf can be measured in either units or dollars (cf. Stock-out percentage).

**PERFORMANCE EFFICIENCY** A ratio, usually expressed as a percentage, of actual output to a benchmark or standard output.

**PERFORMANCE STANDARD** A criterion or benchmark with which actual performance is compared.

**PERIOD COSTS** All costs related to a period of time rather than a unit of product; e.g., marketing costs, property taxes.

**PERIODIC ORDER SYSTEM** *See* Fixed interval reorder system.

**PERIOD ORDER QUANTITY (POQ)** A lot-sizing technique under which the lot size will be equal to the net requirements for a given number of periods (e.g., weeks) into the future (cf. Fixed order quantity, Lot-for-lot).

**PERPETUAL INVENTORY** Usually used to describe an inventory record-keeping system where each transaction in and out is recorded and a new balance is computed (cf. Physical inventory).

**PERPETUAL INVENTORY RECORD** A computer record document on which each inventory transaction is posted so that a current record of the inventory is maintained.

**PHANTOM BILL OF MATERIAL** *See* Transient bill (of material).

**PHYSICAL DISTRIBUTION** The combination of activities associated with the movement of material, usually finished products, from the manufacturer to the customer. In many cases, this movement is made through one or more levels of field warehouses (cf. Distribution requirements planning).

**PHYSICAL INVENTORY** The determination of inventory quantity by actual count. Physical inventories can be taken on a continuous, periodic, or annual basis (cf. Cycle counting).

**PICK DATE** The start date of the picking activity for a work order. On this date, the system produces a list of orders due to be picked, a pick list, tags, and turnaround cards.

**PICKING** The process of withdrawing from stock the components to make the products or the finished goods to be shipped to a customer (cf. Kitting).

**PICKING LIST** A document used by operating personnel to pick manufacturing or shipping orders.

**PIECE PARTS** Individual items in inventory at the simplest level in manufacturing; for example, bolts and washers.

**PIECE RATE** The amount of money paid for a unit of production. It serves as the basis for determining the total pay for an employee working in a piecework system.

**PIECEWORK** Work done on a piece rate.

**PILOT LOT** A relatively small preliminary order for a product. The purpose of the small lot is to correlate the product design with the development of an efficient manufacturing process.

**PLANNED ORDER** A suggested order quantity and due date created by MRP processing.

**PLANNING BILL (OF MATERIAL)** An artificial grouping of items in bill of material format used to facilitate master scheduling and/or material planning (cf. Common parts bill, Modular bill, Super bill).

**PLANNING FENCE** A boundary between two periods on the planning horizon with different limitations on schedule changes and different subperiods of the planning horizon.

**PLANNING HORIZON** The span of time from the current to some future date for which plans are generated. It covers at least the cumulative purchasing and manufacturing lead time and usually is quite a bit longer.

**POISSON DISTRIBUTION** This is a statistical distribution similar to the normal distribution except that the standard deviation is equivalent to the square root of the mean.

**POLYNOMIAL** An algebraic expression that contains two or more terms. The dependent variable is represented by a linear combination of powers of the independent variables with the degree of the polynomial determined by the highest power in the expression.

**POPULATION** The entire set of items from which a sample is drawn.

**PRICE PREVAILING AT DATE OF SHIPMENT** An agreement between the purchaser and the vendor that the price of the goods ordered is subject to change at the vendor's discretion between the date the order is placed and the date the vendor makes shipment and that the then-established price is the contract price.

**PRIMARY STORAGE** The memory of a computer where instructions and data being worked upon are contained. Most primary storage today is made up of small iron rings or cores that can be electrically charged; therefore, primary storage is often called core storage.

**PRIORITY** In a general sense, refers to the relative importance of jobs, i.e. which jobs should be worked on and when. It is a separate concept from capacity (cf. Capacity, Scheduling rules).

**PROBABILITY DISTRIBUTION** A table of numbers or a mathematical expression indicating the probability with which each of all possible results of an experiment is expected to occur.

**PROCESS CHART** A graphic representation of events occurring during a series of actions or operations and of information pertaining to those operations.

**PROCESS COST SYSTEM** A costing system in which the costs are collected by time period and averaged over all the units produced during the period. This system can be used with either actual or standard costs in the manufacture of large numbers of identical units (cf. Job order costing).

**PROCESS INDUSTRIES** Businesses that add value to materials by mixing, separating, forming, or chemical reactions. Processes may be either continuous or batch and usually require rigid process control and high capital investment.

**PROCESS SHEET** Detailed manufacturing instructions issued to the shop. The instructions can include speeds, feeds, tools, fixtures, machines, and sketches of setups and semifinished dimensions.

**PROCESS TIME** The time during which the material is being changed, whether it is a machining operation or a hand assembly.

**PROCUREMENT LEADTIME** The time required by the buyer to select a supplier and to place and obtain a commitment for specific quantities of material at specified times (cf. Purchasing lead time).

**PRODUCTION CONTROL** The function of directing or regulating the movement of goods through the entire manufacturing cycle from the requisitioning of raw materials to the delivery of the finished product.

**PRODUCTION REPORT** A formal, written statement giving information on the output of an organization or one or more of its subdivisions for a specified period. The information normally includes the type and quantity of output; workmen's efficiencies; departmental efficiencies; costs of direct labor, direct material, and the like; overtime worked; and machine downtime.

**PRODUCTION SCHEDULE** A plan which authorizes the factory to manufacture a certain quantity of a specific item. Usually initiated by the production planning department (cf. Manufacturing order, Work order).

**PRODUCTION STANDARD** Time standards to produce piece parts and assemblies.

**PRODUCT LOAD PROFILE** A statement of the key resources required to manufacture one unit of a selected item. It is often used to predict the impact of the item scheduled in the master production schedule on these resources (*syn.:* Bill of labor, Bill of resources, Resource profile).

**PRODUCT MIX** The combination of individual product types and the volume produced that make up the total production volume.

**PRODUCT STRUCTURE** The way components go into a product during its manufacture. A typical product structure would show, for example, raw material being converted into fabricated components, components being put together to make subassemblies, subassemblies going into assemblies, etc.

**PROGRESS PAYMENTS** Payments arranged in connection with a purchase transaction requiring periodic payments in advance of delivery for certain amounts or for certain percentages of the purchase price. The whole of the purchase price may be due in advance of delivery or partially after delivery.

**PROJECTED AVAILABLE BALANCE** The inventory balance projected out into the future. It is the running sum of on hand inventory minus requirements plus scheduled receipts.

**PROJECTED FINISH DATE** The date at which a shop order will be completed; calculated by using the remaining lead time and the current date.

**PROJECT EVALUATION AND REVIEW TECHNIQUE (PERT)** A project planning technique similar to the Critical Path Method, which additionally includes obtaining a pessimistic, most likely, and optimistic time for each activity from which the most likely completion time for the project along the critical path is computed (cf. Critical path method).

**PROTECTION TIME** A number of days used as a safety buffer between the date demands are due and the date orders are to be completed.

**PULL DISTRIBUTION SYSTEM** A system for replenishing field warehouse inventories wherein replenishment decisions are made at the field warehouse itself, not at the central supply warehouse or plant (cf. Push distribution system).

**PURCHASE ORDER** The purchaser's document used to formalize a purchase transaction with a vendor. A purchase order, when given to a vendor, should contain statements of the quantity, description, and price of the goods or services ordered, agreed terms as to payment, discounts, date of performance, transportation terms, and all other agreements pertinent to the purchase and its execution by the vendor.

**PURCHASE REQUISITION** A document conveying authority to the procurement department to purchase specified materials in specified quantities within a specified time.

**PURCHASING CAPACITY** The act of buying capacity or machine time from a vendor. This allows a company to use and schedule the capacity of the machine or a part of the capacity of the machine as if it were in their own shop.

**PURCHASING LEAD TIME** The total lead time required to obtain a purchased item. Included here are procurement lead time, vendor lead time, transportation time, receiving, inspection, and put away time.

**PUSH DISTRIBUTION SYSTEM** A system for replenishing field warehouse inventories wherein replenishment decision making is centralized, usually at the manufacturing site or central supply facility (cf. Distribution requirements planning, Pull distribution system).

**QUANTITY PER** The quantity of a component to be used in the production of its parent. It is used when calculating the gross requirements for components.

**QUEUE** A waiting line. In manufacturing, a queue is the line of jobs at a given work center waiting to be processed.

**QUEUEING THEORY** The collection of models dealing with waiting line problems; i.e., problems for which customers or units arrive at a service facility at which waiting lines or queues may build.

**QUEUE TIME** The amount of time a job waits at a work center before setup or work is performed on the job. Queue time is one element of total manufacturing lead time.

**RANDOM** Having no predictable pattern.

**RANDOM ACCESS** Files that do not have to be searched sequentially to find a particular record but can be addressed directly.

**RANDOM NUMBERS** A sequence of integers or group of numbers (often in the form of a table) that show absolutely no relationship to each other anywhere in the sequence. At any point, all integers have an equal chance of occurring, and they occur in an unpredictable fashion.

**RANDOM SAMPLE** A selection of observations taken from all of the observations of a phenomenon in such a way that each chosen observation has the same possibility of selection (cf. Sampling).

**RANDOM VARIATION** A fluctuation in data that is due to random occurrences, and the resulting data are random numbers.

**RANGE** The statistical term referring to the spread in a series of observations.

**RECEIVING** This function includes the physical receipt of material; the inspection of the shipment for conformance with the purchase order (quantity and damage); identification and delivery to destination; and preparing receiving reports.

**RECEIVING POINT** Location to which material is being shipped.

**RECEIVING REPORT** A form used by the receiving function of a company to inform others of the receipt of goods purchased.

**RECONCILING INVENTORY** Comparing the physical inventory count with the inventory record and making any necessary corrections.

**REGEN** Slang abbreviation for Regeneration MRP.

**REGENERATION MRP** An approach where the master production schedule is totally re-exploded down through all bills of material, at least once per week to maintain valid priorities. New requirements and planned orders are completely regenerated at that time (cf. Net change MRP).

**RELEASED ORDER** *See* Open order.

**REORDER POINT** *See* Order point.

**REORDER QUANTITY** *See* Order quantity.

**REPLENISHMENT LEAD TIME** The total period of time that elapses from the moment it is determined that a product is to be reordered until the product is on the shelf available for use.

**REPLENISHMENT ORDER QUANTITY** *See* Order quantity.

**REPLENISHMENT PERIOD** *See* Replenishment lead time.

**RESCHEDULING** The process of changing order or operation due dates, usually as a result of their being out of phase with when they are needed.

**RESCHEDULING ASSUMPTION** A fundamental piece of MRP logic which assumes that existing open orders can be rescheduled into nearer time periods far more easily than new orders can be released and received. As a result, planned order receipts are not created until all scheduled receipts have been applied to cover gross requirements.

**RESERVE STOCK** *See* Safety stock.

**RESERVED MATERIAL** Material on hand or on order that is assigned to specific future production orders (*syn.*: Obligated material; cf. Available material).

**RESOURCE PLANNING** *See* Long-range resource planning.

**RESOURCE PROFILE** *See* Product load profile.

**RESOURCE REQUIREMENTS PLANNING** The process of converting the production plan and/or the Master Production Schedule into the requirements for key resources, such as man-hours, machine hours, engineering capacity, inventory levels, and capital requirements.

**REVIEW PERIOD** The time between successive evaluations of inventory status to determine whether or not to order—in a periodic review system. (Cf. Lead time.)

**RUNNING TIME** The time during which a machine is actually producing product. Running time for a machine tool does include time cutting metal and the time moving into position to cut metal, but running time does not include setup, maintenance, waiting for the operator, etc. (cf. Idle time).

**RUN SHEET** A loglike document used in continuous processes to record raw materials used, quantity produced, in-process testing results, etc. It may serve as an input document for inventory records.

**SAFETY CAPACITY** The planning or reserving for excess work force personnel and equipment above known requirements for unexpected demand. This reserve capacity is in lieu of safety stock.

**SAFETY FACTOR** A multiplying constant used in calculating safety stock. Its value depends on the level of customer service desired and whether MAD or the standard error of forecast errors is being used.

**SAFETY STOCK** A quantity of stock planned to be in inventory to protect against fluctuations in demand and/or supply.

**SAFETY TIME** The difference between the requirement date and the planned instock date is safety time (cf. Safety stock).

**SALES MIX** The combination of individual product types and their sales volume that make up the total sales volume. Differences between sales mix and product mix are the results of changes in inventory or backlog (cf. Product mix).

**SALES ORDER NUMBER** A unique control number assigned to each customer order, usually during order entry. For some make-to-order products it can also take the place of an end item part number by becoming the control number that is scheduled through the final assembly operation.

**SALES REPLACEMENT SYSTEM** Each warehouse periodically, perhaps quarterly, establishes a stocking level for each item based on local demand. Sales at each warehouse are reported to the central warehouse at periods shorter than the normal order interval. Shipments replacing the quantities sold are sent to each warehouse at the end of the replenishment periods. Periods usually are established to obtain economical shipments such as full truck loads.

**SAMPLE** A portion of a universe of data chosen to estimate some characteristic(s) about the whole universe. The universe of data can consist of historical delivery cycles, unit cost, sizes of customer orders, number of units in inventory, etc. (cf. Sampling distribution).

**SAMPLING** A statistical process whereby generalizations regarding an entire body of phenomena are inferred from a relatively small number of observations (cf. Sampling distribution).

**SAMPLING DISTRIBUTION** The distribution of values of a statistic calculated from samples of a given size.

**SCHEDULE** A listing of jobs to be processed through a work center, department, or plant, and their respective start dates as well as other related information.

**SCHEDULING RULES** Basic rules that are spelled out ahead of time so that they can be used consistently in a scheduling system. Scheduling rules usually specify the amount of calendar time to allow for a move and for queue, how load will be calculated, etc.

**SCRAP FACTOR** A percentage factor in the product structure used to increase gross requirements to account for anticipated loss during the manufacture of a particular product (cf. Shrinkage factor, Yield).

**SCRAP RATE** The percentage difference between the amount or number of units of product that is started in a manufacturing process and the amount or number of units that is completed at an acceptable quality level (*syn.:* Shrinkage).

**SEASONAL** Daily, weekly, or monthly sales data that show a repetitive pattern from year to year with some periods considerably higher than others (cf. Anticipation inventories).

**SEASONAL HARMONICS** *See* Harmonic smoothing.

**SEASONAL INVENTORY** Inventory built up in anticipation of a peak season in order to smooth production (cf. Anticipation inventories).

**SECOND ORDER SMOOTHING** A method of exponential smoothing for forecasting trends.

**SEND-AHEAD** *See* Split lot.

**SEQUENCING** Determining the order in which a manufacturing facility is to process a number of different jobs in order to achieve certain objectives (cf. Dispatching).

**SERVICE LEVELS** *See* Customer service.

**SERVICE PARTS** Parts used for the repair and/or maintenance of an assembled product. Typically they are ordered and shipped at a date later than the shipment of the product itself.

**SERVICE-VERSUS-INVESTMENT CHART** A curve showing the amount of inventory that will be required to give various levels of customer service.

**SETUP COST** The out-of-pocket costs associated with a machine setup (*syn.:* Changeover cost).

**SETUP LEAD TIME** The time in hours or days needed to prepare before a manufacturing process can start. Setup time may include run and inspection time for the first piece.

**SETUP TIME** Time required to adjust a machine or line and attach the proper tooling to make a particular product (cf. Idle time).

**SHIP-AGE LIMIT** The date after which a product cannot be shipped to a customer.

**SHIPPING DEPARTMENT** Facilities for the outgoing shipment of parts, products, and components. Packaging, marking, weighing, and loading for shipment are part of its activity.

**SHIPPING LEAD TIME** The number of working days normally required for goods in transit between a shipping and receiving point, plus acceptance time in days at the receiving point (cf. Transit time).

**SHIPPING TOLERANCE** An allowable tolerance the vendor can ship over or under a contract quantity.

**SHOP FLOOR CONTROL** A system for utilizing data from the shop floor as well as data processing files to maintain and communicate status information on shop orders and work centers.

**SHOP ORDER** *See* Manufacturing order.

**SHOP PACKET** A manufacturing order that travels with the job and includes a group of documents like the routings, blueprint, materials requisitions, move tickets, time tickets, etc. Usually many of the documents are in the form of punched cards (cf. Traveler).

**SHOP SCHEDULING** *See* Detailed scheduling.

**SHOP TRAVELER** *See* Traveler.

**SHORTEST PROCESS TIME RULE (SPT)** A dispatching rule that directs the sequencing of jobs in ascending order by processing time. Following this rule, maximum jobs per time period can be processed. As a result, the average lateness of jobs is minimized, although some jobs will be very late (cf. Due date rule).

**SHRINKAGE** Reductions of material quantities of items in stock, in process, in transit. The loss may be caused by scrap, theft, deterioration.

**SHRINKAGE FACTOR** Percentage factors in the Item Master File that compensate for expected losses during the manufacturing cycle either by increasing the gross requirements or by reducing the expected completion quantity of planned and open orders. The shrinkage factor differs from the scrap factor in that the former affects all uses of the part and its components. The scrap factor relates to only one usage (cf. Scrap factor).

**SHRINKAGE RATE** *See* Shrinkage factor.

**SIGMA** A common designation for the standard deviation that is a measure of the dispersion of data or the spread of the distribution (cf. Standard deviation).

**SIGNIFICANT PART NUMBERS** Part numbers that are intended to convey certain information such as the source of the part, the material in the part, the shape of the part, etc. (cf. Nonsignificant part numbers).

**SIMPLEX ALGORITHM** A procedure for solving the general linear programming problem.

**SIMULATION** The technique of utilizing representative artificial data to reproduce in a model various conditions that are likely to occur in the actual performance of a system. Frequently used to test the behavior of a system under different operating policies (cf. Monte Carlo simulation, Model).

**SINGLE LEVEL BILL OF MATERIAL** Shows only those components that are directly used in an upper-level item. It does not show any relationships more than one level down.

**SINGLE LEVEL WHERE USED** Lists each assembly in which a component is directly used and in what quantity. This information is usually made available through implosion.

**SINGLE SMOOTHING** *See* First order smoothing.

**SKEW** The degree of a nonsymmetry shown by a frequency distribution.

**SKU** *See* Stockkeeping unit.

**SLACK TIME** The difference in calendar time between the scheduled due date for a job and the estimated completion date. If a job is to be completed ahead of schedule, it is said to have slack time; if it is likely to be completed behind schedule, it is said to have negative slack time.

**SLOW MOVING ITEMS** Those items in inventory that have infrequent rather than constant demand. For these items, the important aspect of the forecast is when there will be demand rather than what will the demand be.

**SMALLEST PROCESS TIME RULE** *See* Shortest process time rule.

**SMOOTHING CONSTANT** In exponential smoothing, the weighting factor that is multiplied against the most recent error.

**SOFTWARE** Computer programs used in executing management information systems. These include the computer operating system (program), utility programs, as well as the functional application programs.

**SPARE PARTS** *See* Service parts.

**SPLIT DELIVERY** A method by which a larger quantity is ordered on a purchase order to secure a lower price, but delivery is spread out over several dates to control inventory investment.

**SPLIT LOT** A manufacturing order quantity that has been divided into two or more smaller quantities usually after the order is in process. Lots are sometimes split so that a portion of the lot can be moved through manufacturing faster. This portion is called the *send-ahead*.

**SPT** *See* Shortest process time rule.

**STABILIZATION STOCK** A type of fluctuation stock carried to cover variations in manufacturing time.

**STAGING** Pulling the material requirements for an order from inventory before the material is required. This action is taken to protect against inaccurate inventory records, but leads to increased problems in inventory records and availability.

**STANDARD COSTS** The normal expected cost of an operation, process, or product including labor, material, and overhead charges. It is computed on the basis of past performance costs, estimates, or work measurement.

**STANDARD DEVIATION** A measure of dispersion of data or of a variable. The standard deviation is computed by finding the difference between the average and actual observations, squaring each difference, summing the squared differences, finding the average squared difference (called the variance), and taking the square root of the variance.

**STANDARD ERROR** Applied to statistics such as the mean, to provide a distribution within which samples of the statistics are expected to fall.

**STANDARD TIME** **1.** The time that should be needed to set up a given machine or assembly operation. **2.** The time that should be required to run one part/assembly/end product through that operation.

**STANDING ORDER** An order with a vendor to supply a certain amount of material at specified intervals or as released until further notice.

**START DATE** The date that an order should be placed in the shop based upon some form of scheduling rules (cf. Scheduling rules).

**STOCHASTIC MODELS** Models where uncertainty is explicitly considered in the analysis (cf. Deterministic models).

**STOCK** Stored products or service parts ready for sale as distinguished from stores that are usually components or raw materials (cf. Stores).

**STOCKKEEPING UNIT (SKU)** Represents an item of stock at a particular location that is completely specified as to style, size, color, location, etc.

**STOCK ORDER** A manufacturing order to replenish stock as opposed to a production order to make a particular product for a specific customer (cf. Manufacturing order).

**STOCK-OUT** The lack of materials or components that are needed (cf. Back order).

**STOCK-OUT PERCENTAGE** A measure of the effectiveness with which the inventory management system responds to actual demand. The stock-out percentage can be a measurement of total stock-outs to total line item orders, or of line items incurring stock-outs during a period to total line items in the system.

**STOCKPOINTS** Places where items can be stocked and subjected to management control.

**STOCK STATUS** A periodic report showing the inventory on hand and usually showing the inventory on order and some sales history for the products that are covered in the stock status report (cf. Job status).

**STORES** Stored materials used in making a product (cf. Stock).

**SUBASSEMBLY** An assembly that is used at a higher level to make up another assembly (cf. Component).

**SUBOPTIMIZATION** A term describing a problem solution that is best from a narrow point of view but not from a higher or overall company point of view.

**SUMMARIZED BILL (OF MATERIAL)** A form of multilevel bill of material that lists all the parts and their quantities required in a given product structure. (Unlike the Indented Bill it does not list the levels of assembly and lists a component only once for the total quantity used.)

**SUPER BILL (OF MATERIAL)** A type of planning bill, located at the top level in the structure, that ties together various modular bills (and possibly a common parts bill) to define an entire product or product family. Its quantity per relationship to modules represents the forecast percentage popularity of each module. Its master scheduled quantities explode to create requirements for the modules which also are master scheduled (cf. Common parts bill, Modular bill, Planning bill).

**SUPPLIES** Materials used in manufacturing that are not normally charged to the finished production, such as cutting and lubricating oils, machine repair parts, glue, tape, etc. (cf. Floor stocks).

**SYSTEM** A group of elements that may be personnel, machines, and/or physical entities such as energy and information, working in an interrelated fashion toward a set of objectives.

**TARGET INVENTORY LEVEL** The equivalent of the maximum in a min-max system. It is often called an *order-up-to inventory level* and is used in a periodic review system (cf. Min-max system).

**TELEPROCESSING** Processing of data that is received from or sent to remote locations over communications lines; also called *telecommunications*, or simply *TP*.

**TELESCOPING** *See* Overlapped schedule.

**TIME BUCKET** The number of days summarized into one columnar display. A weekly time bucket would contain all of the relevant planning data for an entire week.

**TIME FENCE** *See* Planning fence.

**TIME-PHASED CONTRACT** The practice of showing requirements, scheduled receipts, the projected available balance, and planned order releases (in their proper time relationship to each other) to the vendor.

**TIME-PHASED ORDER POINT (TPOP)** An order release time calculated using MRP logic in an independent demand situation. The order release is planned in the period obtained by subtracting the lead time from the period in which a stock outage is projected.

**TIME SERIES** A set of data that are distributed over time, such as demand data in monthly time period occurrences.

**TIME SERIES ANALYSIS** Analysis of any variable classified by time in which the values of the variable are functions of the time periods.

**TIME STANDARD** The predetermined times allowed for the performance of a specific job. The standard will often consist of two parts, that for machine set up and that for actual running.

**TRACKING SIGNAL** The ratio of the cumulative algebraic sum of the deviations (between the forecast demand and the actual demand) to the mean absolute deviation. Used to signal when the validity of the forecasting model should be questioned.

**TRAFFIC** The department charged with responsibility for arranging the most economical classification and method of shipment for both incoming and outgoing materials and products.

**TRANSIENT BILL (OF MATERIAL)** A bill of material coding and structuring technique used primarily for transient (nonstocked) subassemblies. For the transient subassembly item, lead time is set to zero and lot sizing is lot-for-lot. This permits MRP logic to drive requirements straight through the transient item to its components while retaining its ability to net against any occasional inventories of the subassembly. This technique also facilitates the use of common bills of material for engineering and manufacturing (*syn.*: Phantom bill of material).

**TRANSIT TIME** A standard, arbitrary allowance that is given on any given order for the physical movement of items from one operation to the next.

**TRANSPORTATION INVENTORY** Shipping more than just adequate stock from one of a firm's plants to another for more work, storage, assembly, or distribution to customers so that production and/or distribution are not interrupted. Thus, if it takes two weeks to replenish a branch warehouse, inventory equivalent to approximately two weeks of sales will normally be in transit (cf. Movement inventory).

**TRANSPORTATION METHOD** A linear programming model concerned with the minimization of costs involved in supplying requirements at several locations from several sources with different costs related to the various combinations of source and requirement locations.

**TRAVELER** A copy of the manufacturing order that actually moves with the work through the shop (cf. Shop packet).

**TRAVEL TIME** *See* Transit time.

**TURNAROUND** **1.** The time span in days between receipt of order and shipping date. **2.** The time required to shut down, clean, repair, and start up a processing plant.

**TWO BIN SYSTEM** **1.** Material physically separated into the order point quantity and the remaining units. The latter are consumed first and an order is placed upon their consumption. Material may be placed in different bins or physically separated within the same bin. **2.** Any fixed order system (even when physical "bins" are not used) (cf. Fixed order quantity system).

**UNIT COST** Total labor, material, and overhead cost for one unit of production, i.e., one part, one gallon, one pound, etc.

**UNIT OF MEASURE** The unit in which quantitative data regarding an item are expressed. Examples are each, pounds, gallons, feet, etc.

**UNIT OF MEASURE (PURCHASING)** The unit used to purchase an item. This may or may not be the same unit of measure used in the internal systems. Purchasing buys steel by the ton, but it may be issued and used in square inches.

**UNIT PRICE** The price for each unit.

**UNIVERSE** The population, or large set of data, from which samples are drawn. Usually assumed to be infinitely large or at least vey large relative to the sample (cf. Sampling).

**UNPLANNED ISSUE/RECEIPT** An issue or receipt transaction that updates the quantity on hand but for which no order or allocation exists.

**USAGE** The number of units or dollars of an inventory item consumed over a period of time.

**UTILIZATION** The percentage of time a machine, work center, or line is not down due to equipment failure, lack of material, or lack of an operator.

**VALUE ANALYSIS** The systematic use of techniques that serve to identify the required function, establish a value for that function, and finally to provide that function at the lowest overall cost. This approach focuses on the functions of an item rather than the methods of producing the present product design.

**VARIABLE** A quantity that can assume any of a given set of values (cf. Constant).

**VARIABLE COSTING** An inventory valuation method in which only variable production costs are applied to the product; fixed factory overhead is not assigned to it.

**VARIABLE COSTS** An operating cost that varies directly with production volume, i.e., materials consumed, power, direct labor, sales commissions, etc.

**VARIANCE** **1.** The difference between the expected (or budgeted or planned) and the actual. **2.** In statistics, a measure of dispersion of data (cf., Standard deviation).

**VENDOR** A company or individual that supplies goods or services.

**VENDOR LEAD TIME** The time that normally elapses between the time an order is placed with the supplier and its shipment of the material.

**VENDOR MEASUREMENT** The act of measuring the vendor's performance to the contract. Measurements usually cover delivery, quantity, and price.

**VENDOR SCHEDULER** An individual whose main responsibility is matching vendor performance to the schedule.

**VISUAL REVIEW SYSTEM** A simple inventory control system where the inventory ordering is based on actually looking at the amount of inventory on hand. Usually used for low value items like nuts and bolts (cf. Two bin system).

**WAIT TIME** *See* Queue time.

**WALL-TO-WALL INVENTORY** Production material, parts, and assemblies entering the plant at one end and processed through the plant to end product without ever having entered a formal stock area.

**WAREHOUSE DEMAND** The need for an item in order to replenish a branch warehouse.

**WHAT-IF ANALYSIS** The process of evaluating alternate strategies. Answering the consequences of changes to forecasts, manufacturing plans, inventory levels, cost, etc. Some companies have the capability of submitting various plans as a "trial fit" in order to find the best one (*syn.*: Simulation).

**WORK CENTER** A specific production facility, consisting of one or more people and/or machines, that can be considered one unit for purposes of capacity requirements planning and detailed scheduling.

**WORK-IN-PROCESS** Product in various stages of completion throughout the plant including raw material that has been released for initial processing and completely processed material awaiting final inspection and acceptance as finished product or shipment to a customer. Many accounting systems also include semifinished stock and components in this category (*syn.*: In-process inventory; cf. Movement inventory).

**WORK IN PROGRESS** *See* Work-in-process.

**WORK ORDER** Frequently, orders to the machine shop for tool manufacture or maintenance. *See* Manufacturing order.

**WORK SAMPLING** The use of a number of random samples to determine the frequency with which certain activities are performed.

**WORK STATION** The assigned location where a worker performs her or his job; it could be a machine or a work bench (cf. Work center).

**WORK TICKET** *See* Work order.

**YIELD** The ratio of usable output from a process to the materials input to the process. Yield is usually expressed as a percentage and may be in terms of total input or of a specific raw material.

**YIELD RATE** *See* Shrinkage factor.

# AUTHOR INDEX

# SUBJECT INDEX

## C

## N



## O

## Q

## T



## U



## V